DISTILLED SPIRITS

Science and Sustainability

Distilled Spirits
Science and Sustainability

Edited by

Graeme Walker[1]
Robert Fotheringham[2]
Ian Goodall[3]
Douglas Murray[4]

[1]*Professor of Zymology, Abertay University, United Kingdom;* [2]*Chief Chemist, Chivas Brothers Ltd, Pernod-Richard;* [3]*Senior Scientist, The Scotch Whisky Research Institute;* [4]*Liquid & Process Technology Manager, Diageo*

First published by Nottingham University Press

This reissued original edition published 2023 by 5m Books Ltd www.5mbooks.com

Copyright © The Institute of Brewing and Distilling 2023

All rights reserved. No part of this publication may be reproduced in any material form (including photocopying or storing in any medium by electronic means and whether or not transiently or incidentally to some other use of this publication) without the written permission of the copyright holder except in accordance with the provisions of the Copyright, Designs and Patents Act 1988. Applications for the copyright holder's written permission to reproduce any part of this publication should be addressed to the publishers.

British Library Cataloguing in Publication Data
Distilled Spirits - Science and Sustainability
I. Walker, G. II. Fotheringham, R., III. Goodall, I., IV. Murray, D.

ISBN 9781789182750

Disclaimer

Every reasonable effort has been made to ensure that the material in this book is true, correct, complete and appropriate at the time of writing. Nevertheless, the publishers and authors do not accept responsibility for any omission or error, or for
any injury, damage, loss or financial consequences arising from the use of the book.

Typeset by Nottingham University Press, Nottingham

EU GPSR Authorised Representative
LOGOS EUROPE, 9 rue Nicolas Poussin, 17000, LA ROCHELLE, France
E-mail: Contact@logoseurope.eu

Foreword

This publication is the fourth in the series of World Distilled Spirits Conference proceedings and draws its content from the presentations, discussions and posters of the fourth Worldwide Distilled Spirits Conference held in Glasgow during September 2011. A record figure of over 360 delegates attended the conference which is organised by the Scottish Section of the Institute of Brewing and Distilling. The proceedings are acknowledged as essential reading for those studying and practising in the global spirits industry. As the global spirits industry adapts to external pressures of legislation, climate change and global economics whilst retaining its strong heritage and traditional practices, an understanding of the science which will underpin sustainability becomes an invaluable tool. This publication hopes to help the reader in their search for practical solutions to today's challenges.

It was a pleasure to serve as the chairman of the organising committee for the 2011 conference and I would like to thank the organising committee and their employers for offering up their time, experience and enthusiasm so willingly to make the conference such a success.

I would also like to thank the sponsors and exhibitors for their generous support and I would in particular offer my special thanks to the editing team led by Professor Graeme Walker for their sterling efforts post conference.

Robert Fotheringham

Chief Chemist, Chivas Brothers Limited, Pernod-Ricard.
Chairman of the fourth Worldwide Distilled Spirits Conference Organising Committee

Contents

PART 3: DISTILLATION

PART 4: SCIENCE BEHIND FLAVOURS

PART 5: ANALYTICAL ASPECTS

PART 7: SUSTAINABILITY FOCUS

PART 8: FUTURE TECHNOLOGY

PART 9: CONSUMER PERCEPTION

Chapter 1

Recent progress in the genetics of malting barley

W Thomas[1], J Comadran[1], L Ramsay[1], P Shaw[1] D Marshall[1], A Newton[1], D O'Sullivan[2], J Cockram[2], I Mackay[2], R Bayles[2], J White[2], T Bringhurst[3], J Brosnan[3], R Waugh[1] and the AGOUEB Consortium

[1]The James Hutton Institute, Invergowrie, Dundee DD2 5DA, UK; [2]NIAB, Huntingdon Road, Cambridge CB3 0LE, UK; [3]Scotch Whisky Research Institute, Research Avenue North, Riccarton, Edinburgh EH14 4AP

Introduction and background

Malting barley is a key market for UK agriculture, consuming 30% of UK annual barley production. It underpins the Scotch Whisky industry, which earns over £3 billion in annual exports, and the domestic brewing industry. In Scotland, the average barley growing area over the past 10 years is greater than 300,000 ha with an average annual production of 1.8 million tonnes. Over 75% of the crop is spring sown and Scottish maltsters' annual purchases average over 750,000 tonnes over the same period. Distillers consume the majority of these purchases and the market is therefore driven by varieties that meet their requirements of a high spirit yield, ease of processing and low production of glycosidic nitriles. They are thus keenly interested in the development of a continuing supply of suitable new barley varieties. Over the years, stakeholders have developed robust evaluation systems for new barley varieties, which have been effective (mostly) in encouraging plant breeders to direct their products into these markets.

Barley (*Hordeum vulgare*) is an inbreeding self-fertile diploid with genes carried on 7 pairs of chromosomes. This means that barley varieties do not readily outcross with other varieties and thus breed true to type and that genes that are located close to each other on the same chromosome tend to be inherited together as well. Plant breeders create new genetic combinations by forcibly crossing one parent with another parent that complements the first for desirable characteristics. The segregation of these new characters becomes apparent in the F2 generation, i.e. the second generation after making the cross. The breeder generally begins to select in F2 populations and continues the process over succeeding generations until he/she has identified true breeding lines that meet targets for agronomic and, if appropriate, quality characteristics. Selection has been based upon the observed phenotype, which is the result of genetic and environmental effects upon a character and the interaction between the two. Such selection is most effective when characters are under a high degree of genetic control (high heritability) and least when environmental and interaction effects are stronger (low heritability). Typically, quality characters tend to fall in the latter category, necessitating widespread testing to obtain a better estimate of the genetic potential of a new variety. If, however, one knows which genes contribute to specific characteristics, one can use DNA finger-printing methodologies to directly select for these genes without undergoing extensive trialling in a process called

'Marker-Assisted Selection'. But, before Marker-Assisted Selection can be deployed, one needs to identify specific DNA fingerprints that tag the genes controlling target characters.

This is a similar problem to that faced by human geneticists in attempting to identify the genes responsible for a range of characters, including susceptibility to different types of cancer, and they currently rely upon connecting detailed DNA fingerprints of individuals to phenotypic data sets in association genetics analyses to identify chromosomal regions likely to contain the causal gene. This methodology is now being applied in plant genetics and is based upon the fact that genes located close together on a chromosome are said to be linked so that the same alleles at neighbouring loci tend to be inherited together. If the alleles in the region are at selectively neutral genetic loci, over time recombination between the neighbouring loci will have occurred during the various cycles of crossing and selection from the ancestral gene pool to a contemporary variety. Such a process creates different allelic combinations and the loci in the region will therefore be in Linkage Equilibrium as there are no phenotypic differences between the different allelic combinations. In contrast, if a region contains one or more loci where one or more alleles conferred a phenotypic advantage that had been selected for, the alleles at neighbouring loci that also derive from the same ancestral genotype will predominate in the population and are therefore in Linkage Disequilibrium (LD) (Figure 1). Association genetics searches for such non-random distribution of genes and tests whether any are associated with observed phenotypic differences for characters of interest. LD can, however, arise by chance through the past history of the population, domestication bottle-necks, selection, population structure and diversity and such possibilities need to be accounted for in the analyses.

The power and discrimination of association studies is largely determined by the underlying patterns of LD in the population under study and the size of the effect of allelic differences of underlying genes affecting the phenotype. If LD persists well beyond the causal gene or allelic differences are large, we can identify molecular markers in close proximity to a target gene controlling a specific quality attribute (Figure 2). The precision of the system is dependent on the resolution of the markers, and the more precisely

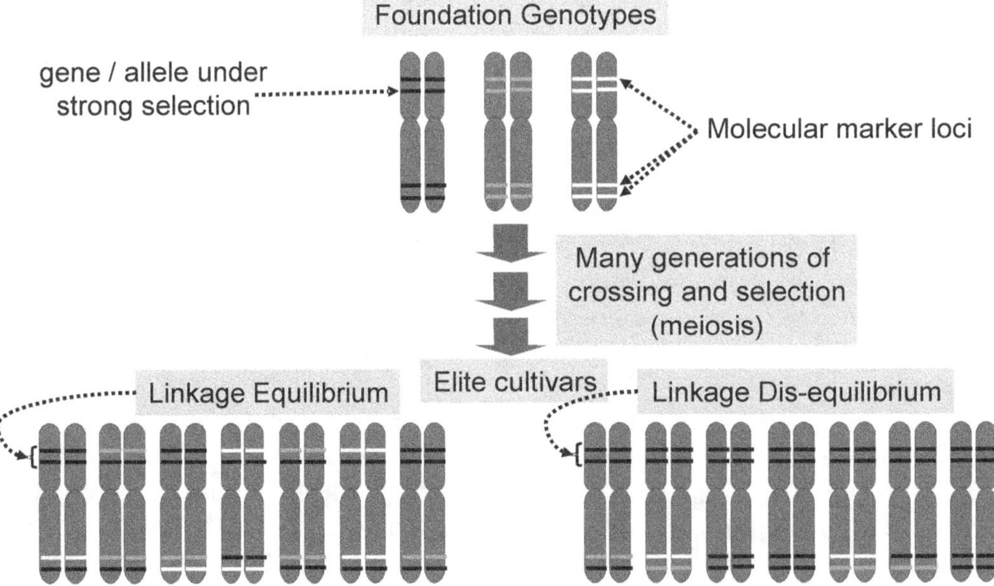

Figure 1. Schematic of chromosome pairs with marker pairs in the short and long arms. Seven individuals derived from the founder pairs are in Linkage Equilibrium (LHS) and Linkage Disequilibrium (RHS) for the markers on the short arm.

these can be resolved, the more easily a target gene can be located. For association genetics to be effective, LD must persist to a greater degree than the average marker density.

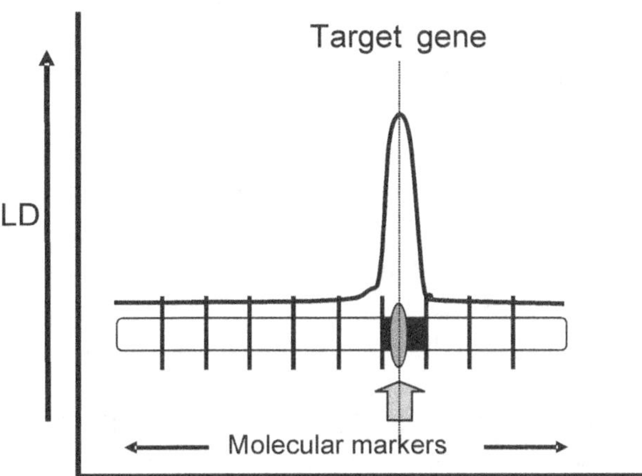

Figure 2. Increase in Linkage Disequilibrium amongst markers distributed along a chromosomal segment in the neighbourhood of a target gene under strong selection.

Different alleles at a genetic locus can represent different functional variants of the gene which can therefore affect the phenotype of the character resulting from the pathway that it is involved in. The differences are due to small variation in the DNA of the gene and are often represented by a difference in one nucleotide in a small segment of sequence of the gene. Such differences are called Single Nucleotide Polymorphisms (SNPs) and are the most abundant marker currently available for barley. Not only can the SNPs be assembled into genetic maps that identify their positions on each of barley's seven chromosomes but, because they are in known genes, their identity and hence function can also be compared to that of sequenced genomes of related species such as rice.

Each year, breeders submit their most promising selections for first year National List trials (NL1). The poorer-performing lines from NL1 trials are discarded or withdrawn and the remainder progress to second year National List trials (NL2) at the end of which, a variety is placed on the National List if passes Distinctness, Uniformity and Stability (DUS) and Value for Cultivation and Use (VCU) tests. Up to 2002, the British Society of Plant Breeders (BSPB) also ran a parallel series of trials to NL1 and NL2 at selected member sites, where NL1 and NL2 entries were generally grown together. Between 1993 and 2002, several of the BSPB sites were officially licensed NL sites and the NL1 and NL2 entries were grown in separate trials at these sites so we have assigned them to the NL1 and NL2 trial series, rather than the BSPB. At the end of NL2, the agronomic data from BSPB, NL1 and NL2 trials is then combined to identify the best performing lines for entry into Recommended List trials (RL). The remaining lines from NL2 are eventually withdrawn from the National List, unless they show promise as a variety in another country. At the end of the first year of RL, candidates that show some advantage over existing varieties on the RL will be give a provisional recommendation (P1). If the provisional recommendation continues to show merit after a second year of RL it continues in trial with a provisional recommendation (P2) and will gain full recommendation after a third year of trials if it continues to show merit that is also reflected in increasing seed sales.

Here we describe association genetics analyses of economically important characters in barley using phenotypic data collected from NL and RL trials and genotypic data collected using SNP markers in a project called Association Genetics of UK Elite Barley (AGOUEB).

Materials and methods

Between 1993 and 2005, 251 and 328 spring and winter barleys had at least completed 2 years of NL trials. A further 18 spring and 28 winter barleys were already in or were selected for recommended list trials in 1993 and 1994 making a total of 625 different barley lines that were available during the survey period. We supplemented this list with some varieties that had been commercially successful during the 1980's and some other key progenitor lines to bring the total to 663 lines. We were not able to source seed of all the lines, especially those originating from the continental breeding programmes, so that we were eventually able to utilise 547 lines for genotyping in what we term the AGOUEB Public Set. The lines that were already in trials in 1993 had been grown in trials in preceding years and we also grew samples of over 60 spring and winter barley lines that represented UK commercial successes and failures since 1980 in a set of new trials during 2006-8 as part of the project. When combined with the historical NL and RL VCU trials, this gave us data from 1988-2008 but none were grown in trials throughout the period and the majority were in trials for two or three years. The winter barley Pastoral was in trial for each year apart from 2004 and 2005 and the spring barley Optic has been in trial each year from 1992.

Cleaned and graded samples from selected plots of the new trials grown in 2006-8 were micro-malted by six companies representing the Maltsters Association of Great Britain; Boortmalt (formerly Greencore), Crisp Malting Group, Diageo Scotland, Molson Coors Brewing Company (UK), Muntons, and Simpsons Malt to provide standard malting and end-user quality data. Each maltster micro-malted a range of spring or winter barley varieties, designed to cover the full range of elite varieties that were grown on the project trial sites and thus provide an unambiguous estimate of genetic changes in malting parameters over time. Additional end-user quality data was supplied by the Scotch Whisky Research Institute and Campden BRI.

When the data from the 2006-8 trials was combined with the historical data gathered during National List and Recommended List trials, we had over 6,300 and 4,500 malt extract data points for spring and winter barley respectively with over 1,000 data points for 23 other germination and malting characters in spring barley and 11 others for winter barley. Gathered over a minimum of two years with multiple sites each year for each variety, this is a far more comprehensive data set than any previous and will provide a major improvement on the precision of previous QTL studies, which were done on a much smaller scale. As most of the table of variety x site x year means was missing because no one variety was tested over the whole of our 20year survey period, we employed state of the art statistical methodology to predict the overall mean of each genotype for each of the characters that we studied.

The challenge of the Association Genetics of UK Elite Barley (AGOUEB) project was to generate detailed genetic fingerprints for elite barley varieties to find individual genetic markers that are in Linkage Disequilibrium with phenotypes of interest. An international effort to improve barley genomics resources identified a number of SNPs for use in fingerprinting barley and the best of these have been used to produce two Barley Oligo Pooled Arrays of 1536 SNPs each (BOPA1 and BOPA2) (Close et al. 2009). We therefore genotyped the lines in the project with BOPA1 and BOPA2 under a commercial contract using the Illumina GoldenGate assay. We then combined these means with the DNA fingerprints of each variety to search for associations of markers with each character in each crop type after accounting for major differences such as two v six-row ear type in the winter barleys.

Results and discussion

Genetic variation in malting quality

Analysis of the whole data set enabled us to determine how much of the variation in each character was due to variation between different barley lines (i.e. genetic), how much was due to variation between sites and seasons (i.e. environmental) and how much was due to interactions between genetic and environmental factors. We detected significant genetic variation for all the germination and malting characters with an average heritability of 36% for the spring crop and 50% for the winter. We found the least genetic variation for germination in 4ml of water for both crops and that malt extract was the second highest. Whilst this suggests that there is still considerable genetic potential for improvement in any one of these characters, the analysis was based upon all lines in trial so not all would be malting varieties, especially in the winter crop. The means and ranges for each character are shown in Tables 1a and b, together with the genotypes representing the extreme expression of each character

Results from the new trials grown in 2006-8 showed an increase in the average malt extract potential of IBD approved varieties over a 25 year range as there were significant regression slopes between the character and the year of a variety being first placed on the UK recommended list (Figure 3). As the varieties were all given the same treatments, these differences are entirely

Table 1. Minima, maxima, overall mean, SED and the extreme genotypes for each of 24 and 12 germination and malting characters measured on spring (a) and winter (b) barley respectively.

(a) Character	*Minimum* Genotype	*Minimum* Value	*Mean*	*Maximum* Value	*Maximum* Genotype	*SED*
D-Power	Georgie	65.53	99.10	136.50	Hanka	6.473
Dorm-4ml	Trinity	84.54	95.38	98.51	Ursa	1.696
Dorm-5ml	Neruda	43.37	84.59	97.60	Henni	3.788
Dorm-8ml	Alliot	17.68	41.13	77.94	Penthouse	7.308
Ferm Extract	Henni	66.57	70.88	72.24	Rummy	0.373
Fermentability	Hart	77.48	86.97	87.99	Flick Sejet	0.378
Friability	Klaxon	65.54	88.76	96.42	Sacha	1.913
GE4ml	Spotlight	93.79	97.73	99.06	Spey	0.445
GE5ml	Alabama	72.47	94.32	99.60	Ricarda	1.220
GE8ml	Blenheim	38.39	67.35	85.03	Ferment	5.282
Homogeneity	Klaxon	81.23	97.33	99.62	Pitcher	0.988
HWE	Digger	291.39	312.11	316.94	Tartan	0.994
Grain N	Talbot	1.42	1.60	1.95	Jersey	0.024
Malt N	Mandolin	1.26	1.51	1.79	Tyne	0.030
PSY	Alexis	398.51	427.30	435.00	Rummy	3.308
TSN	Otira	0.46	0.60	0.76	Goldie	0.018
SNR	Hart	30.81	40.33	45.85	Decanter	1.109
Wort B-Glucan	Toby	59.99	130.56	407.64	Klaxon	27.291
Wort Colour	Tyne	2.07	2.84	4.36	Georgie	0.161
Wort Viscosity	Amber	1.43	1.51	1.96	Klaxon	0.020

(b) Character	*Minimum* Genotype	*Minimum* Value	*Mean*	*Maximum* Value	*Maximum* Genotype	*SED*
D-Power	Peridot	67.83	96.84	151.78	Plaisant	7.506
Friability	Igri	38.01	71.32	92.88	Portrait	3.053
GE4ml	Gypsy	94.29	96.87	98.05	CPBT B66	1.026
GE5ml	Oleron	65.57	95.29	100.00	Jewel	1.531
Homogeneity	Igri	58.09	90.17	98.85	Flagon	1.813
HWE	Majestic	268.45	299.26	309.46	Tiffany	1.742
Grain N	Courtois	1.55	1.74	2.20	Malta	0.043
Malt N	Jessica	1.46	1.71	2.07	Esterel	0.049
TSN	Antonia	0.44	0.56	0.71	Spirit	0.023
SNR	Tallica	24.45	33.65	40.31	Jessica	1.210
Wort Colour	Firefly	2.11	2.62	3.23	Vertige	0.146
Wort Viscosity	Chestnut	1.44	1.70	2.64	Igri	0.046

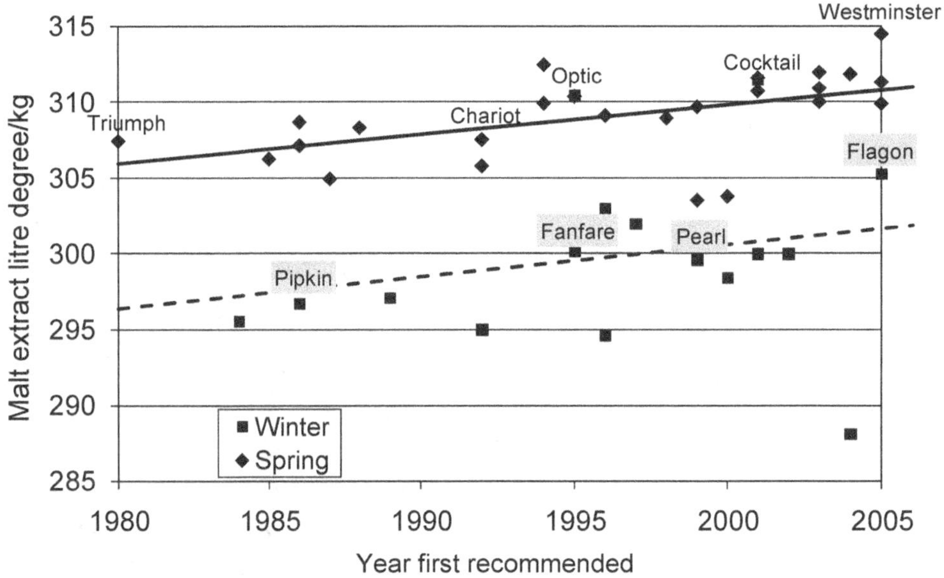

Figure 3. Malt extract of IBD approved spring and winter barley varieties plotted against their first year of recommendation in the UK. Data derived from common trials grown in 2006-8 and provided by MAGB member companies.

genetic and therefore gave us confidence that we could identify the chromosomal segments responsible and, as they were detected amongst IBD approved varieties, that the findings would have value in the future improvement of malting quality.

Marker Phenotype Associations

We found associations of malt extract on each of barley's seven chromosomes for spring and winter barley. In spring barley, the better allele was found in Optic for 19 of the 24 significant associations, reflecting its known quality attributes but also highlighting genetic regions where improvement could be possible by introducing the non-Optic allele. Similarly, we found 25 significant associations with malt extract in winter barley with Intro possessing the better allele in five of them (Figure 4). Whilst Intro was used by maltsters in the mid 1990s, it was never approved by IBD and thus its overall deleterious effect on malt extract is not surprising but it does show that some beneficial characters might still exist in the feed barley gene pool.

The challenge now is to examine all the associations to identify the critical ones that could be manipulated for further improvement in malting quality. Those that are detected in both the winter and spring barley gene pools, such as the region towards the end of chromosome 7H, are most attractive as they are more likely to be effective in different environments. Within each crop type, there are also some interesting targets, such as the specific winter malt extract QTL towards the middle of chromosome 1H that is also associated with processability characters. The beneficial non-Intro alleles in this region are largely fixed in spring barley but are only found in lines with malting potential in the winter crop. Thus, when selecting for the malting market amongst progeny from malting x feed winter barley crosses, breeders can use this information to select lines targeted for either the malting or feed sector. The most significant association with spring malt extract is on chromosome 3H close to the end of the short arm with the Optic allele increasing the character. Whilst the non Optic allele is also found in some IBD accepted malting cultivars (e.g. Triumph), it tends to be

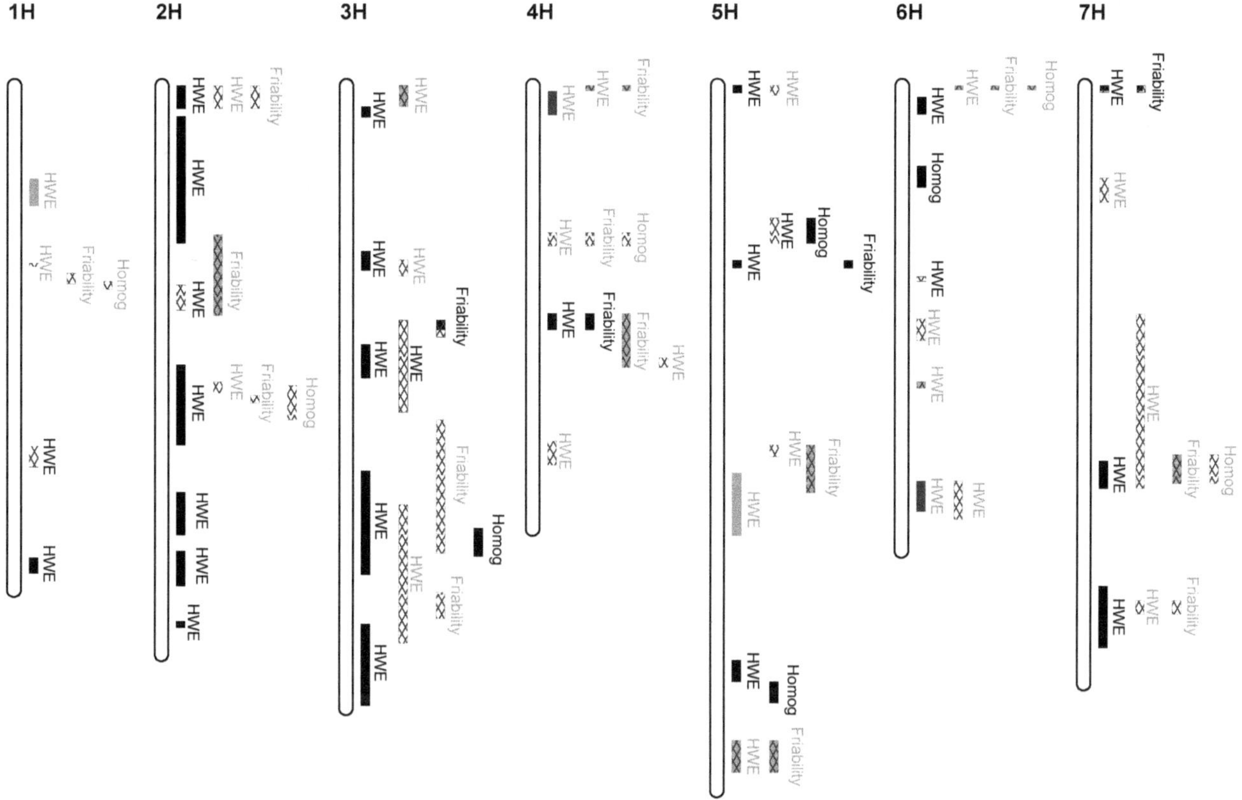

Figure 4. Genetic map of barley's seven chromosomes with significant marker phenotype associations in the coloured boxes alongside. Solid fills and hatched fills indicate associations found in the spring and winter crops respectively. Black indicates beneficial alleles derived from Optic (spring) and Intro (winter) and grey indicates non-beneficial alleles from these two varieties.

found amongst the older spring cultivars and not in the more recent ones. So, if breeders are entirely crossing within UK elite germplasm then the favourable allele is likely to be fixed and MAS is unnecessary. But, if crossing with other germplasm where the allele may not be fixed, then MAS would be worthwhile. It is also noticeable that the Optic allele is found in some winter IBD approved cultivars such as Pipkin and Halcyon but not in more recent ones such as Pearl and Flagon. Combining the Optic allele in this region with the other malting characters found in Pearl and Flagon may be one route towards bridging the gap in malt extract potential between the winter and spring crop.

Acknowledgements

The Association Genetics of UK Elite Barley (AGOUEB) project is a collaborative barley research project funded by the BBSRC, RERAD and the Home Grown Cereals Authority (HGCA) under the Sustainable Arable LINK Programme (LINK SA302/BB/D522003/1). The AGOUEB Consortium represents the Scottish Crop Research Institute (SCRI), Mylnefield Research Services Ltd (MRS), the Maltsters Association of Great Britain (MAGB), Calibre Control International Ltd, Campden BRI, Coors Brewers Ltd, KWS UK Ltd, LS Plant Breeding (SERASEM), the National Institute of Agricultural Botany

(NIAB), RAGT Seeds, Secobra/Dalgety, Groupe Limagrain, Svalöf Weibull AB, Syngenta Seeds Ltd, the University of Birmingham and the Scotch Whisky Research Institute.

References

Close, T.J., Bhat, P.R., Lonardi, S., Wu, Y.H., Rostoks, N., Ramsay, L., Druka, A, Stein, N., Svensson, J.T., Wanamaker, S., Bozdag, S., Roose, M.L., Moscou, M.J., Chao, S.A.M., Varshney, R.K., Szucs, P., Sato, K., Hayes, P.M., Matthews, D.E., Kleinhofs, A., Muehlbauer, G.J., DeYoung, J., Marshall, D.F., Madishetty, K., Fenton, R.D., Condamine, P., Graner, A. and Waugh, R. (2009). Development and implementation of high-throughput SNP genotyping in barley. *BMC Genomics* **10**: 582. DOI: 10.1186/1471-2164-10-582

Chapter 2

Sustainability of grapes as a raw material for distilled spirits

L. Lurton, G. Ferrari, B. Galy, L. Boitaud, V. Dumot
Bureau National Interprofessionnel du Cognac, Station Viticole, BP 18, 16100 Cognac, France

Introduction

Activities in the vine and wine sector are highly dependent on natural resources: solar energy, climate, water, soils, and their successful integration in ecological processes. Therefore, protection and preservation of these natural assets, through environmentally sustainable practices, are imperative for the long-term viability of vitivinicultural activities.

The International Organisation of Vine and Wine (OIV) defines sustainable vitiviniculture as a "Global strategy, on the scale of the grape production and processing systems, incorporating at the same time the economic sustainability of structures and territories, producing quality products, considering risks to the environment, products safety and consumer health and valuing of heritage, historical, cultural, ecological and landscape aspects" (O.I.V., 2008).

This presentation will focus on sustainability of vitiviniculture intended to allow production of distillation wines, through examples from the Cognac production area.

Vineyards dedicated to the production of distilled spirits

Some global vitivinicultural statistics (O.I.V., 2007 and O.I.V., 2011)

In 2010, world vineyards reached a total surface area of 7,586 Mha. After a period of sustained growth which continued until the late 1970s (10,2 Mha between 1976 and 1980), global vineyard acreage declined in the 1980s and 1990s, as a result of extensive vine pull schemes in the European Union (EU) and in the former Soviet Union. Today's level is close to that of the 1996-2000 period (7,705 Mha).

World wine production (excluding juice and musts) can be estimated for 2010 at 260 Mhl. This is a lower global wine production than those of 2001, 2003 and 2007 or 2009. It is similar to 1998 and 2002 harvests.

In 2010 world wine consumption level is estimated at 236Mhl. This result, similar to 2009, is considered by OIV as the sign of a return to the pre-crisis trend in world wine consumption, namely a fairly steady moderate growth.

The International Code of Oenological Practices (O.I.V., 2011) defines the following products, in the category of spirit beverages from vitivinicultural origin : wine spirits, brandy, grape marc spirits, wine lees spirits, grape spirits, and raisin spirits. The same categories can be found in European Regulation N°110/2008 on the definition, description, presentation and labelling of spirit drinks. Statistical data on distilled products are only partly available. In 2006-2007, the volumes used for the production of wine distillates in a set of countries accounting for 74% of world wine production (i.e. EU15 market, Cyprus, Hungary, Czech Republic, Romania, Argentina, Brazil and South Africa) reached approximately 23,7 Mhl, out of 27,8 Mhl of wines used for industrial purposes in the same countries. These figures clearly underestimate the global use of grapes and wines as raw material for spirits production.

Cognac vineyard and production

A delimited production area

The Cognac Delimited Area is located in France, in the north of the Aquitaine basin, along the Atlantic Ocean. The total agricultural acreage of the area is in the order of 700,000 ha among which the total vineyard area covers about 75,000 ha, 96% of which (about 72,000 ha) is used in Cognac production. The production area mainly covers two French departments: Charente Maritime, and a large part of Charente. Some districts in Dordogne and Deux-Sèvres are also part of the area. Figure 1b shows that most of Cognac vineyard is confined to an 80 Km diameter circle, centered near Cognac. The rate of vine cultivation, as a percentage of the total agricultural area, is particularly high in the central part of the vineyard, corresponding to the "crus" of Grande Champagne, Petite Champagne and Borderies, but also on the islands of Ré and Oléron (Figure 1).

In 2010, 7 609 682 hl million hectolitres of wine were produced by a total of 5000 vine-growers and distilled by over 1300 grower-distillers (bouilleurs de cru) and 110 professional distillers.

A production area divided into 6 crus

In the mid-19th century, geologist Henri Coquand (1811-1881) made a very detailed study of the Cognac region's geology (Coquand, 1858). With the help of a taster, he classified the different areas according to the quality of the wine spirits that their soils could produce. Around 1860, their work resulted in the demarcation of different "crus" (growing areas) and served as a basis for the Order of 13 January 1938 delimiting the

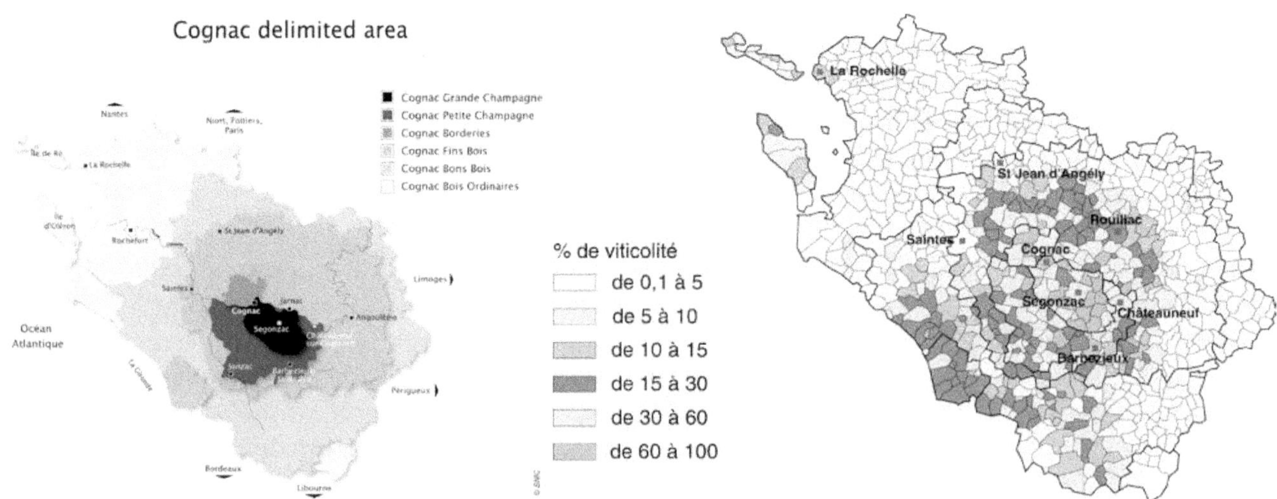

Figure 1. Map of Cognac vineyard : delimitation of the "crus" [left] and percentage of vineyards in administrative districts [right]

"crus" (Figure 1a). Geographical denominations, complementary to the Cognac appellation, still make use of their historical names: "Grande Champagne", "Petite Champagne", "Borderies", "Fins Bois", "Bons Bois, and "Bois Ordinaires".

According to the work carried out at this time, the dominant characteristics of soils typical of each denomination can be described as follows :

- Grande and Petite Champagne : thin argilo-calcareous soils over soft chalky Cretaceous limestone ;
- Borderies : clayey soils containing flint nodules resulting from limestone decarbonation ;
- Fins Bois : largely covered by "groies", thin, stony red argilo-calcareous soils, from Jurassic limestone ;
- Bons Bois and Bois Ordinaires : sandy soils are encountered in coastal areas, certain valleys and over the entire southern part of the vineyard.

Dumot *et al* (1993) give a detailed agronomic description of the main types of soil to be found in Cognac area.

A vineyard with a long history

Grapevines have been grown in Charentes since the end of the 1st century AD. In the Middle Ages, thanks to the River Charente, the town of Cognac was already famous for its wine trade. Wines from the Poitou vineyards, transported in Dutch ships coming to load up with Atlantic coast salt, were much appreciated in the lands lying alongside the North Sea.

In the 16th century, the Dutch began distilling the region's wines to produce "brandwijn" (burnt wine), the origin of the term "brandy". Double distillation made its appearance in the early 17th century, enabling the product to travel in the form of a stable wine spirit much more concentrated than wine itself.

In 1877, the Cognac vineyard covered some 280.000 ha, producing up to 17Mhl of wines in 1875 (59 hl/ha) but only 4.6 Mhl in 1876 (16 hl/ha) (Coussié, 1996).

Around 1875 *Phylloxera vastatrix*, an insect that attacks vines by sucking the sap from their roots, destroyed most of the Cognac vineyards which, by 1893, only covered some 40 600 hectares, as against 280 000 hectares before the phylloxera plague. As elsewhere in Europe, the Charentes vineyards were reconstituted by use of American rootstocks. This episode is an historical example of the role of science in the development of sustainable viticulture. Vineyards replanting schedules led to the creation in 1892 of the Station Viticole, a scientific and technical research centre devoted to Cognac production, which became in 1947 the BNIC technical department.

In the first half of the 20th century, legislation bearing upon Cognac was drawn up in order

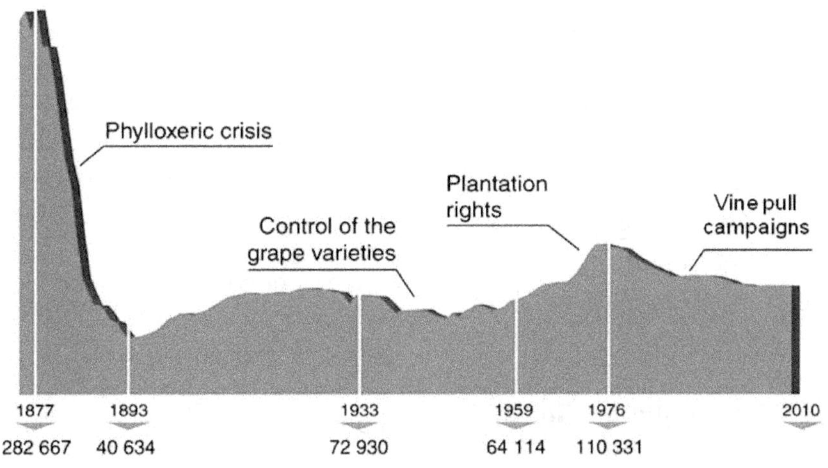

Figure 2. Cognac vineyard historical evolution (BNIC)

to conserve longstanding and unchanging local practices :

- 1909 : delimitation of the geographical production area ;
- 1936 : certification of Cognac as an AOC ;
- 1938 : delimitation of regional appellations.

This regulation remains very stable until now, and the last 2009 decree defining production rules of "Appellation d'Origine Contrôlée Cognac" shows only slight evolutions compared to the 1936 and 1938 texts.

The twentieth century was marked by a constant progression in production levels, linked to technical progress. Vineyard replanting, mainly on the base of Ugni blanc, development of adapted rootstocks, major improvements in vine's protection against pest and diseases, increased the average regional yield up to 50 hl/ha in the 50s. It was only 30 hl/ha during the first part of the century. With 116 hl/ha, 1968 was the first regional harvest beyond the 100 hl/ha threshold. The average was 102 hl/ha in the 70s decade, and 105 hl/ha in the 80s, due to the plantation of new clones issued from sanitary selection and important technical progress in viticulture and pest and diseases management. Since the 90s the average yield is between 110 and 120 hl/ha. The vineyard is now totally planted with selected sanitary clones, and most often favourable climatic conditions allow a good flowering period, propitious to floral induction for the next year.

Encepagement and vineyard management rules

Vines destined for elaboration of Cognac wine spirits come exclusively from the following grape varieties :

- Colombard B, Folle Blanche B, Montils B, Ugni Blanc B and Semillon B ;
- Folignan B, up to 10 % of the regional grape varieties.

Ugni Blanc is the most commonly planted variety and these days accounts for almost 98 % of vines in Cognac area. Its rise in Cognac vineyards began following the phylloxera crisis, about a century ago (Ravaz, 1900). A variety originating in Italy, where it is known as "Trebbiano Toscano", the Cognac region is its northern limit for ripening. In the mid-20th century, it became the first variety for Cognac production, due to its qualities with regard to productivity (its average yield in the Cognac region is between 110 and 120 hectolitres per hectare), late budding, and production of an acidic wine, low in alcohol content, which is particularly suited to production of quality wine spirits.

The Ugni blanc clones currently available in France were selected in the 1970s. They only show little phenotypic variability, which is confirmed by genetic analysis, showing no difference on 38 SSR microsatellite markers. In 2003, the Bureau National Interprofessionnel du Cognac undertook a major research programme in order to preserve the variety's genetic diversity (Dumot *et al*, 2010). A genetic preservation collection, containing more than 800 accessions of Ugni blanc, from Cognac vineyards but also from other French and European (Italy, Portugal) regions was created. In order to address environmental and economical challenges (climate change, sustainable development), a selection programme looking for new clones presenting greater diversity is actually underway.

Rules concerning vineyard management, planting density, distance between rows, pruning techniques, number of buds per hectare, percentage of missing plants, and minimum age of vines also figure in the technical specifications which are annexed to Order n°2009-1146 by the French Ministry of Agriculture, relative to Appellation d'Origine Contrôlée "Cognac". The management methods used by the vine growers tend to reinforce the required balance between high acidity and low alcohol content. Such ripeners standards are specific to distillation wines. High acidity helps wine preservation through the winter months, up to distillation, and low alcohol content enables greater concentration of the wines' aromas in the spirits. Maximum annual production expressed in pure alcohol per hectare is fixed each year by inter-ministerial order.

Vineyard landscapes and tourism

Vineyard and wine landscapes also represent architectural, environmental, economical and patrimonial assets for vitivinicultural regions. Discovery of French vineyards attracts annually more than 7.5 million visitors, including 1/3 of foreigners. Together with nine other vineyards from Burgundy, Loire and Rhône valleys and South West of France, Cognac terroirs were granted the new "Vignobles & Découvertes" label, attributed in October 2010 by Ministries in charge of Agriculture and Tourism. This label, covering a 50 km circle around Cognac city, aims at the promotion of cultural, historical and natural sites, local know-how, leisure facilities, events, accommodations and restaurants, in relation with Cognac vineyard.

Cognac region's economy

The region's economy is historically linked to Cognac's prosperity. Historically a product for export, nowadays more than 95 % of Cognac is consumed outside France. Currently, around 150 million bottles are sent annually to over 160 different countries, where Cognac is recognized as a premium wine spirit, emblematic of the French art of living.

Regionally, over 17000 employments are closely linked to Cognac sector. With 5000 wine-growers, including 1300 grower-distillers, viticulture directly employs 10 500 people. About 110 professional distilleries, and 300 trade companies (Maisons de négoce), provide on their side 2900 direct employments. Besides, many crafts and industries developed around Cognac production and trade companies, creating a professional community accounting for about 3900 people in Cognac Chamber of Commerce and Industry district. These associated activities include cooperage (1000), cardboard and printing houses (800), glass industry (700), freight (400), agriculture and industrial equipments (300), closures (100), tertiary sector, laboratories...

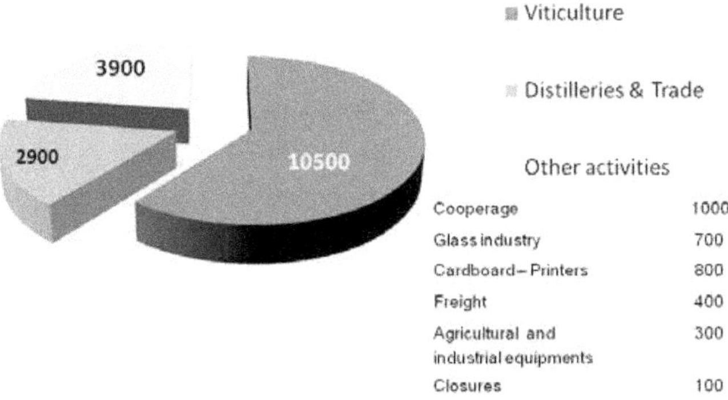

Figure 3. Employment in Cognac sector (BNIC)

Adaptation to climate change

The Cognac winegrowing region enjoys a temperate maritime climate, with little variations except in coastal areas, which get more sunshine and experience a narrower range of temperatures. Because the ocean is so close by, rain, although heavier in winter, may fall at any time of the year. Periods of drought are few, ensuring the vine a regular water supply. The average annual temperature stands at around 13 °C, with fairly mild winters. Temperatures are high enough to ensure good ripening of grapes to be used for wine spirit production, but not high enough to burn them. The Cognac region's climate was described at the beginning of the 20th century by Ravaz (1900), and later on by Lafon *et al* (1964).

A recent study, based on temperature and rainfall data since 1918, was carried out by the BNIC in order to evaluate recent changes in the Cognac region's climate and assess their impact on grape production (Boitaud *et al*, 2010). The 30-years mobile means of average annual temperatures have risen by 1 °C since 1980. The number of hot summer days has also increased. Conversely, the number of frost days and the frequency of spring frosts have diminished. Average annual rainfall has slightly risen over the past 20 years.

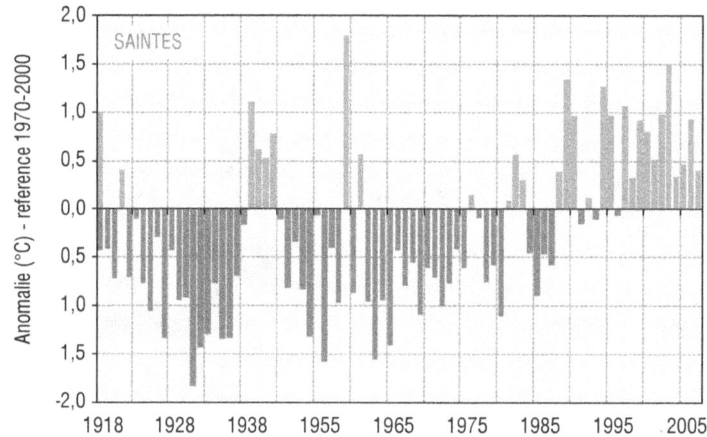

Figure 4. Annual average temperature anomaly relative to 1970-2000 in Cognac vineyard

Huglin (1986) heliothermal index, used to characterise the climate of a wine-producing region, has evolved from a cool climate – up until the 1980s – to a temperate climate. Over the course of time, it could evolve towards a warm temperate climate. Since the 80s, there has been a clear trend towards earlier grape harvests, yet bud break dates have remained relatively stable. A 1 °C rise in maximum daytime temperatures during the vine's growth period (April to August) corresponds to the grape harvest being brought forward by 10 days in the Cognac vineyards (Figure 5) as in most French vineyards (Daux *et al*, 2007).

Climate change is accelerating the maturation process, leading to an increase in sugar content and lower acidity levels. Its impacts on the production of wines and spirits have been evaluated (Figure 6).

Preservation of acidity in grapes and wines is an important research topic for Cognac sector, which concerns as well the selection of new clones and new grape varieties, as vineyard management techniques and winemaking process.

Reduction of viticultural inputs

Input reduction is a fundamental principle of environmentally sustainable production. At

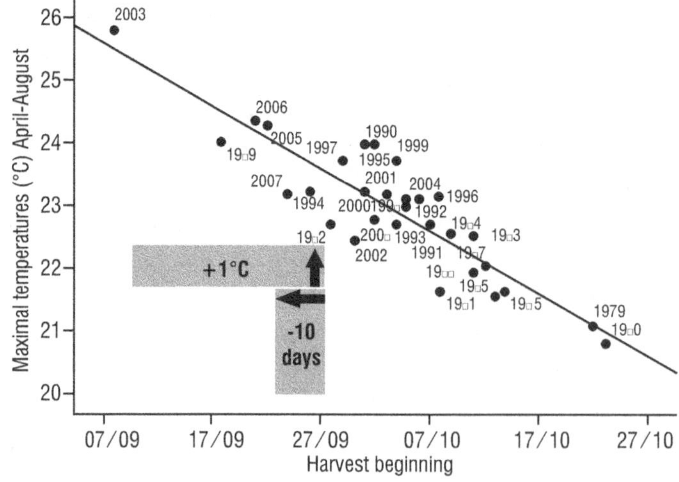

Figure 5. Correlation between harvest date and mean maximal diurnal temperature (april - august) in Cognac vineyard.

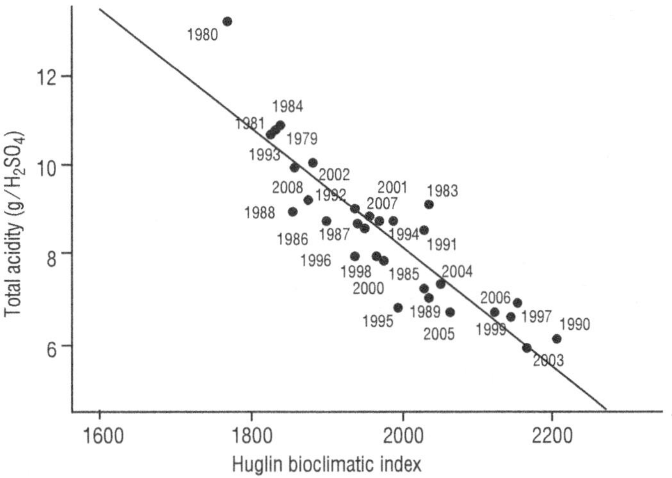

Figure 6. Correlation between grapes total acidity at harvest time and Huglin bioclimatic index in Cognac vineyard.

European level the sustainable use of pesticides is thus one of the seven thematic strategies in the Sixth Environment Action Programme of the European Community 2002-2012. The aim is to achieve "a significant overall reduction in the risks and uses of pesticides consistent with the necessary crop protection". Ecophyto 2018 is the French action plan to reduce pesticides, in compliance with the Sustainable use directive (Directive 2009/128/EC).

Following on from the Grenelle consultation process on environmental issues, the Ecophyto 2018 plan embodies the commitment given by the authorities, industry professionals, and representatives of civil society – the plan's co-authors – to cut the nationwide use of pesticides by 50% in the space of ten years, if possible. The most notable goal of Ecophyto 2018 is to reduce the dependency of farms on plant protection products, while at the same time maintaining agricultural production at a high level in both quality and quantity terms. Cognac sector is very clearly involved in the Poitou Charente regional level of this national action plan. BNIC, together with regional Chambers of Agriculture and National French Institute of Vine and Wine (IFV France) conducts technical programs entering different focuses of Ecophyto 2018 plan, among which :

- Focus 1 : evaluation of progress on reduction of pesticide use is performed by the close monitoring of different farm networks, covering Cognac production area.
- Focus 2 : dissemination of known techniques for economic use of plant protection products is performed through the organisation of technical conferences, the edition of technical guidelines for good viticulture and environmental practices, the conception of an extranet website dedicated to environmental and safety questions and of a self-test diagnostic for vine-growers.
- Focus 3 : research and innovation in low-pesticide technical pathways and cropping systems. Long term research programs, in partnership with French National Institute for Agricultural Research (INRA) are being conducted in order to obtain new high quality grape varieties, with a sustainable resistance to downy and powdery mildew.

These programs use traditional breeding techniques and molecular marker assisted selection, in order to associate several resistance sources naturally present in *Vitis* and *Muscadinia* vines.

Evaluation of greenhouse gas emissions

In 2009, BNIC performed a global evaluation of Cognac sector Greenhouse Gas Emissions. To conduct this study, Cognac production activity was sequenced into three steps :

- vitivinicultural activity : from vineyard implantation to wine production
- distillation activity : from wine to wine spirit
- negoce activity : wine spirits ageing, blending, packaging and shipment

For each activity, detailed flow charts were established, inventorying all the inputs and outputs of each stage and assessing the GHG emissions of each source. As a whole, 162 emission items have been quantified, 63 for vitivinicultural activity, 37 for distillation and 62 for negoce activity. This database is now available to help Cognac sector companies, vine growers, distillers and negociants, to perform their own GHG emissions evaluations, and build their reduction action plans. It can also be used as a basis for other environmental studies on Cognac sector.

Treatment of distillery effluents

Management of effluent, by-products and waste is also a fundamental consideration in environmentally sustainable vitivinicultural activity. The distillation of 1 hl of wine produces 13 litres of wine spirit and 87 litres of distillation waste, known as "vinasses". Each year, between November and March, about 500 000 to 600 000 m^3 of vinasses are produced in Cognac region.

As soon as 1971, several major companies of Cognac area joined together to create REVICO, a wastewater plant dedicated to the treatment of Cognac region distillery effluents.

Today, four 5,000 m^3 anaerobic digesters are installed on REVICO site, near Cognac. They allow to dispose of 300.000 m^3 of vinasses produced each year by 140 distilleries, located within a 50 km radius from REVICO. The plant operates nine months a year – from November to July – processing approximately 80 truckloads of vinasses each day during peak season.

The process to break down the vinasses organic load produces significant amounts of methane biogas: about 1 850 000 m^3 of methane are produced on average every year. Since 1984, REVICO captures the methane and uses it to fuel steam generators which provide heat to the entire facility, including the four digesters and the large nearby greenhouses of Cognac municipality.

The anaerobic digesters allow to decrease by 95% the Chemical Oxygen Demand of the vinasses. The decrease is over 98% at the end of the aerobic finishing process. To complete the process, the final by-product of the digester system (dehydrated sludge) is combined with green waste and composted to be used in agriculture.

In 2008, REVICO decided to complete the facility's onsite-boiler system. A methane-fueled cogeneration system was installed. The innovative energy system now converts methane gas into thermal energy and electricity. It generates 3,300MW-hour per year of clean-and-green electricity and 4,500MW-hour per year of thermal energy, used to heat the four anaerobic digesters and warm Cognac city greenhouses.

The system produces enough electricity onsite to sell power to Électricité de France (EDF) through "Revico Energies Vertes", a joint venture between REVICO and "EDF Energies Nouvelles".

Besides this energetic valorisation, vinasses agronomic use can also be performed, by spreading in vineyards or other agricultural fields as organic fertilizer. The maximum use of 600hl/ha may bring back to the soil 13-17 units of Nitrogen, 10-18 of Phosphorus (P_2O_5), 49-77 of Potassium (K_2O) and 7 of Magnesium (MgO).

Conclusion

Adaptation to climate change, reduction of greenhouse gas emissions and of viticultural inputs, vineyard management in order to achieve economic sustainability, valorisation of effluents, answering safety, quality and environmental societal expectations are among the main challenges of sustainable vitiviniculture for the decades to come. Technical programs conducted by BNIC Station Viticole in these fields contribute to Cognac sector global approach of its sustainable development.

References

Appellation d'origine "Cognac" ou "Eau-de-vie de Cognac" ou "Eau-de-vie des Charentes", Décret n° 2009-1146 du 21 septembre 2009, French regulation.

Boitaud, L., Dumot, V., Ferrari, G., Lurton, L. (2010). Constat et incidences du Changement climatique dans la région de Cognac. Poster. XXXIIIème Congrès Mondial de la Vigne et du Vin, 20-27 juin 2010, Tbilisi (Géorgie).

Commission Regulation (EC) 110/2008 of 15 January 2008 on the definition, description, presentation, labelling and the protection of geographical indications of spirits drinks and repealing Council Regulation (EEC) n° 1576/89.

Coquand, H. (1858). Description physique, géologique, paléontologique du département de la Charente. T1, Besançon, 1858, T2, Marseille, 1860.

Coussié, J.V. (1996). Le Cognac et les aléas de l'histoire. Editions BNIC, Cognac.

Daux, V., Le Roy Ladurie, E., Mestre, O., Chevet, J.M. (2007). Températures et dates de vendanges en France. Actes du colloque «Réchauffement climatique, quels impacts probables sur les vignobles ?», Dijon 2007.

Dumot, V., Lacouture, J., Mazerolles, G., Lurton, L., Chaumet, J., Naullaud, J., Chetaneau, B. (1993). Les principaux types de sols viticoles charentais : observations sur leurs caractéristiques analytiques et agronomiques. In *Elaboration et connaissance des spiritueux*, édition BNIC, diffusion Lavoisier Tec et Doc, 37-47.

Dumot, V., Boitaud, L., Menard, E., Lambert, F., Catté, A., Ferrari, G., Snakkers, G., Lurton, L. (2010). Sélection clonale de l'Ugni blanc pour la production du Cognac. Poster. XXXIIIème Congrès Mondial de la Vigne et du Vin. 20-27 juin 2010, Tbilisi (Géorgie).

Huglin, P. (1986). Biologie et écologie de la vigne. 372 pages. Editions Lausanne, Paris.

Lafon, R., Lafon, J., Couillaud, P., (1964). Le Cognac, sa distillation. J.B. Baillère ed. Paris France.

O.I.V., (2007). World vinivinicultural statistics, 2007., report available on the International Organisation of Vine and Wine (OIV) website, www.oiv.int.

O.I.V., (2008). Guidelines for sustainable vitiviniculture : production, processing and packaging of products, Resolution CST 1/2008., available on the International Organisation of Vine and Wine (OIV) website, www. www.oiv.int.

O.I.V., (2011). State of the vitiviniculture world maket, March 2011, report available on the International Organisation of Vine and Wine (OIV) website, www.oiv.int.

O.I.V., (2011). International Code of Oenological Practices., document available on the International Organisation of Vine and Wine (OIV) website www.oiv.int.

Ravaz, L., (1900). Le Pays du Cognac. L. Cocquemard, imprimeur éditeur à Angoulême, France.

Chapter 3

The impact of peat source on the flavour of Scotch malt whisky

Barry Harrison
Scotch Whisky Research Institute, Riccarton, Edinburgh, EH14 4AP, United Kingdom

Introduction

In Scotch malt whisky production, the burning of peat during the kilning of malted barley is carried out to impart characteristic flavour attributes to certain whiskies (Swan and Howie, 1983). Traditionally, the levels of steam-volatile marker phenols and guaiacols are used as an indicator of peating level (Swan and Howie, 1983). Compounds belonging to these groups are generally considered to be important for peat smoke flavour, though a complete understanding of the compounds contributing to this flavour is yet to be obtained. The phenols and guaiacols found in peat smoke are derived from lignin or similar polyphenolic structural elements found in plants and these polyphenolic structures can vary depending on plant species (Higuchi, 1978; Vanbreemen, 1995; Vanderheijden and Boon, 1994). In addition, the levels of phenols and guaiacols in peat can also be influenced by the level of decomposition which the peat has undergone (Kirk, 1971).

In Scotland there are over one million ha of peatlands. As of 2004, the area of peatland being extracted by the Scotch whisky industry was less than 300 ha (approximately 0.03% of the total area in Scotland) (Harrison, 2007). There is, therefore, a large peat resource available. However, peat forms slowly, taking approximately 3000–4000 years to accumulate a depth of 1 m (Fuchsman, 1980), so particularly in localised areas it may not be considered a renewable resource and it may be the case that malt producers will be required to change their peat source in the future. Also, difficulties in gaining and maintaining planning permission for particular peatland extraction sites may limit the choices of peat source for malt producers.

It has been shown that the peat used for the production of peated whiskies can vary in chemical composition (Harrison, 2009). In that work, the variance in composition was found to be influenced both by the geographical source and the age of the peat. Such variation could ultimately be important for defining the flavour of particular whiskies. Therefore, an improved understanding of the potential flavour impact of whisky source would be useful to the industry should malt producers change their peat source, through choice or necessity, in the future.

In this work, chemically distinct peats from different sources in Scotland have been used to make new make spirit under carefully controlled laboratory conditions. Analysis of the new make spirits was then carried out in order to determine the impact of peat source on whisky flavour.

Materials and Methods

New make spirits

Peated new make spirits were produced on a laboratory scale using peat from six different geographical locations in Scotland which are used by the Scotch whisky industry: Castlehill (Islay), Gartbreck (Islay), Glenmachrie (Islay), Orkney, St Fergus (mainland), Tomintoul (mainland). Additionally, a laboratory scale unpeated new make spirit was produced as a control. New make spirits were all produced using the same green malt and yeast. All kilning, mashing, fermentation and distillation parameters were controlled to ensure that the influence of peat source on spirit flavour and composition could be determined. New make spirits were made in triplicate from each peat to demonstrate the reproducibility of the process.

Sensory analysis

Quantitative Descriptive Analysis (QDA), carried out by the Scotch Whisky Research Institute (SWRI) sensory panel, was used to provide a measure of the relative intensity of a range of pre-determined sensory attributes. The attributes studied were the peaty aromas listed on the SWRI's Flavour Wheel (Jack, 2003), namely: intensity of peaty aroma, burnt, medicinal and smoky. Also, the presence of "other new-make spirit aromas" was used as a single attribute to define any additional aromas. Each test sample was presented in a random order to each assessor, who was asked to score them in terms of intensity of each attribute. Scores were given on a line scale of 0–3 with intervals of 0.1.

Gas chromatography olfactometry/mass spectrometry (GC-O/MS)

New-make spirit samples were extracted into ethanol using solid phase extraction. The extracts were then analysed using a gas chromatograph. The flow from the gas chromatograph was split between an olfactory detection port and a mass spectrometer. The olfactory detection port allowed the detection of aroma active compounds by nose whilst the mass spectrometer was used to determine the identity of these compounds. To help determine which compounds were organoleptically most important, aroma extraction dilution analysis (AEDA) was carried out using dilution factors of 10, 100 and 1000. For quantification of aroma active compounds, the entire flow from the gas chromatograph was passed into the mass spectrometer. Quantification was based on compound peak areas relative to an internal standard peak area.

Results and discussion

Impact of peat source on flavour

Results of the QDA of peated new make spirits were analysed by principal components analysis (PCA) and the results are shown in Figure 1. This plot shows that, as a group, the spirits produced using the Islay peats generally gave the highest scores for peaty aroma attributes and the lowest for other new make characteristics. This was particularly true for Castlehill and Glenmachrie. St Fergus spirit generally scored low for peaty aromas. Tomintoul and Orkney were differentiated by a relatively high medicinal score for Tomintoul and a relatively high smoky score for Orkney. In this way, not only was the overall intensity of peaty aromas influenced by peat source, but also the balance of the individual peaty aroma attributes.

Relationship between new make spirit flavour and composition

Different peats were found to have an influence on new make spirit aroma. The next step was to try and determine the underlying compositional causes of these aroma differences. Therefore,

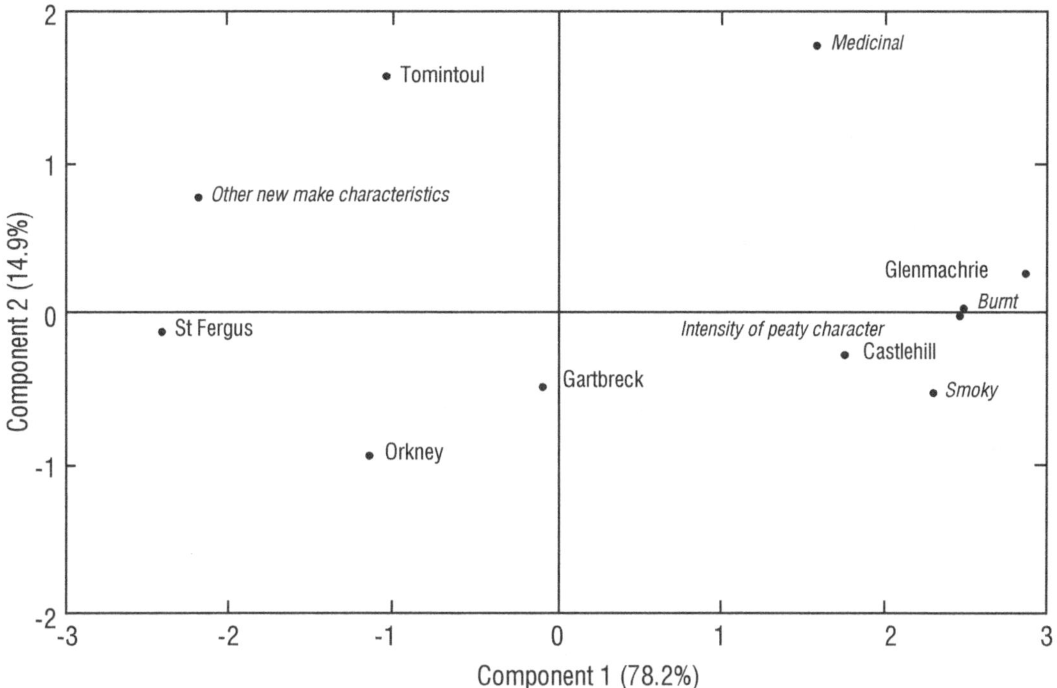

Figure 1. PCA of sensory scores for peaty aromas in new make spirits.

new make spirit samples produced from each of the six peat sources were extracted using SPE and the extracts analysed by GC-O/MS. One hundred and thirty nine aromas were detected in total. The aromas detected in these peated new make spirits were compared with those found in an unpeated new make spirit. In this way, it was possible to determine the aromas which were derived from peat. Seventy five peat-derived aromas were detected (Table 1). The peat-derived aromas represented a large proportion of the total number of aromas. It is clear, therefore, that the use of peat introduces a large number of potential variables which could influence spirit flavour. Forty two of the peat derived aromas had an identifiable compound or a clear mass spectrum associated with them (Table 1). Some aromas were found to have more than one compound eluting at that time making accurate identification difficult so all potential compounds are listed.

The GC-O/MS analysis yielded a large number of aromas derived from peat. To help determine which compounds were organoleptically most important, AEDA was carried out using the extract from the Castlehill spirit. There were 43 aromas with dilution values of 10 or more and compounds co-eluting with these aromas were detected in 33 cases (Table 1). All the identifiable phenols and guaiacols had dilution values of 10 or more. Twenty three aromas had dilution values of 100 or more and 21 of these had associated chromatographic peaks of which 11 were identified as relating to phenols or guaiacols. The four aromas with dilution values of 1000 or more were all identified as being derived from phenols or guaiacols. It was therefore apparent that phenols and guaiacols were major contributors to the peaty aromas of the new make spirits.

To help identify the compounds responsible for the sensory differences detected in the new make spirits, peat derived aroma compound levels were correlated with sensory scores using PCA (Figure 2). For this analysis, only compounds with dilution factors of 10 or over

Table 1. GC-O/MS aromas.

Aroma no. [a]	*Compound*	*Compound group* [b]	*Odour*	*Dilution factor*
1	?		Sulphury, burnt	1
2	1,1-Diethoxyhexane	o	Solvent	10
3	3-Methylcyclopentanone	o	Solvent, stale	10
4	?		Earthy, vegetably, dirty	1
5	?		Earthy, woody, stale	1
6	Ethyl trans-2-pentenoate	o	Earthy, stale	100
7	Styrene	o	Sweet, solvent	1
8	Ethyl 3-hexenoate	o	Sweet, solvent	1
9	?		Sweet, solvent	1
10	?		Earthy, stale	1
11	Ethyl heptanoate	o	Sweet, estery, solvent	1
12	?		Burnt, stale, sulphurs	1
13	?		Earthy, meaty	1
14	3-Ethylcyclopentanone	o	Earthy, solvent, burnt	10
15	Unknown (95,140)	o	Solvent, burnt	100
16	Ethyl 5-heptenoate	o	Sweet, solvent	100
17	?		Earthy, solvent, burnt	10
18	?		Earthy, stale	10
19	Unknown (67,110)	o	Earthy, stale	100
20	Ethyl 7-octenoate	o	Plastic, sweet	10
21	?		Earthy, stale	10
22	6-Hepten-1-ol	o	Green, musty	10
23a	Trimethylcyclopentenone	o	Earthy, stale	1
23b	Acetylfuran	o	Earthy, stale	1
24	2,3-Dimethyl-2-cyclopenten-1-one	o	Earthy, stale	10
25	Ethyl 8-nonenoate	o	Sweet, plasticy	1
26	?		Estery, herbal, sweet, minty, boiled potatoes, waxy	1
27	?		Herbal, plasticy, sweet	1
28	?		Plasticy, solventy	1
29	?		Plasticy	1
30	?		Earthy, stale	1
31	Acetylmethylfuran	o	Earthy, stale, green	100
32	?		Plasticy, herbal, sweet, earthy	1
33	?		Earthy, stale	10
34	Methylfuranylpropanone	o	Earthy, solvent,	100
35	?		Solventy, sweaty, earthy	1
36a	Dimethoxybenzene	o	Burnt, plasticy, sour, oily, solventy	1
36b	Pentanoic acid	o	Burnt, plasticy, sour, oily, solventy	1
36c	Ethyl undecanoate	o	Burnt, plasticy, sour, oily, solventy	1
37	?		Estery	10
38	1-Phenyl-2-propanone	o	Sweet, stale, earthy	1
39	?		Earthy, stale	100
40	Methylacetophenone 1	o	Estery, phenolic	100
41	?		Dirty, sour	1
42	?		Stale, spicy	1
43	Methylacetophenone 2	o	Estery, phenolic	100
44	Dimethoxytoluene 1	o	Burnt	1
45	2-Chlorophenol	p	Medicinal, TCP, plasters	10
46	Dimethoxytoluene 2	o	Smoky, burnt	10
47	Guaiacol	g	Smoky, spicy	1000
48	Unknown (123,138)	o	Spicy, medicinal, sweet	1

Aroma no. [a]	*Compound*	*Compound group* [b]	*Odour*	*Dilution factor*
49	Dimethylphenol 1	p	Plasters	1000
50	Hydroxymethylacetophenone	p	Plasters	10
51	Methoxymethylphenol	g	Smoky, sweet	1000
52	Methylguaiacol	g	Sweet, vanilla	10
53	Quinoline	o	Stale, earthy	100
54	o-Cresol	p	Medicinal	100
55	?		Plasters	10
56	Ethylguaiacol	g	Sweet, spicy	100
57	Unknown (137,152)	o	Sweet, spicy, burnt	100
58	2-Ethylphenol	p	Plasters	100
59	Dimethylphenol 2	p	Medicinal	100
60	Dimethylphenol 3	p	Medicinal	100
61a	p-Cresol	p	Barnyard	1000
61b	m-Cresol	p	Barnyard	1000
62	?		Vegetably, sour, manure	1
63	Propylguaiacol	g	Spicy	100
64	C3 phenol	p	Medicinal, burnt	10
65a	4-Ethylphenol	p	Barnyard, medicinal, spicy	100
65b	Eugenol	g	Barnyard, medicinal, spicy	100
66	3-Ethylphenol	p	Burnt, barnyard, medicinal	10
67	?		Burnt, stale	1
68	?		Plasticy, burnt, earthy	10
69	?		Plasters, burnt electrics	100
70	?		Burnt electrics	1
71	?		Burnt electrics, stale, oily	1
72	?		Burnt	10
73	?		Tarry, burnt	1
74	?		Tarry, burnt	1
75	?		Burnt	1

[a] Where more than one compound coeluted with an aroma, coeluting compounds are indicated by a letter after the aroma number.
[b] Compound groups: g = guaiacol, p = phenol, o = other.

were used in order to focus on the most aroma active compounds in the new make spirits.

The peaty attributes were all co-localised in the upper right quadrant of the plot. This reflected the fact that all of these aromas were generally most intense in the Castlehill and Glenmachrie spirits. Also, along component 2 there was a shift from the top of the component from medicinal aroma down to smoky aroma. This reflected the relatively high score that the Tomintoul spirit gave for medicinal. Compounds co-localising with the aroma descriptors on the PCA plot would be the most likely contributors to these aromas.

As a group, the phenols were found to be the most prominent compounds in the upper right quadrant of the plot. The aromas of the phenols, as described by GC-O/MS analysis, were generally described as medicinal. This result, combined with the fact that these compounds all had dilution factors of 10 or more, suggested that these compounds were major contributors to the peaty aromas, and in particular the medicinal aroma, of the spirits. Para/meta cresol (61a and b) and a dimethylphenol (49) had particularly high dilution factors of over 1000 so might be expected to be of major importance as contributors to aroma. Para and meta cresol eluted from the GC column close together making it difficult to determine which one was the main contributor to the detected aroma. However, analysis by the SWRI sensory panel has shown that para cresol has a lower aroma detection threshold (51 ppb compared to 578

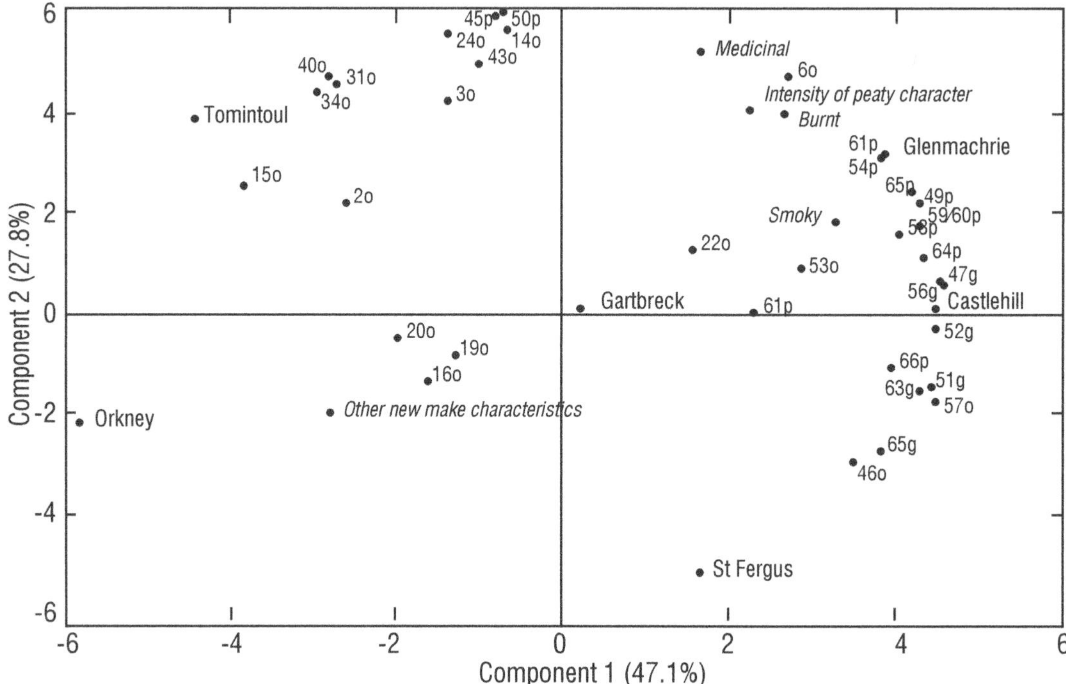

Figure 2. PCA of sensory and GC-O/MS data. Compounds are identified by aroma number and by compound group (see Table 1).

ppb for meta cresol) and was present in greater abundance in the new make spirits making this the more likely compound to have contributed to the strong aroma.

Whilst the phenols appeared particularly good candidates for explaining the medicinal aroma of new make spirit, the shift from medicinal to smoky along component 2 correlated with a shift in composition from phenols to guaiacols. As a group, the guaiacols also had dilution factors of 10 or more and had smoky, spicy or sweet aroma descriptors. Guaiacol (47) itself, along with a methoxymethylphenol (51) were likely to be particularly potent contributors to aroma with dilution factors of over 1000.

An abundance of particular phenols and guaiacols were found to be important for the high levels of peaty aromas in Islay, notably Castlehill and Glenmachrie, spirits. In general terms, the levels of these compounds can be influenced by both peat decomposition level and the type of vegetation contributing to the peat, and a combination of these factors has resulted in the Islay peats being rich in these aroma active compounds. Whilst the exact reason for the high levels of these compounds in the Islay peats was not obvious, some evidence obtained from previous analysis of the peats themselves pointed to potential causes (Table 2). This research suggested that the Islay peats may have contained a relative abundance of grassy vegetation and that this vegetation appeared to have undergone a relatively high level of decomposition compared to the other peats analysed.

The other notable sensory finding was that the new make spirit produced from Tomintoul peat had a relatively medicinal aroma (Figure 1). This was found to be related to a relative abundance of phenols (Figure 2). It is known that *Sphagnum* moss derived peat tends to contain relatively high levels of phenols relative to guaiacols (Vanderheijden and Boon, 1994). On visual inspection, *Sphagnum* remains could be more readily detected in the Tomintoul peat than the others, and this may therefore account

Table 2. Peat compositional data (Harrison, 2007).

Peat	*Lignin/ polyphenol*	*Lignin/polyphenol decomposition*	*Characteristic vegetation*
Islay	High	High	Grass
Orkney	Low	High	Heather
St Fergus	High	Low	Woody plants/trees
Tomintoul	Low	Low	Moss

for the relatively high levels of phenols and, therefore, the particular medicinal note of the Tomintoul new make spirit.

The compositional results for the St Fergus new make spirit were also interesting as this new make spirit generally contained relatively high levels of phenols and guaiacols yet scored low for all the peaty aromas (Figures 1 and 2). From the data in Figure 2 it was apparent that the St Fergus new make spirit was separated from the Islay spirits as it contained a relative abundance of guaiacols, particularly derivatives with long side chains, compared to phenols. This relative abundance probably related to the high level of undegraded woody material detectable in the St Fergus peat (Table 2). It would therefore appear that not only was the overall levels of phenols and guaiacols important for determining the levels of the peaty aromas but also the ratio of these compounds. It may be that a relative abundance of those guaiacols with long side chains which have sweet and spicy aromas decreases the overall perception of peaty aromas in the St Fergus new make spirit. Spiking experiments may help confirm the reason for this finding.

Whilst phenols and guaiacols appeared to play the main role in contributing to peaty aromas in new make spirit, there were a number of other aroma active congeners detected. Figure 2 shows those which had dilution factors of 10 or more. These compounds covered a range of compound families: acetals, alcohols, aromatics, carbonyls, esters and nitrogen compounds. Aromatic compounds imparting burnt, smoky, spicy and sweet aromas (46 and 57) were probably guaiacyl derivatives and may have contributed to the peaty aromas in a similar way to the guaiacols. The remaining compounds, which tended to be relatively abundant in those spirits which contained relatively low levels of phenols and guaiacols (Orkney and Tomintoul), may have contributed a variety of notes to the overall aroma of the spirit: solventy, earthy, burnt, sweet, green and estery. However, as these notes are those that might be expected in an unpeated spirit as well, it would be difficult to determine exactly how much the presence of such notes was due to the presence of these compounds as their perception could also be enhanced by the presence of a relatively low level of phenols and guaiacols.

Conclusions

Producing peated new make spirit on a laboratory scale, it was possible to see that peat source has an impact on spirit flavour. Compositional analysis of these spirits demonstrated that differences in both the overall levels of guaiacols and phenols and in the relative levels of these compounds contributed to the flavour differences. These new make spirit compositional differences could be related directly to the composition of the peat. Therefore, should malt producers change their peat source, they should be aware of the potential impact on spirit flavour.

Acknowledgements

This work was carried out as part of a PhD project funded by Suntory Limited.

References

Collins, E. (1974). Steam volatile components of roasted barley. *Journal of Agricultural and Food Chemistry* **19**: 533-535

Fiddler, W.; Doerr, R. C.; Wasserman, A. E. and Salay, J. M. (1966). Composition of hickory sawdust smoke. Furans and phenols. *Journal of Agricultural and Food Chemistry* **14**: 659-662

Fuchsman, C.H. (1980). *Peat: Industrial Chemistry and Technology*. Academic Press, London.

Harrison, B.M. (2007). *Peat Source and its Impact on the Flavour of Scotch Whisky*. PhD Thesis, Heriot Watt University.

Harrison, B. M. and Priest, F. G. (2009). Composition of peats used in the preparation of malt for Scotch whisky production – Influence of geographical source and extraction depth. *Journal of Agricultural and Food Chemistry* **57**: 2385-2391

Higuchi, T. (1978). Lignin structure and morphological distribution in plant cell walls. In: *Lignin Biodegradation- Microbiology, Chemistry and Potential Applications*. Edited by Kirk, T.K, Higuchi, T and Chang, H-M., CRC Press, Boca Raton, USA, pp 1-20

Jack, F.R. (2003). Understanding Scotch whisky flavour. *Food Science and Technology* **17**: 28-30

Kirk, T.K. (1971). Effects of microorganisms on lignin. *Annual Review of Phytopathology* **9**: 185-210

Swan, J. S. and Howie, D. (1983). Sensory and analytical studies on the regional composition of Scotch malt whiskies. In: *Current Developments in Malting, Brewing and Distilling*. Edited by Priest, F. G. and Campbell, I., Institute of Brewing, London, pp 129-142

Vanbreemen, N. (1995). How *Sphagnum* bogs down other plants. *Trends in Ecology & Evolution* **10**: 270-275

Vanderheijden, E. and Boon, J.J. (1994). A combined pyrolysis mass-spectrometric and light-microscopic study of peatified calluna wood isolated from raised bog peat deposits. *Organic Geochemistry* **22**: 903-919

Wasserman, A. E. (1966). Organoleptic evaluation of three phenols present in wood smoke. *Journal of Food Science* **31**: 1005-1010

Chapter 4

The case of cork

Miguel Cabral, Paulo Lopes & Isabel Roseira
Research & Development, Amorim & Irmãos, S. A. Rua das Meladas, 380, P. O. Box 20, Mozelos, 4536 – 902 Portugal

Introduction

Packaging has an important role in the success of any product. Products can have very high standards of quality but, to be sold, they need an attractive and modern packaging. Beverages in general and spirits in particular are not exception, all companies are trying to get the most attractive and different packaging in order to make a special appeal to the consumer.

The traditional spirits like Port and Cognac and also premium Whiskies have used always cork stoppers to close their bottles. Consumers are used to make the association between cork stoppers and high quality traditional spirits. New brands and also new types of spirits, in their strategy to be recognized as high quality premium beverages mimic packaging trends, where cork stoppers have an important role. This is the reason why more and more labels of Brandies, Tequilas and also Vodkas are using cork stoppers.

Cork industry has been modernized and has improved enormously in recent years. Nowadays, cork taint is not any more the wine defect more frequently recognized. Oxidation and reduction are bigger problems than cork taint. Cork stoppers are sustainable and renewable materials in opposite to the other alternative closures.

Cork industry is clearly prepared to face the challenge that wine and spirits industry makes in order to achieve premium markets. We want to be partners of that effort, and this presentation will show five reasons to believe that cork industry is prepared to face it.

Gas exchanges

After the work of Lopes, *et al.* (2006) it is well known the kinetics of oxygen ingress in a bottle when closed with different type of closures [Figure 1]. In fact three separate groups can be observed. The first group includes technical cork stoppers and screw cap saran tin, the second corresponds to natural cork stoppers and the third group to the synthetic closures.

When stored in horizontal position, technical cork stoppers, such as TwinTop and Neutrocork, introduce 0.7 – 0.8 ml of oxygen in the bottle during the first month of bottling and 0.002 – 0.0011 ml/month from the second up to 36 months of bottling. Screw cap saran-tin, allowed ingress of a mean of 1.1 ml of oxygen over 12 months of storage being 85-90% of the oxygen transferred in the first 2 days after bottling. The natural cork stoppers displayed

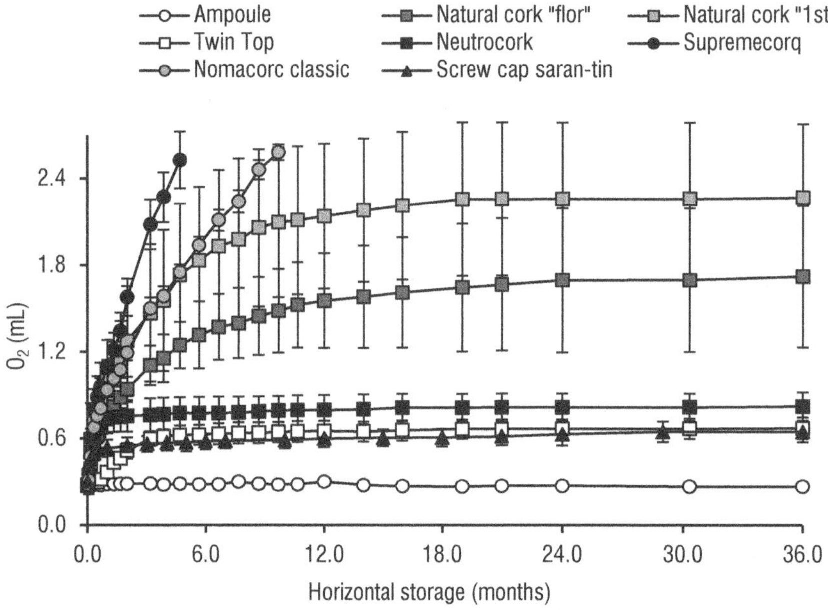

Figure 1. Kinetics of oxygen ingress through different closures into commercial bottles stored horizontally over 36 months. Error bars represent the standard deviation of four replicates

mean oxygen ingresses of 1.7 – 2.3 ml for flor and first grade respectively over 36 months. The ingress of oxygen was greater in the first month of storage, ranging from 0.7 – 1.3 ml of oxygen representing 28-53% of the overall ingress up to 36 months. Between the second and the 12th month the amount of oxygen that entered into the bottle varied between 0.03 to 0.17 ml of oxygen/month. Finally after the first 12 month in bottle, oxygen ingress/month ranged from 0,002 to 0,07 ml up to 36 months. Synthetic closures had high oxygen permeation reaching 2.5 ml of oxygen (limit of quantification) within 140 and 290 days after bottling. Respectively 35 and 45% of this oxygen ingress was observed during the first month, and 0.3 to 0.4 ml of oxygen/month in the others.

The main routes of oxygen ingress through wine bottles, was studied (Lopes, *et al.* 2007) using three type of closures, natural cork stoppers, technical cork stoppers and synthetic closures with three conditions each: normal closure introduced in the bottle; a ring of impermeable varnish between the cork glass interface and the top of the closures completely covered with a layer of impermeable varnish and a plate of glass glued in the top in order to prevent the air to enter the closures. These bottles were stored during 24 months in horizontal position and in a controlled atmosphere. The results clearly indicates that technical cork stoppers were essentially impermeable to atmospheric oxygen, natural corks diffuses oxygen, slowly but continuously, over the first 12 months of storage and no permeation was found between the cork glass interface and finally synthetic stoppers were completely permeable to oxygen mainly after the first month of storage.

A similar trend of oxygen ingress in bottle was found with closures used to seal white spirits. A microagglomerate cork (Neutrotop) a Bartop cork (Top Series) and two synthetics T corks (Ribbeb and Supremecorc) were used to check the oxygen ingress in bottle using the same method described by Lopes *et al.* in 2005. After 9 months in bottle the synthetics allowed a double oxygen ingress than the cork stoppers, confirming the same trend found when using closures for wine.

Exogenous compounds, like 2,4,6-trichloroanisole (TCA), 4-ethylphenol (EP) and 4-ethylguaiacol (EG) can be present in wine cellars or in transport containers, so they can contaminate wine and spirit bottles, if they can penetrate throughout the closures. Two experiments were made to access this hypothesis. In the first experiment (Lopes, *et al.* 2011), bottles with wine model solution were closed with microagglomerate Neutrocork and natural cork stoppers and with the synthetic Nomacorc classic and were stored separately in a contaminate environment with deuterium-labeled TCA (d5- TCA). After 24 months high concentrations of d5-TCA were found in the wine stimulants closed with synthetic stoppers but none was detected in bottles closed with both type of cork closures [Figure 2].

In the second experiment, bottled wine sealed with natural and microagglomerate cork stoppers, two types of synthetic closures with different levels of permeability and screw caps saranex were stored under a contaminated environment with d5- TCA, d4- EP and d4-EG. Over a period of 12 months the wine was accessed for these compounds, and they were found in wine sealed with screw cap saranex and Nomacorc light, but again no compounds were found in wine sealed with cork stoppers. The closures were divided in three parts and analyzed for the presence of the same contaminated compounds. These were found in the top of all the cylindrical closures, because of the exposure of this area to the contaminated environment, but in the middle of the cylindrical closures, just the synthetics were contaminated, indicating that the contamination of the wine with these compounds is a matter of time (Lopes *et al.* 2011).

In conclusion it is clear that synthetic stoppers allow not just oxygen but also other volatile compounds to ingress throughout the closure and be found in the wine. Conversely, cork stoppers are not permeable to any of these compounds, and the oxygen that diffuses into wine comes from the cell structure of the cork stoppers

Off – flavors

In the nineties, cork stoppers had significant problems of off-flavors, mainly TCA, that were responsible for a new born of the industry. In fact, cork industry had two alternative ways to go: or keep the same way as ever, and the result would be their dead, or change in the way of dealing with raw material, innovate in processes and in products and, of course, try to solve the TCA problem. This was the way how the industry went, and this work will present the results already achieved.

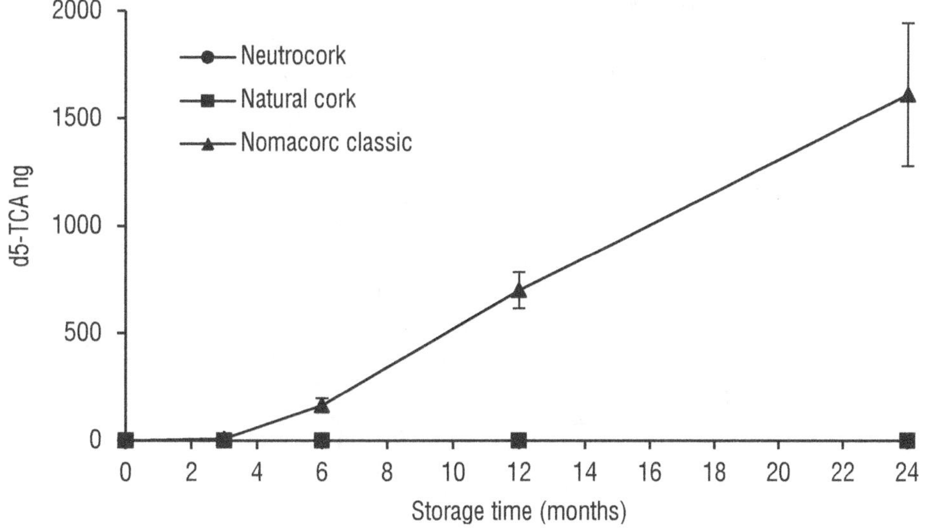

Figure 2. D5-TCA in bottled wine model solutions sealed with different closures during 24 months. Values per each analysis point an per closure are the mean of five replicates

According to the different type of products, different curative processes are used to extract TCA. INOS II is used since 1998 and contributes to the extraction of TCA in cork disks used in the production of Champagne corks and Twintop corks and also in Top Series corks used in spirits. The process uses different cycles of pressure and vacuum in order to profit of the elastic characteristics of cork, allowing hot water to come in and out of the cork holes. This process reduces in average 40% of TCA present in cork disks. ROSA, Rate of Optimal Steam Application, is applied in cork granules since 2004. TwinTop, Neutrocork and Neutrotop cork stoppers are made using these treated granules. The process is a basic steam distillation that reduces, in average, 80% of the TCA present in cork granules. ROSA Evolution is a curative process applied to natural corks since 2007. This process is able to extract the same amount of TCA in natural corks as ROSA in cork granules, but has the advantage of preventing the deformation of the stoppers, through a smooth but efficient decontamination treatment. Vaporization is a process used in cork bark. Before punching, cork bark is vaporized to extract TCA and also to homogenize the humidity. We have got around 40% of TCA reduction with this treatment. In complement to the curative processes, a very thigh quality control, where all lots of cork granules, disks and natural stoppers are analyzed by Gas Chromatography was implemented. Around 600 cork soaks are analyzed for releasable TCA in a daily base in 10 Gas Chromatography equipments.

In summary, it is clear that the strategy that cork industry implemented against TCA was responsible for the improvement in quality of the products, as ever happen. This is shown by results carried out at ETS laboratories who found a reduction of 82% of TCA in natural corks arrived in USA being 90% of the samples bellow 1ng/l, in 2011 (http://www.corkqc.com/newsandpress/cnews 2.htm) [Figure 3].

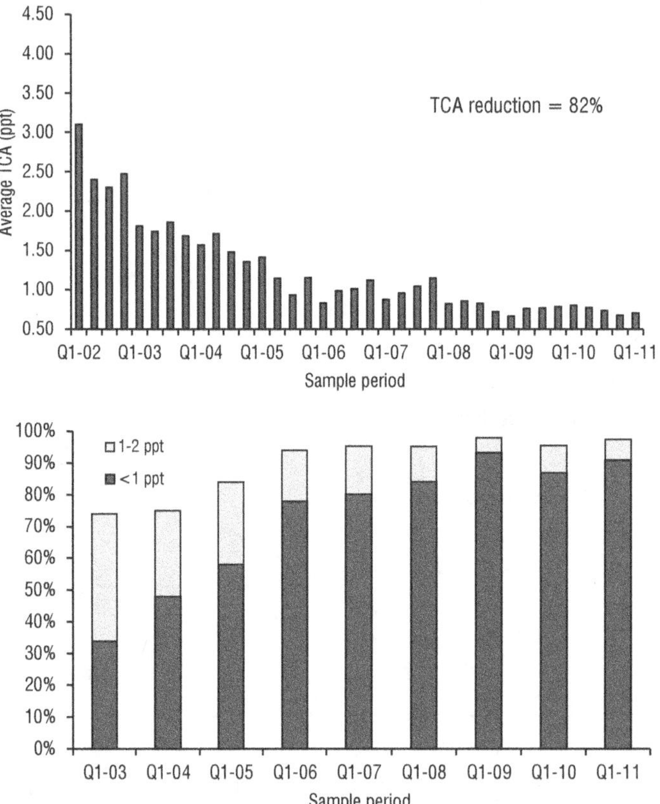

Figure 3. TCA results obtained by ETS laboratories analyzing natural cork stoppers shipments of the members of Cork Quality Council in the United States

Mechanical properties

Physical- mechanical parameters of cork stoppers, used to seal spirit bottles, were not extensively studied. Specific weight could be a predictive marker for cork performance. We launch a bottling experiment using TopSeries Natural cork and Neutrotop cork stoppers belonging to 3 different groups of specific weight. Natural corks have specific weights between < 140 kg/m^3; 165 - 175 kg/m^3 and > 200 kg/m^3 . Neutrotop ranged between < 270 kg/m^3; 300 - 310 kg/m^3 and > 335 kg/m^3. The corks sealed bottles with 50% ethanolic solution were stored upright and in inverted position. After 6 and 12 months the absorption and the extraction strength was measured in 10 bottles each. The results already indicate that, as expected, absorption is higher in natural corks than in Neutrotop corks and is higher when bottles are stored in inverted position. Normally higher densities gave less absorption.

In conclusion, it was not possible to obtain a clear different performance of spirit corks, neither natural nor technical, based on specific weight. It is necessary to wait until the 18th month of analysis to see if a clear difference is going to appear, allowing specific weight to be used as a quality differentiation tool in TopSeries corks.

Sustainability

Nowadays, the trend for natural products is a reality of the modern societies. Packaging assumes the same rule, and the return to cork is a clear assumption of this trend by the market. Since the beginning of the XXI century, technical corks have increased their presence in the market due to their very interesting technical performance and price range. To be in line with the market trend for natural products, cork industry has the objective of producing a 100% natural technical cork stopper, so new natural agglomeration glues and natural surface treatments has been seached.

The agglomeration polyurethane-based glues used in technical cork stoppers have some specifications, very difficult to comply. They need to be reactive with cork, compressible, chemically stable in long time contact with ethanolic solutions, sensorial inert and approved to be in contact with food materials. Different products have being tested, so far, but practically none of them were able to meet the requirements. To be approved after production, cork stoppers must be submitted to hard physical mechanical tests, based on ISO norms. Just starch based glues were able to pass this strict quality control program, however, in bottle, these corks were absorbing significant amounts of liquid responsible for a certain extent of leakage. At this stage, none of the products tested can be used as an alternative natural adhesive.

Surface treatments are used to lubricate corks stoppers during bottle insertion and extraction. The normal surface treatments used are based on paraffin and silicones but some natural waxes aspire to be natural alternatives to them. Bee or Candelilla waxes are among these products, which are being tested in bottling experiments. New products need to have sensorial inertia, being able to gave normal extraction strength and keep as low as possible the absorption.

In conclusion, cork industry is not too far for being able to produce a 100% natural technical cork stoppers. Projects for natural agglomeration glues are under way, but some difficulties seem to appear in reaching the expected performance. More easy seems to be the natural surface treatments, where different products can be use to replace the paraffin's and silicones probably already during the next year.

Colour migration

White spirits, like Vodka, Tequila, Gin, Genebra, Rum, etc. have some constrains in the use of natural cork stoppers, because of the extraction of colour phenolic compounds. In fact it is well known the yellowish colour presented by these beverages when cork stoppers are used to close their bottles.

With the objective of solving this problem, we were hardly searching for treatments that can be applied to the surface of cork stoppers acting as mechanical barriers for those compounds. After a significant number of treatments tested, we arrive to a product that was applied to Top Series natural corks and was able to fulfil the specifications required: impermeable to colouring matter, chemically stable, with thermal and mechanical resistance, transparent, flexible and with adherence to cork. After fine tuned the industrial application of this treatment to cork stoppers, bottling experiments were made to see the efficacy of the treatment in cork stoppers closing bottles of Tequila, Vodka and Gin. After 383 days in accelerated conditions, 35°C with manual agitation, the white spirits keep their colorless which was not the case of the same beverages when closed with cork stoppers without this treatment [Figure 4].

Conclusion

Increasing knowledge about cork stoppers, how they perform, their advantages, their limitations, etc. is an objective that we pursue to be able to supply top quality corks into the market.

Knowing better the permeability of corks and comparing it with alternative closures; making cork better than ever, avoiding TCA or off-flavour compounds; creating new attributes in the product like a new classification based on physical–mechanical performance, making corks a 100% bio product and catering new markets. We are making important steps forward to the success of the strategy we have defined.

Already in the market for centuries, we are sure that all the present innovation will guarantee a bright future for this natural and renewable product for next generations

References

Paulo Lopes Juliana Marques, Cátia Alves, Maria Pimenta, Isabel Roseira, Adélio Mendes, Miguel Cabral (2011). Permeation of volatile phenols and haloanisoles via vapor phase through different closures into wine. *In XXXIV World Congress of vine and wine June 20-27, Porto, Portugal*

Lopes, P.;Marques, J. Lopes, T.; Lino, J.; Coelho, J.; Alves, C., Roseira, I., Mendes, A.; Cabral, M.(2011). Permeation of d_5-2,4,6-trichloroanisole via vapor phase through

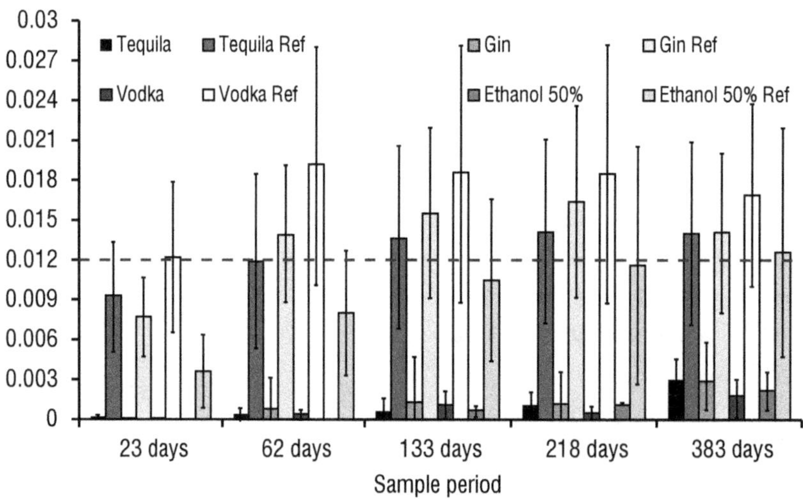

Figure 4. Color results obtained in Tequila, Vodka, Gin and Hidroalcoholic solution sealed with Top Series Natural corks treated and untreated with the color barrier treatment. Each bar corresponds to the average of 10 bottles. The dashed line represents the visual threshold.

different Closures into Wine Bottles during 24 Months of Storage. Am. *J. of Vit. and Enol.*, 62, 245-249.

Lopes, P.; Saucier, C.; Teissedre, P.L.; Glories, Y. (**2006**). Impact of storage position on oxygen ingress through different closures into wine bottles. *J. Agric. Food Chem.*, *54*, 6741-6746

Lopes, P.; Saucier, C.; Teissedre, P.L., Glories, Y. (**2007**). Main routes of oxygen ingress through different closures into wine bottles. *J. Agric. Food Chem.*, *55*, 5167-5170.

Chapter 5

Near Infrared Reflectance (NIR) used as a predictive tool for Canadian Whisky Ageing

Don Livermore

Pernod Ricard United States – Canada Technical Centre, Windsor, Ontario, Canada

Introduction

The current quality assurance test used in the Canadian whisky industry for cask management is visual appearance (Brown, L. 1994). There is not a developed analytical procedure which determines cask quality. The overall aim of this study was to be able to predict the wood extract potential of a whisky cask prior to filling with Canadian base (grain) whisky by using a rapid, non-destructive analytical technique. The goal was to optimize the management of cask inventories at a Canadian whisky distillery. Wood extractives which are considered important for the quality casks in other spirits and wines are 5-hydroxymethylfurfural, furfural, 5-methylfurfural, furfuryl alcohol, cyclotene, guaiacol, 4-ethylguaiacol, *cis*-whisky lactone, *trans*-whisky lactone, creosol, maltol, eugenol, 4-ethylphenol, syringol, vanillin, and syringaldehyde (Otsuka, K., *et al.* 1974; Nishimura, K. *et al.* 1983; Piggott, J.R, Lee, K.Y., and Paterson. A. 2001). Therefore, it was decided to focus on these compounds for Canadian whisky.

The first part of the study was to establish a "real time" profile of wood extractives entering base Canadian whisky over a three year time period – the minimum age requirement according to Canadian law (Health Canada 2010). The flexibility of the Canadian whisky law allows for different types of casks to be used. The rates of the migration of wood extractives into the spirit may vary with the type of cask. Typical casks used for the Canadian whisky industry include casks which have been used multiple times, casks with various char depths, once used American bourbon casks, refurbished casks that have been recharred, and casks with that have been filled with other wines or spirits. Wood extraction fundamentals are important knowledge for each type of cask treatment to better understand the maximum potential yield of oak wood for blending Canadian whisky.

The difficulty with wood cask research is the time it takes to achieve results. If subsequent trials are required based on the results from the first experiment it could take years to produce final conclusions. To expedite research time a bench top ageing procedure which mimics a cask environment using wood discs with various charring treatments was developed, compared, and extrapolated to the "real time" three year ageing study. Wood extracts from the bench top ageing procedure were measured by gas chromatography mass spectrometry (GCMS) methods used for other spirits or wines (Gonzalez-Arjona, D., *et al.* 1999; Guillen,

M.D., and Manzanos, M.J. 2002; Perez-Coello, M.S., *et al.* 1997; Garde-Cerdan, T., *et al.* 2004).

Extraction fundamentals would be better understood if component concentration of oak wood were known prior to the ageing process. The components which can be measured by chemical digestive means are neutral detergent solubles (NDS), hemicellulose, lignin, cellulose, and char. Standard wet chemical procedures have been developed for wood analysis, however these methods are destructive and wood samples cannot be used for further ageing experimentation after digestion (Hatfield, R., and Fukushima, R.S. 2005; Goering, H.K., and Van Soest, P.J. 1975; Van Soest, P.J. 1967; Saeman, J.F., *et al.* 1944). A non-destructive technique such as NIR equipped with fibre optics to measure wood components is ideal for a comparison study.

If NIR calibration models for wood components on charred casks can be developed it could be possible to study correlations between the wood component concentration measured by NIR prior to ageing, and the wood extract potential measured by GCMS after the ageing process. Wood extractives which are lignin derived are vanillin, guaiacol, cresol, 4-ethylguaiacol, eugenol, 4-ethylphenol, syringol, and syringaldehyde (Piggott, J.R, Lee, K.Y., and Paterson. A. 2001). Via regression analysis the lignin component measured by NIR prior to ageing could be compared to the total lignin derived extractives measured by GCMS after the ageing process. Likewise, hemicellulose derived products includes furfural, 5-methylfurfural, furfuryl alcohol, cyclotene, maltol, and 5-hydroxymethylfurfural extracted could be compared via regression analysis to the hemicellulose component prior to ageing (Nishimura, K., *et al.* 1983). If a correlation could be established with the NIR results and the GC extract results, the NIR can be used as a rapid predictability test.

Wood extractives are at concentration levels less than 0.01% (w/v) in various alcoholic beverages (Garde-Cerdan, T., and Ancin-Azpilicueta, C. 2006; Caldeira, I., *et al.* 2006). To develop reliable NIR calibration models guidelines typically dictate the component of interest should be above 0.1% (EMEA 2003). On the surface of oak casks, wood extractives may be at high enough concentrations to be quantifiable by NIR. An additional aim of the study was to develop NIR calibration models directly to the total wood extractives. Wood extractives are developed either by thermal degradation prior to ageing or from ethanolysis during the ageing process (Mosedale, J.R. and Puech, J.L. 1998; Mosedale, J.R. and Puech, J.L. 2003). The NIR measurement could only measure the thermally degraded wood extractives not extractives developed by ethanolysis. Therefore calibration models a various time intervals during the ageing process would have to be developed in order to determine the point where extraction from ethanolysis surpasses extraction from thermal degradation. If the total wood extract calibration models are reliable then the need for NIR calibration models for wood components (NDS, hemicellulose, lignin, cellulose, and char) would not be required for the determination of overall cask quality.

Materials and methods

GC analysis

The chromatographic analyses were carried out using a Varian CP-3800 gas chromatograph connected to a Varian 2200 Saturn mass spectrometer (Palo Alto, California, U.S.A.). A VF-WAXms capillary column of 30 m X 0.25 mm ID and 0.50 μm film thickness from Varian (Palo Alto, California, U.S.A.). Helium with the purity of 99.999% from Praxair (Danbury, Connecticut, U.S.A.) was the carrier gas with a constant flow of 1.5 mL/min with a split injection setting of 2. As the helium enters the injector, it was heated to 250°C. Initial oven temperature was set at 35°C and held for 2 min; then an increase of temperature of 7.5°C/min to 60°C and held for 0.50 min; then an increase in temperature of 15°C/min to 150°C and held for 0.75 min; then an increase in temperature of 15°C/min to 240°C and held for 14.42 min.

Three year ageing trial in 197 L casks

Four cask types used in the Canadian whisky industry were chosen for this study. Oak wood casks were designated as cask type 1 through 4. Barrels were placed upright on a pallet of six. Therefore, in total there were 24 barrels in the study. Bung holes were located on the side of the cask placed there from the original design of the cask manufacture. A second bung hole was cut through the top barrel head to fill upright on a pallet. All casks were standard American bourbon barrels in size, which had contained 197 L of spirit. The storage conditions were held close to room temperature (20°C), with some fluctuation with the heating and cooling system.

The spirit that was selected for the cask was a typical double distilled (DD) base whisky spirit that was distilled to 94.8% alcohol by volume at the Hiram Walker distillery (Walkerville, Ontario, Canada) but reduced to cask strength before it was filled. Sampling of the spirit occurred at 30, 60, 120, 365, 730, and 1095 days of age and was measured by the GCMS for 5-hydroxymethylfurfural, furfural, 5-methylfurfural, furfuryl alcohol, cyclotene, guaiacol, 4-ethylguaiacol, *cis*-whisky lactone, *trans*-whisky lactone, creosol, maltol, eugenol, 4-ethylphenol, syringol, vanillin, and syringaldehyde.

NIR

All the analyses of wood samples were performed on a Bruker Equinox 55 NIR (Ettlingen, Germany) spectrometer. The accessory used was a fibre optic fused silica cable that had a core diameter of 600 μm.

Wood samples were presented to the fibre optic probe without sample preparation. Spectral measurements were carried out by moving the tip of the fibre probe along the surface of interest, with a light to moderate pressure applied against the wood surface. It was important that the probe remained in contact with the surface during the time allotted for scanning, yet not to move the probe with such force to dislodge sections of the wood sample. This was particularly difficult when scanning the inside surface of the stave which had blistered, or thick char due its fragile nature. After the scan was completed, the spectrum was reviewed to determine if there was excess spectral noise from the measurement. This was evident if the spectrum that had sharp, random peaks, as opposed to smooth rounded peaks. Spectral noise was typical when pieces of char were trapped between the probe tip and the wood sample as the probe was moved along the wood surface, or if the probe did not maintain a tangential angle to the sample, or if the probe was lifted from the surface of the wood sample. If spectral noise was evident, a second measurement was made and the first spectrum was discarded. All wood samples that were scanned by the fibre optic probe were at room temperature, and ambient humidity.

The spectral measurements were measured in triplicate, and averaged using the commercial software program OPUS version 4.0 (Bruker, Ettlingen, Germany). To create a calibration model, four spectral scans were used for development – the average spectrum, and the three spectra that made up the average. All four samples were entered into the calibration model were defined as the same wet chemistry result. Whenever possible, a full range of expected wet chemical values were added to the calibration to optimize and develop a robust model.

To properly optimize a calibration model a number of frequency ranges and data preprocessing methods were used and determined empirically by trial and error. For all the calibration models 40 – 50 different combinations of frequency ranges, and data preprocessing steps were evaluated. The OPUS software determined the optimal number of partial least squares (PLS) ranks used for the cross validation. The root mean square error of cross validation (RMSECV), coefficient of determination (R^2), ratio error ranges (RER), and ratios of performance deviation (RPD) were also used as indicators of the accuracy of the calibration model.

The American Association of Cereal Chemists set calibration model performance criteria for RER guidelines: ≥ 4 the model is acceptable for screening, ≥ 10 the model is acceptable for quality control, and ≥ 15 the model is acceptable for quantification (AACC 1999). A suggested rule by the agro market for NIR analysis of wheat is that when a RPD between 2 and 3 the calibration model is OK for rough screening. RPD > 3 the calibration model is OK for screening; RPD > 5 the calibration model is good for quality control. An RPD > 8 indicates that the calibration model is excellent for analytical tasks (Williams, P.C. 1997). The larger the RER and RPD indicates reliability of the calibration model.

In order to determine the robustness and to validate NIR calibration models, an external test set validation system was used. For an external test set validation, two sets of independent sample sets from the developed calibration models were used. One sample set was used as a calibration, and the other sample set was used to validate the corresponding calibration model. To obtain two independent sample sets, the developed calibration models were randomly split in half and compared against the cross validations to determine the root mean square error of prediction (RMSEP). It was ensured that calibration test sets covered the full variation of sample set in order to present a meaningful challenge to the calibration model.

Wet chemistry for wood component Analysis

The wet chemistry used for NIR calibration of neutral detergent solubles (NDS), hemicellulose, lignin, cellulose, and char was determined using a VELP Scientfica (Usmate, Italy) FIWE 3 extraction unit. The instrument was outfitted with three condenser tubes that held three glass crucibles. A sequential analysis system was used to determine wood components where a 1 g sample was used to determine the concentration of wood components. Prior to the wet chemical measurement, the NIR spectrum was determined in the area of interest which included the outside of cask, inner charred surface, below the charred surface, or the edge. The first component measured was NDS and the residue following the measurement was used for hemicellulose determination. Likewise, the residue following hemicellulose was used for lignin extraction by permanganate, then a 72% (w/w) sulfuric acid extraction for cellulose. The final residue after NDS, hemicellulose, lignin, cellulose extractions was determined as char.

The rapid 60 day bench top wood ageing trial

Circular discs from various whisky staves were manufactured for the purpose of ageing in ethanol (Figure 1). Staves were selected from cask type 1, 3, and 4. One surface of the disc was charred, and the opposite surface was non-char which had never been exposed to a flame. The surface area of the discs was calculated.

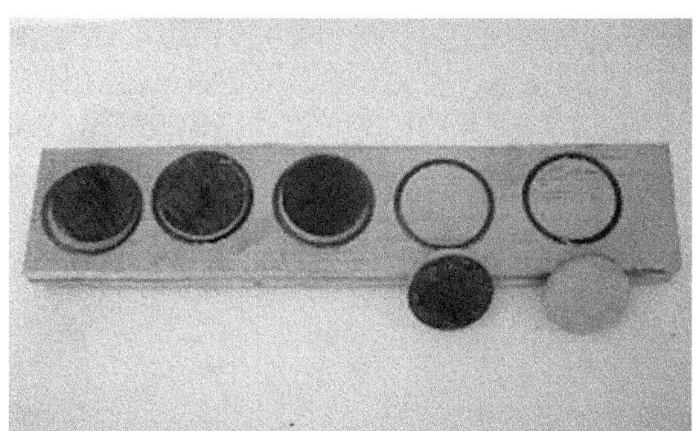

Figure 1. A stave during the manufacturing of the discs for the rapid 60 day ageing trial. Discs were 32 mm in diameter and ranged 2 – 7 mm in thickness.

Prior to exposing the discs to ethanol each surface was analyzed with the NIR fibre optic probe. Discs were then placed in 100 mL of ethanol at 60% (v/v) (Figure 2). At the 10, 30, and 60 day interval the wood extractives were measure using the GCMS protocol for furfural, 5-methylfurfural, furfuryl alcohol, cyclotene, guaiacol, *cis*-whisky lactone, creosol, *trans*-whisky lactone, maltol, 4 ethyl-guaiacol, eugenol, 4-ethylphenol, syringol, hydroxymethylfurfural, vanillin, and syringaldehyde. The spirit was also analyzed for total tannin content using wet chemical methods.

Figure 2. A representation of the rapid 60 day wood ageing trials at various stages. The first bottle is base whisky. The middle bottle is day 1 and the last bottle is at the end of the ageing process.

After the ageing process the discs were removed from the spirit, dried in an oven for a short period of time, and left over night at room temperature to cool. The discs were analyzed again by the NIR probe, and the changes in neutral detergent solubles, hemicellulose, lignin, cellulose, and char were determined over the 60 day period. A regression analysis was used to determine if the NIR calibration models could be used as a predictive tool. Also, NIR calibration models for total wood extract were developed for the char, non char, and averaged char – non char surfaces, in order to predict the performance of a cask.

Results

Three year ageing trial in 197 L casks

The total wood extractives were plotted versus time. A logarithmic, linear, exponential, and power trend lines for each barrel type was calculated. The trend line which had the R^2 closest to 1 was determined to be optimal. In the case of total wood extractives for each cask type the power trend line was chosen and an equation with its R^2 was determined (Figure 3).

At the end of the three year period there was a significant difference in total wood extractives of all four barrel types Cask type 1 had the highest total extract on day 1095 with 90000

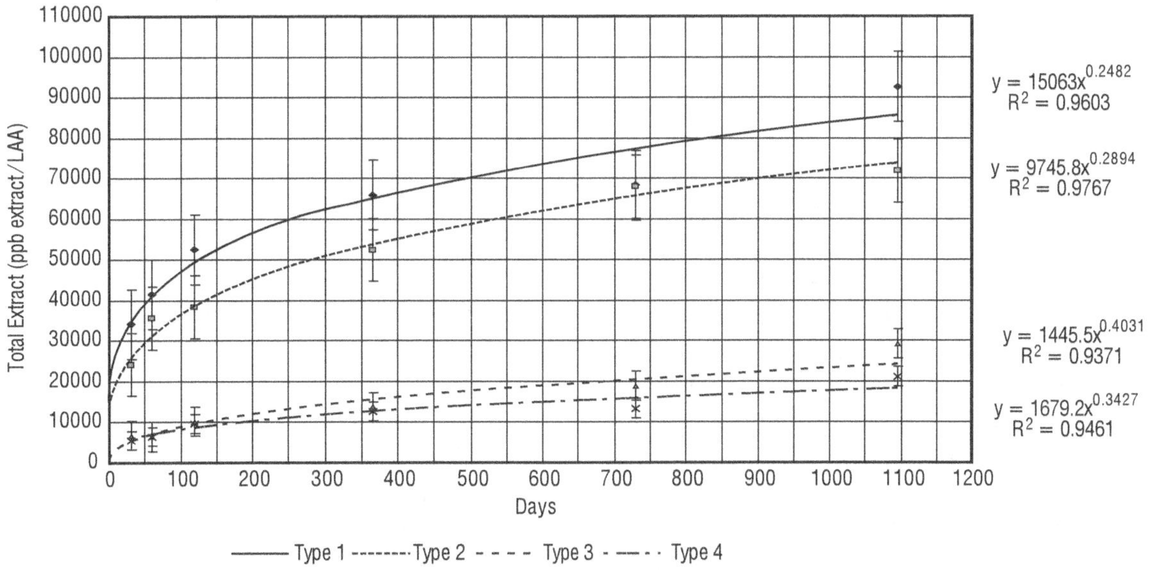

Figure 3. The total wood extractivess on a ppb absolute alcohol basis versus time in four types of Canadian whisky barrels. The wood extracts include furfural, 5-methylfurfural, furfuryl alcohol, cyclotene, guaiacol, *cis*-whisky lactone, creosol, *trans*-whisky lactone, maltol, 4 ethyl-guaiacol, eugenol, 4-ethylphenol, syringol, hydroxymethylfurfural, vanillin, and syringaldehyde. Each point represents the average of 6 casks with a calculated standard error bar.

ppb extract/LAA (litres of absolute alcohol) compared to cask type 2 with 70000 ppb extract/LAA. Cask type 3 total wood extract was slightly higher than the cask type 4 with 30000 ppb of extract/LAA compared to 18000 ppb of extract/LAA. There could be as much as three to five times more total wood extractives from one cask type to another by the end of a three year period. This is a significant concentration difference for a Canadian whisky blender when devising formulations based on wood content and demonstrates the variability in casks sold in the market place.

For all four cask types the wood extractives quickly enter the whisky and slow over time. Depending on the barrel type the deceleration phase for cask type 3 and 4 started between days 20 to 30, and for cask type 1 and 2 the deceleration commences at days 50 to 60. Within the deceleration phase the balance of wood extract from thermal degradation versus ethanolysis changes. The thermal degradation process creates "free" by-products and migrates out of the wood cask and dissolves into the spirit quickly. After deceleration phase, the total wood extract continues to increase in time. However, it is much slower because of the ethanolysis process – where ethanol acts as a solvent and cleaves free ends off the cellulose, hemicellulose, and lignin molecules to contribute to the total wood extract.

NIR calibration of wood components

The wood components NDS, hemicellulose, lignin, cellulose, and char were determined using the wet chemical methods. Samples were taken at various locations of the cask including the char and non-char surfaces and the heads and bottoms of the cask. The number of samples used in the calibration model after removing the outliers was 640. It is evident that it is possible to calibrate the NIR to measure neutral detergent solubles, hemicellulose, lignin, cellulose, and char; but only for screening purposes (Table 1). The models were not reliable for quality control purposes since the RPD and RER were below guidelines. The order of reliability for the calibration models was hemicellulose, char, cellulose, lignin, and then NDS. The accuracy of the NIR calibration models may be improved if different wet chemical methodologies, or different NIR measurement techniques.

Thermal degradation of staves can be controlled by temperature and length of burn. Extractable material such as hemicellulose, lignin, and cellulose converts into non-extractable material such as char (Di Blasi, C. 2009). When a barrel is thermally degraded, it cracks, blisters, and becomes brittle, thus opening it up for the spirit to come into contact with the slightly charred or non-charred layers underneath and the extractable material into the spirit. A longer or hotter burn will create a thicker layer of char which has converted the hemicellulose, cellulose, and lignin which is not efficient in terms of wood extraction yields. Char is a form of activated carbon that has absorptive properties (Suhas, *et al* 2007). This can have benefits for subtractive reactions in a cask which is not necessarily detrimental to the overall quality of whisky. Samples from the NIR calibration data were divided into three categories: less than 25% char, 25 – 50% char, and greater than 50% char (Figure 4). As the level of thermal degradation increased, the component which was most susceptible to heat was hemicellulose as it had the greatest relative change when the relative char level increased. The wood component order of thermal susceptibility is hemicellulose, cellulose, NDS, and then lignin.

The rapid 60 day bench top wood ageing trial

The manufactured oak wood disc samples come from a number cask types and location within the cask. Also the depth and degree of char varied. Total extractives for each individual cask treatment were measured by the GCMS at day 10, 30, and 60. The intention of the experiment was to determine if the disc study could replicate or predict a three year ageing process of a 197 L

Table 1. The standard error of performance and external validation of the neutral detergent solubles, hemicellulose, lignin, cellulose, and char NIR calibration models. For brevity only the optimal calibration models are shown.

Calibration method	*Data range (%)*	*Data pre-processing*	*Frequency range (cm^{-1})*	*PLS factors*	*Cross validation*				*First test set validation*				*Second test set validation*			
					RMSECV	*R^2*	*RPD*	*RER*	*RMSEP*	*R^2*	*RDP*	*RER*	*RMSEP*	*R^2*	*RPD*	*RER*
Neutral detergent solubles	15.57	FD sp% + VN	8000-4300	4	2.65	57.14	1.53	5.88	2.68	56.21	1.51	5.81	2.64	56.94	1.52	5.90
Hemicellulose	25.98	SD sp 17	8000-4300	5	2.13	92.86	3.74	12.20	2.17	92.56	3.67	11.97	2.04	93.43	3.90	12.74
Lignin	21.45	SD sp 21	8000-4300	6	2.42	70.30	1.83	8.86	2.42	70.02	1.83	8.86	2.50	68.47	1.78	8.58
Cellulose	52.72	SD sp 17	8000-4300	5	7.22	78.15	2.14	7.30	7.43	76.82	2.08	7.10	7.02	79.37	2.20	7.51
Char	84.68	FD sp5 + VN	8000-4300	6	7.07	91.38	3.41	11.98	7.16	91.18	3.38	11.83	6.90	91.78	3.50	12.27

SD = Second Derivative; VN = Vector Normalisation; FD = First Derivative; MinMax = Minimum Maximum Normalisation; MSC = Multiplicative Scatter Correction; sp = smoothing points

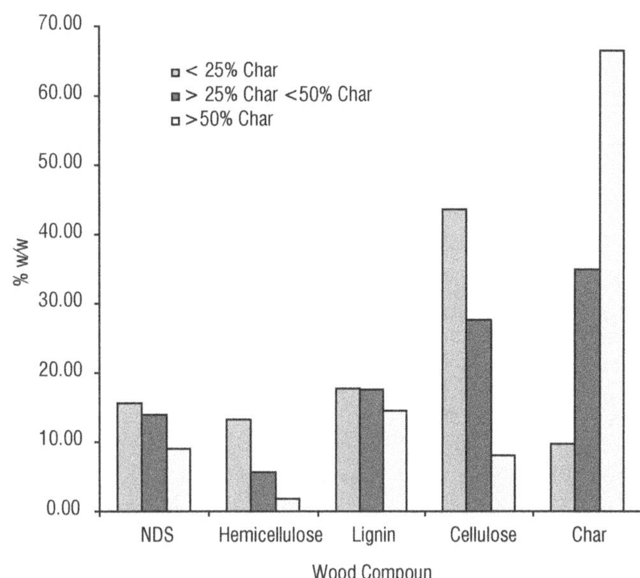

Figure 4. The NIR data set sorted by degree of char. The samples were separated in three char levels: less than 25%, between 25% and 50%, and greater than 50%.

American Bourbon cask with an internal area of 1.81 m^2 from the developed trend line equation in the "actual" three year ageing experiment (Figure 3). In that experiment it was determined that total wood extractives followed a power type trend equation. The data from the 10, 30, and 60 day study could be extrapolated to 1095 days (three years).

The GCMS data was first sorted into the three general types of casks that were used for the 3 year ageing study – cask type 1, 3, and multi-used cask type 4 (Figure 5). Multi-used casks are casks which have been exposed to alcohol for repeated fills and an unknown period of time. There were 47 disc samples for the multi-used cask type 4, 20 disc samples for cask type 3, and 6 samples for cask type 1.

For the discs from cask type 1 the rapid 60 day ageing study year predicted a total extractive level of 87000 ppb/LAA (Figure 5) and the actual three year study yielded 90000 ppb/LAA (Figure 3). The cask type 3 discs predicted 30000 ppb/LAA in the rapid 60 day ageing study, and in the real-time study it achieved 25000 ppb/LAA; however the upper limit for the standard error

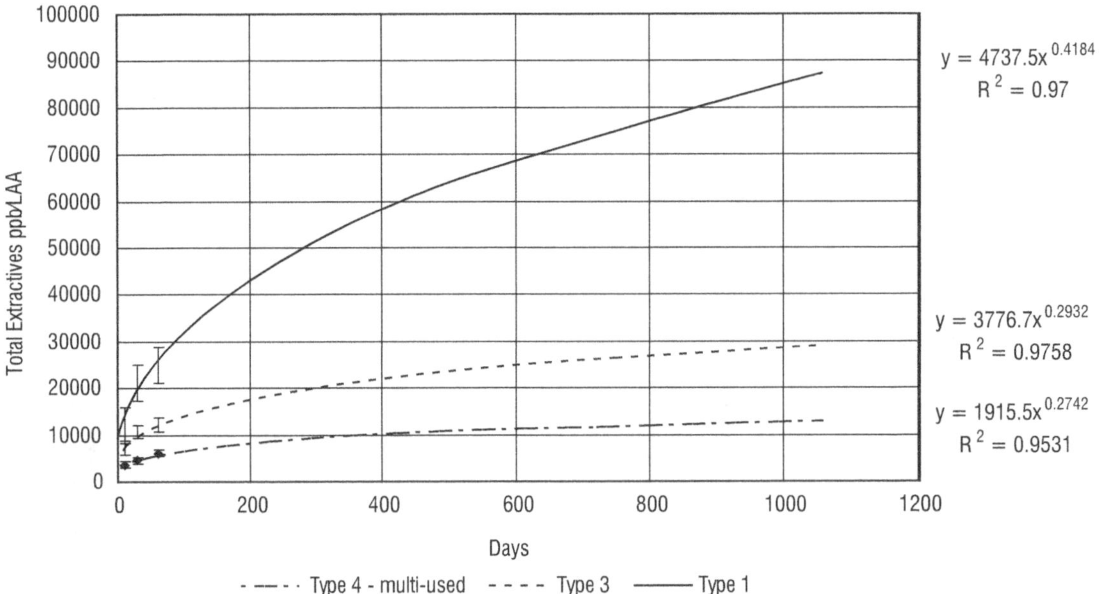

Figure 5. Extrapolated total hemicellulose derived extractives from the 60 day disc study to predict three years of ageing in cask types 1, 3, and multi-used cask type 4.

was 32000 ppb/LAA. Multi-used cask type 4 discs predicted a three year level of 13000 ppb/LAA of total wood extractives for the rapid 60 day ageing study which was less the actual 18000 ppb/LAA from the real-time study. This result was to be expected since the discs came from used wood. The more wood is exposed to ethanol the less the expected wood extractives. Although the rapid 60 day disc study was not exactly the actual real time study it can be still used as an effective screening tool to determine differences within wood samples from different cask types and can potentially predict differences in the total wood extractives for three years of ageing.

To determine if the NIR calibration models that were developed for hemicellulose, lignin, and NDS could be used as a predictor of ageing they were correlated with the extractive data from the GCMS 60 day disc study. A regression analysis was used to ascertain if the NIR calibration models could predict wood derived extractives from hemicellulose, lignin, and NDS. The wood extractives that were derived from hemicellulose were compared to the hemicellulose component value from its corresponding NIR calibration model. Likewise lignin derived extractives were compared to the lignin NIR calibration model and NDS was compared to the total wood extractives. Exponential, logarithmic, linear, and power regressions were calculated and the regression analysis which had the R^2 closest to 1 was determined to be optimal.

The wood discs were measured with the NIR fibre optic probe on both surfaces, where one surface was thermally degraded to some extent which was referred to as charred, and the other surface was not thermally degraded which was referred to as non-charred. Some of the discs used in the study were not charred on either surface. Using the OPUS software the spectral average of the char and non-char surface could be calculated. A regression analysis of the 60 day GCMS wood extractive data was determined for the non-charred surface, charred surface, and the combined spectral average of both surfaces (Table 2).

It could be concluded that using the developed NIR calibration models for lignin, hemicellulose, and neutral detergent solubles for the non-charred, charred, and spectral average of the charred and non-charred surface prior to

Table 2. Regression analysis of NIR calibration models hemicellulose, lignin, and NDS versus its relative derived extractives (measured by GCMS) from the 60 day ageing study.

Component	*Surface*	*R^2*	*Equation*
Hemicellulose	Non Char	0.0109	y=-0.0001x+22.317
Lignin	Non Char	0.008	y=-0.0001x+13.068
NDS	Non Char	0.004	y=-0.00005x+18.362
Hemicellulose	Char	0.0531	y=-0.5323Ln(x)+4.5715
Lignin	Char	0.0179	y=0.4421Ln(x)-3.2026
NDS	Char	0.1371	y=1.3307Ln(x)-10.209
Hemicellulose	Non Char/Char Spectral Average	0.0002	y=-0.00005x+15.762
Lignin	Non Char/Char Spectral Average	0.0017	y=-0.00005x+14.977
NDS	Non Char/Char Spectral Average	0.0679	y=-0.7123Ln(x)+22.271

the ageing process was not comparable to the respective GCMS extract values. The highest R^2 value was 0.1371 which was considered a poor correlation. The possible explanation for not correlating could be due to the RMSECV of the hemicellulose NIR calibration model was 2.13, lignin calibration model was 2.42, and the neutral detergent solubles calibration model was 2.89. The GCMS measures the wood extraction values are magnitudes lower which was in the ppb range or 0.001%; therefore, the NIR calibration models developed for the lignin, hemicellulose, and neutral detergent solubles could not be sensitive enough for concentration changes. Also the rate of extraction of hemicellulose, cellulose, and lignin derived components occurred at different rates, thus the relative concentration of each component prior to the ageing process cannot not be used as a predictor.

Total wood extract NIR calibration models

Since measuring the lignin, hemicellulose, and neutral detergent solubles with the developed NIR calibration models did not correlate with the respective wood extractives a more direct method was employed. Instead of attempting correlation analysis with existing calibration models the total wood extraction data from the GCMS was directly cross validated with the NIR spectra even though the wood extraction into the spirit was far below the limits of detection of typical NIR calibration models.

The NIR spectra used for the direct cross validation was analyzed at day 0, prior to the ageing process. Each side of the disc, the char and non-char surface was analyzed in triplicate using the fibre optic probe. Selections of discs from all four cask types were used. The RMSECV, R^2, RPD, RER, and rank were used as tools to determine optimal calibration models and two independent sample sets were investigated to ensure the robustness of the developed models. A number of calibration models were attempted, where the GCMS data was calibrated at 10 days, 30 days, and 60 days, as well as the spectra of each wood surface including the char side, non-char side, and the spectral average of each side (Table 3).

In this study the calibration model that was the most robust and accurate was the 30 day model developed from the spectra from the non-char surface. The RMSECV was 914 ppb, the R^2 was 93.68, the RPD was 3.98, and the RER was 32.52 which indicate that the NIR calibration model is acceptable for screening or quantification purposes. The other noteworthy fact was that the calibration models developed from the charred surface were not acceptable even for screening purposes. This demonstrates two conclusions: the light from the NIR fibre optic probe cannot penetrate the char surface of a whisky cask and the surface below the char layer contributes to the wood extractives that enter the spirit. In previous studies infrared light has been shown only to penetrate a few millimeters into wood (Murphy, G., and Acuna, M.A. 2006).

Table 3. Validation of the optimized total wood extracts calibration models from the disc study.

Calibration modle	Data range (ppb)	Data pre-processing	Frequency range (cm^{-1})	PLS factors	Cross validation				First test set validation				Second test set validation			
					RMSECV	R^2	RPD	RER	RMSEP	R^2	RDP	RER	RMSEP	R^2	RPD	RER
10 day char-nonchar average	17586	FD sp17+MSC	9000-5300	6	1800	66.41	1.73	9.77	1950	54.99	1.54	9.02	1830	69.06	1.82	9.61
30 day char-nonchar average	29729	FD sp5	9000-5300	6	3750	48.52	1.40	7.93	4140	25.89	1.16	7.18	3860	52.42	1.46	7.70
60 day char-nonchar average	24522	FD sp13+MSC	9000-5300	7	2470	76.54	2.07	9.93	3310	47.43	1.42	7.41	2860	73.69	1.95	8.57
10 day char	17586	FD sp5	9000-5300	11	1830	43.92	1.34	9.61	1970	35.25	1.24	8.93	2030	31.16	1.21	8.66
30 day char	29729	VN	9000-5300	12	3170	61.62	1.62	9.38	3170	61.50	1.61	9.38	3230	60.11	1.58	9.20
60 day char	24522	FD sp5+VN	9000-5300	12	3260	54.35	1.48	7.52	3390	50.72	1.43	7.23	3410	50.09	1.42	7.19
10 daynon-char	17586	FD sp5+VN	9000-5300	17	846	92.50	3.65	20.79	939	90.81	3.31	18.73	995	89.55	3.19	17.67
30 day non-char	29729	FD sp5+VN	9000-5300	17	914	93.68	3.98	32.53	990	92.85	3.75	30.03	977	92.48	3.67	30.43
60 day non-char	24522	FD sp5+VN	9000-5300	16	1460	90.97	3.33	16.80	1520	90.18	3.24	16.13	1520	90.18	3.24	16.13

SD = Second Derivative; VN = Vector Normalisation; FD = First Derivative; MinMax = Minimum Maximum Normalisation; MSC = Multiplicative Scatter Correction; sp = smoothing points

As previously discussed wood extractives enter the spirit in two ways, either by thermal degradation of wood components during the char process or by ethanolysis whereby ethanol acting as a solvent slowly degrades the wood components over time. At day 0 the NIR spectra that was obtained could have only measured the wood extractives that were created by thermal degradation. Since the R^2 values at 10 day was 92.50, and at 30 day was 93.68, and at 60 day was 90.97, it would indicate that majority of wood extractives from thermal degradation entered the spirit was closest to the 30 day mark, but at some point between day 10 and 60 the majority wood extractives which entered the spirit from ethanolysis over took the wood extractives from thermal degradation. It was noted that extractives from newer discs (staves that had little to no previous exposure to ethanol) took longer reach its half way extraction point than discs from multi-used casks. The wood extracts from thermal degradation versus ethanolysis may take longer to disperse into the spirit from newer wood than from used wood. This could be a source of error from the developed calibration models in this study. Accuracy may be improved if calibration models were split into two calibrations - a used and newer wood model since the NIR could only measure extractives from thermal degradation.

If NIR were to be used in a production environment a system would have to be devised to remove the top char layer to obtain spectra from the underneath surfaces. Char could be scraped at specific locations in a cask. NIR measurements could be collected and averaged together to get an indication of the quality of cask. Another alternative would be to design a fibre optic device that could penetrate just below the char layer to obtain spectral information that is pertinent to wood extraction.

Calibration models developed from the disc ageing study proved that NIR could be used as a rapid tool to predict the quality of a cask; however, it must be kept in mind that the NIR spectra were obtained from discs that were air dried to the 3 – 5% (w/w) moisture content. In a practical setting on a drain in fill production line, casks are drained and filled almost immediately and casks that are purchased from American Bourbon suppliers are wet from previous alcohol fills. To increase the robustness of the non-char calibration models from the disc study the discs would have to be soaked in ethanol prior to the NIR measurement to develop calibration models that are practical to industrial settings. Further study should be carried out whereby discs should be soaked for a couple of hours at various strengths of alcohol in the range of 50% to 80% (v/v) to accommodate all possible situations. The dried discs should also remain in the NIR calibration model since the top portion and heads of the barrel dry out after several years of non-contact in a cask and remain relevant after a second fill.

Conclusions

Casks used for Canadian whisky production are shown to have variability, thus the importance for a rapid non-destructive quality measurement. It was found that the components of wood thermally degrade at different rates and the corresponding extractives dissolve at different rates into the whisky spirit. Previous exposure to ethanol would also contribute to the rate of extractives which dissolved into the surrounding spirit. It is possible to develop NIR calibration models to wood components on oak wood staves including charred and non-charred sections of the stave. However, it was found that these calibration models were suited for screening purposes. Direct NIR calibration to total wood extractives which were developed by thermal degradation could be used as a quality control tool for cask management.

References

AACC. 1999. Near Infrared Methods: Guidelines for Model Development and Maintainence. AACC Method 39-00. Approved Methods of the American Association of Cereal Chemists. St. Paul Mn.

Brown, L. 1994. The Story of Canadian Whisky. Canadian Whisky: 200 years of Tradition The Seagram Museum. p. 1 – 35.

Caldeira, I., Climaco, M.C., Bruno de Sousa, R., and Belchior, A.P. 2006. Volatile Composition of Oak and Chestnut Woods Used in Brandy Ageing: Modification Induced by Heat Treatment. *Journal of Food Engineering*. **76**, 202 – 211.

Di Blasi, C. 2009. Combustion and Gasification Rates of Lignocellulosic Chars. *Progress in Energy and Combustion Science*. **35**, 121 – 140.

EMEA (The European Agency for the Evaluation of Medicinal Products). 2003. Note for the Guidance on the Use of Near-Infrared Spectroscopy by the Pharmaceutical Industry and the Data Requirements for New Submissions and Variations. London, UK. EMEA/CVMP 961/01. p 1 – 14.

Health Canada. 2010. Food and Drug Regulation. C.R.C., c.870. Division 2. Alcoholic Beverages. B.02.020 [S]. Canadian Whisky, Canadian Rye Whisky, or Rye Whisky. p. 216 – 217.

Garde-Cerdan, T., and Ancin-Azpilicueta, C. 2006. Effect of Oak Barrel Type on the Volatile Composition of Wine: Storage Time Optimization. *LWT*. **39**, 199 – 205.

Garde-Cerdan, T., Torrea Goni, D., and Ancin Azpilicueta, C. 2004. Accumulation of Volatile Compounds During Ageing of Two Red Wines with Different Composition. *Journal of Food Engineering*. **65**, 349 – 356.

Goering, H.K., and Van Soest, P.J. 1975. Forage Fiber Analysis. Approaches, Reagents, Procedures, and Some Applications. *Agriculture Handbook* Number 379379. USDA-ARS, US Gov. Print. Office, Washington, D.C.

Gonzalez-Arjona, D., Gonzalez-Gallero, V., Pablos, F., and Gonzalez, A.G. 1999. Authentication and Differentiation of Irish Whiskys by Higher-Alcohol Congener

Analysis. *Analytica Chimica Acta.* **381**, 257 – 264.

Guillen, M.D., and Manzanos, M.J. 2002. Study of the Volatile Composition of an Aqueous Oak Smoke Preparation. *Food Chemistry.* **79**, 283 – 292.

Hatfield, R., and Fukushima, R.S. 2005. Can Lignin be Accurately Measured? *Crop Science.* **45**, 832 – 839.

Mosedale, J.R. and Puech, J.L. 1998. Wood Maturation of Distilled Spirits. *Trends in Food Science and Technology.* **9**, 95 – 101.

Mosedale, J.R. and Puech, J.L. 2003. Wines, Spirits, and Other Beverages. UMR Sciences Pour L'oenolgie, Montpellier, France. Elsevier Science Ltd. p. 393 – 402.

Murphy, G., and Acuna, M.A. 2006. Estimating Internal Wood Properties of Logs Based on Real-Time, NIR Measurements of Chainsaw Wood Chips from a Harvester/Processor. Proceedings of the International Precision Forestry Symposium, South Africa. p 1 – 10.

Nishimura, K., Ohnishi, M., Masuda, M., Koga, K. and Matsuyama, R. 1983. Flavour of Distilled Beverages. J.R. Piggot (ed.). Ellis Horwood, Chichester. p. 241 – 255.

Otsuka, K., Zenibayashi, Y., Itoh, M. and Totsuka, A. 1974. Presence and Significance of Two Diastereomers of ß-methyl-γ-octalactone in Aged Distilled Liquors. *Agriculture and Biological Chemistry.* **38**, 485 – 490.

Perez-Coello, M.S., Sanz, J., and Cabezudo, D. 1997. Analysis of Volatile Components of Oak Wood by Solvent Extraction and Direct Thermal Desorption-Gas Chromatography-Mass Spectrometry. *Journal of Analytical Chromatography.* **778**, 427 – 434.

Piggott, J.R, Lee, K.Y., and Paterson. A. 2001. Origins of Flavour in Whiskies and a Revised Flavour Wheel: a Review. *Journal of the Institute of Brewing.* **107**, 287 – 313.

Saeman, J.F., Bubl, J.L., and Harris, E.E. 1944. The Quantitative Saccharification of Wood and Cellulose. United States Department of Agriculture Forest Service. Forest Product Laboratories. Madison, Wisconsin. p. 1 – 10.

Suhas, P.J., Carrott, M.M.L., and Carrott, R. 2007. Lignin – From Natural Adsorbent to Activated Carbon: A Review. *Bioresource Technology.* **98**, 2301 – 2312.

Van Soest, P.J. 1967. *Journal of Animal Science.* **67**, 119.

Williams, P.C. 1997. Recent Advances in Near Infrared Application for the Agriculture and Food Industries. Proceedings: International Wheat Quality Conference. Manhattan, Kansas. Grain Industry Alliance.

Chapter 6

Reducing the need for new wood by regenerating and re-using casks

John Conner, Mark Patterson, Craig Owen and John Freeman
The Scotch Whisky Research Institute, The Robertson Trust Building, Research Avenue North, Riccarton, Edinburgh EH14 4AP

Introduction

Scotch whisky companies will always need a regular supply of new wood for maturation. Maturation is an essential step in creating the character of Scotch whisky and has been a legal requirement since 1915. Casks for whisky maturation do not last forever: with each fill the levels of colour and flavour compounds extracted from the cask decrease until a point is reached where the cask becomes practically inert and the spirit does not mature within an economical time frame. At this point the distiller will either replace the cask with a new one, or prolong the life of the cask through a regeneration treatment. In the past, this decision would have been an economic one based on the relative costs of new casks and the regeneration treatment. With the publication of the Scotch whisky industry's Environmental Strategy consideration should also be given to the sustainability of the oak used to make the new casks and whether regeneration contributes to the efficient use of raw materials. In this respect, the outcomes of regeneration treatments must be critically appraised as to whether it extends the life of a cask and/or re-creates enough of the character of a first fill cask that it will reduce distillers' need for new casks. This paper collates some of the background information that should be considered when making decisions about cask regeneration with respect to the current situation and what impact developments in cooperage technology may have in the future.

Casks used for Scotch whisky maturation

The overwhelming majority of whisky is matured in casks originating from the Bourbon industry. Bourbon casks are made from American white oak (*Quercus alba*) that comes from forests in the eastern part of the USA including Arkansas, Missouri, Kentucky and Tennessee (Swan, 1994). Casks are either imported and used as standing barrels (190 litres) or imported as stave shooks and re-assembled to hogshead size, with the addition of new oak ends (250 litres).

A small proportion of whisky is matured in Sherry casks, estimated at only 5% of malt spirit fillings (Gray 2010) and these may be made of oak from either Spain or America. Sherry producers favour the use of casks made from imported American white oak and any cask actually used in the production of sherry is likely to be American oak. The use of American oak casks for Sherry production was established in the 17th century and Sherry producers have only used their native oaks for casks when trade with America has been disrupted (González Gordon, 1990). Historically, the Sherry casks used by the Scotch whisky industry were made from pedunculate (*Quercus robur*) or sessile oaks (*Quercus petraea*) grown in north-western Spain and used to transport Sherry to the United Kingdom for bottling. When the definition of Spanish Sherry changed to include a requirement for bottling in Spain, the source of this type of Sherry cask disappeared and required whisky producers to deal directly with sawmills and Sherry producing bodegas for the supplies of the required timber (Ramsay, 2008).

In the US and Spain, trees are harvested by selective felling of mature trees in natural forests. The removal of mature trees creates space on the forest floor for re-growth. The majority of forests in both countries are in private ownership (Robak and Vignas, 2003; Smith et al., 2009), with cooperages and stave mills buying logs rather than managing their own forests. The new casks are first used to mature Bourbon or seasoned with Sherry before they are shipped to Scotland. Both the US and Spain are committed to the sustainable management of their forests and are developing broadly similar criteria and indicators for assessing forest management decisions and outcomes (USDA Forest Service, 2011; MCPFE, 2011). However, as the vast majority of wood used for the maturation of Scotch whisky (>97%) is sourced from the United States, the consideration of the sustainability of oak supplies will focus on the United States.

The sustainability of oak supplies

The definition of sustainability with respect to forests has its origins in the 1992 United Nations Conference on Environment and Development (also known as the "Earth Summit"). From this summit a definition has evolved that goes beyond the measurement of forest areas and balancing growth and removals and includes factors such as the conservation of biological diversity, forest ecosystem health and vitality, soil and water resources, contributions to global carbon cycles and the multiple socioeconomic benefits of forests (USDA Forest Service, 2011; MCPFE, 2011). Indicators of these additional criteria are still being developed and in this paper, consideration of the sustainability of oak wood supplies is limited to an analysis of forest resources. However, as the additional indicators are developed, more information will become available that will allow the industry to monitor the future sustainability of its wood supplies using the broadest possible definition of sustainability.

The first step in evaluating the sustainability of oak supplies is to estimate the Scotch whisky industry's annual need for new wood. Little information appears to be available on the amount of harvested green wood that is required to make one cask. This volume was estimated for a barrel (190 litres) and a hogshead (254 litres), the two most frequently used American oak casks. This estimation is based on the dimensions of the finished casks (Philp, 1989) and the area of stave wood required to make this cask is estimated as the largest circumference of the cask (bilge) by its height. This rectangular area includes wood lost when jointing and shaping staves. Similarly ends are assumed to be cut from a square of wood the size of the largest diameter of a cask. Wood for 4 ends is included for a hogshead: two ends for its first use as a bourbon barrel and two ends for when it is remade as a hogshead. Volume for both is calculated using an assumed stave thickness of 30 mm, again to account for losses when shaping the staves. This gives a wood volume of $0.076m^3$ for a barrel and $0.128m^3$ for a hogshead. The volume of quarter sawn green timber required to produce this wood is estimated based on the following losses.

1. An additional 10% wood is lost during shaping and jointing of staves and ends.
2. The volumetric shrinkage during kilning is calculated using the formula in Glass and Zelinka (2010).

3. Losses due to trimming of stave blanks after kilning to remove split ends is calculated using the relative lengths of stave bolts (39 inches in Slusher, 1993) and staves (34 inches in Philp, 1989).

This estimated the volume of green wood prior to seasoning is $0.111m^3$ for a barrel and $0.186m^3$ for a hogshead. All American oak is sawn, which recovers about 50% usable timber from a log (Schahinger and Rankine, 1992) and this gives the "log" volume for a barrel of $0.222m^3$ (= 7.8 cubic feet) and $0.372m^3$ (= 13.2 cubic feet) for a hogshead. Applying these values to the International Rule Table in Slusher (1993) gives yields of between 0.8 and 6.6 barrels per tree depending on the diameter and height. Yields for hogsheads are lower at between 0.5 and 4 per tree.

In this paper the annual requirement for new wood is based on replacing 10% of the casks emptied in a year, though the actual number of casks will vary from year to year depending on production, price and availability. The number of casks emptied was estimated from the overall consumption of Scotch whisky, which was equal to 330.15 million litres of pure alcohol in 2009 (Gray, 2010). This would require approximately 3.4 million barrels or 2.5 million hogsheads, assuming a strength of 60% abv at the end of maturation, an average age of 7 years and a loss in volume of 2% per annum. Replacing 10% of these casks with new barrels or hogsheads would need wood for 340,000 barrels or 250,000 hogsheads and require an estimated harvest of 2.6 or 3.3 million cubic feet of oak trees in the United States. The median productivity of oak-hickory forests in the North Central (including Missouri) and South Central (including Arkansas, Kentucky and Tennessee) sub regions of the Eastern USA is between 50 and 84 cubic feet per acre per year (Smith et al., 2009). Introducing this level of new wood would require the harvest from between 30,000 and 52,000 acres of oak forest for barrels and between 39,000 and 66,000 acres for hogsheads. There are approximately 78 million acres of oak-hickory forest in the two sub regions of the Eastern USA, with over 21,000 million cubic feet of select white oaks growing on timberland. The growing stock of select white oaks in these sub-regions has increased from 16,744 million cubic feet in 1997, giving an average annual increment of 485 million cubic feet (Smith et al., 2009). Replacing 260,000 hogsheads would require less than 1% of the average annual increment in the growing volume of select white oaks.

This estimation suggests that the amount of oak required by the Scotch whisky industry represents only a small proportion of the annual increment in growth and therefore would be sustainable. Additionally, the harvest of oak for cooperage represents only a small proportion of the total hardwood harvest: Cooperage products were included with poles, pilings and other miscellaneous products and accounted for 36,551,000 cubic feet out of a total hardwood harvest of 8,235,000,000 cubic feet from the eastern USA (<1%) (Smith et al., 2009). This level of harvest appears to be sustainable as there was no evidence that forests were being used up, with the total forest area stable and the volume of wood recorded on it increasing (USDA Forestry Service, 2011). The sustainability of US forests in the past has been largely characterised as a balancing act between nature and timber harvests, but the most recent National Report on Sustainable Forests (2011) uses a much broader definition and some of the additional indicator statistics are described as "less promising". Concerns are expressed with regard to the fragmentation of forest lands and declines in the diversity of forest flora and fauna, though many of these concerns are based on declines in the management of working forests and a steady demand of land for housing development. As monitoring of the indicators for these concerns develops, the Scotch whisky industry should review the available information at regular intervals to provide a broader context to the sustainability of its wood supplies.

The casks used for the production of Scotch whisky are not purchased directly from cooperages in the United States but are first used for the maturation of Bourbon. The producers of other whiskies, rums and tequilas also use ex-Bourbon casks for the maturation of their products and the availability and price of Bourbon barrels is therefore dependent on the relative outputs of the Bourbon industry and other distillers. While the evidence suggests that supplies of wood to make casks are sustainable, changes in the relative outputs of the different distillers could lead to increased competition for the available casks. This, rather than the sustainability of oak supplies, is likely to be the biggest driver that will require greater utilisation of existing casks and the increased use of regeneration.

Cask regeneration

The standard procedure for regenerating exhausted Scotch whisky casks is to remove the original char layer using a rotating brush or flail system and to rechar the exposed wood using a gas burner. The key element of this regeneration process is the charring of the inner surface, which thermally degrades lignin and hemicelluloses to give colour and flavour compounds, and creates an active char layer important for the removal of sulphides and immature characters from new make spirit. In sensory terms, the advantages of regeneration are obvious: when whiskies matured in regenerated casks are compared with the same distillate matured in refill casks, the regenerated cask samples are given significantly higher scores for mature characters, such as sweet, woody and fruity, and lower scores for immature characters such as feinty and sulphury (Figure 1). This indicates that regeneration is a valid option for prolonging the life of a cask.

When compared to the same age distillate matured in first fill ex-bourbon casks, the regenerated cask samples were significantly less sweet, woody and fruity. The reasons for these differences lie in the origins of the different flavour compounds present in cask wood. Some flavour compounds (e.g. oak lactones) are natural constituents of the heart wood and are not regenerated by heat treatment of exhausted wood (Figure 2).

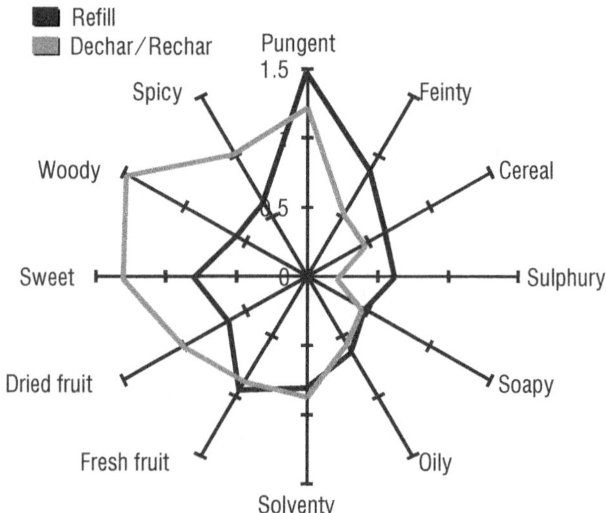

Figure 1. Mean panel scores for the same age distillate matured in refill and dechar – rechar casks.

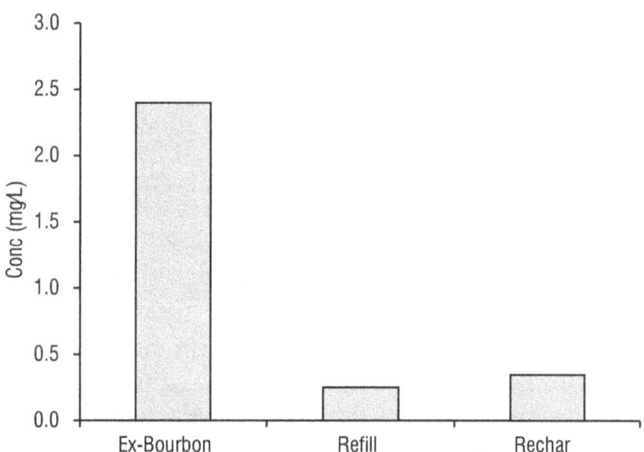

Figure 2. Cis oak lactone concentrations (mg/L) in ex-Bourbon, refill and recharred cask samples.

The concentrations of other flavour compounds (e.g. eugenol) are greatly increased by heat treatment, but this is dependent on the presence of specific precursors in the wood. Repeated use of a cask greatly reduces the level of precursors present in exhausted wood and in their absence, re-charring fails to generate the concentrations present new wood. Consequently, while de-char/re-char casks produce whisky that has greater maturity and is of better quality than that produced by refill casks, it may lack some of the character of whisky matured in a first fill cask.

Regenerating casks through a dechar-rechar process will prolong the active life of the cask, but may not reduce the requirement for new wood, if the mature character of the product requires a balance from first fill casks.

Developments in cooperage technology

There have been a number of developments in cooperage technology, mainly for the production or regeneration of wine casks that could be exploited for the regeneration of whisky casks. These are based on two possible mechanisms:

1. removing more of the exhausted wood to allow maturing spirit to penetrate and extract from deeper layers in the stave
2. having greater control over the heat treatment process for the break down of structural elements of the wood into colour and flavour compounds.

The rotating brush or flail system currently used by the Scotch whisky industry does not remove sufficient exhausted wood to allow the maturing spirit to access deeper layers of the wood. Extraction and analysis of wood from different depths within a stave have shown that, in exhausted staves, it is only the inner part of the stave that is depleted of extractives and that deeper layers can yield substantial levels of colour and extractives (Figure 3).
Analysis of the extractives from these deeper layers has shown that they contain constituents of the wood, such as oak lactones and tannins that are not normally regenerated by the dechar-rechar process (Figure 4).

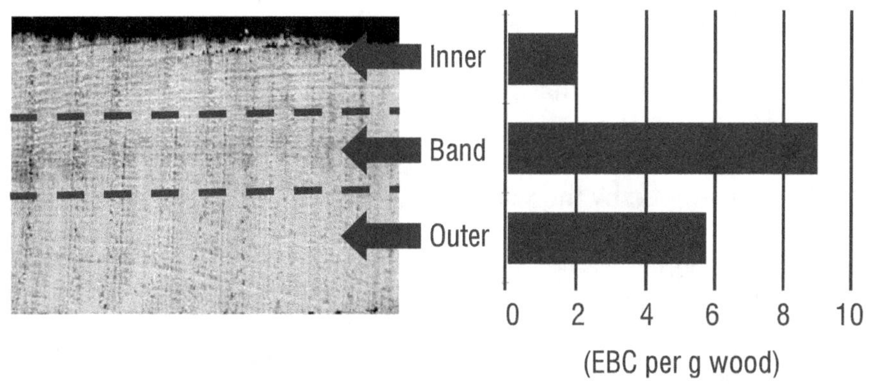

Figure 3. The extraction of colour from different depths in an exhausted whisky cask stave

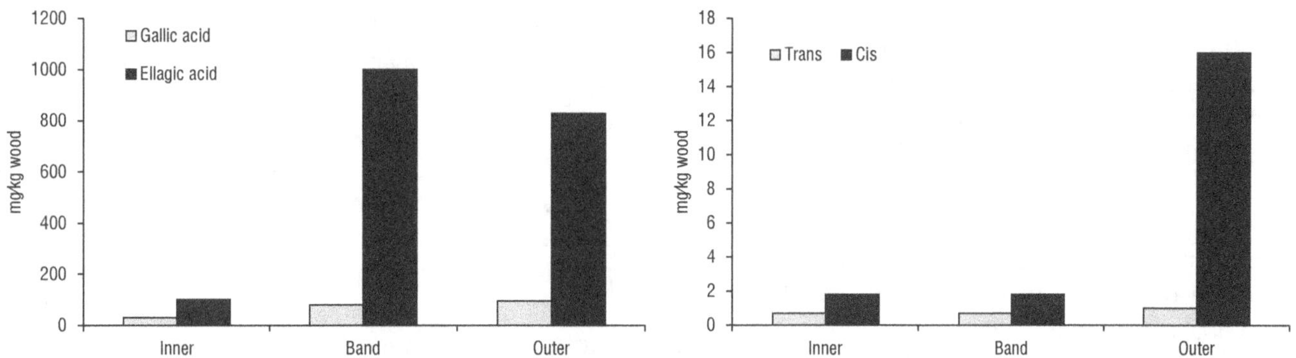

Figure 4. Levels of tannins and oak lactones in extracts of wood from different depths within a stave. Values are the averages for 3 staves.

The potential of removing exhausted wood to increase first fill characteristics in regenerated casks is supported by trials using precision cutting tools to remove up to 8 mm of old wood from the inside surface of an intact cask (Wickham, 2009). Combined with toasting of the exposed wood, this has been reported to restore 85% of the activity of a new cask (Smith, 2010). Removing 8mm from a 25mm Bourbon stave would give a markedly thinner stave and likely to have an impact on structural integrity leading to increased evaporative losses, particularly over the longer timescales of Scotch whisky maturation. The loss of this amount of wood could not be repeated and when the cask becomes exhausted after this regeneration treatment, it would need to be replaced. An alternative strategy to introduce "new wood" characters is to replace the ends of the cask, possibly in combination with a dechar-rechar process. This has the advantages of repeatability and retaining the structural integrity of the cask. The choice between the two strategies must weigh the increase in the life span of the cask body against the use of a proportion of new wood.

The other area being developed by the wine industry is better control of the heat treatment process. Control of heat treatment is essential for consistent maturation, whether using re-charred whisky casks (Perry et al., 1990) or toasted wine casks (Spillman et al., 2005). Toasting casks has the potential to generate higher concentrations of colour and extractives than charring, as the formation of a char layer results in the loss of colour and flavour compounds by volatilisation and degradation. Traditionally toasting uses wood braziers and coopers find it difficult to produce casks with consistent toast levels. This can be overcome by monitoring the toasting intensity and grading casks after they have been toasted (Chatonnet, 1999) or by the use of alternative and potentially more controllable methods of toasting such as infra red heating (Wickman, 2009) or hot air convection (Fernandez-Mesa and Fantoni-Salas, 2010). Infra red toasting was pioneered by the Scotch whisky industry, but the first instruments could only handle flat staves and so could only be used for toasting new wood or the regeneration of ends. The technology has now advanced to the stage that intact cask shells may be heat treated, opening up new possibilities for its use in whisky cask regeneration.

Better control of heat treatment and the removal of exhausted wood will produce more consistent results from the regeneration of whisky casks and open up the possibilities for tailoring regeneration treatments to give specific mature characteristics. To make full use of these advances, whisky producers will need to understand the origins of the mature characters in their products. This combination of a better understanding of mature quality and greater control over regeneration should lead to increased utilisation of existing casks and reduce the need for new wood.

Conclusions

National reports on sustainable forest management suggest that the oak forests of eastern USA are a sustainable source of timber. The USA uses the criteria and indicators of the Montreal Process to monitor the sustainable management of its forests and the Scotch whisky industry should make use of this information in the future to assess the sustainability of its oak supplies.

Regeneration techniques used for Scotch whisky casks may prolong the active life of a cask but may not reduce the industry's requirement for new wood, as they often fail to regenerate the character of a first fill cask. Advances in cooperage technology now offer the potential for tailoring regeneration treatments to restore a greater proportion of the first fill activity of casks. Use of these treatments for whisky casks has the potential to reduce the industry's requirement for new wood.

References

Chatonnet, P. (1999). Discrimination and control of toasting intensity and quality of oak wood barrels. *American Journal of Enology and Viticulture*, **50**(4), 479 – 494.

Fantoni-Salas, A.; Fernandez-Mesa, A. (2007). Process and apparatus for inner wall toasting of casks for wine guard by hot air convection. *United States Patent*: US 7 179 082 B2.

Glass, S.V. and Zelinka, S.L. (2010). Moisture Relations and Physical Properties of Wood. *Wood Handbook:* Chapter 04. U.S. Department of Agriculture, Forest Service, Forest Products Laboratory, Madison, WI, USA. http://www.fpl.fs.fed.us/documnts/fplgtr/fplgtr190/chapter_04.pdf

Gray, A.S. (2010). *Scotch Whisky – Annual Review of the Industry*; Thirty Third Edition. Sutherlands, Edinburgh, UK.

González Gordon, M.M. (1990) *Sherry: The Noble Wine* (Revised and edited by John Doxat) Quiller Press, London.

MCPFE (2011). *State of Europe's Forests 2011*: Status and Trends in Sustainable Forest Management in Europe. Ministerial Conference on the Protection of Forests in Europe, Forest Europe Liaison Unit, Oslo, Norway. http://www.foresteurope.org/filestore/foresteurope/Publications/pdf/Forest_Europe_report_2011_web.pdf

Perry, D., Ford, A. and Burke, G. (1990) Cask Rejuvenation, in *Proceedings of the Third Aviemore Conference on Malting, Brewing and Distilling*, (ed I. Campbell), Institute of Brewing, London, pp. 464 – 467.

Philp, J.M. (1989). Cask quality and warehouse conditions, in *The Science and Technology of Whiskies*, (eds J.R. Piggott, R. Sharp, and R.E.B Duncan), Longman Scientific and Technical, Harlow, pp. 264-94.

Ramsay, J. (2008). Getting the Right Wood. *The Brewer and Distiller International*, **4**(9), 46 – 47.

Robak, E.W. and Vignas, J. A. (2003). Sustainable Forest Management for a Region of Small Private Ownerships. Paper submitted to XII World Forestry Congress, 2003, Quebec City, Canada. http://www.fao.org/DOCREP/ARTICLE/WFC/XII/0300-C2.HTM

Schahinger, G. and Rankine, B. (1992) *Cooperage for Winemakers*: A Manual on the Construction, Maintenance and Use of Oak Barrels. Ryan Publications, Adelaide.

Slusher, J.P. (1993). How to Measure Trees and Logs. School of Forestry, Fisheries and Wildlife, University of Missouri Extension. http://extension.missouri.edu/p/G5050

Smith, F. (2010) DBS helps wineries roll out "almost new" barrels. *Australian & New Zealand Grapegrower & Winemaker* No. 552, 50–51

Smith, W. B., Miles, P. D., Perry, C. H., Pugh, S. A., (2009). Forest Resources of the United States, 2007. *Gen. Tech. Rep. WO-78*. U.S. Department of Agriculture, Forest Service, Washington, DC. http://www.fs.fed.us/nrs/pubs/gtr/gtr_wo78.pdf

Swan, J.S. (1994). Sourcing oak wood for the distilling industries, in *Proceedings of the Fourth Aviemore Conference on Malting, Brewing and Distilling*, (eds I. Campbell and F.G. Priest), Institute of Brewing, London, pp. 56 - 70.

Spillman, P. J.; Sefton, M. A.; Gawel, R. (2004). The effect of oak wood source, location of seasoning and coopering on the composition of volatile compounds in oak-matured wines. *Australian Journal of Grape and Wine Research* **10** (3) 216–226

Wickham, N. (2009). American, French oak trials support Phoenix revolution. *Australian & New Zealand Grapegrower & Winemaker* No. 548, 112–114

USDA Forest Service (2011). National Report on Sustainable Forests – 2010. United States Department of Agriculture, Forest Service, Arlington, VA. http://www.fs.fed.us/re0search/sustain/2010SustainabilityReport/documents/2010_SustainabilityReport.pdf

Chapter 7

Evaluation of oakwood potential for aging of wine and spirits: comparison of physicochemical, sensory and molecular approaches

E. Guichoux[1,2,3] and R. J. Petit[1,2,3]

[1] *INRA, UMR 1202 Biodiversity Genes & Communities, F- 33610 Cestas, France;* [2] *Univ. Bordeaux, UMR1202 Biodiversity Genes & Communities, Bordeaux, F-33400 Talence, France;* [3] *Pernod Ricard Research Centre, F-94000 Creteil, France*

Introduction

The sensory characteristics of wines and spirits are significantly improved during aging in oak barrels (Boidron et al 1988). When aging in oak barrels, wine and spirits undergo a series of processes that cause important improvements in wine aroma, taste, astringency and colour (Jarauta et al 2005). Since the Gallo-Roman period, this maturation has been performed in oak barrels. Recently, alternative methods have started to emerge, using either oak planks, staves, chips, cubes, powder or shavings, which can be added to wine or spirits held in tanks made of any inert material (Del Alamo Sanza et al 2004, Young et al 2010). These techniques allow a better control of aging and reduce production cost (Spillman 1999). In this context, precise characterization of wood aromatic properties appears to be particularly relevant. But anticipating the aromatic contribution of a barrel or of some oak chips is difficult in practice.

The most common oak species used in spirits maturation are *Quercus alba* (American white oak), *Q.robur* (pedunculate oak) and to a lesser extent *Q.petraea* (sessile oak). For wine maturation, the majority of winemakers insist on using French oak (*Q. robur* and *Q. petraea*) for its typical aromatic contribution (Boidron et al 1988) but a growing minority uses American white oak (*Q. alba*) for the crafting of barrels. Still today, a noticeable proportion of oak woods are primarily selected based on their grain size and geographic origin (Mosedale and Ford 1996, Feuillat et al 1998, Ancin et al 2004, Spillman et al 2004). Yet, several studies have shown that the major effect explaining aromatic differences among wood batches depends on the botanical species (Doussot et al 2000, Doussot et al 2002, Guchu et al 2006, Prida and Puech 2006, Prida et al 2007). For example, American oaks are characterized by lower levels of polyphenols and higher amounts of volatiles than the European species (Mosedale 1995). Recent studies have also confirmed differences between the two European species, with *Q. petraea* possessing characteristics similar to those of American oak, while *Q. robur* is characterized by high levels of ellagitannins but often negligible amounts of volatiles such as whisky-lactone (Mosedale et al 1998, Feuillat et al 1997b, Doussot et al 2000). This molecule (ß-methyl-γ-octalactone), also known as quercus lactone, provides typical aromas of coconut, resin and celery (Boidron et al 1988), and is one of the most aromatic molecules described to date. If *Q.*

robur wood has only traces of whisky-lactone, *Q. petraea* wood often presents high amounts of this compound (Prida et al 2007). Hence, the ability to sort wood-lots according to the species will allow better anticipation of the aromatic contribution of wood.

Species identification based on wood anatomy is complex and sometimes impossible in the case of taxonomically related species that have similar wood structure (Feuillat et al 1997a, Deguilloux et al 2002, Lens et al 2005). Chemical analyses can be effective at differentiating species but remain expensive and often suffer from the high level of variability among populations or samples (Deguilloux et al 2002, Gougeon et al 2009). Tree species can also be differentiated by near-infrared reflectance spectroscopy (Atkinson et al 1997, Humphreys et al 2008) but this technique requires samples with similar preparation conditions and is highly sensitive to ascertainment bias (Russ et al 2009). Thus, wood identification methods relying on molecular markers have recently been investigated (Eurlings et al 2010, Finkeldey et al 2010).

For two decades, genetic analyses on fresh tissues such as leaves, bud or cambium are commonplace and technological improvements allow the retrieval of DNA from most tree species (Doyle and Doyle 1990, Lin and Walker 1997, Csaikl et al 1998). But the retrieval of DNA from wood itself is more complex because wood properties differ from fresh tissues (Rachmayanti et al 2009). Once a tree is cut, the quantity and quality of DNA that can be retrieved quickly diminish and the size of fragments that can be amplified decreases after the death of the wood tissue (Bär et al 1988, Lindahl 1993, Cano 1996, Deguilloux et al 2002). Furthermore, some species, like oaks, have high levels of polyphenols and ellagitannins, which are known to inhibit DNA amplification (Cooper and Poinar 2000). Amounts of water-soluble ellagitannins increase during wood drying (Mosedale et al 1998), which could be problematic for genetic analyses targeting aged wood-lots.

In this study, we illustrate the wood-based DNA identification approach using as a case study two interfertile oak species, *Q. robur* and *Q. petraea*. The first successful DNA isolation from dry wood was notably achieved on these species in 1999 (Dumolin-Lapègue et al 1999). Genetic markers have been efficiently used for differentiating the species using DNA isolated from fresh material (Bodénès et al 1997, Samuel 1999, Bakker et al 2001, Gömöry et al 2001, Muir et al 2001, Coart et al 2002, Mariette et al 2002, Scotti-Saintagne et al 2004, Lepais et al 2006, Guichoux et al 2011).

The ability to identify oak species from dry wood would have major consequences. In the first place, it could contribute to improving the control of the maturation processes of wine and spirits by selecting woods based on their aromatic contribution. But it could also allow *a posteriori* certification of wood-lots when no traceability evidence is present, contributing to the combat of fraud (Degen and Fladung 2008, Finkeldey et al 2008, Tacconi 2008).

We therefore developed DNA-based methods of identification of oak species from dry wood samples. We paid particular attention to DNA isolation and purification protocols to recover high-quality DNA. We also adapted published microsatellite markers (also known as SSRs - Simple Sequence Repeats) to maximise amplification success on dry wood and accurately identify the two species using assignment analysis.

Material and methods

Wood sample collection

Seven pieces of internal wood (100mm x 50mm x 30mm) were sampled in barrel staves after 18 months of seasoning. Species status (*Q. robur* or *Q. petraea*) had been previously provided by the cooper. Prior to experiments, all samples were sanded on each side, were cleaned with 10% bleach to remove contaminants and over 2mm of the external surface of wood was removed with a scalpel.

DNA isolation

All DNA isolation steps were carried out in a separate dedicated lab under high-pressure, with strict experimental precautions, following Deguilloux et al (2006). About 50mg of wood shavings obtained with a scalpel were added to 2ml tubes with two 3mm tungsten beads. Tubes were frozen in liquid nitrogen for 2min before disruption into fine powder using a Mixer Mill MM300 (Retsch, Germany), for 4min at 30Hz. DNA was isolated with a modified CTAB protocol (Doyle and Doyle 1990), which is available from the authors upon request. All DNA extracts were purified with the OneStep PCR Inhibitor Removal Kit (Zymo Research, USA). For each sample, DNA was isolated twice in separate experiments and each duplicate was used for further DNA amplifications to test the reproducibility of the results.

Microsatellite genotyping

To enhance microsatellite genotyping success on wood samples, we redesigned primer pairs previously published by Guichoux et al (2011). Two strict criteria were followed: amplicon size below 100bp and primer melting temperature over 55°C. Redesigned primers were all labelled with an "A-" prefix (Figure 1). DNA amplifications were performed following the method of Deguilloux et al (2006). PCR (Polymerase Chain Reaction) products were separated on 3% agarose gel stained with GelRed (Biotium, USA), diluted 25 times in ultrapure water and run on ABI-3730 (Applied Biosystems, USA), with LIZ600 as internal lane size standard. Size fragment analysis was performed with Genemapper (Applied Biosystems, USA).

Species identification of wood samples

We used assignment methods based on Bayesian clustering approaches to confirm the species of wood samples. The admixture proportion of each sample was estimated using STRUCTURE v.2.3.3 (Pritchard et al 2000, Falush et al 2003), with a burn-in of 50,000 steps followed by 50,000 Markov chain Monte Carlo repetitions. We calculated the average result over 10 runs with *K* (number of clusters) set to two, corresponding to the two species. Samples were classified as purebreds if their admixture proportion was over 0.875 for one of the two clusters (Guichoux et al 2011). Fresh samples (24 *Q. robur* and 24 *Q. petraea*) have been previously assigned to one species using all published microsatellites (Guichoux et al 2011) and 273 samples from both species. Here, we repeated this analysis with seven loci to test the assignment stability of the 48 fresh samples using a subset of markers. To allow comparison of genotypes obtained from wood samples generated with the redesigned primer, we genotyped the same 48 fresh samples with the redesigned primers and estimated size shifts for each locus. This way, we could integrate the genotypes generated with the redesigned primers in our genetic database of 273 samples of both species (Guichoux et al 2011).

Results and discussion

Microsatellite genotyping

Despite the use of optimized protocol (modified CTAB in combination with OneStep PCR Inhibitor Removal Kit), preliminary tests on wood samples with original primers (Guichoux et al 2011) were inconclusive, confirming the necessity to design dedicated primers for amplification of degraded DNA. With an appropriate primer redesign, we successfully genotyped all wood samples at seven nuclear microsatellites except one locus that failed to amplify on all *Q. robur* samples. Although one locus had a very low melting temperature (49°C), missing data ratio was low (on average <15%). We noticed discrepancies between some duplicates, resulting most of the time in the absence of one allele, a phenomenon called

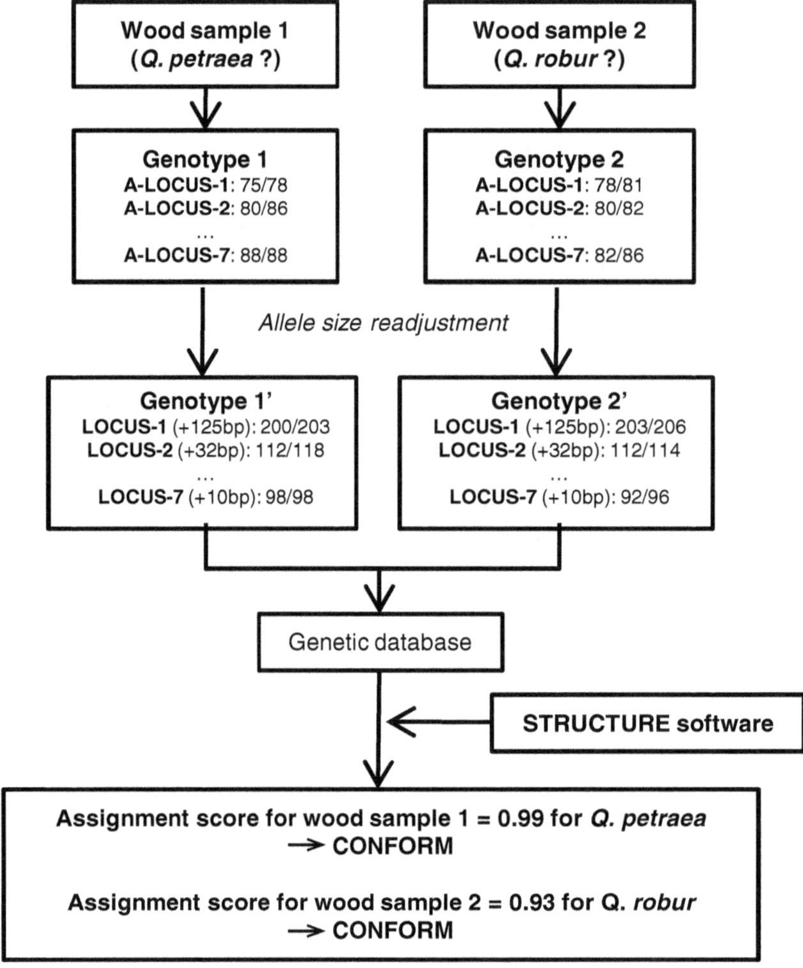

Figure 1. Species conformity methodology with the example of two samples from both species genotyped at seven microsatellites.

allelic dropout that has been described previously (Soulsbury et al 2007, Tvedebrink et al 2009). We also detected sporadic profiles with unexpected peaks (artefacts or extra allele). By repeating these ambiguous profiles three to five times, a consensus genotype could be retrieved in most cases.

Species identification of wood samples

Using seven microsatellites and a threshold value of 0.875 for the targeted purebred cluster, the admixture proportion of the 273 samples from the reference genetic database was still accurate (in comparison to all markers). In particular, all 48 samples used for allele size synchronization between datasets remained strongly assigned to one species (>0.875 for the targeted cluster). Genotyping of the 48 fresh samples with redesigned primers at seven nuclear microsatellites allowed the determination of size shift between original and redesigned primers (between 0bp and 125bp). Thus, multilocus genotypes of wood samples were transformed to allow their integration into the reference genetic database (Figure 1). Assignment results for the seven wood samples were consistent with the species announced by the cooper. In all cases, assignment scores were high (>0.875) except for one sample (assignment value of 0.850), maybe due to missing data at one locus that has high species discriminatory power (Scotti-Saintagne et al 2004).

Conclusion and perspectives

In this study, we proved that DNA-based certification of oak species from dry wood samples is possible provided some precautions are taken. First, contamination must be avoided, so all experiments prior to DNA amplification have to be done in a dedicated clean lab. Second, primers must be chosen on their ability to amplify short fragments, given that wood contains only largely degraded DNA. Third, the reference genetic database used for assignment analysis should be as complete as possible to allow accurate estimation of admixture level of wood samples when they are integrated. Following this methodology, we successfully confirmed the species of wood samples dried for 18 months.

However, some limits were identified in this study, and these will have to be taken into account in the future. Despite precautions, standardization of wood sample preparation remains difficult and could lead to different amplification success rates. Thus, high number of replicates (same samples extracted many times) should be used.

Microsatellites genotyping on degraded DNA underlined the limits of multiallelic markers for species identification of wood samples. Despite optimized DNA isolation and purification protocols and the use of efficient primers, we repeatedly found ambiguous profiles (with triple bands or showing allelic dropout), which obliged us to perform up to five repetitions to obtain reliable genotypes. Assignment results may have been different if such precautions had not been taken, potentially compromising assay quality.

Given the technical limits for isolation of longer DNA fragments inherent to dry wood, di-allelic markers such as Single Nucleotide Polymorphisms (SNPs) appear promising (Asari et al 2009, Ogden et al 2009). Genotyping errors are more limited with only two alleles and amplicons can be further shortened, down to a minimum of 45-50bp. Hence, amplification success should be higher than with microsatellites. On the other hand, assignment methods with SNPs will require more markers (Glover et al 2010, Haasl and Payseur 2011) unless more differentiated loci can be identified. The generalization of next-generation sequencing on non-model species will soon allow the detection of such informative markers. In view of our efforts to optimize DNA amplification and of the many SNP genotyping techniques currently available (High-Resolution Melting analysis, allele specific PCR, Derived Cleaved Amplified Polymorphic Sequences), we are optimistic that accurate DNA-based identification of species from dry wood samples might be feasible at acceptable cost in the near future, thus providing efficient tools to improve the evaluation of oakwood potential for aging of wine and spirits.

Acknowledgments

Wood samples were provided by the Research Centre of Pernod Ricard with the contribution of Petitrenaud sawmill (Dirol, France). Genotyping was performed in the Genome-Transcriptome facility of the Functional Genomic Centre of Bordeaux. Experiments were funded by the Research Centre of Pernod Ricard (CRPR) as part of Erwan Guichoux's PhD.

References

Ancin, C., Garde, T., Torrea, D. and Jimenez, N. (2004). Extraction of volatile compounds in model wine from different oak woods: effect of SO2. *Food Research International,* **37**: 375-383

Asari, M., Watanabe, S., Matsubara, K., Shiono, H. and Shimizu, K. (2009). Single nucleotide polymorphism genotyping by mini-primer allele-specific amplification with universal reporter primers for identification of degraded DNA. *Analytical Biochemistry,* **386**: 85-90

Atkinson, M.D., Jervis, A.P. and Sangha, R.S. (1997). Discrimination between *Betula pendula*, *Betula pubescens*, and their hybrids using near-infrared reflectance spectroscopy. *Canadian Journal of Forest Research,* **27**: 1896-1900

Bakker, E.G., Van Dam, B.C., Van Eck, H.J. and Jacobsen, E. (2001). The description of clones of *Quercus robur* L. and *Q. petraea* (Matt.) Liebl. with microsatellites and AFLP in an ancient woodland. *Plant Biology,* **3**: 616-621

Bär, W., Kratzer, A., Mächler, M. and Schmid, W. (1988). Postmortem stability of DNA. *Forensic Science International,* **39**: 59-70

Bodénès, C., Joandet, S., Laigret, F. and Kremer, A. (1997). Detection of genomic regions differentiating two closely related oak species *Quercus petraea* (Matt) Liebl and *Quercus robur* L. *Heredity,* **78**: 433-444

Boidron, J.N., Chatonnet, P. and Pons, M. (1988). Influence du bois sur certaines substances odorantes des vins. *Connaiss. Vigne Vin,* **22**: 275-294

Cano, R.J. (1996). Analysing ancient DNA. *Endeavour,* **20**: 162-167

Coart, E., Lamote, V., De Loose, M., Van Bockstaele, E., Lootens, P. and Roldan-Ruiz, I. (2002). AFLP markers demonstrate local genetic differentiation between two indigenous oak species [*Quercus robur* L. and *Quercus petraea* (Matt.) Liebl] in Flemish populations. *Theoretical and Applied Genetics,* **105**: 431-439

Cooper, A. and Poinar, H.N. (2000). Ancient DNA: Do it right or not at all. *Science,* **289**: 1139

Csaikl, U.M., Bastian, H., Brettschneider, R., Gauch, S., Meir, A., Schauerte, M., Scholz, F., Sperisen, C., Vornam, B. and Ziegenhagen, B. (1998). Comparative analysis of different DNA extraction protocols: A fast, universal maxi-preparation of high quality plant DNA for genetic evaluation and phylogenetic studies. *Plant Molecular Biology Reporter,* **16**: 69-86

Degen, B. and Fladung, M. (2008). Use of DNA-markers for tracing illegal logging. IN DEGEN, B. (Ed.) *Proceedings of the International Workshop Fingerprinting Methods for the Identification of Timber Origins.*

Deguilloux, M.F., Bertel, L., Celant, A., Pemonge, M.H., Sadori, L., Magri, D. and Petit, R.J. (2006). Genetic analysis of archaeological wood remains: first results and prospects. *Journal of Archaeological Science,* **33**: 1216-1227

Deguilloux, M.F., Pemonge, M.H. and Petit, R.J. (2002). Novel perspectives in wood certification and forensics: dry wood as a source of DNA. *Proceedings of the Royal Society B-Biological Sciences,* **269**: 1039-1046

Del Alamo Sanza, M., Fernandez Escudero, J.A. and De Castro Torio, R. (2004). Changes in phenolic compounds and colour Parameters of red wine aged with oak chips and in oak barrels. *Food Science and Technology International,* **10**: 233-241

Doussot, F., De Jeso, B., Quideau, S. and Pardon, P. (2002). Extractives content in cooperage oak wood during natural seasoning and toasting; Influence of tree species, geographic location, and single-tree effects. *Journal of Agricultural and Food Chemistry,* **50**: 5955-5961

Doussot, F., Pardon, P., Dedier, J. and De Jeso, B. (2000). Individual, species and geographic origin influence on cooperage oak extractible content (*Quercus robur* L. and *Quercus petraea* Liebl.). *Analusis,* **28**: 960-965

Doyle, J.J. and Doyle, J.L. (1990). Isolation of plant DNA from fresh tissue. *Focus,* **12**: 13-15

Dumolin-Lapègue, S., Pemonge, M.H., Gielly, L., Taberlet, P. and Petit, R.J. (1999). Amplification of oak DNA from ancient and modern wood. *Molecular Ecology,* **8**: 2137-2140

Eurlings, M.C.M., Van Beek, H.H. and Gravendeel, B. (2010). Polymorphic microsatellites for forensic identification of agarwood (*Aquilaria crassna*). *Forensic Science International,* **197**: 30-34

Falush, D., Stephens, M. and Pritchard, J.K. (2003). Inference of population structure using multilocus genotype data: linked loci and correlated allele frequencies. *Genetics,* **164**: 1567-1587

Feuillat, F., Dupouey, J.L., Sciama, D. and Keller, R. (1997a). A new attempt at discrimination between *Quercus petraea* and *Quercus robur* based on wood anatomy. *Canadian Journal of Forest Research-Revue Canadienne De Recherche Forestiere,* **27**: 343-351

Feuillat, F., Keller, R. and Huber, F. (1998). Grain and quality of cooperage oak (*Quercus robur* L. and *Q. petraea* Liebl.): myth or reality? *Revue des Oenologues et des Techniques Vitivinicoles et Oenologiques*: 11-15

Feuillat, F., Moio, L., Guichard, E., Marinov, M., Fournier, N. and Puech, J.L. (1997b). Variation in the concentration of ellagitannins and cis- and trans-beta-methyl-gamma-octalactone extracted from oak wood (*Quercus robur* L., *Quercus petraea* Liebl.) under model wine cask conditions. *American Journal of Enology and Viticulture,* **48**: 509-515

Finkeldey, R., Leinemann, L. and Gailing, O. (2010). Molecular genetic tools to infer the origin of forest plants and wood. *Applied Microbiology and Biotechnology,* **85**: 1251-1258

Finkeldey, R., Rachmayanti, Y., Nuroniah, H., Nguyen, N.P., Cao, C. and Gailing, O. (2008). Identification of the timber origin of tropical species by molecular genetic markers - the case of dipterocarps. IN DEGEN, B. (Ed.) *Proceedings of the International Workshop Fingerprinting Methods for the Identification of Timber Origins.*

Glover, K.A., Hansen, M.M., Lien, S., Als, T.D., Hoyheim, B. and Skaala, O. (2010). A comparison of SNP and STR loci for delineating population structure and performing individual genetic assignment. *BMC Genetics,* **11**: 2

Gömöry, D., Yakovlev, I., Zhelev, P., Jedinakova, J. and Paule, L. (2001). Genetic differentiation of oak populations within the *Quercus robur/ Quercus petraea* complex in Central and Eastern Europe. *Heredity,* **86**: 557-563

Gougeon, R.D., Lucio, M., Frommberger, M., Peyron, D., Chassagne, D., Alexandre, H., Feuillat, F., Voilley, A., Cayot, P., Gebefugi, I., Hertkorn, N. and Schmitt-Kopplin, P. (2009). The chemodiversity of wines can reveal a metabologeography expression of cooperage oak wood. *Proceedings of the National Academy of Sciences of the United States of America,* **106**: 9174-9179

Guchu, E., Diaz-Maroto, M.C., Diaz-Maroto, I.J., Vila-Lameiro, P. and Perez-Coello, M.S. (2006). Influence of the species and geographical location on volatile composition of Spanish oak wood (*Quercus petraea* Liebl. and *Quercus robur* L.). *Journal of Agricultural and Food Chemistry,* **54**: 3062-3066

Guichoux, E., Lagache, L., Wagner, S., Léger, P. and Petit, R.J. (2011). Two highly-validated multiplexes (12-plex and 8-plex) for species delimitation and parentage analysis in oaks (*Quercus* spp.). *Molecular Ecology Resources,* **11**: 578-585

Haasl, R.J. and Payseur, B.A. (2011). Multi-locus inference of population structure: a comparison between single nucleotide polymorphisms and microsatellites. *Heredity,* **106**: 158-171

Humphreys, J.R., O'reilly-Wapstra, J.M., Harbard, J.L., Davies, N.W., Griffin, A.R., Jordan, G.J. and Potts, B.M. (2008). Discrimination between seedlings of *Eucalyptus globulus, E. nitens* and their F-1 hybrid using near-infrared reflectance spectroscopy and foliar oil content. *Silvae Genetica,* **57**: 262-269

Jarauta, I., Cacho, J. and Ferreira, V. (2005). Concurrent phenomena contributing to the formation of the aroma of wine during aging in oak wood: An analytical study. *Journal of Agricultural and Food Chemistry,* **53**: 4166-4177

Lens, F., Jansen, S., Caris, P., Serlet, L. and Smets, E. (2005). Comparative wood anatomy of the primuloid clade (*Ericales* s.l.). *Systematic Botany,* **30**: 163-183

Lepais, O., Léger, V. and Gerber, S. (2006). Short note: High throughput microsatellite genotyping in oak species. *Silvae Genetica,* **55**: 238-240

Lin, H. and Walker, M.A. (1997). Extracting DNA from cambium tissue for analysis of grape rootstocks. *Hortscience,* **32**: 1264-1266

Lindahl, T. (1993). Instability and decay of the primary structure of DNA. *Nature,* **362**: 709-715

Mariette, S., Cottrell, J., Csaikl, U.M., Goikoechea, P., Konig, A., Lowe, A.J., Van Dam, B.C., Barreneche, T., Bodenes, C., Streiff, R., Burg, K., Groppe, K., Munro, R.C., Tabbener, H. and Kremer, A. (2002). Comparison of levels of genetic diversity detected with AFLP and microsatellite markers within and among mixed *Quercus petraea* Liebl. and *Quercus robur* L. stands. *Silvae Genetica,* **51**: 72-79

Mosedale, J.R. (1995). Effects of oak wood on the maturation of alcoholic beverages with particular reference to whisky. *Forestry,* **68**: 203-230

Mosedale, J.R., Feuillat, F., Baumes, R., Dupouey, J.L. and Puech, J.L. (1998). Variability of wood extractives among *Quercus robur* and *Quercus petraea* trees from mixed stands and their relation to wood anatomy and leaf morphology. *Canadian Journal of Forest Research,* **28**: 994-1006

Mosedale, J.R. and Ford, A. (1996). Variation of the flavour and extractives of European oak wood from two French forests. *Journal of the Science of Food and Agriculture,* **70**: 273-287

Muir, G., Fleming, C.C. and Schlotterer, C. (2001). Three divergent rDNA clusters predate the species divergence in *Quercus petraea* (matt.) liebl. and *Quercus robur* L. *Molecular Biology and Evolution,* **18**: 112-119

Ogden, R., Mcgough, H.N., Cowan, R.S., Chua, L.L., Groves, M. and Mcewing, R. (2009). SNP-based method for the genetic identification of ramin *Gonystylus spp.* timber and products: applied research meeting CITES enforcement needs. *Endangered Species Research,* **9**: 255-261

Prida, A., Ducousso, A., Petit, R.J., Nepveu, G. and Puech, J.L. (2007). Variation in wood volatile compounds in a mixed oak stand: strong species and spatial differentiation in whisky-lactone content. *Annals of Forest Science,* **64**: 313-320

Prida, A. and Puech, J.L. (2006). Influence of geographical origin and botanical species on the content of extractives in American, French, and East European oak woods. *Journal of Agricultural and Food Chemistry,* **54**: 8115-8126

Pritchard, J.K., Stephens, M. and Donnelly, P. (2000). Inference of population structure using multilocus genotype data. *Genetics,* **155**: 945-959

Rachmayanti, Y., Leinemann, L., Gailing, O. and Finkeldey, R. (2009). DNA from processed and unprocessed wood: Factors influencing the isolation success. *Forensic Science International-Genetics,* **3**: 185-192

Russ, A., Fiserova, M. and Gigac, J. (2009). Preliminary study of wood sepcies identification by NIR spectroscopy. *Wood Research,* **54**: 23-32

Samuel, R. (1999). Identification of hybrids between *Quercus petraea* and *Q. robur* (*Fagaceae*): results obtained with RAPD markers confirm allozyme studies based on the Got-2 locus. *Plant Systematics and Evolution,* **217**: 137-146

Scotti-Saintagne, C., Mariette, S., Porth, I., Goicoechea, P.G., Barreneche, T., Bodenes, K., Burg, K. and Kremer, A. (2004). Genome scanning for interspecific differentiation between two closely related oak species [*Quercus robur* L. and *Q. petraea (*Matt.) Liebl.]. *Genetics,* **168**: 1615-1626

Soulsbury, C., Iossa, G., Edwards, K., Baker, P. and Harris, S. (2007). Allelic dropout from a high-quality DNA source. *Conservation Genetics,* **8**: 733-738

Spillman, P.J. (1999). Wine quality biases inherent in comparisons of oak chip and barrel systems. *Australian and New Zealand Wine Industry Journal,* **14**: 25-33

Spillman, P.J., Sefton, M.A. and Gawel, R. (2004). The effect of oak wood source, location of seasoning and coopering on the composition of volatile compounds in oak-matured wines. *Australian Journal of Grape and Wine Research,* **10**: 216-226

Tacconi, L. (2008). *Illegal logging: law enforcement, livelihoods and the timber trade,* Earthscan

Tvedebrink, T., Eriksen, P.S., Mogensen, H.S. and Morling, N. (2009). Estimating the probability of allelic drop-out of STR alleles in forensic genetics. *Forensic Science International-Genetics,* **3**: 222-226

Young, O.A., Kaushal, M., Robertson, J.D., Burns, H. and Nunns, S.J. (2010). Use of species other than oak to flavor wine: an exploratory survey. *Journal of Food Science,* **75**: S490-S498

Chapter 8

Kiwi spirits: first results

Francisco López[1], Laura García-Llobodanin[1], Ricardo Pérez-Correa[2], Pilar Blanco[3], Cristina López-Vázquez[3], Ignacio Orriols[3]

[1]Departament d'Enginyeria Química, Facultat d'Enologia, Universitat Rovira i Virgili, Av. Països Catalans 26, Campus Sescelades, 43007 Tarragona, Spain; [2]Departamento de Ingeniería Química y Bioprocesos, Pontificia Universidad Católica de Chile, Casilla 306, Santiago 22, Chile; [3]Estación de Viticultura y Enología de Galicia (EVEGA)-Ingacal, Ponte San Clodio, 32427 Leiro, Spain

Introduction

Kiwi or kiwi fruit, botanically known as Actinidia chinensis, originates from the Yangtze River valley of China (Luh and Wang, 1984). In recent years, due to the development of cultivation techniques and production management, in Spain (mainly Galicia) and other countries kiwi production has increased significantly leading to an excess of supply, hence, new forms of use need to be developed. Spanish kiwi production, over 10,000 tonnes, is mainly located in Galicia, where more than 60% of the 900 hectares grown in Spain is concentrated. Consequently, despite the fact that kiwi is still mainly consumed fresh; there is an increasing trend to develop new kiwi based products, such as nectar, jams and preserves. Moreover, in recent years some kiwi wine studies have been developed, especially in some places of Asia. This opens up the possibility of developing kiwi distillates. Nevertheless academic research on kiwi wine and distillates is scarce. Our literature search found only two papers on kiwi wine in Europe (Sensidoni, Da Porto, Dalla Rosa and Testolin, 1997 and Soufleros, Pissa, Petridis, Lygerakis, Mermelas, Boukouvalas, and Tsimitakis, 2001) and one on kiwi distillates (Sensidoni et al 1997). Consequently, this research aims to provide fundamental knowledge that will help developing kiwi distillates that meet market standards.

Materials and methods

Kiwi fruits of the Hayward variety, grown in the southwest of Galicia (Spain), harvested in November 2009, were used in this work. Kiwi fruits were sorted by size and washed with plenty of running water in order to remove foreign material from the skin (pesticides, hairs, particles). Next, the kiwi fruits were crushed, and the mash obtained, treated with a pectolytic enzyme to favour juice extraction. The mash obtained was divided into 6 batches of 55 kg and put in 6 fermentation tanks of 50 L. The kiwi mash was fermented using two different strains of *Saccharomyces cerevisiae*: L1 (*S. cerevisiae* ALB-6 from yeast collection of EVEGA) and L2 (*S. cerevisiae* Uvaferm BDX from Lallemand), and then 50 kg of fermented kiwi mash was distilled in a 50 L copper Charantais alembic. The first 300 mL of distillate was collected as head, the heart was collected until the final concentration reached 40 °A, and the tail was distilled until the final ethanol concentration reached 28 °A. Distillations for both types of yeast were carried out in triplicate.

The distillates were submitted to analysis of the volatile compounds by GC-FID, with direct injection of the rough distillate. Analyses were carried out using two different columns. A capillary column CP-WAX-57 CB (Varian) was used for evaluation of the macroconstituents according the method given in a previous study (López-Vázquez, Bollaín, Bertsch, and Orriols, 2010). The other compounds were analysed using a Supelcowax 10 capillary column, and the method used was the one described by López-Vázquez, Bollaín, Moser, and Orriols, 2010.

Statistical analysis. One-way analysis of variance (ANOVA) was applied to the data obtained from the GC analysis to determine significant differences (at 5% level) between the kiwi spirits produced with the two different yeast strains. All the statistical analyses were performed with the SPSS statistical package (version 17.0).

Results and discussion

Fermentation process

The characteristics of the initial mash and the final kiwi ferments are summarized in Table 1. Fermentation runs took around six days to complete, although fermentation conditions were maintained for four additional days. The fermentation temperature was maintained at 12 ± 1°C.

Fermentations carried out with yeast L1 (ALB 6) showed a slightly lower alcohol content, a lower total acidity and a lower citric and malic acid concentration than fermentations conducted with L2 yeast ($p<0.05$). The volatile acidity and pH were slightly higher in L1 yeast fermentations.

Aroma analysis

Table 2 shows the average concentration of macroconstituents for the spirits obtained. They are grouped according to the yeast used in the kiwi fermentation. The heart ethanol contents for yeasts L1 and L2 were 41.5 ± 0.9 %v/v and 42.3 ± 1.6%v/v, respectively.

In all cases methanol concentrations surpassed the legal limit (1000 g/hL a.a.) for general fruit spirits. However, the values are similar to those obtained by Sensidoni et al 1997 in a distillation column operating at atmospheric pressure. However, our kiwi distillates are within the methanol limits of such fruit distillates as plum, mirabelle, quetsch, apple, pear (except for Williams pears), raspberry, blackberry, apricot and peach (1200 g/hL a.a.) and below the limits of Williams pears, redcurrants, blackcurrants, rowanberries, elderberries, quinces and juniper berries (1350 g/hL a.a., Council Regulation EC No. 110/2008).

Table 1. Characteristics of initial mash and final kiwi ferments

	Initial mash	*L1 yeast*		*L2 yeast*	
		mean	*sd*	*mean*	*sd*
Citric acid (g/L)	7.60	6.40	0.53	7.27	0.76
Density (g/mL)	1.0415	1.012	<0.001	1.014	0.004
Alcoholic strength (%vol.)	5.4[a]	4.63	0.06	4.80	0.10
Reduced sugars (g/L)*	59.6	2.70	0.10	2.40	<0.01
Total acidity (g/L tartaric acid)*	11.4	9.63	0.15	10.37	0.15
Volatile acidity (g/L acetic acid)*	nd	1.39	0.06	1.26	0.03
pH*	3.54	3.88	0.03	3.76	0.03
Malic acid (g/L)*	nd	3.53	0.32	4.60	0.26

[a]: probable alcohol strength. * indicate significant differences ($P < 0.05$) between yeast used. sd: standard deviation

Table 2. Content of macroconstituents (g/hl a.a.) present in distillates obtained from kiwi. (Σ Total higher alcohols: 1-propanol, 2-methyl-1-propanol, 1-butanol, 2-butanol, 2-methyl-1-butanol, 3-methyl-1-butanol).

	L1 yeast		*L2 yeast*	
	Mean	*sd*	*Mean*	*sd*
ethanol %v/v	41.5	0.9	42.3	1.6
Methanol	1236.6	76.4	1137.3	47.4
Ethyl acetate	46.4	8.9	33.0	0.3
Acetaldehyde	153.9	38.0	212.2	41.6
Acetal	51.9	10.6	65.5	16.3
1-propanol	49.57	2.19	50.32	5.17
2-methyl-1-propanol	70.20	1.28	75.30	13.09
1-butanol*	1.12	0.06	0.62	0.05
2-butanol*	1.80	0.84	0.41	0.09
2-methyl-1-butanol*	40.07	0.73	52.83	7.45
3-methyl-1-butanol*	154.53	3.27	194.58	14.84
Σ Total higher alcohols*	317.30	4.37	374.06	28.91
Ethyl lactate*	6.48	2.45	1.86	0.67
1-hexanol*	6.27	0.55	4.13	0.22
Isobutyraldehyde	0.27	0.04	0.26	0.03
Ethyl formate	1.32	0.31	1.17	0.26
Methyl acetate	2.62	0.34	2.27	0.22
Acrolein	4.48	0.80	5.27	1.13

* indicate significant differences ($P < 0.05$) between yeast used. sd: standard deviation

Acetaldehyde is mainly produced by yeast during the fermentation process (Apostolopoulou, Flouros, Demertzis, and Akrida-Demertzi, 2005) and when the distillates obtained with both yeasts were compared, it was seen that yeast L1 produced lower amounts of acetaldehyde than yeast L2, although the differences were not statistically significant.

The average concentration of ethyl acetate in the samples studied ranged between 33.0 and 46.4 g/hL a.a., which is much lower than the perception threshold of 180 g/hL a.a. (Soufleros, Mygdalia, and Natskoulis, 2004).

Ethyl lactate is also linked to bacterial spoilage, specifically to lactic acid bacteria (Apostolopoulou et al 2005). The distillates obtained presented low concentrations of this compound in all cases, which indicated that there was no spoilage.

Higher alcohols are mostly formed during fermentation. They make an important contribution to the aroma profile of distillates, imparting a positive aroma and essential character (Soufleros et al 2004). The values are lower than those of Sensidoni et al, 1997, in the order of 50-60% and 30-40%, when distillation is carried out at atmospheric pressure and under vacuum, respectively. When the two yeasts were compared, it was observed that yeast L1 produced slightly fewer higher alcohols than yeast L2. Finally, 1-hexanol may have a partly varietal origin. It plays a positive role in spirits, but when it exceeds 10-15 g/hL a.a., its strong herbal smell becomes unpleasant (Cantagrel, Lurton, Vidal, and Galy, 1997).

Table 3 shows the average concentration of microconstituents for the spirits obtained, then we analyse the most significant results. Higher alcohol acetates are of fermentative origin and supply the distillates with apple and banana scents, especially isoamyl acetate (Versini, Franco, Moser, Barchetti, and Manca, 2009). The amounts found of isoamyl acetate in our distillates are notably lower to the values found by Sensidoni et al 1997.

C4-C12 ethyl esters come from the fruit and are also produced during fermentation. The values obtained are about 50% lower than those

Table 3. Content of microconstituents (g/hl a.a.) present in distillates obtained from kiwi. S Ethyl esters C6-C12: ethyl hexanoate, ethyl octanoate, ethyl decanoate, ethyl dodecanoate, ethyl palmitate. S Ethyl esters C14-C18: Ethyl tetradecanoate, Ethyl hexadecanoate, Ethyl octadecanoate, Ethyl 9-octadecenoate, Ethyl 9,12-octadecadienonate, Ethyl 9,12,15-octadecatrienoate. S Minor alcohols: 1-pentanol, 1-heptanol, 1-octanol, 1-nonanol, 1-decanol. S monoterpenols: trans-furan linalool oxide, cis-furan linalool oxide, linalol, a-terpineol, Citronellol, Nerol, Geraniol, Hotrienol

	L1 yeast		*L2 yeast*	
	Mean	*sd*	*Mean*	*sd*
Isoamyl acetate	0.02	0.00	0.03	0.02
Hexyl acetate	<LOD		<LOD	
Ethyl butyrate	0.09	0.04	0.08	0.04
Σ Ethyl esters C6-C12	2.14	1.06	2.04	1.00
Σ	0.44	0.42	0.44	0.75
trans-3-hexen-1-ol	0.03	0.01	0.02	0.01
cis-3-hexen-1-ol*	0.14	0.02	0.08	0.02
trans-2-hexen-1-ol	0.03	0.01	0.01	0.01
1-pentanol	0.23	0.02	0.19	0.03
1-heptanol*	0.05	0.00	0.03	0.01
1-octanol*	0.11	0.03	0.04	0.00
1-nonanol	0.04	0.00	0.03	0.01
1-decanol*	0.03	0.01	<LOD	
Benzylic alcohol	0.05	0.01	0.03	0.01
2-phenylethanol	0.76	0.11	1.09	0.43
Σ Minor alcohols*	0.45	0.03	0.30	0.04
Benzaldehyde*	0.01	0.00	<LOD	0.00
Furfuraldehyde	1.56	0.28	1.40	0.52
3-ethoxy-1-propanol	0.04	0.03	0.03	0.00
1-octen-3-ol*	0.02	0.00	<LOD	
3-hydroxy-2-butanone*	1.43	1.12	0.05	0.04
trans-furan linalool oxide	0.26	0.03	0.23	0.06
cis-furan linalool oxide	<LOD		<LOD	
linalol	0.76	0.19	0.44	0.08
α-terpineol	0.19	0.02	0.16	0.03
Citronellol*	0.19	0.01	0.07	0.02
Nerol	<LOD		<LOD	
Geraniol	<LOD		<LOD	
Hotrienol[d]	0.21	0.02	0.18	0.04
Σ monoterpenols*	1.61	0.20	1.07	0.22

* indicate significant differences ($P < 0.05$) between yeast used. LOD = detection limits.
d Quantification as linalol. (RF = 1.02). sd: standard deviation

obtained for kiwi distillates by Sensidoni et al 1997, nevertheless the levels of C4-C12 ethyl esters are similar for both yeasts tested.

C14-C18 ethyl esters are high molecular weight compounds that are dependent on the yeast level in the fermented pomaces, yeast type and nutrition factors (Versini et al, 2009). In our distillates, levels were similar with the two types of yeasts used. Nevertheless, the concentration of ethyl tetradecanoate, the only C14-C18 ethyl ester identified by Sensidoni et al (1997) in kiwi distillates is lower.

Hexenols are usually called 'leaf alcohols' because of the flavour they impart to spirits when present at relatively high concentrations (Versini et al, 2009). The concentrations of cis-

3-hexen-1-ol are higher for yeast L1 ($p<0.05$). In our kiwi distillates, the concentrations of these alcohols are low, and the cis-3-hexen-1-ol concentration is 4-5 times higher than that of trans-3-hexen-1-ol.

Linear alcohols from C7 to C10 are rather fruity-floral compounds derived from the decomposition of fatty acids during the fermentative process (Versini et al, 2009). Their concentration in the kiwi distillates is quite low for both of the yeasts. However, 1-pentanol showed significantly higher concentrations than the other linear alcohols.

Among the minor alcohols present in the kiwi distillates, 2-phenylethanol shows the highest concentration, ranging from 0.76 to 1.09 g/hL a.a. for yeast L1 and L2, respectively. The differences, however, are not statistically significant (see Table 3). The levels found in our distillates (around 1 g/hL a.a.) indicate a good separation of the tail fraction. In addition, the yeasts used did not significantly affect the amount of 2-phenylethanol produced, the levels of which are lower than those found by Sensidoni et al, 1997 for kiwi distillate..

Terpenoids play an important role in the flavour profile of fruits and fruit distillates, even when present at low concentrations. In our distillates, the so-called 'skin monoterpenols' (geraniol, nerol, and citronellol) had lower concentrations than linalool. Sensidoni et al, 1997 detected a similar trend, but at generally lower concentrations and they identified fewer compounds than in our distillates. It should be pointed out that the distillates obtained from the kiwi fermented with yeast L1 presented a significantly higher concentration of monoterpenols than distillates obtained with yeast L2

In our distillates, furfuraldehyde shows a very low concentration. Therefore, it can be concluded that the separation of the tail fraction was good, which confirms the results obtained for the 2-phenylethanol.

The ANOVA tests focused on comparing the differences between the kiwi spirits obtained with yeast L1 and L2. For yeast L1, the concentrations of 2-methyl-1-butanol, 3-methyl-1-butanol and the total higher alcohols were significantly lower ($p < 0.05$). On the other hand, the concentrations of 1-butanol, 2-butanol, ethyl lactate, 1-hexanol, cis-3-hexen-1-ol, 1-heptanol, 1-octanol, benzaldehyde, 1-octen-3-ol, citronellol and the sum of monoterpenols were significantly higher ($p < 0.05$). All other compounds underwent no significant changes in their concentration. From this series of ANOVA tests, it can be concluded that yeast L1 gives a kiwi spirit with fewer total higher alcohols, although in the range normally found in other fruit spirits. In addition, the higher concentration of monoterpenols obtained with L1 yeast is positive for the aromatic profile of the kiwi spirit.

To conclude, then, kiwi fruit can be a good raw material for obtaining spirits. Nevertheless, additional studies with other yeasts, distillation systems or enzymatic treatment are necessary if products are to be distinctive and accepted by consumers (i.e., lower levels of methanol and higher levels of higher alcohols, ethyl esters C6-C12 and monoterpenols).

Acknowledgements

J.R.P. appreciates the support of AGAUR from the Generalitat de Catalunya through grant 2007PIV-00017 and the Pontificia Universidad Católica de Chile for financial support for a sabbatical visit at the Department d'Enginyeria Química of the URV. C.L.-V. acknowledges the Ph.D. fellowship from INIA. The reported research has been funded by FEDER and INIA (Instituto Nacional de Investigación y Tecnología Agraria y Alimentaria) (RTA2009-00123-C02-01).

References

Apostolopoulou, A.; Flouros, A.; Demertzis, P.; Akrida-Demertzi, K. (2005) Differences in concentration of principal volatile constituents in traditional greek distillates. Food Control **16**: 157-164.

Cantagrel, R., Lurton, L., Vidal, J. P., Galy, B. (1997). From vine to cognac. In: Fermented Beverage Production, 1st ed., Edited by Lea, A. G. H., Piggott, J. R., Blackie Academic and Professional, London, UK, pp. 208-228

López-Vázquez, C.; Bollaín, M. H.; Bertsch, K.; Orriols, I. (2010) Fast determination of principal volatile compounds in distilled spirits. Food Control **21**: 1436–1441.

López-Vázquez, C.; Bollaín, M. H.; Moser, S.; Orriols, I. (2010) Characterization and Differentiation of Monovarietal Grape Pomace Distillate from Native Varieties of Galicia. Journal of Agricultural and Food Chemistry **58**: 9657-9665.

Luh, B. S., Wang, Z. Kiwifruit (1984) Advances in Food Research **29**: 279–307

Sensidoni, A.; Da Porto, C.; Dalla Rosa, M.; Testolin; R. (1997) Utilisation of reject kiwifruit fruit for alcoholic and non-alcoholic beverages. Acta Horticulturae **444**: 663-670

Soufleros, E.H.; Mygdalia, A.S.; Natskoulis, P. (2004) Characterization and safety evaluation of the traditional Greek fruit distillate "Mouro" by flavor compounds and mineral analysis. Food Chemistry **86:** 625-636.

Soufleros, E.H.; Pissa, I.; Petridis, D.; Lygerakis, M.; Mermelas, K.; Boukouvalas, G.; Tsimitakis, E. (2001) Instrumental analysis of volatile and other compounds of Greek kiwi wine; sensory evaluation and optimisation of its composition. Food Chemistry **75**: 487-500.

Versini, G.; Franco, M.A.; Moser, S.; Barchetti, P.; Manca, G. (2009) Characterisation of apple distillates from native varieties of Sardinia island and comparison with other Italian products. Food Chemistry **113**:1176-1183.

Chapter 9

Potential of Conference pear variety to produce pear spirits: influence of the raw material and distillation system on the final quality of the spirits

Francisco López[1], Yanine Arrieta-Garay[1], Laura García-Llobodanin[1], Ricardo Pérez-Correa[2], Pilar Blanco[3], Cristina López-Vázquez[3], Ignacio Orriols[3]
[1]Departament d'Enginyeria Química, Facultat d'Enologia, Universitat Rovira i Virgili, Av. Països Catalans 26, Campus Sescelades, 43007 Tarragona, Spain; [2]Departamento de Ingeniería Química y Bioprocesos, Pontificia Universidad Católica de Chile, Casilla 306, Santiago 22, Chile; [3]Estación de Viticultura y Enología de Galicia (EVEGA)-Ingacal, Ponte San Clodio, 32427 Leiro, Spain

Introduction

Spain is the second largest pear producing country in the European Union; the Conference variety is the most abundant. The development of a pear spirit using local varieties of pear such as Conference can help to reduce the surplus of this fruit, while providing a product with high added value. The possibility of using pear juice concentrate as the raw material for the process has two logistic advantages compared to the raw fruit or juice: the storage space needed is smaller, and it is less likely to spoil. However, the process of concentration can cause loss of aroma, so the addition of aromas recovered in the concentration step may allow obtaining spirits that are more similar to those obtained from the natural juice. The volatile composition of a distilled beverage is a complex matrix of different compounds and depends not only on the material used, but also on the distillation processes (Hernández-Gómez, Úbeda and Briones, 2003, Rodriguez –Madrera, Blanco-Gomis, and Mangas-Alonso, 2003).

In this study we have compared the aromatic profile of pear brandy produced from pear juice concentrate (with and without addition of aroma recovered), and natural pear juice of the Conference variety with two different distillation equipments.

Materials and methods

Pear juice preparation

The natural pear juice, and pear juice concentrate from the Conference variety, were produced and donated by Nufri S.A. (Lleida, Spain). They were all obtained from the same production batch, in order to assure comparable results. The natural juice was a concentration of sugars of 43.4 g/L, and the concentrated juice, of 71 °Brix, was diluted with water until a sugar concentration of 35.6 g/L. The dilution was done before the fermentation. Total sugars were measured using a GAB kit for sugar analysis (GAB Sistemática Analítica S.L., Spain).

Fermentation process

A volume of 150 L of both pear juices natural and concentrated previously diluted were equally divided into three stainless steel fermentation tanks of 100 L capacity each. The pH of the pear juice was adjusted to 3.2 using concentrated sulphuric acid. An inoculum of a commercial strain of *Saccharomyces cerevisiae* (Enoferm BDX, Lallemand, Switzerland), prepared according to the instructions provided by the supplier, was added to the fermentation tanks in a dose of 25 g /hL. Fermentations were carried out at room temperature (14 ºC) until the concentration of total sugars was lower than 3.0 g/L. The ethanol content was determined by High Performance Liquid Chromatography as described by García-Llobodanin, Achaerandio, Ferrando, Güell and López, 2007. Once the fermentation finished, the pear wines obtained were mixed and kept in a glass fibre tank until distillation.

Distillations with traditional alembics

The pear wine was double-distilled, in the presence of its lees, to obtain the pear spirit. A volume of 12 L of pear wine was first distilled in a 20 L copper Charentais alembic, heating the base of the boiler with an electric heater and using tap water to cool the total condenser. The heater was set to obtain an average distillation rate of 14 mL/min approximately. The first 1.2 L distilled were collected and used for the second distillation, which was carried out in a 2 L copper Charentais alembic. In this case, the electric heater was set to obtain an average distillation rate of 3 mL/min. The first two samples collected were 25 mL each, followed by samples of 50 mL each, until a total volume of 450 mL had been distilled. Distillations and re-distillations were performed in triplicate, although the products of the first distillations were combined and then split into three equal volumes before re-distillation. Once a distillation had finished, the alembic was allowed to cool. Then, it was washed and left to dry before the next distillation was performed. Usually only one distillation was performed per day. The ethanol content of each sample was determined by gas chromatography (GC). Based on sensory analysis, the fraction of the head is defined as the first fraction of 25 ml for both the natural and concentrate juice, the fraction of the heart included samples from 25 to 300 ml and 25 to 250 ml, for natural (Al-nat) and concentrate (Al-conc) juices, respectively, the rest of fractions till 450 ml was the tail.

Packed column distillations

The packed column distillations consists of a 50-L cylindrical stainless steel boiler with two 1.2 kW electric heaters, a copper rectification column (5.25 cm OD) packed with 10 cm of copper mesh (Amphora Society, http://www.amphorasociety.com/). The column also included a partial condenser as well as a total condenser and a condensate reservoir (2 cm height). A more detailed description of the equipment and distillation conditions can be found in García-Llobodanin, Roca, López, Pérez-Correa and López, 2011.

The boiler was loaded with 36 L of pear wine with its lees. First, four samples of 25 mL of distillate were collected, followed by samples of 50 mL each, until a total volume of 900 mL was reached. Two distillations were performed. The ethanol content of each sample was determined by GC. Based on an organoleptic analysis of the different samples, the head fraction was defined as the first 25 mL for natural and concentrate wine pear (Col-nat and Col-conc-1) and the first 50 mL for the concentrate wine pear with aromas (Col-conc-2). The heart fraction included samples from 25 to 650 mL for all the distillations. In all cases, the rest was the tail fraction.

Statistical analysis

One-way analysis of variance (ANOVA) was applied to assess if there were significant differences (at 5% level) between the different Conference pear spirits obtained. Principal components analysis (PCA) was performed to determine the differentiation degree due to the raw material and the distillation system used. All the statistical analyses were performed by means of SPSS statistical package (version 15.0).

Sensory evaluation

The pear distillates were diluted with demineralised water to an ethanol content of 40% (v/v), Then, they were tasted for their flavour quality using order-of-preference tests. Sensory evaluation was conducted with a panel of 28 consumers, whom were asked to evaluate separately the smell and the taste of the spirits. The results were analyzed using the Friedmann statistic test, described by Jellinek, 1981.

Results and discussion

Conference pear juices were fermented according to the procedure described in the fermentation process, and the total duration was 8 days. The six fermentations showed the same behaviour throughout the process, so the fermented pear juices from natural and concentrated were mixed for further distillation. The final total amounts of sugar were 2.6 g/L and 0.8 g/L for the natural and concentrated juice, respectively, and the final ethanol concentrations were 16.3 and 19.2 g/L for the natural and concentrated juice, respectively. The pear wine was stored at 4 °C until distillation.

Table 1 shows the volatile composition and ethanol content of the different pear spirits.

Table 1. Concentrations (g/hL a.a.) of the main volatile compounds present in the heart fractions obtained [(1)].

Compound	*Al-nat*	*Al-conc*	*Col-nat*	*Col-conc-1*	*Col-conc-2*
acetaldehyde	36.1 ± 1.3 ^{a,A}	25.9 ± 1.6 ^{b,B}	20.7 ± 1.0 ^{a,B}	8.3 ± 0.1 ^{b,B}	63.6 ± 0.7 ^{c,C}
acetal	7.4 ± 0.2 ^{a,A}	5.2 ± 0.3 ^{b,A}	3.3 ± 0.6 ^{a,B}	1.9 ± 0.1 ^{b,B}	11.0 ± 0.5 ^{c,C}
methanol	997.3 ± 2.7 ^{a,A}	270.5 ± 9.3 ^{b,A}	905.0 ± 10.4 ^{a,B}	45.6 ± 0.6 ^{b,B}	282.0 ± 2.3 ^{c,A}
furfural	1.6 ± 0.1 ^{a,A}	2.1 ± 0.2 ^{b,A}	1.7 ± 0.1 ^{a,A}	4.0 ± 0.0 ^{b,B}	4.1 ± 0.1 ^{c,B}
1-propanol	40.9 ± 2.1 ^{a,A}	38.4 ± 3.1 ^{a,A}	42.4 ± 1.5 ^{a,A}	43.3 ± 1.8 ^{a,B}	45.0 ± 0.0 ^{a,B}
2-methyl-1-propanol	52.7 ± 1.5 ^{a,A}	51.9 ± 0.0 ^{a,A}	67.8 ± 1.5 ^{a,B}	59.3 ± 1.0 ^{b,B}	57.1 ± 0.6 ^{c,C}
1-butanol	3.2 ± 0.1 ^{a,A}	15.5 ± 0.3 ^{b,A}	3.6 ± 0.2 ^{a,A}	0.3 ± 0.0 ^{b,B}	15.7 ± 0.0 ^{c,A}
2-butanol	<LOD	0.5 ± 0.0 ^{b,A}	0.1 ± 0.0 ^{a,B}	1.7 ± 0.2 ^{b,B}	1.4 ± 0.0 ^{c,C}
2-methyl-1-butanol	35.0 ± 0.4 ^{a,A}	31.6 ± 0.2 ^{b,A}	48.7 ± 1.4 ^{a,B}	43.7 ± 0.0 ^{b,B}	39.5 ± 0.1 ^{c,C}
3-methyl-1-butanol	189.8 ± 6.2 ^{a,A}	194.2 ± 2.6 ^{a,A}	252.4 ± 6.2 ^{a,B}	277.2 ± 2.1 ^{b,B}	241.8 ± 1.0 ^{c,C}
phenethyl alcohol	0.7 ± 0.0 ^{a,A}	0.5 ± 0.1 ^{b,A}	0.3 ± 0.0 ^{a,B}	0.4 ± 0.0 ^{b,B}	0.3 ± 0.0 ^{a,B}
total higher alcohols[(2)]	**321.6 ± 5.6 ^{a,A}**	**332.1 ± 5.6 ^{a,A}**	**415 ± 9.4 ^{a,B}**	**425.5 ± 4.9 ^{b,B}**	**400.5 ± 1.7 ^{c,C}**
methyl acetate	3.5 ± 0.1 ^{a,A}	1.8 ± 0.1 ^{b,A}	10.0 ± 0.6 ^{a,B}	0.6 ± 0.0 ^{b,B}	2.5 ± 0.2 ^{c,A}
ethyl acetate	16.5 ± 0.1 ^{a,A}	15.5 ± 0.1 ^{a,A}	102.9 ± 3.5 ^{a,B}	59.2 ± 0.9 ^{b,B}	61.0 ± 1.2 ^{c,B}
ethyl hexanoate	0.4 ± 0.0 ^{a,A}	<LOD	1.0 ± 0.1 ^{a,B}	0.3 ± 0.0 ^{b,B}	2.2 ± 0.1 ^{c,C}
ethyl octanoate	0.3 ± 0.0 ^{a,A}	0.1 ± 0.0 ^{a,A}	0.7 ± 0.3 ^{a,B}	0.4 ± 0.0 ^{a,A}	0.3 ± 0.0 ^{b,A}
ethyl decanoate	0.2 ± 0.0 ^{a,A}	0.5 ± 0.0 ^{a,A}	1.8 ± 1.1 ^{a,B}	1.7 ± 0.0 ^{a,B}	1.6 ± 0.1 ^{a,A}
ethyl myristate	<LOD	<LOD	0.047 ± 0.001 ^{a,B}	<LOD	0.004 ± 0.000 ^{b,A}
ethyl palmitate	<LOD	<LOD	0.309 ± 0.098 ^{a,B}	0.205 ± 0.029 ^{a,B}	0.020 ± 0.005 ^{b,A}
total ethyl esters[(3)]	**0.9 ± 0.0 ^{a,A}**	**0.6 ± 0.0 ^{b,A}**	**3.5 ± 1.3 ^{a,B}**	**2.4 ± 0.2 ^{b,B}**	**4.1 ± 0.2 ^{c,C}**

LOD = detection limits.

(1) Different superscript small letters in the same row indicate a significant difference ($P \leq 0.05$) for the pear spirits produced with the two different raw matters for every distillation methods. Different superscript capital letters in each row indicate significant difference ($P \leq 0.05$) for the spirits produced with the same raw matter and different equipment.

(2) Σ 1-propanol, 2-methyl-1-propanol, 1-butanol, 2-butanol, 2-methyl-1-butanol, 3-methyl-1-butanol

(3) Σ ethyl hexanoate, ethyl octanoate, ethyl decanoate, ethyl myristate, ethyl palmitate

The concentration of methanol in all the spirits obtained do not exceeded the legal limit of 1000 g/hL a.a. imposed by the European Council Regulation 110/2008. The concentrations of methanol are significantly higher in the distillates from natural pear juice compared to the ones from concentrate. Similar results were obtained with Blanquilla pear variety by Garcia-Llobodanin, Ferrando, Güell and López, 2008. This may be due to the low amount of pectic substances in the pear concentrate, because the methanol is produced by enzymatic degradation of pectic substances present mainly in the skin of the fruits (Da Porto, 2002). The concentration of methanol is lower in the spirits distilled with the column, nevertheless the spirit obtained with the concentrate juice with aroma addition shows similar levels of methanol than the obtained with alembic without addition of aromas.

In the distillates, the total amount of higher alcohols ranged between 321 and 426 g/hL a.a. The distillates obtained with the column have a higher concentration of total higher alcohols, and the effect of the raw material employed is not significant.

On the other hand, the sum of the ethyl esters is present in higher concentrations in the distillates from concentrate pear juice with addition of aromas, but the distillates from natural pear juice in both system is higher than the distillates from concentrate pear juice. The ethyl ester concentration is higher in the spirits distilled with the column.

A principal components analysis (PCA) was performed on all the data obtained, except ethyl and methyl acetates, in order to check for differences among the distillates. The PCA separates the compounds in three main components. The first two principal components (PC1 and PC2) are plotted in Fig. 1 and they explain 71.7% of the variance. PC1 is composed by 2-methyl-1-butanol (0.968), 2-methyl-1-propanol (0.940), 3-methy-1-butanol (0.867), phenethyl alcohol (-0,828), ethyl decanoate (0.798), ethyl octanoate (0.796), ethyl palmitate (0,767), ethyl myristate (0.742), and 1-propanol (0,583), PC2 is composed by 2-butanol (0.981), methanol (-0.948), and furfural (0.944). PC3 is composed by acetaldehyde (0.977), acetal (0.932), ethyl hexanoate (0.837), and 1-butanol (0.650).

From Figure 1 we can clearly differentiate between the distillates obtained from pear juice concentrate from the distillates obtained with

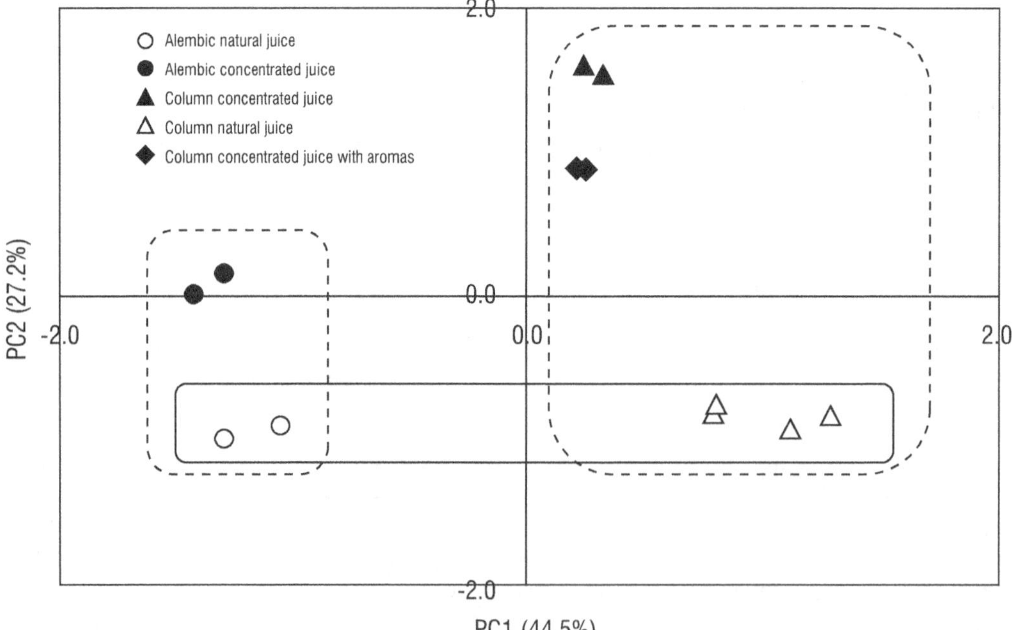

Figure 1. Principal components analysis (PCA) of the main volatile compounds in the pear spirits.

natural pear juice, and we can also differentiate between the distillates obtained by column or alembic. PC1 mainly differentiates the system of distillation, while PC2 mainly differentiates the raw material used.

The sensory evaluation showed that for the smell and taste, the spirits from natural pear juice were the preferred ones, not finding significant differences between the distillates obtained by alembic or column. The addition of aromas to the concentrated juices represents an improved acceptance of the spirit, being preferred to the spirit obtained with the concentrated juice without addition of aromas, but the difference is not significant.

In conclusion, the Conference pear was a suitable raw material for the production of pear spirits. However, the spirit made from juice concentrates are of lower quality than that obtained from fresh juice, even though the addition of aromas to the juice concentrate can improve its quality. The concentration of positive compounds as ethyl esters is higher in the spirits obtained with the column against the alembic.

Acknowledgements

Y.A.G greatly acknowledges to Universitat Rovira i Virgili (URV) for a financial support provided for performing the master's degree in Enology. J.R.P. appreciates the support of AGAUR from the Generalitat de Catalunya through grant 2007PIV-00017 and the Pontificia Universidad Católica de Chile for financial support for a sabbatical visit at the Department d'Enginyeria Química of the URV. C.L.-V. acknowledges the Ph.D. fellowship from INIA. The reported research has been funded by FEDER and INIA (Instituto Nacional de Investigación y Tecnología Agraria y Alimentaria) (RTA2009-00123-C02-01).

References

Da Porto, C. (2002). Volatile composition of 'grappa low wines' using different methods and conditions of storage on an industrial scale. International Journal of Food Science and Technology **37**: 395-402.

Garcia-Llobodanin, L., Achaerandio, I., Ferrando, M., Güell, C, López, F. (2007). Pear distillates from pear juice concentrate: effect of lees in the aromatic composition. Journal of Agricultural and Food Chemistry **55**: 3462-3468.

Garcia-Llobodanin, L., Ferrando, M., Güell, C, López, F. (2008). Pear distillates: influence of the raw material used on final quality. European Food Research and Technology **228**: 75-82.

García-Llobodanin, L.; Roca, J.; López, J.R..; Pérez-Correa, J.R. López, F. (2011). The lack of reproducibility of different distillation techniques and its impact on pear spirit composition. International Journal of Science and Technology 46: 1956-1963

Hernández-Gómez L, Úbeda J, Briones A (2003) Melon fruit distillates: comparison of different distillation methods. Food Chemistry **82**:539–543

Jellinek, G. (1981). Sensorische Lebensmittelprüfung. Verlag D&PS, Germany.

Rodríguez-Madrera, R.; Blanco-Gomis, D.; Mangas-Alonso, J.J. (2003) Influence of Distillation System, Oak Wood Type, and Aging Time on Volatile Compounds of Cider Brandy. Journal of Agricultural and Food Chemistry **51**: 5709-5714.

Chapter 10

Creating better cereal varieties for the sustainability of the distilling industry

T.A. Bringhurst, R.C. Agu, J.M. Brosnan
The Scotch Whisky Research Institute, The Robertson Trust Building, Research Avenue North, Riccarton, Edinburgh, EH14 4AP

Introduction

At the 2008 Worldwide Distilled Spirits conference James Brosnan outlined the Scotch whisky industry's aspirations for new wheat varieties that were required to meet its future sustainability and the involvement of the Scotch Whisky Institute in the distilling wheat selection process and supply chain projects designed to facilitate the development of new tools to fulfil these requirements (Brosnan et al 2010). We are now in a position to follow on from this, to highlight the successful selection, within the last few years, of three new distilling wheat varieties (Denman, Viscount and Beluga), each of which offers a significant increase in distilling quality compared with established varieties.

Unlike Scotch Malt Whisky, which is produced exclusively from malted barley, Scotch Grain Whisky and neutral spirits for vodka and gin manufacture can be produced from a range of unmalted cereals. Originally Scotch Grain Whisky spirit was produced from a mixture of malted and unmalted barley (as well as oats or rye) (Hume and Moss 2000)), but from the late 19th century until the 1980's US maize was the main unmalted cereal that was used. However since the mid 1980's, soft winter wheat has been the major cereal raw material for the production of Scotch Grain Whisky, although some maize is still used by at least one Scotch Whisky distillery. The changeover from maize to wheat was a result of its relatively low cost and local availability on the local market. The main disadvantages of wheat are its reduced alcohol yield compared with maize, and its association with processing problems, particularly in terms of the downstream viscosity, which has a strong impact on the efficiency of the systems that are used to recover valuable co-products such as dark grains and spent wash syrups. However, the 'local' availability of good quality distilling wheat and its relative cost continue to make this cereal attractive to distillers as a raw material. Until the advent of the bio-ethanol industry, the demand for distilling wheat represented a small, but significant niche market, and Scotch Whisky distillers use around 700,000 tonnes of wheat per year (HGCA 2011) out of a total production of around 15M tonnes. This demand is quite low compared with that from the potential demands of bioethanol processors, who are looking for supplies in excess of 2M tonnes for each individual plant. It is thus essential that the Scotch Whisky industry has a strong input into the selection of new wheat varieties, in order to ensure an ongoing, sustainable supply of suitable wheat raw materials to support its future production requirements (Brosnan et al 2010). To secure this, together with other major wheat supply chain representatives the Scotch Whisky industry, represented by the Scotch Whisky Research Institute (SWRI), is a strong participant in the UK selection process for new wheat varieties.

The official Home Grown Cereals Authority (HGCA) (National List/Recommended List) selection process for UK wheat, in which SWRI participates, helps to identify new distilling wheat varieties which are better suited for the production of potable spirits. The selection process for new wheat varieties includes the major commercial UK end-users of wheat, such as flour millers, bread producers, biscuit manufacturers as well as distillers (and bio-ethanol producers). Each of these has specific quality requirements for different types of wheat varieties which are officially classified into 4 separate groups by the National Association of British and Irish Millers (NABIM) (Table 1).

Scotch whisky distillers would use soft wheat varieties from groups 3 and 4, and an important function of the Scotch Whisky Research Institute is to provide distilling performance data, (alcohol yield and potential for downstream process problems) that can be used to select and promote new varieties that are particularly suited for distillers. Distillers quality requirements for wheat for potable ethanol (Scotch grain spirit and neutral spirit) production are well defined, (Bringhurst et al, 2008) these are, soft wheat, of low nitrogen/high starch content with easy processing characteristics (low viscosity). Hard wheats and soft wheat varieties containing the 1b1r rye gene translocation are not suitable for Scotch whisky distilling since they are associated with high viscosity and hence are more likely to result in processing problems.

Distillers are particularly interested in new wheat varieties that are capable of producing high levels of alcohol yield (litres of alcohol per tonne), and have over the last decade been able to encourage Plant Breeders to invest in the development of new varieties for this market. As a result, the current UK selection systems have been successful in generating a steady supply of suitable distilling varieties that provide an attractive return for growers. Table 2 shows the current SWRI classification of new wheat varieties for Scotch whisky production.

Table 1. NABIM Classification for UK Winter wheat (HGCA 2010)

NABIM Group	*Type*	*Principal application*	*Quality criteria*
1	Hard	Milling and Baking	Premium quality, consistent milling and baking performance, meeting specific quality requirements (Specific Wt (76 kg/hl), Protein (13%), HFN (~250) (Varieties not interchangeable- Depend on end user requirements)
2	Hard	Milling and Baking	Variable premium, breadmaking potential, some consistent but not as good as Gp 1. Others perform inconsistently or are suited to specialist flours, lower protein than Gp 1.
3	Soft	Biscuit, Cake, Distilling	Soft varieties for biscuit, cake and other flours, will also include some distilling varieties. Quality requirements include soft milling characteristics, low protein, good extraction rates and an extensible but not elastic gluten.
4s / h	Soft/Hard	Distilling, General purpose, Feed	Non-premium varieties mainly grown as feed varieties, but may be used by millers for some general purpose grists. Distillers will use certain soft varieties

Table 2. Current SWRI quality ratings for distilling wheat (modified from Bringhurst et al 2008)

Rating	*Definition*
Good	Established soft wheat variety producing consistently good laboratory distilling yield as well as giving good distilling performance
Medium/Good	Newer soft wheat variety producing consistent, good laboratory results or established variety giving satisfactory laboratory and distillery performance
Medium	Soft wheat variety with acceptable, but average results or laboratory distillery performance
Medium/Poor	Soft wheat with below average laboratory or distillery performance
Poor	Soft wheat with significantly below average laboratory or distillery performance, or which shows potential viscosity issues. Also includes all hard wheat or soft wheat carrying the 1b1r rye gene classification

As well as meeting alcohol production targets, initiatives to reduce the carbon footprint of the industry and address other sustainability issues have come to the fore over the last few years and this is now an important consideration for all stakeholders interested in the development of new wheat varieties. The Green Grain Project, which was led by ADAS (formerly the Agricultural Development Advisory Service, but privatised in 1997) together with the Scotch Whisky Research Institute, the Scottish Crop Research Institute (now the James Hutton Institute), Syngenta Seeds, the Home-Grown Cereals Authority (HGCA), and a number of other partners ((Foss (UK), Wessex Grain and Grampian Country Foods (VION Food Group)) aimed to identify an ideotype for distilling wheat that would address sustainability targets, such as reduced nitrogen inputs and environmental emissions, but which would also meet primary end-user requirements for high alcohol yield and desirable processing characteristics. The project was designed to develop improved tools that could be used by plant breeders to select suitable varieties directed at meeting these requirements. This project was very successful and one of the outputs was a new variety, Denman, which was identified as having a high potential for producing a high alcohol yield, as well as showing other important agronomic advantages.

Plant breeding and genetics

Plant breeders still take a 'classical' Mendelian approach to breeding new wheat varieties in which they select parental varieties with desirable properties (traits), which they hope to pass on to future generations to provide new improved varieties that are better suited for particular end-user markets. In practice this means screening and crossing potential parent varieties to provide a very large number of progeny, which need to be tested to identify those that are most suited for a particular application. These are assessed for a wide range of attributes, including agronomic performance (grain yield), disease resistance and potential end-user quality. In practice this means growing and evaluating many thousands of individual plants grown on trial plots. As a result, breeding of new wheat varieties is a time consuming and expensive, high risk business, and it can take up to 15 years to develop a new wheat variety, with no guarantee of success.

A more modern approach is to study the genetics of wheat to identify genes (Quality Trait Loci (QTL)) associated with desirable traits in potential parental varieties (genotypes). These can then be selected and crossed 'classically' to provide improved offspring in which these traits are expressed (phenotypes), and which are more suited for particular end user applications, such as alcohol production. This is the approach that was used in the GREEN Grain project. It is important to emphasise that this is not a genetic modification approach.

Each year wheat breeders will enter potential new varieties into wheat evaluation trials which are operated in the UK by the Home Grown Cereal Cereals Authority (HGCA).

HGCA (RL) evaluation of new wheat varieties

The HGCA conduct a series of annual harvest trials to evaluate new and upcoming wheat varieties, and the data generated are assessed by the HGCA Wheat committee, representing the major stakeholders in the wheat supply chain, including plant breeders, agronomists, growers and representatives of the main end-user groups. This Committee will make decisions regarding whether new varieties should progress through the assessment process for Recommendation, or be rejected.

The HGCA trials process is a two tier system which comprises National Level (NL) and Recommended Level (RL) trials. The NL trials, provide data covering 2 harvest years (NL1, NL2), comparing the performance of wheat varieties that have been entered by plant breeders with established control varieties. This is primarily used as a screening process to highlight their suitability for growing in the UK, in terms of agronomic performance, disease resistance, and suitability for particular end-user markets, and is mainly used to "weed out" varieties that would be unsuited for growing in the UK, or which might have other problems associated with them. In addition, the NL trials are used to highlight any specific qualities that might be useful in particular end-user markets.

Varieties that are successful in the NL trials are then progressed to more complex RL trials, where they are planted on a wide range of trial plots distributed geographically throughout the UK, providing a range of environmental growing conditions, nitrogen fertiliser applications and fungicide treatments. These trials provide a large amount of robust performance data that can then be used to inform decisions regarding whether an individual variety can be Recommended (i) for growing in the UK; or (ii) for a range of particular end-user applications. Decisions are based primarily on agronomic performance, and potential for disease resistance, but end user quality traits such as specific weight, Hagberg Falling number (HFN) (potential for sprouting) and distilling performance are also of major importance. It is important to note that varieties with good agronomic characteristics will not necessarily give the best balance of end-user traits, hence input by technical experts representing end user groups, such as distillers, is an essential feature of the decision making process. Once a RL trial candidate has been successful its performance is usually monitored for at least 1 further year, before being fully recommended.

Recommendations are normally for the UK, but under certain circumstances a variety may be given a specific regional recommendation, for example, if it performs poorly in some regions, but still shows quality characteristics that would be important to growers and end-users in certain regions. Similarly certain varieties may be given specific recommendations for certain end-user applications, such as distilling, or biscuit making.

The principal role of the Scotch Whisky Research Institute in the HGCA RL Wheat Trials process is to provide analytical data on a wide range of potential distilling wheat varieties grown on trial sites throughout the UK (particularly in Scotland). The most important of these is the generation of wheat alcohol yield data, which is determined using a standard reference method, based on a model grain distillery process (Agu et al 2006). This is supplemented with additional data relating to downstream viscosity, which gives an indication of the probability of a particular wheat variety giving serious processing problems in the distillery. This data is included in the HGCA evaluation, and is an important factor in the selection of potential distilling wheat varieties.

The GREEN Grain Project

The GREEN Grain Project, officially titled *"Genetic Reduction of Energy use and Emissions of Nitrogen through cereal production: GREEN grain"* was jointly funded by the HGCA, the Department for Environment, Food and Rural Affairs (Defra) and the Scottish Government through the Sustainable Arable LINK programme, and cost £2.67M and ran from July 2004 until September 2009. The final report (HGCA Project Report No. 468) (Sylvester-Bradley et al 2010) was published in June 2010. This was a collaborative LINK project and research partners included ADAS, Scottish Crop Research Institute (James Hutton Institute), Syngenta Seeds, Scotch Whisky Research Institute, School of Biosciences, University of Nottingham, VION Food Group, Fairview, and Wessex Grain Ltd.

The main aim of the GREEN grain project was to initiate the development of a new wheat ideotype for the UK distilling and non-ruminant feed market which would address sustainability requirements by providing new tools to facilitate the development of high-energy wheat varieties with reduced input requirements, especially of fertiliser N, thus reducing the costs of growing wheat with reduced emissions of nitrate, ammonia and nitrous oxide and hence with less environmental impacts, while improving the value of UK wheat for these and other markets. The project was also directed at providing knowledge about the structure and properties of wheat that could be used to refine the specifications and devise protocols for the production of wheat grain for distilling (and for non-ruminants feeding), and to set targets for plant breeders developing new wheat varieties, that are better suited to alcohol production and livestock feeding, that would bring benefits for growers as well as processors.

One of the main objectives of the project was to identify suitable germplasm that could be used to identify gene-based markers for positive GREEN grain characteristics suited to ethanol production, such as high alcohol yield, as well as to establish any associations with other aspects of varietal performance such as a low propensity for processing problems. This was done by identifying gene-based markers that could be used to monitor the segregation of GREEN grain and alcohol yield characteristics across a wide range of germplasm, and which can be used by plant breeders in the 'classical' selection of new grower- and user- friendly wheat varieties.

The project was highly successful and had shown that the genetic variation indicated potential to breed varieties with the 'GREEN grain' ideotype with both low canopy nitrogen and low grain protein. Varieties with lower grain protein tended to have higher grain yields when nitrogen was withheld. Grain protein content was identified as the most important, readily measurable wheat quality trait and had much greater heritability and, breeding for low grain protein appears to offer the greatest scope to reduce N fertiliser requirements (Sylvester-Bradley et al 2010).

Grain protein is easily measured by Near Infrared Spectrometry (NIR), and comparison with reference alcohol yield data supplied by SWRI resulted in the development of more accurate NIR models relating protein content with alcohol yield. The well known inverse relationship between protein content and alcohol yield was confirmed, but it was also clear that there was a consistent genetic variation in alcohol yield of up to 50 litres per dry tonne that was unrelated to protein content. This means that alcohol yield potential has a strong genetic component, and confirms that certain wheat varieties will be associated with significantly higher high alcohol yields than others.

The project also showed that the varieties with the best alcohol yields (e.g. Glasgow, Denman, Zebedee, Istabraq) tended to have high grain yields and low grain protein, making them attractive to growers as well as distillers. Maximum alcohol yields in the project were in excess of 480 litres per dry tonne, giving agronomic (grain yield) better than 4,600 litres per hectare. If these levels of alcohol yield, can be sustained, the performance of wheat would be comparable to that of maize.

Emergence of Denman

A new potential soft distilling wheat variety, c.v. Denman was identified during the GREEN Grain project. This was associated with a very high alcohol yield and subsequent trials identified some other important agronomic advantages that stood out from some of the other varieties that were looked at in the project. Denman is the progeny of Alchemy and Glasgow, both of which were previously identified as potentially good distilling varieties. Alchemy has been on the HGCA Recommended List since 2006, and is well established as a 'medium' quality variety for Distilling. Glasgow on the other hand was initially identified as a 'good' distilling variety, but was agronomically unsuited for growing in the North (Scotland), although it remains on the HGCA list.

Denman was first noted as a result of its performance on two GREEN grain trial sites grown at different nitrogen (protein) levels during 2008. The results had shown that it had consistently given a high alcohol yield, and one of the samples had given the highest alcohol yield that had been observed in the GREEN Grain project, both in terms of grain weight (383 litres of alcohol per tonne (dry)) (Figure 1), and in terms of grain yield (4,638 litres of alcohol per hectare). The samples in these Green Grain trials had very low nitrogen treatments and showed that on the whole Denman provided more alcohol, than other varieties at similar nitrogen levels and that Denman gave particularly good performance at such low nitrogen levels (1.1 - 1.5% (dry)). Denman had an alcohol yield advantage of almost 20 litres of alcohol per tonne compared with the average of all the varieties. This equates to a potential increase in alcohol production of almost 4.5 percent, which represents a very significant improvement in distillery performance.

Comparison of Denman with its closest peers (Glasgow and Zebedee) in the Green Grain trials (Figure 2) shows that it is comparable with both of these varieties, which were the only 'established' varieties approaching the performance of Denman. In the past, both Glasgow and Zebedee have given very high alcohol yields in HGCA RL trials and were initially identified as potentially very 'good' distilling varieties, but for various reasons, relating to agronomy and market performance, neither Glasgow nor Zebedee became successful distilling varieties. Both Zebedee and Glasgow, are on the current HGCA Recommended list for winter wheat (HGCA 2010), but are not suited

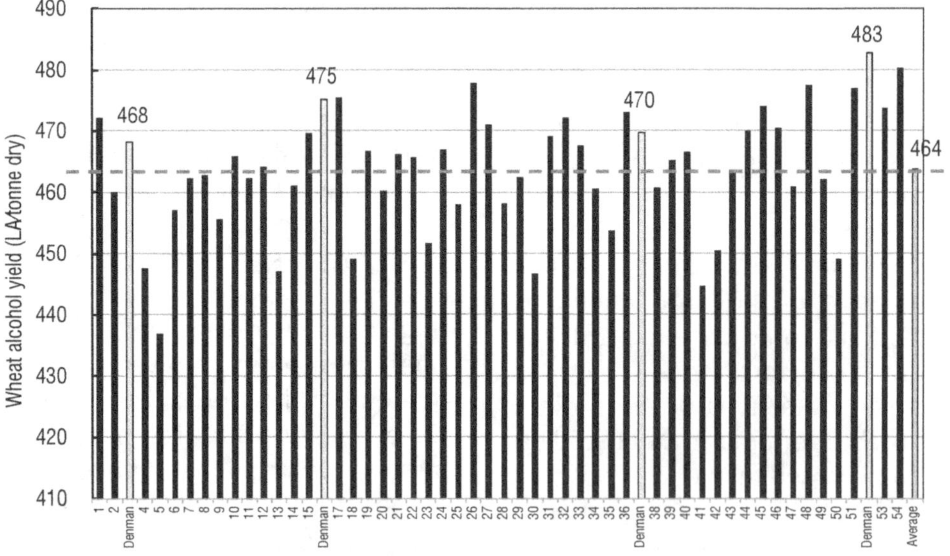

Figure 1. Performance of Denman in green grain trials (2008: Sites 8Sp; 8Tp)

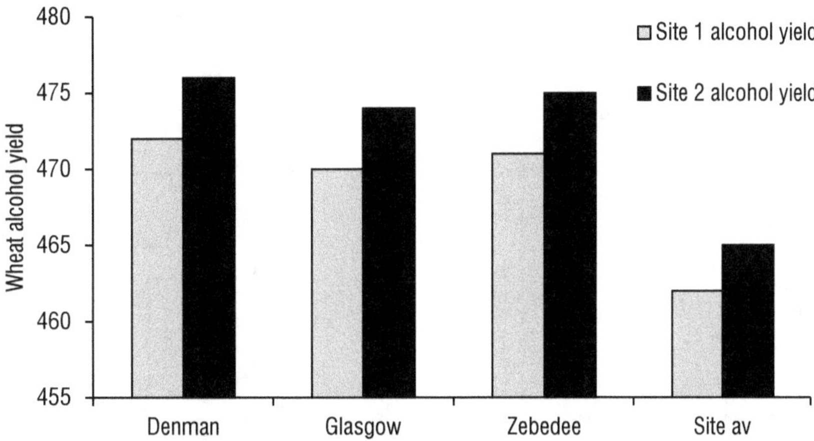

Figure 2. Average alcohol yield performance of Denman and other varieties against the site average for both sites (Green Grain Trials).

for growing in Scotland (Zebedee was removed from the list in 2011 (HGCA 2011)).

On the basis of its high level of performance in the Green Grain project, Syngenta Seeds, decided to accelerate Denman into commercial production and this variety was placed into the HGCA NL1 Trials in 2008, with NL2 following 1 year later. The results of these trials (Figure 3) highlight the promise of Denman as a consistently good wheat variety over a series of harvest years on several different sites, giving alcohol yields that were well above the site controls and consistently higher than its closest peers (Gymnast and Tuxedo). This indicates that Denman is a particularly robust wheat variety, able to perform well over a wide range of environments.

More recently Denman was successful in the HGCA RL trials for the 2010 harvest. These trials are more complex than the NL trials, since they were based on distilling performance on five different trial sites, located throughout the UK. These included 3 Scottish sites (Lothian, Borders, and Aberdeenshire) and 2 sites in North England (North Yorkshire and North Lincolnshire). The sites were all close to the main catchment areas for commercial supplies to the Scotch whisky industry (and bio-ethanol producers).

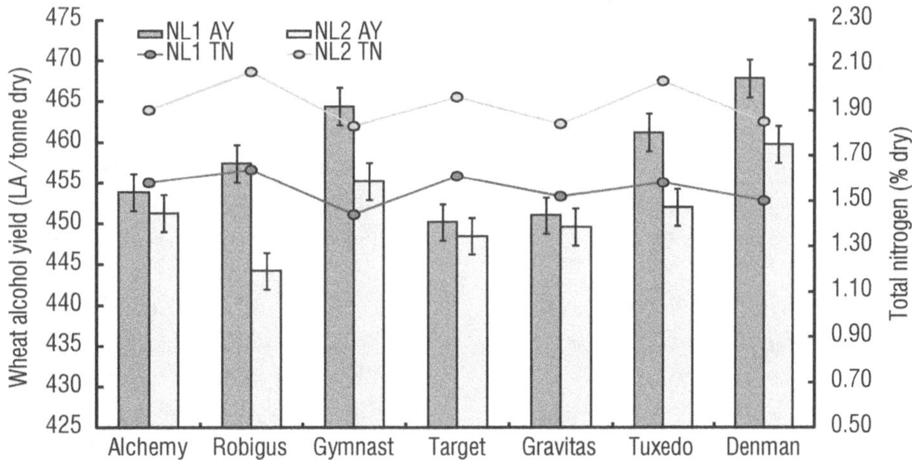

Figure 3. Performance of Denman at NL1 (2008) and NL2 (2009) in HGCA Trials (Error bars set at +/- 0.5%)

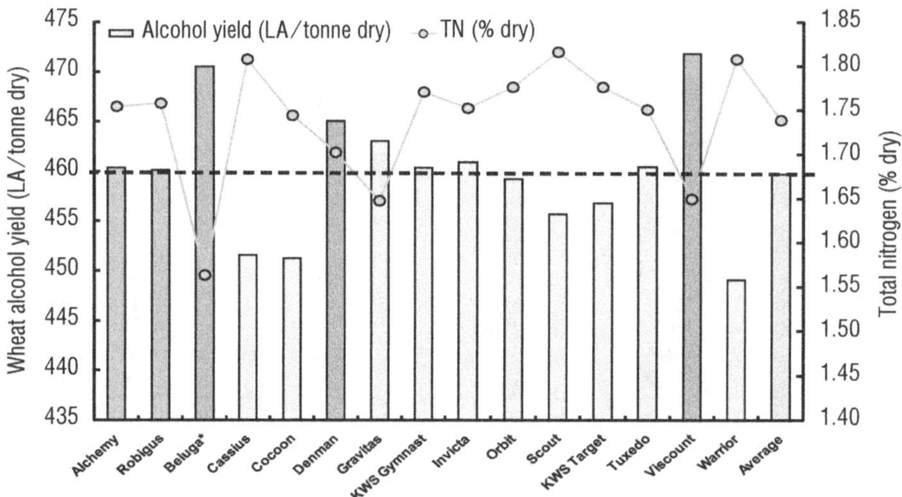

Figure 4. Performance of Denman, Viscount and Beluga in HGCA Recommended List Trials (2010) (Average of 5 sites)

Denman performed very well in comparison with the other varieties in the RL trials (Figure 4), again providing well in excess of the alcohol yields of the control varieties (Alchemy and Robigus), both of which are established distilling varieties. The two exceptions were Viscount and Beluga, which are recently recommended distilling wheat varieties. These varieties are particularly interesting because they were both identified as exceptional distilling varieties, each providing a significant step change in the alcohol yield performance of distilling wheat. Viscount is particularly good for distilling, and is generally the top performing distilling variety in recent RL trials. Beluga also performs very well, but is less consistent, and is more prone to the effects of pre-harvest sprouting. Viscount can also be affected by sprouting, but the problem is less of an issue with this variety.

Both Viscount and Beluga emerged through the standard HGCA Trials systems. Viscount, a NABIM Group 4 (soft) wheat, developed by KWS, was originally aimed at the market for high yielding UK feed wheat, but has since been shown to be associated with excellent distilling properties, having both high alcohol yield and good processing characteristics, both for Scotch whisky distillers and bio-ethanol producers. During RL trials Viscount consistently gave the highest alcohol yield on the sites on which it was grown, and has given a 'step increase' in alcohol yield compared with established distilling varieties, such as Alchemy and Invicta, to set a new standard in distilling wheat performance. Although not originally targeted at the market for biscuit and cake baking wheat Viscount has successfully been used in both applications, making it an extremely versatile wheat variety, and as a result Viscount is now the most widely grown and popular UK winter wheat variety, both in terms of agronomic performance and end user market potential.

Beluga, which was developed by Senova also has an interesting history. This was a soft NABIM Group 4 variety that looked like it would be unsuccessful, since agronomically it offered nothing special, until it was identified as a potential 'good' distilling variety. Subsequent trials have shown that it gives a similar advance in distilling quality to Viscount. Beluga is more susceptible to pre-harvest sprouting than Viscount and Denman, which would make it less attractive to growers, but its exceptional distilling quality was a major factor in securing its successful Recommendation by the HGCA wheat committee.

In the case of Denman, the most recent trials have shown that at the nitrogen levels in the trial, although Denman gave alcohol yields that were slightly lower than Viscount and Beluga it gives a similar 'step up' in alcohol yield in comparison with the other trial varieties, and will hence provide an additional, and robust choice for distillers. The consistent performance of Denman in all its trials, will continue to make it an attractive option for both distillers and for growers, and the continuing availability of this variety will help to support a sustainable supply of high quality wheat for distillers, and bio-ethanol processors.

Conclusions

Denman, Viscount and Beluga are all exceptional wheat varieties for distilling, both in terms of alcohol production, and also in terms of agronomic features. Together, these varieties, Viscount and Beluga provide distillers with an unprecedented choice of very high performance distilling wheat varieties that will enable them to draw from a pool of sustainable wheat raw materials which will realise the potential for higher alcohol yields, improved processing properties, and reduced energy requirements, which will help distillers address their sustainability objectives.

Clearly the results from the 2010 RL trials indicate that Denman is a variety that is not quite as good in alcohol yield terms as Beluga and Viscount, although it does fit comfortably into the same high quality range for 'good' distilling wheat. However, Denman shows some additional agronomic advantages over these varieties. It has a high agronomic yield (treated and untreated) and has a higher Hagberg falling number (HFN) than either Beluga or Viscount, which indicates an improved resistance to sprouting compared with these varieties. Denman also has a sound disease profile with improved disease resistance to Yellow Rust and Septoria in comparison with Viscount (NIAB 2011). Hence Denman provides a potentially more rounded 'package' in terms of what distillers want, as well as strong agronomic features that will also appeal to growers. These advantages will all contribute to the long term potential for Denman to become established as a successful distilling wheat variety.

While at current agronomic nitrogen levels there appears little advantage in alcohol yield performance between Denman and the best of the other current varieties (Viscount and Beluga), there is strong evidence that Denman can perform exceptionally well if it is grown under tightly controlled, low nitrogen conditions, as it was designed to do. Commercially, the use of this variety is still in its infancy and it is probable that more experience with Denman, will ultimately bring its use closer to the aspirations of the GREEN Grain ideotype, by contributing to the reduction of farming emissions, and facilitating distillers to meet their own sustainability targets in achieving lower energy requirements and will contribute to ensuring a sustainable supply of high quality wheat for the future production of both Scotch whisky and other potable spirits as well as for bio-ethanol processors.

The importance of Denman is not simply that it could deliver another step increase in alcohol yield performance compared with other varieties, but that it offers a robust addition to Beluga and Viscount, which will help to ensure the availability of a wider range of suitable high quality distilling wheat varieties, both in response to more challenging growing/harvest conditions, and in response to the challenges arising from the recent expansion of the bio-ethanol industry. This will help to increase the choices that distillers have in maintaining suitable supplies for potable alcohol production, while allowing growers to improve the management of their crops to spread the risks of their production.

Originally Denman was identified in the parental population that was studied in the Green Grain Project, and as such provides only the initial development arising from this project, the information developed in the project is expected to lead to the development of future varieties that will ultimately provide further improvements, both in terms of increased alcohol yield and reduced nitrogen requirements for growing. These improvements will contribute to ensuring the sustainability of Scotch whisky production by helping to reduce its environmental impact and carbon footprint by ensuring the on-going development and continuing availability of new distilling wheat varieties that can give higher levels of alcohol production, which will further increase the scope for reduced energy usage by distilleries.

It must be emphasised that while Denman is the first promising variety to come out of the GREEN Grain project, one of the principal aims of the project was to develop tools that would help plant breeders generate more wheat varieties meeting the GREEN Grain ideotype, and the project outputs in terms of improved knowledge of the factors influencing alcohol yield and the genetics controlling them, will surely lead to a better understanding of the development of future distilling wheat varieties and will ultimately result in the emergence of new varieties that will potentially maximise the available alcohol yield, as well as meet the future sustainability of the UK distilling industry.

Acknowledgements

The authors would like to thank Gordon Steele, Director of Research, and the other Directors of the Scotch Whisky Research Institute for permission to publish this paper. We would also like to acknowledge contributions from Richard Weightman and his team from ADAS, Stuart Swanston and Bill Thomas of The James Hutton Institute, Tracy Creasy (Syngenta Seeds) and other Project Partners.

References

Agu, R.C., Bringhurst, T.A. and Brosnan, J.M., (2006), Production of grain whisky and ethanol from wheat, maize and other cereals, *Journal of the Institute of Brewing*, 2006, 112(4), 314-323.

Bringhurst, T.A., Agu, R.C., Brosnan, J.M., and Fotheringham, A.L., (2008), Wheat for Scotch whisky production: Broadening the horizon, in *Distilled Spirits, Production, Technology and Innovation, the Proceedings of the Worldwide Distilled Conference (2005),* Edited by Bryce, J.H., Piggott J.R. and Stewart, G.G., Nottingham University Press, Nottingham, UK, pp. 51-66

Bringhurst, T.A., Fotheringham, A.L. and Brosnan J.M., (2003), Grain Whisky: Raw materials and Processing, in *Whisky: Technology, Production and Marketing,* Edited by Russell, I., Academic Press, London, UK. pp. 77-115

Brosnan, J.M., Bringhurst, T.A. and Agu, R.C., (2010), Growing sustainability in the wheat supply chain, in *Distilled Spirits, New horizons: Energy, Environment and Enlightenment,* Edited by Walker, G. and Hughes, P.S., Nottingham University Press, Nottingham, 27-32.

Home Grown Cereals Authority (2010), *HGCA Recommended List 2010/11 for cereals and oilseeds*, Agriculture and Horticulture Development Board, Kenilworth, UK.

Home Grown Cereals Authority (2011), *HGCA Recommended List 2011/12 for cereals and oilseeds*, Agriculture and Horticulture Development Board, Kenilworth, UK.

Hume, J.R. and Moss, M.S., (2000), *The Making of Scotch Whisky,* Canongate Books Ltd, Edinburgh, UK.

National Institute of Advanced Botany (NIAB) (2011), *NIAB TAG Network Varietyadvantage, Cereals, Oilseeds, Pulses, Autumn 2011,* NIAB, Cambridge, UK, February 2011.

Sylvester-Bradley, R., Kindred, D., Weightman, R., Thomas, W.T.B., Swanston, J.S., Thompson, D., Feuerhelm, D., Creasy, T., Argillier O, Melichar, J., Brosnan, J.M., Agu, R.C., Bringhurst, T.A., Foulkes, J., Pask, A., Cowe, I., Hemingway, D., Robinson, D., and Wilcox (2010), *HGCA Project Report No. 468, Genetic Reduction of Energy use and Emissions of Nitrogen through cereal production: GREEN grain*, Home Grown Cereals Authority (HGCA), Agriculture and Horticulture Development Board, Kenilworth, UK. Published June 2010.

Chapter 11

Geometric features of oak casks I. Modelling shape and derivation of surface areas and volumes

Paul. S. Hughes[1] *and James A. Hughes*[2]

[1] *International Centre for Brewing and Distilling, Heriot-Watt University, Edinburgh, EH14 4AS, UK;*

[2] *School of Mathematical Sciences, Science Laboratories, South Road, Durham University, DH1 3LE, UK*

Introduction

It is likely that the wooden barrel derived from an extension of techniques developed for the manufacture of buckets and tanks (Jackson, 2008). Various ancient illustrations (eg a drawing at the tomb of Hsi-Re, *ca* 2630 – 2611 BC (Quibell, 1913) and a painting in the tomb of Rekh-Mi-Re at Thebes from around 1400 BC (Davies, 1935)) clearly show that wood has long been appreciated as a material of choice for the storage of liquids and solids. However, the first unequivocal evidence of wooden cooperage for the storage of wine dates from the Roman era (Jackson, 2008).

It is commonly agreed that cooperage and the development of the oak cask for the storage of wine was developed, or at least popularised, during the latter stages of the Roman Empire. However, some contend that the development of the oak cask should be attributed to the Gauls some several hundred years earlier (www.snooth.com).

The process of whisky maturation is reliant on several parameters, which may be considered to be either environmental or cask-specific (Table 1). Given that whisky maturation is characterised by changes in the flavour qualities and the extraction of colour from the wood of the cask, it is clear that interactions between the spirit and wood are essential for the creation of the eventual brands or the blending elements for eventual sale. Whilst this is self-evident, it highlights the importance of developing a more detailed understanding of the cask itself. In this paper, as part of an ongoing programme to

Table 1. Factors affecting whisky maturation

Environmental	*Cask-specific*
Temperature and temperature cycles	Internal surface treatment
Humidity and humidity changes	Fill cycle
Ventilation	Surface area/volume ratio
Altitude	Cask condition (eg leaks)
Cask orientation in warehouse	Liquid movement in cask (eg convection)
Duration of the maturation process	

develop a modular whisky maturation model, we evaluate several models of cask geometry and propose a convenient accurate geometry that can be solved analytically for a full range of cask dimensions.

Methodology

Three models for the derivation of surface areas and volumes of smooth[1] casks have been considered here. In order of increasing complexity, the simplest model was that of a cylinder, which has simple solutions for both surface area and volume. The other two models required the stating of functions, which can then be used to derive surface areas and volumes of revolution.

For what we term the linear model, a function of the form of *equation 1* was used:

$$y = c - |mx| \tag{1}$$

where (x, y) are the coordinates of the function that is to be rotated about the x-axis and therefore trace the boundaries of the cask model. The modulus term ensures that the function has a maximum at x = 0 when m ≠ 0 (Fig. 1). Variation of m allows for an approximate accommodation of a discontinuous bend in the cask wall. The resulting three-dimensional shape resembles two identical truncated cones joined at their bases.

For what is termed here the non-linear model, a function of the form of *equation 2* was used:

$$y = c - lx^2 \tag{2}$$

As before, (x,y) are the coordinates of the function that traces the curved boundaries of the cask model. Variation of *l* allows the curvature of the cask staves to be accounted for more fully than in the case of the non-linear model. A graphical comparison of the three functions indicates how they approximate the conventional cask geometry (Fig. 1).

There are standard procedures to derive surface areas and volumes of revolution (mathworld.com). For the former, the expression given in *equation 3* was evaluated:

$$Curved\ surface\ area = 2\pi\int_0^x y\sqrt{1+\left(\frac{dy}{dx}\right)^2}.dx \tag{3}$$

For all the models considered here, an additional contribution from the circular ends of all three models needs to be added in (*ie* $2pr^2$, where r is equivalent to the radius of the end of the cask; *ie* a minimum value of y for given values of x, c and *l*).

[1] The term "smooth" in this context indicates that the geometry being considered has no roughness, ie that the calculated surface areas and volumes are at a minimum

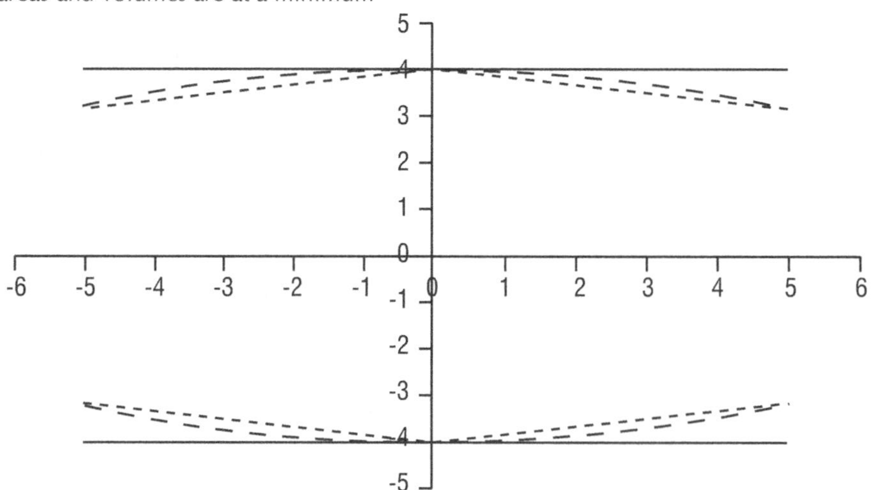

Figure 1. A comparison of the three models used to estimate surface areas and volumes of casks. Note that the functions are symmetric around the *y* = 0 axis.

To derive volumes of revolution, the expression given in *equation 4* was evaluated:

$$Volume = 2\pi\int_0^x y^2.dx \tag{4}$$

A final calculation was required to determine the length of the joins between adjacent staves. Mathematically this can be derived by solving *equation 5*:

$$Length\, of\ arc = 2\int_0^x \sqrt{1+\left(\frac{dy}{dx}\right)^2}.dx \tag{5}$$

Equations 3, 4 and *5* deviate slightly from the standard format, in that there is a factor of two before the integral. This is because all of the functions considered here are symmetric about the $x = 0$ axis and so are integrated between 0 and x and then doubled, whilst the general solution requires integration from $-x$ to x'.

The derived linear and non-linear models were tested for their veracity by confirming that they simplified to the cylindrical model when $m = 0$ (for the linear model) or $l \Rightarrow 0$ for the non-linear model, and as the values of m and l were increased monotonically in the positive domain the volumes and surface areas derived changed smoothly (*ie* demonstrated no discontinuities).

Results and discussion

The expressions for the three models are presented without proof in Table 2.

As the solution of the integral for the surface area and length of joins between staves for the non-linear model are more complex, their derivation is shown in full in Appendix 1. To test the veracity of the models, it is clear by inspection of the volume expressions in Table 2 that setting l or m to zero results in expressions that are identical to that of the cylinder volume. Similarly, when $m = 0$, the surface area for the linear model again simplifies to that of the cylinder. For the non-linear model, this approach is not so straightforward. As $l \Rightarrow 0$, the initial multiplier term, $\pi/16l^2 \Rightarrow \infty$. However, it is clear (Fig. 2) that as $l \Rightarrow 0$, the surface area for the non-linear model does indeed approach that of a cylinder.

To apply these models, particularly if surface area/volumes are to be derived, it is essential that the units of measurement and of the curvature parameter for the non-linear model (which has units of distance $^{-1}$) are consistent. In this paper all units are based on the decimetre, primarily because the most common unit of volume for casks is the litre (*ie* dm^3).

A comparison of surface areas and volumes for the three models (Table 3) indicates that, relative to the non-linear model, the cylinder overestimates volumes, whilst the linear model underestimates volumes for a given bilge radius. Interestingly, the surface area/volume calculations imply that the non-linear model, arguably the closest to actual cask geometries, has the most modest surface area/volume ratio, implying that from a maturation viewpoint, such a shape is less efficient than the other models.

Table 2. Expressions for the three cask geometry models

	Arc length	*Surface area*	*Volume*
Cylinder	$2x$	$2\pi c(2x+c)$	$2\pi c^2 x$
Linear model	$\sqrt{1+m^2}$	$2\pi\left(\sqrt{1+m^2}\left(2cx-mx^2\right)+(c-mx)^2\right)$	$2\pi\left(c^2x-cmx^2+\frac{m^2x^3}{3}\right)$
Non-linear model	$\frac{1}{2l}\left(2lx\sqrt{1+4l^2x^2} + ln\left\|\sqrt{1+4l^2x^2}+2lx\right\|\right)$	$\frac{\pi}{16l^2}\left(\left(16cl+1\right)\left(2lx\sqrt{1+4l^2x^2} + ln\left\|\sqrt{1+4l^2x^2} + 2lx\right\|\right) - 4lx\left(1+4l^2x^2\right)^{3/2}\right) + 2\pi(c-lx^2)^2$	$2\pi\left(c^2x-\frac{clx^3}{3} + \frac{l^2x^5}{5}\right)$

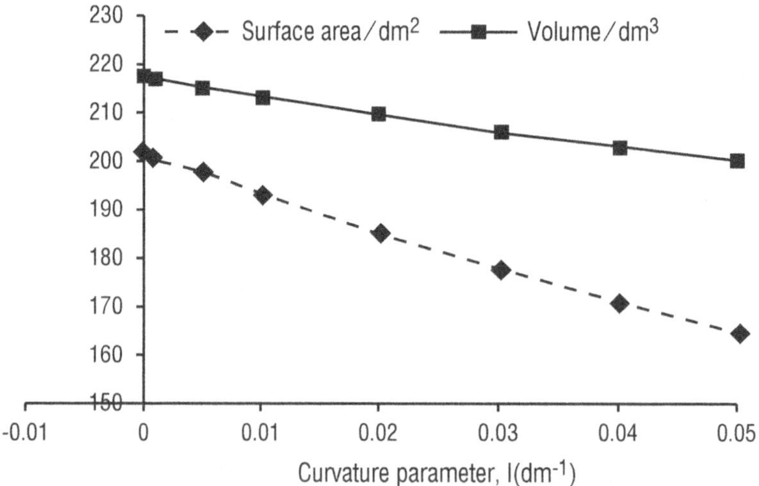

Figure 2. Graphical demonstration of the smooth approach of surface areas and volumes to the cylindrical case as curvature approaches zero. In this case the cask had a fixed internal height of 8.128 dm and a fixed bilge radius of 2.921 dm. Head diameter varied as a function of the curvature parameter. A curvature of 0.030 dm^{-1} results in a cask of 206 litre volume, close to that expected for a US bourbon cask.

Table 3. An example comparing the performance of the three models of cask geometry. The cask parameters are based on typical measurements of an American Standard Barrel (200 litres)

	Radius (bilge, head; dm)	*Half-height (dm)*	*Surface area (dm^2)*	*Volume (dm^3)*	*Surface area/ volume (dm^{-1})*
Cylinder	2.858	4.064	197.2	208.5	0.946
Linear model	2.858, 2.477	4.064	175.3	181.9	0.964
Non-linear model	2.858, 2.477	4.064	178.8	200.0	0.894

Here, we are advocating a cask geometry based on the rotation of a function of the form $y = c - mx^2$, which can be used to develop expressions for both surface areas and volumes of smooth casks. By comparison of this model with simpler models we find that, despite the undoubted utility of the overall geometry of the oak cask in terms of the convenience of handling, there is a minor adverse consequence in terms of reducing the available surface area for a given contained volume. However, the overall length of the arcs of wood joins between staves lengthen with stave curvature, whilst the length of head joins (both with the body of the cask and between the head pieces) reduces. In a future manuscript we will explore the distribution of the path lengths of the contained liquid to the cask wall, and consider the relative rates of diffusion through stave and head joints, and the apparent "translocation" of ethanol and water through remnants of the oak phloem vessels.

References

Davies, N. de G., The Tomb of Rekh-Ri-Me at Thebes, Arno Press, New York, 1935, plate 15.

Jackson, R.S., Wine Science: Principles and Applications, 3rd edition, p. 452, Academic Press, San Diego, CA.

http://mathworld.wolfram.com/SurfaceofRevolution.html, accessed 2nd June 2011.

http://www.snooth.com/articles/the-history-of-wine-part-ii-wine-storage-barrels/, accessed 30th June 2011.

Quibell, J.E., Excavations at Saqqara, 1911-12: the tomb of Hesy, Impr. de l'Institut Français d'Archéologie Orientale,1913.

Appendix 1

Non-linear model: Surface area

The following solution is valid where *l* >0 (*ie* a convex geometry) and where c > l/x^2. The latter constraint prevents the function $y = c - lx^2$ from crossing the $y = 0$ axis. At $c = l/x^2$ the diameter of the model cask head = 0.

$$Surface\,area,\ S = 4\pi\int_0^x (c - lx^2)\sqrt{1+4l^2x^2}\,.dx$$

Substituting for *x*:

$$x = \frac{\tan(a)}{2l} \Rightarrow dx = \frac{sec^2(a)}{2l}da$$

$$\Rightarrow S = 4\pi\int\left(c - \frac{tan^2(a)}{4l}\right)\sqrt{1+tan^2(a)}\left(\frac{sec^2(a)}{2l}\right)da$$

$$sin^2(A) + cos^2(A) = 1 \Rightarrow \underline{\tan^2(A) + 1 = sec^2(A)}$$

$$\Rightarrow S = \frac{4\pi}{2l}\int\left(c - \frac{tan^2(a)}{4l}\right)sec^3(a)da$$

$$= \frac{2\pi}{l}\left(\int c\,sec^3(a)da - \int\frac{tan^2(a)sec^3(a)}{4l}da\right)$$

$$= \frac{2\pi}{l}\int c\,sec^3(a)da - \frac{2\pi}{4l^2}\int\left(sec^2(a)-1\right)sec^3(a)da$$

$$= \frac{2c\pi}{l}\int sec^3(a)da - \frac{\pi}{2l^2}\int sec^5(a)da + \frac{\pi}{2l^2}\int sec^3(a)da$$

$$= \left(\frac{2c\pi}{l} + \frac{\pi}{2l^2}\right)\int sec^3(a)da - \frac{\pi}{2l^2}\int sec^5(a)da \qquad [1]$$

The integration of higher orders of powers of sec (a) requires integration by parts:

$$\int sec^n(a)da = \int sec^2(a)sec^{n-2}(a)da\ , n \geq 2$$

$$u = sec^{n-2}(a),\ dv = sec^2(a)da \Rightarrow v = tan(a),\ du = (n-2)sec^{n-2}(a)tan(a)da$$

$$\Rightarrow \int sec^n(a)da = sec^{n-2}(a)tan(a) - \int(n-2)sec^{n-2}(a)tan^2(a)da$$

$$= sec^{n-2}(a)tan(a) - (n-2)\int sec^n(a)da + (n-2)\int sec^{n-2}(a)da$$

$$\Rightarrow(n-1)\int sec^{n}(a)da = sec^{n-2}(a)tan(a)+(n-2)\int sec^{n-2}(a)da$$

$$\Rightarrow\int sec^{n}(a)da = \frac{1}{(n-1)}\left(sec^{n-2}(a)tan(a)+(n-2)\int sec^{n-2}(a)da\right)$$

Substituting the general solution above into [1] gives:

$$S=\left(\frac{2c\pi}{l}+\frac{\pi}{2l^2}\right)\int sec^3(a)da-\frac{\pi}{2l^2}\int sec^5(a)da$$

$$=\left(\frac{2c\pi}{l}+\frac{\pi}{2l^2}\right)\int sec^3(a)da-\frac{\pi}{2l^2}\frac{1}{(5-1)}\left(sec^{5-2}(a)tan(a)+(5-2)\int sec^{5-2}(a)da\right)$$

$$=\left(\frac{2c\pi}{l}+\frac{\pi}{2l^2}-\frac{3\pi}{8l^2}\right)\int sec^3(a)da-\frac{\pi}{8l^2}sec^3(a)tan(a)$$

$$=\left(\frac{2c\pi}{l}+\frac{\pi}{2l^2}-\frac{3\pi}{8l^2}\right)\frac{1}{(3-1)}\left(\sec^{3-2}(a)\tan(a)+(3-2)\int\sec^{3-2}(a)da\right)-\frac{\pi}{8l^2}sec^3(a)tan(a)$$

$$=\left(\frac{16c\pi l}{16l^2}+\frac{4\pi}{16l^2}-\frac{3\pi}{16l^2}\right)\left(\sec(a)\tan(a)+\int\sec(a)da\right)-\frac{\pi}{8l^2}sec^3(a)tan(a)$$

$$\int\sec(a)da=\int\frac{\sec(a)(\sec(a)+\tan(a))}{(\sec(a)+\tan(a))}da$$

$$b=\sec(a)+\tan(a)\Rightarrow db=\left(\sec(a)\tan(a)+\sec^2(a)\right)da=\sec(a)(\sec(a)+\tan(a))da$$

$$\Rightarrow\int\sec(a)da=\int\frac{1}{b}db=\log_e|b|=\underline{\log_e|\sec(a)+\tan(a)|}$$

$$\Rightarrow S=\left(\frac{16c\pi l+\pi}{16l^2}\right)\left(\sec(a)\tan(a)+\log_e|\sec(a)+\tan(a)|\right)-\frac{\pi}{8l^2}sec^3(a)tan(a)$$

$$=\frac{\pi}{16l^2}\left((16cl+1)\left(\sec(a)\tan(a)+\log_e|\sec(a)+\tan(a)|\right)-2\,sec^3(a)tan(a)\right)$$

$$x=\frac{\tan(a)}{2l}\Rightarrow\underline{\tan(a)=2lx}$$

$$\Rightarrow S=\frac{\pi}{16l^2}\left((16cl+1)\left(2lx\sec(a)+\log_e|\sec(a)+2lx|\right)-4lx\,sec^3(a)\right)$$

$$\tan(a)=2lx=\frac{2lx}{1}=\frac{opp}{adj}\Rightarrow\cos(a)=\frac{adj}{hyp}=\frac{1}{\sqrt{(2lx)^2+1^2}}\Rightarrow\underline{\sec(a)=\sqrt{1+4l^2x^2}}$$

$$\square \quad \boxed{S\square \frac{\square}{16l^2}\left((16cl\square 1)\left(2lx\sqrt{1\square 4l^2x^2}\square\log_e\left|\sqrt{1\square 4l^2x^2}\square 2lx\right|\right)\square 4lx\left(1\square 4l^2x^2\right)^{3/2}\right)}$$

Non-linear model: Arc length

The solution of this integral applies ideas derived in the previous solution. Briefly:

$$Arc\,length,\ A = 2\int_0^x \sqrt{1+4l^2x^2}\,.dx$$

$$x = \frac{\tan(a)}{2l} \Rightarrow dx = \frac{sec^2(a)}{2l}da$$

$$\Rightarrow A = 2\int\sqrt{1+tan^2(a)}\left(\frac{sec^2(a)}{2l}\right)da$$

$$sin^2(A)+cos^2(A)=1 \Rightarrow \underline{\tan^2(A)+1=sec^2(A)}$$

$$\Rightarrow A = \frac{1}{l}\int sec^3(a)da$$

The integration of higher orders of powers of sec (a) requires integration by parts (see above), so that:

$$\Rightarrow A = \left[\frac{1}{2l}\left(\sec(a)\tan(a)+\log_e\left|\sec(a)+\tan(a)\right|\right)\right]_0^a$$

But:

$$\tan(a) = 2lx = \frac{2lx}{1} = \frac{opp}{adj} \Rightarrow \cos(a) = \frac{adj}{hyp} = \frac{1}{\sqrt{(2lx)^2+1^2}} \Rightarrow \underline{\sec(a) = \sqrt{1+4l^2x^2}}$$

So substituting for *tan(a)* and *sec(a)* gives:

$$\therefore \quad \boxed{A = \frac{1}{2l}\left(2lx\sqrt{1+4l^2x^2}+\log_e\left|\sqrt{1+4l^2x^2}+2lx\right|\right)}$$

Chapter 12

Production of a cassava based potable spirit

*Bhavya Mandanna; **Paul Hughes; **James H. Bryce
*Molson Coors Brewing Company (UK), Station Street, Burton upon Trent, DE14 1BG' **The International Centre for Brewing and Distilling (ICBD), Heriot-Watt University, Riccarton, Edinburgh EH14 4AS

Introduction

Cassava (*Manihot esculenta* Crantz) is a tropical root crop capable of producing a high percentage of easily extractable starch (~81%), with a low percentage of other compounds like proteins (~1%), minerals (~1%), and lipids (~0.4%) (Karuri *et al.*, 2001; Westby, 2000). The maximum amount of starch gelatinisation occurs between 65°C and 70°C, similar to that of barley malt (Karam, 2005).

Cassava contains the cyanogenic glucosides linamarin and lotaustralin, which makes it toxic when consumed raw or inadequately processed. Under suitable conditions, it can bring about self-detoxification, mediated by an inherent, intracellular enzyme called linamarase (Piyachomkwan, *et al.*, 2005; O'Brien *et al.*, 1991; Cooke, 1978). Currently, a number of processing techniques involving varied physical, mechanical and chemical treatments are used in the production of cassava products that are safe for consumption (Cooke and Maduagwu, 1978). Cassava flour is the dried root that is ground into flour, while cassava starch is the refined starch extracted from the root.

Efforts have been made for industrial ethanol production from cassava, though no significant work has been published on the production of potable spirit from it. The limiting factor is most probably the presence of traces of cyanide in the alcohol produced. However, this is a character that can be controlled by appropriate process conditions such as temperature and pH.

Cassava promises to be a good substrate for alcohol production due its convenient and abundant availability, high fermentable sugar content, stable shelf-life and lower cost when compared to other raw materials such as barley malt, maize, rice and wheat (significantly cheaper locally; global prices subject to currency fluctuation) (Grace, 1977). It is also known to contain a wide range of flavour compounds including a number of esters and aromatic hydrocarbons (Dougan *et al.*, 1983) (Appendix). It should hence be recognised as a potential sustainable raw material for the future.

Scope

This exploratory piece of work was carried out to establish the feasibility of producing an acceptable cassava based potable spirit. The focus is therefore on the production and quality of the potable new make spirit fraction.

This work was conducted as a follow-on from original research on using cassava as an adjunct in beer production. Hence the beers produced were used in the distillation process, rather than a conventional distillation wash. However, a conventional distillation process was followed for spirit production.

Method

Brewing

Conventional brewing techniques were used in the International Centre for Brewing and Distilling (ICBD)'s 2 hL pilot brewery to produce 150 L of wort (OG 1040). Refined cassava starch and unfermented cassava flour were used as adjuncts at the rate of 40% (w/w) of the total grist composition. The former was used as a mash tun adjunct (65°C 60 minutes and 76°C 1 minute) while the latter was cooked, to enhance cyanide detoxification, prior to being mashed in (48°C 10 minutes, 65°C 60 minutes and 76°C 1 minute) with the pale ale malt. These two regimes were designed to determine the impact of linamarase induced self-detoxification of cassava on the final cyanide content of the beer.

Bittering Tomahawk hops were added at the rate of 30 mg/L of iso-α-acid at the start of boil. Fermentation was carried out using a brewery ale yeast. The beers produced were then degassed in preparation for distillation.

Distillation

The degassed cassava starch and flour adjunct beers were subjected to a conventional double pot still distillation in the ICBD pilot distillery. The same procedure was followed in both cases.

Wash still distillation

50 L of wash were distilled to obtain low wines. Samples of low wines were collected every 100 ml, and the sample density measured and %ABV calculated.

Spirit still distillation

11.2 L of low wines were distilled in the spirit still. Samples of foreshots were collected every 100 ml. The first cut was taken after 200 ml based on a volume collected, which in previous work has shown adequate clearance of foreshots and fusel oils. Subsequently, new make spirit samples were collected every 250 ml. The second cut was taken once the %ABV dropped below 50, and samples of the feints were collected every 500 ml. At the time of collection of each sample, the density was measured and %ABV calculated.

Analytical tests

All samples were subjected to headspace-gas chromatography and cyanide (both free and bound) analyses.

Results

Wash still distillation

The degassed cassava starch and flour adjunct beers (Table 1) were used as the charge in the initial, individual, wash still distillations to produce low wines (Table 2).

Spirit still distillation

The low wines produced from the wash still distillation were used in the spirit still to produce the foreshots, new make spirit and feints (Figures 1 and 2, Table 3).

Flavour analysis - New make spirit

The final new make spirits obtained from the cassava starch and cassava flour adjunct distillations had different flavour profiles (Figure 3). In both spirits, acetaldehyde and ethyl acetate were present at concentrations much higher than

Table 1. Analysis of charges fed into the wash still.

Charge	*PG (Degrees)*	*%ABV*	*pH*	*Bitterness (IBU)*	*Cyanide (mg/L)*	
					Free	*Bound*
Cassava starch adjunct wash	11.1	3.86	3.90	30.24	ND	ND
Cassava flour adjunct wash	8.4	4.36	4.54	32.40	0.0004	0.006

Table 2. Analysis of the low wines obtained from the wash still distillations.

Low Wines Type	*%ABV*	*Cyanide (mg/L)*	
		Free	*Bound*
Cassava starch adjunct distillation	17.68	0.006	0.175
Cassava flour adjunct distillation	20.47	0.027	0.116

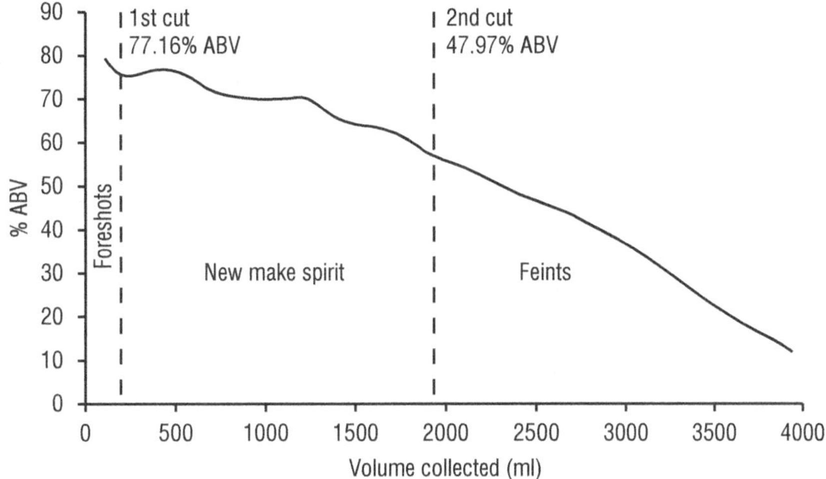

Figure 1. Sample alcohol percentage-volume graph for the cassava starch adjunct spirit still distillation.

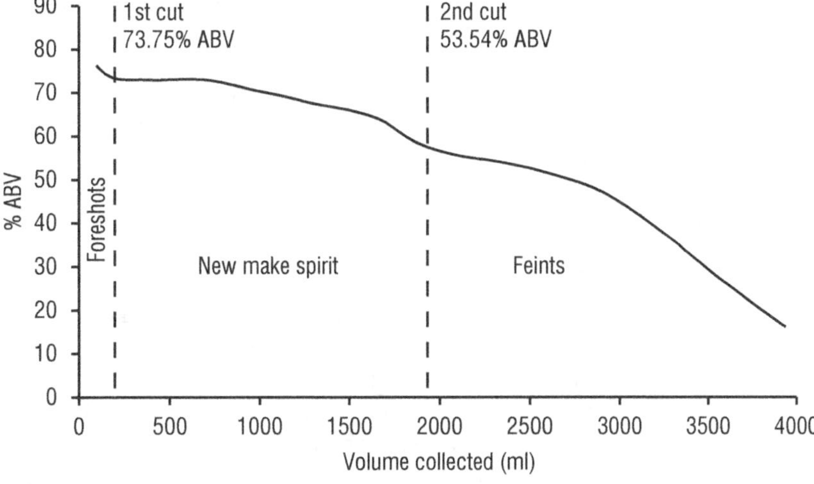

Figure 2. Sample alcohol percentage-volume graph for the cassava flour adjunct spirit still distillation.

Table 3. Analysis of the spirit fractions obtained on spirit still distillation of cassava starch and flour adjunct low wines.

Spirit Still Distillation	*Spirit Fraction*	*%ABV*	*Cyanide (mg/L)*	
			Free	*Bound*
Cassava starch adjunct distillation	Foreshots	75.6	0.007	0.135
	New Make Spirit	66.4	ND	0.468
	Feints	36.3	ND	0.172
Cassava flour adjunct distillation	Foreshots	77.2	0.008	0.122
	New Make Spirit	68.6	ND	0.123
	Feints	38.3	0.008	0.190

their individual threshold values, while isoamyl acetate was found at a concentration below its threshold value. Isobutyl acetate, ethyl octanoate, ethyl butyrate, and ethyl hexanoate were found at concentrations higher than their individual threshold values in the spirit from the cassava starch charge, while they were not detected in the spirit from the cassava flour charge. All the higher alcohols analysed, except propanol, were found at concentrations above their thresholds in both spirits, however, it must be noted that they indicated higher concentrations in the spirit from the cassava flour adjunct charge, than in that from the cassava starch adjunct charge.

Cyanide analysis - New make spirit

The new make spirit obtained from the cassava starch adjunct distillation indicated a significantly higher concentration of bound cyanide (0.46 mg/L) than in that from the cassava flour adjunct distillation (0.12 mg/L). Free cyanide was not detected in both spirits (Figure 4).

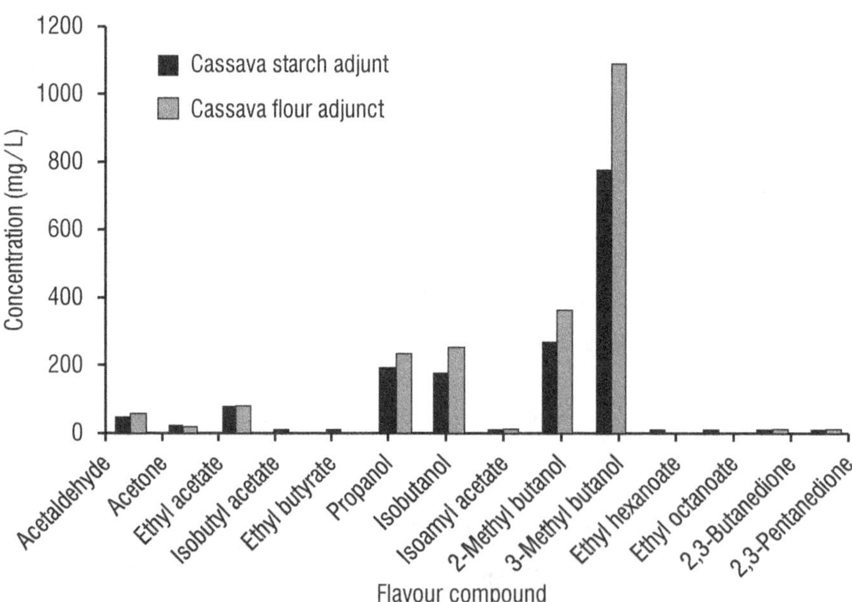

Figure. 3. Comparison between the final new make spirit samples obtained from the cassava starch and flour adjunct distillations.

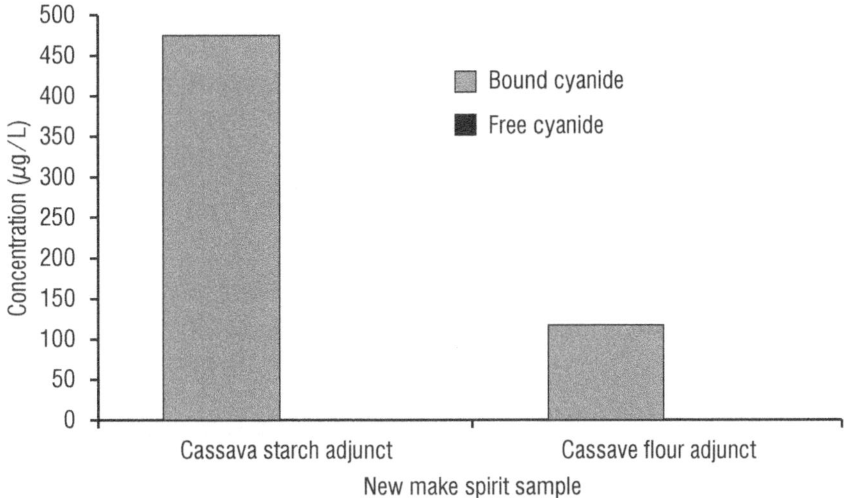

Figure 4. Comparison between the cyanide content in the final new make spirit obtained from the cassava starch and flour adjunct distillations.

Discussion

Distillation

Similar conventional procedures were used in the distillations of both, the cassava starch and flour adjunct charges. In the wash still, low wines collection started at ~ 57% ABV and continued till it dropped to about ~5%ABV. However, in order to obtain the required volume for spirit still distillation, low wines were collected from the cassava starch adjunct wash distillation till about ~2%ABV. Hence it showed a slightly lower total %ABV.

The low wines, in each case, were subjected to distillation in the spirit still. The first foreshots sample, in both cases, failed to mist, indicating a minimal concentration of fusel alcohols left behind from the previous distillation. However, from past experience of these stills, 200 ml of foreshots were collected in each case, before taking the first cut for the collection of the new make spirit (Figures 1 and 2). This was done to reduce the concentration of low boiling point compounds such as methanol, acetone, aldehydes and other volatiles, in order to produce a cleaner spirit. New make spirit, the potable fraction, was collected up to the second cut at ~50%ABV (Figures 1 and 2), in order to manage the concentration of fusel oils. The spirit collected was clear and bright in appearance. The feints were subsequently collected until the alcohol content was at or below ~20%ABV.

The cassava flour adjunct based spirit still distillation took place at a steadier rate in comparison to that of the cassava starch adjunct based one, which took place at a faster, more irregular rate. This could be attributed to the higher rate of heat input in the latter when compared to the former. This occurred due to the poor control mechanism of the spirit still, and was not part of the experimental design.

Flavour analysis – New make spirit

It was found that, apart from the higher alcohols, isoamyl acetate and ethyl hexanoate, all the other compounds indicated dissimilar behavioural patterns in both distillations. In the distillation of new make spirit from the cassava flour adjunct charge, it was found that the esters isobutyl acetate, ethyl octanoate and ethyl butyrate were distilled off at a faster rate than in that of the new make spirit from the cassava starch adjunct charge. A slower rate of distillation allowing an enhanced separation of the components could help to better understand the behaviour of the various flavour compounds in the distillate.

On comparing the flavour profiles of the final new make spirit samples from both the cassava starch and flour adjunct distillations; it was found that the former had a higher concentration of esters making it more sweet, fruity and floral in aroma, while the latter had a higher concentration of higher alcohols, giving it a stronger alcoholic aroma.

Cyanide analysis

The main purpose of this analysis was to establish the long-term potability of a cassava based spirit, without causing any of the potential health problems associated with chronic cyanide poisoning. The analysis was conducted at regular intervals to better understand those parts of the process where maximum detoxification took place.

In both distillations, as expected, the cyanide levels showed a drop in concentration as the process progressed. This is due to the hydrolysis of the cyanogenic glucosides (bound cyanide) to their respective cyanohydrins, and further, their thermal degradation to form volatile hydrocyanic acid (free cyanide) (Westby, 2000).

On comparing the final new make spirit samples from both distillations; no free cyanide was detected in either of them. The cassava starch adjunct spirit had a significantly higher level of bound cyanide than the cassava flour adjunct spirit. This appears to be odd considering the fact that to begin with, no cyanide, neither free nor bound, was detected in the cassava starch adjunct wash. This indicates the occurrence of a possible 'cyanide formation' process which appears to take place in parallel with the cyanide removal process. The former could be attributed to the presence of undetectable cyanogenic precursors which undergo thermal conversion to form detectable forms of cyanide.

Another point to note is that the cassava flour based spirit still distillation took place at a more steady rate in comparison to the cassava starch based one, which appeared to take place at a faster, and more irregular rate (Figures 1 and 2). This piece of information points towards a steady distillation being key to the balance between cyanide formation and removal, and possibly the occurrence of the latter at a greater magnitude. Further research in this area will be needed to better understand this process, as temperature is key to cyanide detoxification. The cyanohydrins have a boiling point of the order of 82°C, which must be exploited to increase the rate of the cyanide removal process (Westby, 2000).

Conclusion

The potential for the production of a potable spirit from cassava is highlighted in this piece of work. The spirits produced were clear and bright in appearance, and had good flavour profiles. The cassava starch based spirit had a slightly higher cyanide content, restricting its potability in line with the US EPA (United States Environmental Protection Agency) MCL (Minimum Consumption Level) regulation of 0.2 mg/L cyanide (in water) to prevent chronic cyanide toxicity, while the cassava flour based spirit was potable under the same (Consumer fact sheet, National Primary Drinking Water Regulations). However, it is important to understand that cyanide levels in the spirit can be potentially controlled with adequate knowledge of the process, to produce potable spirits well within specifications. A suitable mashing regime, accommodating a ~50°C linamarase stand to intensify the innate cyanide degradation process, can be devised to bring about maximum detoxification early on in the brewing process. Apart from temperature control in conventional pot stills, a fractionating column could be used during distillation to selectively remove the cyanide fraction.

The nature of cassava and its wide range of flavour constituents present a number of opportunities to produce low cost, neutral and/or flavoured spirits with appropriate process control. Moreover, cassava is a globally easily accessible, consistent and plentiful source of good quality raw material. In the tropical and sub-tropical regions of the world where it is abundantly produced and consumed as a staple food, local populations can enjoy additional advantages such as foreign exchange conservation, and increased employment opportunities, which could potentially serve to improve local industries and aid their economy.

This is a largely unexplored area of research. Considering all the advantages involved in the use of cassava as a raw material, efforts must be made to better understand all the aspects of its use in the process. An understanding of the behaviour of the various flavour compounds and cyanide (both and free and bound) is essential for this. Also, it is known that the processed waste, like the flour, can be used as cattle feed. However, a better understanding of the composition of the pot ale and spent lees will be critical to its method of disposal and hence environmental sustainability.

Bibliography

Cooke, R.D., (1978). An enzymatic Assay for the Total Cyanide Content of Cassava (*Manihot esculenta* Crantz). *Journal of the Science of Food and Agriculture,* 29, 345-352.

Cooke, R.D., and Maduagwu, E.N., (1978). The effects of simple processing on the cyanide content of cassava chips. *Journal of Food Technology*, 13, 299-306.

Consumer Fact Sheet on: Cyanide. *National Primary Drinking Water Regulations*. US EPA. Available: http://www.epa.gov/safewater/pdfs/factsheets/ioc/cyanide.pdf. Last accessed 25 July 2011.

Dougan, J., Robinson, J.M., Sumar, S., Howard, G.E., and Coursey, D.G., (1983). Some Flavouring Constituents of Cassava and of Processed Cassava Products. *Journal of the Science of Food and Agriculture* **34:** 874-884.

Grace, M.R., (1977). *Cassava Processing – FAO Plant Production and Protection Papers – 3*. Available: http://www.fao.org/docrep/x5032e/x5032E01.htm#Introduction. Last accessed 20 June 2010.

Karam, L.B., Grossmann, M.V.E., Silva, R.S.S.F., Ferrero, C., and Zaritzky, N.E., (2005). Gel Textural Characteristics of Corn, Cassava and Yam Starch Blends: A Mixture Surface Response Methodology Approach. *Starch/Stärke* **57:** 62-70.

Karuri, E.E., Mbugua, S.K., Karugia, J., Wanda, K., and Jagwe, J., (2001). *Marketing Opportunities for Cassava Based Products: An Assessment of the Industrial Potential in Kenya*. University of Nairobi. Available: http://www.foodnet.cgiar.org/Projects/Cas_Demand_Kenya.pdf. Last accessed 15 August 2010.

O'Brien, G.M., Taylor, A.J., and Poulter, N.H., (1991). Improved Enzymatic Assay for Cyanogens in Fresh and Processed Cassava. *Journal of the Science of Food and Agriculture* **56:** 277-289.

Piyachomkwan, K., Wanlapatit, S., Chotineeranat, S., and Sriroth, K., (2005). Transformation and Balance of Cyanogenic Compounds in the Cassava Starch Manufacturing Process. *Starch/Stärke* **57:** 71-78.

Westby, A, (2000).*Cassava Utilisation, Storage and Small-scale Processing*. International Center for Tropical Agriculture. Available: http://www.ciat.cgiar.org/downloads/pdf/cabi_08ch5.pdf. Last accessed 08 August 2010.

Appendix

Compound	*Peak number*
Hydrocarbons	
Ethylbenzene	3
A trimethylbenzene	7
Iso-propylbenzene	5
A tetramethylbenzene	10
Naphthalene	18
A methylnaphthalene	22
An ethylnaphthalene	26
A dimethylnaphthalene	27
Diphenyl	28
A dichlorobenzene	11
A dibromochloromethane	8
Alcohols	
Pentan-2-ol	2
Aldehydes	
Hexanal	1
Heptanal	4
A deca-2,4-dienal	20
Benzaldehyde	12
Phenylacetaldehyde	16
A cholorobenzaldehyde	19
Ketones	
A decanone	30
A di-*tert*-butylbenzoquinone	21
Lactones	
δ-decalactone	33
Esters	
Methyl hexadecanoate	35
Ethyl hexadecanoate	36
Methyl octadecanoate	38
A methyl octadecadienoate	39
Diethyl phathalate	37
Furans	
2-Pentylfuran	6
Sulphur compounds	
Benzothiazole	26

Compounds identified by combined gas chromatography-mass spectroscopy in fresh cassava roots (Dougan *et al.*, 1983).

Chapter 13

Chinese white spirit

Dong Lin
Sichuan Swellfun Co. Ltd, Admin Office 4F, 9 Quanxing Road, Chengdu 610036, China

Introduction

Chinese white spirit (CWS) is very popular in China over a wide range of the population. The production of CWS has reached 890 million litres in 2010 (Figure 1).

High quality starch-providing cereal grains and the traditional Qu, the Chinese Spirit Saccharification-fermentation agent, are the main raw materials in Chinese white spirit production. CWS refers to spirit which is produced through various processes: solid state fermentation (semi-solid or liquid state fermentation for some exceptional spirits), distillation, storage or maturation, blending and aging.

CWS has the following characteristics:

1. Raw materials

   Raw materials used in white spirit production include spirit producing materials and Qu-producing materials. Solid state fermentation requires main materials such as sorghum, rice, wheat, sticky rice and corn whereas semi-solid state fermentation requires rice as the main component, and rice and corn are needed for liquid state fermentation. Qu-producing materials include wheat, barley, beans and wheat bran etc.

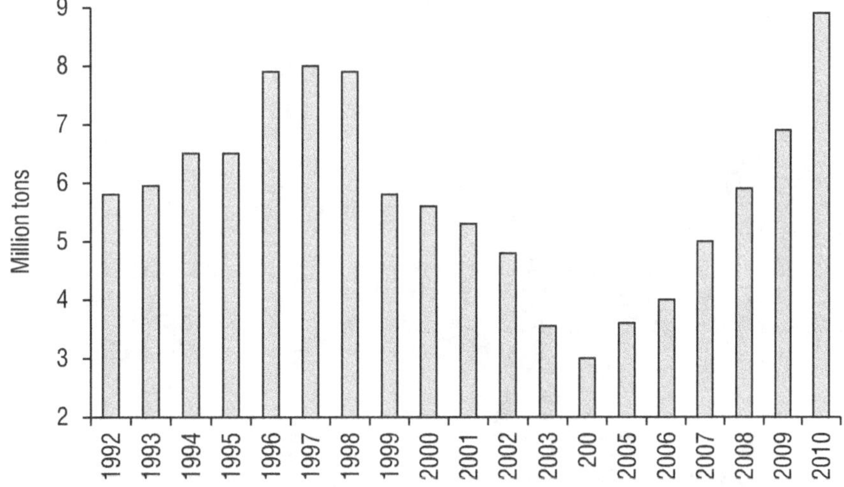

Figure 1. Chinese White Spirit nationwide annual total out put (Wang.Y.C, 2010)

2. Saccharification-fermentation agents

   Apart from yeast, the Saccharification-fermentation agents used in CWS are different types of Qu made from wheat, barley or rice. For strong aromatic CWS, median or high temperature Big Qu (Da-Qu made of wheat) is used; for soy saucy aromatic style CWS, high temperature Big Qu is used, for mild aromatic style, low temperature Big Qu is used; for rice aromatic style CWS, Small Qu (Xiao-Qu made of rice) is used.

3. Fermentation

   CWS undergoes bilateral fermentation: during CWS solid fermentation saccharification and fermentation is completed in one-go

4. Production

   In the production of CWS, the fermentation process is mostly solid state and is based on wheat-made Qu, barley-made Qu or various microorganisms. Some other spirits use semi-solid or liquid state fermentation.

5. Fermentation period

   The fermentation period for CWS is relatively long. For example, Strong aromatic style CWS is fermented for 30-90 days; Mild aromatic style CWS is fermented for about 28 days and Soy sauce aromatic style CWS has a fermentation period of 30 days per cycle, and the whole fermentation period lasts for a year.

6. Fermentation facilities

   Fermentation of CWS mainly takes place in pits and underground cylinders. Strong aromatic style CWS uses clay pit; Soy sauce aromatic style uses a semi-stone pit and Mild aromatic style CWS uses an underground pottery cylinder.

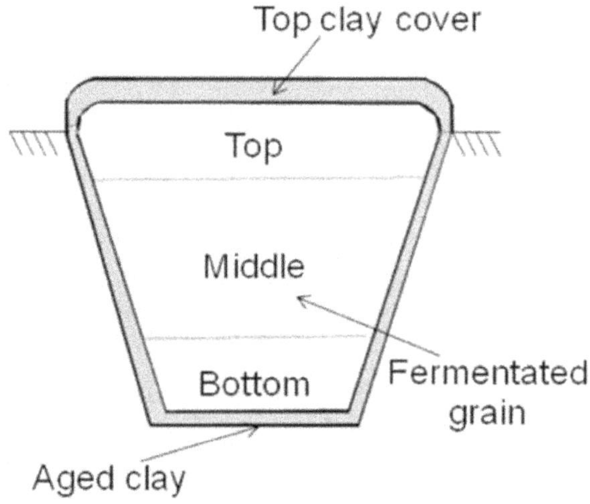

Figure 3. Typical CWS fermentation facility (clay pit)

Figure 2. Picture showing the a whole process of Big-Qu preparation (Xu.G..R., Bao.T.F. (1988))

7. Distillation

   A steaming bucket call "Zeng" is used in distillation of CWS. Steaming bucket is a unique distillation facility and is different from other distillation kits. It is a special tower design based on solid state fermentation. Zheng has higher efficiency in alcohol concentration enabling 5% (alcohol content) fermented grain to be distilled to CWS with about 70% alcohol content.

8. Maturation Storage

   CWS is usually stored in pottery jar and stainless steel tanks. On average, a pottery jar has 1-4% volume lost annually through pottery micro-holes. Freshly made spirit must be stored for a certain period. Different spirits have different storage periods depending on flavours and quality. For example, Soy sauce aromatic style CWS requires a storage period of over 3 years; Strong aromatic style and Mild aromatic style CWS require at least 1 year storage time and high-end premium CWS requires at least 3 years storage time.

Figure 5. Typical CWS maturation container (pottery jar)

9. Blending and flavouring

   Blending in CWS production is one of the most important techniques to achieve high quality finished CWS. Blending is a process that turns different types of original spirit into final blends, depending on sensory characters, pits and class grade. Flavouring is the last liquid modification in the production

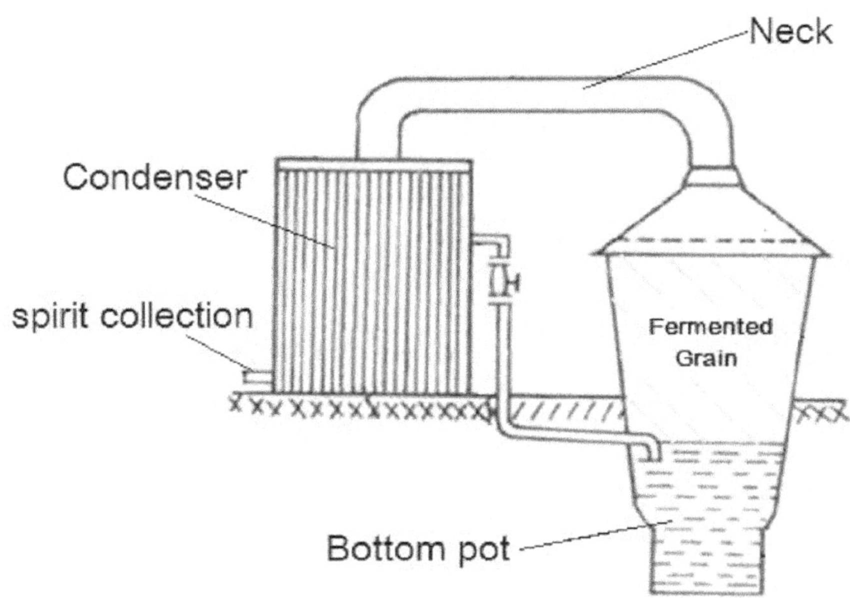

Figure 4. Typical CWS distillation equipment (Zeng) (Shen.Y.F, 2009)

of CWS. To meet the standard requirements of premium CWS, a small amount of essence flavouring spirit or spirit with characterised flavours is used to enhance the aroma and taste of the final blends.

10. Trace congener contained in CWS

CWS contains various trace compounds including acids, esters, aldehydes, alcohols, ketones and aromatic compounds and other aromatic substances; generally speaking low fat ethyl ester is the majority aroma compound in CWS. These flavour compounds are formed during the production of Qu and microbial metabolism in fermentation, as well as through steaming, distilling and maturation. Some of the flavour compounds are directly from the raw materials. These trace congeners have significant impact on the flavour of CWS.

With such a historic background, different white spirit types have unique character. There are 12 categories: Strong aromatic white spirits, Soy Sauce aromatic white spirits, Mild aromatic white spirits, Rice aromatic white spirits, Feng white spirits, Mixed aromatic white spirits (a mixture between Strong aromatic and Soy Sauce aromatic white spirits), Herbs aromatic white spirits, Fermented-bean aromatic white spirits, Sesame aromatic white spirits, Special aromatic white spirits, Fuyu aromatic white spirits and Laobaigan.

Soy Sauce flavor, Strong flavor, Mild flavor and Rice flavor are the basic flavors, which independently exist in a variety of flavors. The other eight types are based on the four basic types, which are mixed with one, two or more types to produce the desired type.

The flavour characteristics are developed from various materials during fermentation such as grains, Qu, fermentation container, production craft, storage, maturation and blending as well as environmental and geographical factors. The following is a summary of those flavour characters.

1. **Strong aromatic style**
   Raw material:
   - Single-grain style: Sorghum
   - Multi-grain style, Sorghum, Rice, Sticky Rice, Wheat, Maize

   Qu used: Middle high temperature Da Qu

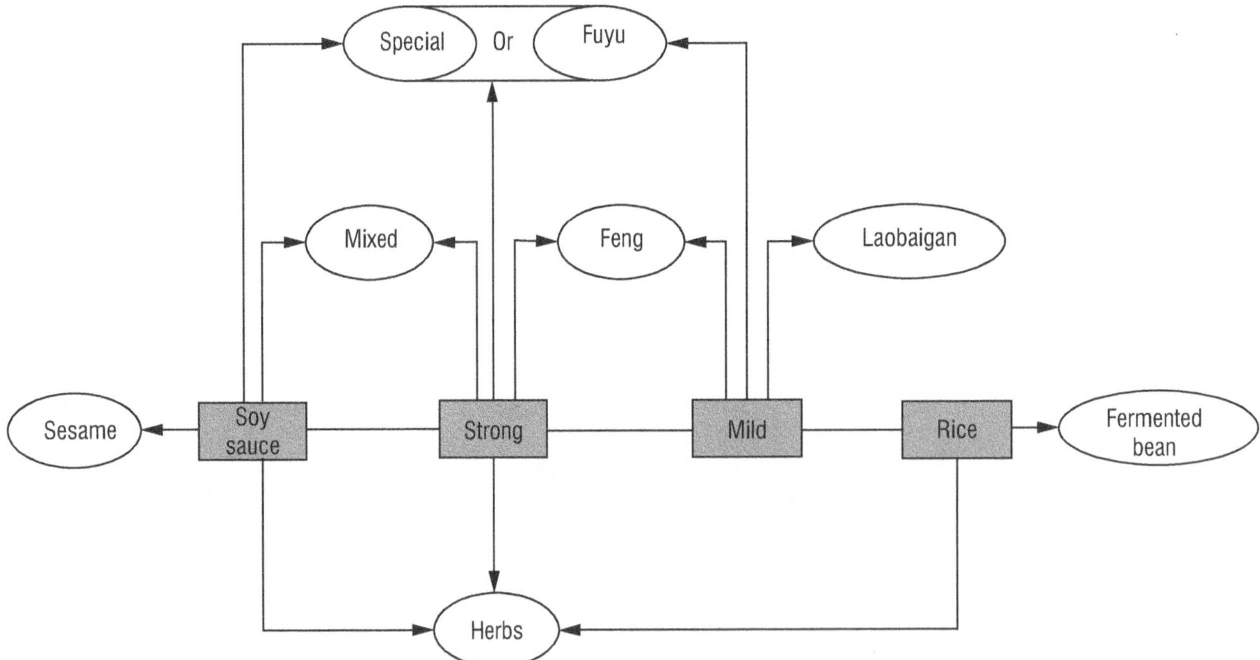

Figure 6. Chinese White Spirit classification by flavour categories (Lai.D.Y & Lin.D, 2007)

Fermentation style: solid fermentation
Fermentation facilities: clay pit
Fermentation time: 60—90 days
Processing characteristics: pit solid fermentation, continue fermentation, combine cooking grain and distillation in one go

2. **Soy sauce aromatic style**
   Raw: Sorghum
   Qu used: High temperature Da Qu
   Fermentation style: solid fermentation
   Fermentation facilities: semi-stone pit,
   Fermentation time: Eight rounds, each round lasts for a month
   Processing characteristics: accumulation multiple rounds of solid fermentation

3. **Mild aromatic style**
   a. Wheat-made Qu
      Raw material: sorghum
      Qu used: low temperature wheat-made big-Qu
      Fermentation facility and state: ceramic pit, solid state
      Fermentation period: ~28 days
      Process characteristics: grain cooking and distillation carry on separately
   b. Bran-made Qu
      Raw material: sorghum
      Qu used: bran yeast Qu
      Fermentation facility and state: concrete ponds, solid state short-term fermentation
      Fermentation period: 4-5 days
      Process characteristics: grain cooking and distillation carry on separately
   c. Barley-made Qu
      Raw material: sorghum
      Qu used: barley-made big -Qu
      Fermentation facility and state: concrete ponds or small cans, solid state short-term fermentation
      Fermentation period: Sichuan barley-made Qu is 7 days; Yunnan barley-made Qu is 30 days
      Process characteristics: grain cooking and distillation carry on separately

4. **Rice aromatic style**
   Raw materials: Rice
   Qu: Xiao Qu
   Fermentation style: semi-solid fermentation
   Fermentation facilities: metal tank or pottery jar
   Fermentation time: one week
   Processing characteristics: short fermentation period fermentation

5. **Feng aromatic style**
   Raw material: Sorghum
   Qu used: Middle high temperature Da Qu
   Fermentation facilities: new clay pit
   Fermentation style: solid fermentation
   Fermentation time: 28 – 30 days
   Processing characterizes: recycle fermentation and mixed with new raw materials, combining cooking grain with distillation

6. **Herb aromatic style**
   Raw materials: sorghum
   Qu used: mixed big and small Qu
   Fermentation facilities: combining use of different types and materials of pit
   Fermentation style: big and small Qu separated solid fermentation
   Fermentation time: small Qu fermentation 7 days / big Qu fermentation approx eight months
   Processing characteristics: mixed big and small Qu fermented grain distillation

7. **Fermented bean aromatic style**
   Raw: Rice
   Qu used: small Qu
   Fermentation facilities: underground pottery cylinder
   Fermentation style: liquid fermentation
   Fermentation time: 20 days
   Processing characteristics: soaked with matured pork fat

8. **Sesame aromatic style**
   Raw materials: Sorghum
   Qu used: mixed of low, middle and high temp Da Qu

Fermentation facilities: Concrete pond
Fermentation style: solid fermentation
Fermentation time: 30 – 45 days
Processing characteristic: continue fermentation, combine cooking grain and distillation in one-go

9. Special aromatic style
Raw materials
Qu used: big Qu
Fermentation facilities: stone pit
Fermentation style: solid fermentation
Fermentation time: 45 days
Processing characteristics: continue fermentation, combine cooking grain and distillation in one-go

10. Mixed (strong and soy sauce aromatic style)

a. Major Soy sauce minor strong aromatic
Raw material: sorghum
Qu used: high temperature wheat-made big Qu
Fermentation facility and state: concrete pond, solid state
Fermentation period: 9 cycles (one cycle per month)
Process characteristics: multi-cycle solid state fermentation, 1-7 cycles for saucy and 8-9 cycles are mixed processes for strong aromatic.

b. Major Strong minor Soy sauce aromatic
Raw material: sorghum
Qu used: high temperature wheat-made big-Qu
Fermentation facility and state: concrete pond and clay pit, solid state fermentation
Fermentation period: 60 days for strong aromatic; 30 days for soy sauce
Process characteristics: separate fermentation and storage for each type, then blend into mixed styled spirit

11. Laobaigan aromatic style
Raw materials: Sorghum
Qu used: mild-temp big Qu
Fermentation facilities: underground pottery cylinder
Fermentation style: solid fermentation
Fermentation time: 15 days
Processing characteristic: short fermentation time, continue fermentation, combine cooking grain and distillation in one go

12. Fuyu aromatic style
Raw materials: sorghum, rice, sticky rice, maize and wheat
Qu used: big and small Qu combining used
Fermentation facilities: clay pit
Fermentation: solid fermentation
Fermentation time: 30-60 days
Processing characteristics: using whole grain, big and small Qu combining used, grain cooking and distillation carry on separately

Reference

Xu.G..R., Bao.T.F. (1988) Jiuqu making technology: Grandiose Survey of Chinese Alcoholic Drinks and Beverages. China alcoholic drinks industry association

Wang.Y.C, (2010) China Wine-making industry association(Liquor Branch) Working Report 2011No.6 (Tol.204):116-121

Shen.Y.F, 2009 Chinese white spirit production and technology, China light industry press. 2009.9.p853.

Lai.D.Y, Lin.D, 2007 Research on Technological Feature and Flavor Characteristics of Six World Famous Distilling Liquors, LIQUOR MAKING No.3 (Tol.34): 106-110

Chapter 14

Analysis of a distiller's yeast during industrial grain fermentation

R. Hansen[1,2], F. Moffat[1], and D. J. Jamieson[1]
[1]*School of Life Sciences, Heriot-Watt University, Edinburgh EH14 4AS, UK;*
[2]*Current address: Syngenta, Jealott's Hill International Research Centre Bracknell, Berkshire RG42 6EY, United Kingdom*

Introduction

The distilling strain of *Saccharomyces cerevisiae* named 'M' is widely used in the production of whisky due to its ability to convert wort sugars into ethanol under changing conditions without developing off-flavors. 'M' yeast is thought to be a hybrid of *Saccharomyces cerevisiae* and *Saccharomyces diastaticus*, a strain that differs from *S. cerevisiae*, in that it contains a gene for ß-amylase (Kunze et al. 1993). Industrial grain fermentation is a challenging environment for *S. cerevisiae* 'M' as it is exposed to many stress factors such as high osmotic pressure, hydrostatic pressure, nutrient limitations, high ethanol concentration and rising temperature. Furthermore, as the wort is not boiled prior to fermentation, wild yeast and lactic acid bacteria found in the natural flora around distilleries are present in the fermentation (van Beek and Priest 2002). The ability of *S. cerevisiae* 'M' to protect itself and ferment efficiently relies on its stress responses. The stress response in *S. cerevisiae* involves regulation of gene expression, protein expression and post-translational modifications, protein targeting to organelles and proteolytic activity.

The stress response in industrial yeast has been subject for a number of DNA array experiments for measuring changes in gene expression. Recently, a transcription profile of brewers yeast under fermentation conditions was generated that showed a complete repression of many stress response genes (James et al. 2003). A transcription profile of wine yeast in synthetic must showed that entry to stationary phase was a key event involving induction of many TOR target genes (Rossignol et al. 2003). DNA array technology was also applied to investigate dynamics in the transcriptome of *Saccharomyces carlsbergensis* during production-scale lager beer fermentation. This study showed the complexity of the yeast response under industrial conditions as it was not possible to group related genes into clusters showing identical expression pattern (Olesen et al. 2002). A wealth of information about yeast stress responses has also been gained from controlled laboratory experiments, which has focused on altering a single parameter to dissect the effect of each stressor on transcription (Alexandre et al. 2001; Causton et al. 2001; Gasch et al. 2000; DeRisi et al. 1997). Recently, proteomic studies on industrial yeasts have been carried out (Trabalzini et al. 2003; Hansen et al. 2006).

Here we present an analysis of a distilling strain of *Saccharomyces cerevisiae* called 'M' during industrial grain fermentation. Quantitative PCR was used to measure the expression of selected genes during fermentation to complement and validate our earlier protein expression data (Hansen et al. 2006). Insights into maltose metabolism, heat shock protein expression, TOR pathway activity, which may be used for future optimization of distilling yeast performance that can lead to improvements in fermentation robustness, ethanol yield and flavor development in the whisky industry.

Materials and methods

Strains, media and growth conditions

The distilling yeast strain 'M' (Kerry Ingredients and Flavours Ltd) was used throughout this study, supplied in compressed format. Fermentations were carried out in 400,000 l mechanically agitated steel washbacks. The wort contained 15% malted barley and 85% pre-boiled maize which had been heated to 62 °C. After two hours, the wort was cooled. At the time of transfer to the washbacks, the wort had a specific gravity of 1.060 kg l^{-1}. Fermentations were pitched with a yeast cell density of 1 g l^{-1}.

Sampling was done from the bottom of the washback and 50 ml samples were collected and filtered though a 0.5 mm mesh to remove solids and centrifuged at 3000 g for 5 min. The cell pellet was washed once with cold phosphate buffered saline (PBS), while the supernatant was stored frozen at -20°C until required for HPLC analysis of carbohydrate, acetic acid and lactic acid content.

HPLC analysis of carbohydrates, lactic acid, acetic acid and ethanol

Supernatants from the fermentation samples were diluted and used for detection of carbohydrates, ethanol and lactic- and acetic-acids. Carbohydrate analysis was performed by high performance anion exchange (HPAE) separation using a Dionex Carbopac PA-100 column coupled to a Dionex PAD detector. Lactic and Acetic acid was extracted from samples using a Phenomenex Strata SI-2 column and a Varian SAX column and separated using a Phenomenex Synergi 4u hydro-RP 80A column connected to a Waters 484 tunable wavelength detector. Ethanol was measured by direct sample injection into a Chrompack CP9000 Gas Chromatography instrument with a FID detector using a CP SIL 5CB column.

Free Amino Nitrogen (FAN) analysis

Samples withdrawn from the fermentations were diluted 100-fold, and free amino nitrogen was measured with ninhydrin (Sigma) using glycine as a reference (Moore and Stein 1954).

Yeast and bacterial enumeration

Samples withdrawn from the fermentations were and diluted in PBS buffer and yeast viability measured using methylene blue. Yeast cell counts were also performed by plating serial dilutions onto YPD plates containing 20 g l^{-1} glucose, 20 g l^{-1} peptone, 10 g l^{-1} yeast extract and 10 mg l^{-1} tetracycline. Lactic acid bacteria were enumerated by plating on MRS plates (52 g l^{-1} MRS 10 g l^{-1} Brain heart infusion, 10 g l^{-1} Maltose) containing 100 mg l^{-1} cycloheximide.

RNA extraction

Samples were solubilised in cold DMPC-treated water, and filtered though a 0.5 mm mesh to remove solids. Samples were then centrifuged, and suspended in RNA buffer (500 mM NaCl, 10 mM EDTA, 1% SDS, 200 mM Tris-HCl, pH 7.5). A mixture of phenol:chloroform (1:1) was mixed 1:1 with the RNA buffer, and glass beads were added. The cell suspension was vortexed for 4 min, and then centrifuged at 10000 g for 2 min. The aqueous phase was transferred to fresh eppendorf tube, and RNA was precipitated in 70% ethanol. After incubation on ice for 15 min, RNA was recovered by centrifugation at 10000 g for 10 min. The RNA pellet was washed once with 70% ethanol, and solubilised in DMPC-treated water. RNA was further purified using RNeasy Mini Spin Columns (Qiagen) according to manufacture's instructions. The integrity, purity and quantity of purified RNA were estimated by running 1% Agarose gels.

cDNA synthesis and Quantitative PCR

Contaminating DNA was removed from RNA samples by 30 min incubation in RNAse-free DNAse (Amersham Biosciences) at 37°C in a DNAse buffer containing RNAsin (Invitrogen). To prevent degradation of RNA, EDTA was added to a concentration of 40 mM prior to DNAse heat inactivation, which was performed at 75°C for 10 min. cDNA was synthesized using Iscript cDNA synthesis kit (BioRad) according to manufacture's instructions. To quantify cDNA, quantitative PCR (qPCR) was carried out on a Icycler iQ real-time detection system with iQ SYBR Green Supermix (BioRad) and ABsolute QPCR SYBR Green Flourescein Mix (ABgene) according to manufacturer's instructions. Primers were designed with Primer3 software. All qPCR assays was run with the same program (40 cycles of 20 s at 95°C, 30 s at 58°C, 20 s at 72°C) and a control for contaminating DNA was performed for each sample. Melt-curve analysis was done for each qPCR assay to detect primer dimer formation. Obtained Ct-values was normalized to actin cDNA and relative quantification was carried out using the $2^{-\Delta\Delta C_T}$ method (Livak and Schmittgen 2001).

Results

In order to further characterise distillers yeast during industrial fermentations and in the hope we would uncover indications of post-transcriptional control we examined the expression of several key genes encoding proteins we had previously shown were up or down regulated in a proteomic study, Table 1 and Table 2. In addition we also investigated the transcriptional response of several key genes whose products were not identified in our proteomic study, Table 2.

Table 1. Selected M-yeast Proteins identified by proteomics

Gene	*ORF*	*Gene description*	*Induction fold*				*Abundance* (%)*
			0 h	*24 h*	*48 h*	*72 h*	
Heat shock Proteins							
Hsp104p	YLL026W	Chaperone	-	-	-	Present	0.19
Ssa1p	YAL005C	Chaperone with ATPase activity	1	-	-	9.4	0.36
Hsp60p	YLR259C	Mitochondrial Chaperone	2.6	1	1	2.2	0.65
Hsp31p	YDR533C	Chaperone and cysteine protease	1	3.2	5.3	5.7	0.21
Maltose metabolism							
Mal12p	YGR292W	Maltase	1	10.6	5	1.8	0.77
Ygr287cp	YGR287C	Similar to maltase	1	17.5	12	4.9	1.23
TOR pathway regulated proteins							
Pep4p	YPL154C	Vacuolar aspartyl protease	1	8.2	17.8	20.7	1.66
Prb1p	YEL060C	Vacuolar serine protease	1	2.9	2.9	4.6	1.36

* Abundance is measured as the volume of the protein spot divided with the total volume of all protein spots in the gel (time), where the normalised protein volume was highest.
Present indicates that the protein was identified but that the levels were too low for accurate quantification.
Adapted from Hansen et al 2006

Table 2. Genes selected for transcript analysis, and their function.

Gene	*Encoded Protein*	*Activity / Function*
ACT1	Actin 1	Structural protein involved in cell polarization, endocytosis, and other cytoskeletal functions
AIF1	Apoptosis initiating factor 1	Mitochondrial cell death effector, Nuclease activity
ATG1	AuTophaGy related protein kinase 1	Required for autophagy and for the cytoplasm-to-vacuole targeting
ATH1	Acid trehalase 1	Acid trehalase required for utilization of extracellular trehalose
HSP26	Heat shock protein 26	Small heat shock protein with chaperone activity
HSP42	Heat shock protein 42	Small cytosolic stress-induced chaperone
HSP60	Heat shock protein 60	Mitochondrial chaperonin required for ATP-dependent folding of precursor polypeptides
HSP104	Heat shock protein 104	Chaperone required refolding and reactivating previously denatured, aggregated proteins; responsive to stresses including heat and ethanol
NTH1	Neutral Trehalase 1	Neutral trehalase required for thermotolerance, mediate resistance to other cellular stresses
NTH2	Neutral Trehalase 2	Putative neutral trehalase, required for thermotolerance
PEP4	Proteinase A	Vacuolar aspartyl protease
PRB1	Proteinase B	Vacuolar proteinase B (yscB), a serine protease of the subtilisin family
SSA1	Stress-seventy subfamily A, Heat shock protein 70 family member	ATPase involved in protein folding and translocation
UTH1	yoUTH, mitochondrial membrane protein	Oxidative stress response, life span during starvation, mitochondrial biogenesis, and cell death
YCA1	Yeast Caspase 1	Cysteine protease similar to mammalian caspases

Sugar uptake and metabolism

Maltose and maltotriose are the most abundant sugars in grain wort. Mal11p or Mal31p are the major transporters responsible for maltose and maltotriose uptake. Using RT-qPCR, it was found that *MAL31* was expressed at a 6 to 8 -fold higher level at the beginning and 24 h of fermentation compared to at 48 and 72 hours, Figure 1. *MAL11* was not regulated at transcriptional level. The fact that expression of *MAL31* is occurring in presence of glucose in the beginning of the fermentation suggests that no glucose repression of maltose metabolism is present in 'M' yeast strain. Higher initial gene expression was also obtained for *MAL12*, a maltase responsible for converting maltose to glucose. However, protein levels of Mal12p showed a different pattern with the lowest level of Mal12p in the beginning of fermentation, indicating a lag in translation of *MAL12* mRNA. The protein expression pattern of Ygr287cp, a maltase showing high sequence similarity to Mal12p, is similar to that of Mal12p, whereas transcription levels did not show major regulation (data not shown). Messenger RNA encoding the low-affinity hexose transporter, Hxt1p, could not be detected at any time during fermentation, whereas mRNA for the high-affinity hexose transporter, Hxt2p, was highly induced at the beginning and at 24 hours of fermentation, suggesting that Hxt2p is involved in uptake of glucose, when glucose is present at low concentrations, Figure 1.

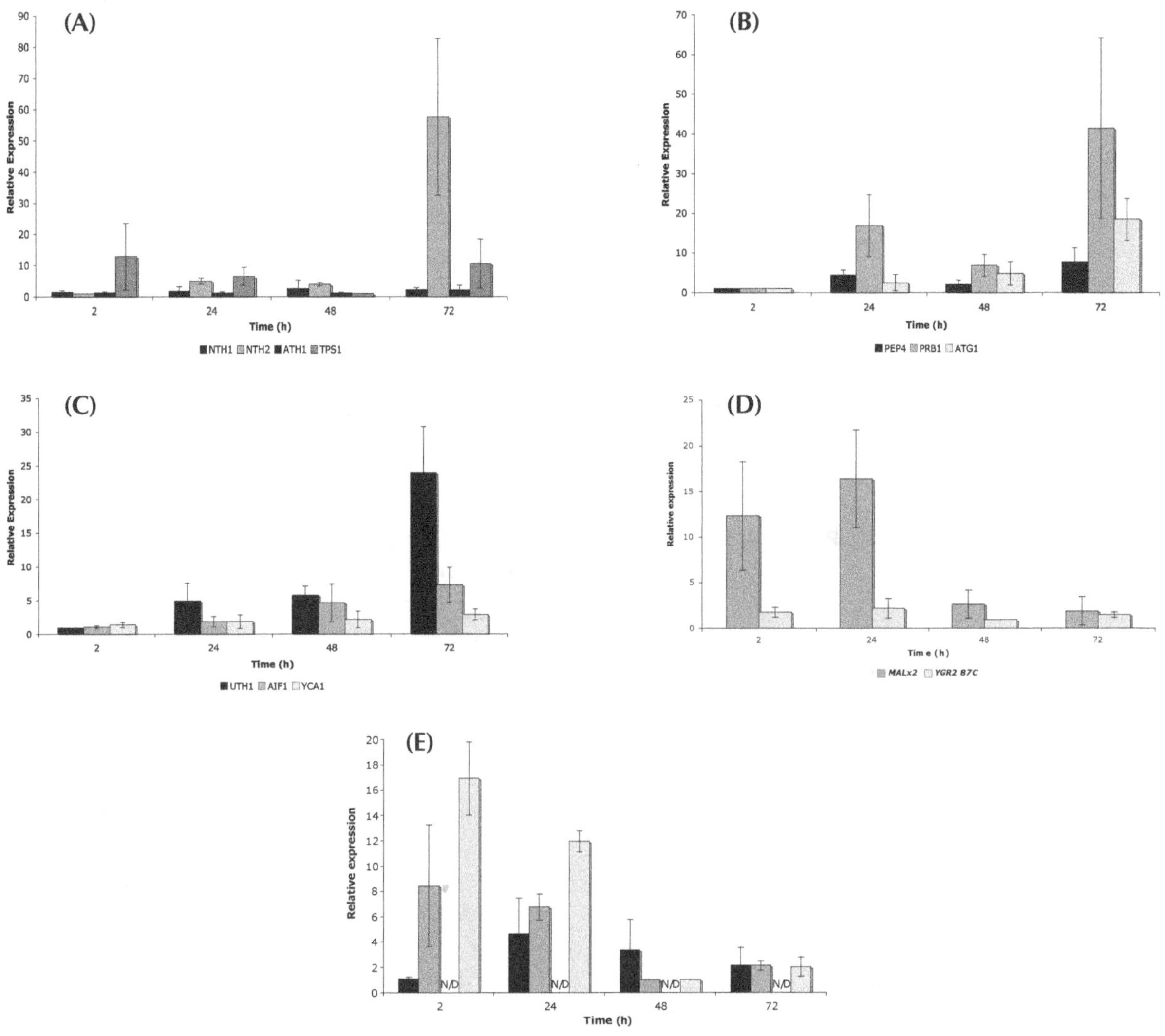

Figure 1. Examination of the relative expression levels of key genes during grain fermentation, in all cases the levels of the *ACT1* gene was used for normalization. A; Transcript levels of genes encoding proteins involved in trehalose metabolism. B: Transcript levels of autophagy-related proteins. C: Transcript levels of apoptosis- and autophagy-related cell death mediators. D: Transcript levels of *MALx2 and YGR287C*. E: Transcript levels of genes encoding membrane permeases involved in sugar uptake (*HXT1* = N/D, not detected).

Trehalose is a key protection agent against environmental stressors, such as heat and ethanol, acting by increasing structural integrity and protein stability in addition to providing a reserve carbon source (Singer and Lindquist 1998). Trehalose is produced by a complex of proteins, of which the protein encoded by *TPS1* is an important subunit, expression of the *TPS1* gene was at its highest at 72 h, where it was on average 10- to 12-fold higher compared to 48 h. Surprisingly, examination of the expression of the genes encoding the three different yeast trehalases, *ATH1*, *NTH1* and *NTH2* revealed that only *NTH2* expression was significantly up-regulated, 57-fold at 72 h compared to 0 h, Figure 1.

Activation of TOR target genes upon FAN depletion

Yeast growth arrested after 24 h as a result of poor nitrogen availability. Low nitrogen sources have been shown to trigger expression of genes subjected to nitrogen catabolite repression, a mechanism controlled by the TOR pathway. In accordance with this, protein levels of vacuolar proteases, Pep4p and Prb1p, increased during fermentation, Table 1. The up-regulation of Pep4p and Prb1p, which are controlled by the TOR pathway though transcription factor Gln3p, might enable yeast metabolism by recycling endogenous amino acids. Analysis of *PEP4* and *PRB1* gene expression mirrored the protein levels and increased as the fermentation progressed, Figure 1. Interestingly, induction of *PRB1* expression appeared to be higher than *PEP4* at 72 h, whereas the relative protein levels of Pep4p were higher than for prb1p, thus suggesting that post-transcriptional mechanisms regulate protein levels of Pep4p. Despite extensive searches several key TOR pathway controlled proteins that are involved in autophagy and autophagy-related cell death, Atg1p and Uth1p respectively, were never detected. However expression of the *ATG1* and *UTH1* genes were induced during fermentation, Figure 1.

Heat Shock proteins

Heat Shock Proteins (HSPs) play a major role in yeast stress defense and are though to be important during fermentations. The levels of Hsp31p and Ssa1p proteins increased during fermentation indicating that yeast were stressed during the industrial fermentations. Gene expression studies revealed a major increase in expression of all analysed HSPs at 72 h, at which stage available sugars were limited and cells were effectively in stationary phase, Figure 1. In particular the expression of *HSP26* was found to increase by 17000-fold at 72 h *vs.* 0 h.

Discussion

Transcription of proteinase genes is regulated by the TOR pathway, specifically, deactivation of TOR kinases releases the repressor Ure2 from the transcription factor Gln3, which then transcribes its target genes, which includes proteinase A (*PEP4*) and proteinase B (*PRB1*) (Beck and Hall 1999). Moreover, growth arrest caused by nitrogen depletion has been shown to trigger de-activation of TOR pathway, leading to transcription of *PEP4* and *PRB1* (Hardwick et al. 1999). The significant increase in the protein and transcription levels of Pep4 and Prb1 during fermentation in this study is another indicator of nitrogen depletion. A similar up-regulation of *PEP4* and *PRB1* gene expression upon growth arrest has been observed during wine yeast fermentations (Rossignol et al. 2003). The TOR pathway has major regulatory roles in autophagy-related degradation and recycling of organelles and cytosolic proteins, which is sequestered within vesicles and delivered to the vacuole for final proteolytic digestion by PEP4 and PRB1 (Klionsky 2005). Autophagy has been found to be required for maintenance of amino acid levels and protein synthesis under nitrogen synthesis (Onodera and Ohsumi 2005). The activity of agt1 is required for the induction of autophagy, and its transcription has been correlated with inhibition of TOR kinases (Hardwick et al. 1999). Our results showed that the expression of *AGT1* increased in similar manner to *PEP4* and *PRB1*, further suggesting a shared regulating mechanism. Uth1p is an autophagic-related cell death effector, which is triggered in response to starvation and oxidative stress (Bhatia-Kissova and Camougrand 2010). We found that *UTH1* was highly induced towards the end of fermentation, indicating that Uth1p might contribute to lower yeast viability in the late stage of fermentation.

The work presented here is in agreement with earlier studies using micro-arrays on brewers yeast in industrial settings, showing that the expression of many heat shock proteins was repressed during fermentation (Brosnan et al. 2000; James et al. 2003). However, upon entering stationary phase at the end of the fermentation, the complete set of heat shock proteins were detected, in agreement previous findings in laboratory yeast (Sanchez et al. 1992). In agreement with proteomic data, the study of gene expression showed high induction of heat shock proteins. Among other HSPs, gene expression of hsp26 was highly induced. The high expression of hsp26 might, as a result, prevent cell death under conditions with high stress levels and low ATP availability such as late-stage grain fermentation. Furthermore, a recent study has linked Hsp26 expression to autophagy-related degradation upon nitrogen starvation (Onodera and Ohsumi 2005).

Trehalose is stress-protective as it promotes survival during heat shock. It is thought that trehalose can stabilise the native folded state of proteins, and thereby prevent aggregation (Singer and Lindquist 1998). The neutral trehalases encoding genes, *NTH1* and *NTH2*, have both been shown to be induced by heat and nutrient limitations (Nwaka and Holzer 1998). A third trehalase Ath1p in contrast has shown enhanced survival to ethanol and other stresses (Singer and Lindquist 1998). In the present study, *NTH2* gene expression was highly induced at 72 h, whereas expression of both *NTH1* and *ATH1* was low throughout the fermentations.

In conclusion, our previous use of 2D gels and Peptide Mass Fingerprinting has allowed quantification and identification, respectively, of proteins up and down regulated during industrial grain fermentations a comparison of those result with our transcription studies shown here suggests there may be some post-transcriptional regulation involved in controlling the levels of key fermentation proteins.

Acknowledgments

The funding given by the BBSRC and the Scotch Whisky Research Institute is gratefully acknowledged. Many thanks are also due to Carole Judd from North British Distillery Ltd. for assistance with sampling and data collection.

References

Alexandre H, Ansanay-Galeote V, Dequin S, Blondin B, 2001 Global gene expression during short-term ethanol stress in Saccharomyces cerevisiae. *FEBS Lett* **498**: 98–103.

Beck T, Hall M, 1999 The TOR signalling pathway controls nuclear localization of nutrient-regulated transcription factors. *Nature* **402**: 689-692.

van Beek S, Priest F, 2002 Evolution of the lactic acid bacterial community during malt whisky fermentation: A polyphasic study. *Applied and Environmental Microbiology* **68**: 297-305.

Bhatia-Kissova I, Camougrand N, 2010 Mitophagy in yeast: actors and physiological roles. *FEMS Yeast Research* **10**: 1023-1034.

Brosnan MP, Donnelly D, James TC, Bond U, 2000 The stress response is repressed during fermentation in brewery strains of yeast. *J Appl Microbiol* **88**: 746–755.

Causton H, Ren B, Koh S, Harbison C, Kanin E, Jennings E, Lee T, True H, Lander E, Young R, 2001 Remodeling of yeast genome expression in response to environmental changes. *Molecular Biology of the Cell* **12**: 323-337.

DeRisi J, Iyer V, Brown P, 1997 Exploring the metabolic and genetic control of gene expression on a genomic scale. *Science* **278**: 680-686.

Gasch A, Spellman P, Kao C, Carmel-Harel O, Eisen M, Storz G, Botstein D, Brown P, 2000 Genomic expression programs in the response of yeast cells to environmental changes. *Molecular Biology of the Cell* **11**: 4241-4257.

Hansen R, Pearson SY, Brosnan JM, Meaden PG, Jamieson DJ, 2006 Proteomic analysis of a distilling strain of Saccharomyces cerevisiae during industrial grain fermentation. *Applied Microbiology and Biotechnology* **72**: 116-125.

Hardwick J, Kuruvilla F, Tong J, Shamji A, Schreiber S, 1999 Rapamycin-modulated transcription defines the subset of nutrient-sensitive signaling pathways directly controlled by the Tor proteins. *Proceedings of the National Academy of Sciences of the United States of America* **96**: 14866-14870.

James TC, Campbell S, Donnelly D, Bond U, 2003 Transcription profile of brewery yeast under fermentation conditions. *J Appl Microbiol* **94**: 432–448.

Klionsky D, 2005 Autophagy. *Current Biology* **15**: R282-R283.

Kunze G, Kunze I, Barner A, Schulz R, 1993 Classification of *Saccharomyces cerevisiae* strains by genetic and biochemical methods. *Monatsschrift fur Brauwissenschaft* **46**: 132–136.

Livak K, Schmittgen T, 2001 Analysis of relative gene expression data using real-time quantitative PCR and the 2(T)(-Delta Delta C) method. *Methods* **25**: 402-408.

Moore S, Stein WH, 1954 A modified ninhydrin reagent for the photometric determination of amino acids and related compounds. *J Biol Chem* **211**: 907–913.

Nwaka S, Holzer H, 1998 Molecular biology of trehalose and the trehalases in the yeast Saccharomyces cerevisiae. In: *Progress in Nucleic Acid Research and Molecular Biology, Vol 58*, Progress In Nucleic Acid Research And Molecular Biology., pp. 197-237.

Olesen K, Felding T, Gjermansen C, Hansen J, 2002 The dynamics of the Saccharomyces carlsbergensis brewing yeast transcriptome during a production-scale lager beer fermentation. *FEMS Yeast Research* **2**: 563-573.

Onodera J, Ohsumi Y, 2005 Autophagy is required for maintenance of amino acid levels and protein synthesis under nitrogen starvation. *Journal of Biological Chemistry* **280**: 31582-31586.

Rossignol T, Dulau L, Julien A, Blondin B, 2003 Genome-wide monitoring of wine yeast gene expression during alcoholic fermentation. *Yeast* **20**: 1369–1385.

Sanchez Y, Taulien J, Borkovich KA, Lindquist S, 1992 Hsp104 is required for tolerance to many forms of stress. *EMBO J* **11**: 2357–2364.

Singer M, Lindquist S, 1998 Thermotolerance in Saccharomyces cerevisiae: the Yin and Yang of trehalose. *Trends in Biotechnology* **16**: 460-468.

Trabalzini L, Paffetti A, Scaloni A, Talamo F, Ferro E, Coratza G, Bovalini L, Lusini P, Martelli P, Santucci A, 2003 Proteomic response to physiological fermentation stresses in a wild-type wine strain of Saccharomyces cerevisiae. *Biochemical Journal* **370**: 35-46.

Chapter 15

The tolerance of *Saccharomyces cerevisiae* distilling and bioethanol strains to ethanol

Annie W.Y. Cheung[1], James M. Brosnan[2] and Katherine A. Smart[1*]

[1]*Bioenergy and Brewing Science, School of Biosciences, University of Nottingham, Sutton Bonington Campus, Loughborough, Leics, LE12 5RD, UK;* [2]*The Scotch Whisky Research Institute, The Robertson Trust Building, Research Avenue North, Riccarton, Edinburgh, EH14 4AP, UK; * Corresponding author*

Introduction

Scotch whisky fermentations commonly employ worts with standard gravities (1.060 to 1.070). Table 1 summarises the expected ethanol yield of worts with different original gravities. For high gravity (HG) fermentations, they may be expected to yield at least 10% (v/v) ethanol (Briggs *et al.*, 2004). Recent trends in the distilling industry suggest that "very high gravity" (VHG) fermentations employing worts with a gravity of 1.097 or more might begin to be adopted by the sector because of their capacity to yield at least 15% (v/v) ethanol (Bai *et al.*, 2004). High gravity fermentations are also employed for the production of bioethanol. Both distilling and bioethanol industries utilise the yeast *Saccharomyces cerevisiae*. However, Neto *et al.* (2009) compared the Brazilian fuel alcohol and Scotch whisky fermentation yeasts and identified several key differences that would impact on strain selection. Bioethanol fermentations tend to be thermally controlled at around 30°C but for most Scotch whisky fermentations temperature is allowed to increase naturally as fermentation progresses. Bioethanol fermentations are typically much faster, with some requiring only 6 to 10 hours to complete whilst whisky fermentations can take more than 72 hours.

Increasing the specific gravity at the start of fermentation has the potential to improve the energy and water footprints of the final product providing that the volumetric and specific productivity are not adversely affected. In essence the advantages centre on the capacity

Table 1. The expected ethanol yield of worts with different original gravities.

	Original gravity (OG)	*°Plato*	*Cane sugar (% (w/w) concentration equivalent**	*Expected ethanol yield*	*References*
Low gravity (LG)	1048	12°P	11.7%	4%-5%	Dragone *et al.*, 2003
Standard gravity (SG)	1060-1070	15-17°P	14.7% - 17%	7.5%	Gibson *et al.*, 2007
High gravity (HG)	1080	20°P	19.3%	10%	Briggs *et al.*, 2004
Very high gravity (VHG)	1097	> 24°P	> 25%	> 15%	Bafrncova *et al.*, 1999, Bayrock and Ingledew, 2001, Bai *et al.*, 2004

* Cane sugar % w/w represents g per 100 g of solution

to produce more ethanol, maximising plant fermentation capacity. Moreover, high ethanol content leads to a more efficient distillation process which is important for both whisky and bioethanol production. In addition, there are reductions in the volume of waste produced per unit ethanol and in the labour and space required in the plant, which in turn reduces production costs (Stewart, 2010).

One of the main drawbacks of HG and VHG fermentations is the elevated stress experienced by the yeast cells throughout fermentation. For example, HG wort exhibits an increased osmolarity (4 x 10^6 Pa) at the beginning of fermentation due to the higher concentration of sugars and other solutes (Briggs *et al.*, 2004) posing an osmotic challenge to yeasts. Similarly, the higher level of ethanol that is accumulated towards the end of fermentation can be toxic to yeasts as the expected ethanol yield of VGH fermentations is two fold higher than that of SG fermentations (Table 1). Ethanol stress in *S. cerevisiae* has recently been reviewed by a number of authors (Gibson *et al.*, 2007, Ding *et al.*, 2009, Stanley *et al.*, 2010). Yeast exposed to high levels of ethanol are challenged with respect to maintenance of viability, efficient uptake of glucose and other wort sugars, and fermentation rate (Pascual *et al.*, 1988, Fernandes *et al.*, 1997). Distilling and bioethanol strains suitable for HG and VHG fermentations must therefore be able to tolerate both osmotic and ethanol stress. To identify strain traits that might be beneficial in surviving stress, knowledge regarding the strain-dependent tolerance is critical so that target sites leading to damage and death can be effectively identified.

Ethanol tolerance in *S. cerevisiae* laboratory and industrial strains has been widely studied, although little has been reported concerning the tolerance of distilling or bioethanol strains to ethanol. Where tolerance has been investigated in laboratory strains, assessments have typically involved exposure of yeast cells to exogenous ethanol followed by measurement of viability and/or cell growth. The former has been typically investigated by microscopy using vital stains (Chi and Arneborg, 1999) and the latter by optical density (Teixeira *et al.*, 2009) or inhibition spot plates (Abe *et al.*, 2009). Most ethanol tolerance assessment has been conducted in aerobic conditions; yet strains not exhibiting respiratory deficiency are able to utilise the ethanol as a carbon source potentially mitigating the negative effects of this stress. Furthermore, ethanol accumulates during fermentation and is most concentrated in the anaerobic phase of fermentation when yeast may exhibit a modified response due to the up-regulation of anaerobic gene families (Lawrence and Smart, 2007). In this study, bioethanol and distilling *S. cerevisiae* strains were assessed for their tolerance to exogenous ethanol under anaerobic conditions. Tolerance was assessed as the capacity of the strains to: recover, grow and develop colonies on spot plates; maintain viability; and retain genetic integrity in liquid culture during exposure to exogenous ethanol stress.

Materials and methods

Yeast strains and maintenance of cultures

Eight *Saccharomyces cerevisiae* strains commonly utilised for either distilling (SWRID1, SWRID2, SWRID3 and SWRID4) or bioethanol fermentations (SWRIB1, SWRIB2, SWRIB3 and SWRIB4) were used in the current study (Table 2), all the strains were provided by the Scotch Whisky Research Institute, U.K.. Media components were obtained from Oxoid (U.K.) unless otherwise specified.

Active dried yeasts (1 g) were rehydrated in 20 ml of 30°C sterile water; the mixture was mixed and incubated at ambient temperature for 20 minutes. The rehydrated active dried yeasts and yeasts supplied in other formats were all routinely grown in YPD (w/v: 1% yeast extract, 2% neutralised bacteriological peptone, 2% D-glucose (Fisher Scientific, U.K.) and solid media was prepared by the addition of 1.3% (w/v) agar technical no.3. Strains were stored on YPD agar slopes at 4°C. Yeast cell suspensions

Table 2. The *S. cerevisiae* strains used in this study.

Background	*S. cerevisiae strains*	*Designation of isolates*	*Physiological state when supplied*
Distilling	SWRID1 isolate 1	SWRID1a	Active dried yeast
	SWRID1 isolate 2	SWRID1b	Active dried yeast
	SWRID1 isolate 3	SWRID1c	Cream yeast
	SWRID2 isolate 1	SWRID2a	Yeast cake
	SWRID2 isolate 2	SWRID2b	Cream yeast
	SWRID3 isolate 1	SWRID3a	Yeast slurry
	SWRID3 isolate 2	SWRID3b	Cream yeast
	SWRID4	/	Active dried yeast
Bioethanol	SWRIB1	/	Slope
	SWRIB2	/	Active dried yeast
	SWRIB3	/	Active dried yeast
	SWRIB4	/	Active dried yeast

were prepared by inoculating a single colony from a YPD streak plate into 10 ml of YPD medium; the culture was incubated at 30°C and shaken at 120 r.p.m. in an orbital shaker for 48 hours. This culture was then decanted into 100ml of fresh YPD medium and incubated in the same conditions for 48 hours.

Inhibition spot plates

Yeast cell suspensions were diluted using sterile deionised water to achieve concentrations of 10^6, 10^5, 10^4 and 10^3 cells ml^{-1}. A 10 μl aliquot was removed from each cell concentration and spotted onto a minimal medium plate (w/v: 0.67% yeast nitrogen base (Formedium, U.K.), 2% glucose and 1.2% agar technical no.3) containing the required concentrations of ethanol (Fisher Scientific, U.K.) (v/v): 0%, 5%, 10%, 12% and 15%. The plates were incubated anaerobically at 30°C for 96 hours in a sealed rectangular box, containing two AnaeroGen packs and an anaerobic indicator to ensure the atmosphere inside the box was anaerobic. The plates were photographed with a digital camera after 96 hours.

Ethanol stress test

Yeast cell suspensions were inoculated into 50 ml of water or ethanol solution (v/v: 10% or 15%) in a flask to achieve a final concentration of 1 x 10^7 cells ml^{-1}. The cultures were incubated anaerobically at 30°C and shaken in an orbital shaker at 120 r.p.m. for 96 hours. The flasks were incubated in a sealed rectangular box containing two AnaeroGen packs and an anaerobic indicator to ensure the atmosphere inside the box was anaerobic. At designated intervals, 1 ml aliquot was removed from each flask and the cell suspension assessed for viability using the methylene blue staining technique as described in Smart *et al.* (1999).

Statistical analysis

The percentage viabilities and percentage of mutants presented in this study represent the means of triplicate analyses. Standard errors were expressed as error bars where appropriate. The statistical analysis of variance (ANOVA) and T-test were performed with SPSS to determine the significance between sample groups.

Results and discussion

The ability of yeast cells to tolerate stress during fermentation conditions is critical. Various authors (Rose, 1993, Chi and Arneborg, 2000, Stanley *et al.*, 2010, Zheng *et al.*, 2011) have suggested that ethanol tolerance is strain dependent; to address the hypothesis that ethanol tolerance in bioethanol and distilling yeast is strain dependent, sensitivity to exogenous ethanol in anaerobic conditions was assessed.

Impact of ethanol stress on growth of yeasts

Impact of ethanol stress on growth of S. cerevisiae bioethanol strains

The ability of yeast cells to recover and grow on minimal medium in the presence of ethanol is shown in Figure 1A. Relative ethanol tolerance of the bioethanol strains can be differentiated by applying an ethanol concentration exceeding 10% (v/v). Growth was inhibited when the ethanol concentration reached 15% (v/v) and above (data not shown). In the presence of 12% (v/v) ethanol, abundant growth was observed for all the bioethanol strains except SWRIB4. This suggested that SWRIB4 had a lower capacity to recover and grow after exposure to ethanol.

Impact of ethanol stress on growth of S. cerevisiae distilling strains

All the distilling strains grew well in the presence of 5% (v/v) ethanol (Figure 1B). When the concentration of ethanol was elevated to 10% (v/v) and 12% (v/v), all distilling strains exhibited weaker growth but no significant differences were observed between the strains. In the presence of 15% (v/v) ethanol, growth of all distilling strains was prevented.

Impact of ethanol stress on viability of yeasts

The ability of yeast strains to maintain viability throughout fermentation is critical since

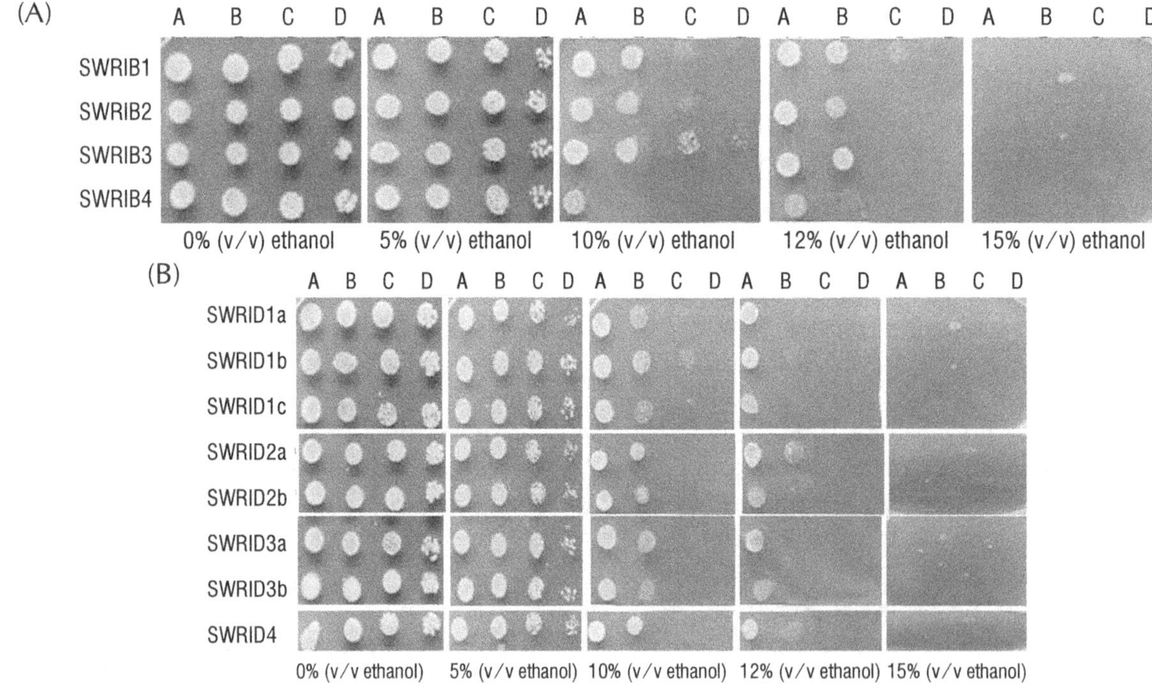

Figure 1. Growth of *S. cerevisiae* (A) bioethanol and (B) distilling strains on minimal medium plates in the presence of ethanol (0- 15% v/v). *S. cerevisiae* SWRIB1, SWRIB2, SWRIB3, SWRIB4, SWRID1, SWRID2, SWRID3 and SWRID4 were spotted onto minimal medium plates contained different concentrations of ethanol (v/v): 0%, 5%, 10%, 12% and 15%. The plates were incubated anaerobically at 30°C for 96 hours. A 10 μl aliquot of cell suspension comprising (A) 10^6 cells ml^{-1}, (B) 10^5 cells ml^{-1}, (C) 10^4 cells ml^{-1} and (D) 10^3 cells ml^{-1} for each strain was inoculated onto the plates. Visible growth was assessed.

yeast populations exhibiting low viabilities may demonstrate a reduced fermentation performance. With regard to the capacity to maintain viability during anaerobic exposure to exogenous ethanol, SWRIB2 and SWRID1c were observed to be the most ethanol tolerant whilst SWRIB1 and SWRID4 were the most ethanol sensitive.

Impact of ethanol on the viability of S. cerevisiae bioethanol strains

When the concentration of ethanol was 10% (v/v) and 15% (v/v), strain dependent differences in ethanol tolerance became more distinct. When the ethanol concentration was 10% (v/v), the percentage viabilities of SWRIB1 and SWRIB3 declined below 10% (v/v) after 72 hours whilst those of SWRIB2 and SWRIB4 were 92.1% and 88.4% respectively (Figure 2A). In the presence of 15% (v/v) ethanol, the percentage viabilities of the four bioethanol strains declined below 10% albeit at different rates: SWRIB1 at 24 hours, SWRIB2 and SWRIB4 at 40 hours and SWRIB2 at 72 hours (Figure 2B). These results suggest that SWRIB2 and SWRIB1 were the most and least ethanol tolerant bioethanol strains, respectively.

Impact of ethanol on the viability of S. cerevisiae distilling strains

Some yeast isolates, SWRID1a, SWRID1b, SWRID2 and SWRID3, exhibited viabilities of less than 10% after exposure to 10% (v/v) ethanol for 96 hours and 15% (v/v) ethanol for 24 hours (Figure 3, 4). In contrast, SWRID1c exhibited a viability of 12.7% after similar duration of exposure to both ethanol concentrations (Figure 3). Of the four distilling strains examined SWRID4 was the most sensitive to ethanol. After 48 hours exposure to 10% (v/v) ethanol, the percentage viabilities of SWRID1b, SWRID1c, SWRID2 and SWRID3 isolates were above 20% whilst those of SWRID1a and SWRID4 were 13.7% and 11.6% respectively (Figure 3B and 4A). When the ethanol concentration was increased to 15% (v/v), the percentage viabilities of the isolates of SWRID1, SWRID2 and SWRID3 declined below 5% after 24 hours; whilst that of SWRID4 was below 5% after only 16 hours (Figure 3C and 4B).

Ethanol tolerance in yeast is strain dependent

These results support the hypothesis that ethanol tolerance is strain dependent in *S. cerevisiae*. The ethanol stress in this study was induced by exposing yeast cells to exogenous ethanol, but it has been proposed that differences in relative tolerance of *S. cerevisiae* strains might occur when cells are exposed either to exogenous ethanol (ethanol stress test) or to ethanol generated by the yeast itself during fermentation (Watson and Cavicchioli, 1983). In addition, viability as an assessment of ethanol sensitivity can be misleading since cells assessed as viable

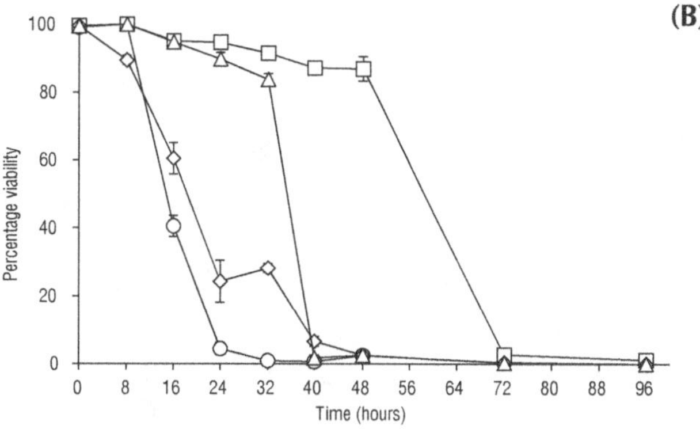

Figure 2. Maintenance of viability of bioethanol strains in the presence of ethanol. The viabilities of SWRIB1 (○), SWRIB2 (□), SWRIB3 (◇) and SWRIB4 (Δ) were assessed following exposure to (A) 10% (v/v) and (B) 15% (v/v) ethanol for 96 hours at 30°C in anaerobic conditions. Percentage viabilities represent the mean of triplicate analysis and the standard errors were shown as error bars.

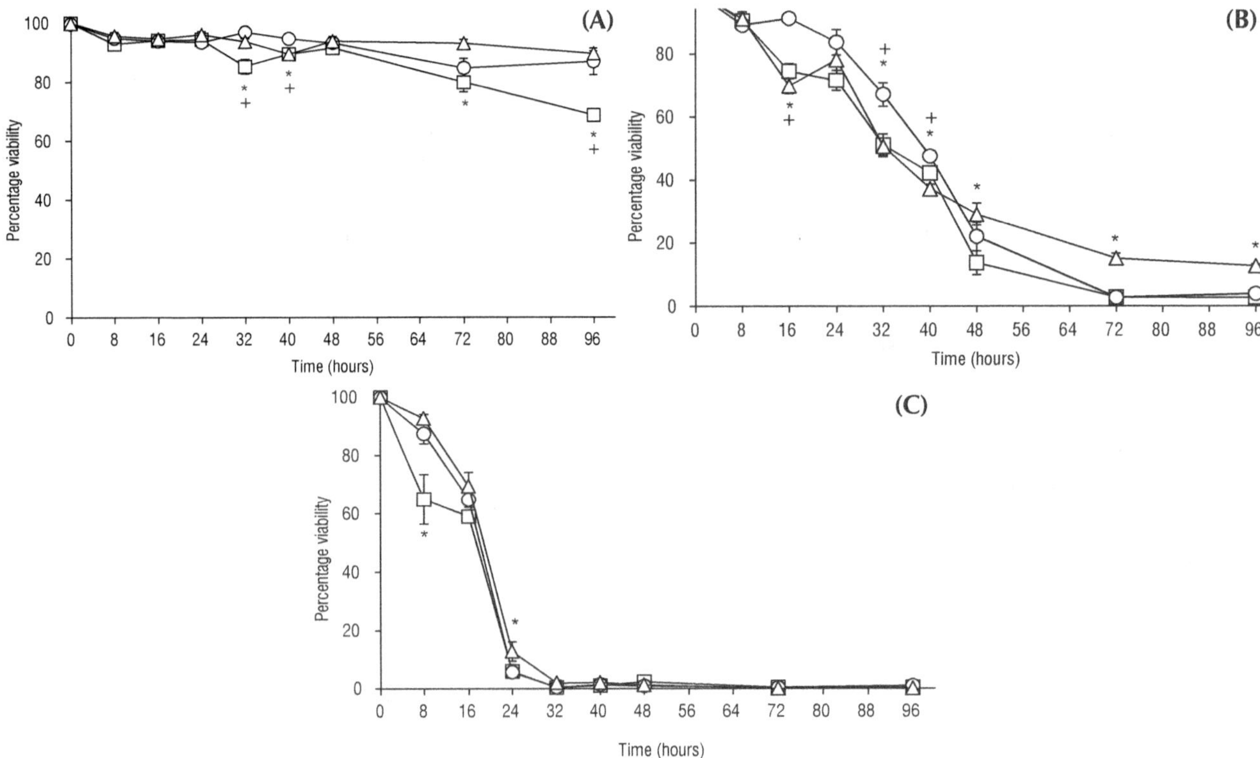

Figure 3. Maintenance of viability of distilling strains in the presence of ethanol. SWRID1a (□), SWRID1b (○) and SWRID1c (Δ) were exposed to (A) 5% (v/v), (B) 10% (v/v) and (C) 15% (v/v) ethanol for 96 hours at 30°C in anaerobic conditions. The percentage viability was assessed using the methylene blue staining technique. ANOVA was used to compare the percentage viabilities of SWRID1a, SWRID1b and SWRID1c. A significant difference is indicated by (*). The t-test was used to compare the percentage viabilities of SWRID1a and SWRID1b, a significant difference in viabilities is indicated by (+). Percentage viabilities represent the mean of triplicate analysis and the standard errors were shown as error bars.

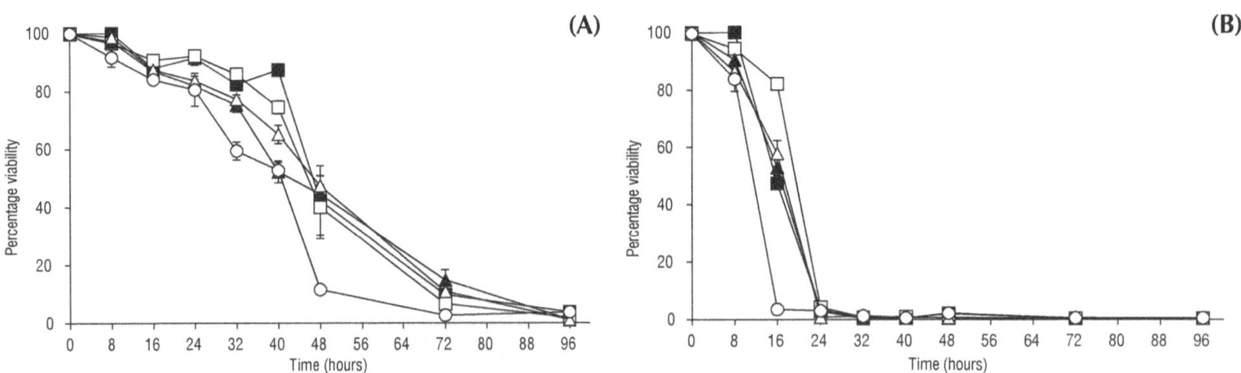

Figure 4. Maintenance of viability of distilling strains to ethanol. The viabilities of SWRID2a (■), SWRID2b (□), SWRID3a (▲), SWRID3b (Δ) and SWRID4 (○) were assessed following exposure to (A) 10% (v/v) and (B) 15% (v/v) ethanol for 96 hours at 30°C in anaerobic conditions. The percentage viability was assessed using the methylene blue staining technique. Percentage viabilities represent the mean of triplicate analysis and the standard errors were shown as error bars.

may also be damaged beyond repair and in the process of dying. It is proposed that viability in this context serves to identify strains severely impacted by exogenous ethanol and cannot be used as an indicator of ethanol tolerance during fermentation where other conditions may moderate or exacerbate ethanol induced cell death. In addition to ethanol toxicity, osmotic stress, heat stress, oxidative stress, pH shift and depletion of nutrients are commonly associated with fermentation (Gibson *et al.*, 2007). Among these stresses, heat tolerance, a characteristic that is beneficial to both bioethanol and distilling strains, has been suggested to be closely related to ethanol stress as the potential target site of both stresses is the plasma membrane, and where fluidity maintenance has been identified as a critical element for tolerance (Jeffries and Jin, 2000). A multi-stress simulation would provide more insight into the response of yeast cells under fermentation conditions and this is the subject of current investigation in our laboratory.

Ethanol tolerance in distilling yeast is dependent on source of yeast inoculum

The Scotch whisky industry does not practice "serial repitching", where yeast is collected at the end of fermentation, washed by acids, stored and repitched into subsequent fermentations (Briggs *et al.*, 2004), each fermentation requires an inoculation of fresh yeast, usually supplied by a third party in dried, pressed or creamed format. Therefore it is critical to ensure that the yeast culture inoculated is consistent. Variations between yeast inocula can occur despite being undesired. To investigate the consistency of ethanol tolerance between yeast populations with differing physiological histories, three isolates of the distilling strains SWRID1 (Table 2) were obtained. Two of the SWRID1 isolates (SWRID1a and SWRID1b) were active dried yeasts inocula while SWRID1c was creamed yeast that had been stored at chilled temperatures. The three isolates were all maintained in laboratory conditions as described in Materials and Methods.

Impact of dried and creamed yeast on ethanol tolerance

SWRID1 a and b were both supplied in dried format, yet the percentage viability of SWRID1a was significantly lower ($P \leq 0.05$) than that of SWRID1b when exposed to 5% (v/v) ethanol for 32, 40 and 96 hours and 10% (v/v) ethanol for 16, 32 and 40 hours (Figure 3A, 3B). In the presence of 15% (v/v) ethanol, the percentage viabilities of both isolates declined below 5% after 16 hours (Figure 3C) and no significant differences in percentage viabilities were observed. These results suggested inconsistency in ethanol tolerance depending on the batch of dried yeast assessed. Interestingly SWRID1c, which was supplied as creamed yeast, was observed to be more ethanol tolerant than the other two SWRID1 isolates. In the presence of 5% (v/v), 10% (v/v) and 15% (v/v) ethanol, significant differences ($P \leq 0.05$) in percentage viabilities between SWRID1a, SWRID1b and SWRID1c were observed (Figure 3). After exposure to 10% (v/v) ethanol for 48 hours, the percentage viabilities of SWRID1c was significantly higher ($P \leq 0.05$) than that of SWRID1a and SWRID1b; by 96 hours, only SWRID1c retained viability above 10% (Figure 3B). Similarly, after 24 hours exposure to 15% (v/v) ethanol, SWRID1c exhibited a percentage viability of 12.7% while those of SWRI1a and SWRID1b were below 5% (Figure 3C).

These data clearly demonstrate the impact of yeast culture supply on ethanol tolerance. It has been reported (Gibson *et al.*, 2007) that during the preparation of dried yeast various stresses including heat stress, oxidative stress, osmotic stress and nutrient starvation are experienced by the yeast. Assuming that the stress levels are sub-lethal during dried yeast production it would be likely that the yeast would elicit responses to these stresses which might prepare the cells for subsequent ethanol stress. However, the data presented in the current study does not support this hypothesis. One possible explanation for this is that cells surviving the dehydration and rehydration process might incur sub-lethal genome damage which subsequently reduces stress tolerance.

Conclusions

The ethanol tolerance of eight yeast strains commonly used for bioethanol or Scotch whisky fermentations has been assessed in anaerobic conditions. Ethanol tolerance was strain dependent suggesting that VHG distilling fermentations may require appropriate strain selection to be fully successful. Ethanol tolerance was also dependent on the mode in which the strain was supplied with creamed yeast appearing to exhibit enhanced ethanol tolerance. Whilst the reasons for this are not known, it was interesting to note that physiological state of the fermentation inocula (pitching yeast) may influence the capacity of a strain to tolerate fermentation stress and therefore potentially to perform. It is not suggested that creamed yeast offers distinct advantages *per se*, more that changes in yeast supply modes may lead to unexpected differences in tolerance and/or performance, highlighting the requirement for quality assurance of yeast intake for the distilling sector.

Acknowledgments

The authors would like to thank the Directors of the Scotch Whisky Research Institute (SWRI) for permission to publish this manuscript. Annie Cheung is supported by a University of Nottingham and SWRI PhD Scholarship. All three authors are part of and gratefully acknowledge the support of the BBSRC Sustainable Bioenergy Centre Programme Lignocellulosic Conversion To Ethanol (BB/G01616X/1). Katherine Smart is the SABMiller Professor of Brewing Science and is grateful to SABMiller for this support.

References

abe, H., Fujita, Y., Takaoka, Y., Kurita, E., Yano, S., Tanaka, N. and Nakayama, K. 2009. Ethanol tolerant *Saccharomyces cerevisiae* strains isolated under selective conditions by overexpression of a proofreading deficient DNA polymerase delta. *Journal of Bioscience and Bioengineering* 108(3):199-204.

Bafrncova, P., Smogrovicova, D., Slavikova, I., Patkova, J. and Domeny, Z. 1999. Improvement of very high gravity ethanol fermentation by media supplementation using *Saccharomyces cerevisiae*. *Biotechnology Letters* 21(4):337-341.

Bai, F.W., Chen, L.J., Zhang, Z., Anderson, W.A. and Moo-Young, M. 2004. Continuous ethanol production and evaluation of yeast cell lysis and viability loss under very high gravity medium conditions. *Journal of Biotechnology* 110(3):287-293.

Bayrock, D.P. and Ingledew, W.M. 2001. Application of multistage continuous fermentation for production of fuel alcohol by very-high-gravity fermentation technology. *Journal of Industrial Microbiology & Biotechnology* 27(2):87-93.

Briggs, D.E., Boulton, C.A., Brookes, P.A. and Stevens, R. 2004. Brewing: Science and Practice. Cambridge, U.K.: Woodhead Publishing Ltd.

Chi, Z. and Arneborg, N. 1999. Relationship between lipid composition, frequency of ethanol-induced respiratory deficient mutants, and ethanol tolerance in *Saccharomyces cerevisiae*. *Journal of Applied Microbiology* 86(6):1047-1052.

Chi, Z. and Arneborg, N. 2000. Saccharomyces cerevisiae strains with different degrees of ethanol tolerance exhibit different adaptive responses to produced ethanol. *Journal of Industrial Microbiology & Biotechnology* 24(1):75-78.

Ding, J.M., Huang, X.W., Zhang, L.M., Zhao, N., Yang, D.M. and Zhang, K.Q. 2009. Tolerance and stress response to ethanol in the yeast *Saccharomyces cerevisiae*. *Applied Microbiology and Biotechnology* 85(2):253-263.

Dragone, G., Silva, D.P., Silva, J. and Lima, U.D. 2003. Improvement of the ethanol productivity in a high gravity brewing at pilot plant scale. *Biotechnology Letters* 25(14):1171-1174.

Fernandes, L., Cortereal, M., Loureiro, V., Loureirodias, M.C. and Leao, C. 1997. Glucose respiration and fermentation in *Zygosaccharomyces bailii* and *Saccharomyces cerevisiae* express different sensitivity patterns to ethanol and acetic acid. *Letters in Applied Microbiology* 25(4):249-253.

Gibson, B.R., Lawrence, S.J., Leclaire, J.P.R., Powell, C.D. and Smart, K.A. 2007. Yeast responses to stresses associated with industrial brewery handling. *Fems Microbiology Reviews* 31(5):535-569.

Jeffries, T.W. and Jin, Y.S. 2000. Ethanol and thermotolerance in the bioconversion of xylose by yeasts. *Advances in Applied Microbiology* 47221-268.

Lawrence, S.J. and Smart, K.A. 2007. Impact of CO_2 induced anaerobiosis on the assessment of brewing yeast flocculation. *Journal of the American Society of Brewing Chemists* 65(4):208-213.

Neto, H.B.D., Yohannan, B.K., Bringhurst, T.A., Brosnan, J.M., Pearson, S.Y., Walker, J.W. and Walker, G.M. 2009. Evaluation of a Brazilian fuel alcohol yeast strain for Scotch whisky fermentations. *Journal of the Institute of Brewing* 115(3):198-207.

Pascual, C., Alonso, A., Garcia, I., Romay, C. and Kotyk, A. 1988. Effect of ethanol on glucose transport, key glycolytic enzymes and proton extrusion in *Saccharomyces cerevisiae*. *Biotechnology and Bioengineering* 32(3):374-378.

Rose, A.H. 1993. Composition of the envelope layers of *Saccharomyces cerevisiae* in relation to flocculation and ethanol tolerance. *Journal of Applied Bacteriology* 74S110-S118.

Smart, K.A., Chambers, K.M., Lambert, I., Jenkins, C. and Smart, C.A. 1999. Use of methylene violet staining procedures to determine yeast viability and vitality. *Journal of the American Society of Brewing Chemists* 57(1):18-23.

Stanley, D., Bandara, A., Fraser, S., Chambers, P.J. and Stanley, G.A. 2010. The ethanol stress response and ethanol tolerance of *Saccharomyces cerevisiae*. *Journal of Applied Microbiology* 109(1):13-24.

Stewart, G.G. 2010. High-gravity brewing and distilling-past experiences and future prospects. *Journal of the American Society of Brewing Chemists* 68(1):1-9.

Teixeira, M.C., Raposo, L.R., Mira, N.P., Lourenco, A.B. and Sa-Correia, I. 2009. Genome wide identification of *Saccharomyces cerevisiae* genes required for maximal tolerance to ethanol. *Applied and Environmental Microbiology* 75(18):5761-5772.

Watson, K. and Cavicchioli, R. 1983. Acquistion of ethanol tolerance in yeast cells by heat shock. *Biotechnology Letters* 5(10):683-688.

Zheng, D.Q., Wu, X.C., Tao, X.L., Wang, P.M., Li, P., Chi, X.Q., Li, Y.D., Yan, Q.F. and Zhao, Y.H. 2011. Screening and construction of *Saccharomyces cerevisiae* strains with improved multi-tolerance and bioethanol fermentation performance. *Bioresource Technology* 102(3):3020-3027.

Chapter 16

Selecting new distilling yeasts for improved fermentation and for sustainability

Graeme Walker[1], James Brosnan[2], Tom Bringhurst[2] and Frances Jack[2]
[1]Yeast Research Group, School of Contemporary Sciences, University of Abertay Dundee, Dundee DD1 1HG; [2]Scotch Whisky Research Institute, Research Avenue North, Riccarton, Edinburgh, EH14 4AP

Introduction

Yeast is essential for the production of all distilled spirits and as such has provided much interest at previous Worldwide Distilled Spirits Conferences (Walker 2010a). The strain of yeast employed in potable spirit fermentations is crucially important not only for yielding high levels of ethanol, but also for production of minor yeast metabolites which collectively contribute to the development of spirit flavour (Watson 1981). Distillers must therefore pay careful attention to the type of yeast used to ensure consistency of fermentation performance in terms of both of these parameters (Watson 1984). Walker (1998) has provided a fundamental and detailed review of the physiology and biochemistry of yeast and Campbell (2003) concisely summarised yeast and fermentation aspects with regard to Scotch whisky production.

Watson (1984) has highlighted a number of yeast characteristics that are important in determining the efficiency of fermentation. These include carbohydrate utilisation, rate of fermentation, alcohol tolerance and culture stability. Scotch whisky distillers are strongly interested in extending this list of desirable yeast attributes.

Over the last decade or so, there has been a high level of interest in new distilling yeasts, and there has been much research into new strains and different types of yeast by distillers, yeast scientists in academia and yeast manufacturers. This expansion of research has become more important now that distillers are increasingly seeking initiatives that fulfil the sustainability requirements of the industry.

With the emergence of a rising awareness of environmental issues, such as global warming and climate change, distillers now have to take a longer term perspective on issues that will impact on the sustainability of their respective industries. These present challenges for distillers to meet through initiatives to reduce demands for energy, use less water and improve the utilisation of co-products. This means that Scotch whisky distillers will have to think 'out of the box' (Ingledew 2009) when considering new yeasts. As a result distillers' expectations for their yeast supplies are changing, with a greater requirement for efficient fermentation performance under more highly stressful conditions. Hence, it is essential to stimulate research into developing new yeast strains that will be capable of fulfilling these objectives.

Yeast producers already have research programmes that have the potential to deliver new types of yeast, capable of efficiently fermenting a much wider range of substrates. While many of these developments are directed principally at the burgeoning biofuels (fuel alcohol, or bioethanol) sector, there are clearly lessons to be learned from these applications and from the technology that has been developed along with it, that would also be of benefit for potable spirits distillers. It is therefore essential that lines of communication between yeast producers and distillers are kept open so that there continues to be an on-going dialogue to ensure that the distilling industry is able to achieve not only its production objectives, but also to address sustainability issues.

This paper highlights the priorities of the Scotch whisky industry, while also comparing and contrasting their yeast requirements with those of other potable spirit manufacturers and biofuel producers.

There are a very large number of potential substrates and processes for the production of spirit beverages and Watson (1984) summarised the main substrates used for a range of different spirits. Buglass et al (2011) provided a more recent, detailed review of a wide range of products. For the purposes of this paper we have just highlighted a small number of the important ones.

The present contribution aims to provide a stimulus for discussion, which will encourage yeast producers and researchers to look more closely at the desirable attributes of yeast directed at the market for distilled beverages, to ensure that specific requirements over the whole range of products are considered when developing new distilling yeast strains.

Scotch Whisky distilling yeast

Although there is now, in theory, a large selection of potential yeast strains available to distillers, in reality the bulk of the standard distilling strains of *Saccharomyces cerevisiae* used by the Scotch whisky industry are supplied from two major sources: Kerry Ingredients and Flavours (Glenochil, Menstrie) who produce 'M' and 'MX' strains, and Mauri Products (Hull) who produce Pinnacle yeast. Some distillers, particularly those producing grain whisky and neutral spirit also use yeast supplied by Lallemand Ethanol Technology (LET) from the former British Fermentation Products (BFP) plant (Felixstowe), which is now part of the Lallemand Group who also own Anchor Yeast, a South Africa based company specialising in dried yeast. LET has a range of yeasts (under the DistillaMax® brand) for different types of distilled spirit production and is now a supplier of cream yeast to grain distilleries in Scotland. LET also supplies both malt and a grain distillers yeast under the Anchor brand, both in dried form, which and are being used by some distillers to deliver natural flavour complexity, as well as high alcohol yield. All of these yeast manufacturers are developing new distilling yeasts, so there will always be potential for novel strains that will suit distillers.

The yeast strains used are based on a small number of stable commercial *S.cerevisiae* strains, primarily deriving from a baking/brewing (ale) yeast heritage. Scotch whisky distillers currently use yeast in three main formats; cream yeast, pressed (or cake) and dried yeast. Distilling yeast differs from brewing yeast in that it is expected to ferment the wort more completely, fully utilising the fermentable sugars deriving from starch (mainly maltose, glucose and maltotriose). The production of Scotch whisky differs from brewing in that the wort is not boiled, so sufficient enzyme activity will survive into fermentation, to provide secondary conversion of oligosaccharides to fermentable sugars.

The ability to efficiently ferment maltotriose in cereal based worts is considered to be an important characteristic of yeasts suitable for Scotch whisky production (Korhola et al 1989; de Amorim Neto et al 2009), and the presence of unfermented maltotriose in the co-products can cause serious problems (Stewart 2010). This contrasts with the yeasts for sugar and fruit based fermentations which are developed to ferment sucrose, fructose and glucose. Jones (1999) has described the former yeasts as "maltose + oligosaccharide type" and the latter yeasts as "sucrose + glucose" type.

Producers of similar products to Scotch whisky, such as bourbon, often propagate their own proprietary yeast strains, something that Scotch whisky distillers do not commonly do. Although there is no technical reason for them not to propagate their own yeast, the relatively small size of a typical Scotch malt whisky distillery makes this uneconomic. In addition, most Scotch malt whisky distilleries are in close proximity to yeast suppliers, so obtaining fresh yeast direct from them makes more sense in terms of both quality assurance and cost effectiveness.

Scotch malt whisky production

Scotch malt distilleries, which traditionally used pressed yeast, are increasingly moving over to cream yeast, which is, at least in theory, easier to handle and store. While there is a capital cost involved in the changeover, since it requires the installation of custom made handling facilities, this is more than offset by improved yeast storage conditions, and more precise control over subsequent inoculation (pitching) rates and temperature.

Malt whisky distilleries do not normally propagate yeast but add it to the wort, by injecting it into the wort line, putting it directly into the washback (fermenter), or adding it via a slurry tank. Pitching rates can vary but are normally in region of 0.4 percent (w/v). There is normally no temperature control. Control of fermentation is achieved by adjusting the wort to a suitable pitching temperature (typically 16 - 19°C). This is sufficient to achieve a maximum temperature (32 - 33°C) which is necessary to ensure efficient fermentation. Fermentation normally takes 2 - 3 days, depending on distillery capacity. A small number of malt distilleries have a pre-multiplication conditioning step to help maximise the vigour of the yeast to encourage it to begin fermenting more rapidly, particularly if a high original gravity (>1070) is used. Scotch whisky distilleries do not recycle their yeast, in the way that brewers do. Instead the full contents of the fermenter are transferred to the wash still for distillation. This practice is considered to be fundamentally important from a flavour point of view.

The use of dried yeast is *essential* for a small number of remote malt distilleries, such as those in the Highlands and Islands of Scotland, where delivery of regular supplies of fresh yeast would be difficult. Although pressed and cream yeasts are most prevalent, dried yeast is also useful as a backup in case of disruption of other supplies. Use of certain dried yeasts can give distinctive sensory characteristics, hence providing an opportunity to diversify spirit flavour.

Until fairly recently, distillers used a proportion of brewers' yeast (typically 30 - 50 percent of the pitching rate) obtained from the recycling of aged yeast from brewery fermentations. This was acid washed, repackaged and supplied to distilleries, and was considered to provide a useful supplement to normal distillers' yeast, in terms of supporting fermentation performance and providing additional flavour complexity (Watson, 1981). More recent work reported at the 2005 Worldwide Distilled Spirits Conference (Yomo et al 2008; Noguchi et al 2008) confirmed the synergistic effects of using a mixture of distilling and brewers' yeast and highlights the flavour benefits of using brewer's yeast in providing 'richer', 'full bodied' and 'more complex' characters. However, the use of brewer's yeast was largely phased out by Scotch whisky distillers (Munro 2008) during the last decade, when it was realised that the quality, consistency and keeping properties of commercially available material from breweries, had declined to such an extent that it no longer provided significant benefits. Nonetheless, a small number of distilleries do still use it for 'traditional' reasons.

Scotch grain whisky production

In some ways, the yeast and fermentation requirements of Scotch whisky grain distilleries are similar to those of malt whisky distillers. The main difference is one of scale, since the aim of these production units is to produce the maximum quantity of alcohol from the raw materials, within the confines of the legal definition of Scotch whisky production. One of the ways of doing this is to ferment cereal derived worts in larger batches, but with less yeast. In grain distilleries pitching rates (eg. 0.1% v/v using cream yeast) are generally about 25 percent of that used in a malt distillery. Although the flavour attributes of grain spirits are important, there is greater separation of flavour congeners from alcohol in a grain still than in a malt whisky still, making flavour control in many ways easier to achieve. Consequently this puts fewer constraints on the available options for increasing production efficiency, provided that they are consistent with the legal definition of Scotch whisky. This means that grain distillers can operate closer to the process limits, particularly in terms of wort specific gravity, where wort concentrations approaching 1080°IBD (19 - 20°Plato) can be used.

Currently, nearly all Scotch whisky grain distilleries are using cream yeast, although they could use other formats (pressed or dried) if necessary. Because of the scale of production, there is often some form of yeast propagation, multiplication or conditioning. Grain distillery fermentations may operate under more stressful conditions, such as high original gravity (> 1080°IBD), higher alcohol strength (>10 percent v/v) and at elevated temperatures, and it is essential for yeasts to have the ability to perform efficiently under these conditions. Some, but not all grain distilleries, have at least some capacity for temperature control of washbacks. Due to the (semi) continuous nature of grain whisky production, it is desirable that fermentations are as short as practically possible. Hence, as well as using the standard malt whisky yeasts, grain distillers may use additional strains, that are better adapted to these conditions.

Neutral spirit (vodka and gin)

Scotch whisky grain distilleries may also produce neutral (or plain) spirit for vodka or gin production, using a fermentation process that is similar, if not identical, to that for grain whisky. The main difference is that the production of neutral spirit is not constrained by the Scotch whisky definition, so a wider range of processing options is available. The most important of these is that distillers producing neutral grain spirits are allowed to add food grade enzymes to degrade starch to ease the processing of cereals and produce as much ethanol as possible. Hence the composition of the initial substrate can be slightly different.

The process used in the production of neutral spirit will give even greater separation of flavour congeners from alcohol than in grain whisky production, the aim being to reduce the level of flavour compounds to below the limits of sensory detection. Hence, there is no requirement for the yeast to provide any specific flavour congeners, although distillers have to ensure that the selected strains do not produce any unusual or undesirable flavours that could potentially pass through the process.

Other sugar/fruit based spirits (rum, tequila, and cognac/brandy)

Sugar and fruit based spirits use a wide range of yeasts for their fermentation processes. Some more specialised products (eg. tequila/mescal, cachaça etc) may use spontaneously fermenting indigenous microflora, or local yeast cultures isolated from previous fermentations. Producers of the major spirit types (Cognac, brandy, rum) prefer to use specific, pure or cultivated yeast strains. In all cases, as with Scotch malt whisky, flavour is an important consideration and the selection of suitable strains is vital in determining the flavour profile of these spirits.

Other fruit and pomace spirits are prepared by fermenting the fruit pulp and/or juice, and are distilled from the fermented fruit wine (or cider, perry). These are mostly fermented by *S. cerevisiae* cultures, but some products use the natural microflora (ie. wild, or non-*Saccharomyces* yeasts), associated with the fruit skins, or present in the must. In some cases the naturally occurring microflora has to be supplemented with cultured yeast to ensure complete fermentation.

Fuel alcohol (bioethanol)

Walker (2010b; 2011) has reviewed bioethanol fermentation processes and compared fuel and potable ethanol production.

Global bioethanol production in 2008 was 65.7 billion litres and this will soon exceed 100 billion litres, with the largest increases in the US (using maize) and Brazil (using sugarcane). In Europe, bioethanol production is increasing sharply and the main producers are France, Germany and Spain using primarily feedstocks of cereals (mainly wheat) and sugarbeet. *First-generation* bioethanol feedstocks refer to plant biomass sources that are also sources of human and animal nutrition (namely: cereal starches and sugar crops), whilst *second generation* raw materials for bioethanol production typically refer to non-food biomass sources, mainly lignocellulosic biomass (eg. biowastes, woody residues, energy crops etc). The predominant microorganism responsible for first generation bioethanol fermentations is the yeast species, *Saccharomyces cerevisiae*, but other yeasts and certain bacteria have future potential for cellulosic second generation fermentations (see Walker, 2010b). Microbes for lignocellulosic hydrolysate fermentations are subject to intense research activity (Mousdale, 2008), mostly involving genetically engineered yeasts and bacteria. When cellulose and hemicellulose polymers are hydrolysed, the resultant monomeric sugars represent a mixture of C5 (pentose) and C6 (hexose) sugars. Conventional distilling strains of yeast are unable to metabolise pentose sugars such as xylose and arabinose. However, GM strains of yeast and bacteria are being developed to ferment both C5 and C6 sugars (see Walker, 2011). To achieve efficient fermentation of lignocellulose hydrolysates, it is necessary to further develop stress-resistance in industrial yeast strains, particularly with regard to the ability to withstand chemical inhibitors such as acids, phenols and furans.

The undesirability of production of secondary fermentation metabolites (notably glycerol) in bioethanol plants leads to potential loss of ethanol and efforts are made to dissipate this, including simultaneous saccharification and fermentation (SSF) processes to prevent osmotic pressure stress on yeast cells. Construction of yeast strains with reduced glycerol production is also possible (eg. Guo et al, 2009).

For first generation bioethanol processes (using starch and sugar based feedstocks), commercially available strains of *S. cerevisiae* have now been developed that can produce >10%v/v ethanol and can ferment effectively in high (>20%) solids. For example, through careful attention to yeast nutritional physiology, it is now possible to produce over 20%v/v ethanol in high gravity wheat fermentations (Thomas and Ingledew, 1992).

Some bioethanol distilleries operate yeast recycling and this circumvents the need to regularly purchase new batches of yeast from commercial suppliers. Other plants conduct their own aerobic yeast propagation in order to boost biomass required as starter cultures for fermentation. To maximise bioethanol production, it is important to ensure yeast is highly viabile and vital and also to minimise levels of contaminant bacteria – especially *Lactobacillus* spp. that can subtract significantly from bioethanol yield.

Aspirational targets for distilling yeasts

In the past Scotch whisky distillers have consulted with yeast experts, both within academia and individual yeast companies, to develop a 'wish list' for new distilling yeast strains (Walker et al 2008). In 2003 the Scotch Whisky

Research Institute hosted a Yeast Workshop, which included a wide range of stakeholders representing each of the above groups. The aim of this workshop was to identify and prioritise the main attributes of yeast that would be of most benefit to Scotch whisky distillers, so that they could be targeted by manufacturers and researchers when looking at new developments in distilling yeast.

The 2003 Yeast Workshop identified 6 key attributes (Table 1) for new distilling yeast strains that could be prioritised to deliver strong potential benefits for distillers, namely (1) consistency of flavour, (2) temperature tolerance, (3) increased fermentation rate, (4) increased alcohol tolerance, (5) increased substrate tolerance and (6) increased substrate utilisation. While the main focus of this workshop was on yeasts for Scotch whisky production, it was clear that many of these attributes are also highly relevant both for other potable distilled spirits, as well as potentially for bioethanol production.

Table 1. Aspirational targets for new distilling yeasts (from the 2003 Yeast Workshop at SWRI)

Consistency of flavour:- Consistently having the sensory characters associated with Scotch whisky
Temperature tolerance:- Have the ability to withstand and operate efficiently at temperatures up to 37 -38°C (aspiring to 40°C)
Increased fermentation rate:- The ability to reduce fermentation times substantially, perhaps to less than 30h
Increased alcohol tolerance:- Display increased alcohol tolerance and be able to produce up to 15 percent (v/v) alcohol (or higher) (12 percent (v/v) for malt distilleries)
Increased substrate tolerance:- Capable of operating efficiently at higher original gravities up to 1080 or even 1100° IOB
Increased substrate utilisation:- Reduce biomass and waste (co-) product production and form more alcohol

Since this list was compiled, time and technology have moved on, primarily as a result of the research initiatives that have been stimulated, individually and collectively by distillers, yeast suppliers, and importantly in the academic sector. Partly this has been driven by the emergence of the bioethanol sector. While the 2003 targets are still considered to be highly relevant, recent years have seen the increasing importance of other sustainability issues, as described earlier. This has resulted in a growing awareness that distillers should revisit the criteria for selecting new distilling yeasts, so they can take into account the increasing priority of these aspects.

Options open to Scotch whisky distillers to address sustainability issues include, operating their distilleries to give increased wort concentration (specific gravity), higher alcohol strength, as well as aiming to ferment at higher temperatures to reduce the need for cooling. All of these place additional stresses on the yeast, compromising their fermentation performance. Addressing these issues requires a focus on specific yeast attributes, such as increased stress tolerance (thermotolerance, osmotolerance, alcohol tolerance). However, any developments need to take into account the impact on spirit flavour, which remains of primary importance.

In revisiting the targets for new yeasts, the need to widen our horizons to address not only the requirements of Scotch whisky distillers, but also for those of other distillers, became apparent. The continuing emergence of the fuel alcohol sector will drive the development of new yeasts for this market, so it is essential that distillers of potable spirits continue to communicate with those involved to ensure that their own specific requirements are not overlooked.

Priorities for distilling yeasts

Although the previous sections of this paper have shown that there are many similarities in yeast requirements between different distilling sectors, there are also some important differences.

Discussions between the University of Abertay Dundee and the Scotch Whisky Research Institute have resulted in the development of a convenient check-list (Table 2) which summarises these requirements. This highlights what we consider to be the key desirable properties of yeast strains employed for various types of alcohol fermentations: whisky and neutral spirit fermentations based on starchy/cereal substrates; rum and cognac fermentations based on sugar and fruit; and provides a comparison with fuel alcohol fermentations based on starch, sugar and cellulose substrates.

The aim of the check-list is to stimulate discussion between distillers (in all sectors), yeast manufacturers and academic yeast experts on the options that are available. This should help to ensure that future research resources effectively address the needs of all end users, to provide the distilling industry with a variety of new yeast strains that are tailored to specific individual needs.

Table 2. Distilling yeast desired attributes: Qualitative criteria

Yeast attributes	Malt whisky fermentations	Grain whisky fermentations	Neutral spirit fermentations	Sugar-based fermentations	Fuel alcohol fermentations		
			Grain/Molasses	Sugar crops /Fruits	Starch	Sugar	Cellulose
Rapid fermentation (eg. 1-2days)	**	****	****	****	*****	*****	*****
Continuous fermentation	*	**	***	**	***	*****	*****
Alcohol yield	****	****	****	****	*****	*****	*****
Acceptable spirit character	*****	****	**	*****	*	*	*
Maltotriose utilisation	****	****	**	*	*****	*	*
Less yeast biomass	**	***	***	**	**	*****	**
Stress tolerance							
High gravity	***	****	****	**	*****	*****	*****
Temperature	***	****	****	****	*****	*****	*****
Ethanol	****	****	****	****	*****	*****	***
Competitive (v. bacteria)	***	***	****	***	*****	*****	***
Consistency of fermentation							
Yield	****	*****	*****	*****	*****	*****	*****
Flavour	*****	***	***	****	*	*	*
Yeast vitality	*****	*****	*****	*****	*****	*****	*****
Available Format							
Cream/liquid yeast	***	*****	*****	***	*****	**	***
Cake/pressed yeast	***	*	**	***	***	**	**
Dry yeast	***	*	**	**	***	**	**
Freshly propagated	**	****	****	**	***	**	*****
Recycled	*	*	***	*	**	*****	**

*****	= very high priority (or essential)
****	= high priority
***	= moderate priority
**	= low priority
*	= very low priority (or not applicable)

Defining yeast fermentation performance

As with the development of our understanding of yeast and fermentation, recent years have seen an expansion in the analytical techniques that are available to researchers and distillers to assess the performance of new yeast strains (Table 3). While some of these are well established, modern techniques, such as flow cytometry are coming forward, which are able to provide an unprecedented level of detail regarding yeast viability, vitality and performance during fermentation. Additionally there have been advances in our understanding of the genetic aspects of yeast, and this will ultimately allow yeast researchers to select for more specific quality and performance traits (Ingledew et al 2009). This will help to provide distillers with a palette of yeasts that can be selected to meet their specific requirements. In addition such advances will not only help to ensure consistent spirit quality for existing products, but should also result in a wider choice of strains that will give specific desired flavour attributes.

Conclusions

Research into new distilling yeast strains has progressed significantly over the last decade. Distillers now have a much clearer idea of the desirable attributes that they would like to see in new yeasts, while the direction of research and improved analytical techniques is in the fulfilment of these wishes. However, as seen previously with the emergence of sustainability issues, distillers' requirements can change. It is vital to communicate these changing needs to the other stakeholders in the supply chain, so that they can develop strains with the required characteristics.

Effective communication on distillers yeast matters has proved to be useful in the past. Some areas of interest originally identified by the 2003 Yeast Workshop are now being actively studied by multidisciplinary groups (e.g. the BBSRC Sustainable Bioenergy Centre, based at the University of Nottingham). Although some research is focussed primarily on bio-ethanol, this shares some of the key targets for improved distilling yeasts, such as maximising ethanol production and improved process tolerance (osmo-tolerance, ethanol tolerance, thermo-tolerance and pH tolerance). In addition, investigations of the genetic aspects controlling yeast attributes will ultimately result in a more fundamental understanding of yeast physiology during industrial fermentations (Ingledew et al 2009), and will help to identify potential new strains that are more suited to these environments.

Finally, and with specific regard to Scotch whisky production, this continues to be a 'traditional' industry with a strong cultural and regional identity, and is enshrined in its legal definition. Consequently, the options available to Scotch whisky distillers to address sustainability issues and deliver production improvements are

Table 3. Distilling yeast fermentation performance: quantitative criteria

Criteria (fermentation performance)	*Analytical method (examples)*
Spirit yield	Calculations based on conversion of cereal starch to ethanol
Carbon dioxide evolution rate	Gas flow meter
High gravity fermentation	Original Gravity, yeast viability, pH decline
Sugar utilisation spectrum (eg. maltotriose)	HPLC
Spirit character (off-notes, fusel oils)	Sensory panel evaluation, GC
Yeast viability/vitality	Flow cytometry
Response (s) to stress	" "
Yeast cell cycle characteristics	" "
Distillery/Product/Application specific attributes*	Genetic Markers

(* Possibility of 'designing' yeast with attributes for specific applications/product profiles/processes)

constrained by the limits set out in the regulations, in ways that other distillers are not. Improving raw materials, such as developing new yeast strains, offers one of the few realistic options for delivering the necessary improvements in production performance, while at the same time addressing the industry's sustainability targets. It is hoped that the information will provide useful qualitative guidance for distillers and yeast suppliers in selecting new yeast strains that will enable them to fulfil their needs.

References

de Amorim Neto, H.B., Yohannan, B.K., Bringhurst, T.A., Brosnan, J.M., Pearson, S.Y., Walker, J.W. and Walker, G.M., (2009). Evaluation of a Brazilian fuel alcohol yeast for Scotch whisky fermentation. *Journal of the Institute of Brewing,* **115** (3): 198-207.

Buglass, A.J., McKay, M. and Lee, C.G., (2011). Distilled Spirits. In: *Handbook of Alcoholic Beverages, Volume 1*. Edited by Buglass, A.J., John Wiley and Sons, Chichester, pp. 555-627.

Campbell, I., (2003). Yeast and Fermentation. In: *Whisky: Technology, Production and Marketing*. Edited by Russell, I., Academic Press, London UK, pp. 117-153.

Guo, Z.P., Zhang, L., Ding, Z.Y., Wang, Z.X. and Shi, G.Y,. (2009). Interruption of glycerol pathway in industrial alcoholic yeasts to improve the ethanol production. *Applied Microbiology and Biotechnology,* **82**: 287-292.

Ingledew, W.M., (2009). Yeasts: Physiology, nutrition and ethanol production. In: *The Alcohol Textbook, Fifth Edition*. Edited by Ingledew, W.M., Kelsall, D.R., Austin, G,D. and Kluhspies, C., Nottingham University Press, Nottingham, UK, pp. 101-113.

Ingledew, W.M., Austin, G.D. and Kraus J.K.,(2009). Commercial yeast production for the fuel ethanol and distilled beverages industries. In: *The Alcohol Textbook, Fifth Edition*. Edited by Ingledew, W.M., Kelsall, D.R., Austin, G,D. and Kluhspies, C., Nottingham University Press, Nottingham, UK, pp. 127-144.

Jones, R.C., (1999). Distillery yeast technology. In: *Proceedings of the 5th Aviemore Conference on Malting, Brewing and Distilling*. Edited by Campbell, I. and Priest, F.G., Institute of Brewing, London, pp. 65-77.

Korhola, M., Harju, A.K., Lehtonen, M., (1989). Fermentation. In: *Science and Technology of Whiskies*. Edited by Piggott, J.R., Sharp R. and Duncan, R.E.B., Longman Scientific and Technical, Harlow, UK, pp. 89-117.

Mousdale, D. M., (2008). *Biofuels, Biotechnology, Chemistry and Sustainable Development*. CRC Press, Boca Raton.

Munro, R., (2008). Opportunities for improved yeast supplies in whisky and related spirits production. In: *Distilled Spirits, Production, Technology and Innovation*. Edited by Bryce, J.H., Piggott, J.R. and Stewart, G.G., Nottingham University Press, Nottingham UK, pp. 133-138.

Noguchi, Y., Urasaki, K., Yomo, H. and Yonezawa, T., (2008). Effect on new-make spirit character due to performance of brewer's yeast – (II) various yeast strains containing commercial strains. In: *Distilled Spirits, Production, Technology and Innovation*. Edited by Bryce, J.H., Piggott, J.R. and Stewart, G.G., Nottingham University Press, Nottingham UK, pp. 110-116.

Stewart G.G., (2010). High-Gravity Brewing and Distilling – Past experiences and future prospects. *Journal of the American Society of Brewing Chemists* **68**(1): 1-9.

Thomas, K.C. and Ingledew, W.M., (1992). Production of 21% (v/v) ethanol by fermentation of very high gravity (VHG) wheat mashes. *Journal of Industrial Microbiology* **10**: 61-68.

Walker, J.W., Pearson, S.Y., Bringhurst, T.A. and Brosnan, J.M., (2008). Towards improved distilling yeast: effect of wort gravity and pitching rate on fermentation performance. In: *Distilled Spirits, Production, Technology and Innovation*. Edited by Bryce, J.H.,

Piggott, J.R. and Stewart, G.G., Nottingham University Press, Nottingham UK, pp. 127-132.

Walker, G.M., (1998). *Yeast Physiology and Biotechnology*. John Wiley and Sons, Chichester, UK.

Walker, G.M., (2010a). Distiller's yeast discussion forum. In: *Distilled Spirits, New Horizons: Energy, Environment and Enlightenment*. Edited by Walker, G.M. and Hughes, P.S., Nottingham University Press, Nottingham, UK, pp. 101-104.

Walker, G.M., (2010b). *Bioethanol: Science and Technology of Fuel Alcohol*. Ventus Publishing ApS, Copenhagen. ISBN 978-87-7681-681-0 [http://bookboon.com/int/student/chemical/bioethanol-science-and-technology-of-fuel-alcohol]

Walker, G.M., (2011). Fuel alcohol: current production and future challenges. *Journal of the Institute of Brewing* **117**: 3-22.

Watson, D.C., (1981). The development of specialised yeast strains for use in Scotch whisky fermentations. In: *Current Developments in Yeast Research. Advances in Biotechnology*. Edited by Stewart G.G. and Russell, I., Pergamon Press, Oxford, pp. 57-62.

Watson, D.C., (1984). Distilling Yeasts. *Developments in Industrial Microbiology* **25**: 213-220

Yomo, H., Noguchi, Y. and Yonezawa, T., (2008). Effect on new-make spirit character due to performance of brewer's yeast – (I) physiological changes of yeast during propagation and brewing. In: *Distilled Spirits, Production, Technology and Innovation*. Edited by Bryce, J.H., Piggott, J.R. and Stewart G.G., Nottingham University Press, Nottingham UK, pp. 110-116.

Chapter 17

Current challenges and future opportunities for distillers yeast: discussion forum

Reporter: G M Walker

Forum panel members: Prof Mike Ingledew (University of Saskatchewan)
Prof Graham Stewart (GGStewart Associates)
Dr Mike Walsh (AB Mauri Global Technology Group)
Mr Jonathan Miles (Anchor Yeast/Lallemand)

Chair: Graeme Walker (University of Abertay Dundee, UK)

Introduction

The Chair introduced the panel of experts who represented expertise in yeast science, fermentation technology, and the yeast supply sector of industry. This Distiller's Yeast Discussion Forum followed similar events held previously at the Scotch Whisky Research Institute (SWRI) in 2003 and the previous Worldwide Distilled Spirits Conference (WDSC) in 2008, to discuss key scientific and technological issues regarding yeast for the distilling industry. Table 1 summarises the main discussion points of these previous meetings

Some of the aspects outlined in Table 1 are still being considered by the distilled spirits industry at the present time. Therefore, current challenges and future opportunities for distillers yeast were firstly reviewed by the Chair who indicated there were different priorities for end-users (distillers), suppliers (yeast companies) and researchers (yeast academics). Key questions relevant to modern distilling, and which impact on the activities of the distiller, yeast supplier and researcher were considered to include the following:

Is it possible to obtain >20% v/v ethanol by fermentation? Are there very stress-tolerant yeasts available for industrial fermentations operating at higher temperatures, elevated wort gravities etc? Can yeasts be provided that consistently yield flavoursome fermentations? Is there a simple, and rapid, vitality test available for distiller's yeast? How can genomics and proteomics be of practical value for the distiller, and will the sector ever embrace GM yeasts?

The concept of the *ideal* distillers yeast (Fig 1) was then raised in which multiple attributes

Table 1. Distiller's Yeast Discussion Forums 2003 & 2008

2003 Yeast Workshop at SWRI – Distiller's yeast attributes	*2008 Yeast Forum at WDSC – Key yeast questions raised*
1. consistent flavour congener production	1. what can GM yeasts do?
2. temperature tolerance	2. sources of innovative Scotch whisky yeasts?
3. faster fermentation	3. thermotolerant yeasts for tropical distilleries?
4. increased alcohol tolerance	4. is there a good vitality test for yeast?
5. increased substrate tolerance	5. matching yeasts strains with barley varieties?
6. increased substrate utilisation	6. liquid, cake or dried yeast formats?

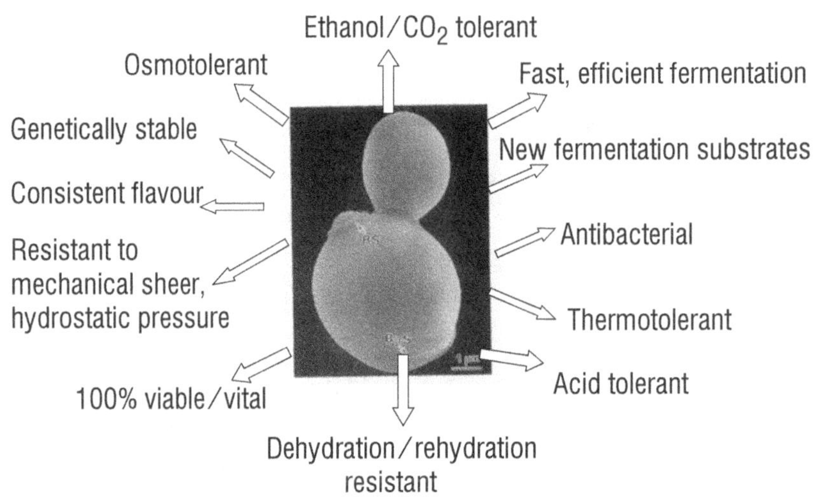

Figure 1. Conceptual aspects of the *ideal* distiller's yeast.

would be combined, but the Chair concluded such "super-yeasts" were not yet available for practical exploitation in all types of industrial fermentation processes.

The Chair then thanked conference delegates for their following questions to the panel.

Questions to the panel

Q1 What is the key desired attribute for a distilling yeast strain? (Tom Bringhurst – SWRI)

The panel commented that flavoursome fermentations as well as ethanol production were key attributes for distiller's yeast strains. Dr Jamieson (Heriot-Watt University) had already considered some of these attributes in his presentation to this conference (see Chapter 14). A multi-purpose distiller's yeast would be one that was equally effective in fermenting both malt-based sugars (primarily maltose) and sucrose (from sugar cane and beet). Maintenance of high viabilities and vitalities was also deemed to be a valuable attribute, especially in the fuel alcohol sector where some biofuel producers (especially in Brazil) conduct yeast recycling (a process uncommon in the distilled beverage sector). The attribute of high vitality (as a measure of yeast cells' physiological fitness or fermentation vigour) was deemed to be more important than viability (as a measure of yeast cells' reproductive capabilities). However, it should not be forgotten that yeast growth and fermentation are closely integrated activities. For some processes, it would be very desirable to achieve fast and predictable (i.e. minimal batch-to-batch variation) fermentations that reached over 20% v/v ethanol – these levels can be obtained by paying close attention to aspects of yeast nutrition. Professor Ingledew indicated that levels of 23.8% ABV have previously been achieved using very high gravity fermentation (VHG) technology. A small Scottish brewing company (Brewdog, Aberdeenshire) had recently claimed to reach 28% ABV by fermentation but unlike most breweries the yeast is not recycled.

Q2 Are heat-tolerant yeasts as efficient in alcohol production at higher temperatures (40°C) compared with lower temperatures (25-30°C)? (Dennis Watson, Pernod Ricard)

The panel indicated that *efficiency* in this context required definition. Fermentation rates will be higher at 40°C than 30°C, but although yeast will ferment at the higher temperature, yeast growth would be compromised. In addition, at this high temperature there would be volatilisation and loss of product. Dr Walsh commented that in work with bioethanol yeast strains showed that higher ethanol levels can be obtained at temperatures <27°C. However, yeast will experience thermal stress, but with simultaneous saccharification and fermentation (SSF) systems, osmotic stress problems would be minimised. The added expense on effective cooling systems also requires careful consideration. Professor Stewart indicated that for some industrial fermentations, combined stresses on yeast will prove lethal, but this may not be problematic if yeast were not to be recycled following fermentation. The practice of over-pitching may compensate for yeast viability loss during stressful fermentations.

Q3 – What is the best yeast format for whisky fermentations – cake, cream or dried? (Jason Bennett, Abertay University)

Mr Miles commented that the choice of yeast format depended quite a lot on the location of the distillery. For example, creamed is ideal if the yeast supply company is in relative close proximity to the end-user. For the use of dried yeast preparations, it is very important to conduct rehydration protocols carefully to maintain cells' physiological state and high viability. In terms of fermentation performance, dried, pressed or cream yeast all compare favourably.

Q4 Is there a "reference method" for sampling of yeast from grain fermentations? (John Carvell, Aber Instruments)

The panel commented that such sampling is very difficult and lacks reproducibility. The presence of suspended solids in fermentation broths is particularly problematic for yeast enumeration. Dr Walsh indicated that when taking samples from 8 points in a 3000 hL fermentation vessel, a distinct lack of homogeneity can be observed. Professor Stewart mentioned, in relation to brewing practice, that wort clarity distinctly influences final beer flavour due to lipid and carbon dioxide effects, with some companies showing striations in multi-brew fermentations.

Q5 Is there more interest in yeast strain diversity for distilling in USA compared with Europe? (Tim Dolan)

Mr Miles commented that there is much diversity when considering yeast strain usage in the US. For example, some Kentucky distilleries have their own specific yeasts, and North American craft distillers are prepared to use any yeast to get diverse and interesting products. Some distillers are currently experimenting to get different flavours but many of the world's distillers are reticent to change from their currently employed yeast strain(s). Professor Smart (from the audience) commented that Dr Ed Louis at the University of Nottingham had a very large yeast culture collection tracing stains back to continent of origin. In Brazilian fuel alcohol plants, there was evidence of yeast strain diversity in fermentation processes based on sugar cane molasses. Dr Watson (from the audience) commented that for Scotch whisky processes there were strict definitions to abide by and the use of complex substrates without addition of enzymes. There was, nevertheless, potential to consider yeast strain "blends" in distillery fermentations.

Q6 Can we use nitrogen-assimilation characteristics as a distilling yeast attribute? (Luc Lurton, BNIC)

Professor Ingledew commented that attention to nitrogen nutrition for distiller's yeast was very important. Urea supplementations are beneficial for fuel alcohol fermentations, but such practices are not tolerated for potable spirits due to production of potentially carcinogenic ethyl carbamate. Of course, for Scotch whisky, no nutritional supplements are permitted in the fermenters. With regard to amino acid utlisation by yeast, Professor Smart (from the audience) commented that ale and lager brewing yeast strains differed in their amino acid uptake profiles. For example, it was now known that lager yeast strains have the ability to utilise the amino acid proline, previously considered to be poorly assimilated by brewing strains. There is a need for further research into nitrogen nutrition in yeast strains specifically for distilled spirits. Other nutritional factors for distiller's yeast were also considered important, notably phosphorous, sulphur, magnesium and zinc. The latter was emphasised by Professor Stewart who indicated that zinc plays an important role in maintenance of yeast health, and some brewing companies add this nutrient to maintain the health of its 'old' yeast. Dr Walsh commented that a procedure called "accelerated evolution" may be employed to alter the physiological characteristics of yeast, including nutrient uptake capabilities (as has been reported for brewer's yeast).

Q7 Are "floc" yeasts more stress-tolerant than "non-floc" yeasts? (Dennis Watson, Pernod Ricard)

Professor Stewart commented that this question was somewhat provocative, but it was unclear if this was the case. Perhaps (but not proven) yeasts flocculate as a response to environmental stress? Dr Walsh indicated that nutrient limitation plays a role and there is a difference in cells nutrient status from the outside to the centre of the yeast floc. Epigenetic factors may also be involved. For example, the presence of repetitive sequences may relate to loss of flocculation characteristics with too many generations. There are 11 FLO genes identified, but why so many when only three seem to be active?

Q8 Are yeast suppliers reaching the end of the line in terms of yeast strain development, and will we now seriously need to consider the use of GM strains? (Tom Bringhurst, SWRI)

Mr Miles commented that there were numerous GM yeast strains sitting in laboratory culture collections that are not being used in industry due to current adverse consumer perceptions. Nevertheless, research by yeast suppliers continues to seek new yeast varieties of potential value to the distilled spirits and other sectors. Dr Walsh indicated that GM technology had the capability to solve many problems, but inventors require protection for their invention by patent. The appeal is that you can "paste" whatever gene you want, but there are different rules and conventions in different countries. Dr Walsh noted a new phrase – gene repair – relating to the addition of a particular gene to a yeast that has not got one. This is different from cloning. However, do not be fooled as it is GMO and such yeasts are widely used in the enzyme industry. Professor Ingledew mentioned that GM technology was widespread for research currently, but practical advances will soon accelerate in the bioethanol industry, especially for lignocellulose-derived fuel alcohol and biobutanol. In the US, GM corn is used in the biofuel industry which shows distinct benefits. Professor Stewart concluded the discussion on GM yeasts for distillers by commenting: never say never!

Chapter 18

Modelling methanol recovery in wine batch distillations using rectification columns

J. Ricardo Pérez-Correa*; Raúl Munizaga-Miranda; Claudio A. Gelmi
Department of Chemical and Bioprocess Engineering, Pontificia Universidad Católica de Chile, Av. Vicuña Mackenna 4860, Macul, Santiago, Chile.
** Corresponding author*

Introduction

Pisco brandy is one of the most popular alcoholic beverages in Chile: a young distillate from Muscat wine with a distinctive fruity character produced since colonial times. Like other spirits, pisco's characteristics depend on the raw materials, fermentation process, distillation method and ageing. All these will determine the content of minor volatile components, so called congeners, in the distillate. Congeners can be favourable (terpenes, esters and some high alcohols at very low concentrations), off-flavours (fatty acids), or if present at high concentrations toxic (methanol, acetaldehyde and furfural). During the last decade, several studies have been carried out to define and enhance the aromatic quality of this beverage, improve process operation and reduce costs.

Mathematical modelling has been crucial in the development of efficient and reproducible distillation processes to obtain spirits with a pre-defined aromatic characteristic (Osorio et al., 2004). Indeed, process engineers can use simulations to explore many distillation operational strategies, predict the impact of changes in raw materials on spirit quality, and design new control methods (Batista et al., 2009). Nevertheless, minimization of toxic compounds, such as acetaldehyde and methanol, has not received major attention yet, despite being regulated in most countries. In Chile, the concentration of methanol in alcoholic beverages should be less than 1.5 g/L of absolute alcohol (a.a.).

Within this context, the objective of this work was to develop an effective mathematical model to simulate reliably the entire batch distillation process (from the head to the tail cut) of the ternary water-ethanol-methanol mixture, to explore in the future operating strategies for reducing methanol content in wine distillates with minimum ethanol and aroma losses. Simulations obtained with the proposed model have been compared with experimental data obtained in our laboratory and with a previous model developed to simulate the head cut (Carvallo et al., 2011).

Mathematical model

The following assumptions were used in the construction of our model, which are also available in Carvallo et al. (2011):

- Wine has been modelled as a ternary mixture of ethanol, water and methanol with methanol the minority compound.
- Due to the low methanol concentration, the physical properties of the ternary mixture were obtained from ethanol-water correlations.
- The partial condenser and the boiler are in thermodynamic equilibrium.
- The column operated under atmospheric pressure, hence the vapour phase was assumed ideal.
- Plug flow was assumed for vapour and liquid phases, therefore temperature and composition radial gradients were not considered (Hitch et al., 1987).
- Pressure drop through the column is very small, and therefore it was neglected and total pressure was assumed constant (Hitch et al., 1987).
- No heat transfer resistance in the vapour and liquid phases were considered, therefore, bulk vapour and liquid temperatures were equal to the equilibrium temperature in the interface.
- Equimolar counter diffusion was assumed.
- The partial condenser operates at pseudo steady state condition (very fast dynamics).
- The column is assumed thermally insulated, except for the boiler supports.

Additionally, in order to better predict the dynamics of the distillation during the head cut, in this work the dynamics of the packed column and the heating of the packing was taken into account.

Balances in the boiler

Total mass balance:

$$\frac{dM_B}{dt}=L_1-V_B \tag{1}$$

Ethanol balance:

$$\frac{dx_{1,B}}{dt}=\frac{1}{M_B}\cdot\left(L_1\cdot\left(x_{1,1}-x_{1,B}\right)-V_B\cdot\left(y_{1,B}-x_{1,1}\right)\right) \tag{2}$$

Methanol balance:

$$\frac{dx_{2,B}}{dt}=\frac{1}{M_B}\cdot\left(L_1\cdot\left(x_{2,1}-x_{2,B}\right)-V_B\cdot\left(y_{2,B}-x_{2,B}\right)\right) \tag{3}$$

Energy balance:

$$\frac{dh_B}{dt}=\frac{1}{M_B}\cdot\left(L_1\cdot\left(h_1-h_B\right)-V_B\cdot\left(H_B-h_B\right)+Q_B-Q_p\right) \tag{4}$$

Bosley and Edgar (1994) proposed to compute the boiler molar flow V_B from Eq. (4) using the derivative of the enthalpy with respect to time. The liquid in the boiler is at its bubble point; therefore its enthalpy depends only on the molar fraction of ethanol present in the mixture (Carvallo et al., 2011; Osorio et al., 2004). Thus, after some mathematical manipulations, V_B can be written as follows:

$$V_B=\frac{L_1\cdot\left(\left(\frac{\partial h_B}{\partial x_{1,B}}+\frac{\partial h_B}{\partial T_B}\cdot\frac{dT_B}{dx_{1,B}}\right)\cdot\left(x_{1,1}-x_{1,B}\right)+\left(h_1-h_B\right)\right)+Q_B-Q_p}{\left(\frac{\partial h_B}{\partial x_{1,B}}+\frac{\partial h_B}{\partial T_B}\cdot\frac{dT_B}{dx_{1,B}}\right)\cdot\left(y_{1,B}-x_{1,B}\right)+\left(H_B-h_B\right)} \tag{5}$$

Random packed column

Total mass balance:

$$\frac{\partial M'}{\partial t}=\frac{\partial L}{\partial z}-\frac{\partial V}{\partial z} \tag{6}$$

Ethanol mass balance:

$$\frac{\partial x_1}{\partial t}=\frac{1}{M'}\cdot\left(L\cdot\frac{\partial x_1}{\partial z}-V\cdot\frac{\partial y_1}{\partial z}+\left(x_1-y_1\right)\cdot\frac{\partial V}{\partial z}\right) \tag{7}$$

Methanol mass balance:

$$\frac{\partial x_2}{\partial t}=\frac{1}{M'}\cdot\left(L\cdot\frac{\partial x_2}{\partial z}-V\cdot\frac{\partial y_2}{\partial z}+\left(x_2-y_2\right)\cdot\frac{\partial V}{\partial z}\right) \tag{8}$$

Ethanol mass balance, vapour phase:

$$0=-V\cdot\frac{\partial y_1}{\partial z}-y_1\cdot\frac{\partial V}{\partial z}+S\cdot N'_1 \tag{9}$$

Methanol mass balance, vapour phase:

$$0=-V\cdot\frac{\partial y_2}{\partial z}-y_2\cdot\frac{\partial V}{\partial z}+S\cdot N'_2 \tag{10}$$

Energy balance:

$$\frac{\partial T}{\partial t}=\left(M'\cdot\frac{\partial h}{\partial T}+m'_{pack}\cdot c_{p,pack}\right)^{-1}\cdot\left(L\cdot\frac{\partial h}{\partial z}-V\cdot\frac{\partial H}{\partial z}+(h-H)\cdot\frac{\partial V}{\partial z}-\frac{\partial h}{\partial x_1}\cdot\left(L\cdot\frac{\partial x_1}{\partial z}-V\cdot\frac{\partial y_1}{\partial z}+(x_1-y_1)\cdot\frac{\partial V}{\partial z}\right)\right) \quad (11)$$

Partial condenser

Total mass balance:

$$0=V_N-L_C\cdot\left(1+\frac{1}{R_f}\right) \quad (12)$$

Ethanol mass balance:

$$0=V_N\cdot y_{1,N}-L_C\cdot\left(x_{1,C}-\frac{y_{1,D}}{R_f}\right) \quad (13)$$

Methanol mass balance:

$$0=V_N\cdot y_{2,N}-L_C\cdot\left(x_{2,C}+\frac{y_{2,D}}{R_f}\right) \quad (14)$$

Energy balance:

$$0=V_N\cdot H_N-L_C\cdot\left(h_C+\frac{H_D}{R_f}\right)-Q_C \quad (15)$$

Constitutive equations

Several constitutive relations were used in our models. Most of them were a function of the ethanol molar fraction (Carvallo et al., 2011; Osorio et al., 2004). The liquid-vapour equilibrium (LVE) was calculated using the NRTL coefficient activity model as described in Carvallo et al. (2011). The direct dynamic derivatives (DDD) functional approach of Bosley and Edgar (1994) was applied to solve the resulting implicit algebraic equations. This technique avoids the need for sophisticated and expensive DAE solvers, and has been successfully applied in our previous works (Carvallo et al., 2011; Osorio et al., 2004).

In order to model the hydraulic behaviour of the packed column, the hold-up and the retained liquid was related using the following expression (Peng et al., 2003):

$$h_L=\frac{M'\cdot\overline{PM}}{S\cdot\rho}\times 10^{-6} \quad (16)$$

The specific liquid load was computed using the correlation developed by Billet and Schultes (1991, 1993):

$$u_L=\left(\frac{h_L^3\cdot g^{1.2}\cdot(\rho\cdot 1000)^{0.7}}{12\cdot C_h^2\cdot a_{ef}^{1.9}\cdot\mu^{0.7}}\right)^{\frac{1}{1.7}} \quad (17)$$

Where C_h is a constant that depends on the type of packing used in the column (in our case, this value was equal to 1.094). a_{ef} corresponds to the interfacial effective area, which is the product between the packing specific area per volume (771 m^2/m^3) and the interfacial effective factor (fixed to 0.83).

Finally, the liquid flow through the column was computed using the following expression:

$$L=\frac{u_L\cdot\rho\cdot S}{\overline{PM}}\times 10^6 \quad (18)$$

The resulting partial differential equations were solved using the Method of Lines (see for example Schiesser and Griffiths, 2009). This method use finite difference relationships for the spatial derivatives and ordinary differential equations (ODE's) for the time derivative. And its implementation requires a convenient ODE solver package. In this work, the computational package of MATLAB® was used.

Model parameters

The unknowns in the model were fitted using a calibration set from an experimental batch distillation column (50 L capacity), located in the Chemical and Bioprocess Engineering Department at the Pontificia Universidad Católica de Chile. Specifically, three unknowns were fitted: (i) the effective power supplied by the heaters, (ii) the effective power removed by the partial condenser and (iii) the interfacial area factor. Through a sensitivity analysis (± 10% of the nominal value) in the head and heart stages, we concluded that the latter parameter was not sensitive. Therefore, it was set at 0.83, the value obtained in a previous work (Carvallo et al., 2011).

In order to calibrate the *effective cooling power*, we built a proportional-integral feedback control system (PI) in the model, which manipulates the cooling power to control the alcoholic content of the distillate, minimizing the error between the simulated and measured experimental data. The controller was tuned by trial-and-error, resulting in a proportional constant Kc of 900 and an integral time τ_i of 20455. The fitting error was low: 0.09% for the head cut and 0.14% for the heart cut (0.14% for the whole distillation); well below the 6.7 and 1.0% obtained in a previous work (Carvallo et al., 2011).

Then, with the PI controller tuned, we proceed to calibrate the *effective heating power* using a similar trial-and-error procedure. In this case, the square error of the distillate volume was minimized. For the distillation head cut (first 8.87 min), an optimal value of 1000 W was found (equal to the nominal value), with an error of 20.4% in the estimated distillate volume (in Carvallo et al. this error was 39.7%). It is possible that the true heating power is higher than the value indicated by our data acquisition system. For the heart cut, the procedure was repeated and an optimal value of 597 W was found (735 W nominal power). In this case, the average error in the simulated distillate volume was 6.2%, lower than the obtained by Carvallo et al. (10.5%).

The power supplied by the electric heaters was corrected by heat losses, because the supports of the boiler are not thermally insulated. The losses were modelled by the following relationship, which depends on the boiler temperature (TB) and the average ambient temperature (T∞):

After proper calibration, Figure 1 shows an almost perfect agreement between our model and the alcohol content data from Carvallo et al. (2011).

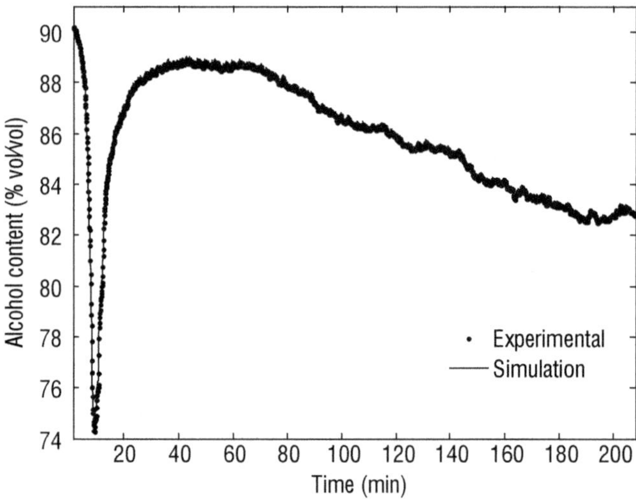

Figure 1. Distillate ethanol content evolution in a standard distillation run.

Figure 2 shows the fitted power removed by the partial condenser for the same calibration data.

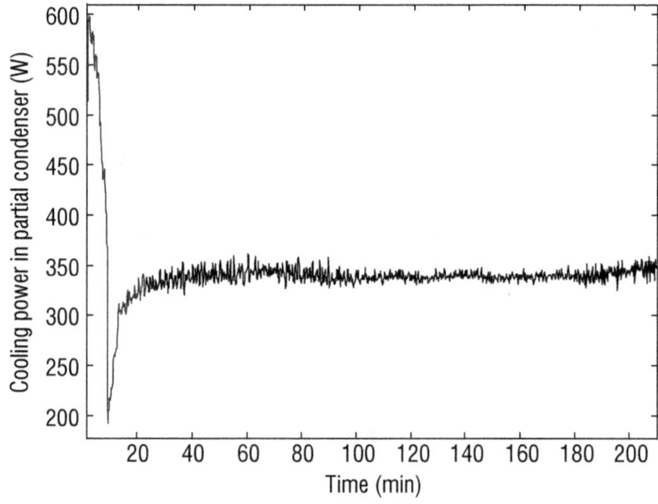

Figure 2. Predicted cooling power in the partial condenser according to the PI calibration procedure in a standard distillation run.

$$Q_p = -190.45051 + 0.027736447 \cdot T_B^{1.5} - 0.00069779137 \cdot T_\infty^2 + \frac{31705.067}{T_\infty} \tag{19}$$

Results and discussion

The fitted model was compared with three experimental series with slightly different conditions (boiler load, initial molar fraction of ethanol and methanol as well as the average ambient temperature) performed by Carvallo et al. (2011). In all these cases, the feedback control system reproduced closely the ethanol evolution in the distillate (see Model Parameters section). In Table 1 we compare the experimental data with our simulations and the predictions using the model developed by Carvallo et al. (2011).

Table 1. Comparison between experimental data and mathematical models.

Variable	*Average error of our model*	*Average error Carvallo et al.*
Alcohol content (series 1)	0.17%	1.79%
Alcohol content (series 2)	0.17%	2.60%
Alcohol content (series 3)	0.18%	5.08%
Distillate volume (series 1)	5.84%	10.34%
Distillate volume (series 2)	2.90%	11.88%
Ethanol recovery (series 1)	5.24%	10.26%
Ethanol recovery (series 2)	3.05%	12.83%
Methanol recovery (series 1)	20.81%	27.60%
Methanol recovery (series 2)	4.35%	11.62%

Table 1 shows that our model reproduces the total recovery of ethanol, methanol and distillate better than Carvallo et al. In general, this is explained due to a much better predictive capability of our model during the head cut, where the errors were substantially lower than those using Carvallo's model (in the head cut : methanol recovery error, 20.45% vs. 40.94%; distillate volume error, 14.06% vs. 36.72%; ethanol recovery error, 12.20% vs. 38.09%).

The better performance of our model can be explained by the inclusion of the random packing dynamics, the packing thermal effects during the first cut period and the PI controller. The latter, behaved very well in all 3 experimental series (see for example, the errors in alcoholic content), despite variations in the initial conditions of distillation. Still, we will have to speed up simulations using better numerical methods. Also, better prediction of activity coefficients at infinite dilution for relevant congeners is necessary. In future work, the PI controller will help us in experimental distillations to track optimal policies that minimize methanol in the heart cut. In addition, we have available now a new fully instrumented column, where cooling power and heating power will be measured and strictly controlled. Hence, we expect to reduce model fitting and enhance its predictive capability.

Acknowledgements

This work was supported by project FONDECYT 1100357.

Nomenclature

a	Interfacial area, m2/m3
aef	Effective interfacial area, m2/m3
cp	Heat capacity, J/g K
ct	Concentration, mol/mL
g	Gravity constant, m/s2
H	Enthalpy vapour phase, J/mol
h	Enthalpy liquid phase, J/mol
hL	Liquid hold-up, m3/m-3
L	Molar flow in liquid phase, mol/s
M	Moles of retained liquid, mol
M'	Moles of retained liquid per meter of packing, mol/m
m'	Mass per meter of packing, g
MW	Molecular weight, g/mol
$\overline{MW}$	Molecular weight of the mixture, g/mol
Q	Heat, W
Rf	Reflux ratio
S	Cross section of the column, m2
T	Temperature, K
t	Time, s
uL	Specific liquid load, m3/m2 s
V	Molar flow in gas phase, mol/s
x	Molar fraction in liquid phase
y	Molar fraction in gas phase
z	Column height, m
μ	Viscosity, kg/m s
ρ	Density, g/mL

References

Batista, F.R.M., Scanavini, H.F.A., Batista, E.A.C., Ceriani, R., Meirelles, A.J.A., and Luz, L.F.L. (2009). Chapter 3. Distillation applied to the processing of spirits and aromas. In M. A. A. Meireles (Ed.), Extracting bioactive compounds for food products: theory and applications. CRC Press.

Billet, R. and Schultes, M. (1991). Modelling of pressure drop in packed columns. Chemical Engineering and Technology **14**: 89-95.

Billet, R. and Schultes, M. (1993). Predicting mass transfer in packed columns. Chemical Engineering and Technology **16**: 1-9.

Bosley, J.R. and Edgar, T.F. (1994). An efficient dynamic model for batch distillation. Journal of Process Control **4**: 195-204.

Carvallo, J., Labbé, M., Pérez-Correa, J.R., Zaror, C. and Wisniak, J. (2011). Modelling methanol recovery in wine distillation stills with packing columns. Food Control **22**: 1322-1332.

Hitch, D.M., Rousseau, R.W. and Ferrell, J.K. (1987). Simulation of Continuous-Contact Separation Processes: Unsteady-State, Multi-component, Adiabatic Absorption. Industrial and Engineering Chemistry Research **26**: 1092-1099.

Osorio, D., Pérez-Correa, J.R., Belancic, A. and Agosin, E. (2004). Rigorous dynamic modelling and simulation of wine distillations. Food Control **15**: 515-521

Peng, J., Edgar, T.F. and Eldridge, R.B. (2003). Dynamic rate-based and equilibrium models for a packed reactive distillation column. Chemical Engineering Science **58**: 2671-2680.

Schiesser, W.E. and Griffiths, G.W. (2009). A Compendium of Partial Differential Equation Models: Method of Lines Analysis with Matlab. Cambridge University Press, New York.

Chapter 19

New Scotch grain whisky distillery design and build – Starlaw Grain Distillery, Bathgate

Ian Palmer[1], Gary Gibson[2] and Filippo Cannoni[3]
[1]Glen Turner Company, Starlaw Road, Bathgate, West Lothian; [2]Colorado Group, Rosyth, Fife; [3]Frilli Impianti SRL, Monteriggioni, Italy

Background

As part of our shareholders' long held strategy of owning and operating the principal production assets for its key products, it was agreed in 2007 to build a grain distillery in Scotland. This was to secure the supply of Scotch Grain Whisky (SGS) for our branded blended whiskies and Grain Neutral Spirit (GNS) to supply the rapidly growing vodka brand. This decision followed the start of the construction of the final phase of the maturation warehouse construction on the bottling facility site.

This paper sets out the development and delivery of the project and the challenges faced and also the design considerations in the selection of the distillation system. This project was the first green-field grain distillery construction project since the mid 1960's.

Project objectives

The brief for the project was to build a 25.0 M litres alcohol grain distillery that would deliver the current and future volumes for the company and to produce a spirit style that closely matched the spirit that was currently being used in the brand blends. The spirit also had to be acceptable to the wider whisky industry as the grain whisky would be used in reciprocal deals for new malt whisky.

Cost was a major driver in the overall design with more emphasis being placed on the on-going operational costs as opposed to the initial capital cost. In order to defray the initial cost, speed of delivery of the project was important.

Location

A number of locations were examined in detail with only two being considered as feasible. Taking into account the primary objective of reducing production costs it was agreed to build the distillery on an adjacent site to the maturation and bottling facility. The benefit of doing so was two-fold, the elimination of all spirit transport costs while being cost neutral for cereal and other consumables and the ability to manage the distillery from, and share resources with, the bottling and maturation facility. This location would help to create a full supply chain process on the one site - cereal to cased goods.

However the site did bring its challenges, namely: the location was in a known shale oil mining area, part of it was a designated flood plain, the area was out with the local plan designated development area, and the local effluent plant was near to capacity. Despite this it was agreed to proceed with this location.

Principal design considerations

The big question was the management of the co products - Dried Distillers Grains and Solubles (DDGS) or Bio mass energy generation. At the time of this internal discussion there was a great deal of discussion within the industry on the matter. The decision was taken to proceed with the DDGS solution. The reasons for this were:

- The DDGS technology was well known and understood, while the biomass options were not so well known nor were they proven.
- The installation of biomass energy generation represented a risk to the delivery of the project.
  - ◇ Technology not well understood
  - ◇ Impact on the time of delivery of the whole project
  - ◇ Absorption of project management resource.
- Despite views expressed to the contrary the capital costs of DDGS was not high compared to Bio mass plants.
- The operational costs and revenue balance was still favourable with the selected technology despite the contrary industry views expressed at the time.

We appeared to be swimming against the tide!

Energy is the second largest direct cost in the production of grain spirit and having discounted biomass energy generation the installation of a gas fired Combined Heat and Power plant (CHP) was considered. The decision was taken not to install initially but to build in the capability for later installation. This included the construction of a larger boiler house and the installation of a power cable with the appropriate switching at both ends to accommodate power travelling in either direction.

As there was a capacity restraint at the local effluent treatment works and to reduce our effluent costs, it was agreed to install our own on-site treatment and an anaerobic / aerobic treatment plant was selected and installed.

In order to keep the building costs low, ensure a very high level of natural ventilation in the distillation Atex area, and to reduce the impact on the sky line, the distillation area was not enclosed in a building.

The DDGS drier was enclosed in a building but only on three sides while the evaporator was not enclosed like the distillation plant and for the same reasons.

Regulatory approval

Planning permission

Planning permission was sought after very detailed consultation with the local council officials and there was a very satisfactory outcome. The general design concept was to keep the same theme as the current site in terms of general shape and colour. The height of the columns was a consideration, but it was agreed to build an earth screen on the edge of the site next to the public road. To achieve this cost effectively, it was agreed to use the spoil from the distillery construction and from the construction of the maturation warehouses, which was being undertaken on the adjacent site. Combined this provided the 40,000 m^3 of material to create the screen of sufficient height and length. Trees were salvaged from the construction area and relocated on to the bunds to provide further screening. The final approved planning permission included approval to build more maturation warehouses and a malt distillery. At the time of writing only the additional maturation warehouses are being built and at present there is no business requirement for the malt distillery.

Building regulations (building warrant)

Seeking approval for the detailed building design was achieved in phases as and when each part of the building was designed. The early decision to keep the building a separate construction to the process equipment allowed the design and construction of the building to proceed quickly which then provided a weather proof envelope to protect the process plant assembly, in particular the onsite construction of the fermentation vessels. Keeping the building and process plant interface to a minimum made the civil design easier to develop.

The support, cooperation and professionalism of the local council officials, West Lothian Council, must be acknowledged at this point.

Upper tier COMAH site (Control of Major Accident Hazards)

Due to the adjacent bottling plant and maturation area holding in excess of 50,000 tons of whisky, it was already classified as an upper tier COMAH site and the construction of the distillery was treated as a major change to the existing site safety report. The competent authority was consulted very early in the project and before planning permission was sought. A process was agreed where the safety report could be submitted in phases allowing the work to proceed before the final report was submitted.

As this was a new build there was an expectation by all of the regulatory authorities that the design would meet all of the standards for such a plant. This presented a number of issues as the majority of the equipment was sourced in Europe where the standards used were European, which did not always have equivalent British Standards. To make the situation worse some suppliers used their own country's standards, Germany in particular. Some other suppliers with a high level of international business adopted some US standards, in particular those of the American Petroleum Institute (API). Matching the standards was possible to a certain extent, but there were gaps. However, the different standards did not present any practical integration issues.

The principal environmental concerns were over loss of containment and the management of fire water run-off. The site was adjacent to a small burn, with associated flood plain, which also ran through the middle of the existing maturation site. This burn had to be protected from the runoff water. This protection was complicated by the fact the area next to the burn also had to be kept available for flooding in the event of a serious storm. This was achieved by building a 2 meter high earth bund along the edge of the burn with automatic sluice gates that would control the flow of Sustainable Drainage System (SUDS) water off the site, while preventing the flow of contaminated water off the site. Allowance also had to be made for the safe removal off site of any fire water or other liquid.

Environmental consents

Due to the size of the distillery, the decision to install a DDGS plant and an Anaerobic digester resulted in the need to apply for an Environmental Permit known as a Part B process licence .

The main issues here were the possible smell from the drier exhaust and the smell from the anaerobic digester. The smell from the drier was easily resolved with a combination of the following operating parameters:

- The scrubbing of the vapour directly off the drier before passing the vapour onto the evaporator as its main heat source.
- The condensing of most of the vapour in the evaporator
- Relatively low operating temperature and low oxygen levels in the drier itself.

More importantly, this was not a new process or technology for the regulatory authority, but the anaerobic digester was, however, an issue due to the relatively recent introduction of the process to the industry. Where this process had been installed there was a very wide range of application and technologies used and the plant installed on this occasion added to this range. The digester was only being used to treat the spent lees from the distillation plant and the foul condensate from the evaporator. This feed stock had very low levels of sulphur but there was an insistence on the installation of an H_2S monitor on the gas coming off the digester.

Application was made to burn the Fusel oil and the head and tails from the GNS production in the boilers, but due to a policy review this part of the application was refused. At the time of writing the policy review is still not complete.

General impact of the regulations

Working within such a highly regulated environment with a large number of different design standards and the requirement to design and construct to these standards meant there was very little room available for much innovation. The main innovation effort was directed in meeting the regulations and achieving the design standards, while still having an operating distillery that was commercially viable. Many suppliers, while working to the correct standards and the application of those standards, were being independently verified. However, they found it incredulous that we should ask for the detail behind their application of the standards and many stated that the level of detail required put at risk their intellectual property rights.

Detailed design

Civil Works

The plant was laid out in such a way that the risk areas were separated from each other and the control room was located such that it was protected from these areas - the hazardous areas being the mill house, distillation area and the DDGS drier. These areas were further protected by fire walls. The detailed work that was carried out in modelling the major accident hazards for the COMAH safety report was used in designing these areas. To support this approach inventory of materials was kept to a minimum - 4 days of cereal, 6 hours of spirit and 12 hours of DDGS meal.

Process

The design cereal was wheat with high enzyme malt inclusion to aid starch conversion with the option to change to maize if commercial terms made this a more attractive feed stock. Both the wheat and the malt are hammer milled before being passed into the conversion area. The conversion process is a continuous process made up of 4 different vessels - wheat wetting tank, wheat cooker, malt slurry tank and conversion vessel. All of the vessels operate on a residence time philosophy with the capability of altering the flow rate and any of the temperature parameters.

The batch fermentation process is based on nine 450,000 litre fermentation vessels. The cream yeast is injected into the wort line shortly after charging the fermentation vessel. The setting temperature is 30°c and each of the fermenters has its own shell and tube heat exchanger used for temperature control. The temperature of the fermenting wash is automatically controlled by pumping as necessary round the vessel via the coolers. The fermentation is completed long before the planned 72 hours.

The distillation plant discussion is dealt with below.

The DDGS process is a normal centrifuge, evaporator and drier configuration but no pellet mill. The centrifuged spent wash is used initially in the stripping column re-boiler before be sent to the evaporator.

The waste water treatment plant as stated above is a single vessel anaerobic / aerobic reactor with sand filtration following the reactor.

The main challenge with this process was the weakly buffered and highly degradable feedstock that made pH control difficult and with most of the COD removal occurring in the anaerobic section leaving little to be done in the aerobic section. The boiler burner design was modified to allow for the untreated methane from the treatment plant to be burnt in the boiler.

The recovery of the fermentation CO_2 was discounted due to the poor financial return

The Construction

The contractual arrangements for the project were not the traditional Principal Contractor style but the Construction Management Contractor arrangement. This was chosen for two reasons, the need to develop a one team approach with a holistic view of the project and the complexity of the project where the civil construction and the process plant installation and construction were interdependent and the contractors were on site together.

The chosen site presented a significant geological problem that being the general area was formerly a shale oil mining area and two mines were very close to the chosen site. A very detailed site investigation was undertaken, which established the safe area and the orientation of the buildings that maximised that area.

The extensive use of 3D modelling helped the project team to develop the layout in both general terms and in the detail. The detailed 3D modelling was very useful in the initial setting out of the process equipment, ensuring there were no clashes with steel work etc, but it was also very useful in ensuring the equipment was accessible throughout the whole equipment life cycle - access for operational reasons, maintenance and replacement.

Managing Health and Safety was a main priority for the project and this required significant investment of time and effort before any work was undertaken on site. Health and Safety and the CDM regulations were managed throughout the project jointly by the construction management team and client who created one set of standards that were equally and pragmatically applied over the civil and process works. The project was a very European project with suppliers and contractors being sourced from 9 different countries with 9 different cultures and 4 different working languages. An induction video and a 'cardinal rules' document in the 4 different languages proved a very useful tool. This resulted in an accident frequency rate measure of AFR 1.73, which is significantly better than the construction industry norm of 4.8.

There was only one project plan that covered every activity necessary for the delivery of the project and this plan was driven by the civil construction team. This plan was reviewed every two weeks and a detailed two week look-ahead program issued every week. The critical path in the plan was the construction of the fermentation vessels, which had to be constructed on site. Due to the project timing and the prevailing weather conditions, the fermentation hall building had to be built first and then the fermentation vats built inside the building.

In order to meet the time schedule the civil design and procurement was carried out in small packages that allowed the construction to proceed without all of the detailed design having being completed. Also late design challenges were easily managed as all of the commitments were not made at the start of the project.

The weight and height of some of the process equipment presented a number of changes, in particular the height of the distillation columns and the weight of the DDGS drier. The distillation plant was designed so that they were all supported from the foundation with no high level supporting steel work, this resulted in the need for very significant foundation works.

A group of common contractors were used by all of the other suppliers and contractors for example scaffolding, process support steel work, process plant lifting and location team. This reduced coordination problems and maintained a common standard throughout the site.

All of the building steelwork and process equipment support steel work were constructed in galvanised steel.

Distillation plant

A number of matters had to be considered during the selection of the outline distillation solution:

- Energy consumption
- The need to produce both SGS and GNS.
- Integration with the rest of the process.
- Spirit quality
- Ethyl Carbamate levels in the final spirit.
- Ability to turn down the capacity.

Considering the height of the columns was not necessary as the planning permission was granted for the worst case scenario. The options considered were:

- Two separate distillation streams, one for the SGS and one for the GNS
- Two steams but with a shared stripping (mash column) column
- Direct steam injection with thermal recompression
- Vacuum column with spent wash re-boiler
- GNS with or without a methanol column
- Use of a degasser or not.

The final choice was to install a one stream system, with de-gasser and spent wash re-boiler. This was selected for the following reasons.

- Commercially it was agreed that there was no need for the plant to produce both GNS and SGS simultaneously, therefore, the need for two separate streams was rejected. The two different products would be produced in campaigns as the wider business has the storage capacity for the GNS. A single stream was agreed upon with isolation of the GNS sections from the SGS steam using spectacle pieces. The spectacle pieces isolation was selected as it was agreed that closing down the plant to change over between products maintained the integrity of the SGS product.
- The sharing the stripping column option was chosen for economic reasons as the column could be designed and constructed with consideration for the different operating parameters associated with production of SGS and GNS, principally pressure, with little additional costs.

A whole distillery approach was taken when considering the energy consumption in the distillation stream. The use of a re-boiler and vacuum operating running pressures was selected due to the lower energy demand of such a system when integrated with the DDGS plant. The re-boiler would use centrifuged spent wash as opposed to the spent wash direct from the column. There were a number of reasons for this decision. Due to the lower solids content in the spent wash the lower cost and more efficient plate heat-exchangers could be used and the flashing in the re-boiler acted as a first effect for the evaporator, concentrating the spent wash prior to the evaporator. The indirect steam usage kept the concentration of the spent wash higher and the return of the hot steam condensate to the boilers all combined to create a lower net distillery energy demand.

A degasser section in the stripping column was selected to ensure that all the odours from the wash and in particular any dissolved CO_2 was removed before the vapour was passed into the rectifier. This is supported by the use of copper plates in the de-gasser section to assist in the removal of some of the sulphur compounds.

The rectifier was extended with the addition of a lutter column section connected directly below the rectifier. This lutter column removes the alcohol from the rectifier feints as opposed to feeding the feints back into the stripping column. This configuration keeps the concentration of the spent wash high reducing the energy demand in the DDGS plant.

In order to keep the ethyl carbamate levels low in the finial spirit the trays in the rectifier were made of copper and the main condenser on the rectifier is also made of copper. The trays were mounted in such a way that they could be easily removed and replaced. This replacement work will only take 48 hours to complete and the necessary safe access and egress for the confined space work was designed in.

In order to meet the GNS quality parameters a five column configuration was agreed on for the GNS stream:

- Stripping column
- Hydroselection column
- Rectifier column
- Methanol column and
- Heads and tails concentration column

The plates in all the columns are simple two stage valve trays allowing for a 50% down turn in the production volumes.

The fusel oil extraction was designed on the basis of a decanter only as the higher amyl content of such a system was acceptable to the spirit style.

One of the main criteria for the distillation process was the ability of the distillery to produce a spirit that matched the style of the companies principal blended whisky, Label 5. In order to achieve this, the ability to modify the running conditions was designed in. There is the ability to change the spirit take off plate and to withdraw heads off the rectifier as well as off the stripping column and the ability to create more copper exposure.

Operating under a vacuum carries the inherent risk of alcohol loss due to the lower condensing temperature and carryover into the vacuum pumps. The vacuum system included a scrubbing column which recovers any alcohol carryover into the pumps. Each of the condensers which operate under vacuum has a guard condenser which is cooled with recirculating chilled water.

As described earlier the distillation plant is not enclosed in a building. This arrangement provides a number of advantages:

- Very high levels of natural ventilation reducing the Atex area.
- Equipment can be easily installed and removed using cranes.
- The fundamental self-supporting design of the columns did not require the columns to be supported by any other supporting steel frame work.

Although the Atex area was reduced by the non-enclosed location this did not remove the need for other protection systems. The distillation area was bunded, but the bund naturally drained to a remote retention tank. The effect of this is to remove the liquid from below the equipment so that in the event of a pool fire the fuel is being drawn away to a safe location. This bunding arrangement was supported by low level ethanol vapour detection and infrared/ultraviolet flame detection. The external location also requires a high level of poor weather protection including the trace heating of some of the pipe work and instruments.

The entire distillery process was subject to a full HAZOP study and in particular the distillation process. The main risks identified during the HAZOP study were then followed up by a quantitative layer of protection analysis, which identified all of the key protections systems. Also the quantitative approach identified that there was no need for any formal Safety Instrumented Systems. All of the different layers of protection have been catalogued and are now protected by a change management process as well as planned maintenance and inspection routines.

Conclusion

The major design issue had been the decision to build a new distillery with a DDGS solution for the co-products. Some plants have converted to biomass energy while others have invested in digestion processes all of which implies a lack of confidence in the future for DDGS. Our view was that there is a future for DDGS as a viable co-product within the design life of the new plant. However, time will be the true arbiter in this matter. The impact of the current legislative environment, while not being a major impediment, required a lot of resources which diverted the project team from the main task in hand. The project team was very small and the decision to defer non-essential elements of the project has proven to be correct. The spirit, although not yet matured, is proving to be within the style envelope that was initially specified. The project, although exhausting to deliver, has proven to be a success and all of the indications are that it will continue to provide the volume and style demanded by our branded whiskies.

Chapter 20

Ethyl carbamate distribution in pot still Cachaça

A.R. Alcarde[1], L.S. Marelli[1], A.E.S. Belluco[2], B.M.S. Monteiro[1]
[1]*University of São Paulo, College of Agriculture "Luiz de Queiroz", Av. Pádua Dias, 11, CP 9, 13418-900, Piracicaba/SP, Brazil;* [2]*Federal University of São Carlos, DTAiSER, Rodovia Anhanguera, km 174, 13600-970, Araras/SP, Brazil*

Introduction

Ethyl carbamate (EC), also known as urethane ($C_3H_7NO_2$), is a carbamic acid ethyl ester. Its boiling point is 184°C. It is known as a carcinogenic compound, soluble in water and ethanol, with low volatility in hydro alcoholic solutions and found in different alcoholic beverages and in some fermented foods (Lachenmeier, Frank and Kuballa 2005).

The production and origin of EC in sugar cane substrates is not well elucidated. Some studies have reported that reactions responsible for formation of the EC in fermentation processes are influenced by nutrients added and type of yeast (Monteiro and Bisson, 1992), ethanol concentration (Stevens and Ough, 1993), acidity and temperature (Zimmerli and Schlatter, 1991). It is reported that the degradation of amino acids may produce EC through the reaction between ethanol and nitrogen precursors, such as urea, carbamyl phosphate and cyanide. This last one is considered a precursor of ethyl carbamate during and after distillation (Stevens and Ough, 1993).

The EC concentration in beverages should be kept at a technically possible lowest level. To achieve this objective is essential to understand how EC is formed during fermentation, its volatilization in distillation and its distribution in distilled fractions in sugar cane spirit production. According to this approach, the kinetics of volatilization of EC during double distillation of sugar cane wash was investigated.

Materials and methods

Sugar cane juice from the variety SP 81-3250, standardized at 18° Brix, was fermented by the addition of 3 g/L (dry weight) of yeast *Saccharomyces cerevisiae*, strain CA-11. Fermentation was carried out at 30°C for 24 h. The distillations took place in a copper pot still of 37 L capacity.

Doubled distillation was carried out following the methodology used for production of *single malt whisky* (Piggott, 2003). During the distillations the distilled liquid was collected in fractions of 500 ml in which the quantification of EC was carried out. In second distillation fractions were separated as "head" (2% of total boiler volume), "heart" (distilled recovered after "head" and until the distillate recovered from outlet condenser presented 60% v/v ethanol) and tail (distilled recovered after "heart" and until the distillate recovered from outlet condenser presented 3% v/v ethanol).

The samples, without prior treatment, were analyzed in a Shimadzu gas chromatograph (model GCMS-2010) equipped with a Shimadzu mass detector (model QP 2010Plus), with ion source of electron impact at 70 eV, operating with monitoring mode SIM, selecting the ion m/z 62 (ethyl carbamate) and m/z 75 (methyl carbamate – internal standard). A capillary column of polar phase of esterified polyethylene glycol (HP-FFAP, 50 m x 0.20 cm x 0.33 μm) was used to separate the compounds. The oven temperature was programmed to 90°C (1min), raised at 10°C/min to 150°C (0 min) and then raised at 30°C/min to 220°C (2 min). The temperature of the injector was 240°C and that for interface and ion source was 220°C. A sample aliquot of 1.0 μL was injected in "splitless" mode. The carrier gas was He at a flow rate of 1.2 mL/min.

A standard calibration curve (10, 30, 60, 90, 120 and 150 μg/L) was prepared from a stock solution of ethyl carbamate in hydro alcoholic solution (ethanol 40% v/v). Methyl carbamate was used as an internal standard.

By plotting the relative peak areas against the standard and internal standard concentrations, the quantifications of EC in the samples were performed by constructing a calibration curve obtained by regression analysis. Its correlation was verified by linear regression. The linear correlation coefficients of the calibration curves (R^2) ranged from 0.9959 to 0.9988. The standard curves and the sample analysis were carried out in triplicate.

Results and discussion

By investigating the EC formed during the first distillation (Table 1) it may be observed that approximately 87% of EC was collected in *low wines* and 13% remained in the stillage.

Along the second distillation only a small proportion (approximately 6%) of EC was collected in the "heart" fraction. EC was not detected in the "head" fraction. The "tail" fraction accumulated 61% of the EC formed and the remaining 33% of EC was detected in the stillage.

Riffkin *et al* (1989) observed that only 1% of EC formed in the first distillation accumulated in the *whisky* produced by the second distillation. The "tail" fraction accumulated 15% and the stillage retained 84% of EC present in the second distillation.

References

Lachenmeier, D.W., Frank, W. and Kuballa, T. (2005). Application of tandem mass spectrometry combined with gas chromatography to the routine analysis of ethyl carbamate in stone-fruit spirits. *Rapid Communications in Mass Spectrometry* **19**: 108-112

Monteiro, F. and Bisson L. (1992). Utilization of arginine by yeast during grape juice fermentation and investigation of the possible role of arginine as a precursor of urea. *American Journal of Enology and Viticulture* **43**: 18-22

Piggott, J.R. and Conner, J.M. *Whiskies*. In: *Fermented beverage production*. Edited by Lea, A.G.H. and Piggott, J.R., Klumer Academic/Plenum Publishers, New York, USA, pp. 239-262

Riffkin, H.L., Wilson, R., Howie, D. and Muller, S.B. (1989). Ethyl carbamate formation in the production of pot still whisky. *Journal of the Institute of Brewing* **95**: 115-119

Stevens, D.F. and Ough, C.S. (1993). Ethyl carbamate formation: reaction of urea and citrulline with ethanol in wine under low to normal temperature conditions. *American Journal of Enology and Viticulture* **44**: 309-312

Zimmerli B. and Schlatter J. (1991). Ethyl carbamate: analytical methodology, occurrence, formation, biological activity and risk assessment. *Mutation Research* **259**: 325-350.

Table 1. Concentration of ethyl carbamate (EC) in each distillate fractions during the first and second distillations.

First distillation			*Second Distillation*		
	Distillate fractions	*EC (μg/L)*		*Distillate fractions*	*EC (μg/L)*
Low wines	1	<LD	"Head"	1	<LD
	2	<LD	"Heart"	2	<LD
	3	<LD		3	<LD
	4	<LD		4	<LD
	5	<LD		5	<LD
	6	<LD		6	<LD
	7	<LD		7	<LD
	8	<LD		8	<LD
	9	<LD		9	<LD
	10	<LD		10	<LD
	11	<LD		11	<LD
	12	<LD		12	<LD
	13	12		13	<LD
	14	15		14	<LD
	15	25		15	<LD
	16	22		16	<LD
	17	31		17	13
	18	44		18	11
	19	62		19	17
	20	75		20	14
				21	19
			"Tail"	22	17
				23	21
				24	23
				25	29
				26	35
				27	42
				28	46
				29	55
				30	62
				31	77
				32	87
				33	94
				34	106
Stillage		41			375

LD = detection limit (10.0 μg/L)

Chapter 21

Ethyl carbamate formation in Cachaça produced from different sugar cane varieties

A.R. Alcarde, L.S. Marelli, B.M.S. Monteiro
University of São Paulo, College of Agriculture "Luiz de Queiroz", Av. Pádua Dias, 11, CP 9, 13418-900, Piracicaba/SP, Brazil

Introduction

Cachaça is a spirit produced by distillation of fermented sugar cane juice. Its alcoholic concentration is about 40% (v/v).

Sugar cane is a cyanogenic plant which contains the active ingredient hydrogen cyanide (HCN) linked to carbohydrates called cyanogenic glycosides (Andrade-Sobrinho *et al*, 2009) that are soluble in water and potentially release hydrogen cyanide when sugar cane is crushed. The cyanogenic glycosides in the presence of water are enzymatically hydrolyzed by beta-glycosidases (Amorim, Medeiros and Riet-Correa, 2006) and may release cyanide. Cyanide is oxidised to cyanate in a reaction catalyzed by Cu^{2+}, which reacts with ethanol leading to ethyl carbamate (Nagato, Novaes and Penteado, 2003).

As there are many available varieties of sugar cane in Brazil to produce cachaça, the aim of this study was to investigate the formation of ethyl carbamate (EC) in cachaça produced from different varieties of cane sugar.

Materials and methods

Juices from 14 different varieties of sugar cane were fermented by the addition of 3 g/L (dry weight) of yeast *Saccharomyces cerevisiae*, strain CA-11. Fermentation was carried out at 30°C for 24 h. The distillation took place in a laboratory copper distiller following the traditional methodology of single distillation used for cachaça production.

The spirits, without prior treatment, were analyzed in a Shimadzu gas chromatograph (model GCMS-2010) equipped with a Shimadzu mass detector (model QP 2010Plus), with ion source of electron impact at 70 eV, operating with monitoring mode SIM, selecting the ion m/z 62 (ethyl carbamate) and m/z 75 (methyl carbamate – internal standard). A capillary column of polar phase of esterified polyethylene glycol (HP-FFAP, 50 m x 0.20 cm x 0.33 μm) was used to separate the compounds. The oven temperature was programmed to 90°C (1min), raised at 10°C/min to 150°C (0 min) and then raised at 30°C/min to 220°C (2 min). The temperature of the injector was 240°C and that for interface and ion source was used 220°C. A sample aliquot of 1.0 mL was injected in "splitless" mode. The carrier gas was He at a flow rate of 1.2 mL/min.

A standard calibration curve (10, 30, 60, 90, 120 and 150 μg/L of EC) was prepared from a stock solution of ethyl carbamate in hydro alcoholic solution (ethanol 40% v/v). Methyl carbamate was used as an internal standard.

By plotting the relative peak areas against the standard and internal standard concentrations, the quantifications of EC in the samples were performed by constructing a calibration curve obtained by regression analysis. Its correlation was verified by linear regression. The linear correlation coefficients of the calibration curves (R^2) ranged from 0.9959 to 0.9988. The analytical curves and the sample analysis were made in triplicate.

Results and discussion

The concentrations of EC in the cachaças coming from the 14 studied varieties of sugar cane ranged from 49.0 to 77.5 μg/L (Tabel 1). The results indicate that all cachaças were within the maximum limit of 150 μg/L established by Brazilian legislation (Brasil, 2005).

Table 1. Concentration of ethyl carbamate (EC) in cachaças produced from different varieties of sugar cane.

	Sugar cane spirit	
Sugar cane variety	*Ethanol (%v/v)*	*EC (μg/L)*
SP 89-1115	47.08	54.4
RB 86-7515	46.08	69.2
RB 83-5054	49.72	68.3
SP 81-3250	41.42	49.0
CTC 14	41.83	65.2
RB 85-5453	46.59	77.5
RB 85-5536	47.56	69.6
RB 92-5211	41.68	73.5
SP 79-1011	48.89	72.3
SP 83-2847	45.42	68.8
RB 85-5156	43.43	75.9
CTC 6	43.50	68.5
CTC 8	44.70	70.1
RB 72-454	42.79	70.4

These results demonstrate that the variety of cane sugar used for the production of cachaça did not influence significantly the levels of EC in the distillate. The formation of EC in distillates may occur before, during and after the distillation process, including in the storage of the spirit, by the reaction of ethanol with some nitrogen compounds (Nagato, Novaes and Penteado, 2003). The EC formed before distillation is almost entirely removed by distillation. Therefore, the EC levels in distilled beverages are associated with nitrogen precursors that appear before and during distillation (Aresta, Boscolo and Franco, 2001).

The levels of EC in cachaça are largely dependent of the configuration of the distillation equipment and also the distillation process. It was observed that the formation EC by nitrogen precursors during the distillation is favored by high temperatures and also by inadequate rates of reflux (Andrade-Sobrinho *et al*, 2009).

References

Andrade-Sobrinho, I.G., Cappelini, I.T.D., Silva, A.A., Galinaro, C.A., Buchviser, S.F., Cardoso, D.R. and Franco, D.W. (2009). Teores de carbamato de etila em aguardentes de cana e mandioca - Parte II. *Quimica Nova* **32**: 116-119

Aresta, M., Boscolo, M. and Franco, D.W. (2001). Copper(II) catalysis in cyanide conversion into ethyl carbamate in spirits and relevant reactions. *Journal of Agricultural and Food Chemistry* **49**: 2819-2824

Amorim, S.L., Medeiros, R.M.T. and Riet-Correa, F. (2006). Intoxicações por plantas cianogênicas no Brasil. *Ciência Animal* **16**: 17-26

Brasil. (2005). *Instrução Normativa N° 13*. Ministério da Agricultura, Pecuária e Abastecimento, Brasília, Brasil, Diário Oficial da União 30/06/2005

Nagato, L.A.F., Novaes, F.V. and Penteado, M.D.V.C. (2003). Carbamato de etila em bebidas alcoólicas. *Ciência e Tecnologia de Alimentos* **37**: 40-47

Chapter 22

From nature to bottle: How to create authentic flavour profiles

Stephan Haiber
Givaudan, Huizerstraatweg 28, 1411 GP Naarden, The Netherlands

Introduction

Aroma, taste and irritant effects represent the magic triangle of flavour research. The right balance of these three factors is crucial to create a high quality flavour. Consistent analytical data obtained for the original target material are therefore necessary as a starting point to create flavours which come close to the original target material. An appropriate analytical approach has to be followed, focusing on both volatile aroma compounds as well as non-volatile taste compounds. Furthermore, irritants which might be found in both categories have to be taken into account. The composition of volatiles can be quite efficiently analysed by GC-MS and GC-MS-olfactometry. The contribution of non-volatiles is more challenging and is usually carried out by a taste guided HPLC (High Performance Liquid Chromatography) fractionation.

As soon as unknown compounds with a high flavour impact are observed in a chromatogram the material has to be isolated from the natural source material and the chemical structure elucidated, usually by NMR (Nuclear Magnetic Resonance Spectrometer). Once the structure has been identified the flavour effect is confirmed by a synthesized version of the same molecule. This approach is valid for the creation of flavour solutions for a whole range of applications, such as sweet and savoury flavours, but also for dairy applications, soft drinks and distilled spirits.

This approach has been applied to different types of distilled spirits with a focus on whiskies. A cluster analysis has been carried out to evaluate how well analytical results correspond with sensorial similarities between different types of distilled spirits and within the class of whiskies (González-Arjona, López-Pérez, González-Gallero and González, 2006). The same exercise has been applied to a set of vodka samples. In this case, the sensorial variations could be linked to the content and distribution of minerals.

Materials and methods

The following samples have been investigated: Talisker (10 years old), Caol Ila (12 years old), Johnnie Walker (Red Label), 100 Pipers Scotch Whisky, Laphroaig (10 years), Lagavulin (16 years), Highland Park (12 years), Frontier (Bourbon whiskey), Regency Brandy from Thailand, Hennessy Cognac VSOP and Viceroy Brandy. Furthermore the following vodkas were purchased: Ketel One, Grey Goose, Russian Standard, Belvedere and Finlandia. The investigated distilled spirit samples were commercially available in retail stores in the Netherlands. The only exception to this was the Regency Brandy from Thailand which was obtained via colleagues from Bangkok.

Samples were prepared for GC analysis using two methods in parallel: a) by concentration with SPE (solid phase extraction) and subsequent elution with dichloromethane and b) by dilution with methanol. GC olfactometry was carried out by an experienced flavourist. Cations were determined in the vodka samples by ICP-OES analysis. Statistical evaluation of the data was carried out with OPUS software (Bruker Optics, Ettlingen, Germany). Data have been evaluated regarding the heterogeneity of classes using a Ward's algorithm without any further data pre-treatment. Furthermore a PCA (principle component analysis) has been carried out. The 30 most varying chromatographic peaks were taken into account. A maximum of 4 principle components was considered. The odour activity values of flavour compounds were determined by dilution series. These values were recalculated for the typical environment of a distilled spirit by proprietary software.

Results and discussion

Whiskies and brandies

All whisky and brandy samples were pre-treated in the same way. The very polar principal compounds were measured after direct injection of a sample diluted in methanol. For the less polar compounds including trace compounds the data were obtained by solid phase extraction followed by elution with DCM. This is because the polar compounds are underestimated by the SPE approach.

Routinely in a GC-MS run 419 compounds are determined. In the investigated whisky and brandy samples 239 different compounds could be identified. Figure 1 shows all data displayed for the above mentioned sample set. The 239 components are numbered in ascending order.

To the whole dataset a Ward's algorithm was applied to cluster groups according to their heterogeneity. By doing this, samples which are close to each other show low heterogeneity values and form a group. The resulting dendrogram is displayed in Figure 2.

According to this evaluation, the 100 Pipers and Johnnie Walker samples form a group. The Scotch Whiskies are all close to each other. Only

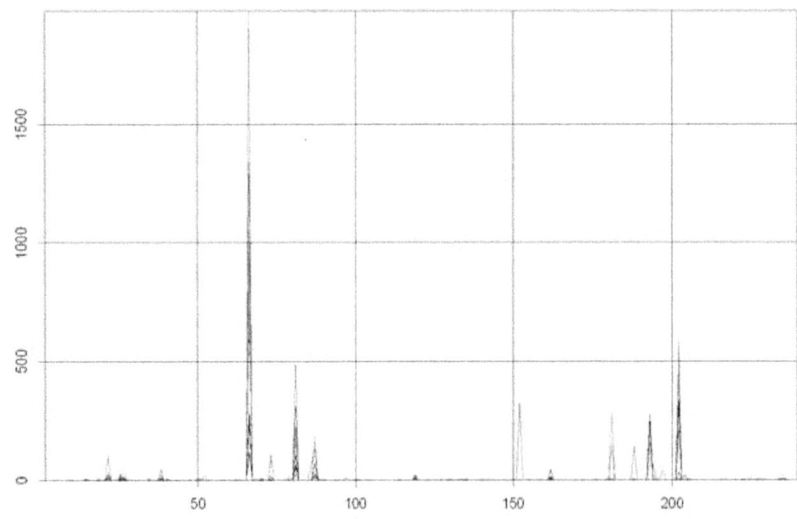

Figure 1. Distribution of 239 compounds in 11 different distilled spirits

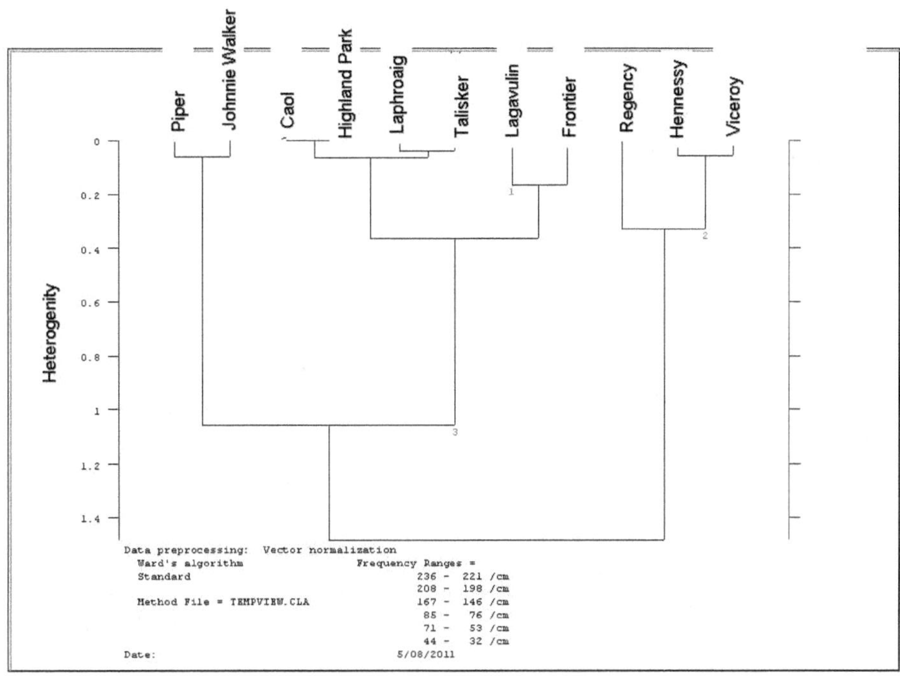

Figure 2. Dendrogram based on the GC-MS data of 11 distilled spirits

the Lagavulin shows some similarities to the Frontier Bourbon. Within the group of brandies the Regency shows the strongest deviation. In a similar way, the data form clusters when a principle component analysis is carried out after a vector normalization of the data (see Figure 3).

It can be clearly observed in the PCA plot of factor 2 versus factor 1 that the blended Whiskeys, the 100 Pipers and the Johnnie Walker, fall close to each other. The single malt Scotch Whiskies form 2 groups. The Frontier is now located somewhere between the single malt

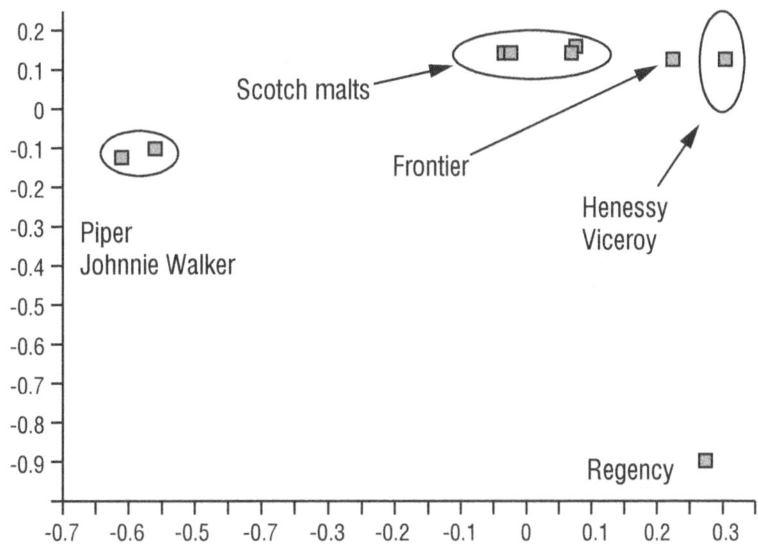

Figure 3. PCA analysis score plot (Score 2 versus 1) of 11 distilled spirits.

Scotch Whiskies and the Cognac/ Brandy group. Only the Regency Brandy shows an extremely strong deviation. Looking at the values which are responsible for this outlier, the deviation can be assigned to a considerable amount of propylene glycol.

Within the cluster of single malt Scotch Whiskies, 2 sub clusters are formed. This is mainly related to the concentration of phenolic (peaty, smoky) compounds, the concentration of ethyl esters, ethyl acetyls and iso-amyl alcohol. The next step was a GC-O/MS evaluation of a single malt whisky to clearly assign the compounds with the strongest impact.

Figure 4 illustrates the principle setup. At the end of the GC column the carrier gas stream is split by a ratio of 70: 30 to a nose interface and to a MS detector, respectively. In this way the 2 GC traces are measured in parallel.

Figure 5 illustrates the detection traces of the chromatographic run, one is the total ion current of the mass spectrometer, the other one is the push button signal of the flavourist. Whenever the flavourist perceives an effect, he/ she pushes the button of a counter and provides a corresponding aroma description into a voice recorder.

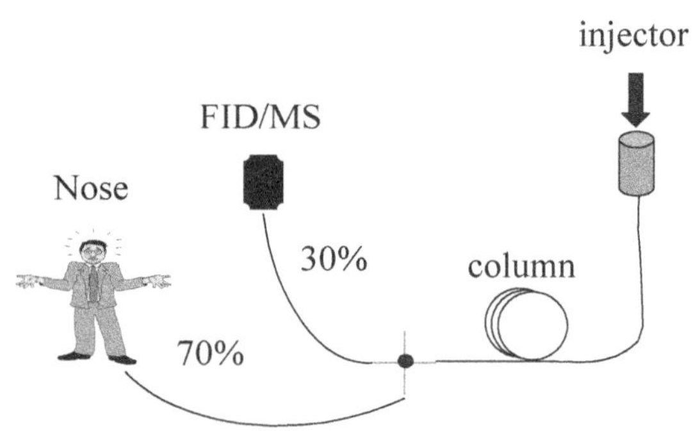

Figure 4. Principle setup of the GC-O/MS system used for the analysis of distilled spirits

Together with the aroma description of each recognized peak this gives a clear picture of the strong aroma contributors of a whisky, 46 compounds out of 239 contributed significantly to the overall aroma profile. Based on these data, a reconstitution of the distilled spirit could be prepared by using single flavour ingredients.

Vodka analysis

A similar approach has been applied to a set of high quality vodka samples. In this case almost no

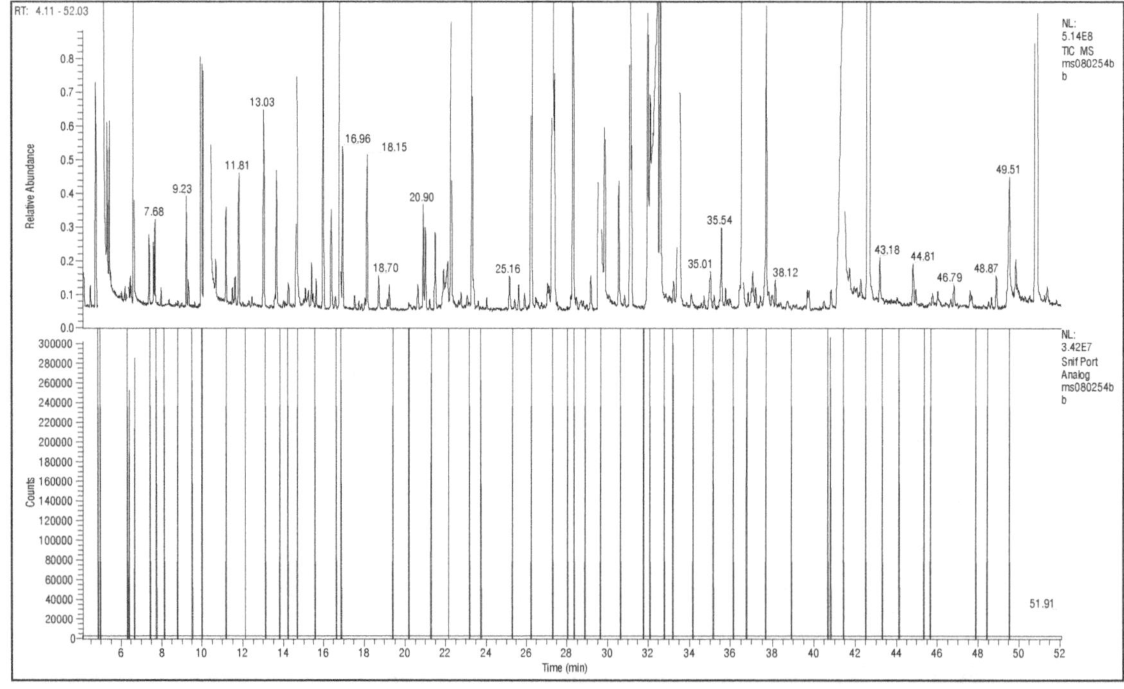

Figure 5. GC-MS and GC-O push button signal obtained for a single malt Scotch

volatiles could be observed. Whereas for whiskies and brandies the concentration is given in parts per million, here only traces of volatiles at the low parts per billion level could be found (see Table 1). Only one vodka shows additional signals, but these compounds are due to sugar breakdown products. Obviously some sugar was added to this brand. Basically vodka consists of ethanol and water. The question in this case was why some vodka brands tend to be smoother than others. Smoothness, in this context, means that the irritating effect of ethanol is less perceivable. Also non-volatile organic compounds could not be identified in considerable amounts, except the sugar. High volumes of vodka (4 L each) have been distilled to quantify and identify the dry residues (Table 2). These analytical results show that the only difference between these samples can be assigned to the minerals introduced by the water (Table 3). Smoothness was rated by a panel of 5 as followed: Finlandia > Grey Goose = Belvedere > Russian Standard = Ketel One.

These findings hint at the fact that a high calcium and a low sodium concentration of the water might be beneficial for the smoothness of a vodka. The addition of sugar does not show any positive effects on the smoothness.

Conclusions

Matching an authentic flavour profile requires considerable efforts to quantitatively analyse

Table 1. Volatiles in 5 Vodka brands, only trace levels can be identified

Name	*ppb*	*ppb*	*ppb*	*ppb*	*ppb*
Formic acid		trace			
Glycol aldehyde			65		
Acetic acid	6	32	69	295	17
Acetol			180		
Furan		4			
Gualacol		2			
Alpha-hydroxy-gamma-butyrolactone			48		
Nor-furaneol			440		
5-hydroxy-5, 6-dihydromaltol			3110		
5-(hydroxymethyl)-2-furfural			18888		
5-(acetoxymethyl)-2-furfural			56		

Table 2. Dry matter content of 5 Vodka brands

	Ketel one	*Grey Goose*	*Russian standard*	*Belvedere*	*Finlandia*
Name	%	%	%	%	%
Dry matter	0.00058	0.00055	0.043	0.00035	0.00093

Table 3. Dry matter content and concentration of cations in 5 Vodka brands

	Ketel one	*Grey Goose*	*Russian standard*	*Belvedere*	*Finlandia*
Name	*ug/L*	*ug/L*	*ug/L*	*ug/L*	*ug/L*
Aluminium	25	5	13	30	8
Calcium	213	583	124	201	2230
Magnesium	11	37	19	19	840
Potassium	17	26	66	201	650
Sodium	1510	1330	5890	1040	1760
Copper	<1	3	2	5	<1
Barium	<1	13	5	4	1
Zinc	<1	<1	5	4	<1
Iron	<1	<1	2	2	<1

original food sources for aromatic, taste and irritant compounds. Only an in-depth understanding of the contribution of a single flavour component to the overall profile allows us to reduce the complexity of a flavour mixture. In the case of whiskies and brandies the concentration of iso-amyl alcohol, a set of ethyl esters, as well as phenols and cresols determined how products were grouped using cluster formation. In the case of vodkas, the analysis of the concentration of volatiles did not correlate with the sensorial properties of interest, basically because of their absence. Also non-volatile organic compounds could not be identified. The only difference from an analytical point of view could be assigned to the content and distribution of minerals.

References

González-Arjona, D., López-Pérez, G., González-Gallero V. and González, A.G. (2006), Supervised Pattern Recognition Procedures for Discrimination of Whiskeys from Gas Chromatography/ Mass Spectrometry Congener Analysis. *J. Agric. Food Chem.* **54**: 1982-1989

Chapter 23

The impact of increased wash fatty acid levels on the nutty/cereal aroma volatile composition of new make malt spirit

E. L. Boothroyd[1], F. Jack[2], B. Harrison[2] and D. J. Cook[1],
[1] *University of Nottingham, Division of Food Sciences, Sutton Bonington Campus, LE12 5RD;* [2] *The Scotch Whisky Research Institute, The Robertson Trust Building, Research Avenue North, Riccarton, Edinburgh, EH14 4AP*

Introduction

Relatively little is known about the origins of the nutty/cereal flavour character in new make whisky spirit. Sensory profiling of a range of whiskies found that nutty, malty or buttery flavours were associated with a deluxe spirit (Lee, Paterson, Piggott and Richardson, 2001), emphasizing the potential commercial significance of these attributes. Flavour consistency is an important consumer quality attribute of premium products such as malt whisky. Improved understanding of the origins of flavour congeners which together impart nutty or cereal characters should help improve the industry's ability to control these characters during manufacture.

It has been suggested anecdotally that a cloudy or turbid wash helps to impart a nutty character to new make spirit (Lindsay, 2009). Differences in milling and mashing practices between distilleries will affect the turbidity of the mash. For example a finely ground grist would tend to increase wash turbidity, whereas use of a membrane mash filter (rather than a mash or lauter tun) will produce a clearer, brighter wash. The amount of solids or particulate matter such as grain or lipid sent forward to the wash still, is highly likely to influence product quality. During distillation a range of thermally induced chemical reactions take place which impact upon the volatile composition of the distillate. These include Maillard reaction chemistry (initiated by the reaction between a reducing sugar and an amino compound), lipid oxidation and the myriad of interactions which occur between the precursors and products of both (Farmer and Mottram, 1994; Hidalgo and Zamora, 2004).

Volatile aroma products of the Maillard reaction are known to impart nutty/cereal characters in other food/ beverage systems. For example, heterocyclic nitrogen compounds such as pyrroles, pyrazines and pyridines have been found to exhibit nutty aroma in malt (Tressl, Bahri and Helak, 1983) roasted cocoa (Bonvehi, 2005) and Chinese liquors (Fan, Xu and Zhang, 2007). Strecker degradation of amino acids gives rise to Strecker aldehydes, such as 2-methylpropanal, 2-methylbutanal and 3-methybutanal, which have been shown to contribute to the perceived nuttiness in cheddar cheeses (Avsar *et al.*, 2004). Unsaturated fatty acids also undergo major effects when heated, forming secondary carbonyl products such as aldehydes and ketones (Lingnert, Eriksson and Waller, 1983). These secondary lipid oxidation products are often characterised by low aroma thresholds, therefore their formation, even in small amounts, is likely to impact on the overall aroma of the spirit (Belitz, Grosch and Schieberle, 2009; Farmer and Mottram, 1994).

In distillation research, the products of the Maillard reaction have been shown to be highly dependent on temperature. Triangle tests of spirits which were distilled under reflux at different temperatures revealed that with each 20 °C increase in temperature there was a significant increase in heavy, cereal, sulfury notes perceived (Jack *et al.,* 2008).

The research reported here was designed to investigate the impacts of wash fatty acid content and of wash still distillation temperature on the chemical composition and sensory characteristics of new make spirits, with particular focus on the nutty/cereal flavour characters thought to be influenced by Maillard and lipid oxidation chemistry.

Methods

Analysis of the fatty acid profile of fermented wash

Fermented wash (10 mL) sourced from a Scotch whisky distillery was exhaustively extracted into dichloromethane (DCM)/methanol (2:1), concentrated under a stream of nitrogen gas and made up to a final volume of 1 mL in DCM. Internal standards (methyl tridecanoate and glyceryl triheptadecanoate) were added and the extracts were subsequently methylated using Trimethylsulfonium hydroxide (TMSH) reagent and quantified by GC-MS of the Fatty Acid Methyl Esters (FAMEs).

Experimental design to investigate the flavour impacts of changing wash fatty acid levels and of wash distillation temperature

To determine the gross impacts of higher wash lipid levels on the sensory character of new make spirit, a comparison was made between distillates prepared from the control wash (as sourced) and wash which had been spiked with an additional 100 μg/mL of both oleic and linoleic acids.

Further to this, a designed experiment was constructed to test the impacts of more subtle variations in wash lipid composition and also of distillation temperature on the volatile flavour profiles of the resulting spirit samples. Design Expert v 8.0, (Stat-Ease, Mn, USA) was used to create a design yielding 18 experimental distillates varying in respect of spiked linoleic/oleic acids (to give samples containing between 1-8 times the analysed concentrations of oleic and linoleic acids in fermented wash) and distillation temperature (2 levels – either the control still temperature or a higher temperature setting; Table 1.).

Laboratory scale distillations

Wash samples (1.65 L) were double distilled using miniature copper wash and spirit stills (2L and 1L capacity respectively) with copper shell and tube condensers, cooled with glycol to 5 °C. The temperature of the wash still mantle was set at two levels: the control and a higher setting. To represent this difference in heat input, temperature was measured at the outer side of the still using a thermocouple sensor. Average time/temperature data for distillations conducted under these two conditions were as recorded in Table 1.

Sensory evaluation

The resulting distillates were submitted for sensory evaluation by the Scotch Whisky Research Institute (SWRI) trained Sensory Panel (n = 16) using Quantitative Descriptive Analysis to rate 13 key new make spirit aroma characteristics. Samples were blind coded and diluted to 20% abv prior to assessment.

Table 1. Average wash still temperatures and their durations during distillation.

	Control Temperature			*Higher Temperature*		
Timings (mins)						
Time at which low wines collection started (t_1)	41.2	±	0.7	34.6	±	2.3
Time at which low wines collection ended (t_2)	119.8	±	2.5	97	±	1.8
Total time of collection for low wines (t_2-t_1)	78.6	±	2.3	62.4	±	1.3
Distillation rate (ml/min)	7	±	0.2	8.8	±	0.2
Temperatures (°C)						
Temperature of still before mantle switched on (T_0)	23.8	±	0.9	24.3	±	0.7
Temperature at which low wines collection started (T_1)	102.2	±	1.9	105.1	±	2.9
Temperature at which low wines collection ended (T_2)	109.7	±	1.7	112.9	±	3.7
Maximum temperature reached during distillation (T_{max})	110.1	±	2.1	113.4	±	4.3

Extraction and analysis of distillate aroma volatiles

Solid Phase Extraction (SPE) cartridges (LiChrolut EN; Merck) were used to adsorb and fractionate volatile compounds from the distillate samples. The fraction eluted from LiChrolut EN cartridges using DCM was concentrated by evaporation under a stream of nitrogen and analysed by GC-O-MS. Panellists sniffing at the GC odour port (n = 7) generated descriptors for any odours perceived, whilst noting the chromatographic run-time and rating each odour intensity on a scale from 1 to 3 (1 = weak, 2 = clear but not intense, 3 = intense). Subsequently GC-O peak assignments were made on the basis of a combination of mass spectral library matching (NIST), comparison of Kovat's linear retention indices (LRI) with prior published data, the odour character reported by the panel in a particular chromatogram region, and wherever possible by chromatographic similarity with authentic standards.

Results and discussion

The predominant fatty acids in fermented wash were analysed as oleic (5 μg/mL) and linoleic (7 μg/mL) acids.

Sensory evaluation of distillates

In order to ascertain the impacts of the investigated variables on the perceived sensory characteristics of new make spirit, Quantitative Descriptive Analysis (QDA) was employed. Intensity scores generated by the panellists for each selected attribute were averaged and ANOVA carried out to test for significant differences between sample treatments. The extreme effect of increasing wash fatty acid concentrations can be seen by comparing spider plots of the mean QDA data between the control and maximum added lipid concentration (Figure 1).

The lipid spiked spirit was scored as significantly higher than the control for both nutty ($p = 0.0203$) and oily ($p = 0.0034$) aroma characters. This supports the hypothesis that a higher level of lipid in the wash produces spirit richer in these characteristics. Whilst perception of some aroma characters (solventy, floral, green, sweet, sulfury) was clearly unaffected by the addition of 100 μg/mL linoleic and oleic acids to the wash, there were (non-significant) trends towards increasing soapy, feinty, cereal, sour and buttery notes with this high level of added unsaturated fatty acids. When the 18 distillates prepared for the designed experiment (varying both fatty acid concentration and wash still temperature) were evaluated sensorially,

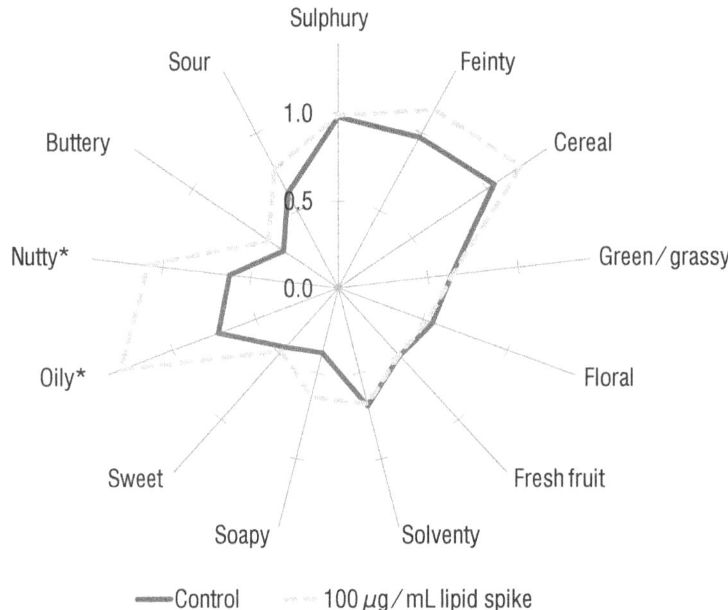

Figure 1. Sensory spider plots comparing the mean perceived flavour profile of the control distillate as compared to the distillate resulting when wash was spiked with 100 μg/mL of both oleic and linoleic acids. *denotes a significant difference in mean sensory scores ($p < 0.05$).

similar trends were observed in the spider plots as illustrated in Figure 1. However, perhaps because of the lower amounts of oleic and linoleic acids added in these experiments, the increase in mean sensory scores for nutty/oily aromas did not reach significance ($p > 0.05$).

Gas Chromatography-Olfactometry

Extracts of all spirit samples were submitted for GC-O analysis. Regions of the chromatograms associated with nutty/cereal/oily aroma descriptors were identified (Table 2). In order to give an indication of the impact of higher concentrations of wash fatty acids on these flavour attributes, the perceived intensity scores awarded by each panellist to the relevant odour active areas of the chromatogram were summed for each sample treatment. The data in Table 2 specifically compare GC-O analysis of the control (fermented wash as sourced) and maximum lipid spike (100 μg/mL of oleic and linoleic acids) distillates. Similar odour active regions were in general also observed at varying intensities in the 18 samples of the designed experiment, but comparison of the 'top and bottom' samples facilitates an easier analysis of the impacts of increased wash fatty acid concentrations.

From the data in Table 2 it is apparent that the odour-active areas with nutty, cereal or oily descriptors were in general scored as more intensely perceived in the lipid spiked sample as compared to the unspiked control. This is consistent with the sensory data for nosing of the distillates (Figure 1).

The carbonyl compounds (E,E)-2,4-heptadienal, (E,E)-2,4-decadien-1-al and 1-octen-3-one are all known to arise as a direct result of lipid oxidation, and in particular the oxidation of linoleic acid (Belitz, Grosch and Schieberle, 2009). The amount of 1-octen-3-one in the final spirit showed a significant positive correlation with the addition of fatty acids to the wash (Table 3) which gives further weight to this hypothesis. A compound well known for its 'nutty/popcorn' aroma is 2-acetylpyrroline (Schieberle, 1991). All three panellists that were able to perceive this aroma awarded it a maximum intensity score,

Table 2. Odour-active areas of the chromatogram which may contribute to nutty/oily aroma character.

#	*LRI*	*GC-O descriptors*	*Compound identity*	*Sum of intensity scores**		*ID confirmed by*
				Control	*Spiked*	
1	1000	butter, caramel	2,3-butanedione	11	14	LRI, odour
2	1325	mushroom, earthy, raw vegetable, cereal	1-octen-3-one	9	12	LRI, odour
3	1370	nutty, malty, musty, nuts/ popcorn/savoury	2-acetylpyrroline	9	9	LRI, odour
4	1421	musty, nut, caramel, meaty sulfur	oct-1-en-3-ol	6	7	LRI, odour
5	1462	peaty, walnut, compost, shoes, savoury, vegetables, plastic, musty earthy, green	(E,E)-2,4-heptadienal	18.5	19	LRI, odour
6	1496	malty, savoury, baked, oaty, roast potatoes, oily	furfural	15	18	LRI, odour, MS
7	1536	raw nut, snickers, green vegetable, earthy, nutty	not identified	4	6	n/a
8	1625	green, caramel, meaty	5-methylfurfural	np	5	LRI, odour, MS
9	1710	beefy, musty, bovril, yeast extract, meaty, savoury, nutty, earthy, old socks	not identified	17	17	n/a
10	1748	seafood, caramel, malty, oily, aldehyde	not identified	np	11	n/a
11	1762	chlorine, chips, cooked	not identified	np	6	n/a
12	1817	musty, leather, nutty, cooked, crispy, pyrazine	(E,E)-2,4-decadien-1-al	6	9	LRI, odour

Areas of the chromatogram were considered odour-active when 3 or more panellists (out of 7) detected an odour.

*The sum of intensity scores given by panellists describing corresponding attributes in the same region, within 0.05 seconds of one another.

np = the odour was not perceived by panellists in the corresponding region of the chromatogram.

which is indicative of its low aroma threshold (reported to be as low as 0.01 ppb in cooked rice (Buttery, Turnbaugh and Ling, 1988). It is perhaps surprising that certain panellists did not record the odour at all, although with GC-O work this can relate to the ability of the panellist to note and record changing aromas individually in busy regions of a chromatogram.

Quantitative analysis of extracted compounds

Chromatogram peak areas were integrated and expressed relative to that of the internal standard for all distillate samples. Concentrations were modelled against the factors 'wash fatty acid concentration' and 'distillation temperature'. Table 3 lists compounds for which there was a significant effect of either or both factors, as well as indicating the direction of the effects. For example, 1-octen-3-one, which was associated with mushroom, earthy, raw vegetable/cereal characters (Table 2) increased significantly in concentration with the addition of oleic/linoleic acids to the wash.

Furfural levels were reduced as the wash still temperature increased ($p < 0.0001$, Table 3). Since the mean temperature difference between

Table 3. Compounds whose concentrations in new make spirit were significantly impacted upon by the factors: wash fatty acid concentration and wash still temperature.

Compound name	*Significant factor(s)*	*p-value*	*Optimum condition for formation*	*Identity confirmed by*	*LRI*
ethyl hexanoate	Wash fatty acids & distillation temperature*	0.0041	high fatty acids, low temperature	LRI, MS, odour	1260
1-octen-3-one	Wash fatty acids	0.0318	high fatty acids	LRI, MS, odour	1325
furfural	Distillation temperature	<0.0001	low temperature	LRI, MS, odour	1496
ethyl decanoate	Wash fatty acids & distillation temperature*	0.0449	high fatty acids, low temperature	MS	n/a
diethyl butanedioate	Wash fatty acids & distillation temperature*	0.0051	high fatty acids, low temperature	MS	n/a

Quantification was by comparison with an internal standard (3-heptanone).
A p-value of < 0.05 indicates that the specified factor had a significant impact on concentrations of this compound in distillates across the 18 sample design space.
*the significant factor in each case was the interaction term between wash fatty acid level and distillation temperature.

the two wash still temperature settings was only of the order of 3°C (Table 1), it is unlikely that the difference in distillate furfural concentration would relate to a direct impact of temperature on furfural formation pathways. More likely it relates to changes in the rate and cut-points of distillation at the different temperature control settings. On average, the rate of distillation of the low wines distilled at the higher mantle setting increased by 1.8 mL/min as compared with the lower 'control' setting (Table 1). Thus, at the higher still temperature setting, distillation process times to collect the specified volume of low wines were shorter, allowing less time for reactions catalysed by copper still surfaces. This would be anticipated to impact upon the volatile composition of the spirit as is evident from the significant effect of still temperature setting on the concentrations of several volatile compounds listed in Table 3.

2-acetylpyrroline was a compound which was clearly associated with a nutty/popcorn-like character in GC-O studies. However, whilst detectable by the human nose due to its low odour threshold, as already noted, the SPE extraction coupled with Total Ion Chromatogram (TIC) GC-MS analysis were not sensitive enough to quantify 2-acetylpyrroline. Hence correlations with lipid concentrations or still temperature could not be sought for this compound.

Conclusions

Spiking oleic and linoleic acids into the wash at concentrations of 100 μg/mL each was shown to significantly increase the perceived nutty/oily aroma characteristics of new make malt spirit. These findings are consistent with the hypothesis that increasing levels of lipid in the fermented wash results in a spirit which is perceived to be significantly richer in nutty and oily characters. Furthermore, GC-O was used to identify the congeners which potentially contribute to these characters. Some of these congeners (e.g. 1-octen-3-one) were found to increase in concentration as a result of adding oleic/ linoleic acids to the wash. The nutty/cereal flavor character of whisky appears to be of complex origins, which is perhaps not surprising, bearing in mind its likely origins in Maillard chemistry and the evident interactions with fatty acid concentrations.

References

Avsar, Y. K., Karagul-Yuceer, Y., Drake, M. A., Singh, T. K., Yoon, Y. and Cadwallader, K. R. (2004). Characterization of nutty flavor in Cheddar cheese. *Journal of Dairy Science* **87**(7): 1999-2010

Belitz, H.-D., W. Grosch and Schieberle, P. (2004). Lipids. *Food Chemistry*. Berlin, Springer: 157-245.

Bonvehi, J. (2005). Investigation of aromatic compounds in roasted cocoa powder. *European Food Research and Technology* **221**(1-2): 19-29.

Buttery, R.G., Turnbaugh, J.G. and Ling, L.C. (1988). Contribution of volatiles to rice aroma. *J. Agric. Food Chem.*, **36**(5): 1006-1009

Fan, W. L., Xu Y., and Zhang, Y. H. (2007). Characterization of pyrazines in some Chinese liquors and their approximate concentrations. *Journal of Agricultural and Food Chemistry* **55**(24): 9956-9962.

Farmer, L. J. and D. S. Mottram (1994). Lipid-Maillard interactions in the formation of volatile aroma compounds. *Trends in Flavour Research*. H. Maarse and D. G. van der Heij. Amsterdam, Elsevier: 313-326.

Hidalgo, F. J. and R. Zamora (2004). Strecker-type Degradation Produced by the Lipid Oxidation Products 4,5-Epoxy-2-Alkenals. *Journal of Agricultural and Food Chemistry* **52**(23): 7126-7131.

Jack, F. R., Brosnan, J. M., Campbell, K. A., Fagnen, O., Fotheringham, R. N. and Goodall, I. C. (2008). Sensory Implications of Modifying Distillation Practice. *Worldwide Distilled Spirits Conference: Production, Technology and Innovation*. Nottingham University Press: 205-211.

Lee, K. Y. M., Paterson A., Piggott J. R., Richardson G. D. (2001). Sensory discrimination of blended Scotch whiskies of different product categories. *Food Quality and Preference* **12**(2): 109-117.

Lindsay, R. (2009). Focus on Fermentation Factors: The Scotch Whisky Wash from a Brewer's Viewpoint. *Brewer & Distiller International.*

Lingnert, H., Eriksson C. E. & Waller, G.R. (1983). Characterization of Antioxidative Maillard Reaction Products from Histidine and Glucose. *The Maillard Reaction in Foods and Nutrition*. G. R. Waller and M. S. Feather. Washington, D.C., American Chemical Society.

Schieberle, P. (1991). Primary odorants in popcorn. *Journal of Agricultural and Food Chemistry* **39**(6): 1141-1144.

Tressl, R., Bahri, D., and Helak, B. (1983). Flavours of Malt and other Cereals. *Flavour of Distilled Beverages Origin and Development*. J. R. Piggott. Chichester, Ellis Horwood: 9-32.

Chapter 24

Understanding the aroma of gin: a Gas Chromatography-Olfactometry approach

P. Dussort[1,2], N. Deprêtre[1], E. Bou-Maroun[1], P. Brunerie[2], E. Guichard[1], C. Fant[3], Y. Le Fur[1], J.-L Le Quéré[1]

[1]Centre des Sciences du Goût et de l'Alimentation, UMR 6265 CNRS, UMR 1324 INRA, Université de Bourgogne, AgroSup Dijon, 17 rue Sully F-21000 Dijon; [2]Centre de Recherche Pernod Ricard, 120 av. Maréchal Foch, 94015 Créteil; [3]Agrosup Dijon, 26 boulevard Petitjean BP 87999 21079 - DIJON cedex

Introduction

Gin is a distilled spirit obtained by the aromatisation of ethyl alcohol with flavouring substances/preparations such that the dominant flavour is juniper ((EC) No 110/2008 of the European Parliament and of the Council of 15 January 2008). As long as this condition is fulfilled, distillers can add ingredients, such as coriander or orange and use different distillation parameters in order to create a unique gin with its own typicity.

Even though sensory tests have shown aromatic differences between gins from different origins (Riu-Aumatell et al., 2008), only a few studies have focused on the analysis of the gin volatile fraction (Clutton and Evans, 1978; Guerra-Hernandez, 2003; Vichi et al., 2005; Vichi et al., 2008). Different extraction procedures were used for these studies, from liquid-liquid extraction (Clutton and Evans, 1978; Guerra-Hernandez, 2003) to solid-phase micro-extraction (Vichi et al., 2005; Vichi et al., 2008). The identification of the isolated compounds by Gas-Chromatography Mass-Spectrometry (GC-MS) showed that the volatile fraction is mostly composed of mono or sesqui-terpenoids (Clutton and Evans, 1978; Guerra-Hernandez, 2003; Vichi et al., 2005; Vichi et al., 2008).

Although it has been shown that less than 5% of volatile compounds actually influence the perception of the aroma (Grosch, 2001), no study has ever focused on these key aroma compounds in gin. This work has previously been performed on other alcoholic products, such as wine (Ferreira, Ortega, Escudero and Cacho., 2002 ; Lorrain et al., 2006, Sarrazin, Dubourdieu and Darriet, 2007 ; Noguerol-Pato, González-Barreiro, Cancho-Grande and Simal-Gándara., 2009 ; Barata et al., 2011) or spirits and liquors (Ferrari et al., 2005; Fan and Qian, 2005 ; de Souza et al., 2006 ; Poisson and Schieberle, 2008). For several years Gas-Chromatography Olfactometry (GC-O) has become a necessary step in identifying the key aroma compounds in food products (Van Ruth, 2001; Delahunty, Eyres and Dufour, 2006) and in alcoholic beverages (Plutowska and Wardencki, 2008). Among the several strategies that exist for GC-O, the detection frequency procedure (Linssen, Janssens, Roozen and Posthumus, 1993; Pollien et al., 1997) has been shown to be fast, repeatable and to correlate with the intensity of the compounds (Van Ruth, 2001, Plutowska and Wardencki, 2008).

The aim of our study was to identify the potential key aroma compounds of gin. For this purpose we used GC-O with the detection frequency procedure on two commercial gins of different origins.

Material and methods

Gin samples

We used two commercial gins for our study, one from the "London dry gin" type and the other from the "Distilled gin" type, as described by the Regulation (EC) No 110/2008. Three bottles of each were tested in GC-MS in order to validate their robustness. A mixture of two bottles of each was used for the extraction procedure.

Liquid-liquid extraction conditions

The extraction procedures used for gin analysis are multiple (Clutton and Evans, 1978; Guerra-Hernandez, 2003; Vichi et al., 2005). This is also true for other alcoholic beverages. Solid Phase Micro Extraction (SPME) has been used for the analysis whisky (Camara et al., 2007), cachaça (Cardeal and Marriot, 2009), brandies (Zhao et al., 2009); Liquid-Liquid Extraction (LLE) with dichloromethane has been used for Cognac (Ferrari et al., 2005; Ledauphin et al., 2004), Calvados (Ledauphin et al., 2004): LLE with diethyl-ether, hexane or pentane for calvados (Guichard et al., 2003), moutai (Zhu et al., 2007) or whisky (Poisson and Schieberle, 2008). Several studies showed that a LLE using dichloromethane gave the best results on alcoholic beverages (Riu-Aumatell et al., 2008 ; Caldeira et al., 2007), hydro-alcoholic systems (Ferreira et al., 2000), wine vinegar (Charles et al., 2000) and for monoterpenes extraction (Lopez, Aznar, Cacho and Ferreira, 2002). For these reasons we decided to use a LLE with dichloromethane. Two hundred millilitres of gin was mixed with 200ml of ultra pure water and 20 g of sodium chloride in a 500mL flask. Thirty millilitres of dichloromethane was then added and the mixture was stirred magnetically for 5 min. The two layers were separated in a 500mL separating funnel. The organic layer was dried on magnesium sulphate. After filtration on deactivated glass wool, extracts were concentrated to 1mL and to 250μL using a Kuderna-Danish apparatus. The concentrated extracts were then stored at -18 °C prior to analysis.

GC-O analysis

Detection Frequency was used to identify the potential key aroma compounds of gin extracts.

We used a Hewlett-Packard 5890 gas chromatograph equipped with a 30m, 0,320 μm, 0.5μm fused silica capillary column (DB-5-MS).

One micro-litter of each extract was injected into the GCO in splitless mode. The injector was held at 225°C. The GCO was held at 40 °C for 3 minutes following sample injection, then the temperature increased at 3 °C/min to 250 °C and held at 250°C for 10 minutes. Both FID and Olfactometric detectors were held at 225°C. Helium with a velocity of 32cm/s constant flow mode was used as a carrier gas. Humidified air was used to prevent dehydration of the nasal mucosa.

The extracts were sniffed in duplicate by a panel composed of 10 untrained assessors (5 males, 5 females), with prior experience in GC-O. They were asked to push a button as soon as they perceived an odour and to release it immediately. In addition, they gave a descriptor of the perceived odour as precise as possible. As a full run lasted one hour, it was divided into two 30 minute sessions in order to prevent the assessors from becoming tired.

The data were recorded with the Aquisniff® software. They have been analysed and regrouped into Odorant Areas (OA) by our home designed software (Blanquet, AgrosupDijon).

Statistical analysis

In order to discriminate the OA, a non parametric Wilcoxon test for p values of <0.05 was used with the StatXact ® software.

Results and discussion

Frequency detection analysis

The 10 assessors sniffed the extract of the two gins at the two concentrations and in duplicate. During the 80 GC-O runs, 2589 buzzes were generated by the assessors, which corresponded to an average of 32 buzzes per run. To each buzz was associated a Linear Retention Indice (LRI) and the descriptor given by the assessor. The buzzes were then regrouped by our home-designed software (Blanquet, AgrosupDijon) into 209 Odorant Areas. An OA was thus composed of buzzes with close LRI. In order to discard the OA corresponding to noise, a threshold of 25% was used (Ballester, 2004). Therefore, only the OA perceived at least 5 times for each extract were retained. Sixty-one OA were above this threshold (table 1).

A non parametric Wilcoxon test was conducted on these data in order to characterise the potential differences between the two products at each concentration of the extract. Over the two concentrations, twenty-four areas appeared to be significantly different between the two products (table 2). Fourteen showed higher intensity for the gin A and 10 for the gin B.

Table 1. Results of the detection frequency analysis: Number of buzzes per extract for each OA above the threshold

OA number	*A 1000µl*	*A 250µl*	*B 1000 µl*	*B 250 µl*	*OA number*	*A 1000µl*	*A 1000µl*	*B 1000µl*	*B 250µl*
3	4	3	0	5	69	6	9	3	2
8	4	4	5	5	71	31	44	14	16
9	3	2	5	1	72	11	19	15	14
10	2	5	2	5	73	10	18	7	7
13	11	12	16	19	74	1	2	1	9
17	7	9	9	11	75	7	8	4	4
19	14	22	17	13	76	1	2	3	5
22	2	2	7	10	79	4	7	4	5
23	2	1	6	1	80	4	14	13	23
24	9	19	5	6	81	3	2	13	19
28	7	14	15	16	82	7	9	3	2
29	3	6	2	6	86	4	9	2	6
33	4	5	1	5	88	2	10	0	0
38	5	4	4	7	92	6	18	13	23
43	17	18	20	18	93	6	15	4	6
44	11	6	3	6	94	2	0	5	0
48	12	23	4	10	97	7	15	4	4
49	22	27	18	23	99	6	8	0	4
50	5	7	11	18	100	7	18	10	14
53	0	1	2	5	101	3	5	6	9
54	9	23	17	29	102	0	5	0	0
55	7	7	5	3	105	1	0	2	12
56	9	9	8	17	106	1	0	4	6
58	5	8	1	0	115	2	6	5	3
59	7	16	11	21	117	10	8	5	4
60	5	14	1	4	120	1	1	3	7
61	24	37	32	44	123	5	4	7	13
62	6	12	5	9	125	4	5	0	0
63	5	9	5	5	126	1	6	3	0
65	6	2	7	14	133	1	5	2	3

Among the 61 selected OA, 37 are thus common to the two products and could correspond to compounds composing a "gin base". Gin A and gin B could gain their typicity respectively from the 14 and the 10 compounds perceived more intensely.

Table 2. Results of the Wilcoxon test for the comparison of the GC-O results.

OA number	*A vs B*	*OA number*	*A vs B*
3	A	69	ns
8	ns	71	A
9	ns	72	ns
10	ns	73	ns
13	B	74	ns
17	ns	75	ns
19	A	76	ns
22	ns	79	ns
23	ns	80	ns
24	A	81	B
28	B	82	ns
29	ns	86	ns
33	ns	88	A
38	ns	92	ns
43	ns	93	A
44	ns	94	ns
48	A	97	ns
49	A	99	A
50	B	100	ns
53	ns	101	ns
54	ns	102	ns
55	ns	105	B
56	ns	106	B
58	A	115	ns
59	ns	117	ns
60	A	120	B
61	B	123	B
62	ns	125	A
63	ns	126	A
65	B	133	ns
68	A		

"A" means that A is perceived as being significantly more intense than B in this OA, at a level of 5%. The reverse applies for "B"
"ns" means that no significant difference was perceived between the two products for this OA, at a level of 5%.

The OA have been associated with compounds identified in GC-MS both by mass spectra and LRI (material and methods not presented here). Among the 13 OA with the highest GC-O scores, most of the compounds have been previously identified in gins (table 3). Linalool, which is mainly derived from coriander (Ravi and Bhat, 2007) is the compound the most intensely perceived in GC-O.

Analysis of the given descriptors

All the assessors were asked to describe the odour they perceived as precisely as possible. Nevertheless, important differences in terms of precision appeared between the given descriptors, with more than 130 different words used. As an example, to describe a fruity odour, the given descriptors could be 'strawberry", "red fruit" or only "fruit". In order to give these descriptors the same level of precision, we categorised them using odour classification wheels (Noble et al., 1987; Meilgaard, Dalgliesh and Clapperton, 1979). Thirteen categories were used to regroup the descriptors. Thus, we obtained a sensory profile for all the 61 selected OA based on the citation percentage of the descriptors in each category (table 4).

Two types of profile can be distinguished:

- OA with a category above 50% (OA 9,13,17...) which can thus be characterised by a main odour;
- OA without a category above 50% (OA 3, 8, 22...), which can be characterised by several odours.

For this last category, the lack of consensus can either be explained by the limited experience of the assessors in odour recognition or by the presence of several compounds in the same OA. This second case is more likely for an OA with high citation percentages in 2 or 3 categories. Thus, the OA 8 perceived at 38% fruity and at 38% floral, could represent two different compounds in coelution. These eventual coelutions will be revealed by further GC-MS analysis.

Table 3. Association of the identified compounds with the 13 OA with the highest scores obtained in GC-O

OA number	*Compound*	*LRI DB5-MS*	*Total buzzes*
13	Hexanal	767	58
43	α-pinene (1-2-3)	926	73
49	ß-myrcene (1-2-3)	993	90
48	ß-pinene (1-2-3)/sabinene (1-2-3)	977/986	49
50	l-phellandrene (1-2-3)	1014	41
54	limonene (1-2-3)/ß-phellandrene (1-2-3)	1045/1045	78
56	γ-terpinene (1-2-)	1068	43
59	α-terpinolene (1-2-3)	1093	55
61	linalool (1-2-3)	1123	137
71	Pinocarvone	1180	105
73	terpinen-4-ol (1-2-3)/α-terpineol (1-2-3)	1194/1201	59
80	d-carvone (3)	1258	54
100	geranyl acetate (1-2-3)	1382	49

The compounds have been previously identified either in gins (1: Clutton and Evans, 1978; 2: Vichi et al., 2005) or in botanicals used for gin aromatization (3: MacNamara, Howell, Huang and Robbat, 2007).

Conclusion and perspective

GC-O analysis applied to two commercial gins resulted on the identification of 61 OA corresponding to potential key aroma compounds identified by GC-MS. For each of these OA, an aromatic profile was generated, based on the descriptors obtained in GC-O.

One of the main limitations of GC-O is the perception of compounds separated from each other, without taking into account the potential effect between them in mixture (Van Ruth, 2001). For this reason, a recombination study of selected compounds will follow this study. A first step will be to reconstruct the gins based on the frequency detection results, by adding to a gin base typicity markers of each product. The selection of compounds for the recombination will be based both on the sensory data presented and on physico-chemical parameters gathered from databases.

References

Ballester, J. (2004). Mise en évidence d'un espace sensoriel et caractérisation des marqueurs relatifs à l'arôme des vins issus du cépage Chardonnay. Unpublished Doctorat en co-tutelle, Universidad politecnica de Valencia UMR Arômes INRA/ENESAD, Valencia.

Barata, A., Campo, E., Malfeito-Ferreira, M., Loureiro, V., Cacho, J., & Ferreira, V. (2011). Analytical and Sensorial Characterization of the Aroma of Wines Produced with Sour Rotten Grapes Using GC-O and GC-MS: *Identification of Key Aroma Compounds. Journal of Agricultural and Food Chemistry,* **59**: 2543-2553.

Caldeira, M., Rodrigues, F., Perestrelo, R., Marques, J. C., & Câmara, J. S. (2007). Comparison of two extraction methods for evaluation of volatile constituents patterns in commercial whiskeys Elucidation of the main odour-active compounds. *Talanta,* **74:** 78-90.

Camara, J. S., Marques, J. C., Perestrelo, R. M., Rodrigues, F., Oliveira, L., Andrade, P., et al. (2007). Comparative study of the whisky aroma profile based on headspace solid phase microextraction using different fibre coatings. *Journal of Chromatography A* **1150:** 198–207.

Cardeal, Z. L., & Marriot, P. J. (2009). Comprehensive two-dimensional gas chromatography–mass spectrometry analysis and comparison of volatile organic compounds in Brazilian cachaça and selected spirits. *Food Chemistry,* **112:** 747-755.

Table 4. Sensory profile of the selected OA obtained in GC-O

OA no.	*Caramelized*	*Chemical*	*Earthy*	*Floral*	*Fruity*	*Microbiological*	*Nutty*	*Pungent*	*Spicy*	*Unknown*	*Unpleasant*	*Vegetative*	*Woody*
3	14	0	0	14	29	29	0	0	0	0	14	0	0
8	0	0	0	38	38	0	0	0	0	0	13	13	0
9	0	0	20	0	60	0	0	0	0	0	0	20	0
10	0	0	0	33	50	17	0	0	0	0	0	0	0
13	13	4	0	8	75	0	0	0	0	0	0	0	0
17	0	0	6	13	63	6	0	0	6	0	6	0	0
19	3	5	0	21	63	0	0	3	0	0	3	3	0
22	0	0	0	25	0	0	0	25	0	0	0	25	25
23	0	33	0	0	33	0	0	0	33	0	0	0	0
24	0	43	7	14	11	4	0	0	0	14	0	4	4
28	0	0	0	16	63	0	0	0	5	0	0	11	5
29	0	10	10	10	60	10	0	0	0	0	0	0	0
33	0	0	0	25	38	0	0	0	13	13	0	0	13
38	10	20	0	10	30	0	0	0	0	10	10	10	0
43	0	11	6	14	6	0	0	3	9	3	6	9	34
44	0	11	0	26	42	0	0	0	0	0	0	5	16
48	0	3	37	6	14	0	0	0	14	6	0	9	11
49	0	16	16	9	4	11	0	4	9	5	4	21	2
50	0	17	8	17	42	0	0	8	0	0	0	8	0
53	0	0	0	50	0	0	0	50	0	0	0	0	0
54	0	7	0	7	38	0	0	0	14	0	3	21	10
55	0	7	14	7	21	14	0	0	0	7	0	29	0
56	0	13	13	13	13	0	0	0	6	13	0	19	13
58	0	0	25	17	33	0	0	0	0	8	0	0	17
59	0	4	24	0	8	0	0	0	0	16	0	28	20
60	0	6	6	6	39	6	0	0	6	0	22	6	6
61	3	6	6	42	27	0	0	0	2	2	0	9	3
62	0	22	0	39	6	0	0	6	0	11	0	11	6
63	0	0	38	23	8	0	0	8	0	8	8	8	0
65	0	0	0	25	25	13	0	0	13	13	0	13	0
68	0	9	4	30	9	0	0	0	13	4	0	9	22
69	5	21	0	5	11	16	0	0	0	26	0	16	0
71	1	22	4	17	17	1	8	0	8	3	1	14	3
72	0	14	24	3	3	7	0	0	10	10	7	17	3
73	6	3	6	23	45	0	0	3	6	0	3	3	0
74	50	50	0	0	0	0	0	0	0	0	0	0	0
75	0	23	8	8	8	0	0	8	8	0	8	8	23
76	0	0	0	0	0	0	0	50	0	50	0	0	0
79	11	0	22	22	22	0	0	0	0	11	0	11	0
80	7	21	0	14	14	0	0	0	7	7	0	14	14

Table 4. Contd.

OA no.	*Caramelized*	*Chemical*	*Earthy*	*Floral*	*Fruity*	*Microbological*	*Nutty*	*Pungent*	*Spicy*	*Unknown*	*Unpleasant*	*Vegetative*	*Woody*
81	0	0	25	50	0	0	0	0	25	0	0	0	0
82	0	8	33	8	8	0	0	8	8	8	0	8	8
86	0	8	15	23	23	0	0	0	8	0	0	23	0
88	0	8	0	8	17	8	0	0	8	17	0	17	17
92	0	14	0	5	18	0	5	0	14	9	9	23	5
93	0	10	50	0	5	10	5	5	0	5	0	10	0
94	0	0	0	100	0	0	0	0	0	0	0	0	0
97	0	12	4	24	12	0	4	0	16	4	0	16	8
99	0	25	6	25	19	0	0	6	0	0	0	19	0
100	4	0	8	19	27	4	0	4	4	0	0	23	8
101	0	0	0	29	57	0	0	0	14	0	0	0	0
102	0	20	0	0	40	0	0	0	20	0	0	20	0
105	0	0	100	0	0	0	0	0	0	0	0	0	0
106	100	0	0	0	0	0	0	0	0	0	0	0	0
115	14	14	0	14	29	0	0	0	0	29	0	0	0
117	0	17	0	11	22	0	0	0	22	11	0	17	0
120	50	0	0	0	0	0	0	0	0	0	0	0	50
123	0	11	0	11	33	0	0	11	0	0	0	33	0
125	0	11	0	33	11	11	0	11	0	22	0	0	0
126	0	14	0	29	43	0	0	14	0	0	0	0	0
133	0	33	0	17	0	0	0	17	0	0	0	17	17

Charles, M., Martin, B., Ginies, C., Etiévant, P., Coste, G., & Guichard, E. (2000). Potent aroma compounds of two red wine vinegars. *Journal of Agricultural and Food Chemistry*, **48:** 70-77.

Clutton, D. W., & Evans, M. B. (1978). The flavour constituents of gin. *Journal of Chromatography*, **167:** 409-419.

de Souza, M. D. C. A., Vasquez, P., del Mastro, N. L., Acree, T. E., & Lavin E.H. (2006). Characterization of Cachaça and Rum Aroma. *Journal of Agricultural and Food Chemistry*, **54:** 485-488.

Delahunty, C. M., Eyres, G., & Dufour, J.-P. (2006). Gas chromatography-olfactometry. *Journal of Separation Science*, **29:** 2107-2125.

Fan, W., & Qian M.C. (2005). Headspace Solid Phase Microextraction and Gas Chromatography-Olfactometry Dilution Analysis of Young and Aged Chinese "Yanghe Daqu" Liquors. *Journal of Agricultural and Food Chemistry*, **53:** 7931-7938.

Ferrari, G., Lablanquie, O., Cantagrel, R., Ledauphin, J., Payot, T., Fournier, N., et al. (2004). Determination of key odorant compounds in freshly distilled Cognac using GC-O, GC-MS and sensory evaluation. *Journal of Agricultural and Food Chemistry*, **52:** 5670-5676.

Ferreira, V., Ortega, L., Escudero, A., & Cacho, J. F. (2000). A Comparative Study of the Ability of Different Solvents and Adsorbents to Extract Aroma Compounds from Alcoholic Beverages. *Journal of Chromatographic Science*, **38:** 469-476

Ferreira, V., Ortín, N., Escudero, A., López, R., & Cacho, J. (2002). Chemical Characterization of the Aroma of Grenache Rosé Wines: Aroma Extract Dilution Analysis, Quantitative Determination, and Sensory Reconstitution Studies. *Journal of Agricultural and Food Chemistry*, **50:** 4048-4054.

Grosch, W. (2001). Evaluation of the key odorants of foods by dilution experiments, aroma models and omission. *Chemical Senses*, **26:** 533-545.

Guerra-Hernandez, E. (2003). Gin/ composition and analysis. *Encyclopedia of Food Sciences and Nutrition (Second Edition)*, 2894-2898

Guichard, H., Lemesle, S., Ledauphin, J., Barillier, D., & Picoche, B. (2003). Chemical and sensorial aroma characterisation of freshly distilled calvados.1. Evaluation of quality and defects on the basis of key odorants by olfactometry and sensory analysis. Journal *of Agricultural and Food Chemistry*, **51:** 424-432.

Ledauphin, J., Saint-Clair, J. F., Lablanquie, O., Guichard, H., Fournier, N., Guichard, E. and and Barillier, D. (2004). Identification of trace volatile compounds in freshly-distilled Calvados and Cognac using preparative separations coupled with GC-MS. *Journal of Agricultural and Food Chemistry*, **52:** 5124-5134.

Linssen, J. P. H., Janssens, J. L. G. M., Roozen, J. P., & Posthumus, M. A. (1993). Combined gas chromatography and sniffing port analysis of volatile compounds of mineral water packed in polyethylene laminated packages. *Food Chemistry*, **46:** 367-373.

Lopez , R., Aznar, M., Cacho, J., & Ferreira, V. (2002). Determination of minor and trace volatile compounds in wine by solid-phase extraction and gas chromatography with mass spectrometric detection. *Journal of Chromatography A*, **966:** 167–177.

Lorrain, B., Ballester, J., Thomas-Danguin, T., Blanquet, J., Meunier, J. M., & Le Fur, Y. (2006). Selection of potential impact odorants and sensory validation of their importance in typical Chardonnay wines. *Journal of Agricultural and Food Chemistry*, **54:** 3973-3981.

MacNamara, K., Howell, J., Huang, Y., & Robbat JR., A. (2007). Analysis of gin essential oil mixtures by multidimensional and one-dimensional gas chromatographymass spectrometry with spectral deconvolution. *Journal of Chromatography A*, **1164:** 281–290.

Meilgaard, M. C., Dalgliesh, C. E., & Clapperton, J. F. (1979). Beer flavour terminology. *Bios*, **10:** 23-31.

Noble, A. C., Arnold, R. A., Buechsenstein, J., Leach, E. J., Schmidt, J. O., & Stern, P. M. (1987). Modification of a standardized system of wine aroma terminology. *American Journal of Enology and Viticulture*, **38:** 143-146.

Noguerol-Pato, R., González-Barreiro, C., Cancho-Grande, B., & Simal-Gándara, J. (2009). Quantitative deferrtermination and characterisation of the main odorants of Mencía monovarietal red wines. *Food Chemistry*, **117:** 473–484.

Plutowska, B., & Wardencki, W. (2008). Application of gas chromatography-olfactometry (GC-O) in analysis and quality assessment of alcoholic beverages - A review. *Food Chemistry*, **107:** 449-463.

Poisson, L., & Schieberle, P. (2008). Characterization of the key aroma compounds in an American Bourbon whisky by quantitative measurements, aroma recombination, and omission studies. *Journal of Agricultural and Food Chemistry,* **56:** 5820-5826.

Pollien, P., Ott, A., Montigon, F., Baumgartner, M., Muñoz-Box, R., & Chaintreau, A. (1997). Hyphenated headspace-gas chromatography-sniffing technique: screening of impact odorants and quantitative aromagram comparisons. *Journal of Agricultural and Food Chemistry*, **45:** 2630-2637.

Ravi, R. P., M. ; Bhat, K.K. (2007). Aroma characterization of coriander (Coriandrum sativum L.) oil samples. *European Food Research and Technology* **225:** 367–374.

Riu-Aumatell, M., Vichi, S., Mora-Pons, M., Lopez-Tamames, E., & Buxaderas, S. (2008). Sensory Characterization of Dry Gins with Different Volatile Profiles. *Journal of Food Science*, **73:** 286-293.

Sarrazin, E., Dubourdieu, D., & Darriet, P. (2007). Characterization of key-aroma compounds of botrytized wines, influence of grape botrytization. *Food Chemistry*, **103:** 536–545.

Van Ruth, S. M. (2001). Methods for gas chromatography-olfactometry: a review. *Biomolecular Engineering,* **17:** 121-128.

Vichi, S., Riu-Aumatell, M., Mora-Pons, M., Buxaderas, S., & Lopez-Tamames, E. (2005). Characterization of Volatiles in Different Dry Gins. *Journal of Agricultural and Food Chemistry*, **53:** 10154-10160.

Vichi, S., Aumatell, M. R., Buxaderas, S., & López-Tamames, E. (2008). Assessment of some diterpenoids in commercial distilled gin. *Analytica chimica acta* **628:** 222-229.

Zhao, Y., Xu, Y., Li, J., Fan, W., & Jiang, W. (2009). Profile of Volatile Compounds in 11 Brandies by Headspace Solid-Phase Microextraction Followed by Gas Chromatography-Mass Spectrometry. *Journal of Food Science*, **74:** 90-99.

Zhu, S. K., Lu, X., Ji, K. H., Guo, K. F., Li, Y. L., Wu, C. Y., et al. (2007). Characterization of flavor compounds in Chinese liquor Moutai by comprehensive two-dimensional gas chromatography/time-of-flight mass spectrometry. *Analytica Chimica Acta*, **597:** 340-348.

Chapter 25

Profiling Scotch malt whisky spirits from different distilleries using an electronic nose and an expert sensory panel

A. Aranyos[1], F. Ayouni[1], M. Bonnefille[1], F. Jack[2], H. Lechat[1]
[1]*Alpha MOS, 20 avenue Didier Daurat – 31400 Toulouse - France;* [2]*The Scotch Whisky Research Institute - Research Avenue North - Riccarton - Edinburgh - EH14 4AP – United Kingdom*

Introduction

Spirits from different Scotch malt whisky distilleries exhibit distinct sensory characteristics. To ensure the future diversity of this spirit category and sustainability of individual distilleries, it is vital that such differences can be maintained. Flavour is complex, with differences being due to variations in composition resulting from the processing parameters and raw materials used in their manufacture. In this research the characteristics of spirits from six distilleries were profiled using an electronic nose (e-nose) and by an expert sensory panel.

Materials and methods

Samples

A total of 58 samples of unmatured malt whisky spirits were collected from six different distilleries (A to F). Sample codes and alcohol strengths are shown in Table 1.

Equipment and analytical conditions

The analysis was conducted using a HERACLES Electronic Nose. This instrument is based on ultra fast chromatography and includes two short columns (2m) of different polarities (DB5 apolar and DB1701 slightly polar), coupled to 2 Flame Ionization Detectors (FID). Therefore, 2 chromatograms are obtained simultaneously.

A Tenax trap located before the columns allows pre-concentration of the injected fraction before rapid thermo desorption.

Data acquisition and processing was operated with the electronic nose Alphasoft software.

Sampling was achieved with an HS100 autosampler. Each sample was injected on the Heracles electronic nose in triplicate using the same optimized method (Table 2).

Sensory evaluation

Sensory evaluation was carried out by an expert panel. Composite samples from each distillery were prepared. These were diluted to 20% abv using water and presented in blind coded glasses to the panel. Panelists were asked to score the spirits according to intensity of 16 aromas listed below, which from previous experience have been found to be the key attributes of unmatured malt whisky spirits: pungent, sulfury, meaty, solventy, fruity/estery, green/grassy, floral,

Table 1. Sample description

Sample	*% of Alcohol*	*Sample*	*% of Alcohol*	*Sample*	*% of Alcohol*
A1	69.7	C1	70.4	E1	70.8
A2	68.8	C2	70.0	E2	70.8
A3	68.8	C3	70.0	E3	71.0
A4	69.8	C4	69.9	E4	71.0
A5	69.8	C5	70.5	E5	70.6
A6	69.8	C6	70.5	E6	70.6
A7	69.8	C7	70.5	E7	70.3
A8	69.8	C8	69.9	E8	70.3
A9	69.8	C9	70.1	E9	70.6
A10	69.8	C10	70.1	E10	70.7
B1	68.1	D1	72	F1	69.2
B2	68.4	D2	72.6	F2	68.9
B3	63.5	D3	71.8	F3	69.3
B4	68.4	D4	72.1	F4	69.1
B5	68.4	D5	72.3	F5	69.3
B6	68.4	D6	71.9	F6	69.2
B7	67.9	D7	71.7	F7	68.9
B8	68.2	D8	70.7	F8	69.3
B9	68.4			F9	69.3
B10	68.4			F10	69.3

Table 2: HERACLES electronic nose parameters for spirits analysis (headspace injection)

Quantity of sample	1g in a 10mL vial
Sample incubation	10 min at 100°C
Syringe temperature	110°C
Injected volume	5mL
Sampling time	23s
Trap temperature	40°C
Trap pre-purge time	30 s
Trap desorption temp.	250°C
Trap purge time	60 s
Injection time	2000 ms
Injector temperature	200°C
Column temperature program	40°C (2s) to 220°C (2s) @ 3°C/s
Column pressure	16 psi
FID temperature	230°C
Acquisition time	50 s

cereal, sweet, soapy, peaty, feinty, oily, sour, stale and clean.

A 0-3 line scale was used for scoring. Analysis of Variance (ANOVA) was carried out to determine which, if any, of the attributes differed among the samples. Data were then summarized by calculating average scores across the panel.

Results and discussions

Electronic nose measurements

Analysis of the spirits showed globally similar profiles at low retention times (between 0 and 10s) for the main volatile compounds (Figure 1).

The chromatographic profile could be represented as an odour map using a Principal Component Analysis (PCA, Figure 2).

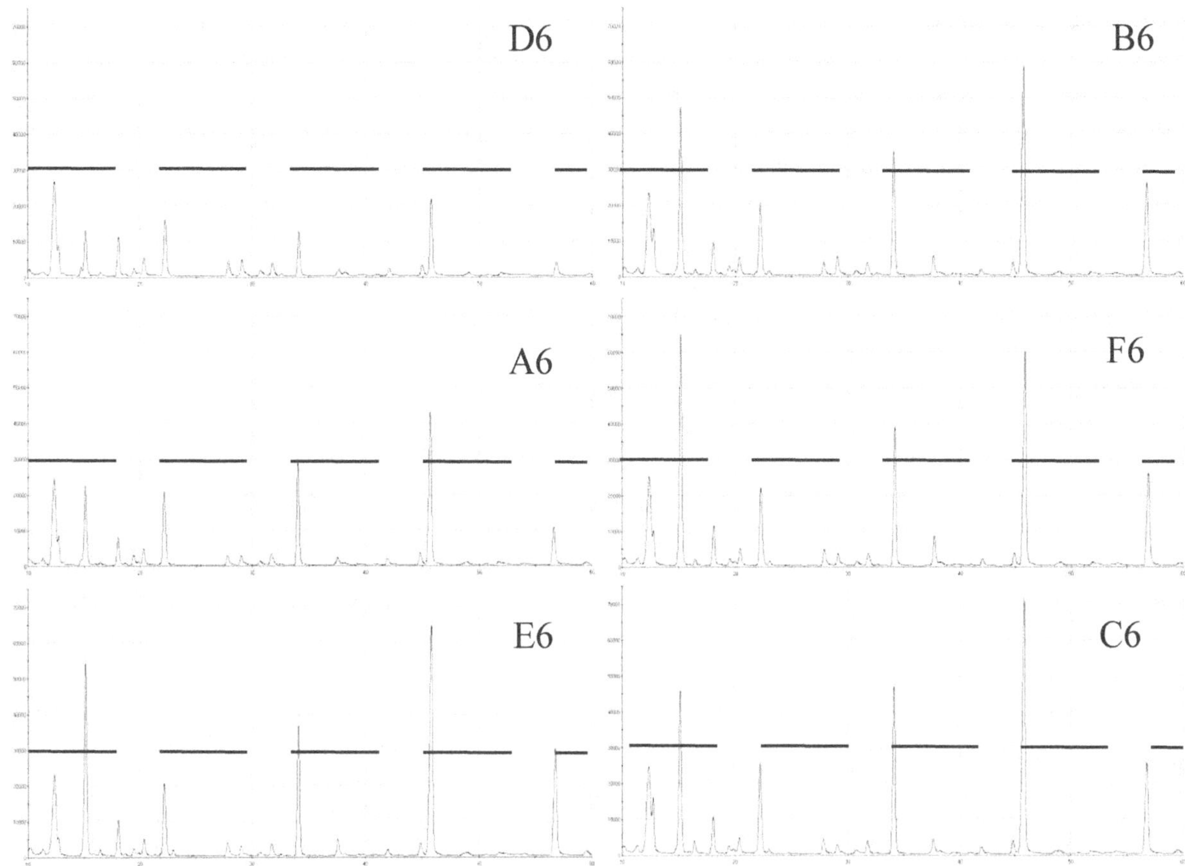

Figure 1. Heracles electronic nose chromatograms for the 6 types of whisky spirit - Focus on 10 to 60 s on DB5 column

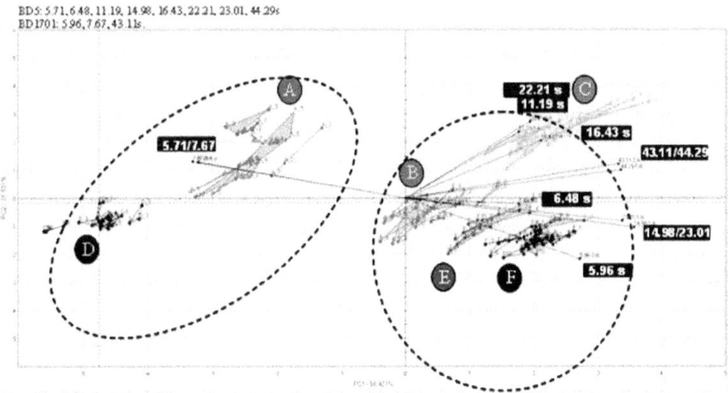

Figure 2. Odour map (Principal Components Analysis) of whisky spirit samples on Heracles electronic nose

The various samples are represented according to their relative volatile contents on a 2-axis graph with PC1 explaining 56% of the variance and PC2 22%. This PCA plot showed clustering of the samples from each distillery, indicating that the instrument could discriminate spirits according to their origin. Samples dispersion was relatively homogeneous, except for Distillery E which showed two distinct subgroups of samples: E8 to E10, which were close to Distillery F (appearing superimposed in Figure 2), and samples E1 to E7, which were closer to Distillery B. Samples were numbered in chronological order according to date of production, so this change in composition may be due to a change in the production parameters or raw materials at a particular point in time.

Additionally, two groups could be distinguished:

- Group 1: Distilleries A and D
- Group 2: Distilleries B, E and F and Distillery C slightly discriminated on the PC2 axis.

Sensory evaluation results

The average panel scores were further summarized using PCA (Figure 3).

Comparison of this PCA plot with the one obtained for the Heracles electronic nose data (Figure 2) showed that the distribution of samples was different. This indicates that the two techniques are complementary.

Correlation between electronic nose and sensory evaluation results

Correlation coefficients between the Heracles and sensory panel data are shown in Table 3. Peak 16.43 showed a good correlation with many sensory attributes: sulfury, meaty and feinty descriptors (+ve) and fruity, green and floral (- ve).

The fact that a number of sensory descriptors, rather than a single flavour, correlated with this peak is due to the inter-relationships among sensory attributes, i.e. as heavy (sulfury, meaty, feinty) aromas increase, lighter (fruity, green, floral) aromas tend to decrease. GC-MS analysis identified Peak 16.43 as furfuryl ethyl ether.

Conclusion

A combination of sensory and electronic nose techniques gives a more comprehensive profiling of malt whisky spirit than either technique can produce in isolation.

Some important sensory attributes such as sulfury, meaty, feinty, fruity, green and floral were highly correlated (positively or negatively) with the Heracles data.

From GC/MS analysis, it appeared that furfuryl ethyl ether seemed to be one of the most important molecules for explaining the characteristic differences in odor between spirits from different distilleries, though other molecules such as sulfides may also be important.

Such a combined approach can have a number of potential applications including competitive benchmarking, descriptive and compositional comparison, or origin authentication.

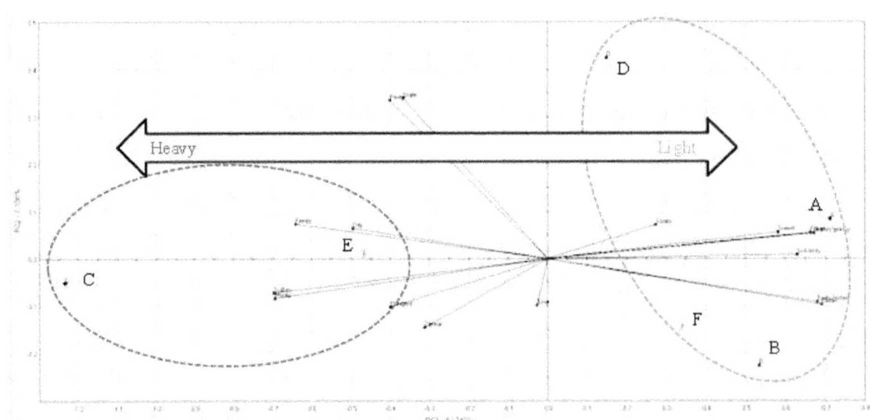

Figure 3. Principal Components Analysis of sensory results

Table 3. Correlation coefficient between area of Heracles peaks and sensory data

Peak	*5.71**	*6.48**	*11.19**	*14.98**	*16.43**	*22.21**	*23.01**	*44.29**	***5.96*****	***7,67*****	***43,11*****
Pungent	-0.54	0.46	0.22	0.38	0.64	0.35	0.24	0.45	0.20	-0.48	0.46
Sulfury	-0.42	0.32	0.36	0.43	0.89	0.49	0.54	0.64	0.11	-0.43	0.65
Meaty	-0.49	0.40	0.32	0.50	0.86	0.47	0.59	0.68	0.20	-0.50	0.68
Solventy	0.41	-0.13	-0.04	-0.31	-0.77	-0.10	-0.41	-0.34	-0.17	0.40	-0.35
Fruity/estery	0.06	-0.21	-0.22	-0.04	-0.82	-0.38	-0.19	-0.36	0.25	0.06	-0.37
Green/grassy	0.32	-0.34	-0.40	-0.38	-0.83	-0.55	-0.51	-0.65	-0.04	0.35	-0.66
Floral	0.53	-0.39	-0.19	-0.44	-0.85	-0.33	-0.46	-0.53	-0.20	0.50	-0.54
Cereal	-0.68	0.26	0.04	0.47	0.51	0.04	0.35	0.32	0.44	-0.61	0.33
Sweet	0.63	-0.40	0.06	-0.54	-0.65	-0.06	-0.55	-0.44	-0.43	0.61	-0.43
Soapy	0.19	0.42	-0.18	-0.06	-0.50	0.03	-0.15	-0.06	-0.02	0.17	-0.09
Peaty	0.39	0.00	-0.33	-0.51	0.35	-0.16	-0.39	-0.32	-0.55	0.43	-0.31
Feinty	-0.15	0.35	0.24	0.06	0.84	0.44	0.10	0.37	-0.24	-0.12	0.39
Oily	0.04	0.46	0.34	0.08	0.56	0.61	0.18	0.47	-0.27	0.01	0.48
Sour	-0.24	0.21	0.31	0.05	0.32	0.34	-0.17	0.17	-0.07	-0.16	0.21
Stale	0.31	0.15	-0.55	-0.33	0.14	-0.32	-0.19	-0.30	-0.30	0.31	-0.32
Clean	0.18	-0.30	-0.06	-0.13	-0.78	-0.25	-0.25	-0.34	0.10	0.17	-0.34

*Retention Time of peaks on column DB5 - **Retention Time of peaks on column DB1701

Chapter 26

The behaviour of whisky lactone isomers in Japanese oak casks

Yushi Noguchi[1], Minako Koike[1], Paul Hughes[2], John Conner[3], and Frances Jack[3]

[1] *Suntory Liquors Limited, Osaka, JAPAN;* [2] *International Centre of Brewing and Distilling, Heriot-Watt University, Edinburgh, UK;* [3] *The Scotch Whisky Research Institute, Edinburgh, UK*

Introduction

Whisky or wine is matured in casks made of oak. During the maturation, various wood components are extracted that contribute to mature flavour. Some of these components have been identified, with *cis*- and *trans*-whisky lactone being well known wood extractives responsible for coconut flavour in whisky (Masuda and Nishimura, 1971).

At the Worldwide Distilled Spirits Conference in 2008, we reported that whisky matured in Japanese oak casks had more active coconut flavour and contained a higher concentration of *trans*-lactone than whisky from American oak casks (Noguchi et al, 2008).

Since lactones are important in giving the distinctive character of Japanese oak matured whiskies, this further study was carried out to examine the effects of heating conditions and other factors on their levels. We also report a comparison of the lactone extraction from different depths within the stave.

Method

Stave cut into slices

Staves were collected from the bottom of a refill Japanese oak cask. These staves were cut into slices using a wood slicer. A series of 1mm slices were collected, starting from the inner surface of the stave. These slices were then cut into chips.

Wood chip heat treatment

4.0 g samples of wood chip were heated in an oven for 30 minutes at 100, 150, 180 and 200°C respectively.

Charring or toasting of the staves

The charring of staves was carried out using a burner or toasted using a toaster. The heating strength of light or heavy charring was decided by visual observation. The toasting of staves was carried out by placing on a hot plate at 250°C for 30 minutes.

Wood components: Extraction from wood chips

For the chemical analysis of woods, the wood components were extracted with 20 mL of 60% (v/v) ethanol solution from 2.0 g samples of wood chip for three days at room temperature.

Whisky samples

Whisky samples were selected as being typical Yamazaki whiskies of either 9 or 10 years old, matured in either untreated or re-charred Japanese oak refill casks.

Colour measurement

The colour of the extracted solution (in EBC colour units) was measured by the UV-Visible Spectrophotometer (Shimadzu, Kyoto, Japan).

Chemical analysis

The lactones and phenolics analysis of whisky and wood extracts was carried out by GC-MS (Agilent, Tokyo, Japan) and HPLC (Shimadzu, Kyoto, Japan). These concentrations are shown at the sample strength.

Results

The effect of the heating conditions

To provide information on the regeneration of old casks or the optimisation of conditions for stronger flavour activity of Japanese oak, we studied the effect of different heating conditions on whisky lactone concentrations in oak chips,. No significant difference in either isomer was shown between all conditions tested, including the untreated control (Figure 1). In the next stage, we studied whiskies. When whiskies of the same age, matured in either untreated or re-charred casks, were compared, again no significant difference in lactone levels was observed (Figure 2). However, the whiskies matured in re-charred casks showed elevated concentrations of phenolics (Figure 3).

Lactone extraction from different depths within the stave

The depth of visual whisky penetration into this stave was around 9 mm from the internal surface (Picture 1). Analysis of the wood chips from different depths within the stave showed that the colour was most intense at the soaking depth of 9 mm. On the other hand, the behaviour of lactones and other phenolics (with the exception of vanillin) was quite different from the colour. They were extracted consistently with no relation to the visual depth of whisky soaking (Figure 4). No change was observed in the lactones ratio. This indicates that shaving of the insides of the cask would not to be efficient for the activation of the extraction of lactones and phenolics.

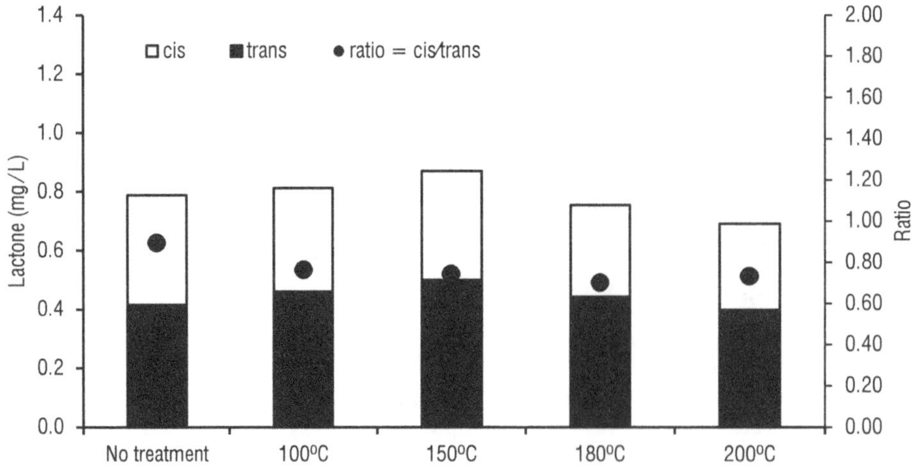

Figure 1. The effect of heating conditions on oak chip lactones

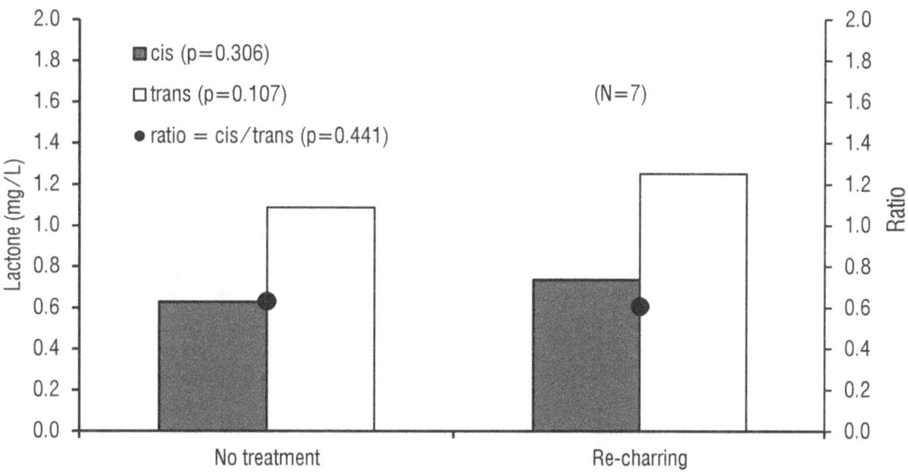

Figure 2. The effect of re-charring conditions on lactones in whisky

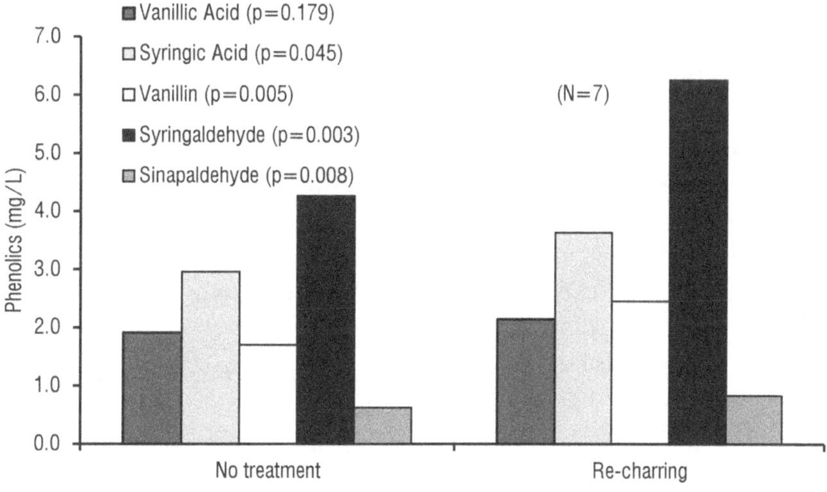

Figure 3. The effect of re-charring conditions on phenolics in whisky

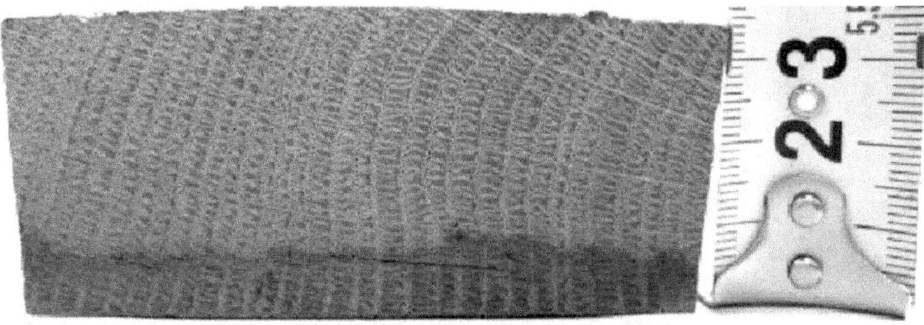

Picture1. Visual whisky soaking into the stave

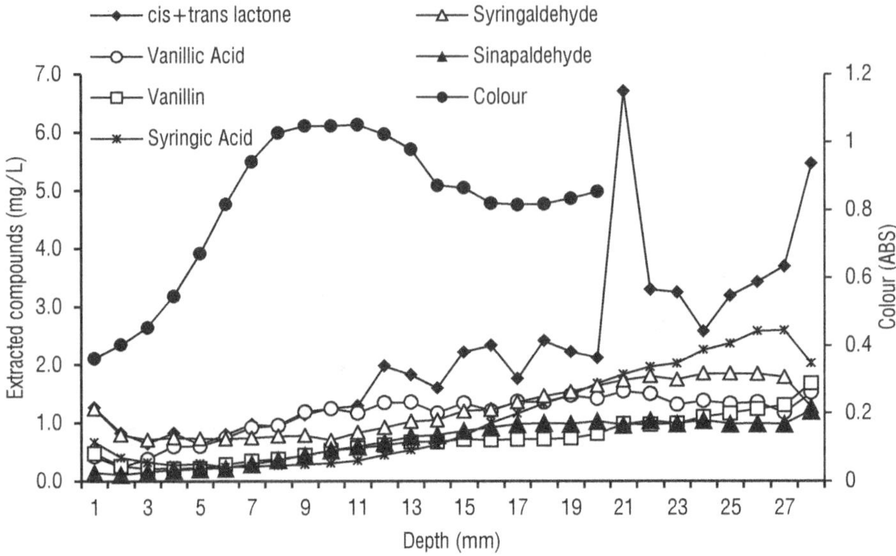

Figure 4. The behaviour of colour and extracted compounds within stave

Heating effect on the regeneration at different depths within a stave

Next, we studied the effects of various heat treatments; light charring, heavy charring, or toasting. None of these heat treated staves showed any activation of lactones, with both the levels of lactones and their ratio being unaffected (Figure 5). However, the regeneration of the colour (Figure 6) and phenolics (Figure 7-11) at the surface was shown. In particular, toasting gave deeper regeneration of phenolics. This indicates that the flavours derived from phenolics, vanilla, woody, etc., are enhanced by heat treatment, while the coconut flavour from lactone is not. In other words, the heat treatment during cask regeneration is selective.

Conclusions

We studied the behaviour of whisky lactones from Japanese oak under various heat treatments and compared the lactone extraction from different

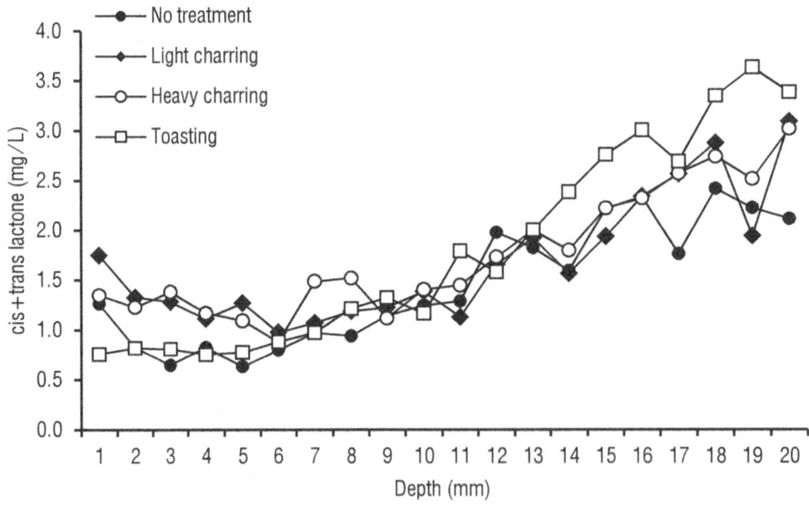

Figure 5. Heating effect on lactone concentrations at different stave depths

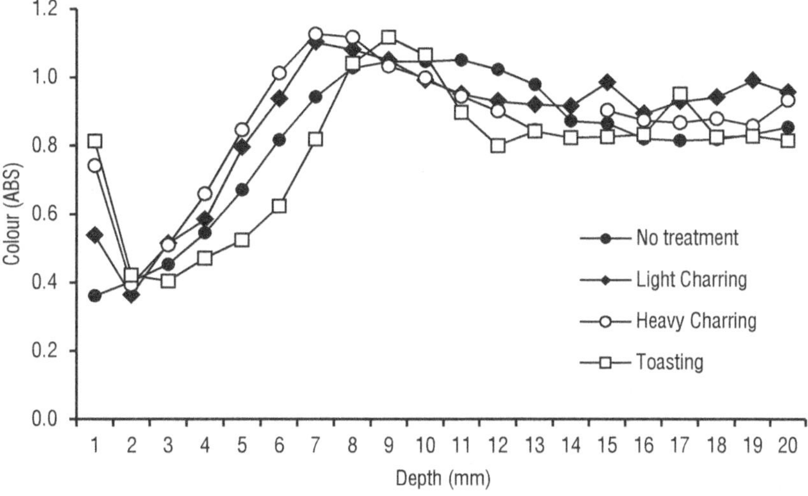

Figure 6. Heating effect on colour at different stave depths

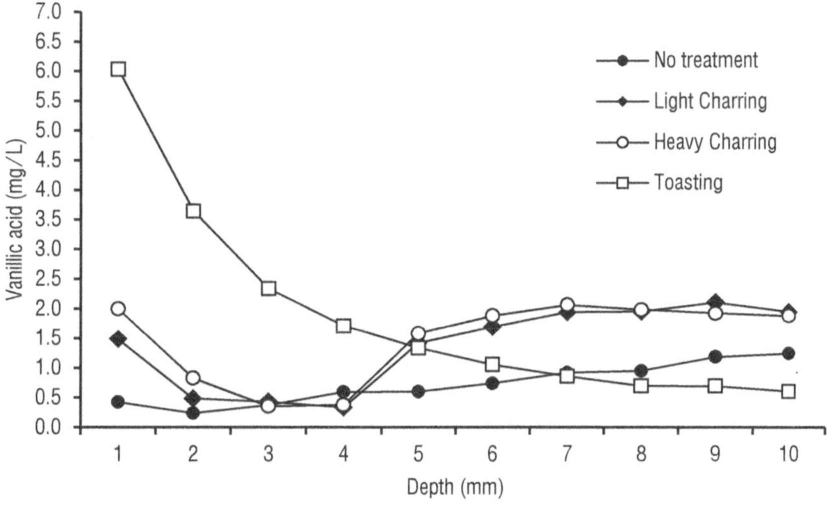

Figure 7. Heating effect on Vanillic acid at different stave depths

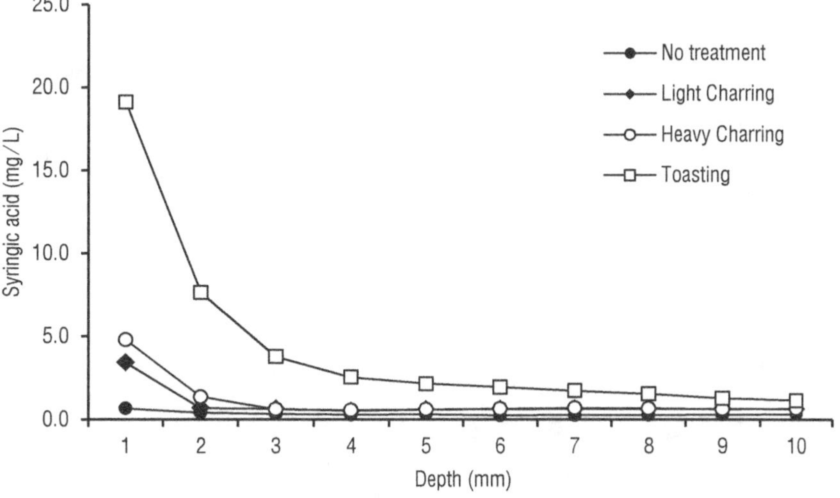

Figure 8. Heating effect on Syringic acid at different stave depths

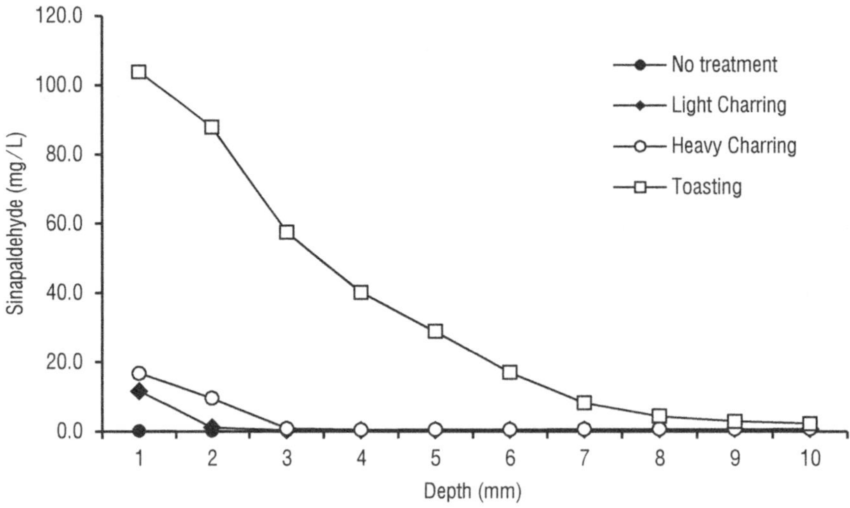

Figure 9. Heating effect on Sinapaldehyde at different stave depths

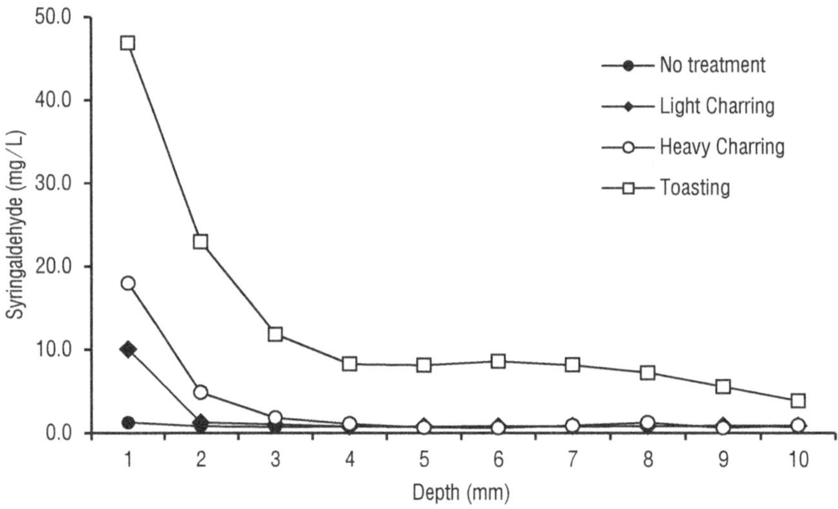

Figure 10. Heating effect on Syringaldehyde at different stave depths

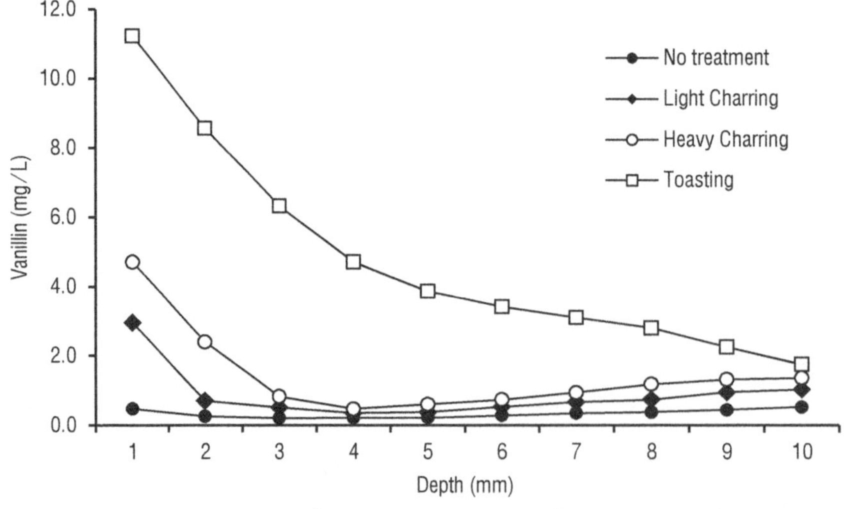

Figure 11. Heating effect on Vanillin at different stave depths

depths within the stave. From our observations, heat treatments are effective for the regeneration of phenolics. In contrast, they are not effective for the activation of lactones. Although our findings show that lactones are likely to continue to be extracted with no treatment, they are not enhanced by heat treatment or shaving. Hence, in order to obtain the aroma associated with Japanese oak, it is important that the lifetime of the cask is evaluated carefully. Finally, although the regeneration of Japanese oak casks will give renewed maturation capabilities, it will not recreate the distinctive coconut aromas associated with Japanese oak.

Acknowledgements

The authors would like to thank their SWRI and Suntory colleagues for their helpful and informative discussions.

References

Masuda, M. and Nishimura, K., (1971). Branched Nonalactones from Some Quercus Species. Phytochemical Reports 10: pp1401-1402.

Noguchi Y., Hughes P. S., Priest F. G, Conner J. M, and Jack F. (2008). The influence of wood species of cask on matured whisky aroma - the identification of a unique character imparted by casks of Japanese oak. In: Proceedings of the Third Worldwide Distilled Spirits Conference, Edited by Walker G. M. and Hughes P. S., Institute of Brewing, London, pp243-251.

Chapter 27

Creating various whiskies utilizing differences in warehouse conditions in Japan

Masaaki Nakajima, Takahisa Fujii
Suntory Liquors Limited, Yamazaki Distillery, 5-2-1 Yamazaki, Shimamoto-cho, Mishima-gun, Osaka, 618-0001, Japan

Introduction

Recently, Japanese whiskies have received many awards in international whisky competitions. Manufacturing processes of Japanese whiskies are fundamentally similar to those of Scotch whiskies, but we have been trying to employ various conditions at each step of the manufacturing process in order to create many whisky characters at one distillery. Of particular interest is the influence of maturation in wooden casks on whisky quality, which is much stronger in Japan than in Scotland because of the temperature difference between the two countries.

Firstly, we report our observation that there are significant differences between the upper and lower tiers of a warehouse in spirit strength changes during maturation.

Secondly, we present the effect of microclimate conditions in our warehouses on the quality of Japanese whiskies. Flavour characteristics of our whiskies are obviously different between upper and lower tiers, particularly in multi-tiered warehouses.

Finally, we introduce some of our efforts to create various types of whiskies and our research on their maturation mechanisms.

Materials and ethod

Whisky samples

Malt whisky samples matured in puncheons, selected as 18 year old Yamazaki whiskies, were taken from tiers at the top, middle and bottom of the same racked Omi warehouse. Three samples from each tier were obtained and used for sensory and chemical analysis.

Environmental measurement

Temperature and relative humidity data at Osaka in Japan and Aberdeen in Scotland were obtained from the website 'Weatherbase' (http://www.weatherbase.com/). The data in the Omi warehouse were recorded using data loggers (T & D, Nagano, Japan). The average monthly temperature and relative humidity were calculated from the data.

Sensory analysis

Sensory analysis was carried out using Quantitative Descriptive Analysis by 5 well trained blenders in Suntory. Attributes were scored using a scale of 0.0 to 2.0 and average scores calculated across the panel. Whiskies were reduced to about 20% (v/v) alcohol strength before nosing.

Chemical analysis

Analyses of volatiles and phenolic compounds in whiskies were carried out using GC-MS (Shimadzu, Kyoto, Japan) and HPLC (Shimadzu, Kyoto, Japan). All component concentrations are shown at sample strength.

Results and discussion

Environmental difference between Japan and Scotland

Due to the higher temperature in Japan, the influences of the cask and warehouse condition on the whisky characters during the maturation seems to be much stronger than in Scotland (Figure 1).

Varieties of warehouse conditions

Even within the same warehouse, the temperatures and relative humidity were very different between the upper and lower tiers. Therefore we can create various whiskies by utilizing these environmental differences (Figure 2).

Correlation between the change in spirit strength and warehouse condition

The spirit strengths of the whiskies stored on the upper tiers increased during maturation, contrary to the strengths on the lower tiers which decreased relative to the filling strength (Figure 3). This correlates with humidity, spirit strength decreasing during maturation under the more humid conditions, however increasing when the average humidity is less than 75% (Figure 4).

General chemical analysis

The whisky stored on upper tiers had higher concentrations of the following compounds relative to those stored on lower tiers: total esters, total fusel alcohols and total phenolic components (Figure 5). Two possibilities are put forward to explain this difference. Firstly, the esterification and extraction of wood components might proceed faster in the upper tiers due to the higher-temperature conditions (Reazin, 1981). Another possibility is the result of

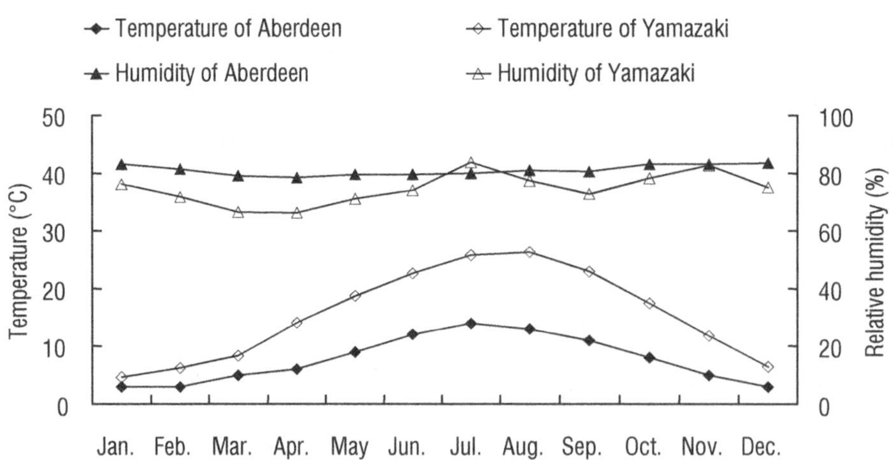

Figure 1. Average monthly temperature and relative humidity in Aberdeen and Yamazaki.

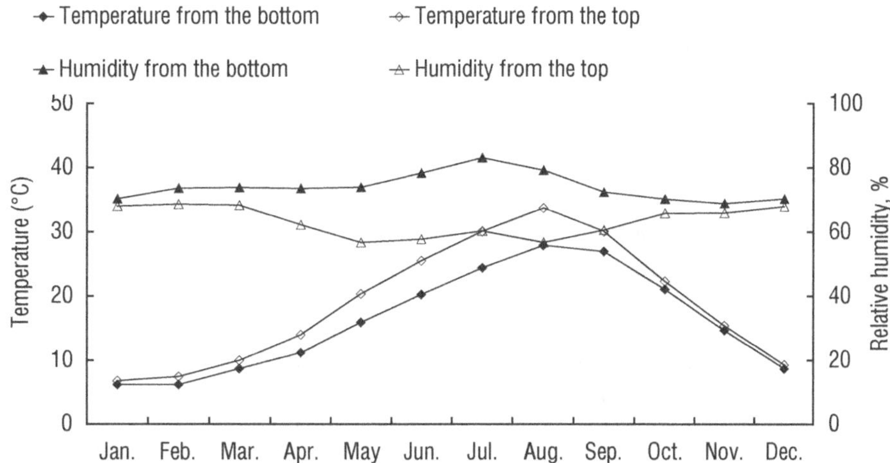

Figure 2. Average monthly temperature and relative humidity of upper and lower tiers in the same warehouse. Six-tiered warehouse D located in Omi is shown.

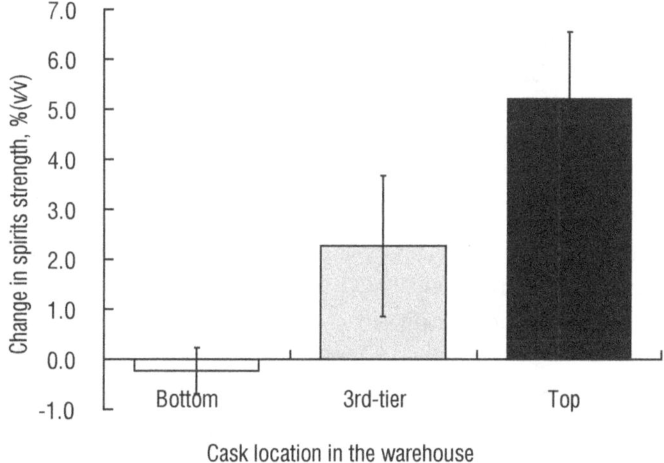

Figure 3. Change in spirits strength compared with the filling strength and cask location. Data presented are means ± SD (n = 3).

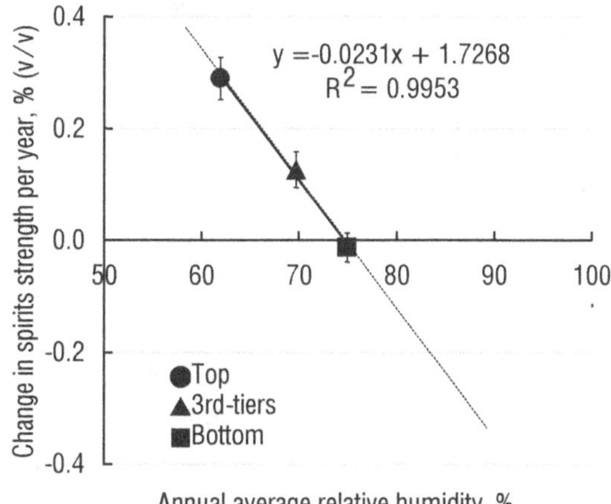

Figure 4. Correlation between the annual average change in spirit strength and the annual average relative humidity. Data presented are means ± SD (n = 3).

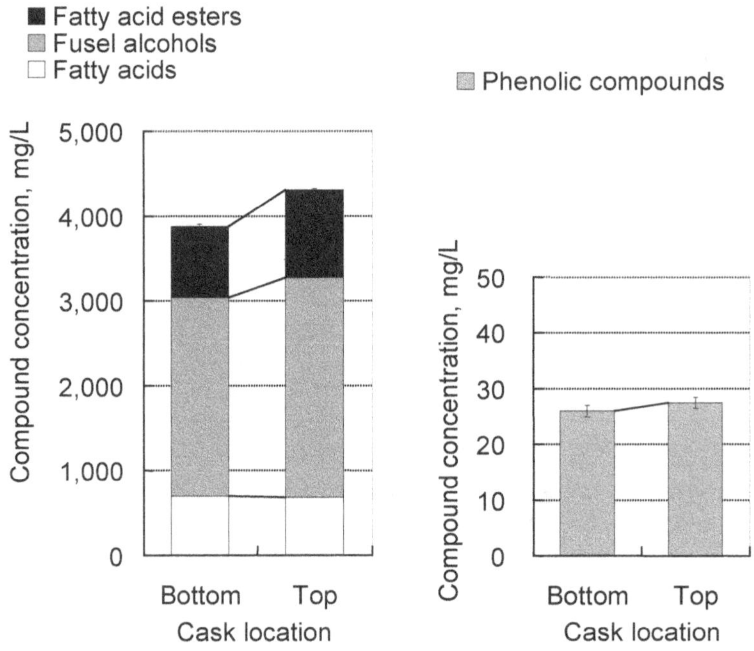

Figure 5. Result of general chemical analysis. Data presented are means ± SD (n = 3).

differences in evaporative losses; the evaporative losses in upper tiers are greater than those in lower tiers leading to an increased concentration effect.

Sensory analysis using general flavour descriptions

The whisky from upper tiers tended to have the following features: woody, vanilla, fruity/estery, floral, pungent and meaty. In contrast, the whisky stored on the lower tiers was found to have the following features, green/grassy, cereal, creamy, feinty, sour and clean (Figure 6).

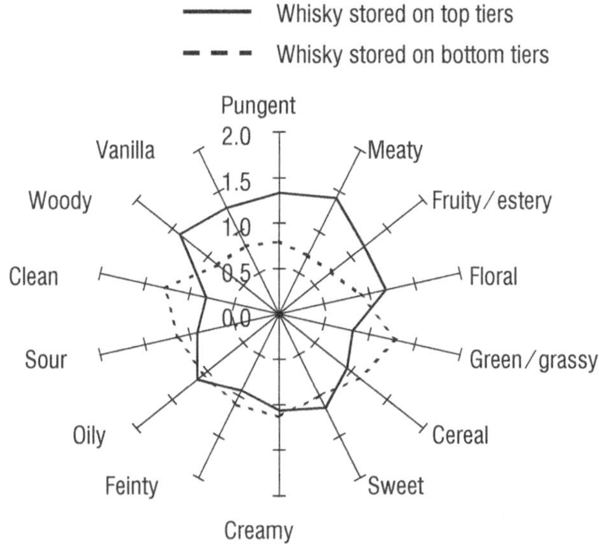

Figure 6. Result of general sensory analysis.

Conclusions and further work

In this report, it was shown that the warehouse conditions in Japan strongly affect both the spirits strength and characteristics of matured whisky.

The spirit strength decreases during maturation under the more humid conditions, although it increases when the humidity is less than 75%.

The whisky stored on upper tiers had higher concentrations of the following compounds, relative to those stored on lower tiers: total esters, total fusel alcohols and total phenolic components.

The whisky from upper tiers tended to have the following features: woody, vanilla, fruity/estery, floral, pungent and meaty. In contrast, the whisky stored on the lower tiers was found to have the following features: green/grassy, cereal, creamy, feinty, sour and clean.

Additionally, it is thought that the influence of the wooden cask on whisky quality is much greater in Japan than Scotland. Therefore, in our research we have focused on the diversity of wood species used for casks. For example, whiskies matured in Japanese cedar or in Japanese oak casks made of Mizunara have unique flavour characteristics (Noguchi et al, 2008). The Mizunara whisky has recently received awards in international whisky competitions (Figure 7). We have also devoted considerable attention to the study of maturation. In order to elucidate the various factors influencing whisky maturation, we have developed small casks for laboratory trials (Figure 8).

In the future, we will investigate the optimal combinations of wooden casks and warehouse conditions to create many types of Japanese whisky.

References

Noguchi Y., Hughes P. S., Priest F. G, Conner J. M, and Jack F. (2008). The influence of wood species of cask on matured whisky aroma - the identification of a unique character imparted by casks of Japanese oak. In: *Proceedings of the Third Worldwide Distilled Spirits Conference - New Horizons: Energy, Environment and Enlightenment,* Edited by Walker, G.M and Hughes P. S., Nottingham University Press: 243-251.

Reazin, G. H. (1981). Chemical mechanisms of whisky maturation. *American Journal of Enology and Viticulture* **32**: 283-289.

Figure 7. Trees for the Japanese original casks, and the Mizunara whisky.

Figure 8. Small casks for laboratory trial.

Chapter 28

Aromatic and flavourful distillates from different malt beer specialities

J. Voigt[1], A. Richter[2]
[1]TU München, Wissenschaftszentrum Weihenstephan, Freising, Germany
[2]Weyermann, Specialty Malting, Bamberg, Germany

Introduction

Specialty beers as a basis for the production of beer distillates are not very common in the distilling world. Such distilled products are more often produced from standard or lower quality beers which are distilled and made into beer distillates like German "Bierbrand" or "Bierschnaps". The character of such products is driven by the taste of the originating beer and they have to be made solely from fresh beer in order to transfer the taste and flavour attributes of the beer. By law, the minimum concentration of spirit must be 38% v/v. This paper describes the methods of making the spirit from different primary beers. Four different specialty beers were produced: a wheat bock, rye malt bock, smoked beer bock and a red malt bock. All beers and distillates were analysed and tested for their sensory qualities.

In a subsequent trial, the products were distilled in order to produce distillate products that can be used as flavourings. The process of distilling was performed in a column, varying the number of trays and flow rates and other process parameters. The resulting distillates were characterised by sensory methods; the characters of the spirits were obviously different.

This chapter shows clearly the wide range of characters achievable in beer distillates by altering the malt basis.

Targets

The project was set up in order to investigate the influence of different base beers on the production of beer distillates. The way that the different malt varieties influence the flavour of fresh, unaged and unblended distillates was determined.

Brewing methods

Beers (Figure 1) were produced in 2.5 hl pilot scale brewery in the Weyermann Research Brewery (Figures 2a and 2b). The raw materials were milled and mashed in an infusion mashing programme with a 52°C mash-in temperature, 35 mins at 64°C, 5 mins at 68°C, 20 mins at 72°C. The gravity of the cast-out wort was 17% OG. Boiling was for 70 minutes, with bitter hopping after 10 minutes and aroma hopping

Figure 1. Colours of original beers

Figure 2a. Brewhouse

Figure 2b: Brewhouse

at 60 minutes. Wheat and Rye beers were fermented at warm temperatures, Red and Rauch beers at 12°C.

Brewing raw materials and brewing parameters

The raw materials used for brewing are shown in Table 1. Brewing parameters are shown in Table 2.

Distilling methods

The beers from the brewing trials were distilled in a pilot scale 150 litre still (Figure 3) with 3 bottoms, dephlegmator and a separator. First runs were stopped at 1.3 l, second runs were collected at 80 to 75% vol. alcohol and last runs from 5 to 15%. Samples were taken from all distillates of the original beers.

Analysis and Results

The beers were generally of very high quality as shown in Table 3.

Figure 3. Distilling Plant

The four different beer distillates (Figure 4) were diluted to a concentration of 40% alcohol (v/v) and bottled into clear bottles without any aging in vats. The resulting distillates were sensorially tested by a panel of 6 trained tasters. The beer character, smell and taste was

Table 1. Brewing raw materials

	Weyermann® Wheat Malt	*Weyermann® Pilsner Malt*	*Weyermann® Carared®*	*Weyermann® Carawheat®*	*Weyermann®*
Wheat Bock	53%	35%	10%	2%	
	Vienna Malt	Munich T2 Malt	Rye Malt	Melanoidin Malt	Rye Roast Malt
Rye Bock	35%	25%	25%	12%	3%
	Pilsner Malt	Carared®	Melanoidin Malt		
Red Bock	70%	20%	10%		
	Smoked Malt	Caraaroma®			
Rauch Bock	90%	10%			

Table 2. Brewing parameters

	OG[%]	*Wort Colour [EBC]*	*Yeast Type*	*Alc. Beer [%v/v]*	*Fermentation [days]*	*FV Temp [°C]*
Wheat Bock	17,00%	85	WB-06	7,62	4	18-21
Rye Bock	17,12%	235	K-97	7,24	4	18-21
Red Bock	17,00%	55	W-34	7,18	9	12-13
Rauch Bock	16,80%	85	W-34	6,98	9	13-14

Table 3. Beer tasting results

	Colour	*Haze*	*Foam*	*Smell*	*Taste*	*Body*	*Bitterness*
Wheat Bock	4,8	4,6	4,6	4,4	4,2	3,8	4,0
Rye Bock	3,9	4,3	4,4	4,6	4,4	4,4	4,0
Red Bock	3,9	4,4	4,4	4,4	4,4	4,4	4,0
Rauch Bock	4,8	4,4	4,4	4,6	4,4	4,2	4,0

Table 4. Distillate tasting results

	Smell	*Taste*	*Flavour overall*	*Preference*
Wheat Bock	crisp,yeasty	sweet, honeylike	winey	***
Rye Bock	slightly fruity, sharp	sharp, neutral	sulphury	*
Red Bock	fruity, rich, round	mild, aromatic	mellow	***
Rauch Bock	bread, peaty	mild	slight smoke	****

characterised by a numbering system (1 = poor, 2 = low, 3 = medium, 4 = high, 5 = very good). Specific aromas were described verbally with appropriate terminology.

Summary

Sensory results

Highly aromatic malt additions like in the Red Bock result in very fruity but smooth aromas in the distillate. Apparently some yeasty notes are detectable in distillates from the top fermented wheat and rye bock beers. Smoky components can be are noted in the Rauch Beer distillate, but these are very subtle.

Most importantly it must be stated that beers for the use in beer distillates should be prepared specifically for this use. Undesired aromatic flavours are sometimes due to insufficient quality of the original beers.

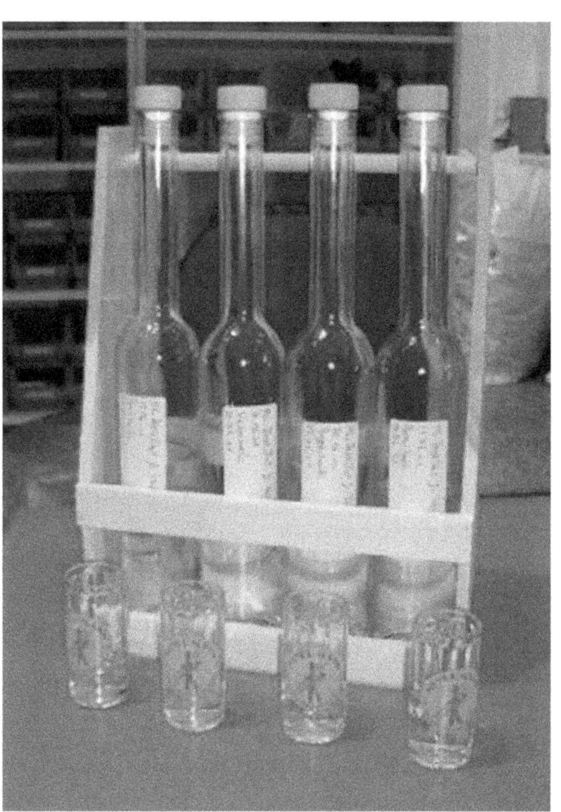

Figure 4. Distillates

Chapter 29

Alert® for methanol, a rapid diagnostic assay to detect methanol contamination in distilled spirits

Sharon Graham[1], Stephen Holmes[1], Brian McGhee[2], Richard Tester[2], Alex Kariagin[3], Brent Steiner[3], Ronald Sarver[3]

[1]Neogen Europe Ltd, The Dairy School, Auchincruive, Ayr, KA6 5HW, Scotland, UK; [2] Glycologic Ltd., c/o Glasgow Caledonian University, Cowcaddens Road, Glasgow, G4 0BA; [3] Neogen Corporation, 620 Lesher Place, Lansing, MI 48912, USA

Introduction

Methanol contamination in illicit, counterfeit or adulterated alcoholic beverages is a potentially serious health hazard in many parts of the world. Effects of methanol ingestion may include confusion, nausea, vomiting, visual problems and abdominal pain, which if left untreated can result in stupor, coma and in the most severe cases death (Ferrari, Arado, Nardo and Giannuzzi, 2003). Methanol poisoning can be difficult to diagnose and treat (Carnero, Nepal and Hartle, 2011; Lushine, Harris and Holger, 2003; Vale and Bradberry, 2009). Methanol contamination of alcoholic beverages is a concern across a broad range of countries. A screening assay that can be rapidly applied on-site to evaluate beverages for methanol contamination is useful for isolating products until additional confirmatory analytical testing can be conducted. Confirmatory analytical testing can require several hours or days to perform since suspect samples need to be sent to analytical laboratories for evaluation.

Materials and methods

Ethanol 95% (Sigma Aldrich, Product # 493538) and methanol (Fisher, Product # A452-4) were used for preparation of control solutions. Alert® for Methanol kits were used for analysis of the control solutions and beverages. Although results can be interpreted visually, for the semi-quantitative results discussed in this work, a spectrophotometer was used.

To determine the precision of the colour generated by the reaction, two sets of six vials of lyophilised enzyme were reconstituted with buffer. Using clean loops, samples of the positive spirit control (1% methanol in 40% ethanol) were added to the reconstituted solutions. Three aliquots of 300 µL were then transferred to microwells. Absorbance values at 650 nm were acquired after 5 min reaction using a Turner Modulus plate reader with the solution in clear flat bottom microwells of a 96 well plate. In addition, linearity of the assay response was determined by similar analysis of control solutions containing the following; 40% ethanol, 1%, 5%, and 10% methanol in 40% ethanol, 30% methanol in water, and 100% methanol.

Absorbance values can also be measured using a StatFax reader which is a general purpose portable spectrophotometer.

Sample analysis procedure for Alert® for Methanol

Each Alert® for Methanol kit contains all the components required to test one sample for the presence of 1% or greater methanol. Two positive control solutions, one for spirits and one for wine are included with each package of kits. The positive control for the beverage type (distilled spirit or beer and wine) should be tested in parallel with each sample tested so the user can compare the colour formation in the sample vial to the colour of the positive control.

The following sampling procedure can be used to evaluate distilled spirits, beer or wine for methanol contamination:

Open the kit's foil packet. Remove the cap and rubber stopper from the glass vial which contains lyophilised enzyme. Then, remove the cap from the plastic tube which contains buffer solution that is used to reconstitute the lyophilised enzyme. Add all the buffer solution to the lyophilised enzyme. Swirl the contents of the vial to ensure full reconstitution. An additional lyophilised enzyme vial should be reconstituted for parallel analysis of the positive control solution. Label the vials accordingly. Then, a sample of the beverage to test is taken by dipping the sample loop into the product. Carefully remove the sample loop so the sample does not get displaced from the loop and place the sample loop into the reconstituted enzyme solution. Stir the loop for 2 s. Using a clean loop, also sample the positive control and dip the loop into another vial of reconstituted enzyme. Stir each for 2 s and withdraw the loops. Cap the vials with the rubber stoppers from each vial and shake the vials for 10 s. Wait 5 min and read the results. A sample containing more than 1% methanol will be as dark as, or darker than, the positive control.

Results

Lyophilised enzyme vials from 12 different kits were reconstituted with buffer and the positive spirit control was added to each vial using a clean sample loop. Absorbance values at 650 nm were collected after 5 min and the results are shown in Table 1a (set 1) and Table 1b (set 2) for triplicate samplings of each solution. Data were collected in two sets of six solutions so the reactions could all be initiated within a 15 s period by addition of 10 μL of 1% methanol in 40% ethanol. The average absorbance for the 1st set of reactions was 0.52 $\pm$ 0.06 with a 12% coefficient of variation. The average absorbance for the 2nd set was 0.50 $\pm$ 0.06 with a 12% coefficient of variation. These data indicated the colour generation for the lyophilised enzyme vials were consistent within the lot and a specification for the permitted variation in colour generation was established at $<20\%$.

Table 1a. Absorbance at 5 min for reconstituted enzyme vials after addition of the positive spirit control (1% methanol in 40% ethanol), set 1.

Triplicate A_{650} for Six Control Samples					
1	*2*	*3*	*4*	*5*	*6*
0.5540	0.5710	0.4434	0.5262	0.5147	0.4218
0.5468	0.5765	0.4374	0.5280	0.5099	0.4165
0.5874	0.6230	0.4854	0.5770	0.5433	0.4647

Table 1b. Absorbance at 5 min for set 2.

Triplicate A_{650} for Six Control Samples					
1	*2*	*3*	*4*	*5*	*6*
0.5667	0.5093	0.5214	0.4504	0.4586	0.4105
0.5999	0.5310	0.5137	0.4759	0.4652	0.4211
0.6012	0.5485	0.5261	0.4947	0.4853	0.4383

The assay's response with increasing concentration of methanol was determined and the results are listed in Table 2 and plotted in Figure 1. Data were fit using a least squares non-linear regression resulting in the following equation, $y = 0.0671\ln(x) + 0.5724$. Since detection of methanol is accomplished through enzymatic reactions, the rate of product formation is controlled by enzymatic reaction rate. The relationship between amount of methanol in the sample and absorbance was not linear but was proportional. The data fit the model with a squared correlation coefficient (R^2)

equal to 0.95. Visually, it was easy to distinguish the colour difference between the negative control containing 40% ethanol in water and the positive control containing 1% methanol in 40% ethanol. Average absorbance values of 0.37 and 0.63 for the negative and positive control solutions, respectively, were consistent with the visual differentiation of the solution colour. Background absorbance can result from low levels of non-specific enzymatic turnover. During the course of the reaction, the colour of the 1% or greater methanol solutions were visually differentiated with the colour generation increasing from lowest to highest methanol concentration. But at 5 min, it was difficult to visually distinguish the colour for the 5% and greater methanol solutions due to the very dark colour formation in all those solutions.

A variety of beverages including beer, hard ciders, wine, and distilled spirits were tested using the assay kits. With the large sample dilution (~200x) there was no significant change in background observed for unspiked beverages that were not contaminated with methanol. This included dark beer, liquor, and red wines. Samples spiked with 1% methanol when tested in the assay generated equivalent dark colour as the matched positive controls. Results for a typical dark beer sample are listed in Table 3. No significant difference in background colour of the unspiked beer samples were observed compared to the negative control of 5% ethanol. Beer samples spiked with 1% methanol showed significantly darker colour compared to the negative control as indicated by the 2x increase in A_{650} within 5 min.

Discussion

Alert® for Methanol provides a rapid method to detect the presence of 1% or greater methanol in beverages. Colour generation is consistent within a lot and is proportional to the methanol concentration, although not in a direct linear relationship. Qualitative assessment of samples

Table 2: Absorbance of Alert for Methanol Solution with Increasing Methanol Concentration.

λ (nm)	*40% EtOH*	*1% MeOH / 40% EtOH*	*5% MeOH / 40% EtOH*	*10% MeOH/ 40% EtOH*	*30% MeOH / Water*	*100% MeOH*
650	0.360	0.619	0.668	0.729	0.780	0.824
650	0.368	0.609	0.653	0.757	0.784	0.814
650	0.388	0.649	0.715	0.801	0.827	0.894
Ave.	0.372	0.626	0.679	0.762	0.797	0.844
S.D.	0.015	0.021	0.033	0.036	0.026	0.044
C.V.	4%	3%	5%	5%	3%	5%

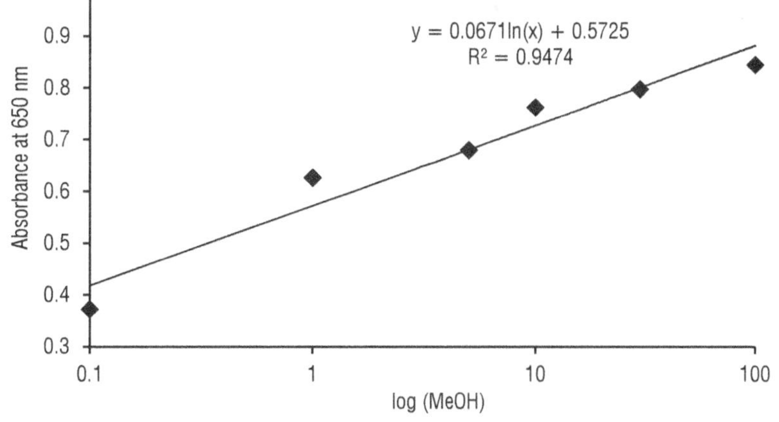

Figure 1. Plot of Absorbance versus methanol concentration

Table 3: Absorbance (650 nm) of Methanol spiked and unspiked Beer samples.

λ (nm)	5% EtOH Blank	Beer Blank	Beer + 1% MeOH Spike	Beer + 5% MeOH Spike	Beer + 30% MeOH Spike
650	0.168	0.137	0.297	0.346	0.428
650	0.162	0.141	0.313	0.357	0.441
650	0.176	0.141	0.314	0.367	0.448
Ave.	0.169	0.140	0.308	0.357	0.439
S.D.	0.007	0.002	0.010	0.010	0.010
C.V.	4%	2%	3%	3%	2%

is performed with visual inspection and semi-quantitative results are obtained using a spectrophotometer that can measure absorbance in the visible spectral region. There is some background colour generated within 5 min for samples that don't contain methanol and the background colour increases with time. Therefore, it is recommended that colour formation is examined up to 5 min. and samples along with the negative and positive control solutions are tested in parallel. Alert® for Methanol is intended as a screening assay for the presence of methanol and all suspect samples should be confirmed by independent methods.

References

Carnero, G., Nepal, M. and Hartle, J. (2011). Severe methanol poisoning requiring recurrent hemodialysis and fomepizole. *American Journal of Kidney Diseases* **57**: B29.

Ferrari, L.A., Arado, M.G., Nardo, C.A., Giannuzzi, L. (2003). Post-mortem analysis of formic acid disposition in acute methanol intoxication. *Forensic Science International* **133**: 152-158.

Lushine, K.A., Harris, C.R. and Holger, J.S. (2003). Methanol injestion: prevention of toxic sequelae after massive ingestion. *Journal of Emergency Medicine* **24**: 433-436.

Vale, A. and Bradberry, S. (2009). Management of poisoning. *Medicine* **37**: 106-108.

Chapter 30

The effect of organic haze on the ethanol determination in whisky

Roman Beneš, Martina Trinkel, Christina Reichart
Anton Paar, GmbH, Anton-Paar Straße 20, 8054 Graz, Austria

Introduction

It is desirable for whiskies to be clear, i.e. without any haze. During the production process, whisky may often be hazy. Haze may be from inorganic and organic substances in whisky.

Inorganic haze derives from the lower solubility of salts in alcohol compared to water. It might be generated during dilution of whisky with water involving ions like calcium and magnesium.

In potable spirits organic haze can be formed by fatty acids, fatty acid ethyl esters, etheric oils, terpenes, higher alcohols, and many other substances. Organic haze typically disappears by the addition of ethanol and/or by increasing the temperature.

Before bottling, whisky is typically chill filtered to get rid of the haze.

The measurement of the ethanol concentration is required during the whole production process, in particular, prior to and after the filtration.

Motivation

The Edrington Group Ltd. reported a discrepancy between the measurement of the ethanol concentration of filtered and unfiltered whiskies measured with the Alcolyzer and the density meter DMA5000 (both from Anton Paar, Austria). The alcohol concentration based on the density measurement is normally lower compared to the ethanol concentration measured with the Alcolyzer. This difference comes from the extract in whisky and is called obscuration. The obscuration should be smaller in filtered whiskies, because they contain less extract than unfiltered samples.

Surprisingly, the obscuration was higher in filtered whisky samples. This phenomenon is illustrated in the Table 1. Two whiskies were analysed before and after filtration. The ethanol concentration measured with the Alcolyzer and with distillation is the same in case of the filtered samples, however, it differs for the

Table 1. Obscuration of filtered and unfiltered whiskies

Sample	*Description*	*Colour*	*Density g/cm³*	*% v/v from density*	*% v/v by alcolyzer*	*% v/v by distillation*	*Obscuration to alcolyzer*	*Obscuration to distillation*
1	Filtered	20.75	0.943197	42.92	43.195	43.15	0.26	0.26
2	Unfiltered	23.8	0.942721	43.19	43.39	43.54	0.2	0.37
3	Filtered	19.1	0.947869	40.11	40.39	40.43	0.28	0.3
4	Unfiltered	23.6	0.947845	40.12	40.31	40.48	0.19	0.36

unfiltered samples. The obscuration related to the distillation has increased for the unfiltered samples whereas the obscuration related to the Alcolyzer has decreased. This effect was studied and is discussed in this report.

Measurements and results

Whisky samples were provided by The Edrington Group Ltd,, United Kingdom. Ten different malt whiskies, as well as filtered and unfiltered samples of each whisky were available. The conditions of the sample filtration were not known to the authors. The ethanol concentration of all whiskies was between 40 % v/v and 43 %v/v. The alcohol concentration in whiskies within this study was measured:

1. by classical distillation as the reference method, and
2. with the Alcolyzer (Anton Paar GmbH), which utilises the absorption of the sample in the near infra-red spectral region to determine the ethanol concentration

Turbidity measurement

The turbidity of the samples was measured with the HazeQC nephelometer (Anton Paar, Austria) using 90° and 25° geometry and the wavelength of 650 nm. The sample chamber of the nephelometer is temperature controlled and the temperature can be varied from -5°C to 40°C. The nephelometer was calibrated with formazine solutions (Hach, USA).

The turbidity at 20°C of the filtered samples was smaller than 0.4 NTU and the turbidity of unfiltered whiskies varied from 10 NTU to 20 NTU.

The turbidity is dependent on the sample temperature (see Figure 1) and on the ethanol concentration (see Figure 2). The temperature dependence was measured in the nephelometer by changing the sample temperature. The same sample remained in the cell during the whole measurement. The temperature range from 15°C to 35°C was investigated and took about 10 minutes to perform and after attemperation the turbidity was stable. In addition, the turbidity change with temperature was reversible.

For the second experiment – ethanol dependence, 50 mL of the sample was diluted with 2 mL and 1 mL of distilled water or with 2 mL and 1 mL ethanol p.a. In this way, the ethanol concentration varied about +/- 2% v/v from untreated sample.

These experiments have clearly proved an existence of an organic haze in the received samples. The same behaviour was observed on 4 randomly selected samples.

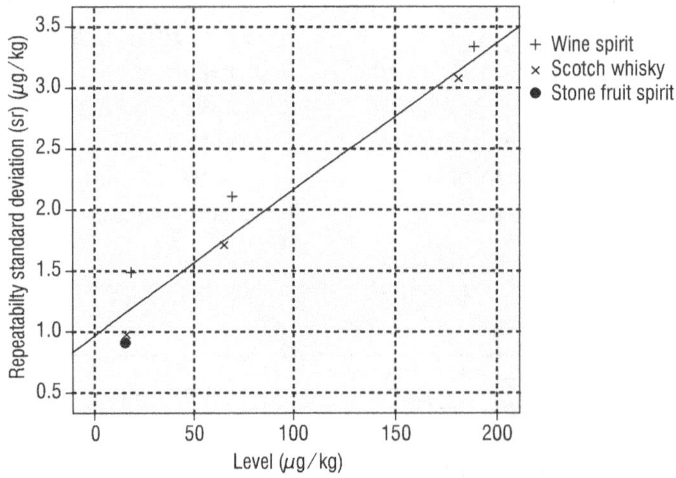

Figure 1. Dependence of turbidity on temperature (unfiltered sample 4064).

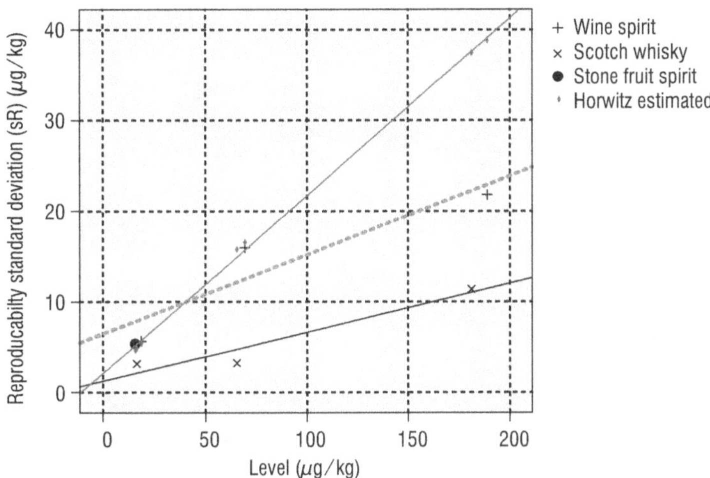

Figure 2. UnfilteredsSample 4064 - addition of 1 and 2 mL of distilled water or ethanol, respectively.

Density measurement

The change of density with temperature of filtered and unfiltered sample has been compared. For this purpose, both the filtered and unfiltered samples Nr. 4069 were slightly diluted with distilled water (approx. 2 mL H_2O into 50 mL whisky). The reason for dilution of the sample was:

1. to generate more haze, and
2. to adjust the density of the filtered and unfiltered sample on the same density value at 20°C.

The temperature dependence was measured with the density meter DMA 5000 by changing the sample temperature; the same sample remained in the cell during the whole measurement. The temperature range from 15°C to 35°C was investigated and took about 15 minutes to perform. As with turbidity, the density change with temperature of both, filtered and unfiltered whisky was found to be reversible. The results can be seen on the Figure 3.

The density changes are different with temperature for filtered and unfiltered samples. When increasing the sample temperature, the density of the unfiltered sample decreased more compared to the filtered one. Because of the constant mass, the volume of unfiltered sample expands more for the same temperature difference. Simultaneously, the haze decreased. This indicates some structural changes of the hazy whiskies that lead to the volume increase accompanied by the decrease of the haze. Even if the density difference between hazy and clear whiskies for $\Delta T = 20°C$ is small, only 4.10^{-5} g/cm^3, this density difference would still express a difference of 0.025 % v/v in terms of the apparent ethanol concentration measured by the density. The apparent ethanol concentration increases with the temperature.

Alcolyzer measurement

First, the Alcolyzer was tested with turbid model samples, which were created by adding of formazine in water and a binary solution. The turbidity was about 100 NTU, i.e. 5-times more than it is in real samples. The measured concentration was not influenced by formazine.

Five samples with varying ethanol concentration were prepared from the hazy sample Nr. 4069 by dilution with water or ethanol. This procedure has been already described in Chapter 3.1. The ethanol concentration and

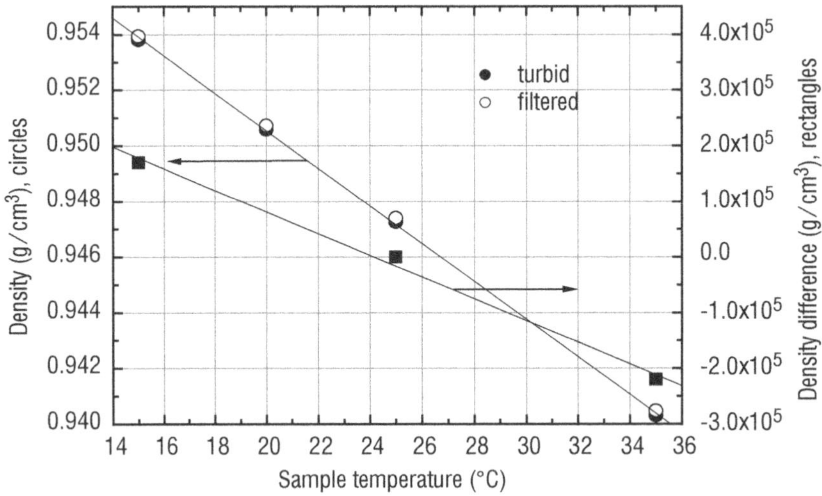

Figure 3. Density change with temperature.

density were measured simultaneously (see Figure 4).

With increasing ethanol concentration the obscuration increases and haze decreases. However, the decrease in haze should increase the sample volume, i.e. the apparent concentration of whisky measured by density and, consequently, the obscuration should decrease (see Chapter 3.2.). This discrepancy can be explained only by spectral changes during the dilution. The expected spectral changes are extremely small and, in addition, overlaid with a huge ethanol absorbance. To be able to detect them, five identically diluted samples were prepared from filtered whisky 4069 and the differences of the absorbance spectra of unfiltered and filtered sample were calculated and evaluated. The absorbance spectra were measured in the region of the second overtone of the symmetrical C-H stretching of the methylene group. The vibration of methylene group reacts sensitively to structural changes, in particular on weak H-bonds between this group and other components. The absorbance differences were pre-processed by a base-line forcing the absorbance at the wavelengths 1177 nm and 1191 nm to be zero. The results are presented on the Figure 5. The discontinuity or "an apparent peak" at 1183 nm is considered to

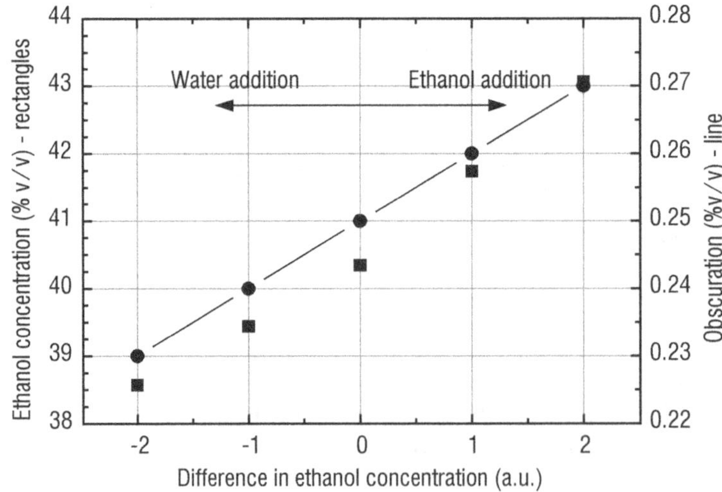

Figure 4. Change of the obscuration as a function of ethanol concentration (unfiltered sample 4069).

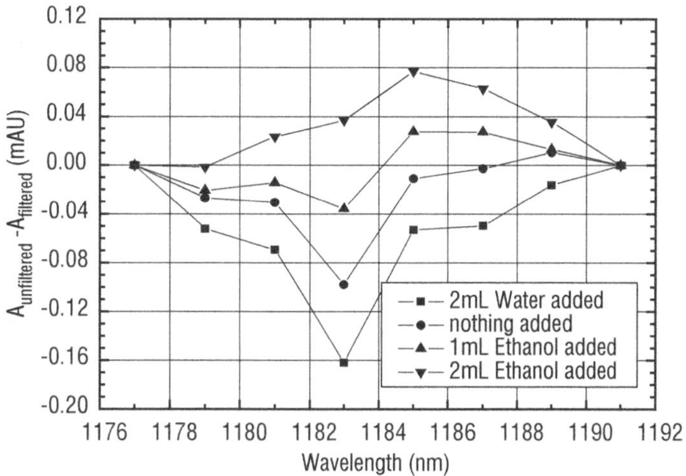

Figure 5. Spectral differences between filtered and unfiltered sample as a function of ethanol concentration.

be an artefact, but even then, a clear tendency in absorbance difference between unfiltered and filtered sample is observed. The spectra of ethanol in water have a form of a peak having its maximum approx. in the middle of the wavelength range, i.e. this form is similar to the absorbance differences from the Figure 5. This means, that by the same ethanol addition the ethanol concentration in hazy samples increases slightly more. Moreover, some systematic difference in the curve form indicates more complex changes in the sample.

The same effect could be expressed in terms of the ethanol concentration measured by the Alcolyzer (see Figure 6). Again, the Alcolyzer measured slightly lower in unfiltered samples where water was added compared to the filtered sample, and, in the contrary, more in case of ethanol addition.

Discussion

Unfiltered whisky is a complicated system, in which the haze obeys equilibrium rules being influenced by the temperature and ethanol concentration.

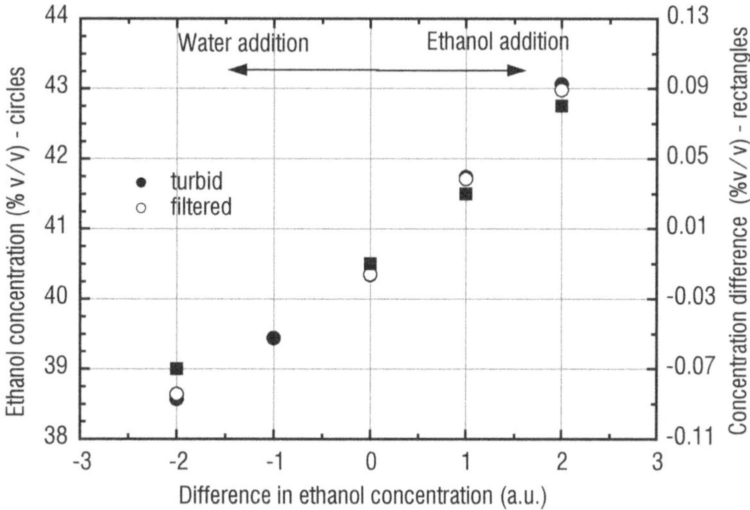

Figure 6. Ethanol concentration measured by alcolyzer of clear and hazy whisky.

Fatty acids react with the ethanol and form ethyl-esters and water (Hauptmann, 1989). The reaction needs free protons, which must be present in the sample. As the pH value of whiskies is normally around pH = 4, free protons are expected to occur. This reaction is reversible, because the water re-hydrolyses the ethyl-esters back to the ethanol and the fatty acid. This equilibrium can be easily influenced by addition of ethanol or water. The temperature will influence the equilibrium, too. Both effects correspond to our observations.

Conclusion

Unfiltered whisky is a complicated system, in which the haze obeys equilibrium rules being influenced by the temperature and ethanol concentration.

The sample temperature and the ethanol concentration change the haze, density and absorption spectrum of the filtered and unfiltered whiskies differently.

The Alcolyzer is not influenced by the light scattering due to the haze presence, but rather by the chemical changes in the whiskies, which are accompanied with haze.

Formation of ethyl-ester from fatty acid may be an explanation for the obscuration changes in the sample during the filtration.

The distillation reference method destroys, due to the high temperature, the equilibrium in the unfiltered sample and, consequently, is not comparable with the Alcolyzer. It is questionable, if the distillation is the correct method for the determination of alcohol strength in the hazy sample before filtration.

The Alcolyzer is believed to be better able to measure the ethanol concentration in the hazy sample, even if the obscuration is lower than expected, because it measures mainly free ethanol and not bonded one in ester. The filtration will remove the ethyl-ester in any case.

Literature

Hauptmann, S (1986). *Einführung in die organische Chemie*. VEB Deutscher Verlag für Grundstoffindustrie, Leipzig, Germany

Chapter 31

Evaluation of the performance of ethyl carbamate determination by GC/MS analysis in spirits

G. Snakkers[1], P. Brunerie[2], S. Muller[3], M. Garden[4], L. Kragelund[5], P. Lockyer[6], K. Mac Namara[7], F. Scanlan[8], I. Tonutti[9]

[1]Bureau National Interprofessionnel du Cognac (BNIC), Station Viticole, 69 rue de Bellefonds, 16100 Cognac France; [2]Centre de Recherche Pernod-Ricard; [3]Edrington Distillers Ltd, 2500 Great Western Road, Glasgow, G15 6RW, Scotland; [4]Scotch Whisky Association; [5]Pernod-Ricard Nordic; [6]Diageo TCE; [7]Irish Distillers; [8]Campari Technical Centre; [9]Analytical Research Lab. Tradall SA Switzerland, Bacardi

Introduction

An inter-laboratory collaborative trial on ethyl carbamate (EC) analysis by GC/MS was performed under the request of CEPS-GPTS (Confédération Européenne des Producteurs de Spiritueux-Group Project Technical Scientific) in order to evaluate the performance of the methods and to allow laboratories to improve their practice. EC concentration is regulated for spirits in Canada with a maximum limit of 125 μg/kg.

Materials and methods

18 laboratories (Table 1) from spirit industry and government control laboratories have participated (Europe and USA). Seven samples were analyzed; three were genuine spirits (a wine spirit, a whisky and a stone fruit spirit) and two were the same wine spirit and whisky spiked with known amounts of pure EC (about 50 and 150 μg/kg). Laboratories were free to use their own method of analysis but were asked to give a full description of the conditions of the sample preparation and the method used.

Results

LOD & LOQ

The study showed that a good precision can be achieved for this analyte without any sample preparation. The LOD or sensitivity of the measurement can be improved by a simple concentration step.

This inter-laboratory trial showed that the limit of quantification varied from 3 to 40 μg/kg (the mean is 13) and the limit of detection from 1 to 12 μg/kg (the mean is 4).

Fidelity

The repeatability standard deviations were homogeneous between samples (figure 1, table 2). The reproducibility standard deviations were about 30 % for a level of 15 μg/kg, 6 % and 12%, respectively for the whisky and wine spirit samples with a EC level of 180 μg/kg (spiked samples) (figure 2, table 2). These values were lower than those estimated by Horwitz' formula.

Table 1. Participants.

Name of correspondant	*Society*	*Country*
Armen MIRZOIAN	Alcohol and Tobacco Tax and Trade Bureau	USA
Craig OWEN	Scotch Whisky Research Institute	Scotland
Emiliana GARBO	Analytical Research Lab. Martini &Rossi	Italia
Carol DRUMMOND	Liquor Control Board of Ontario (LCBO)	Canada
Jean-Charles MATHURIN	Remy Martin	France
Jenny BREEN	Brown-Forman R&D	USA
Joël LAVERGNE	Courvoisier	France
Karen HAGGARTY	Chivas Brothers Ltd. – Pernod-Ricard	Scotland
KEVIN MAC NAMARA	Irish Distillers – Pernod-Ricard	Ireland
Mario GREGORI	Campari Technical Centre	Italia
Nicole OBSCHWALD	SGS Institut Fresenius GmbH	Deutchland
Pascal BRUNERIE	Centre de Recherche Pernod-Ricard	France
Robert FOTHERINGHAM	Chivas, Glen Keith Technical Centre	Scotland
Peter F. LAURSEN	Pernod Ricard Nordic	Denmark
Stéphane VERGER	Martell – Pernod-Ricard	France
Steven MULLER	The Edrington Group Ltd.	Scotland
Sylvie ESTREGUIL	Station Viticole du BNIC	France
Vic CAMERON	Diageo	Scotland

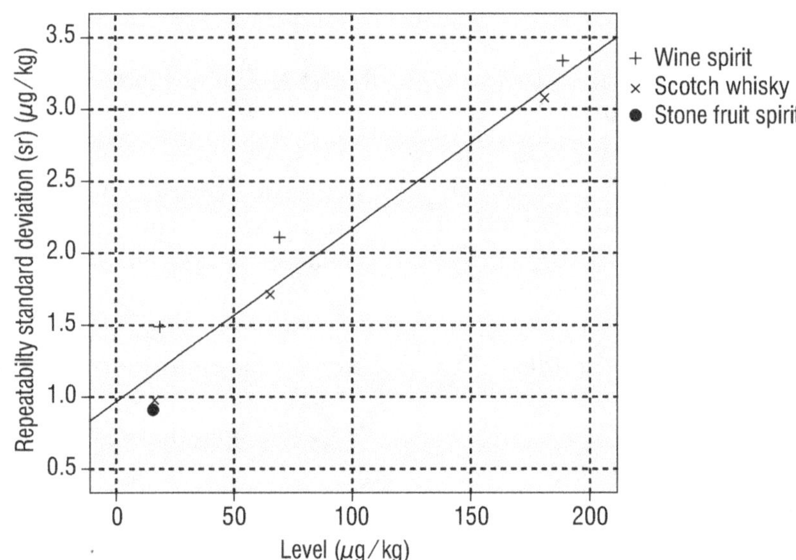

Figure 1. Repeatability standard deviations according to the level.

Table 2 : Linear modelling for fidelity standard deviation

Products	*Standard Deviation (µg/kg)*	*Formula*
Wine spirit Whisky Fruit stone spirit	Repeatability	1.0 + 1.2 %
Whisky	Reproducibility	1.2 + 5.4%
Wine spirit	Reproducibility	6.5 + 8.7 %

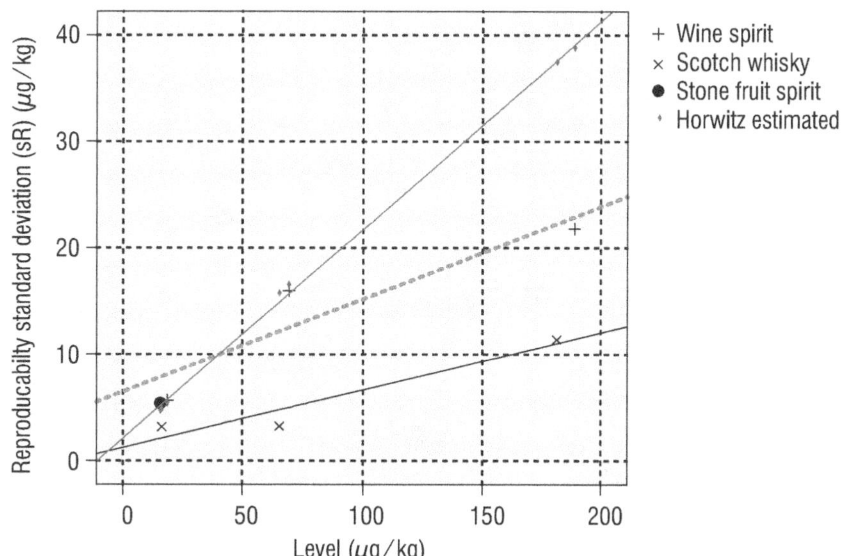

Figure 2. Reproducibility standard deviations according to the level – observed reproducibility, Horwitz estimated reproducibility

Recoveries

For the spikes, mean recoveries range between 96 % and 102 % (table 3).

Table 3. Recoveries based on the samples means.

Sample	Mean (µg/kg) spiked sample	Mean (µg/kg) Based sample	Observed spiked (µg/kg)	Theoretical spiked level (µg/kg)	Recovery (%)	Target level (µg/kg)
W spirit 2	69.3	18.7	50.6	52.6	96%	71.3
W spirit 3	188.7	18.7	170.1	175.5	97%	194.2
Whisky 2	65.4	16.4	49.0	47.9	102%	64.3
Whisky 3	181.1	16.4	164.7	162.8	101%	179.2

Conclusion

These results demonstrate the suitability/reliability of methods using classical GC/MS equipment in Single Ion Monitoring mode to test compliance of the spirits with regulatory limits of 125 µg/kg.

Nevertheless, specific points of EC analysis should be observed :

- The possible generation of EC during injection from interaction of ethanol with the exposed end of the column in the inlet.
- All chemicals used for sample preparation (solvents) and the Internal Standard (especially deuterated EC) have to be free of EC
- Due to the low specificity of EC ions, it is important to check the purity of the qualifier / quantifiers ions and optimise the chromatographic conditions to ensure correct identification and quantification.

Chapter 32

Energy potential and liquid reuse from distillery co-product streams

Jon McAteer
Technical Manager, Veolia Water Solutions & Technologies, Aqua House, 2620 Kings Court, Birmingham Business Park, Birmingham, B37 7YE

Introduction

In the production of whisky there are a few co-products that generally require processing prior to removal from site. The main co-products are

- Draff – the remains of the malt from the lauter tun after the bulk of the sugars have been transferred to the wort,
- Pot Ale – the residue from the first distillation stage (the wash still) containing the yeast and other solids from the fermented wort
- Spent lees – the residue from the second spirit still, with some contamination and high concentrations of copper.

The draff and pot ale have historically been processed to produce animal feed. This is normally done in a dark grains plant. The Draff is dewatered to increase the solids concentration, the pot ale is evaporated to create a syrup and the two can then be combined and further dried to produce dried distillers grain (DDG), sold as animal feed. The dewatered draff and pot ale syrup can however both be sold without blending as animal feeds. The pot ale syrup can only really be used for cattle feed due to its high copper content which would be poisonous to sheep.

The processing of the co-products is energy intensive, utilising both steam and electricity in the dewatering, drying and evaporation processes. Due to fluctuations in price of the animal feeds the dark grain plants are not always a profit centre, although they provide a sustainable discharge route for the co-products produced by the distilling process.

The water evaporated from the pot ale is contaminated with organic pollution and is usually blended with the other low organic strength waste waters and treated in an effluent treatment plant prior to discharge to a river. The general schematic can be seen in figure 1.

Recoverable streams from co-products

Within the draff from a malt distillery there is typically 22-24% dry solids (d.s.). These solids could be anaerobically digested to generate biogas, a renewable source of methane or alternatively the draff can be to be used in a biomass boiler for the generation of steam. Figure 2 shows the potential boiler output from 1 tonne per hour of draff at various dry solids

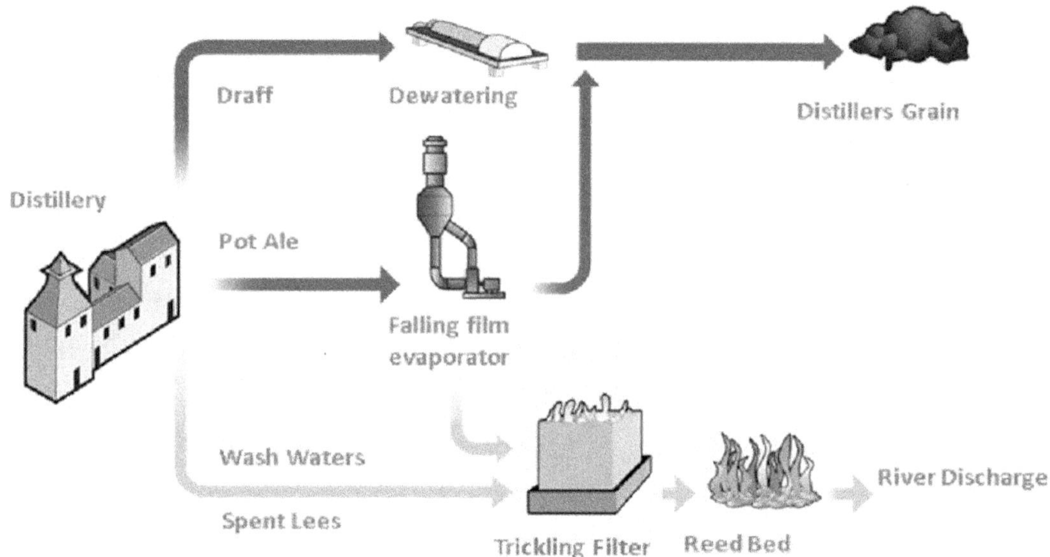

Figure 1. Typical current distillery co-products treatment.

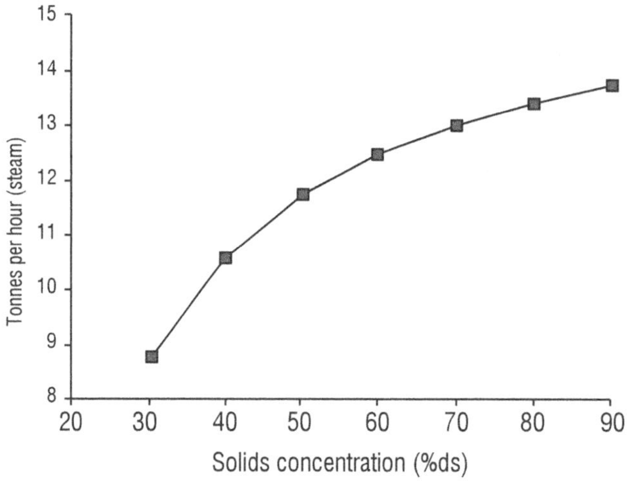

Figure 2. Boiler Output from 1 tph (dry) draff.

concentrations, the dry solids content typically needs to be above 60% to provide efficient steam generation.

Pot Ale has a high Chemical Oxygen Demand (COD) which can be converted to biogas in an anaerobic reactor. Spent wash from a grain distillery has both a high COD concentration and a medium level of suspended solids (SS). Table 1 indicates the typical levels.

From the data in table 1 it can be seen that there is significant water content in the co-products produced. There are many applications where water has been recovered from industrial water treatment plants. This typically involves the use of ultrafiltration and reverse osmosis, applying both biological and physical treatment

Table 1. Typical levels of contamination per mla produced.

	COD, mg/l	*SS*	*Flow*
Draff		22-24%	7.3 tonnes
Pot Ale	57,000	0.9-1.1 %	20.5 m^3
Spent Lees	300	<.01%	10 m^3
Spent Wash	70,000	3.5%	32 m^3

to the impurities in the water. There are even occasions where recovered water has been used as part of the feed to a drinking water treatment facility.

Research was conducted by Veolia into the suitability of various technologies for the treatment of distillery co-products. The investigations were centred on anaerobic treatment as this converts the high COD concentrations to methane rich biogas, with minimal energy and sludge production. With additional BioMethanation Potential (BMP) tests (figure 3), indicating that there is good potential for the digestion of all the distillery co-products, further developments of the technologies have been investigated.

Roseisle Distillery

Diageo have constructed a new malt whisky distillery at Roseisle, on the same site as the Roseisle maltings, to produce approx 12.6 million litres of alcohol (mla) per annum. As part of their commitment to the environment, Diageo's vision was to have a significant amount of the energy required for the distilling process produced from the co-products. *"..an aspiration to deliver a truly sustainable distilling operation, which would be both fossil fuel and water neutral". (Jappy 2010).* An additional benefit of the overall treatment process was the potential to recover water for the maltings process.

Due to the complexity of the project, Veolia Water Solutions & Technologies worked in partnership with Dalkia (Veolia Energy), to deliver and operate the bioenergy and water recovery plant. Veolia's responsibilities include separation of the solids from the aqueous streams, generation of biogas and production of good quality treated water. Dalkia's responsibilities include steam generation from the biomass and biogas and the daily operation of the plant.

All the process stages had been proven in various applications prior to this project, but not all linked together to form the complete facility, shown in figure 4. Various trials were conducted on different technologies and a combination of technologies. This was to ensure that the plant performed as expected when the new build distillery was operational. As the distillery was a new build on a larger scale than has historically been constructed previously, there were some challenges in trialling the processes on representative co-products.

The main process stages are shown in figure 4, with the preparation of the biomass for the biomass boiler occurring in the dewatering/ boiler building. The subsequent aqueous treatment utilises as a first stage, a high rate expanded granular sludge bed, anaerobic reactor to convert the majority of the COD in to biogas ~ 90%. The remainder of the organic pollution

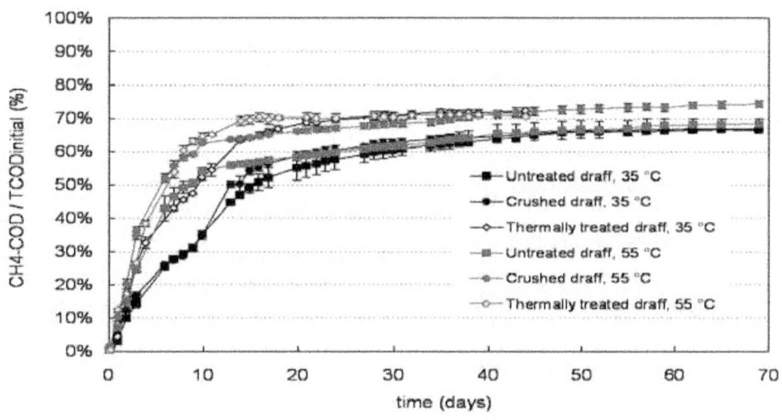

Figure 3. BioMethanation Potential (BMP) Test Results.

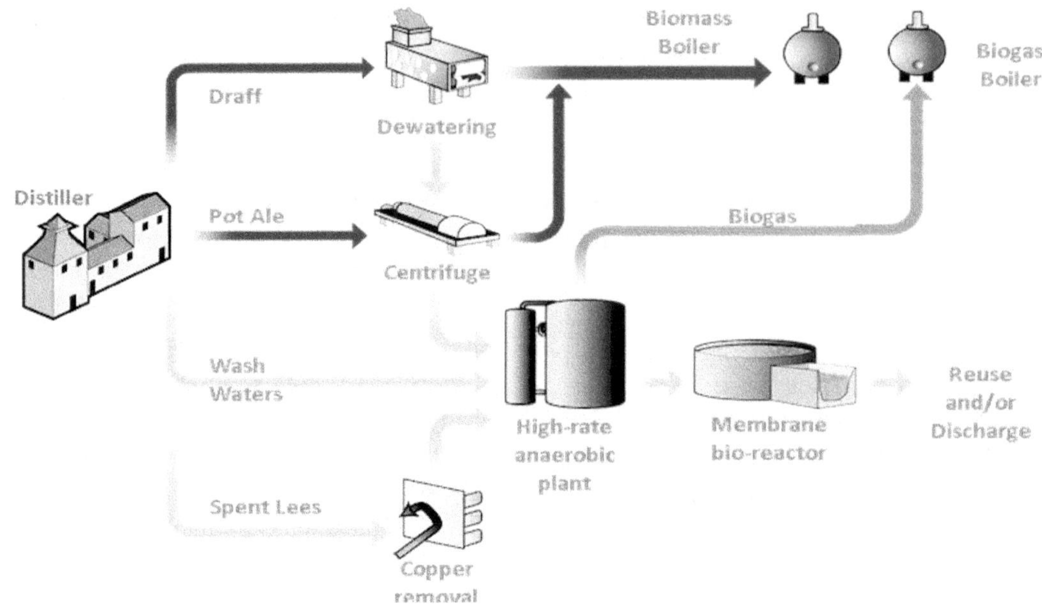

Figure 4. Overall Plant Layout for Roseisle Bioenergy Plant.

is removed through the multistage aerobic plant, culminating with an ultrafiltration membrane to provide a high quality treated effluent.

The Bioenergy facility was commissioned in 2009 to coincide with the start up of the distillery. Overall, the biogas produced from the anaerobic plant has been more than was expected during the design phase. This is attributed to a higher concentration of solids in the feed to the anaerobic reactor. The quality of the treated water has generally been good although to reuse the treated water in the adjacent Maltings plant would require further treatment.

Figure 5 shows how the biogas flow is proportional to the Soluble COD load fed to the anaerobic reactor, with the specific gas yield demonstrating the stability of the process.

The biomass and biogas boiler have been producing steam for the distillery operation, reducing the reliance on heavy fuel oil. During the design, it was anticipated that dust and culms from the adjacent Maltings could be used to aid the dry solids content of the biomass. It has however been found that the dust and culms has a low ash melting point and therefore requires careful monitoring of the feed ratio to minimise clinker production in the ash.

Cameronbridge Grain Distillery

A similar approach to that applied at Roseisle has been developed for the Cameronbridge distillery, shown in figure 6. There is however a major increase in the scale of the facility due to the production capacity of the grain distillery which has been increased from 60 mla to 105 mla and is now the largest grain distillery in Europe. To facilitate this increase in capacity a change in the production method has been implemented, from the historical, cooked process to a Low Temperature and Pressure (LTP) process.

Cameronbridge distillery discharges the liquid waste from site to the Firth of Forth within the permitted consent from SEPA. The increase in the distillery production would also increase the discharge to the Firth of Forth which, whilst within consent would increase the overall BOD discharge from the site. Diageo are focused on reducing their impact on the environment and the installation of the water recovery plant will significantly reduce the BOD in the discharge, leading to a 67% decrease in Diageo's global BOD discharges. (Diageo 2010)

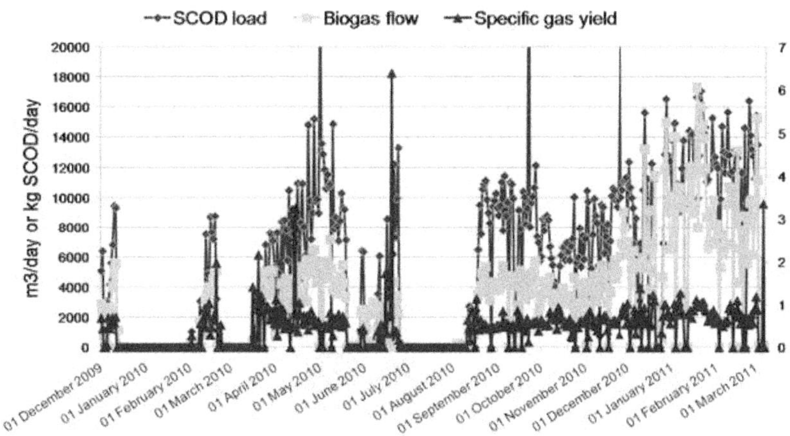

Figure 5. Biogas Yield and Flow.

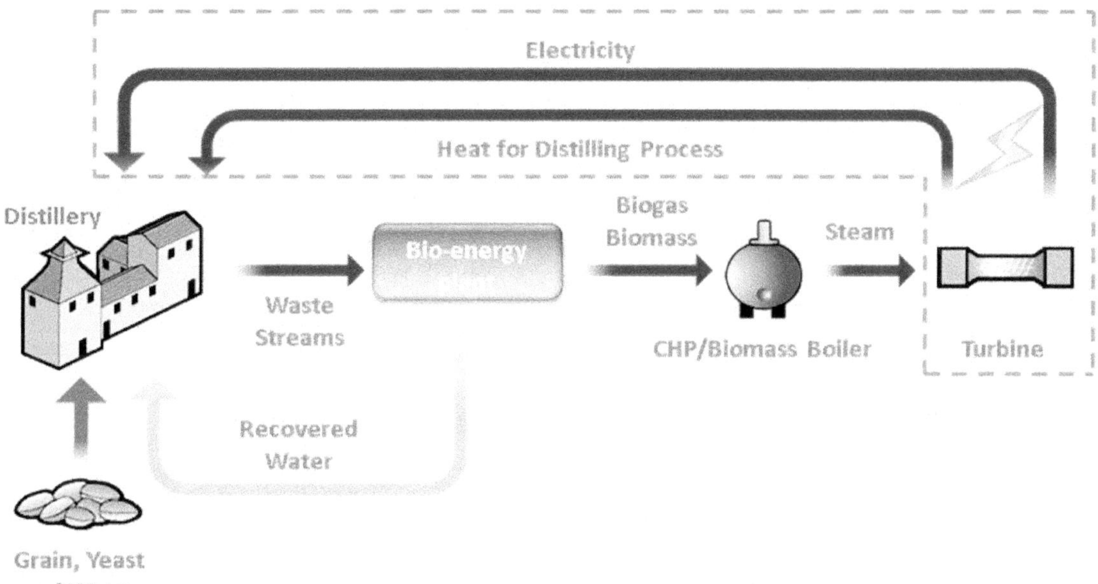

Figure 6. Cameronbridge Bioenergy and Water Recovery Plant.

The bioenergy facility must be able to operate with changeable ratio's of LTP : 'Cooked' through the distillery production. To facilitate the development and security of the scheme, various trials were undertaken at differing LTP ratios. These trials investigated dewatering technologies and anaerobic/aerobic solutions as well as full characterisation of the spent wash.

One of the requirements for the bioenergy plant was to keep the parasitic power to a minimum. The spent grain has historically been separated from the aqueous discharge by centrifuges, however the power consumption on the centrifuges is high. This would also potentially increase by 75% with the increase in production. Continuously running belt presses were investigated and the technology delivered a higher dry solids content of the biomass and a lower solids level in the filtrate compared to the centrifuges. The same was found when comparing the belt presses with screw presses on a high LTP ratio.

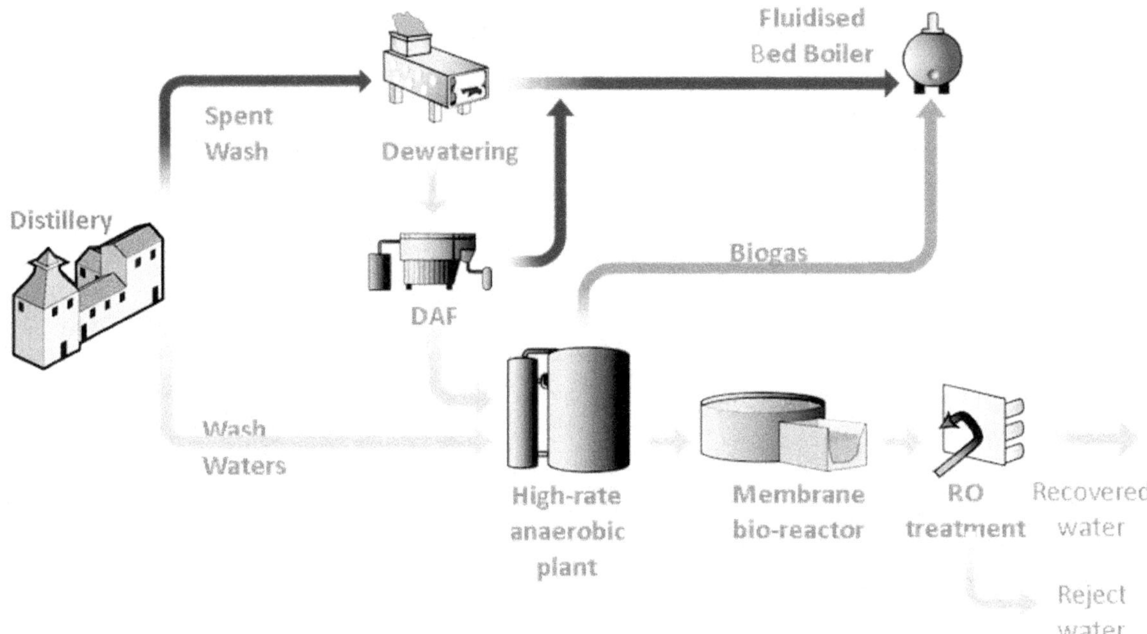

Figure 7. Cameronbridge Co-Product Processing.

The main process units to prepare the biomass and create the biogas out of the aqueous stream are shown in figure 7.

The spent wash from the distillery is first dewatered to 30% ds on belt presses. The filtrate from the presses passes through a Dissolved Air Flotation unit to recover solids and reduce the solids concentration in the feed to the anaerobic reactor. All the biomass removed from the spent wash is then fed to a fluidised bed biomass boiler to raise steam. The steam is then passed to either the distillery or a steam turbine to generate electricity. The biogas produced in the anaerobic reactors is co-fired in the fluidised bed boiler with the biomass to generate steam. The anaerobically treated water now has the majority of the carbon impurities removed and is transferred to the water recovery plant, which consists of an aerobic membrane bio-reactor followed by a reverse osmosis plant. The recovered water will be used in the bioenergy facility and the distillery, reducing the distilleries overall water consumption by 30%.

Commissioning of the dewatering facility and the aqueous treatment plant started mid August 2011. The preliminary results demonstrated that the anaerobic reactor was producing burnable biogas within 24hrs of start up with a methane concentration of 70%.

Further developments

There is significant potential for energy and water to be recovered from distilling co-products as demonstrated on the larger scale with the projects discussed above. There is however a need to make technology suitable for a smaller scale application simplifying the process from a two stage biomass burning and aqueous treatment to a single stage biogas generation process. The latest research being investigated is to blend the draff with the pot ale and convert the organic matter into biogas through anaerobic digestion shown in figure 8.

This method provides a simple treatment route for the co-products and for the utilisation of biogas.

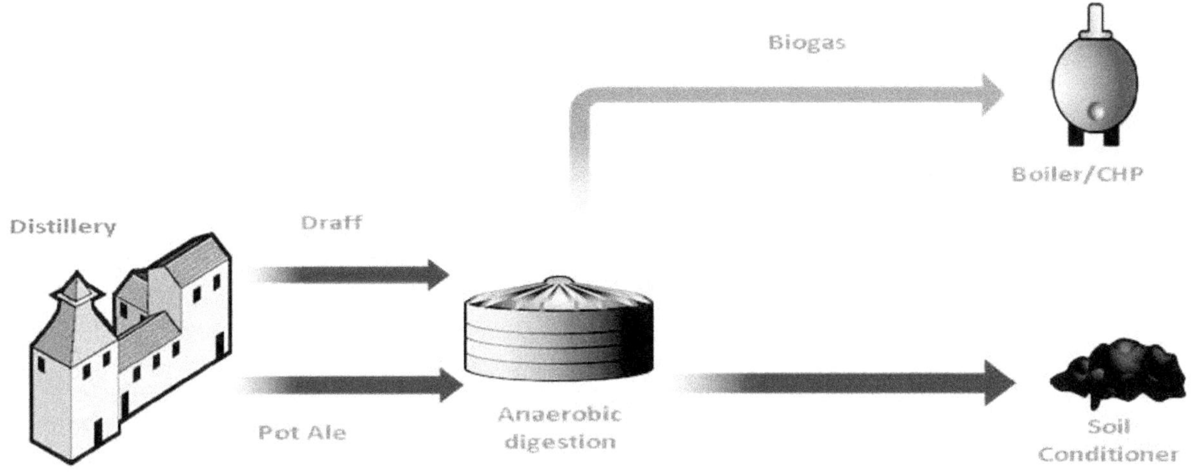

Figure 8. Biogenix Solution.

Conclusion

Energy recovery from distillery co-products is a proven reality. There are different techniques that can be applied, specific to the particular distillery, depending on the main project drivers. This could be to maximise steam or electricity generation, depending on the renewable benefit (FiT, ROC) applied to the project. Water recovery from distillery co-products is deliverable where a high quality final water can be produced for many uses such as ultrapure water for high pressure steam generation.

References

Diageo 2010. Diageo corporate citizenship Report 2010, pp 34.

Jappy, M (2010). New build distilleries – challenges of sustainability. Worldwide Distilled Spirits Conference 2008 Proceedings, Nottingham University Press, pp 105-110.

Chapter 33

Sustainable energy efficient distillation technologies for neutral/potable spirits

S P Singh
Praj Industries Limited, Pune - 411021, India

Background

Praj Industries Limited have been involved in the design and building of hundreds of plants worldwide. This paper outlines some of the innovations that Praj have implemented. The effort has been focused in two broad directions viz. (a) achieving consistent quality of spirits for Rum, new make grain whisky, Vodka etc, and (b) progressively lowering energy consumption. Distilleries are designed in such way that the majority of energy required for the process can be generated through renewable sources like Bio-methanation / Biomass helping to reduce green house gas emissions and CO_2 foot print.

The process of the removal of impurities to produce neutral spirit requires the use of a number of distillation columns. A distillation system consumes high levels of thermal energy, therefore reducing energy use helps reduce cost of production and at the same time make the plant more sustainable.

Introduction

The production of high grade neutral alcohol (potable alcohol) is subdivided into the following four stages:

1. Hydro selection to separate first running's,
2. Rectification to enrich the ethanol to the required concentration,
3. Recovery and conditioning of the ethanol contained in the side draws,
4. Separation of methanol from the concentrated ethanol / water mixture.

Although the design of new energy-saving distillation systems is based on computer simulations, for the production of spirits with very low congener levels, it is necessary to take into account the behaviour and separation of the large number of congeners generally occurring in the system .These could originate from the raw materials used, cooking, saccharification and fermentation techniques or formed during the distillation process. Owing to the uncertainty in the behaviour of minor compounds in the system, and since production scale trials can be very expensive, the best way of investigating the behaviour of a new distillation system and the quality of the product it produces is to gather experience on a sufficiently smaller plant. Praj has built a number of smaller neutral alcohol (potable alcohol) plants. The energy consumption of a distillation system for high-grade alcohol (very low congener levels) has been reduced to 3 Kg steam per litre of product and of course depends upon the level of congeners desired in the end product. Further steam requirement can be reduced by vapour recompression.

Quality and cost are the most important factors that influence the technology choice and which of the various configurations are adopted. Traditionally energy made up only some 10-20% of the total manufacturing costs, and producers were reluctant to try new systems because of fear of adverse effects on quality. However, the rapid rise in energy costs has forced increasing attention to be paid to reducing energy consumption and has led to the design and implementation of energy-saving distillation systems. Distillation and stillage processing are the stages consuming most energy in the alcohol production process. The conventional atmospheric distillation system for potable alcohol with very low congener levels uses about 5 kg steam / litre product. There are various technologies available now to reduce the energy consumption in distillation without affecting the organoleptic quality, these are:

Multi-pressure technologies:

Utilisation of the energy in vapours at the top of a distillation column to meet the energy requirements of another column instead of removing them by cooling water. This is done by operating various columns at different pressures so that the high pressure column(s) can meet the energy requirements of column(s) at lower pressure. In some cases one distillation column can even drive two distillation columns in series. This way, energy saving of about 40 – 50% is possible.

Split distillation technology:

This is a variation of the previous multi-pressure technology wherein the capacity of a column is divided into two lower capacity columns. These lower capacity columns are operated at different pressures so that vapours from the top of one lower capacity column (operating at higher pressure) can meet the energy requirement of the other lower capacity column operating at a lower pressure.

Temperature gradient technology:

This exploits the known property of alcohol-water vapour mixtures i.e. different compositions have different boiling point temperatures. For example in the production of neutral spirit, the hydro-selection column top temperature is in the range of 90-95°C and the simmering column bottom temperature is in the range of 79-80°C allowing the hydro-selection column top vapours to be used to meet the energy requirement of the simmering column although both columns are under the same pressure.

Mechanical Vapour Recompression (MVR) technology:

In this case vapours produced at the top of the column are compressed and then used to provide the energy needs of the same column by condensing in its re-boiler. This could be done on a continuous basis and veritably be termed 'steam less distillation' technology.

Mix of trays and packing:

Since packed columns require lower energy compared to tray columns, one can reduce energy requirements by considering some packed column use where side draws are not required.

Maintaining the desired congener profile in the potable alcohol when using these latest technologies is of the utmost importance.

The congener profiles in the different columns were calculated using a computer program based on simulation software. We have further modified data in the simulation software based on our experience from various plants. The behaviour and quality of products from a distillation system employing a low-pressure mash column have been investigated at length in many of our plants. The organic compounds to be separated from ethanol by distillation are produced in various ways and at various stages during the production process. The raw material itself and the metabolic activity of the fermenting micro-organism give rise to a great number of organic components other than ethanol. Furthermore, the chemical reactions and thermal decomposition taking place during liquefaction, fermentation and distillation produce additional compounds to be separated. The use of simulation software in the design of a distillation system greatly facilitates the calculation of material and energy balances of the distillation process, congener profiles in the columns, flow velocities of liquid and vapour in the columns, column dimensioning etc. However, the ethanol distillation system cannot be designed on the basis of ethanol and water alone. In practice it is also necessary to take into account the behaviour and separation of a large number of impurities in the raw alcohol. It follows that the successful design of an energy-saving distillation system to produce high-grade beverage alcohol requires considerable experience. The number of columns and their interconnections are determined by the quality of the raw material, the required purity of the product and the desired energy consumption of distillation. Various pressures maintained in the column are designed based on energy integration, impurities separation desired etc. Vacuum distillation, as it reduces the operating temperature, is of particular importance in separating many materials which decompose, or tend to polymerize, at their boiling points. Vacuum distillation also helps to obtain increased relative volatility where values are close to unity at atmospheric pressure.

Various important distillation columns

(Please see Figure 3 - Fermented mash to potable alcohol).

Mash/analyser column

In the mash column, alcohol is fractionated from fermented wash so that alcohol vapour with a concentration of 35- 50 % w/w depending upon alcohol concentration in fermented wash is taken at the top and essentially alcohol free stillage is taken at the bottom. Mash column equivalent steam consumption will range between 1.2 kg to 1.7 kg per litre of alcohol depending upon alcohol concentration in fermented wash. The mash fed to the column is generally pre-heated by vapours of either mash column or rectifier column depending upon the scheme selected. Experience has shown that calcium sulphate is precipitated on the upper trays of the mash column when molasses is the feed stock. An increase in alcohol concentration strongly reduces the solubility of calcium sulphate, which explains why calcium sulphate is precipitated on the upper trays of the mash column. The impurities in the mash column vapours include aldehydes, esters, acids, fusel alcohols, diacetyl, methanol, sulphur compounds and nitrogen compounds. The concentration of some of the lighter components depends on the mash column pressure and associated temperature. The content of aldehydes and diacetyl, for example, falls as the boiling temperature of the mash column drops below 90°C. This shows that these compounds are formed partly during the distillation process. Also lower temperature reduces precipitation of calcium sulphate, burnt proteins and residual sugars thus prolonging the intervals between column cleaning.

Extractive distillation (hydro-selection / extraction, also called purifier) column

In principle, components with a volatility greater than that of ethanol can be concentrated by distillation, while less volatile substances pass on from the bottom. The relative volatility of many compounds compared to ethanol is strongly dependent on the ethanol concentration. For example, it is very difficult to separate aldehydes from ethanol by distillation when the ethanol concentration is very high (the relative volatilities are near one), although the separation is possible when the ethanol is diluted. A similar dilution effect is seen in ethanol solutions of diacetyl and 2,3–pentanedione, compounds that are typically present in raw alcohol. In practice, these effects mean that to obtain an effective separation of impurities water must be added to the distillation column to dilute the relatively high ethanol concentration.

If the dilution water is fed to the top of the column and the raw alcohol 15-20 trays lower down, the ethanol concentration in the top product (depending upon no reflux or very little reflux) is low. Most of the highly volatile (e.g. aldehydes) and some of the less volatile (e.g. fusel alcohols) impurities in the raw alcohol feed go to top of column and the remainder of the less volatile components go with the bottom product to be enriched and drawn off at the fusel alcohol zone of the rectification column. This mode of operation is referred to as hydro-extraction. However if a higher concentration of alcohol is desired at the top of column, one reduces dilution and operates the column under reflux. This mode of operation is referred to as a hydro-selection or purifier column. Normally a hydro-extraction column is operated with the dilution ratio of 1:8-9 whereas a purification column (Hydro-selection column) is operated with the dilution ratio of 1:3-4. Separation effects of various impurities are given in Table 1 below:

Rectifier column:

The main purpose of the rectification column is to concentrate the dilute alcohol stream coming out from the bottom of the purifier column (Hydro-extraction or hydro-selection mode). The rectification column normally has 65-72 trays and consumes about 2 Kg steam per litre of neutral/ potable alcohol. At the top of the column, a fraction is taken containing enriched light impurities.

Methanol removal column (simmering column)

A methanol removal column is used to obtain an extremely pure alcoholic distillate by removing methanol and residual impurities (mainly aldehydes) from the product obtained from the rectification column.

Energy saving distillation system for high-grade potable alcohol:

There are various ways of saving energy like multi-pressure distillation, split distillation, mechanical vapour recompression and by taking advantage of temperature gradient etc. Under multi-pressure, we'll talk about columns operating under different pressures, split distillation and temperature gradient advantage.

Table 1. Hydro-extraction vs. Hydro-selection

Impurity	*Hydro-extraction mode % separation*	*Hydro-aelection mode % separation*
Acetaldehyde	100.00	55.81
Methanol	1.00	18.6
Acetone	100	99.65
Ethyl Acetate	100	100
n-Propanol	38.65	0.22
Sec-Butanol	54.69	0.01
Iso-Butanol	11.41	0.00
n-Butanol	24.6	0.00
Amyl Alcohol	6.11	0.00
Acetic acid	-	-
Iso-Propanol	32.19	25.46

Note: Above data relates to steam consumption of 0.6 kg/litre of TS.

Multi-pressure distillation

Multi-pressure distillation technology is based on lowering the pressure of one column and increasing the pressure of another column, hence facilitating the transfer of latent energy from the vapours of the high pressure column to the re-boiler of the column operating under lower pressure.

Figure 1 indicates a simple 2 column based multi-pressure distillation system. Here the rectifier column is operated under pressure and vapours of the rectifier column are boiling the mash column. This scheme simply produces the raw alcohol.

Figure 2 indicates a scheme for producing raw alcohol based on split distillation. Here the mash column is split into two columns and similarly the rectifier column is split into two columns. One mash column is driving another column and similarly one rectifier column is driving another column. By split distillation, we further reduce energy consumption by 30-40% compared with the simple multi-pressure distillation indicated in Figure 1.

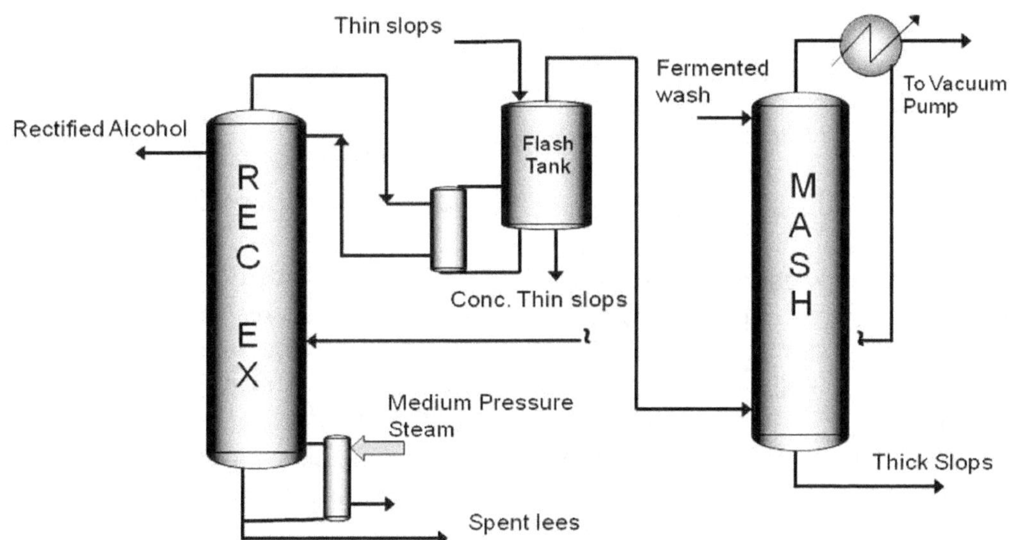

Figure 1. Simple MPR Scheme: Rectifier driving mash column.

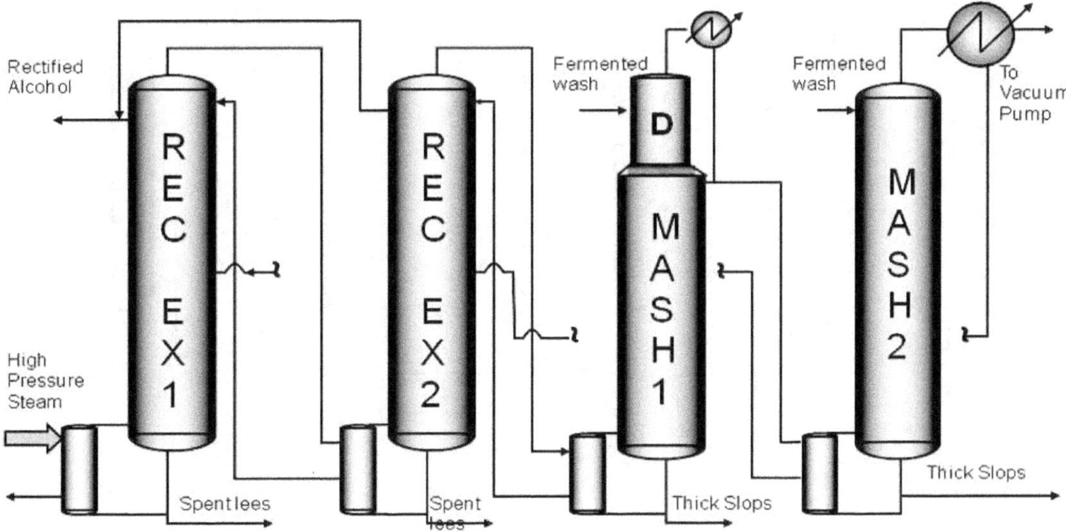

Figure 2. Split distillation

Figure 3 indicates a scheme for wash to potable alcohol using multi-pressure technology, the system consists of seven columns. Raw alcohol from mash and first rectifier is purified by water dilution in the purifier column (hydro-extraction or hydro-selection mode) and concentrated in the rectification column. Remaining impurities are removed in the simmering column (also called methanol column). The dilute pre-distillate of the purifier column along with fusel oil fractions are concentrated in a separate column called the recovery column. In this scheme the rectifier drives the mash column based on multi-pressure and the ED (Extractive Distillation) column drives the simmering column based on a vapour temperature gradient. There is a separate stand alone recovery column for recovering alcohol from the ED column vapour condensate. The mash column is run at so low a pressure that vapours from a rectification column are able to boil it up. Similarly vapour from the purifier column (under hydro-extraction mode) is used to boil up the simmering column. The steam consumption of the system is about 3 kg / litre of potable alcohol with a mash alcohol concentration of about 8% v/v. Furthermore, as has been mentioned previously, using a low-pressure mash column reduces column fouling and improves the quality of the product. The functioning of the systems, energy consumption and quality of the product has been tested in various plants operating world-wide.

Figure 4 indicates the scheme where the required concentration of alcohol in the final product is more than 96.5%. Here we operate the main rectifier under vacuum to increase alcohol concentration in the final product. The mash column drives the main rectifier column. The primary rectifier (indicated as PRC) is operated under higher pressure and drives the ED column and the ED column in turn drives the simmering column. The recovery column is standalone, similar to Figure 3.

Distillation of high-grade alcohol with vapour compression

The energy input to the reboiler of the distillation column is usually similar in magnitude to the latent heat of the vapour leaving from the top of the column. The primary energy requirement of the distillation would be reduced if the energy of this vapour could be returned to the reboiler. In practice this can be achieved with

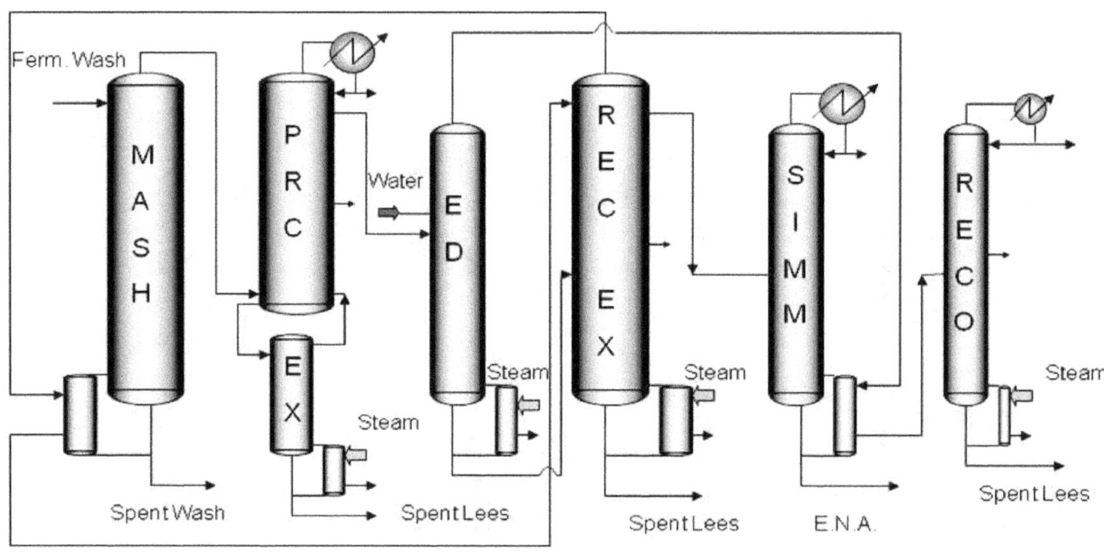

Figure 3. Wash to neutral alcohol (multi-pressure scheme) – Type 1

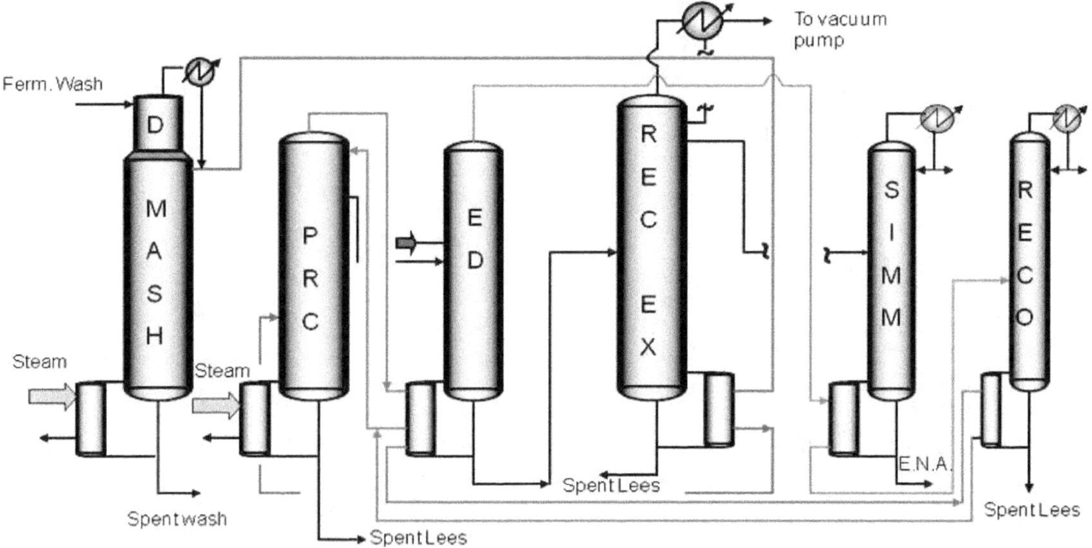

Figure 4. Wash to neutral alcohol – Type 2 (LUX grade)

the aid of mechanical compression. Vapour compression can be applied to distillation in two different ways. In the first case the ethanol vapour from the top of the column is compressed to a higher pressure and used in the reboiler of the column. In the second, the energy of ethanol vapour is first transferred via a heat – exchanger to circulating stillage water (or to the bottom product of the column), and the energy of the vaporized water is then transferred by a compressor as direct steam to the bottom of the column. Compression of ethanol vapour to a high pressure and temperature may result in unexpected off-flavours in the product. Moreover, there is some risk of an explosion as the compressor is started and stopped, and for these reasons compression of the bottom product (or steam) is preferred. Further enthalpy from the alcohol vapour leaving the top of the mash column is transferred to recirculated stillage water. The steam liberated from the stillage water is compressed and fed to the bottom of the mash column as direct steam. Raw alcohol from the mash cum rectifier column goes to the reduced pressure purifier column, where the main parts of the impurities are removed. The purified dilute alcohol stream from the bottom of this column is concentrated in the rectification column. Methanol and residual impurities are removed in a reduced pressure methanol column. Purifier top vapour condensate and fusel alcohol fractions are concentrated in a separate column.

Figure 5 demonstrates the typical scheme of use of mechanical vapour recompression. Here the rectifier column vapours are mechanically compressed and are used to boil the exhaust column as well as the mash column. This scheme is used to produce normal grade rectified spirit. Rectified spirit thus produced can be further purified to produce neutral spirit or potable alcohol. There is steam reduction in the range of 30 % to 70% depending upon level of use of mechanical vapour recompression and quality of product required. This means for potable alcohol from fermented mash, steam consumption can range from 1 to 2 Kg/litres of potable alcohol depending upon number of recompression systems and the quality of product desired.

Conclusion

The distillation of mash to produce different types of beverage alcohol is a complex process. The material to be distilled contains a great number of organic compounds, which must be separated from the ethanol during the

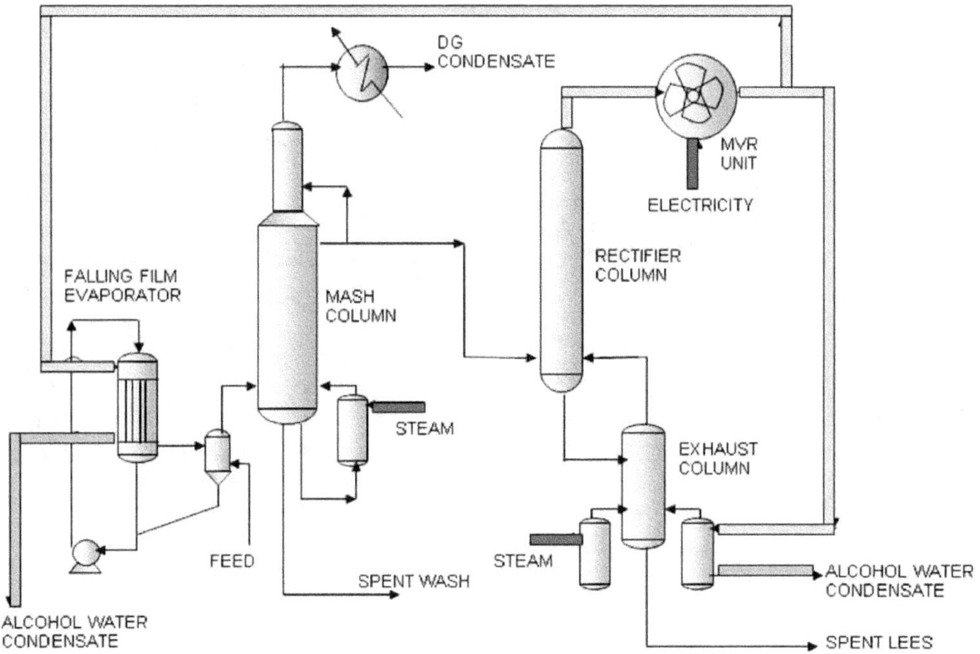

Figure 5. Use of mechanical vapour recompression.

distillation. Chemical reactions taking place during distillation also affect the quality of the final product. The various physical and chemical processes occurring during spirit distillation are still a subject of study, largely because of the number of components involved. The design of new energy-saving alcohol distillation units must therefore be based, in addition to computer simulations, also on reliable practical experience.

References

Aramaki, G., A. Soda (1972) Scale prevention in distillation alcoholic fermentation broth, Japan Patent 7224, 151.

Draft directive council document 7025/83-ENER – Energy group meeting on 11 May 1983, Directorate – General for Energy, Commission of the European Communities.

High vacuum distillation, Chemical Industry Digest, March-April, 2003 : 69-72.

Praj in-house experience.

Ramanarao, B.V. (1964) Scaling in wash columns, Ethyl alcohol production technique, Publ. Noyes Development Co. USA.

Tegtmayer, U (1985) Process Design for energy saving ethanol production, Biotechnology Letters, 7: 129-134.

Chapter 34

Sustainability through process design

M. Phillips, J. A. V. Ludford-Brooks, J. C. Hancock, N. Harlow
Briggs of Burton Plc, Briggs House, Derby Street, Burton-on-Trent, Stafforfdshire, DE14 2LH

Water consumption

Water consumption within a production facility is an important subject area when considering sustainability. A well thought out water strategy and subsequent process balance, has the potential to yield positive results in the areas of environmental impact, production capability and operating costs within any particular facility (Andrews *et al.*, 2011).

The assessment of water consumption from a high level perspective can impact several aspects of the overall process and operational model. This includes the type/quantity of water supplies available, water demand rates, environmental discharge, production capacity, operating costs, seasonality and optimum process mass/energy balances.

Every production plant infrastructure and its associated availability of water is different, meaning that a solution to improve water consumption at one site is unlikely to generate the same benefits at another. Similarly, process solutions for improving water consumption are likely to be different if an existing plant is undergoing modification or if a new plant is being designed from first principles.

One of the most efficient methods of optimising water (and energy) consumption is to use water streams more than once. Many examples of this methodology can and are being used within distilleries such as: -

Cooking flash steam – condensing flash steam from a wheat cooking process and using that as hot water for subsequent cooking.

Weak worts – recovering mash tun sparge water that is not sent forward to fermentation for use as water supply for subsequent mashing.

Backset recovery – using material derived from distillation stillage for use as wort production feed material.

Clean In Place (CIP) water supply – distillery effluent streams that undergo suitable treatment processes can be used as the water source for CIP, which is subsequently used to clean the plant.

Recovery CIP water – re-use of final rinse water from equipment CIP as pre-rinse for subsequent routines.

Wort cooling is a particular example where overall water consumption can vary greatly and can therefore be optimised to suit a particular production facility requirement. Variation in overall water consumption can be attributed to the quantity of wort cooling water that can be re-used for subsequent downstream processes and the use of closed circuit water systems that have the ability to reject heat.

As an example of a water consumption sustainability analysis, consider a single stage wort cooling system versus a multiple stage system that utilises a modular heat exchanger design.

Case study – Cameronbridge Distillery wort cooling

Cameronbridge Grain Whisky Distillery (address in references) is designed to produce 105 million litres of alcohol (mla) per annum. The wort cooling process is continuous such that 180,000 kg/hr of wort requires to be cooled from 62°C to 20°C prior to fermentation resulting in a cooling load of 8,400kW(18).

The site utilises 80,000 kg/hr of process water at 44°C for wort production and equipment flushing. If a single stage wort cooling system were to be used with a cold process water supply, the total amount of water generated at a target temperature of 44°C is calculated as 218,181 kg/hr (Winterton, 1997).

This generates a large constant demand for cold process water and an excess water stream that must be disposed of as shown in Figure 1.

A detailed study of the existing site infrastructure determined that excess cooling capacity within a water ring main system was available. This ring main rejected its low grade heat to river water and cooling towers. This excess cooling capacity was incorporated into the wort cooler design due to its modular nature, such that any number of cooling water streams could be used for wort temperature reduction.

It was therefore possible to design the cold process water section of the system to generate enough water to service subsequent downstream plant demands, utilise excess cooling capacity from the existing site infrastructure and remove the remaining heat from the wort using a new closed circuit chilled water system. This would yield the effect of minimising the overall total water consumption.

A sustainability analysis determined that whilst minimising water consumption was important, the considerable electrical power consumption associated with the new chilled water plant determined that this duty needed to be minimised in order to generate an agreed optimum design. Using the maximum reliable supply of cold process water available within the site infrastructure resulted in the final system design shown in Figure 2.

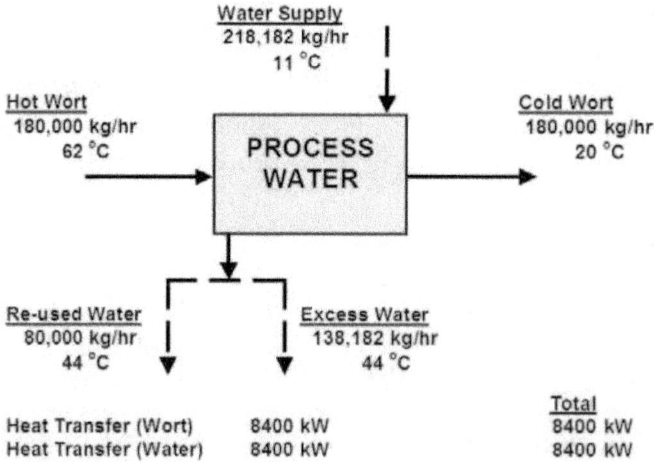

Figure 1. Single stage continuous wort cooling system.

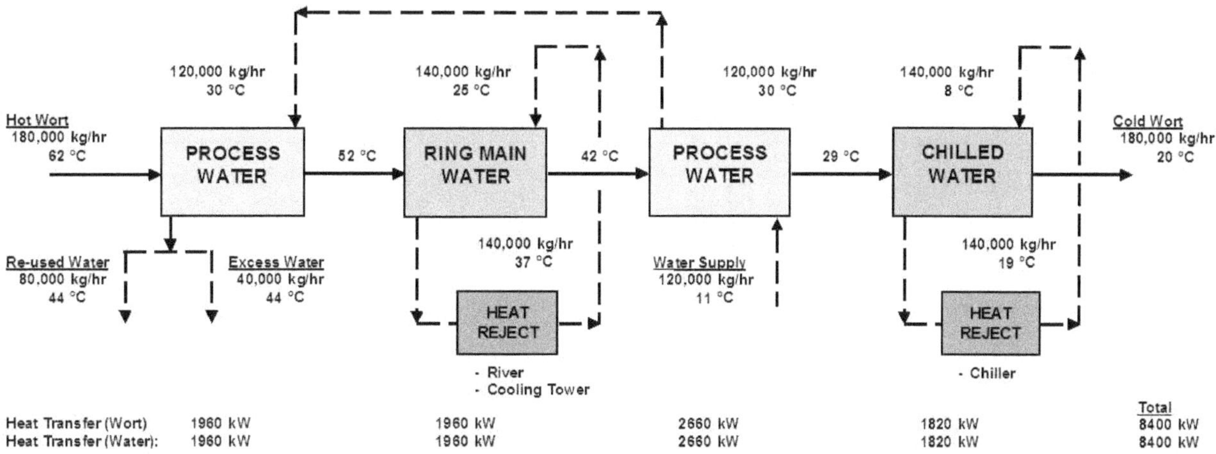

Figure 2. Multi-stage continuous wort cooling system.

Seasonality should also be considered when assessing sustainability in the design of such process systems. The excess cooling capacity of the existing ring main increases significantly during winter due to a lower ambient temperature. By using a modular wort cooler design, it was possible to incorporate this extra capacity to cool wort and subsequently eliminate the need for a chilled water system to meet the pre-fermentation target temperature. By physically connecting the chilled water section of the wort cooling system to the cold process water supply, a big reduction in the use of electrical energy could be made with the overall water consumption remaining constant, as shown in Figure 3.

This case study demonstrates that no single solution fits all applications and that various permutations are frequently available for process design.

Sustainability in pump selection

Pump efficiency at the duty point is often more important than the selection of high efficiency electric motors.

Pump selections made on capital cost grounds alone can have a significant impact on future operational cost for the lifetime of the plant.

In Table 1, both pumps being considered are close-coupled hygienic centrifugal pumps and are from a real case study (Briggs of Burton, 2008).

Pump B – re-quoted pump from less standardised pump range, duty point can be matched and efficiency is 20% better (Table 2).

Based on Qtr 1, 2011 UK Energy prices for a medium sized industrial user (ONS, 2011), the pump installed was more than £400/year cheaper to run, without considering maintenance costs.

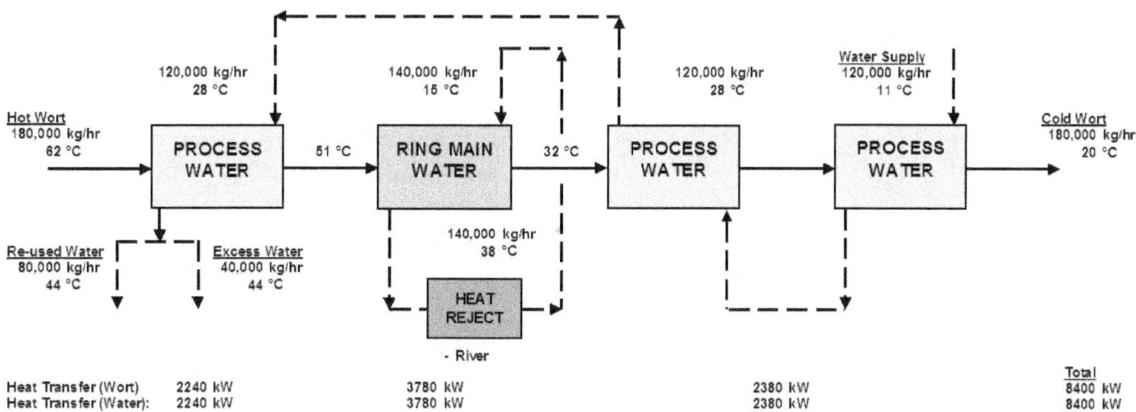

Figure 3. Multi-stage continuous wort cooling system incorporating seasonality.

Table 1 Pump A Offers a significant capital cost saving over Pump B, but is it the best choice? Comparison of Efficiency and operational cost tells a different story.

	Duty	*Head*	*Power Absorbed*	*Efficiency*	*Price*
	m3/hr	*m*	*kW*	*%*	*£*
Duty Required	12	38.9	-	-	-
Pump A	12	45.8*	4.5	30.9	2355
Pump B	12	38.9	2.5	50.5	3145

*Pump A Solution was quoted from a standardised pump range which could not match the duty point required, this, coupled with the efficiency, makes it a less attractive choice in this instance.

This was one of 120 pumps with varying duties purchased for a greenfield site; optimisation of the efficiency for each unit generates a significant operational cost saving from day one.

The duty presented here was for a slightly viscous product where a fixed pressure was required at the point of use – if pressure was not a control parameter it is unlikely that a centrifugal pump would have been used at all, given the generally low efficiencies of both options.

Table 2.

Pump operation	*Unit*	
hours/day	h/day	8
kW difference /year	kW/yr	5476
Price Per kW	p/kWh	7.5
Operational Cost difference/yr	£	411
Payback	Years	1.92

Variable speed drives

The use of variable speed drive (VSD) motors is an effective method of reducing electrical energy consumption. Pump, agitator, conveyor and milling motors are examples that can be operated under VSD control, such that only the amount of energy required to meet a particular process duty is consumed. This philosophy is consistent with maximising sustainability of a process plant.

Process control loops, where a fast speed of response is not required, are excellent candidates for the use of VSDs. Examples of such loops are maintaining a transfer target flowrate, or a level setpoint within a process vessel. A quantitative study into the impact that VSDs has on electrical energy consumption can be made by considering a simple pumping system that has a range of process duties.

Consider an example of discharging from a supply vessel that operates under continuous level control. The conventional method of controlling the level in this vessel would be to utilise a fixed speed pump with a downstream modulating control valve as shown in Figure 4.

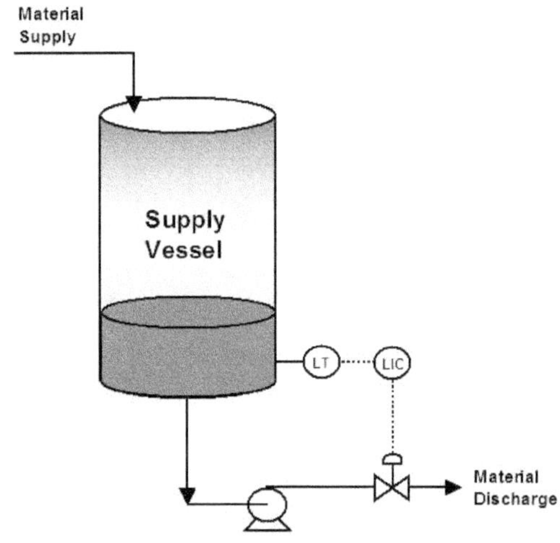

Figure 4. Tank level control using a modulating control valve.

The electrical energy consumed by the pump in this design remains constant, as any variation in process duty is managed by changing the pressure drop over the modulating control valve. An alternative process design for this application is to control the level in the supply vessel using a VSD pump motor as shown in Figure 5.

This system only consumes the amount of electrical energy required to meet the process duty and the requirement for a modulating control valve is eliminated. If the flow entering the supply tank remains constant then the duty point of the pumping system to fill a destination vessel changes as its level rises. A system with a maximum change in static head of 20m is illustrated in Figure 6.

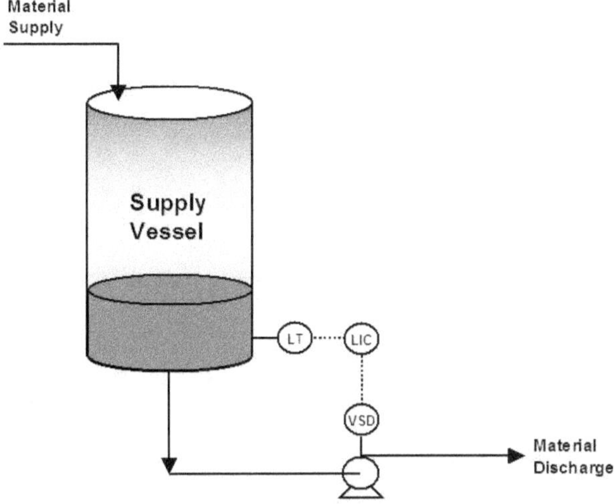

Figure 5. Tank level control using a variable speed pump motor.

If the flow remains constant at 100 m³/hr, then a fixed speed pump would have to be designed for a duty point where the receiving tank is full. If the pressure loss in the system between the two tanks is equivalent to 30m of material head, then a pump duty point of 100m³/hr at 50m is derived when the tank is full. Using a 30kW motor fixed speed pump for this system to fill a tank farm of 300m³ vessels would consume 720kWh of daily electrical energy (Energy Information).

The alternative process design of using a VSD pump motor would consume less electrical energy. Using the affinity characteristics of a typical centrifugal pump curve (Pump Affinity Laws) with the maximum duty point generated at an operating speed of 100%, it is possible to estimate the speed (and therefore power consumption) at which the pump will operate to meet the process duty at different material levels within the destination vessel as shown in Figure 7.

Referring back to Figure 6. Using the average pump power consumed between each of the 25% increments in the destination vessel, the level allows the daily consumption of electrical energy for this system to be estimated as 528 kWh yielding an overall reduction of approximately 26%.

A practical distillery example of this technique is mash tun wort collection, where both head and flow increase through run-off as gravity decreases and washback level increases.

A production facility will house a significant number of pumping and other material processing

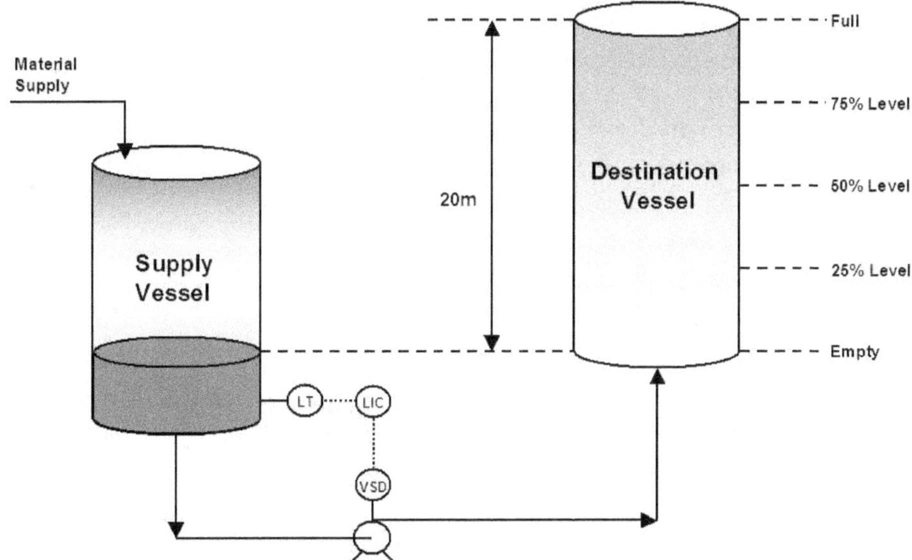

Figure 6. Continuous processing system using a variable speed control loop

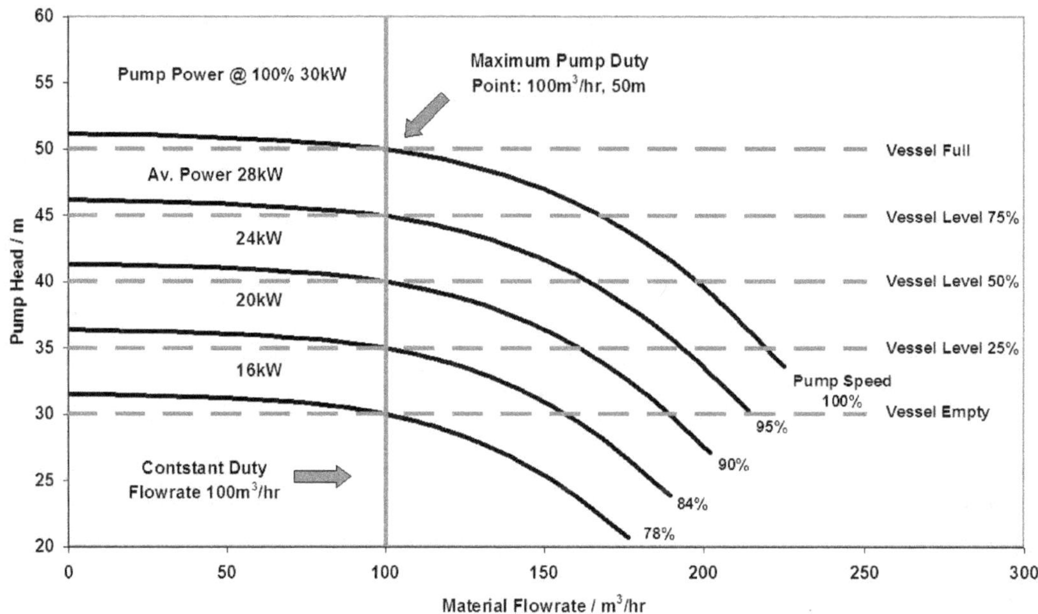

Figure 7. Pump characteristics and power estimation as function of operating speed.

systems. If all systems suitable for VSD motor operation are identified and incorporated into the process design, then considerable optimisation can be made in terms of the consumption of electrical energy and therefore overall sustainability of a production plant.

Sustainable line sizing

As part of any process design or upgrade, consideration to appropriate line sizes should be given. Under-sizing of pipe work has become common in some instances in order to reduce capital cost, an example of typical pipe cost for material and installation is provided as shown in table 3.

Table 3.

Size	*Material And Installation Cost £*
1″ OD	1921
1.5″ OD	2335
2″ OD	2796
2.5″ OD	3220
3″ OD	3854
4″ OD	5482
5″ OD	7533
6″ OD	9252

All costs are based on hygienic 316L austenitic stainless steel descaled tube (Briggs of Burton, 2010). In the following chart, the cost of pipe installation has been plotted against operational cost.

The overall difference in installed cost between pipe sizes is small.

Operational cost of pipework has been calculated from the expected hydraulic pressure drop for a fixed pipe length (100m), assuming electrical energy is used at 7.5p/ kWh to generate the hydraulic head, excluding transmission/ pumping losses. The effect of under sizing can be seen - cost and hydraulic head rise exponentially with a decrease in pipe size for the same mass flow.

This chart is based on pumping water at 1cP viscosity, if the same method was applied to viscous products the effect would be magnified significantly.

Cleaning In Place (CIP)

There have been significant developments in CIP technology as an integral part of the processes that are used to manufacture distilled spirits. CIP

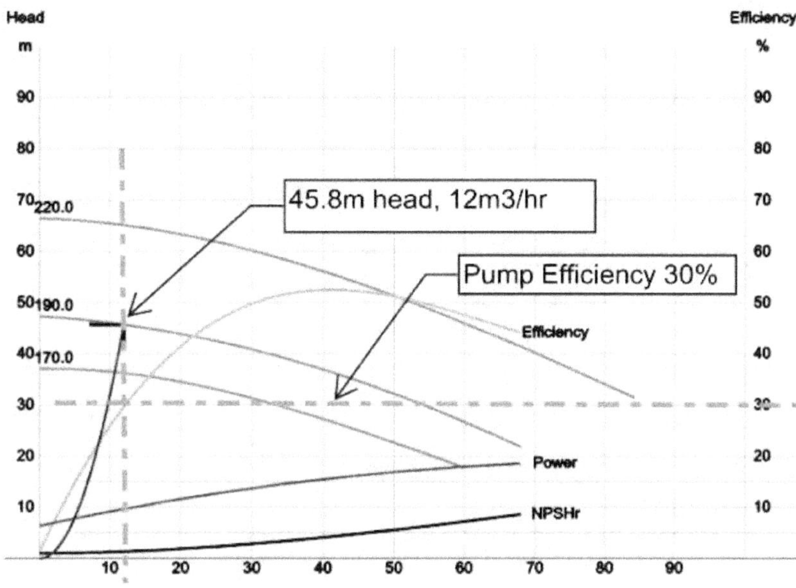

Figure 8. Pump A - Curve (1)

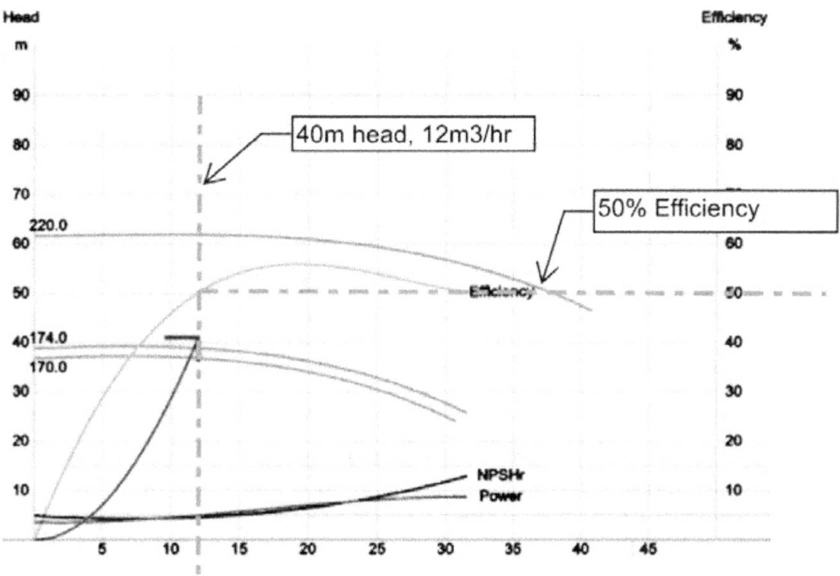

Figure 9. Pump B - Curve (1)

has increasingly played a more important role in new developments, with CIP being built into new and upgraded facilities as a key part of the design, rather than an afterthought. Advances in double seat mixproof valve technology, have allowed systems to be designed with great flexibility, while guaranteeing complete and effective CIP coverage. This is of all (vessel and mains) contact surfaces, with safe separation between product and CIP, and full automation.

The quest for sustainability has emphasised the advantages of effective recovery CIP systems, where detergent, rinse water and detergent interfaces are recovered, with a reduction in water, energy and chemical usage. Effective recipe-based automation has allowed the CIP program to be optimised for each CIP route, and the effectiveness of the CIP to be monitored by return flow, conductivity and, in some cases, by return rinse water quality.

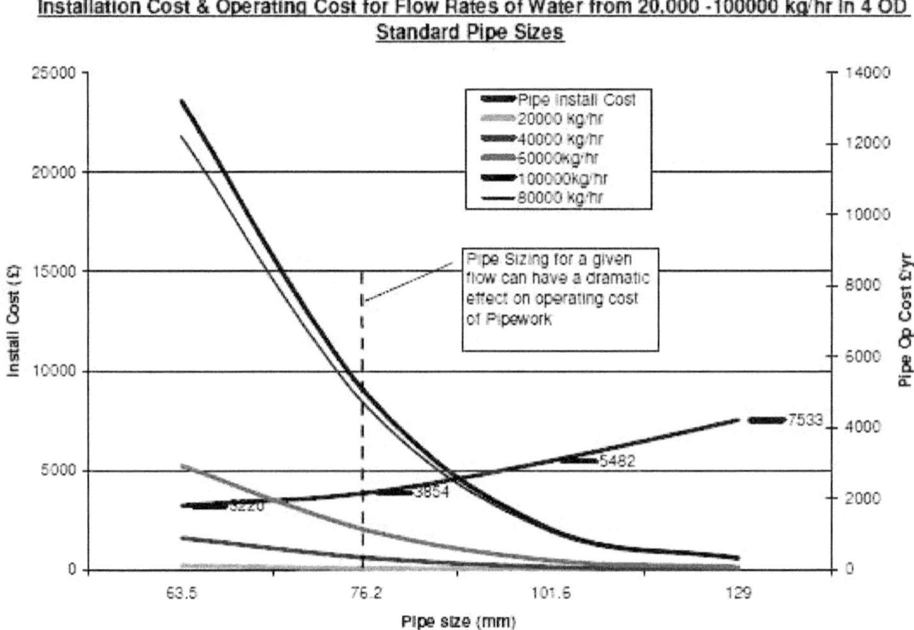

Figure 10. Installation & operating cost of pipework.

High pressure/low flow/high impact, rotating CIP spray heads have allowed very effective CIP of wort production and large fermenting vessels, with low CIP flows, reducing water, energy and chemical costs, as reflected by eligibility for the UK Government Enhanced Capital Allowance (ECA) Scheme (Winterton, 1997). The use of pre-rinse (being effectively a dilute detergent wash using recovered rinse water) both reduces water usage and makes the detergent stage much more economic by maximising soil removal prior to detergent, thereby extending detergent life. By these means, together with high pressure rotating spray heads, it has been possible to re-use detergent even following its use within distilleries for cleaning purposes, as compared with older CIP systems that rely on total detergent disposal or conventional steam sterilisation techniques.

Distillation energy minimisation

Grain and Malt whisky distillation follow different technologies reflecting the product aims and ethos, grain whisky being based on continuous distillation, while malt whisky is based on batch distillation in pot stills.

Whisky distillation, in taking wash at around 8% alcohol, and concentrating this up to around 60%, involves in simplistic terms, evaporating a significant quantity of water, and consequently has a major energy input.

Continuous distillation, by its very nature as a continuous steady state process is more readily and economically adapted to minimise energy input.

Distillation of malt whisky in pot stills, usually in two stages, (Wash and Spirit Stills), but occasionally three stages, is an unsteady state batch process. The design and operation of the stills plays a key role in the development of malt whisky flavour characteristics. As a result, change of any kind has to be undertaken very carefully, so as to ensure there is no change in the spirit quality.

Distillation accounts for a huge proportion (66%) of the energy input in malt whisky production (Chalmers and Hodgett, 1986), of which the majority is in the first stage Wash stills.

It is established practice to recover heat from the pot ale discharged at the end of wash distillation for wash pre-heating, but this is very small compared to the distillation energy input.

There are many well-established and proven engineering techniques for distillation energy efficiency, which simply cannot be used in malt whisky distillation, either because of the batch nature of the process, or because they would (or could) affect spirit quality and character.

Examples of these techniques include continuous distillation itself, and Mechanical Vapour Recompression (MVR). MVR has the benefit of recycling energy within the process, rather than exporting energy. It is obviously not a possibility in this application, as this involves compressing the vapour, which in this case is the product.

During the early 1980s the use of a related technology, the High Temperature Heat Pump (HTHP) was developed for a Malt Whisky application, and a plant installed at the Auchroisk Distillery, Mulben in 1986 (Chalmer and Hodgett, 1986; Energy Efficiency Office, 1985). This was at a time of high energy costs, with an emphasis on energy minimisation, which has some parallels with the current climate, and may be worthy of re-examination.

This system as shown in simplified form in Figure 11, was an indirect system with no changes to the distillation process, as far as the still or distilled vapour was concerned. A key part of this technology was to change the condenser design from the conventional design using cold water on a single pass total loss basis, to using a high flow of recirculated hot water with a relatively low temperature rise across the condenser (Hodgett, 1985). Sub-coolers were added to cool the spirit ex condenser.

This hot water was then flashed at sub-atmospheric temperature into a flash vessel, and this low temperature vapour recompressed using an electrically driven screw compressor to provide steam at 2 bar g to the Wash Still. Essentially this is similar to a refrigeration cycle, but using steam as the working fluid.

The actual installation at Auchroisk comprised a single HTHP system feeding four Wash Stills, Condensers and Sub-Coolers. This system replaced 2,000 kW of thermal energy (fuel oil) with 300 kW of electrical energy (Chalmers and Hodgett, 1986). This system was operational for many years, however its main issues were related to maintaining a large and relatively complex screw compressor.

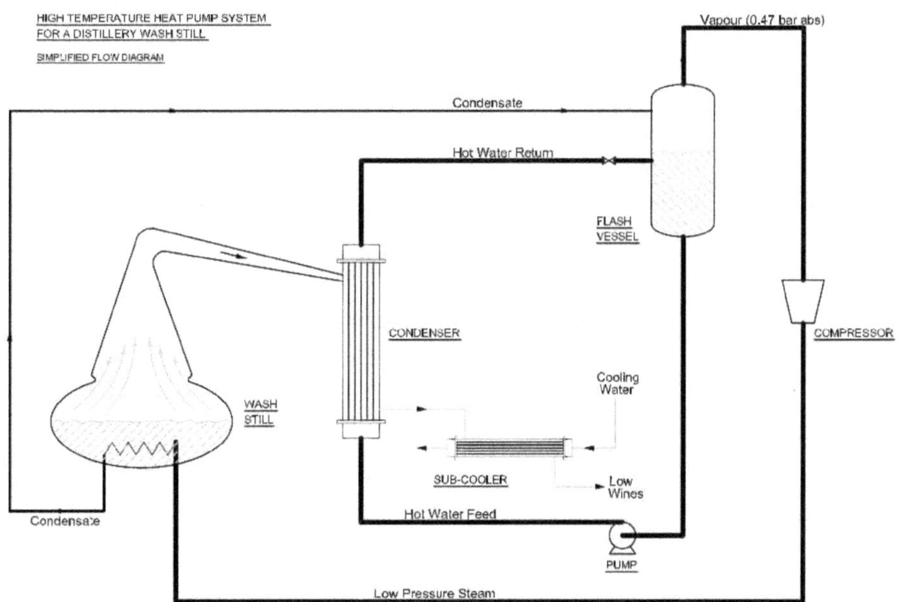

Figure 11. HTHP System.

Another technique explored at Bowmore Distillery in the 1980s, was the use of Thermal Vapour Compression (TVR), where high pressure steam was used in a steam ejector together with high temperature condensers to create steam for still heating (Deakin, 1985). TVR avoids the issues related to steam compressors, but given the high proportion of boiler steam used, has less potential for energy recovery.

It is also possible to examine technologies used in related industries, Brewing being the obvious one. While this does not involve distillation as such, it does involve wort boiling, which has some parallels to pot still heating. Traditionally, Malt Stills are heated by simple internal steam coils. One of the techniques used in wort boiling is the use of a large surface area external heat exchanger on a recirculation loop. This concept has recently been adopted in malt distilleries.

It is also worth noting that the high temperature distillery condenser system above has many similarities with the established Brewery Energy Store type condenser system.

The use of external still heating in turn opens up other opportunities for use of lower temperature heat sources, increasing the possibilities for energy recovery and recycling.

Recent installations have used condensers operating at high temperature, based on the concepts established in the 1980s, together with sub-coolers, to recover or recycle energy. A portion of this energy may be used simply for wash pre-heating, as at Glen Grant.

By splitting the Wash Condenser into two sections, energy may be used both for wash pre-heating, and for still heating. Wash pre-heating may be achieved using warm / hot water circulated through one side of the condenser as a heat source. The other section of the condenser operates under vacuum, and using the distillation energy to evaporate sub-atmospheric pressure steam in a closed loop, this is compressed using a TVR system and used for wash still heating, using external wash heaters (Brotherton, 2010).

Though this avoids a mechanically driven compressor, it is still a complex system. The use of large surface area external still heating, with low pressure steam, would allow the use of a mechanical compressor of a much simpler design and lower energy input than that installed at Auchroisk.

BioEnergy

Increasing energy prices, concerns over security of supply and existing and emerging climate change legislation have all added additional urgency to the constant need to drive down energy usage and operating costs.

Makers Mark In Kentucky, mechanically dewater their whole stillage, the effluent obtained from the mechanical dewatering process has a high COD value 25-30 g/litre which lends itself to treatment in an anaerobic digestion step to recover biogas for use in steam raising, anaerobic digestion typically removes 90% of the incoming COD load. With a methane yield approximately 0.3 –0.35 m^3/ kg of COD presented to the plant, the solids recovered are typically 38-40% dry solids which make it much more suitable for transportation and use as animal feed (Ecolab, 2009).

Two recent projects by Diageo take this a step further and demonstrate a commitment to become more self sufficient in energy use and rely less on outside supplies. Diageo Roseisle are utilising a combination of biomass combustion and anaerobic digestion to recover 8.6mW of energy for re-use in their operations, equivalent to 84% of the total steam load required by the plant.

Meanwhile at Cameronbridge, anaerobic digestion and a CHP plant powered with biomass will account for 80% of site electricity and 98% of the total steam demand (Jappy, 2008).

In both cases the biomass is obtained from spent grains and separated pot ale solids. The solids are concentrated by mechanical dewatering, using belt-press or screw-press technology, before being mixed together and dried prior to combustion. The drying step is energy intensive accounting for approximately

20% of the total energy acquired by the combustion step (Jappy, 2008).

The distillery process generates large volumes of carbon dioxide during fermentation and biomass combustion. Opportunities are being developed to reduce or eliminate these emissions, algae seeded in a photo bio-reactor (PBR) can photosynthesise carbon dioxide in the presence of sunlight to produce solids rich in oils which can be extracted for use as bio-diesel. The main waste gas from the process is oxygen. Glenturret Distillery is one of the first to try this approach (Van Alstyne, 2011).

Active research is progressing to re-use distillers grains to produce more alcohol by fermenting with organisms capable of digesting lignocellulosic material, the ethanol produced can be used as fuel or contribute to the overall alcohol yield from a distillery. TMO Renewables Ltd has developed a thermophillic bacterium (TM242) to convert a wide range of biomass-derived sugars efficiently into ethanol at high yields and temperatures. The process was developed with Briggs and TMO have been testing feedstocks for potential clients since summer 2008 (Andrews and Robinson, 2009).

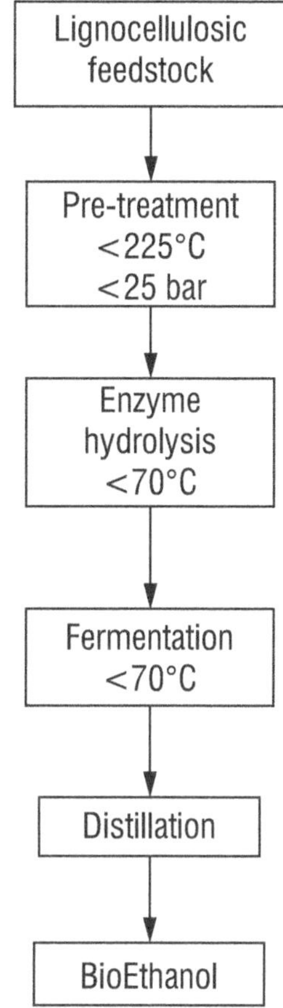

Figure 12. The TMO process

References

Andrews, J.M.H, Hancock, J.C, Ludford-Brooks, J, Murfin, I.J, Houldsworth, L. and Phillips, M. 125th Anniversary Review: Some Recent Engineering Advances in Brewing and Distilling. Journal of the Institute of Brewing, Vol.117, No.1, 2011.

Andrews J and Robinson J, A New Process For the Conversion Of Spent Grain to Ethanol, The Institute Of Brewing and Distilling Africa Sect. 12th Scientific Convention 2009

Briggs Of Burton Plc. Archive Files – 2008.

Briggs Of Burton Plc. Archive Files 2010.

Brotherton F, Heat Recovery in Malt Distilleries, IBD Energy Seminar, 30th September 2010, Dufftown.

Chalmers E.D. and Hodgett D.L, High Efficiency Malt Whisky Production: Reduction in Distillation Energy Consumption by Heat Pumping. Proceedings of the Second Aviemore Conference on Malting, Brewing and Distilling 1986, p381, Institute of Brewing.

Deakin A.W, Reducing Energy Usage in Whisky Distilleries, Brewing and Distilling International, June 1985

Diageo Cameronbridge Distillery, Windygates, Fife, UK, KY8 5RL.

Ecolab and Ecovation - Sustainable Waste Water Management Solutions, February 2009.

Energy Efficiency Office, Energy Efficiency Demonstration Scheme Project Profile 213, Use of a Heat Pump in the Distillation of Malt Whisky, October 1985.

Energy Information - http://www.gcse.com/energy/kWh.htm

Hodgett D.L., A Heat Pump for Batch Distillation, Refrigeration Science and Technology, 1985-3, p 93-102.

Jappy Mike, New Build Distilleries, Challenges Of Sustainability, World Wide Distilled Spirits Conference 14th Oct 2008.

Office Of National Statistics: Quarterly Energy Prices, June 2011.

Pump Affinity Laws - http://www.engineeringtoolbox.com/affinity-laws-d_408.html

UK Government Enhanced Capital Allowances (last accessed August 2010 at www.eca.gov.uk)

Van Alstyne, UK/Spain Algae Biofuels and Other Industrial Applications: Opportunities for Collaboration Repsol Technology Centre, Presentation by Scottish Bioenergy, March 2011.

Winterton, R.H.S. Heat Transfer, Oxford University Press, 1997.

Chapter 35

The real cost of sustainability: Is it possible to reduce effluent and generate green energy while making a profit?

Vinod Ramachandran[1] and Diana Gates[2]
[1]*Ondeo Industrial Solutions, Suez Environnement House, Bo'ness Road, Grangemouth, FK3 9XD;* [2]*Ondeo Industrial Solutions, 530 / 534 Durham Road, Low Fell, Gateshead, NE9 6HU*

Introduction

Over recent years the term 'sustainability' has evolved from a quirky buzzword to an integral part of many company's business strategy. More frequently it is being used to reflect both financial and ecological solutions, rather than in its purest environmental context with manufacturers looking for better ways to manage their co-products and effluent to reduce increasing discharge or disposal costs.

The distilling process uses high volumes of water which is needed for applications such as cooling, heating, and in the product itself. The process generates high flow and strength effluent which has relatively high energy density values, most of which can be recovered. Its strength is measured in terms of Chemical Oxygen Demand or COD and can be used to estimate the amount of chemical energy that could be captured and converted to electricity or heat energy (see table 1).

Table 1. Typical energy captured in distilling effluent/co-products

Industry	*Units*	*Range*
Pot ale	COD in mg/l	40000-60000
Spent Lees	COD in mg/l	3000-6000
Draff	Calorific Value Kcal/Kg	10-16

To encourage recovering this captured chemical energy, the government have put in place many economic and legislative initiatives, creating a market for recovering energy from by-products and waste.

This paper will further discuss the current technologies, the available financial incentives, the associated risks and the importance of establishing a decision making mechanism to aid the decision while using a working example on whether it is both possible and worthwhile to reduce effluent discharge while generating green energy to make a profit.

Financial incentives

The distilling industry is committed to the UK targets of reducing energy usage and CO_2 emissions in line with the UK government pledge to have 15% of all energy production coming from renewable energy by 2020 (Secretary of State, 2009). This has spurred a combination of financial initiatives and legislative drivers creating an emerging market for energy recovery focussed technologies. Some of the drivers for energy recovery from brewing and distilling effluent include Feed-in Tariff, Climate Change Levy, Climate Change Agreements, Renewable Heat Incentive, Enhanced Capital Allowance, Renewable Obligation Certificates and Capital Grant Schemes.

Feed-in Tariff scheme

The Feed-in Tariff (FITs) scheme (Secretary of State, 2011) was introduced in 2010 by the UK government to encourage organisations to invest in small scale (less than 5MW) low carbon electricity generation in return for a guaranteed payment for the electricity they generate and export. The generation tariff and payout period varies depending on the applied technology, where the export tariff is fixed for all applications and currently stands at 3.1p/kWh. The generation tariff from a newly installed anaerobic digestion unit less than 500kW is 12.1p/kWh and those greater than 500kW is 9.4p/kWh. This would be received for 20 years with annual inflation adjustments. Eligible installations have to be completed after 15th July 2009 with the current tariffs to be reviewed in April 2012, although this would not affect installations in the scheme before that time. The FIT scheme is now the primary support for small scale installations (less than 5MW) with large scale renewable initiatives being supported by the Renewables Obligation Certificates (ROC).

Renewable Obligation and Renewable Obligation Certificates

The Renewable Obligation (RO) is the main support scheme for renewable electricity projects in the UK (Secretary of State, 2010). It places an obligation on UK suppliers of electricity to source an increasing proportion of their electricity from renewable sources, currently 12.4% (5.5% in Northern Ireland). In April 2010, the RO was extended from its current end date of 2027 to 2037 to support new projects.

Renewable Obligation Certificates (ROCs) are issued by Ofgem to large renewable energy generators (> 5MW) and are sold in the market for suppliers to fulfil their Renewable Obligation. If their obligation cannot be fulfilled, then the supplier must pay the 'buy-out' price, and this penalty is fed to the 'buy-out fund', which is then recycled to ROCs holders. Currently the 'buy-out' price is around £36.99/MWh. This means that the 'buy-out' price constitutes approximately 70% of the ROCs price (currently around £50/MWh each). The rest of the price is driven by the 'buy-out fund'. Previously, 1 ROC was issued for each megawatt hour (MWh) of eligible generation, regardless of technology, but in April 2009 new reforms meant the introduction of a banding structure where new generators would receive different numbers of ROCs depending on their applied technology to encourage large-scale deployment. Emerging technologies such as anaerobic digestion, gasification and other / advanced technologies are eligible for 2 ROCs, however already existing digestion for Energy from Waste (EfW) with combined heat and power added is only eligible for 0.5 ROC. The bands are currently under review and are expected to be confirmed in the autumn of 2011.

Renewable Heat Incentive

The Renewable Heat Incentive (RHI) is a UK government initiative introduced in July 2011 to provide financial support to encourage organisations to use renewable heat sources (Department of Energy and Climate Change, 2011a). This is being introduced in two phases and the initial part will provide long-term support to industrial customers who have installed an eligible technology after 15th July 2009. The RHI supports a range of technologies and fuels including biomass, solar thermal, heat-pumps, on-site biogas, deep geothermal, EfW and injection of biomethane into the gas grid. The RHI tariff, issued by Ofgem, depends on the application and its size, although all tariffs have a 20 year payout period. For example, biomass installations are split into three tariffs less than 200 kWth, between 200 – 1000 kWth, above 1000kWth and the tariff rate ranges from 1.9 p/kWh to 7.6 p/kWh.

Climate Change Levy

The Climate Change Levy (CCL) is a tax on use of non-renewable energy currently charged at £4.85/MWh (HM Revenue and Customs, 2011) for electricity and £1.69/MWh for gas and rises with inflation. Any energy produced on site will essentially replace energy usage from utility providers thereby reducing the share of CCL/MWh paid by the site.

Climate Change Agreement

Organisations that have a Climate Change Agreement (CCA) with the government can get a 65% reduction on the CCL which is set to increase to 80% on electricity from April 2013 with the overall scheme running until 2023 (Department of Energy and Climate Change, 2011b). CCAs are negotiated by sectors' trade associations and then the individual business. Development of renewable energy could contribute towards achievement of that CCA, in order to help realise the CCL discount for any remaining non-renewable fuel use.

The Scotch Whisky distillers participate in the CCA of the Spirits Energy Efficiency Company (SEEC) and through this have improved their energy efficiency by 18% and reduced emissions of carbon dioxide by 10% on 1999 levels (Scotch Whisky Association, 2010). These have been achieved through capital investments in energy efficient and/or emission reduction technologies.

Capital Grant Schemes

It may be possible to secure a capital grant to promote energy generation from biomass from regional development agencies or enterprise schemes. The UK Government's Bio-Energy Capital Grants Scheme provides grants for up to 40% of the difference between the biomass capital cost and the fossil fuel alternative of biomass-fuelled heat and Combined Heat and Power (CHP) projects, including anaerobic digesters (Department of Energy and Climate Change, 2010). However, accepting a grant will greatly hinder the possibility of receiving the feed-in tariff and may impact on any ROCs received resulting in a reduced incentive.

Enhanced Capital Allowance

The Enhanced Capital Allowance (ECA) scheme, also known as the First Year Allowance, is run by the government and offers a 100% first-year tax allowance for investments in certain water and energy saving equipment. Any eligible equipment such as biomass boilers can be written off against that year's taxable profits (Business Link, 2011).

Management options and available technology

Animal feed

Co-products also have a commercial value as animal feed where they can be sold as wet or dry feed. The moisture content in a wet feed material is around 90% whereas dry animal feed pellets moisture content is around 10-12% and the price varies depending on this. The technologies used to remove moisture are energy intensive and with rising energy prices, a review of all the options is increasingly important. The animal feed prices fluctuate depending on quantity of co-products, location and market economics. Hence the decision between wet or dry feed needs to incorporate projected feed values and also sustainability issues around transportation.

Anaerobic digestion

Anaerobic digestion is a proven, established technology well-suited to treating the effluent arising from many industrial processes and produces valuable energy. The biogas generated in the process is typically rich in methane, (around 60-75%) and its chemical energy can be recovered using a gas engine, gas turbine or gas boiler. A number of criteria should be considered when choosing an anaerobic digester including effluent composition, COD and Suspended Solids (SS) content, volume and temperature of the effluent to be treated, the space available for the equipment, the discharge route for the final effluent, the available sludge disposal options and the biogas use. In addition, the biogas prior to energy recovery needs to be pre treated for contaminants. As there are many anaerobic digestion technologies available, selecting one based on site constraints and waste parameters should be the priority.

Biomass boiler

Biomass can be converted into useful energy (heat or electricity) by thermochemical conversion technologies. These are in varying stages of development, where combustion is most developed and frequently applied. Other thermochemical conversion technologies include gasification and pyrolysis and are becoming more important. The process of biomass combustion involves a number of physical/chemical aspects of high complexity. The nature of the combustion depends both on the fuel properties and its application.

Gas engine

Reciprocating internal combustion engines are the most widespread technology for power generation (World Alliance for Decentralized Technologies (WADE), 2003). Gas Engines are known to have the lowest first cost of CHP systems and high efficiencies at part load operation giving users a flexible power source, which allows for a range of different applications. Also, short start-up times to full loads, make reciprocating engines a favourable source for backup power systems and peak shaving applications, and multiple reciprocating engines can enhance plant capacity and availability. The disadvantages include difficulty in recycling the low grade heat streams, and relatively high vibrations which require support and special foundations with noise shielding. Also, the large number of moving parts increases all-in maintenance costs, offsetting fuel efficiency advantages.

Gas turbine

Combustion or gas turbines are an established power generation technology (Environmental Protection Agency, 2002a). They can produce high-quality heat to generate steam and can burn natural gas, a variety of petroleum fuels, landfill or biogas, or can have dual-fuel capability. Gas turbines are well suited for CHP because their high-temperature exhaust can generate process steam at conditions as high as 82 bar and 540 ^{0}C. Gas Turbines are easier to install than steam turbines and high pressure boilers and are less area intensive with a lower capital cost. Larger systems have high efficiencies with high temperature steam production.

However, gas turbines require clean fuels with relatively constant heat value. The high temperatures limit the type of materials that can be used, therefore raising production costs. There can be issues with reduced efficiencies at part load. Turbine performance is significantly reduced at higher altitudes or high ambient temperatures. Small-capacity system costs are relatively high per installed kW, and efficiencies are lower than some other generation systems.

Steam turbine

Steam turbines generate electricity from the heat (steam) produced in a boiler, converting steam energy into shaft power (Environmental Protection Agency, 2002b). This energy is transferred to the turbine through high-pressure steam that powers the turbine and generator. This enables steam turbines to operate with various fuels including natural gas, solid waste, coal, wood, wood waste, and agricultural by-products. Ideal applications of steam turbine-based CHP systems include medium and large-scale industrial or institutional facilities with high thermal loads, and where solid or waste fuels are readily available for boiler use. Steam Turbines have high overall cogeneration efficiencies of up to 80% and produce high temperature and pressure steam. The disadvantages include low electrical efficiencies, need for expensive high-pressure boilers and equipment, slow start up times and poor part load performance.

Operational considerations

In addition to selecting the appropriate technology, there are various technical considerations. Waste parameters vary depending on factors such as quality of raw materials, quality of water used, production chain and many more depending on site. Appropriate data collation on influent parameters and performance deliverables should be appraised and documented. Typical technical risks include high levels of H_2S expected in biogas, moisture and trace content and suitability for energy recovery systems, the construction material of treatment equipment, a good understanding of treated water quality parameters and the treatment deliverables, additional costs for electricity management such as grid connections for electricity export, power purchase agreements, connection costs, and application of waste incineration directives, fluid selection for heat transfer, and the connection type and generator size will determine the changes to the onsite distribution network. A traffic and transport assessment should also be considered to assess the impact of waste transportation such as sludge.

Decision making methodology

A combination of approaches can be used to manage effluent and co-products. In addition to technology selection based on treatment capabilities it is important to review the technology and treatment chain against stakeholder objectives, commercial risks, sustainability deliverables, financial incentives, legislative framework and whole site economics as a part of a decision making mechanism. Taking a long term view, the establishment of appropriate technology selection criteria and design standards from the beginning adds hugely to the project value and the co-product management.

Ondeo Industrial Solutions, part of the global SUEZ ENVIRONNEMENT, encourages its clients to go through a decision making process to develop a solution that is best for the site(s) in question. The first stage involves defining the problem and stating the objectives. This includes collecting data on existing operations, listing potential technologies and waste management techniques, carrying out stakeholder analysis, describing project location and environment, and reviewing waste source and discharge/outlet routes. This provides an exhaustive list of technologies/treatment chains that can be applied to recover energy from a particular waste source.

A scoring mechanism is developed with the project stakeholders and is divided into key criteria. A high level mass and energy balance is produced for each option which incorporates all raw material inputs, expected outputs and equipment efficiencies. Using a Net Present Value (NPV) change appraisal which takes into account estimated operational expenditure costs (opex), capital expenditure costs (capex), output revenues and financial incentives such as the feed-in tariff, an order of magnitude financial model is developed. This is then used to compare each option while considering the existing plant performance.

A regulatory and environmental review is carried out in parallel and evaluates environmental legislation, planning and permitting issues, air emissions, water management, discharges to land and waste, noise and odour, landscape/visual impact and sustainability.

Monte Carlo analysis is also used to examine the impact of price sensitivity to ensure that the selected approach withstands variance in the market.

Casestudy

Here is working example to show the possibility and financial impact of generating steam and electricity on a distillery. Please be aware that what is shown is very simplistic and is based on an in-depth analysis of the individual site, operating conditions and other influencing factors. The distillery in this example has an effluent treatment plant on site that only requires modifications to its existing systems to generate steam and electricity. These alterations would include installing new equipment to treat the draff with technology such as a screw pump and driers, and modifications to the anaerobic digestion unit so that electricity could be generated from the biogas it produces. In term of the plant size, the flow rate from the pot ale is around $360m^3$/day and $180m^3$/day from the spent lees. It also produces 126 tonnes of draff per day. The revenue figures are based on the current renewable heat incentive and the feed-in tariffs rates.

To implement the necessary modifications would require an approximate capex of around £6.5m which would lend itself to additional operating cost of approximately £140k per year. The new technology enabling renewable energy production would generate revenues of around £1.14m per year from the feed-in tariffs and renewable heat initiative while saving around £0.73m per year in existing energy costs. Based on these simplified figures the payback period is around 4 years.

Other financial incentives that are not included in this example that could be considered are the enhanced capital allowance and a reduction in the sites climate change levy.

Conclusions

During the coming years as there is a government push to reduce industries carbon footprint and improve sustainability in operations, recovering energy from waste offers a great opportunity to work towards, and contribute to, sector and national targets. In this sector, the relatively high energy density in residue materials lends itself to technologies for the recovery of energy. There are a wide range of technologies available, a combination of which can be used to develop treatment philosophies for energy recovery.

Establishing a site specific decision making and technology appraisal methodology is therefore important to develop and deliver a co-product management strategy. The criteria should take a holistic approach to the site economics to develop the best techno-commercial solution. As the FITs and RHI contribute most of the revenue generated from the energy from waste facility, a clear understanding and application of the FITs and RHI economics during the decision making process at an earlier stage of the project ensures long term viability. Developing energy recovery schemes within this framework using a methodical approach ensures that the best techno-commercial solution is developed, thereby creating a viable proposition for long term operations. Financial modelling in terms of variance of important cost and revenue parameters should be carried out to ensure the selected approach for recovering energy from waste withstands these variations, thereby reducing the impact of market factors, prices and other fluctuations.

Ondeo Industrial Solutions works closely with its clients in developing energy recovery from waste and co-products within a decision making framework considering whole site economics. This has also provided our clients, stakeholders and funding agencies information on technical, commercial and other risks involved in a project and the mitigation measures. The establishment of such criteria thereby adds hugely to the value of a project and ensures technical and commercial performance of the developed solution.

In answer to the proposed question, we feel that we have shown that it is possible to reduce effluent and generate green energy while making a profit, though typically with a payback period of a number of years. However, because of the many variables the answer should always be based on an individual site appraisal so the best overall solution is identified and then implemented.

References

Business Link (2011). *First-year allowances - Enhanced Capital Allowances (2011).* http://www.businesslink.gov.uk/bdotg/action/layer?r.l1=1073858808&r.l2=1086692188&r.l3=1086445219&r.s=tl&topicId=1086445242 (accessed 23rd July 2011)

Department of Energy and Climate Change (2011a). *Renewable Heat Incentive.* March 2011.

Department of Energy and Climate Change (2011b). *Climate Change Agreements.* http://www.decc.gov.uk/en/content/cms/emissions/ccas/ccas.aspx (accessed 23rd July 2011)

Environmental Protection Agency (2002a). *Technology Characterization Gas Turbines,* Washington, February 2002.

Environmental Protection Agency (2002b). *Technology Characterization Steam Turbines, Washington March 2002.*

HM Revenue and Customs (2011). *Climate Change Levy 2011.* http://customs.hmrc.gov.uk/channelsPortalWebApp/channelsPortalWebApp.portal?_nfpb=true&_pageLabel=pageExcise_ShowContent&id=HMCE_PROD_009791&propertyType=document (accessed 23rd July 2011)

Scotch Whisky Association (2010). *The Scotch Whisky Industry: Environmental Strategy Report 2010.*

Secretary of State (2009). *The UK Renewable Energy Strategy.* p4.

Secretary of State (2010). *The Renewables Obligation (Amendment) Order 2010.*

Secretary of State (2011). *Feed-in Tariffs (Specified Maximum Capacity and Functions) Order 2010* as amended by the *Feed-in Tariffs (Specified Maximum Capacity and Functions) (Amendment) Order 2011.*

Department of Energy and Climate Change (2010). *Bio-energy Capital Grants Scheme, Round* 6. http://www.bioenergycapitalgrants.org.uk (accessed March 2010)

World Alliance for Decentralized Technologies (WADE) (2003). *Guide to decentralized energy Technologies*, Edinburgh, UK.

Chapter 36

Low-temperature processing of wheat for bioethanol production[1]

G.G. Stewart, S. Cornfine, K.A. Leiper, M. Meidl

International Centre for Brewing and Distilling, Heriot-Watt University, Riccarton, Edinburgh, EH14 4AS, Scotland

Introduction.

Bioethanol is produced by fermentation of sugars extracted from agricultural sources. It is used in a blend with, or in place of, gasoline. As a fuel, it has the advantage of a high octane content, it burns cleanly, and is biodegradable. Ethanol can be used as a blend with gasoline at levels up to 10% without engine modification, whereas levels above 10% require modifications. Although current production is focussed in Brazil and the United States, with the main substrates being sugar (sucrose) and corn (maize) respectively, production of bioethanol in other parts of the globe is rapidly increasing. World ethanol production for transport fuel tripled between 2000 and 2007 from 17 billion litres to more than 52 billion litres per annum. From 2007 to 2008, the share of ethanol in global gasoline type fuel use increased from 3.7% to 5.4%.

In 2010 worldwide ethanol fuel production reached 87 billion litres with the United States as the top producer accounting for 57.5% of global production. Also in 2010 bioethanol fuel in Brazil and the United States together accounted for 88% of world ethanol fuel production. In 1976 the Brazilian government made it mandatory to blend ethanol with gasoline. Since 2007 the legal blend is approximately 25% ethanol and 75% gasoline. In addition, since December 2010 Brazil had a fleet of 12 million flex-fuel automobiles and light trucks and over half a million motorcycles regularly use 100% ethanol fuel (known as E100). In 2010 approximately half of Brazil's sugar cane crop was grown especially for bioethanol production. The Brazilian industry has been particularly successful due to the suitability of the climate and crop, low production costs, and the use of sugar cane waste as a fuel for the distilleries. Currently in the United States, 15% of the national corn crop is being used to produce bioethanol.

Bioethanol production is now expanding in other parts of the globe. The choice of raw material depends on local conditions. As well as sugar cane and corn, other potential substrates include sugar beet, wheat, barley, sorghum, cassava and oats. Materials containing lignocellulose, such as wood, straw, sawdust and grasses, are potential future substrates

[1] Some of the data contained in this paper was presented at the World Grains Summit: Food and Beverages, held in San Francisco, C.A., September 17 to 20, 2006

(Zaldiver, Nielson and Olson, 2001). This is second generation bioethanol. Each source presents technologically unique challenges for commercial-scale production. Wheat is of great interest for use in Northern Europe. In 2009, 682 million tonnes were produced worldwide with a 15% increase in wheat production during the previous decade. Although a few years ago there was a wheat surplus this situation has now reversed with considerable demand for this raw material with considerable price increases. In the United Kingdom, by the end of 2013, the Renewable Transport Fuel Obligation states that UK petrol should contain 5% bioethanol and this percentage will likely rise in subsequent years. Progress towards this goal has so far been achieved largely through imported ethanol (principally from Brazil). However, construction of two plants in England based on wheat as the substrate are nearing completion. One facility is the Ensus plant at Wilton on Teesside and the other the Vivergo plant at Hull. Both plants are scheduled to produce 400 million litres of bioethanol and 350,000 tonnes of distiller's dried grains (DDGS) per annum and each will require 1.2 million tonnes of wheat (Robson, 2010). Also since 2007 there has been an operating bioethanol plant in Norfolk using sugar beet as the feedstock.

The aim of this study was to investigate the use of wheat as a substrate and to develop an appropriate method for the production of bioethanol with it in the United Kingdom and other Northern European countries.

Materials and methods

Wheat. The wheat cv. Riband was the gift of The North British Distillery Co. Ltd. It had moisture and protein contents of 13% and 8.8% respectively. It was stored at 4°C prior to use.

Yeast Strain. Pressed "M" yeast strain of *Saccharomyces cerevisiae* was obtained from Kerry Bio-Sciences. Weekly supplies were obtained and stored at 4°C prior to use.

Enzymes. All enzymes were the gift of Novozymes and were handled and stored according to the manufacturer's specification. Details of the enzymes employed are as follows:

- SAN Super 240L is an aqueous enzyme preparation consisting of a blend of amylase, amyloglucosidase and protease.
- Spirizyme fuel is an aqueous preparation of amyloglucosidase.
- Viscozyme wheat is an aqueous preparation of xylanase endo-1-4-cellulase.
- Liquozyme SC DS is an aqueous preparation of α-amylase.

Determination of α- and β-amylase Activity. The activities of α- and β-amylase in the wheat flavour were determined using the Megazyme Ceralpha (K-CERA 08/05) and Betamyl (K-BETA 12.04) kits (Megazyme International Ltd.).

Chemicals. All chemicals used in this study were of analytical grade or equivalent.

Milling. Wheat was milled in a dry mill to produce a fine grist.

Small-Scale Mashing (200mL). Mashing was carried out using an automated mashing bath (CM4 mashing bath, Canongate Technology). Exogenous enzyme (100μL of SAN Super) was added and the mash was stirred to uniformly distribute the enzyme. To avoid evaporation, the beakers were covered with glass lids. Mashing was conducted for 60 minutes. Sequential samples were taken and supernatants analysed for pH and gravity. This mashing procedure was used to measure water/grist ratios by varying the amount of wheat added, the effects of mashing time, pH and temperature.

Laboratory-Scale Mashing (1L). Mashing was carried out on the 1L scale in 2-L glass beakers in a water bath set at 60°C. Wheat grist was mixed with 1L of water at 85°C and 500μL of exogenous enzymes added and the mash mixed to ensure uniform distribution. Following mashing, a sample was centrifuged and supernatant pH, gravity, sugars and FAN determined. The remainder of the mash (unclarified) was fermented. During backsetting experiments (details later), some of the mashing water was substituted with spent wash.

Wheat Cooking. Wheat was mixed with warm water in 2-L glass beakers and then sealed with foil. These beakers were then cooked for 30 min. at 121°C in an autoclave. Following cooking and cooling to 60°C the wheat was mashed as described above.

Fermentation. The mashes were placed in 2-L glass bottles, cooled to 30°C, a few drops of antifoam added, yeast pitched and fermentation conducted with shaking. After removal of the solid material, the supernatant (250mL) was used for alcohol, gravity, pH, sugars and FAN determination as described previously (Miedl, Cornfine, Leiper, Shepherd and Stewart, 2007).

Production of Spent Wash for Backsetting Experiments. Wash (fermented mash) produced in the fermentation experiments was distilled to produce spent wash for backsetting experiments as described previously (Miedl et al, 2007).

Industrial Trial of Bioethanol Production from Wheat. A trial with uncooked wheat was conducted in The North British Distillery in Edinburgh, Scotland. As well as grain whisky the distillery also produces grain neutral spirit (GNS) from uncooked wheat but with the use of industrial enzymes for starch conversion. Details of the trials conducted have been reported previously (Miedl et al, 2007).

Results

Small-scale mashing (200mL) – optimisation of wheat grist/water ratio, mashing pH and temperatures

A workable wheat inclusion rate was determined. Wheat grist 40-180g in 200mL water was prepared. Mashing was conducted at 63°C for 60 min. with the SAN Super enzyme preparation added (100μL). The higher grist concentrations (100-180g) resulted in too viscous mashes and therefore could not be sampled. Specific gravity during mashing is shown in Figure 1.

As expected, increasing amounts of wheat resulted in higher mash gravities. However,

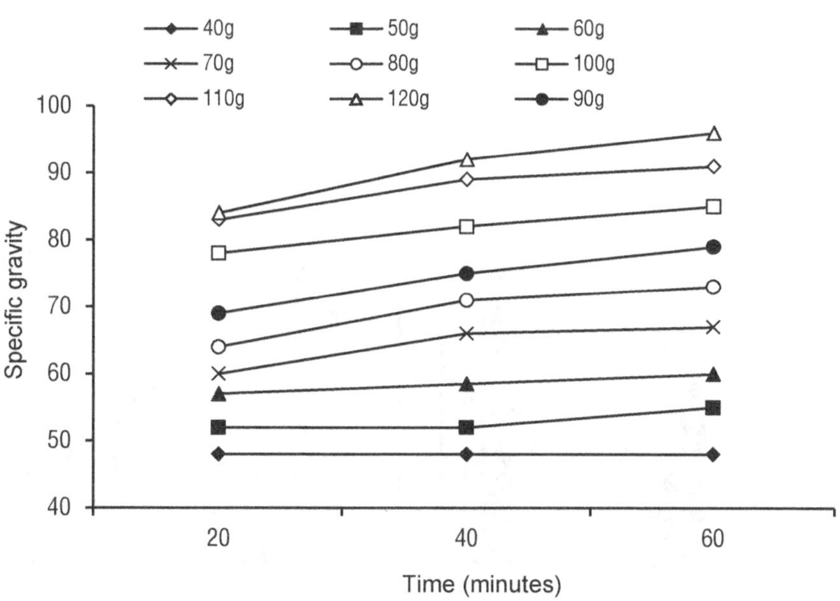

Figure 1. Influence of wheat grist/water ratio and its effect on specific gravity during mashing.

the increase was not directly proportional to the weight of wheat employed. Mash gravity increased during the first hour. Also, mash pH values were between 6.0 and 6.3. Based on these results, wheat grist/water ratios of 70, 80 and 90g wheat/200mL water were selected for subsequent experiments.

The supplier of SAN Super recommended that the optimum pH was 5.5 but the wheat mash pH was 6.0-6.3. An industrial process would be simpler if the need to adjust the pH could be avoided. Therefore, it was of interest to know whether this enzyme preparation could efficiently operate over a wide pH range. As a consequence, the pH values of the wheat mash were adjusted to pH 4.5, 5.0 and 5.5. A further sample was not pH adjusted. All samples were mashed as reported previously. No variation in wort specific gravity was found over the pH range studied (Figure 2). Based on these results, mash pH was not adjusted in subsequent experiments with SAN Super.

The optimum temperature for SAN Super was recommended by the supplier to be 55°C. In order to confirm this fact or otherwise, mashing experiments at 52, 57, 62 and 67°C were conducted. Mash specific gravities were almost identical in the samples mashed at 57-67°C but were lower in the 52°C mashing temperature (Figure 3). It was concluded that the mashing temperature would be 60°C.

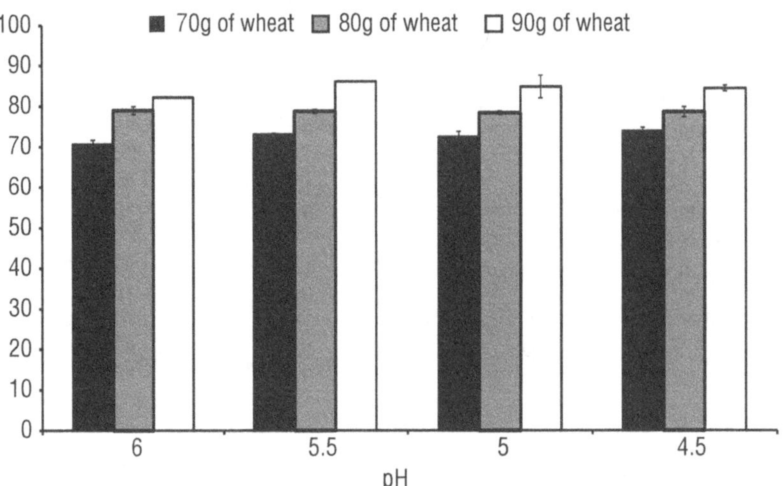

Figure 2. The effect of pH on mash specific gravity.

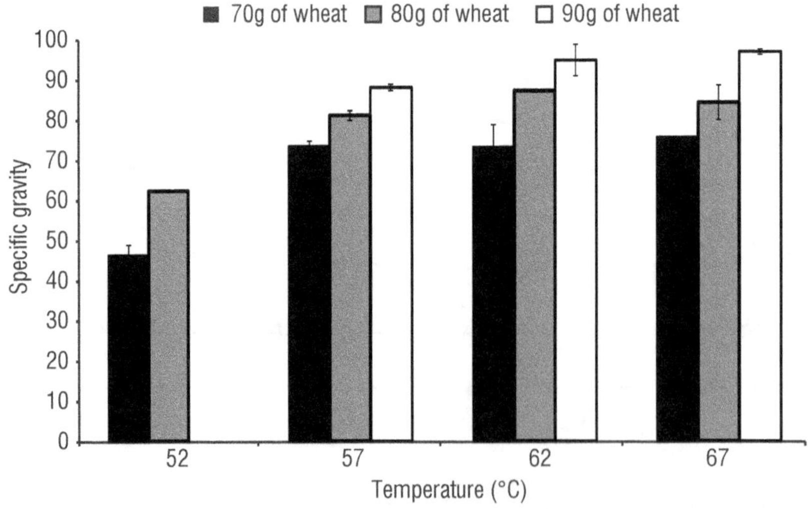

Figure 3. The effect of temperature on mash specific gravity (90g mash at 52°C was too viscous to sample).

Laboratory-scale mashing and fermentation (1L) – optimisation of processing temperature for mashing and fermentation with cooked and uncooked wheat with added enzymes

Following the optimization of mashing parameters at the 200mL scale, further experiments were conducted on a larger (1L) scale. Mashing was conducted at 350, 400 and 450 g/L in duplicate. To one set was added SAN Super and the other set was not enzyme dosed. Following mashing, the samples were cooled and fermented as described.

The specific gravity decreases are shown in Figure 4. As would be expected, initial gravities increased with increasing wheat inclusion.

Interestingly, the samples mashed without enzymes were also high and similar to the samples mashed with added enzymes. During the first 24h of fermentation the gravities decreased rapidly. However, the mashes without added enzymes decreased more slowly. Fermentations with added enzymes were fully fermented by 72h, whereas fermentations without added enzymes were incompletely fermented even after 120h incubation. The pH of the enzyme treated fermentation fell to 4.5 by 72h and rose slightly thereafter whereas the mashes without enzyme addition fell to 4.0 after 72h and then remained constant.

Following fermentation, wash samples were distilled and, as would be expected, the ethanol yield increased with greater wheat inclusion but was not directly proportional to wheat usage (Figure 5).

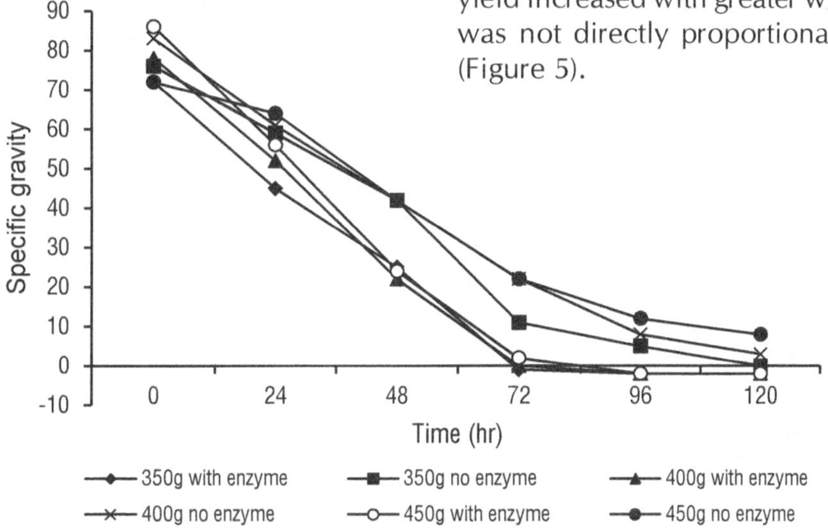

Figure 4. Specific gravity fermentations wheat mashes prepared with and without SAN Super enzyme.

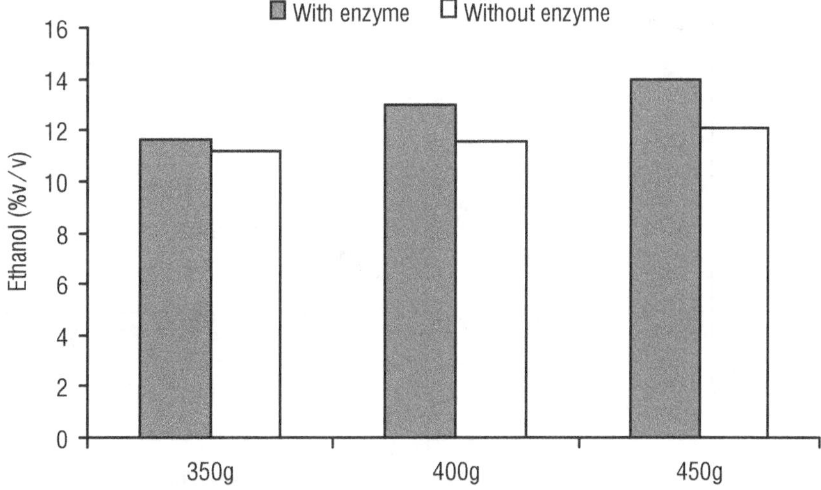

Figure 5. Ethanol concentration of fermentation wheat mashes prepared with and without SAN Super enzyme.

The fermentation with 450g wheat/L mash contained 29% more wheat compared to the 350g wheat/L mash but did not produce 29% more ethanol. This indicates that the preparation with 350g of wheat/L was the most efficient. As would be expected, fermentation with no added enzymes produced slightly lower ethanol yields.

The mashing experiments discussed above were all conducted using uncooked wheat because this is normal practice in potable neutral spirit production in the United Kingdom. In this situation, fine milling of soft wheat is considered sufficient to allow access of exoenzymes to the starch. In contrast, in the Scotch whisky industry wheat for grain whisky production is cooked up to 150°C prior to mashing with malted barley. Could the wheat cooking stage be omitted?

Cooked wheat was mashed with SAN Super along with an uncooked control and both these mashes fermented. Both sets of fermentations had similar (not identical) fermentation patterns (Figure 6) and both were attenuated by 72h with the cooked wheat mash fermenting faster.

The cooked wheat fermentation produced 11.1% (v/v) ethanol and the uncooked fermentation produced 11.8% (v/v) ethanol; indicating that the cooking stage did not result in greater fermentability and should be considered to be omitted during bioethanol production processes.

The exoenzyme preparation employed thus far in this experimental programme was SAN Super. However, an enzyme preparation has now become available specifically designed to produce fuel ethanol. This enzyme preparation consists of three enzyme preparations: Spirizyme, Liquozyme and Viscozyme Wheat. These were tested alongside SAN Super in order to compare their mashing and fermentation characteristics.

Mashes containing 350, 400 and 450g wheat/L were prepared in duplicate and fermented as previously described. One set was mashed with SAN Super and the other with the three enzyme mixtures described above. Specific gravity patterns during fermentation are shown in Figure 7. The specific gravity decreased at similar rates in all the fermentations studied and all attenuated by 70h.

Ethanol content is shown in Figure 8 with the fermentation mashed with the three enzymes producing more ethanol than those mashed with SAN Super.

The fermentation differences observed between the mashes containing either the three enzyme mixture or the SAN Super can, in part, be explained by the sugar profiles in the mash during fermentation. The hexose sugar present in mashes with 450g wheat/L with SAN Super or the three enzymes before and after fermentation are shown in Figure 9.

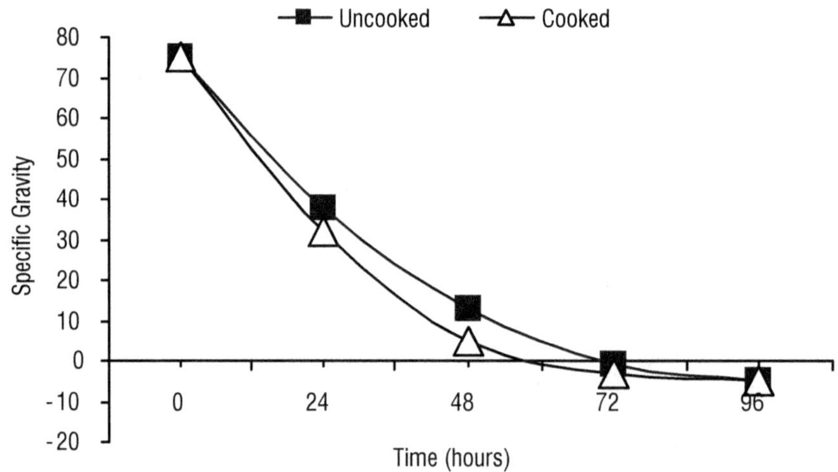

Figure 6. Specific gravity of fermentations with uncooked and cooked wheat mashes.

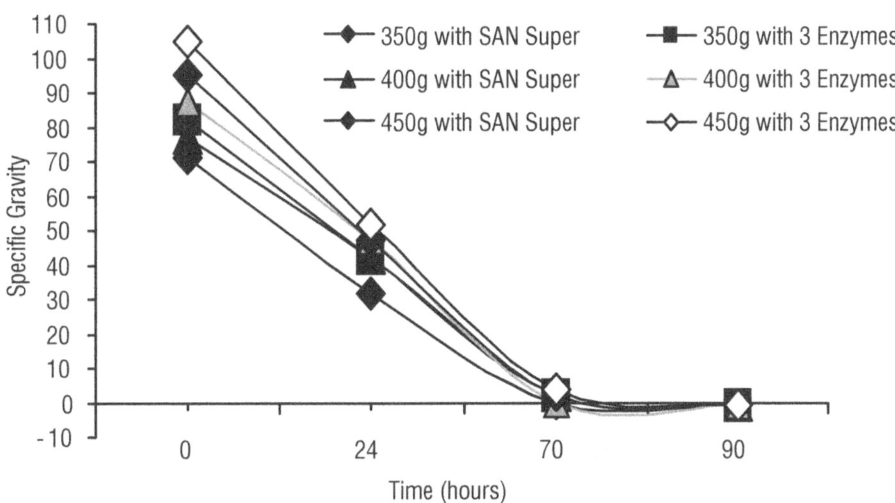

Figure 7. Specific gravity of fermentations with wheat mashes prepared with SAN Super enzyme or a mixture of the three enzymes Spirizyme, Liquozyme and Viscozyme Wheat.

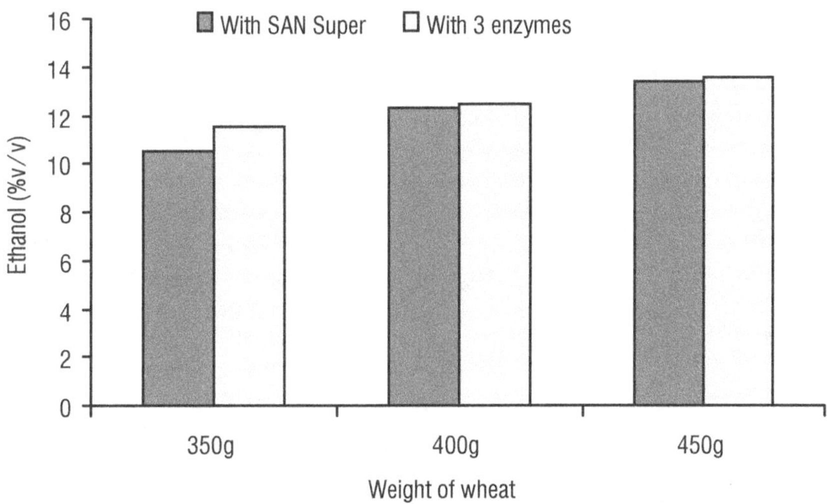

Figure 8. Ethanol concentration of fermentations with wheat mashes prepared with SAN Super enzyme or a mixture of the three enzymes Spirizyme, Liquozyme and Viscozyme Wheat.

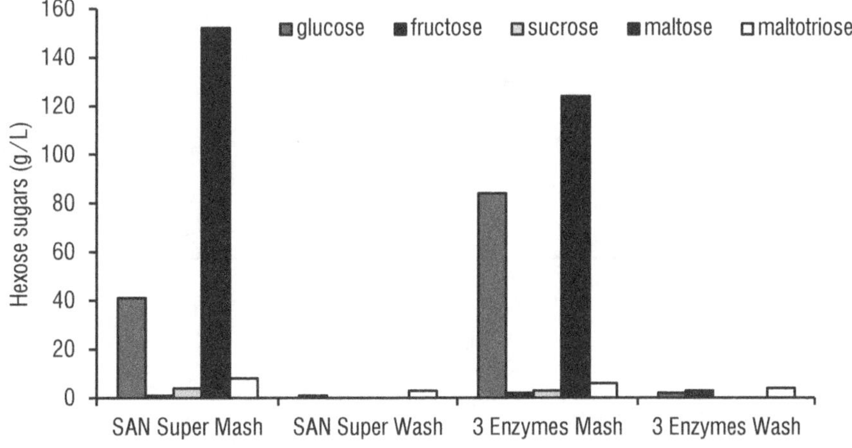

Figure 9. Hexose sugars in mash and wash samples from fermentations of mashes prepared with SAN Super enzyme or a mixture of the three enzymes Spirizyme, Liquozyme and Viscozyme Wheat.

The SAN Super mash contained mostly maltose with some glucose, whereas the three enzymes mashed sample contained maltose and more glucose. This difference was due to glucoamylytic activity in these latter enzyme preparations hydrolising more maltose to glucose than the SAN Super containing mash preparation.

Laboratory-scale mashing and fermentation (1L) with added backset

During the distillation stage (potable or industrial) the ethanol is removed from the fermented media. The material remaining in the still is referred to as spent mash, stillage or vinasse, can be dried in the production of spent grain. This liquid can also be used to replace some of the water utilized at an earlier stage in the process. This is known as "backsetting". This process is of use during wheat-based bioethanol production and experiments have been conducted to investigate the effect of backsetting on ethanol yield.

Mashes containing varying amounts of backset were set up. Although the mash with 70% backset was too viscous to be sampled there were no problems associated with replacing up to 50% of the mashing water with backset. Specific gravity during fermentation is shown in Figure 10.

The original gravities of the mashes increased with high levels of backset. This was caused by the spent wash having a higher gravity than water due to the presence of grist, yeast cell components, and glycerol from previous fermentations. The fermentations with backset proceeded faster than the control, in proportion to the inclusion rate (Figure 10). The 20, 30 and 50% backset fermentations were fully attenuated by 46h. The backset fermentation had higher final specific gravities than the control, due to the presence of unfermentable components such as glycerol.

Ethanol results are shown in Figure 11. Higher than 10% backsetting produced slightly more ethanol. This may be due to the presence of nutrients in the spent wash such as free amino nitrogen (FAN).

The FAN concentration increased in the mash samples as the proportion of the backset became greater (Figure 12). Most of the FAN was taken up by the yeast during the first 22h of fermentation.

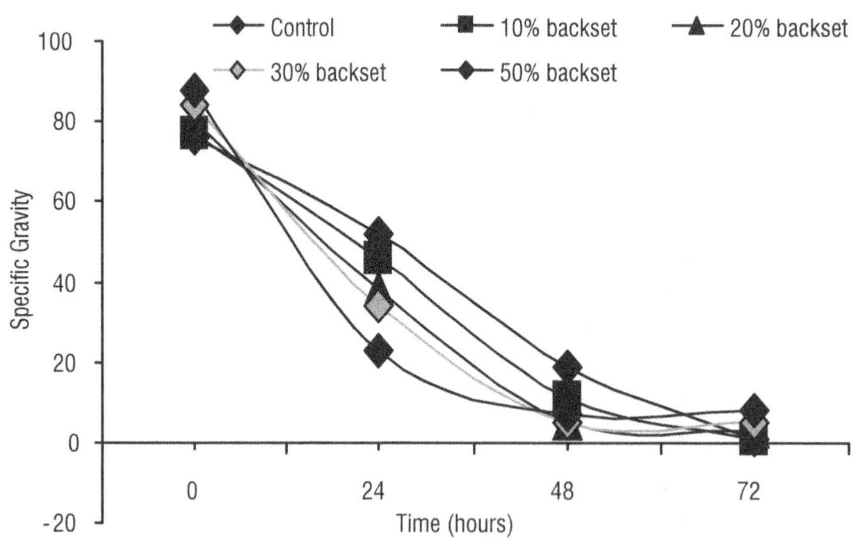

Figure 10. Specific gravity of fermentations of mashes prepared with a mixture of the three enzymes Spirizyme, Liquozyme and Viscozyme without and with varying amounts of backset.

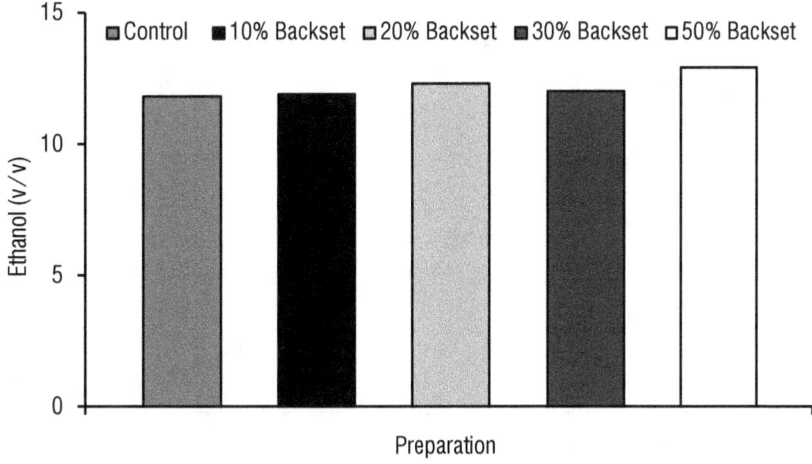

Figure 11. Ethanol concentration of wash produced from fermentations of mashes prepared with a mixture of the three enzymes Spirizyme, Liquozyme and Viscozyme Wheat without and with varying amounts of backset.

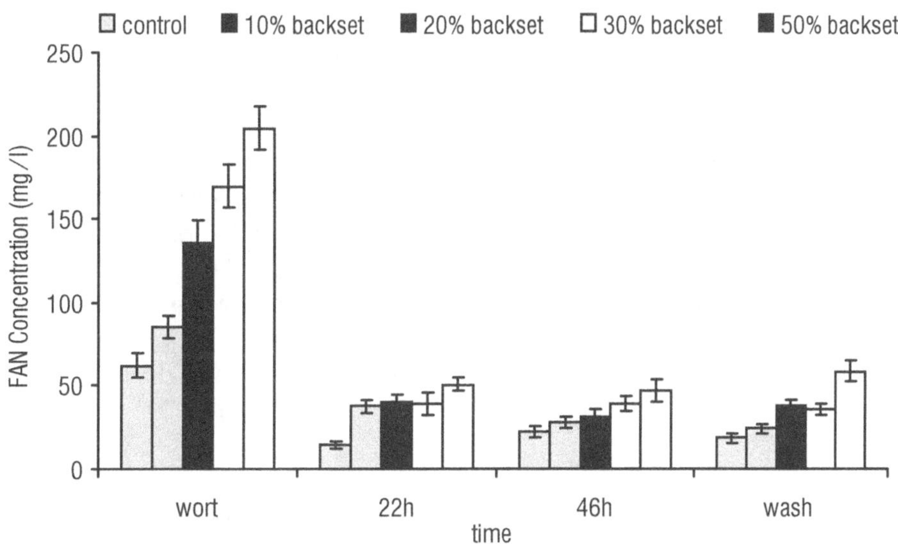

Figure 12. Free amino nitrogen (FAN) concentration during fermentations of wheat mashes prepared with a mixture of the three enzymes Spirizyme, Liquozyme and Viscozyme Wheat without and with varying amounts of backset.

Industrial-scale trials

The initial trial, where the mash was cooled to 25°C, was unsuccessful. A second trial was successfully conducted where the mash was cooled to 30°C and the specific gravity decreases during fermentation in the washbacks are shown in Figure 13. The initial samples (zero time) were taken from the mashing vessels. Fermentation was complete by 48h and an ethanol yield of 8% (v/v) was achieved.

A drawback of this trial was the presence of malt in the grist along with wheat. It was unclear how much even the small amount of malt employed affected fermentability. In order to try to answer this question, laboratory-scale mashing experiments were conducted. Six 1-L mashes with 350g uncooked wheat were conducted. Three mashes were the unheated control and the other three had 13g of malt added in order to simulate the same inclusion rate (3.7%) as the plant trials. The fermentations containing

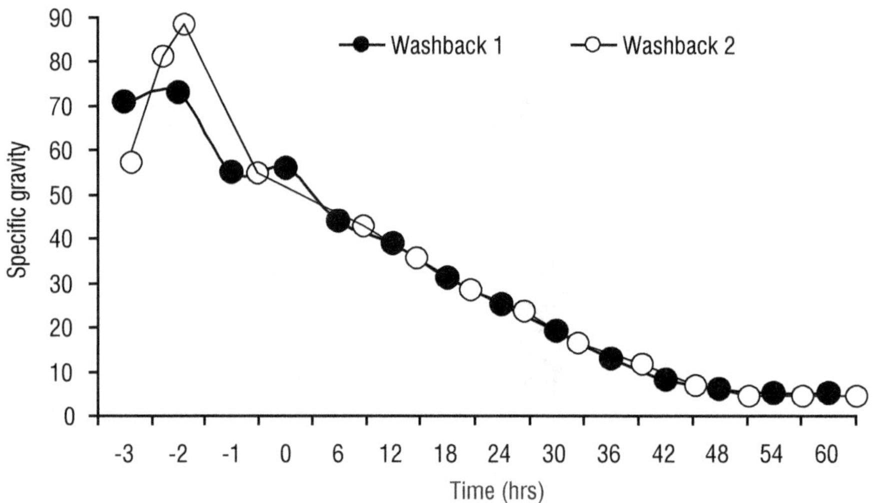

Figure 13. Specific gravity of wheat mash fermentations on the industrial scale.

the malt had a slightly higher original gravity due to the additional starch present (Figure 14).

Apart from this, both sets of fermentation proceeded almost identically with the no malt added samples producing 10.7% (v/v) ethanol and those with malt along with the wheat producing 10.9% (v/v) ethanol. These results show that wheat can be used successfully at a large scale without cooking or the addition of industrial enzymes.

α- and β- Amylase Activity

From the experiments previously discussed, it was assumed that the enzymes needed to hydrolyze the starch were present in the unmalted wheat. In order to confirm this possibility, α- and β- amylase activities were determined in wheat cv Riband before and during mashing (Table 1). Total α- and β- amylase activity was high in the wheat grain and during mashing. β-amylase

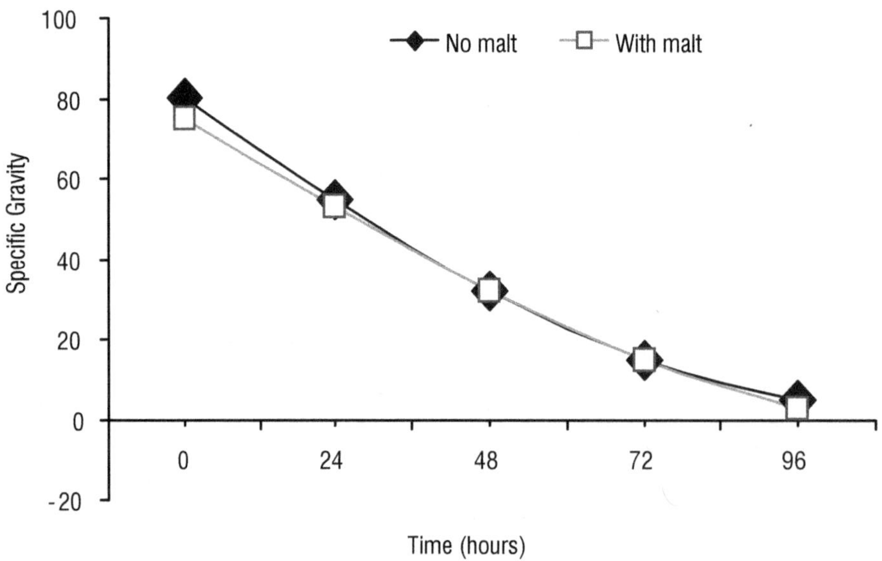

Figure 14. Specific gravity of wheat mash fermentations prepared with and without malt.

Table 1. Activities of α- and β-amylase in unmalted wheat and during mashing.

Unmalted wheat enzyme	*Activity of wheat flour (units/g)*
α-Amylase	0.408
β-Amylase	453.7

Mashing Duration (min)	*α-Amylase (units/L)*	*β-Amylase (units/L)*
0	206	19,706
20	198	10,602
40	192	5,260
60	176	2,800

is a temperature-sensitive enzyme (Merrit and Walker, 1969) and its activity decreased steadily during mashing. Nevertheless, the enzyme level has proved to be sufficient for nearly complete conversion of wheat starch.

Discussion

Research and development on bioethanol production has focussed on all phases and aspects of the process from raw materials to by-product recovery, and has been directed towards improving the fermentation efficiency and reducing the overall cost of ethanol production. There is still considerable scope to develop an efficient and low-cost bioethanol production process. Wheat is currently used for fuel and potable ethanol production (Robson, 2010; Russell, 2003) employing a process that comprises a cooking stage with subsequent addition of exogenous enzymes or barley malt for starch conversion. However, it was proposed that the cooking step could be omitted without a loss in ethanol yield and with savings in energy expenditure.

Laboratory-scale trials showed that fermentation of wheat mash prepared without exoenzymes produced only slightly reduced ethanol than those prepared with exoenzymes. The reduced ethanol production was significant but when set against the cost of purchasing enzymes and enzyme handling equipment this loss may not be critical. Wheat contains sufficient levels of endogenous enzymes to break down starch and protein. In addition, low levels of backsetting were beneficial in terms of fermentation speed efficiency but total ethanol production was unaffected.

These studies enabled the modification of production methods for the production of bioethanol from wheat (Miedl et al, 2007). The major modifications are the omission of industrial enzymes and the higher fermentation temperature. This revised process makes use of finely milled, uncooked wheat mixed with water with a percentage of spent wash at a mashing temperature of 60°C. Also, where possible, hot spent wash (backset) straight from the sills would be used to achieve further energy savings. This mixture will be mashed without exoenzymes and the need for pH adjustment. Following mashing, the mash will be cooled to 30°C and moved to a fermenter. No solid separation takes place similar to the "all grains in" process used in the Scotch grain whisky sector. Fermentaters will be pitched with an appropriate distilling yeast strain. Fermentation vessels do not contain temperature control and be permitted "free rise" to approximately 32°C, depending on the local temperature conditions. Following fermentation, the wash will be distilled in a continuous still (Coffey-type), followed by further rectification and purification to produce pure anhydrous ethanol. No attempt will be made to reuse the yeast. Spent wash will be processed to animal feed and it may be possible to recover the fermentation carbon dioxide.

Conclusions

There is scope for developing an efficient and inexpensive production process for bioethanol. This paper discusses the further development of a process for bioethanol production using wheat as the feedstock. A process with and without the use of exoenzymes is described. These studies were supported with industrial-scale trials. Results showed that the exogenous enzymes are not required with wheat as the feedstock and that the process can be scaled-up without difficulty. These findings have allowed the further development of a low-cost production process with wheat that will be of use in the United Kingdom, other parts of Northern Europe, Central Europe and Canada.

Acknowledgements

We thank the IBD Grants Committee and Green Spirit Fuels Ltd. for providing funding for this project. This project was carried out as part of an exchange program between the Technische Universitat Muchen-Weihanstephan and the International Centre for Brewing and Distilling, Heriot-Watt University, Edinburgh. The authors are grateful to Anne Anstruther for her invaluable assistance with the development of this manuscript.

References

Merrit, N.R. and Walker, J.T. (1969). Development of starch and other components in normal and high amylase barley. *Journal of the Institute of Brewing* **75**: 156-164.

Miedl, M., Cornfine, S., Leiper, K.A., Shepherd, M. and Stewart, G.G., (2007). Low-temperature processing of wheat for bioethanol production. *Journal of the American Society of Brewing Chemists* **65**: 183-196.

Robson, F. (2010). Bioethanol – a new outlet for wheat. *Brewer & Distiller International.* **6(11)**: 58-62.

Russell, I. (2003). *Whisky: Technology, Production and Marketing*, Academic Press, London, UK.

Zaldiver, J., Nielsen, J. and Olson, X., (2001), Fuel ethanol production from lignocellulose: a challenge for metabolic and process integration. *Applied Microbiology and Biotechnology*. **56**: 17-34.

Chapter 37

Adapting liquid digestion systems for distillery co-products

Richard Gueterbock
Marketing Director, Clearfleau Limited, 10 Wellington Street, Cambridge, CB1 1HW

Introduction

On-site treatment of effluents and co-products in the food and drink sector requires technology that will optimise energy output. Other market sectors such as small-scale farm or community projects require different approaches. This paper includes a short overview of the UK AD market and focuses on the opportunities for high-rate digestion on distilled spirit production sites and will cover the following:

- An overview of UK developments with AD solutions and related technologies
- A review of UK Government policy on AD and the application of the Feed in Tariff (FIT) and Renewable Heat Incentive (RHI) support mechanisms
- Several case studies showing technical robustness and payback potential
- Results of recent trials by Clear*f*leau - including with distillery co-products
- Basic design outline for a low cost, high-rate digester for distillery co-products.

One of the case studies will be based on the WRAP/DECC funded, on-site anaerobic digestion plant built for BV Dairy. This has been fully operational since early 2011, digesting processing effluent and dairy co-products, supplying renewable energy to the site while cutting its carbon footprint. This showcase project is demonstrating energy generation from liquid effluents.

UK policymakers and the AD industry seem to be focused on large scale centralised plants with electrical output above 1MW. However, compact AD plants that treat waste and effluents where they are produced will enable the more effective use of the renewable energy (heat and power) in production processes, replacing purchased fossil fuels.

High-rate liquid digestion plants can be installed on confined sites and facilitate reduced effluent treatment and energy costs, whilst generating revenue from the energy produced. They must accommodate flow and load variations and need to optimise biogas (and revenue) generation in order to maximize payback. Post treatment, the process should facilitate grey water recycling for use on site, or possible watercourse discharge.

This paper sets out to address some established preconceptions about Anaerobic Digestion. It examines the scope for adaptation of high-rate liquid digestion to the specific circumstances of the distillery sector. It also highlights some of the ways in which AD technology is being developed and how this might impact on the distilled spirits industry.

Introduction to on-site anaerobic digestion

Anaerobic Digestion (AD) is an established technology, used around the world. However, there are concerns about its adoption in the drinks industry, some of which are specific to the distillery sector and handling of whisky co-products. In this natural degradation process, methanogenic bacteria break down biodegradable materials, that contain organic matter, (sugars, fats and proteins) in the absence of oxygen to produce biogas (mainly methane).

The distillery sector has been slow to evaluate AD, partly because conventional systems cannot cope with relatively dilute feedstocks from distilleries. Also, the established high-rate (suspended media) digestion systems that have been used in the brewery sector, struggle to handle the higher solids in the feedstock (draff squeezings) from, the dark grains plants.

Many distillery sites rely on aerobic bio-plants to treat residues but some are at the end of their life. There are concerns about the level of investment required for AD plants and how long they will take to produce a return on the investment. This is not normally a concept that is associated with disposal of co-products but novel AD technologies that optimise biogas output can benefit from renewable energy incentives to provide a potential IRR of 20%.

The technology has been used for years to treat agricultural or sewage waste but the UK has been a slow adopter. Existing facilities tend to be located away from public gaze and are used to treat municipal waste (they are operated by the waste management industry). Many food and drink businesses are unaware of its benefits. This is partly due to the focus of policy makers on diverting organic materials from landfill. However, a number of issues have restricted the development of AD, not only in the distillery sector but in other industries:

- **Cost and Risk**: recent investment in new anaerobic bio-plants by distillers has not necessarily produced the expected return on investment. To justify investment in an AD plant, plants need to have a realistic payback of less than 5 years. Also the UK was slow to bring in renewable energy incentives that were available elsewhere.

- **Local Impact**: public fears about the impact of renewable energy technologies have been stoked by opponents of wind and incineration technologies. High-rate AD must demonstrate that it does not impact on the lives of those who live close to the plants.

- **Digestate disposal**: disposal of post digestion residues has become an issue mainly due the perception that AD is a technology for handling landfill diverted waste. But digestion of distillery co-products offers a valuable source of crop nutrients for farms.

- **Technology Integration**: there are a range of renewable technologies that can be used on distillery sites (but many have to be imported). On-site AD can be combined with other technologies as a means of creating low or zero carbon production sites.

- **Indigenous Development**: Scotland (as with the entire UK) has lacked the technical skills and economic drivers to facilitate development of sustainable technologies. We are now developing the technical expertise and an indigenous technology base.

While 'political will' also is required to address these issues, commercial drivers are creating opportunities for on-site decentralised renewable energy generation. This will help distillers to reduce energy bills and their environmental impact.

Overview of AD policy framework in the UK and EU

Although the process is a complex one, that needs careful management to optimise outputs, the benefits of AD are clear – generating energy from unwanted or undervalued resources. While energy from biogas has political support, lauded by government and promoted by diverse stakeholders, it must perform commercially. Political enthusiasm for renewable energy must be converted into policies that will encourage the development of an indigenous technology base and a thriving renewables industry. As is often the case, Britain lags behind its EU counterparts in the renewables sector. The UK is now playing catch up.

In June 2011, the Government announced its AD Strategy and Action Plan, but this focus on AD, with politicians and commentators extolling the virtues of the technology, is not delivering many new plants. At present much of the AD sector is hindered by excessive regulation and inability to secure project finance. These are constraints that don't apply to commercial AD projects - where the main challenge is to ensure an attractive ROI, based in part on the delivery of reduced treatment cost and lower fossil fuel consumption.

However, the payback potential for AD is boosted by the availability of specific incentives for renewable energy generators and the inexorable rise in energy prices. The ROCs incentive system was designed for large scale plants but the recently introduced Feed in Tariff (FIT) is now banded to encourage smaller plants (under 500kW electrical output). September 2011 sees the introduction of Renewable Heat Incentive (RHI) for heat from renewable sources.

While it is important to demonstrate how AD fits into a wider resource management picture, some stakeholders have been criticised for presenting it as a 'silver bullet', when in reality it is one of a number of technologies (for instance biomass energy using waste wood has a role to play in Scotland). The development of new renewable energy infrastructure also requires an open and informed debate about the benefits of all the various technologies.

Although the UK Government (DECC and DEFRA) is starting to see its potential application for a wider range of feedstocks, it has not fully grasped the concept of smaller scale AD on farms, in communities and on industrial sites. Also, regulators are reluctant to embrace it as a diverse and low risk renewable energy solution. However, Scotland's authorities seem to be taking a more enlightened approach to the development of anaerobic digestion in rural areas and there will be a range of opportunities to install smaller scale plants in Scotland.

Government and regulators must embrace alternative business models for on-site digestion plants. Smaller plants can be integrated into communities, as well as located on farms or on industrial sites. They may not be able to generate over 1 MW of electricity but they can be located where full use can be made of both electricity and surplus heat (from a CHP engine) or where biogas is fed to an on site boiler or used in district heating schemes. The new RHI will stimulate more effective use of heat, as well as encouraging more community AD plants.

It is disappointing that the British Government's AD strategy review has little to say about opportunities for smaller scale plants. Although this is a growth area, much of the industry seems to be obsessed with very large "merchant" plants that are expensive to build, depend on the road haulage of feedstocks and often are unable to fully utilise surplus heat. Some companies are looking at decentralised plants that make better use of the energy generated from their co-products, to help decarbonise the production process. This is the approach Clear*fl*eau has developed for the distillery sector and the wider food and drink industry.

Developing decentralised renewable energy

The UK has become over reliant on imported technology across the entire renewable sector but with enhanced incentives, British investors are now backing a number of 2nd generation renewables technologies and the AD sector is one of the growth markets in the UK. There is growing interest in plants that treat feedstocks on the site where they are generated – not only on farms or industrial sites, but in communities or institutions like prisons or military sites.

A number of British AD technology providers such as Burdens or Marches Biogas have, like Clear*fl*eau, developed their own technology and design AD plants for a range of potential uses. Smaller scale AD has a number of advantages, including reduced investment risk and greater energy use efficiency. Other UK companies are adapting the technology to suit their target markets, rather than just trying to deploy systems developed elsewhere, such as the German "grow for gas" approach. Development of British renewables technology will have wider economic benefits, including job creation, carbon reduction and export earnings.

Anaerobic Digestion will generate renewable energy from bio-degradable co-products, by converting these organic materials into biogas. Suitable feedstocks can include household and catering wastes, food production residues containing sugar, oils or fat, as well as reject product or discarded ingredients. The biogas produced can be used to generate heat and or power. It can also be fed to the gas grid or used for vehicle fuel with further treatment.

As the disposal of production residues and co-products becomes more expensive and as the regulations becoming more onerous, on-site AD offers an ability to reduce effluent disposal costs and generate value from materials that have the potential to generate energy. Its use in the production process offers greater control of energy costs combined with a reduction in carbon footprint (some clients are investing in converting sites to zero carbon emissions). It also allows businesses to present a more sustainable image to customers and consumers.

The Scottish Government has realised that there are significant opportunities to exploit its natural resources to develop a strong renewable energy sector (unlike North Sea oil - one that it does not have to share with its neighbours). This is not limited to wind and wave power. AD is part of the mix (not just in the distillery sector), as a way of extracting energy from liquid biomass. In Scotland, the drivers for technologies like AD and biomass include:

- Demand for local decentralised sources of energy, particularly in the Highlands.
- The inability of wind or wave power to deliver energy close to where it is consumed.
- Energy needs of industries like Whisky distillation - as they seek to expand output.
- The need for businesses to invest in bio-plant infrastructure to handle residues.
- Availability of unwanted biomass that could be utilised for the generation of energy.

The challenge for renewables in remote areas such as the Highlands of Scotland is distance from energy consumers. However, the distillery sector is a major energy user, with access to materials with significant energy potential. Not just co-products but also waste wood from forest clearance or hydro power. The rest of this paper focuses on the use of liquid digestion in the distillery sector but integration of AD with other renewable systems is also desirable.

Distillery co-products are suited to AD, provided that the technology fits with industry needs and the available feedstocks. Also these co-products (not defined as waste but classified as a resource) have significant biogas potential. The challenge to be addressed by technology suppliers is the design of AD plants that are cost effective and robust enough to optimise energy output.

On-site digestion – high rate technology

Liquid anaerobic digestion systems operate on a confined footprint but not all of them digest fatty materials. These systems should be able to handle materials like sugars, oils and fats, plus reject products or ingredients. In addition to boosting treatment efficiency and providing significant cost savings, renewable energy generated on-site from the biogas can replace fossil fuels while reducing the carbon footprint. Post treatment, the cleansed effluent can be further polished to allow recycling of grey water or discharge to a nearby watercourse.

Clear*fl*eau is a British company that designs robust AD systems for treating liquid feedstocks from the food, dairy and drinks sectors. An award winning plant built for BV Dairy in Dorset, commissioned earlier this year, was funded by the Environment Transformation Fund as a demonstration site for the food processing sector. In addition to winning the "Lets Recycle Award" for Innovation in Design of a Waste Management Facility, we secured recognition in the REA (Renewable Energy Association) Awards for the high-rate plant.

Our plants are designed to accommodate a mix of low strength effluents and higher strength materials. They reduce the COD load by over 95% (COD or chemical oxygen demand also measures biogas potential). The designs are tailored to the specific site and to the specific industry sector.

The AD plant is the first of its type in the UK. It is reducing the site's treatment costs, as well as its energy bill. By digesting trade effluent and co-products (like whey permeate), the bio-degradable materials (fats and sugars) are converted into biogas.

Renewable electricity generated on site is reducing BV Dairy's carbon footprint. The AD process is able to reduce the COD load of the feedstocks by up to 98%. It can also be extended to allow the cleansed liquids to be recycled as grey water or discharged to a watercourse.

The presentation slides accompanying this publication provide additional information on recent trials and other case studies including the distillery sector. Clearly the distillery sector has different requirements from dairy sites. Although there are no fats, the feedstocks contain variable levels of solids that are not easy to digest in other high-rate plants, including Up-flow Anaerobic Sludge Blanket (UASB) or other suspended media systems that have been used in the brewery sector around the world.

Clear*fl*eau are currently looking for a distillery site to undertake trials on pot ale with the mobile trials unit – this containerised system, which can be installed on a distillery site, has already been used to treat a range of materials. An AD plant being built for Diageo will treat draff squeezings and will be the first AD plant in Speyside to do so.

On-site digestion in the distillery sector

The Whisky industry is a key part of the economy in the Scottish Highlands - creating jobs in rural areas and contributing to the wider rural economy (as a buyer of grain and supplier of co-products as cattle feed). As energy becomes more expensive, bio-plants need no longer be production cost. Distilleries can boost generation of renewable energy across the region and also supply valuable crop nutrients, increasing symbiosis with the farming sector.

Potential drivers for upgrading of existing aerobic bio-plants and investing in AD include:

- Increasing energy costs and vulnerability to cost increases and price variability.
- Limited ability to increase output without addressing co-product treatment issues.
- Concern that as production increases sites will exceed effluent discharge consents.
- Risk that effluent disposal costs will increase significantly over the next few years.
- Potential to transform effluent handling system into a revenue generative solution.

Investment in anaerobic digestion will have an impact on the environmental footprint of the site but wider adoption of AD will also help sustain Scottish agriculture, as many producers of Scottish beef feed their cattle on grain co-products (draff) from whisky production.

There are a number of high-rate systems, some of which have been tried in the sector, but while these systems have short overall retention times, they cannot treat higher solids content residual materials generated from the dark grain plants. Clearfleau's design is able to treat the entire range of whisky co-products - by blending them with lower strength feedstocks.

Clear*fl*eau has been in discussion with several distillers since a seminar held in September 2010, at the Glenfiddich distillery. At this event, there was some interest in the potential for AD but also concerns about existing systems and their ability to handle the full range of co-products produced by the industry. Since then Clear*fl*eau has been looking at how our AD process can be adapted to handle these materials and also optimise biogas output.

In autumn 2011, we will embark on a project to build a high-rate AD facility at one of Diageo's Speyside distilleries. It will process co-products from the Dailuaine site, including both draff squeezings and distillery residues. It will replace an existing aerobic bio-plant and generate renewable energy (heat and power) for use in the distillery and reduce the site's COD load by 98%. Residual solids will continue to be land applied but cleansed liquids will be further polished before discharge into the Spey. This will allow bio-plant throughput to be increased, but on a smaller footprint and with no increase in overall load to the environment.

From the outset of this project we have undertaken lab trials to evaluate the digestibility of the feedstocks, as well as bio-solids degradation, COD removal and biogas output. The trials achieved over 95% COD removal and average methane content in the biogas of 69%, with a COD to methane conversion ratio of about 40% (i.e. ratio of the volume of biogas generated from each kilo of COD removed). This exceeded expectations and performance guarantees for the anaerobic bio-plant have been based on these trials.

By retaining bio-degradable solids in the digestion tank for an extended period, the biogas output is optimised. The process also works with a liquid retention time of less than 3 days. Without the proprietary solids management system, the digester tank would be much larger, with higher capex and operating costs. The full scale plant will reduce the COD load of material fed into the digester by up to 98%, which out-performs other high-rate systems on the market. The plant will generate at least 15% more biogas than alternative systems.

In due course, we expect to build other plants in the distillery sector. We are talking to the SWRI about possible collaboration on a full scale trial on pot ale, using our mobile unit that will provide performance data that can be shared across the industry. We hope that distilled spirit manufacturers outside Scotland will be interested in these trials. However, as a small but growing business, we realise that we need to build capacity to operate outside the UK.

Clear*fl*eau is developing routes to market for its innovative AD processes, inside and outside the UK, including a partnership with German based AD company UTS Biogastechnik GmbH. UTS have a complementary process to ours (handling higher solids feedstocks) and serve different sectors. They are building plants across Europe, including in Spain, Italy, Hungary and the Czech Republic. These markets also present opportunities for on-site industrial AD. Clear*fl*eau is already working with several multinational companies and the UTS network will enable us to deliver our technology for clients in the EU and other international markets.

Anaerobic digestion technology will continue to evolve to offer a range of on-site solutions for distillery sites – as well as other industries that have bio-degradable materials. We are developing the system to handle even weaker feedstocks in a more cost effective manner and engineering colleagues are designing a mobile (modular) AD plant for smaller output food processors, dairies and distilleries, plus sites like micro-breweries.

The main driver for optimising biogas output is revenue generation. The payback for on-site AD projects can be less than 5 years. This is based on contributions from several sources:

- Reduced co-product disposal charges - either by cutting costs of running existing on-site aerobic plants or through a reduction in disposal charges for sewer discharge.

- Reduced costs of disposal of the residual sludge from aerobic treatment off site, or from the disposal of higher COD materials generated in the production process.
- Reduced energy costs, as purchased fossil fuels (i.e. as electricity, fuel oils and natural gas) are replaced by renewable energy (biogas) that is generated on site.

AD qualifies for renewable energy incentives and by maximising output of biogas, distilleries can optimise revenue from available payments. The UK Feed in Tariff (FIT) for renewable electricity provides a payment of between 9.4p and 14p per kW generated from biogas. The Renewable Heat Incentive (RHI) when it comes into effect will pay 6.8p per kW of heat used. Payments are index linked and, once registered, are retained for 20 years.

Other countries have different incentives and the actual return on investment will depend on site circumstances and the energy potential of the feedstocks. An operational AD plant will supply nutrient rich bio-solids to the local farmers. Post digestion, these nutrients are more available to boost soil fertility and for uptake by non food crops, thereby reducing reliance upon increasingly expensive fossil fuel derived fertilisers. Distillers can expect to develop this opportunity by convincing local livestock producers of the nutrient value of the solids.

Distillery dector development

There is increasing interest in Anaerobic Digestion and its adaptability to the requirements of the distilled sprits industry and generation of energy from co-products. However, there are a number of issues that must be addressed for the technology to secure wider acceptance.

For companies interested in on-site AD, there are a number of systems to choose from and they must be evaluated on a project by project basis. The industry will be able to learn from early adopters but a number of issues will need to be addressed if AD is to become more widely used (not just in Scotland) and deliver real value to the distilling industry - these include:

- **Digestate Disposal**: AD is not a total treatment solution - once volatile solids have been digested there is still a need to dispose of the residue, which contains nutrients in the form of N, P and K. Disputes about land application of the solid fraction as a fertilizer are inhibiting development of AD. Affected parties (farmers and distillers) need to agree on land application rules for digestate from distillery digestion plants.

- **Watercourse Discharge**: Digestate can be separated into liquid and solid fractions. The solids retain the nutrients and the cleansed liquid fraction can be discharged (even to the river Spey), provided it can be polished to remove residual nutrients. Development of membrane polishing systems will assist this process, helping to protect the fisheries that are also a key part of the rural economy in the Highlands.

- **Energy Optimisation**: Effective use of energy (heat and power) will help enhance the payback. Biogas can be fed to engine generators (CHP units) but the technology is not very efficient. Effective de-centralised generation in remoter locations will benefit from increased CHP efficiency but opportunities exist for more cost effective technologies (such as fuel cells) or direct use of biogas - including as a vehicle fuel.

- **Community Impact**: There are the usual Not in My Back Yard (NIMBY) concerns over the impact of new technologies on the local community (concerns about odour, noise, traffic) and these have to be tackled by distilleries and their technology providers. However, there is no reason why an on-site AD plant, where the feedstocks are pumped to the AD site with a closed loop system need cause any of these impacts on the local community.

BV Dairy's AD plant is reducing the cost of effluent discharge to the local sewage system and there are wider benefits at that site. Installation of the AD plant has removed the need for extending the local sewage plant to accommodate new houses being built in the town. WRAP's support avoided the need to invest a larger sum in upgrading the sewage plant.

Development of production capacity in the distillery sector to meet demand will require new investment in bio-plants. On-site AD can transform co-product management. However, we need a regulatory framework that encourages the industry to consider using AD as part of its energy mix. This means that Governments and regulators need to work with industry to:

- Encourage innovation and development of appropriate AD technologies.
- Reduce regulatory burden imposed on AD plants and digestate disposal.
- Introduce appropriate renewable incentives, based on carbon savings.
- Develop other renewable technologies that are suited to sectors needs.
- Stimulate investment in decentralised energy generation for rural areas.

Chapter 38

Energy saving in Cognac pot still distillation

G. Ferrari, B. Galy and L. Lurton

Bureau National Interprofessionnel du Cognac (BNIC) – Station Viticole, 69 rue de Bellefonds, 16100 COGNAC France

Introduction

Cognac is a wine spirit referenced in the European Regulation (CE) No. 110/2008 on the definition, description, presentation and labelling of spirit drinks. Under French law, Cognac is an AOC, ("appellation d'origine controlée") the rules for production of which are more restrictive, and are laid down in Order no. 2011-685 of 16 June 2011 by the French Ministry of Agriculture, Food, Fisheries and Rural Development. Cognac distillation is also specific: it is the traditional discontinuous double distillation with the charentais pot still, which shape, material (copper), capacity and heating method have been defined since 1936 (Lurton 2012).

Cognac pot stills are heated by naked flame gas burners. In order to save energy and reduce the emission of greenhouse gases, BNIC conducts studies with the cooperation of Cognac distillers and still suppliers (Galy, 2009, Ferrari, 2010). The challenge is to optimize the gas consumption while respecting the quality of the spirit.

State of the art of Cognac distilling

Cognac is distilled either by home distiller (vine growers who distil their own wine production, about 1200 of them, among 4000, have their own pot still) or by industrial distillers (about 110). During the years 2008 and 2009, BNIC conducted an inquiry among the Cognac distillers to update the regional distillation data on practices and devices, and to evaluate the average level of energy consumption. We received data from 1020 stills among the 2734 registered ones. Nowadays, the 25 hl pot still is the most frequently used. The main energy type in use for distilling is gas, with 76% propane and 21% natural gas for home distillers (46% and 54% respectively for the industrial distillers). The other energy types (3%) are wood, charcoal, fuel.

Energy consumption: gas and electricity

First of all, the distilleries gas consumption was recorded. The mean consumption level for 2005-2008 distilling campaigns was 50 kg of equivalent propane for the distillation of one hectolitre of pure alcohol (~640 kwh). The distribution (Figure. 1) is broader for home distillers than for industrial distillers, in relation to the uncertainty of measurements.

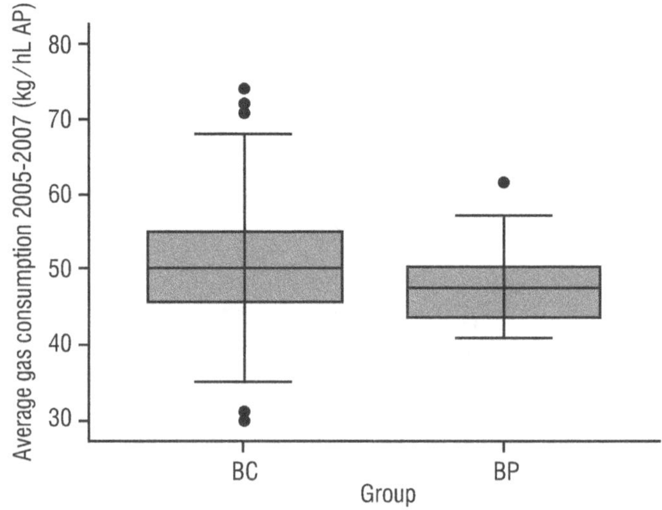

Figure 1. Mean of Gas Consumption for BC (« bouilleurs de crus » = home distillers) and BP (professional distillers). éq. kg propane/hL AP (/hl of pure alcohol) - (*PCI propane = 49 MJ/kg)*

These results show a margin of progress for lowering the gas consumption: 60% of the distilleries are under the mean (23% of which are less than 44 kg).

The mean electricity consumption, among the few distilleries which recorded it, was between 20 and 25 kwh/hl AP. The main use of electricity is for the coolers.

A calculation of the theoretical energy consumption for distilling one hectolitre of pure alcohol (based on Lafon's hypothesis (Lafon 1964) and its distribution was done as shown on Figure 2. Pre-heating of the wine effect was also studied, (Table 1).

Table 1. Theoretical Calculation for a Wine at 15°C, alcohol proof = 8% vol., (Boiling point = 90°C; no alcohol loss; "secondes" recycled with "brouillis").

	Theoretical calculation	
Pre-heating	MJ/hL AP	kg propane/hL AP
None =15°C	2 158	44,0
45°C	1 966	40,1
65°C	1 839	37,5

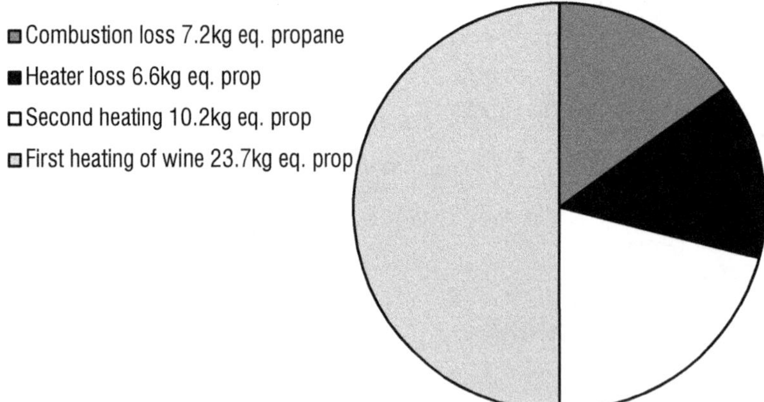

Figure 2. Distribution of energy consumption for the cognac double distillation.

Combustion measurements in distilleries

Measurements of gas combustion were performed in some distilleries and a large amount of data was collected from distillers to check the combustion yield, Figure 3.

It was noticed that the gas burners are generally tuned with a large excess of oxygen (9% in the burned gases) in order to prevent carbon monoxide production. The losses in the smoke gases were about 17%.

Therefore, an optimization of the combustion yield may be possible in some cases by lowering the oxygen amount in the smoke; by the way, it is necessary to keep a safety margin of 3% oxygen (limit for stoechiometric conditions), 5% in practice, in order to stay in the safety area. In this aim, it is proposed to use a probe, measuring online O_2 and CO, in order to manage the burner adjustment during distillation. Such a probe is now on trial in a distillery.

Another way to optimize the consumption of gas could be to replace atmospheric burners with jet air gas burners. The ratio of gas and oxygen is managed online by such burners. Several trials of new air jet gas burners (2 types) have been done during the last distillation campaign. Lowering the gas consumption by at least 10-15% seems to be possible. In order to get more efficiency, it is necessary to upgrade the furnace which has to be airtight and the chimney geometry, because the smoke flow and its temperature are lower.

Calories saving

Another way to save gas is to recover lost calories for heating the wine before distilling. Several means to recover calories during the distilling process are being assessed. Alternative solutions to the traditional wine pre heater, such as tubular or plate heat exchangers using the warm water coming out of the condenser or the hot stillage are currently being investigated. This type of exchanger is used online in order to warm the wine when loading the still.

The source of energy, for a 25 hl still, was estimated at 800 KWh per 24h for warm water (70°C) and 300 KWh / 24h for stillage (95°C). Different trials are now being conducted to evaluate the gas saving and the effect on the spirit quality regarding to the pre-heating temperature level.

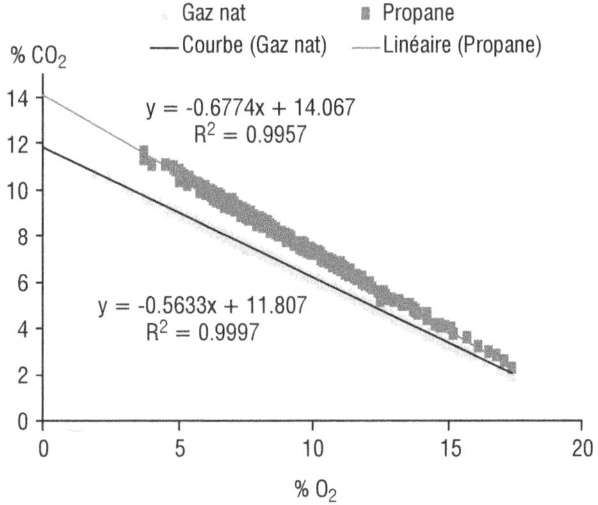

Figure 3. Combustion diagram (Biard) measured in distilleries: O_2/CO_2 for propane and natural gas.

Conclusion

There are two main factors which motivate Cognac distillers to lowering gas consumption: gas price are always going up and the emission of greenhouse gases have to be cut down.

Indeed, the Cognac industry has been involved in sustainable development for many years in order to take into account the society needs and expectations for environmental, economic and social progress and equity. Estimating the levels of greenhouse gas (GHG) emissions is an important element of the efforts to achieve this objective. A global study of Cognac industry GHG emission was performed by BNIC. The objective to reduce gas consumption is a part of the action plan resulting from this study.

References

Ferrari G., Galy B., Lurton L., (2010). Distillation charentaise : les pistes d'économie d'énergie. Conférence VINITECH, 30 novembre 2010, Bordeaux, France.

Galy B. (2009). Distillation et énergie : état des lieux et perspectives. Journée Technique de la Station Viticole du BNIC, 10 septembre 2009, Cognac, France, 65-73.

Lurton L., Ferrari G., Snakkers G., (2012). Cognac. In Alcoholic beverages: Sensory Evaluation and Consumer Research. Edited by Dr John Piggott, University of Strathclyde. Woodhead Publishing Ltd, Cambridge, UK, 242-266.

Lafon R., Lafon J., Couillaud P., (1964). Le Cognac, sa distillation. 4ème édition. J.B. Baillière. Paris.

Chapter 39

Minimisation of water use in the beverage industry

Dan Donnelly

Diageo, Global Beer Technical Centre, Guinness Brewery, St. James' Gate, Dublin 8, Republic of Ireland

Introduction

Easy access to water here in Northern Europe has led us to take water for granted. Easy access, however, does not mean free access. Mains water costs in Ireland and continental Europe are approximately €1.0 / m^3, whereas water abstracted from a borehole costs on average €0.1 / m^3, plus an annual licence fee. Such annual licence fees are generally for a long period time, approximately 30 years; however, such licences are becoming increasingly difficult to obtain, even in Europe. In the recent past beverage companies have lost access to groundwater at certain locations, despite being compliant with local laws. This is because the local authority, when faced with reduced water availability, has reallocated the groundwater to other users (Smith, 2011).

As process water used in a brewery must be of potable quality, the cost of treatment, distribution, maintenance and manning adds a further €0.4 / m^3 to the cost of water to the site.

It is noteworthy that only a small proportion of the water used in a brewery is used directly in the product itself. The vast majority of the water is used in cleaning. This "dirty" water must be discharged to the sewer and the cost of this effluent can be more significant than the cost of potable water. There are generally two sewerage systems on a beverage site: the first handles waste process water and the second, the foul water system, handles sewage and surface run-off from the site.

Brewery effluent costs (process waste water) vary depending on the location, volume, strength and total dissolved solids of the effluent. Charges are calculated using the Mogden formula (Shepherd, 2011). For example, to discharge to the sewer in Ireland, this costs typically €3 / m^3 of waste water. In some cases discharge to a sewer is not an option. This can occur when the amount of effluent produced by a brewery is in excess of what the local authority can deal with in the municipal waste treatment plant. In this case there is no option but to install a waste treatment plant on-site. Again the cost of treating the waste water can be calculated using the Mogden formula.

A good water usage rate in a brewery is 4.5 hl of water per 1 hl of beer produced, however exceptionally low water usage rates of 2.3 hl water / hl beer have been recorded (Brister and Morrow, 2010). The lowest recorded water ratio is at Marten's brewery in Belgium where only 2.1 hl of water is used to make every 1 hl of beer.

At the St. James' Gate brewery in Dublin, total production is 5,000,000 hl of beer, and 2,500 – 3,000 m^3 of waste water are produced per day. The water to product ratio is therefore 3.5. Costs for potable water are €1.4 / m^3 and waste water treatment costs are €3 / m^3. This gives a total water bill of approximately €3.5 million per annum.

The first step in reducing both water and effluent costs is an accurate measurement as to where the beverage alcohol plant is in terms of water usage ratios. Should the usage rate be greater than present good practice, then the approach to be taken is to improve housekeeping and other low cost initiatives. To attain world class ratios, water re-cycle and water re-use for non-ingredient purposes must be considered. Both approaches are considered in this paper.

Materials and methods

Laboratory analysis

All process water samples were analysed for Biological Oxygen Demand (BOD), Chemical Oxygen Demand (COD), pH and Total Suspended Solids (TSS) according to Eaton et al., (2005).

Key Performance Indicators (KPIs) are as follows:

- Water efficiency is expressed as the volume of water (hl) used to produce one hl of beer.
- Water wasted (effluent volume) is the volume (hl) of waste water generated by a site.
- Greenhouse gases (GHGs) are expressed as tonnes of carbon and is calculated using the following formula:

  GHG = electricity [kW hr] (x an energy factor) + all fuel used on the site (converted to kW hr) and converted to GHG using GHG factor. The various energy factors and GHG factors are shown in Tables 1 and 2 respectively.

Table 1. Energy factors for various fuel sources used in the calculation of green house gases used by a site.

Energy factors	
Electricity	1
Natural gas	1
LPG	13.74
Fuel oil	11.953
Diesel	10.952
Kerosene	10.314

Table 2. Factors used in the calculation of green house gases used on a beverage site.

GHC factors	
Imported electricity	0.301
Natural gas	0.184
LPG	0.214
Fuel oil	0.266
Diesel	0.252
Kerosene	0.24
Steam	0
Biodiesel	0
Renewable	0

Process water samples were collected for analyses as follows. Samples of wastewater (500 L to 1000 L) were collected from various process steams in the St. James' Gate brewery in Dublin and stored overnight in a 1000 L portable tank prior to being processed. All samples were pre-filtered using a 100 μm bag filter during collection.

A membrane filtration pilot plant (Koch Membrane Systems UK pilot-scale cross-flow filtration plant) was used to process wastewater using a range of membranes. All wastewater streams were processed in two stages: firstly ultrafiltration followed by either nanofiltration or reverse osmosis – see Table 3 for details. Permeate flux (L/m^2 / min) was measured by collecting the permeate in a graduated cylinder over a period 30 seconds to 1 minute. The pumping pressures employed during all the trials were as follows: ultrafiltration 5 bar, nanofiltration 10 bar, and reverse osmosis 20 bar.

Table 3. Details of membrane filters using during processing trials.

Membrane type	*Description*	*Molecular weight cut off (Daltons)*	*Membrane surface area (m^2)*
Ultrafiltration (UF)	Koch Spiral Membrance 2540-M180-B2V	100,000	1.7
Nanofiltration (NF)	Koch Spiral Membrance TFC 2450-SR100-T	200	2.5
Reverse osmosis (RO)	Koch Spiral Membrance TFC 2540-HR-T	<100	2.5

Results and discussion

Continuous Improvement (CI)

Before discussing KPIs and metrics it is important to understand that ratios are highly dependent on the output of the brewery. A 5,000,000 hl brewery can achieve significantly lower ratios than a 1,000,000 hl brewery because the base load is a lower proportion of total usage. The first step in any initiative to reduce water and effluent costs is to determine the water to product ratio of a site. The second step is to determine the water and effluent charges for that site. Once these facts have been established the cost savings can be calculated and the correct approach then taken to reduce water usage. Should the water ratio be greater than current good practice (Table 4), then implementation will be centred on no-cost water saving measures as shown in Table 5.

Surprisingly, in water-stressed areas in Africa overall awareness of water issues are not commensurate with the importance of water as an essential resource for society and the functioning of industry (United Nations Environment Programme, 2007). From this author's experience in East Africa, making the workforce aware of the need to save water, and changing the culture to one of water conservation, is the most difficult and the single most important water saving initiative. Further afield, in one of our Australian plants, Huntingwood in Sydney, it was the emphasis placed on developing a water conservation culture in the workplace that resulted in saving more than 43% in water usage (Smith, 2011).

Environmental Management Systems (EMS), such as the ISO14000 standard, is a system that uses a CI approach in achieving and demonstrating sound environmental

Table 4. Good and current best practice for water use by area within a brewery.

Department/operation	*Good practice*	*Best practice*
Brewhouse to wort cooling/CIP	1.75	1.48
Fermentation/yesat handling/CIP	0.09	0.05
Maturation/CIP	0.09	0.05
Filtration/BBT/CIP	0.28	0.06
Keg washing, 50% of production	0.23	0.13
Bottle washing, 25% of production	0.34	0.17
Bottle and can pasteurisation, 50% of production	0.16	0.08
General CIP	0.42	0.2
Water treatment conversion	0.2	0.16
Boilers	0.36	0.16
Evap. cooling towers	0.55	0.38
Air compressors and carbon dioxide	0.06	0.04
Domestic	0.07	0.04
TOTAL	**4.6**	**3**

Table 5. List of no/low cost opportunities to reduce water usage rates on a site.

Area	*Description*	*Impact*
Personnel and culture	Insufficient training and awareness regarding water consumption.	Lack of focus on process losses. Liberal approach to water usage.
Monitoring and targeting	Lack of information on water usage throughout the site. No usage targets versus the previous year or current best practice.	Key water loss areas remain unidentified. Lack of focus on actions to drive down water usage.
Identify leaks	Replace leaking valves/identify all leaks including underground leaks.	Allowing valves to leak is not cost effective. Water loss due to underground leak will not be detected.
Reduce water used in cleaning	No hoses/high pressure hoses/ trigger operated hoses/remove unnecessary faucets/optimisation of CIP	Needless waste of water when taps are not turned off. Interfaces between product and push out not detected resulting in losses in product and water push-outs.
Reduce water from water cooling towers	Reduce overflows/reduce bleeds	Cooling by evaporation can leave minerals and scale behind and therefore water has to be bled occasionally from the towers.
Optimize water usage in boilers	Use correct scale inhibitors/ optimize steam traps/minimize	Excess replacement of boiler water with fresh make-up water.

performance. Top Management must be committed to and involved in the design and implementation of the EMS. If for no other reason than to get senior management involved, it is worth implementing the standard, as without senior management sponsorship, no CI initiative will work. They will write the Environmental Policy and be responsible for making sure it is communicated and implemented. Many specific responsibilities are assigned to senior managers to ensure their input and participation. After implementation, a management review will be conducted to ensure continued effectiveness of the system.

Water recycling and reuse

As the current good practice KPIs are approached, water recycle and reuse must be considered. Reclaimed water is primarily used for cooling and process needs. Whether reclaimed water is subject to full (used in the product) or partial reuse depends on the degree of purification to which it is subjected.

Wastewater charges depend on whether a site has an Effluent Treatment Plant (ETP) or whether the waste water is treated by a water company to generate revenue by accepting and treating this waste steam. Wastewater treatment costs vary on the following basis:

- Volume flow (volume per day/month/year)
- COD (Chemical Oxygen Demand)
- TSS (Total Suspended Solids)

Reduction in any or all of the above three variables will lead to reduced charges. The Mogden formula calculates the cost of treating waste water, either in the site's ETP, or the municipal charges that apply to industry for the conveyance and treatment of effluents discharged to the public wastewater network. A Mogden calculator can be used to predict how on-site treatment can be used to reduce costs.

A simple example of how we reduced the volume of waste water at our Mwanza brewery in Tanzania was the installation of simple tanks (see Figure 1) for recovery and re-use of back washing water from the water treatment plant. This "grey water" is now used in the toilets and for gardening. This backwash water thus exits the brewery through the foul sewerage system.

Figure 1. Tanks installed to collect backwash from a filter and to reuse this water in washrooms and gardening.

As the current best practice ratios are approached, technological procedures to not just reuse but to recycle some of the process waste water steams must be considered. Reclaimed water is primarily used for cooling and process needs. Whether reclaimed water is subject to full (used in the product) or partial reuse depends on the degree of purification to which it is subjected. Some applications for recycled water include:

- Dilution water for preparing of chemical cleaning solutions
- Cleaning of crates
- Cleaning of floors, walls and buildings
- Other cleaning purposes
- Other water purposes

Cahill (2011) has examined various wastewater steams at the St. James' Gate brewery in Dublin (see Table 6).

Low strength wastewater (BOD = 14 mg / L) filtered through UF / RO ran without fouling the membrane at the UF stage. The UF stage alone resulted in a reduction of BOD and COD by approximately 30%. In the RO permeate, both COD and BOD levels were reduced by almost 95% compared to the initial waste steam. Ultrafiltration alone reduced heavily contaminated waste water (BOD = 3,246 mg / L) by approximately 20%. Even when RO was applied to this UF permeate, the RO permeate still had a BOD of 750 mg / L. Rainwater on the site was not heavily contaminated and UF combined with RO produced high quality recovered water. Keg plant process water, which was composed of water discharged from the keg washer and keg line lubricant, showed only a limited reduction in both BOD and COD when treated by a combination of UF and NF / RO.

From the above data it can be concluded that process streams with low levels of contamination are effectively treated using two stage cross-flow membrane technology. Water recovered from such streams can be readily reused in various non-process brewery applications. Membrane filtration of highly polluted streams moderately decreased the COD and BOD, however, further treatment of the dewatered steams is essential before any reuse of such can be considered.

Table 6. Description of process water samples used in purification trials.

Trial No.	*Description*	*Stage 1*	*Stage 2*
1	Low strength wastewater, cooling water discharge	UF	RO
2	Combined site waste water before pH balancing	UF	NF and RO
3	Rainwater and yard run-off	UF	RO
4	Keg plant process water	UF	NF and RO
5	Brewhouse process water	UF	RO

Corporate management aspects

Corporate commitment

Global warming is now taken as a fact - the only debate is as to whether human activity is responsible of the warming or not. With this warming we have seen an increasing number of water stressed areas, particularly in Africa. Companies, particularly global companies, are now expected to give back to the communities in which they operate. For example, Diageo with its many operating sites in Africa, have initiated a "water of life" campaign. This gives an undertaking to provide access to clean water to 1 million extra people every year.

Environmental reporting

Diageo has set stretching environmental targets which will be achieved in 2015. These targets were set in 2007 and include

- 30% improvement in water efficiency
- 50% reduction in water effluent (Water stressed sites only)
- 50% reduction in GHG

One of the key drivers for the implementation of such improvement is the intention to change reporting of the company's environmental results, which are currently reported in the corporate citizenship report, to reporting these results as part of the Diageo annual financial statements. The level of assurance associated with publishing these results in the company's financial statement is to be increased and KPMG have audited our sites for the last two years and we have assurance over three of the four main KPI's - water, waste to landfill and GHG's.

Conclusion

Minimisation of water use not only makes sense financially, but it makes sense from a corporate responsibility perspective. Much can be done on this journey by no- / low-cost initiatives, however to arrive at world class standards, capital expenditure is required on technology that is becoming standard in the industry.

References

Bristow, R., Morrow, N., (2010). The use of membranes systems for recovery of waste water to reduce brewery water footprint. Proc. Conv. Inst. Brew. Distill. (Asia Pacific Section) 31: 26 – 52.

Cahill, G., (2011). Purification of brewery process water using membrane technology. Proc. Conv. Inst. Brew. Distill. (Africa Section) in press.

Eaton, A.D., Clesceri, L.S., Rice, E.W., Greenberg, A.E. and Franson, M.H. (2005). Standard methods for the examination of water and wastewater. American Public Health Association, Methods 5210 B, 5220 D, 4500 B and 2540 D.

Shepherd D. (2011). An introduction to waste water treatment http://www.ogdenwater.co.uk/downloads/ogden_water_presentation.pdf

Smith, M.H. (2011) Water efficiency opportunities drink and beverage sector, http://www.environment.gov.au/water/publications/urban/weo-beverage-guide.html

United Nations Environment Programme, (2007). Sustainable water utilization in African breweries. Current practices and prospects. http://www.unep.org/roa/docs/pdf/SustainableWater.pdf

Chapter 40

Cost effective solution for copper removal in distillery effluents

Stephen Walker

B&V Effluent Services Limited, Lamport Drive, Heartlands Business Park, Daventry Northants, NN11 8YH

Introduction

This paper concentrates solely on work undertaken on Scottish Malt Whisky Distilleries; although a team at Penderyn Distillery in Wales have also helped in preparing this paper (however all their effluent is tankered away from that particular site at present). Similarly, at St George's distillery in England, their effluent is tested and sent for land-spreading. Regarding distilling practices in Ireland, this paper will have some relevance with regard to Environment Agency regulations on effluent discharges.

Copper reductions in effluents

Copper within the whisky production industrial sector is traditionally associated with coming from the distillation process. Copper pot stills are used even in the newest malt whisky distilleries for their efficient heat transferring properties, copper also plays a very important role in spirit quality as the spirit vapour comes into contact with the copper still it generally reduces the less desirable sulphur compounds, such as dimethyl trisulphide (DMTS). The greater reactions occur between the copper and the spirit vapour than the copper and spirit still in its liquid form. Although our forefathers could not have known the full benefits of using copper in the manufacturing of pot stills, there is little doubt that overall the use of copper in the distilling process has a positive benefit to whisky production processes.

Nevertheless, copper picked up at this stage of the distilling process is in a soluble form, and although some will be transferred into the final malt whisky, tests show that these levels in Scotch Malt Whiskies to be in the range of 385ng/l – 480ng/l, some copper will pass through the whole of the process and find its way into the final discharge effluent. Additionally, copper is also picked up when various parts of the system are cleaned. Normal cleaning programmes introduce high alkaline detergents (caustic), which pick up the copper as a hydroxide and carry it through into the discharge water. Typical levels of above 10ppm (mg/l) are found in the effluent at this stage.

The traditional way of extracting copper would have been by allowing balancing of the effluent discharge. This means typically having a large enough tank system to be able to hold at least a full day's worth of effluent from the distillery. This then balances out (hopefully) the extremes of pH variation throughout a days' discharge. A lot of sites then have biological processes, to hopefully absorb the high levels of copper. This would be acceptable if the biological plant was efficient enough to cope with the normal standard discharges. However, aqueous discharges with high pH levels from the cleaning process, followed by low buffering capacity, usually resulted in traditional effluent treatment systems failing to remove copper. For example, a balance tank that can only hold 50cum^3 and the site is discharging 200cum^3/per day, then the holding capacity could be as low as 6 hours. If this ties in with a major cleaning programme then the effluent plant would not be capable of balancing out the effluent, including dealing with the copper.

Copper discharge limits

Discharges from distilleries can go to a variety of water courses, e.g. town sewage, river, lake or tidal. Both the Scottish Water (SW) and Scottish Environment Protection Agency (SEPA), driven by European Legislation such as the Priority Substance Directive, have been forced to put pressure on distilleries to clean up their effluent and have amongst these changes requested tighter and tighter discharge consent limits for copper.

The amount of copper allowed in discharges varies tremendously throughout Scotland. For example, those sites discharging to Scottish Water, the discharge consent for copper varies from a high of 40ppm down to a low of 2ppm. This range tends to be in place as some discharges then go for further treatment at Scottish Water run facilities. The norm for SEPA which covers the majority of distilleries, particularly in the high concentration area of Speyside where typically the permitted level for copper discharge is 0.5ppm (mg/l)

Prior to 2001, distilleries certainly in the Spey-side area did not to comply to a copper discharge level and even after the introduction of a discharge level in the range of 2 – 5mg/l for Total Copper there were no major issues with obtaining this first set of discharge limits. Subsequently, however, there have been tighter discharge limits for copper – some being of the order of 0.5mg/l, and this has proved a challenge to most distillers.

Copper removal strategies

Several methods of removing copper have been proposed by a number of companies, and University backed schemes, these have included systems such as reverse osmosis (RO) and electro – coagulation. Although such approaches are good at taking out metals, they are not very good at coping with organic fouling In addition the cost and maintenance of these systems was found to be extremely expensive. This has led to these technologies not being developed further than trials.

For the purpose of our work, once the disadvantages of the aforementioned systems had been looked at, more traditional systems of effluent treatment were accessed. These include the normal way of treating effluent by pH correction, followed by a variety of chemical combinations to reduce the Total Suspended Solids (TSS) and the Chemical Oxygen Demand (COD).

It is known that the maximum solubility of copper is in the range of pH 8 – 8.5 (see Figure 1) Therefore, using samples obtained from within the one of the Scottish distilling companies, initial tests were undertaken to see how much copper could be removed using this pH range as a guide. A range of, metal precipitants, coagulants and polymers were also evaluated to absorb the copper and other solids, once the critical solubility had been obtained. It was found that some coagulants did not work well within this alkaline pH range. Similarly with the metal precipitants, one of which would only work at an acidic pH, this contributed to higher costs for the treatment process, by having to adjust the pH. Likewise there was a variety of success with polymers. However, eventually it was found that aluminium-based coagulants were effective although it was found that the polymer used

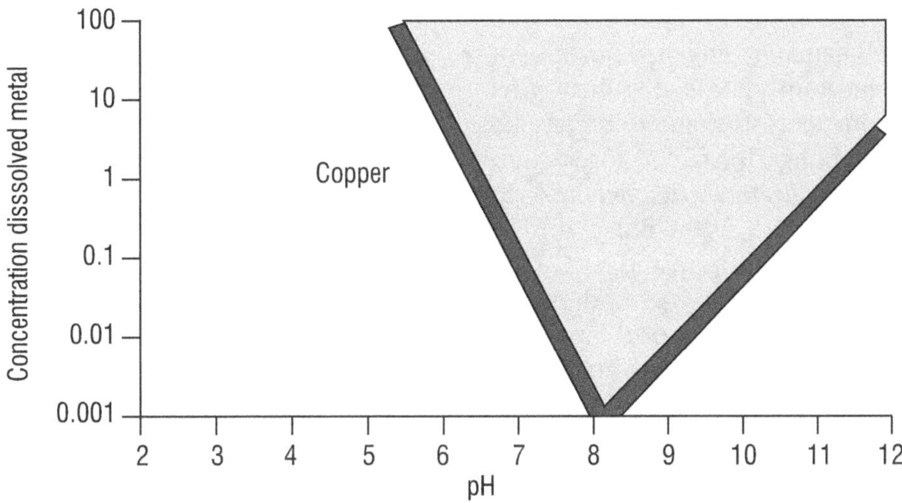

Figure 1. Theoretical solubility of copper hydroxide vs pH

would need to be site-specific. It was additionally found that although the reduction was good (typically above 90% in terms of copper reduction) this process on its own would not be effective in removing all the copper, especially for those distilleries with discharge consents of less than 0.2mg/l. Effluents would still need a further treatment such as biological processing, and this additional treatment in conjunction with the existing biological treatments would be more than adequate to remove residual copper, certainly to levels permitting discharge to a river.

The next stage was to find a physical technology that would assist the chemical process and remove the solids from the effluent water. To this end it was found that Dissolved Air Floatation (DAF) units were effective, and support was obtained from a company to further evaluate this technology. Based on this approach, it was found that the best place to fit in this process would be at the front end of a distillery's effluent treatment. The first set of trials at a test site proved very successful with regular levels of 1ppm copper or less being obtained off the DAF/chemical process for the effluent going onto the biological process. On average, the initial effluent had copper levels of 4ppm; therefore reductions of over 70% in copper were obtained. In addition, as other solids were removed this assisted the biological process by taking off some of the heavier loading from the bio-towers, which follow this new stage. This is because the chemical/physical treatment is only capable of taking out the un-dissolvable Chemical Oxygen Demand (COD); the remaining soluble COD such as sugars have to be taken out by biological treatments. However any solids removed represent the part of the effluent likely to cause solids being deposited on biological towers; therefore their removal would be an added bonus to any treatment processes

As a result of this success, further units were installed in 2 other distilleries. In addition the chemistry part of the process on its own was further applied to a system at another distillery. In this application the treatment was undertaken post-biological to remove the solids, as there was a good balancing system up-front of the Bio-Tower, and the initial driver on this site was to ensure that the site met its discharge consent from Scottish Water of pH within 5 – 11 and Chemical Oxygen Demand (COD) lower than 4,000mg/l. Interestingly, the copper level for this distillery was unusual in that it is required by Scottish Water as 'Soluble Copper' one of only 2 distilleries in Scotland working to this particular discharge requirement with Scottish Water. Currently, all 4 of the systems above are in operation and working successfully.

Based on this work, an enquiry was obtained from another company with a distillery that discharges to a Scottish Water treatment works and, other than a Balancing Tank, had no effluent treatment. Consequently, this distillery was under pressure from Scottish Water to undertake further treatment. Amongst the factors to take into consideration was the limited space available to install any treatment system, as the Balance Tank was situated near to a service road and part of the distillery tour route. Initial tests were undertaken and showed that there was no problem with repeating the successful chemistry employed elsewhere. However, it soon became apparent that the effluent on site could vary, and normally pre-treatment could be in the order of pH 11 – 12 (the discharge from this particular site being a very generous 5 – 11pH from Scottish Water).

Tests were therefore undertaken on distillery effluent, using these high pH's to see if there was still sufficient reduction in copper using the proposed chemical programme to meet a discharge limit of 10ppm (10mg/l) total copper. As can be seen in Figure 2, the level of copper beforehand, on the day of testing was not unduly high (~ 12mg/l) through the day. The pH alteration was achieved by site pumping finished Cleaning in Place (CiP) cleaning solution over to the almost empty balance tank and thereby raising the pH. The main alkaline detergent used on site was caustic soda (32%). If required fine-tuning of the pH was undertaken in the site laboratory.

Overall the results obtained during this experiment (see Figure 2) were as anticipated, and provided a somewhat satisfying trend, in that as the pH rose e.g. from 9 up to 12 the level of copper remaining, increased, although on this particular site, this was still within their discharge consent limits. No other aspect of the chemical treatment, in terms of coagulant and polymer were adjusted during this experiment.

Daily samples were also tested independently at the group's main laboratory and found to be 3.57mg/l. In summary, for the work undertaken at this particular site it was found that the chemical programme on its own exhibited several positive contributions. For example:

- It was able to take the copper to within sites discharge limits for Total Copper
- The pH was typically reduced by 1pH so even at a high pH of 12; the chemical treatment on its own was good enough to take the pH to within discharge consent.
- There was a reduction in Chemical Oxygen Demand (COD), although a generous allowance of 5,000mg/l, a general reduction of the order of 20% means that as the site is under Scottish Water Mogden Formula charging then there is an additional cost saving by reducing the COD

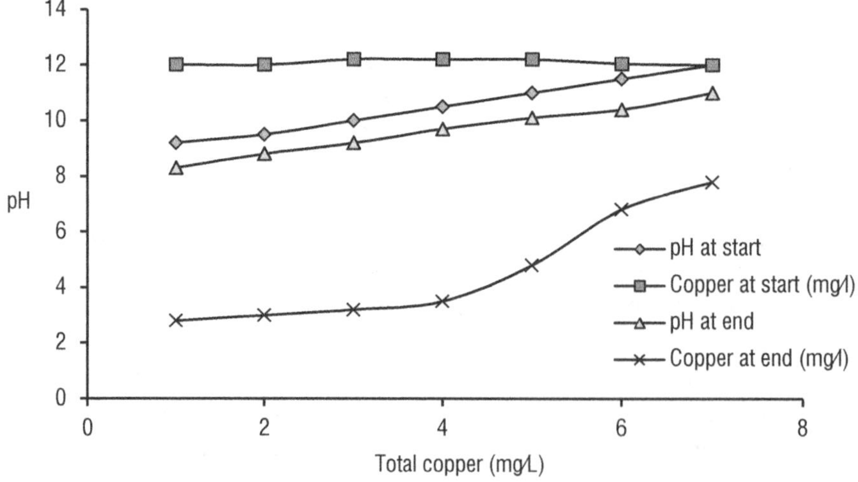

Figure 2. Graph to show comparison between pH and Copper reduction

- The same applies to the Suspended Solids (SS) allowance, again a generous consent of 2,000mg/l, but again as the SS reduction is substantial (65%) then this contributes again to a reduction in the effluent charging to site.

Overall, distillery evaluations have found that the reduction in copper has been in the order of 30%, this mainly being due to working at the high pH values. It was found that in future should distilleries be required to reduce their discharge consent, for example copper from 10mg/l down to 5mg/l, then by refining the pH to within 8 – 9.0 pH would be adequate to strip out more of the copper.

To demonstrate this, samples were taken at various pH's these were then treated at their current pH range, as previously and then as part of the initial treatment, hydrochloric acid (24%) was used to adjust the pH lower followed by the already suggested chemical treatment programme. The results were extremely encouraging and show that maybe stricter copper discharge limits are set by Scottish Water in the future, then this treatment programme would greatly assist with compliance.

Hydrochloric acid was used as there are no issues with chloride consent in the distillery's discharge and 24% is still classed as irritant rather than corrosive at higher HCl concentrations.

Future prospects

With regard to the future using this technology, there is already interest from several other distilling companies to install this system mostly alongside technologies, predominately biological, and usually as an initial treatment stage to take off some of the loading to the biological programme on sites. Nevertheless, there are still several distilleries with currently no effluent treatment, and with the Scottish Water discharge consent being between 5 – 10mg/l, there is no reason why this technology on its own would not be able to assist these sites meet their discharge consents.

Longer term it is felt, that whilst this technology has a place, it is not good enough to entirely strip out the whole of the copper, and certainly in terms of COD reduction 60 – 70% is the maximum ever likely to be achieved. Therefore, should discharge licences be reduced even further in the future, it is suggested that technologies such as micro-filtration, or electro-coagulation might be possible solutions if the effluent is firstly treated by physical/chemical processing to keep the loading off such systems. The process outlined is in itself not reducing the copper, it is merely transferring the copper (and other parts of the effluent) from one area to another, and still has to be disposed of in a sludge form. Although currently the majority of the sludge goes for land spreading there is nothing to say that long term this route may change and as a result the process, whether chemical or physical might have to change also. Alternative processes such as anaerobic digestion, working alongside the technology described in this paper, should be adequate.

We are currently awaiting the full implications of European legislation such as the Priority Substance Directive, and to see how Scottish Water and SEPA interpret this legislation.

Acknowledgements

I would like to thank Farid Turan of Wehlre Environmental who was instrumental in starting this project and to the staff at the various distilleries where this technology is being used for having the confidence to stick by us.

Chapter 41

Characterisation of the pot ale profile from a malt whisky distillery

Jennifer Graham[1], Bob Peter[1], Graeme Walker[1], Alan Wardlaw[2] and Elaine Campbell[2]

[1]School of Contemporary Sciences, University of Abertay Dundee, Bell Street, Dundee DD1 1HG, Scotland; [2] Diageo Global Supply Technical Centre, Glenochil, Menstrie, Clackmannanshire FK11 7ES, Scotland

Introduction

The Scotch Whisky industry is one of the most productive industries in Scotland, second only to oil and gas. Scotch Whisky is one of the few products defined by UK law. Distilleries are often located in scenic areas and their importance is magnified in providing an economic backbone to local communities. The environmental impact of all industrial practices are of paramount importance nowadays, and it is especially important that the Scotch Whisky industry is observed to have minimal deleterious influences on the environment.

During the production of Scotch malt whisky, a large volume of pot ale is produced. Pot ale is a nutrient rich co-product, the residue of fermented wort left in a pot still after the distillation process. (See figure 1) Pot ale is very concentrated and a relatively large volume is produced. For example, for every litre of whisky made, eight litres of pot ale is produced (Mohana, Acharya and Madamwar, 2008). Pot ale is a very complex, caramelised and cumbersome organic turbid liquid residue. It is characterised by a high COD/BOD, possesses dark colour and has a high solids content. In volume and strength pot ale represents the most significant wastewater from the distilling process (Toduka, Fujiwara and Kida, 1999) The composition of pot ale needs to be analysed so that, following its treatment and discharge into watercourses, the environmental impact can be minimised. Many distilleries are located in remote locations in Scotland which need to be protected against any aquatic and terrestrial pollution. This is safeguarded by The Scottish Environmental Protection Agency (SEPA) which ensures effluent emissions comply with legislative requirements. Distilleries' priorities are to discharge effluents that comply with the legal limits of parameters such as BOD, COD and copper content. Distilleries are now additionally looking to find economically viable options to dispose of pot ale. In order to do this the components of pot ale need to be identified to ensure the correct biological treatments provide optimum output and reduce levels of final unfavourable constituents.

This chapter describes research focusing on pot ale from a single distillery, but the findings are pertinent environmentally and economically to the Scotch whisky industry generally. The research employed different techniques to analyse the following constituents of pot ale: BOD, COD, pH, total volatile acids and copper content.

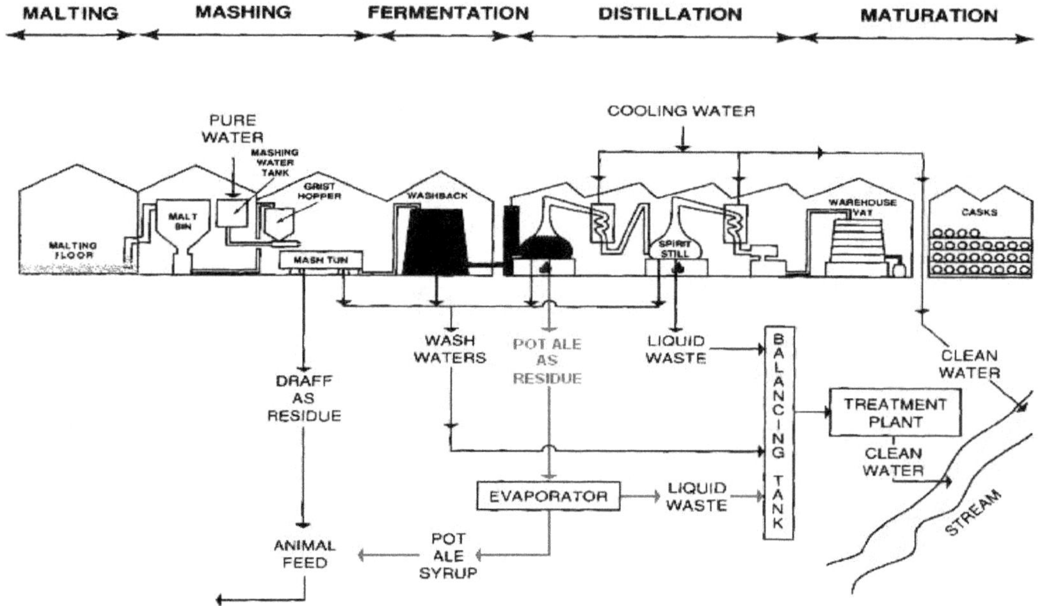

Figure 1. Residues and co- products from the whisky making process (McBoyle 1996)

The aim of the work was to assess (using different analytical techniques) variability in these constituents in pot ale streams from a malt whisky distillery over time.

Materials & methods

Samples were taken weekly from a malt whisky distillery from both the wash still and an external pot ale tank. Comparison between the weekly pot ale compositions could therefore be established. (Refer to figures 2 and 3) In addition, extra samples were taken within the week from the external tank, to test if there were variations within the week.

To characterise pot ale, various analytical techniques were utilised. The organic content of pot ale was examined by measuring the Chemical Oxygen Demand (COD) and the Biological Oxygen Demand (BOD). If pot ale with high COD/BOD values enters the water system, microorganisms metabolise the organic materials present whilst purifying the water, and oxygen in the water will be consumed. Oxygen may not be replaced fast enough to sustain aquatic life so the waterways will deteriorate as a result of the death of aerobic organisms. Thus there is a need to restrict COD/BOD levels (Ansa-Asare, Marr and Cresser 2000) in residues discharged from distilleries, such as pot ale.

COD provides a measure of the oxygen equivalent to that portion of the organic matter in waste water susceptible to oxidation by a strong chemical oxidant. Diluted pot ale was added to a pre-prepared COD vial of reagent solution. The samples were placed in a heating block for 2 hours at 150°C then analysed spectrophotometrically.

BOD relates to the quantity of oxygen (ppm) consumed in waste water by microorganisms measured over a 5 day period. This was completed in defined conditions at 20°C in the dark. An oxygen probe sensor measured the percentage of oxygen in the sample. In order to establish the optimal working range the samples were appropriately diluted.

The copper content of pot ale was measured by ion chromatography (IC) and atomic absorption spectroscopy (AAS). Copper stills are used in the distillation stage. Transfer occurs between the hot still and the refluxing liquid resulting in copper being present in the pot ale. Pot ale has traditionally been used as an ingredient of animal feeds. However, this may be poisonous to sheep as they cannot metabolise copper. Pot ale samples for atomic absorption spectroscopic analysis were pre-digested with nitric acid whereas samples for ion chromatography analysis were pre-filtered to give the copper concentration in the liquid fraction, so a comparison could be made with the AAS results for the complete fraction.

Pot ale contains volatile acids which decrease the effluent pH. If the pot ale sample is fresh, the acetic acid concentration will be ~ 1,000mg/l, but if the sample is sour it will be ~ 10,000mg/l. This is due to bacterial metabolic activity (IBD General Certificate of Distilling 2009). Total acids present in pot ale samples were measured by titration and the individual volatile acids of interest – acetic, lactic and propanoic acid by high performance liquid chromatography (HPLC).

Results and discussion

BOD and COD levels fluctuated significantly throughout the sampling period, as shown in figure 4. The peaks and troughs appear to be at the same positions so the BOD and COD measurements follow the same pattern. More fluctuations are apparent with the external tank samples which could be due to tank heterogeneity (the agitator being out of order) so the sample was unrepresentative. The BOD had an average value of 24,908mg/l with a range of 12,951 to 35,327mg/l. The COD average was 46,854mg/l with a range of 38,476 to 62,948mg/l. The difference between BOD and COD measurements were similar for the weekly sampling period, demonstrated by a correlation coefficient of 0.71. Both BOD and COD levels, which followed similar patterns, exhibited large variations.

A titration technique was used to determine the total acids present in the pot ale samples and

Figures 2 and 3. Wash still (left) and external tank (right)

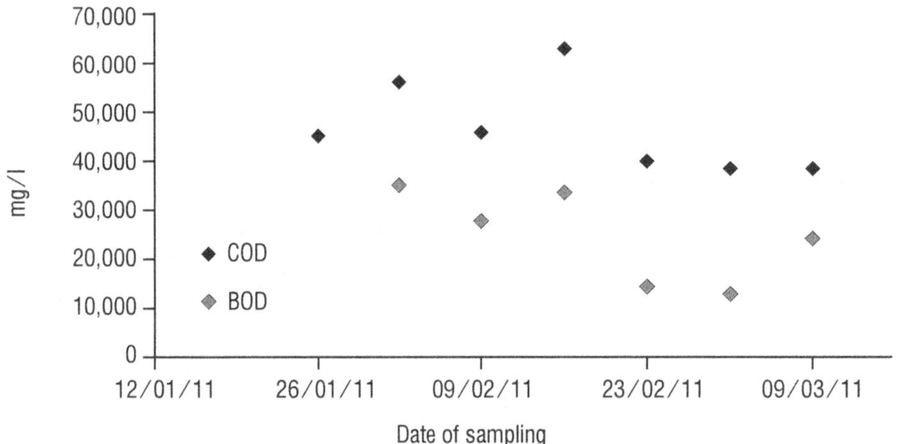

Figure 4. BOD and COD levels in pot ale from a distillery external tank over time

these were also observed to fluctuate over time. The external tank samples contained more acids than the still sample which is due to microbial auto-fermentation (see figure 5).Total volatile acidity values in the pot still samples varied between 3000 to 5040ppm, with an average of 3720ppm. In comparison the external tank measured fluctuated from 3600 to 10560ppm, with an average of 7079ppm which is nearly double the total acids present in the still sample. The pot still samples were more constant over time, while the external tank volatile acidity had a large variation due to tank heterogeneity and unrepresentative sampling. There was no correlation between the external tank and still samples for the total acids present (correlation coefficient of 0.19).

Individual acids analysed included acetic, lactic and propanoic acids with respective analyses of >1000mg/L, 120mg/L and 85mg/l. Acetic acid is high due to microbial conversion from lactic acid during fermentation. Small fluctuations were seen for each sample. Figure 6 shows that the acids varied proportionally (as one acid increased the others also increased).

Regarding pH, small fluctuations occurred at the same points with the sample of pot ale from the still possessing a higher pH for each week analysed. This is due to higher total volatile acidity observed in the external tank which had a range of pH 3.25 to 3.92 and average of 3.54. The still samples were slightly higher with a range of pH 3.34 to 4.13 and an average of 3.81.

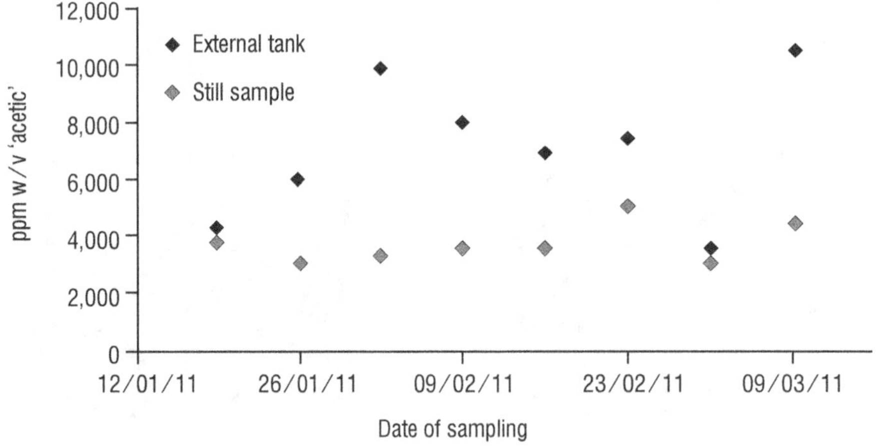

Figure 5. Total volatile acids in pot ale from external tank and still samples over time

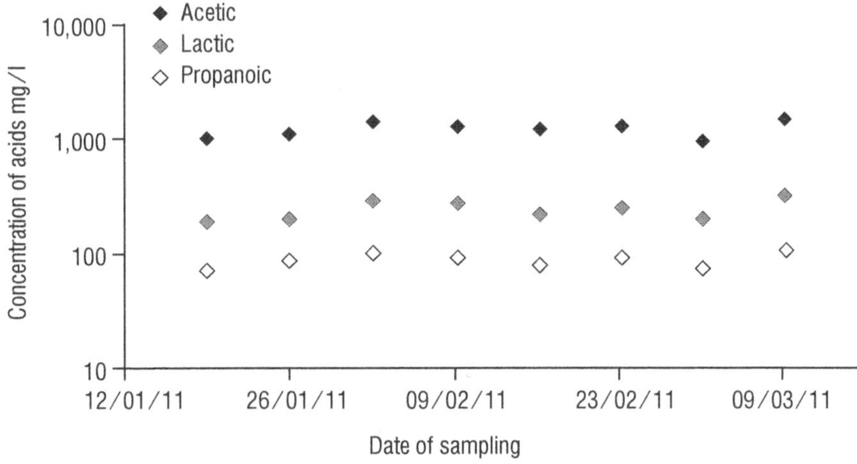

Figure 6. Individual acids in pot ale samples from a distillery external tank over time

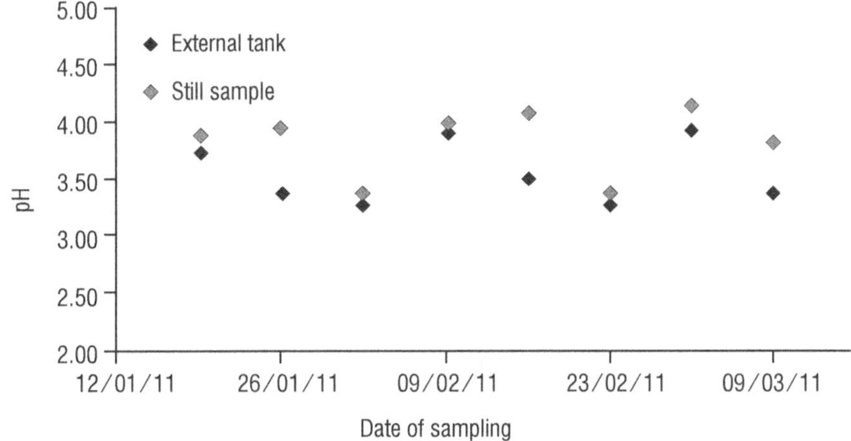

Figure 7. Variation of pH for in pot ale samples from distillery external tank and still over time

With regard to copper analysis, no relationship existed between the samples and copper content (correlation coefficient 0.02). The results varied, with the external tank or still sample occasionally containing more copper. Copper levels in pot ale fluctuated from 2-6ppm throughout the 8 week sampling period. Atomic absorption spectrophotometry (AAS) measures the copper present in the whole pot ale sample whilst ion chromatography measures the soluble copper present in sample filtrates. Figures 8 and 9 show that no relationship was found between the analytical approaches adopted, although more copper was generally found by AAS, which analyses total (bound and soluble) copper in pot ale .

Conclusion

This study has revealed significant inconsistencies in distillery pot ale composition throughout an 8 week sampling period. Care was taken to ensure that replicate samples were removed from the same position each time from both the pot still and the external storage tank. As part of the test regime replicates were taken and averages calculated. Each time the replicates had similar results.

The analytical findings indicate that compositional variation in pot ale was due to inherent differences in pot ale composition, rather than sampling techniques. One of the sources of error may have been that the external

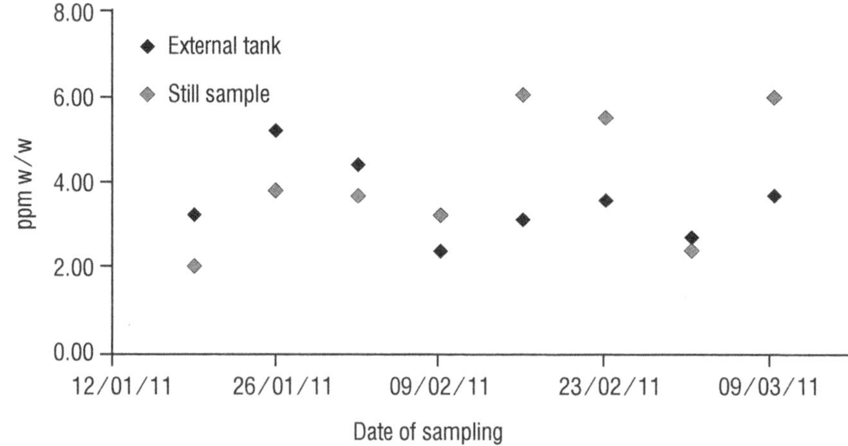

Figure 8. Copper content in pot ale from distillery samples by AAS technique

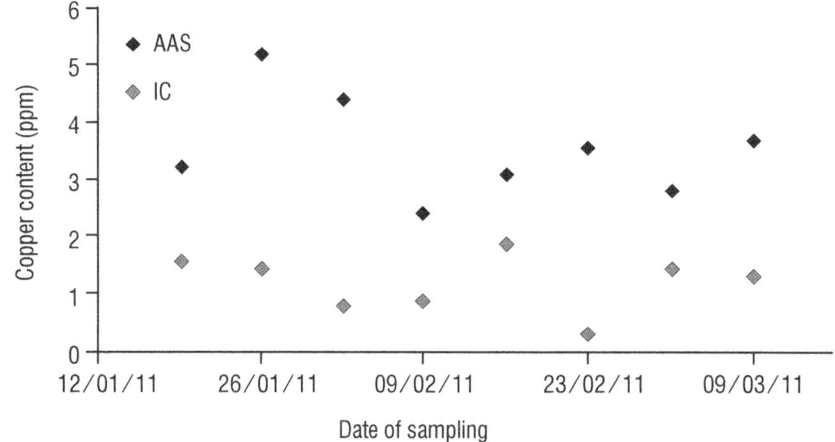

Figure 9. Comparison of copper content in distillery pot ale samples by AAS and IC techniques

tank stirrer was not operational and further work would be required to obtain more homogeneous samples. However, large variations in BOD and COD were observed in the still samples which were unaffected by any lack of stirring.

Whisky raw material ingredients and production processes were constant throughout the sampling period and it was initially assumed that pot ale would not vary during sampling. However, variability in the analysed parameters was observed, although the underlying reasons for this remain unclear. Further research will verify if processing, storage or transportation may account for pot ale compositional differences. This study has highlighted the importance of precise analyses of distillery pot ale residues destined for further treatment or for co-products utilisation in animal feeds.

Acknowledgements

I would like to thank my supervisor Professor Graeme Walker (Abertay University), my industrial placement mentors Elaine Campbell and Alan Wardlaw (Diageo Technical Centre Europe) and technicians Bob Peter and Mike Black (Abertay University).

References

Ansa-Asare, O.D., Marr, I.L., Cresser, M.S. (2000) Evaluation of modelled and measured patterns of dissolved oxygen in a freshwater lake as an indicator of the presence of biodegradable organic pollution *Water research* Vol 34 Issue 4 pages 1079-1088

General Certificate in Distilling GCD (2009) Section 6 Utilities- Effluent The Institute of Brewing and Distilling.

Mc Boyle.G. (1996) Green tourism and Scottish distilleries Tourism management 17(4) pp. 255-263.

Mohana, S, Acharya, B.K and Madamwar, D. (2008). Distillery spent wash: Treatment technologies and potential applications. *Journal of Hazardous Materials*. 163 (2009) pp. 12-25

Toduka, M., Fujiwara, Y. and Kida, K. (1999) Pilot plant test for removal of organic matter, N and P from whisky pot ale. *Process Biochemistry* 35 (1999) pp.267-275

Chapter 42

Anaerobic treatment of Tequila distilling effluent: From pilot to full-scale

Driessen, W., Yspeert, Y., Yspeert, P. and Prins, R.
Paques bv, P.O. Box 52, 8560 AB Balk, The Netherlands

Introduction

Depending on the raw material used, thin-stillage from distilleries is generally well anaerobically biodegraded (Driessen and Yspeert, 2010). Agave is the base ingredient for distilleries producing Tequila. To check the biodegradability of wastewater from a Tequila distillery the wastewater was tested in an on-site pilot trail. The pilot unit including a 60L BIOPAQ IC (Internal Circulation) reactor is depicted in Figure 1.

Figure 1. BIOPAQ® IC pilot plant

As a result of successful pilot trials a combined anaerobic-aerobic effluent treatment plant was constructed comprising an anaerobic IC reactor (Yspeert et al, 2010).

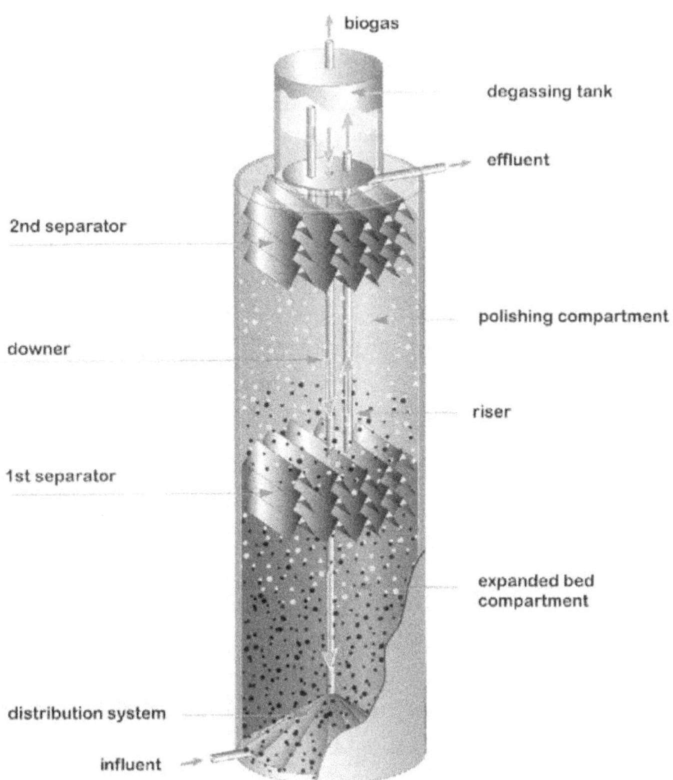

Figure 2. Schematic of BIOPAQ® IC reactor

Materials and methods

The IC reactor, as depicted in figure 2, is characterized by a two-stage biomass separation system for optimal biomass retention and a gas-lift driven internal circulation (IC) for efficient mixing avoiding short circuiting.

The pilot plant was set up as follows. The pilot unit comprised of a 35L conditioning tank and a 60L anaerobic IC reactor. The pilot unit was seeded with 30 liter of granular anaerobic biomass (80 g TSS/L). The wastewater was pre-settled prior feeding it into the pilot unit. The temperature of the wastewater in the pilot unit was kept at around 33 ^{0}C.

Results

Pilot plant

The high strength influent fed into the pilot unit had a typical COD concentration of 30,000 mg/L, while the effluent had a typical COD concentration of 2000 mg/L. The pilot was operated at volumetric loading rates of 20 kg/m3.d indicating stable COD removal efficiencies over 90 %(Yspeert et al, 2010). As the wastewater was pre-settled the recorded COD removal was used as a representative indicator for the soluble-COD removal of the full-scale installation.

After the successful pilot trial confirming the biodegradability of the wastewater, a full-scale effluent treatment plant was constructed.

Full scale

The full-scale treatment plant was designed to treat an overall flow of 1200 m^3/d with a maximum COD load of 42,000 kg/d. The design biogas production was 15,000 m3/d; representing 420 GJ/d.

The Tequila wastewater had a COD concentration of around 30,000-35,000 mg/L. The somewhat higher COD concentration recorded in the full-scale operation as compared to the pilot trial, was due to the higher amount of solids present in the non clarified wastewater. Table 1 presents the typical characterization of the Tequila effluent.

Table 1. Characterization of the Tequila effluent

Parameter	*Unit*	*Raw Effluent*
Flow	m3/d	1200
COD	mg/l	35000
TSS	mg/l	3000
N-total	mg/l	400
P-total	mg/l	100
pH		3.0
Temperature	0C	80

The full-scale effluent treatment plant comprised of a cooling unit, a buffer tank, a conditioning tank, an anaerobic BIOPAQ® IC reactor and an aerobic treatment plant. The full-scale anaerobic IC reactor as shown in figure 3 had a volume of 1700 m^3 (Ø9.5 x 24 m).

Figure 3. Full-scale BIOPAQ® IC Reactor with gas buffer

Figures 4, 5 and 6 present the performance of the full-scale IC reactor.

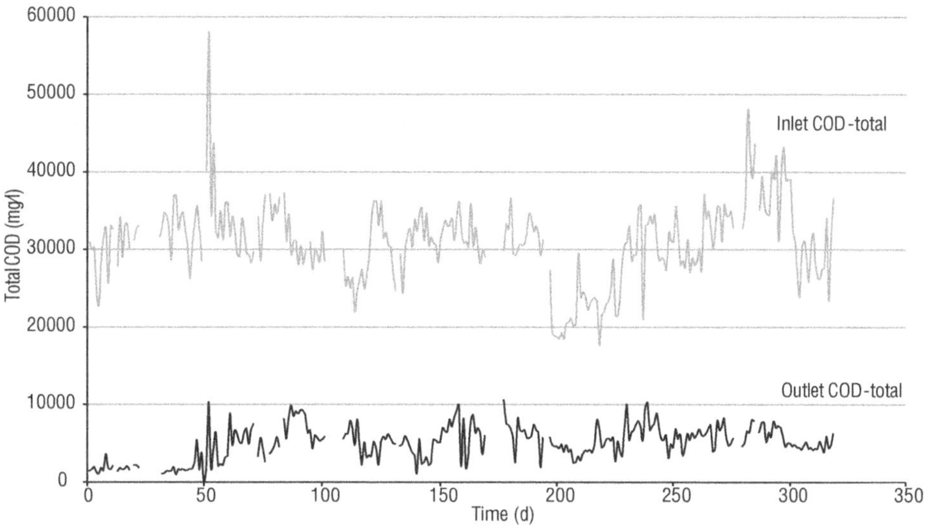

Figure 4. COD of the inlet and outlet

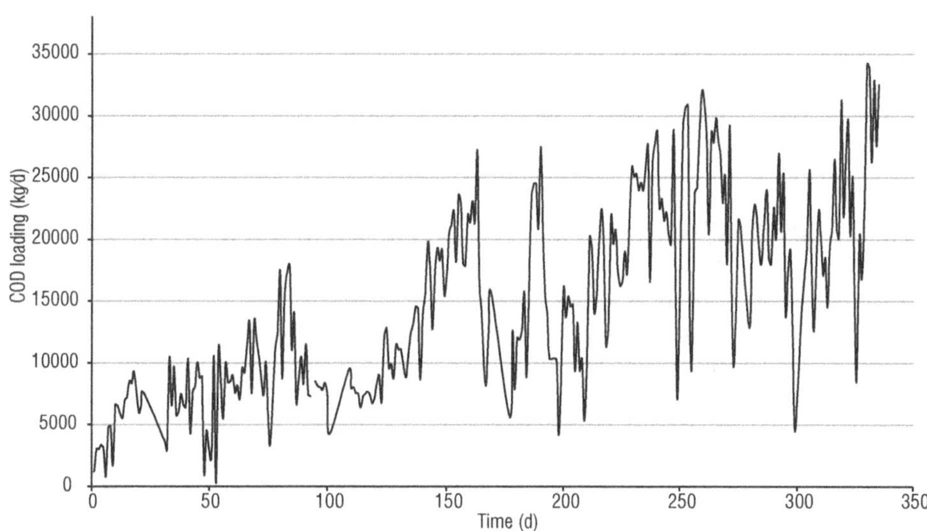

Figure 5. COD removal and COD loading

The results generated from the full-scale IC reactor trial did match the pilot plant performance showing a soluble-COD removal efficiency of typically 95 %. Depending on the concentration of solids in the effluent the total-COD removal in the full-scale installation was typically 85 % (80-90 %).

The treatment plant treats COD loadings up to 32000 kg/d treating all wastewater available. The IC reactor demonstrated stable process performance at fluctuating COD loadings.

Conclusions

- Tequila distilling wastewater is well suitable for anaerobic biodegradation.
- The COD removal efficiency was typically 95 % on soluble-COD and 85 % on total-COD.
- On-site pilot trials proved to be an effective method to confirm anaerobic biodegradability and predict full-scale operation.

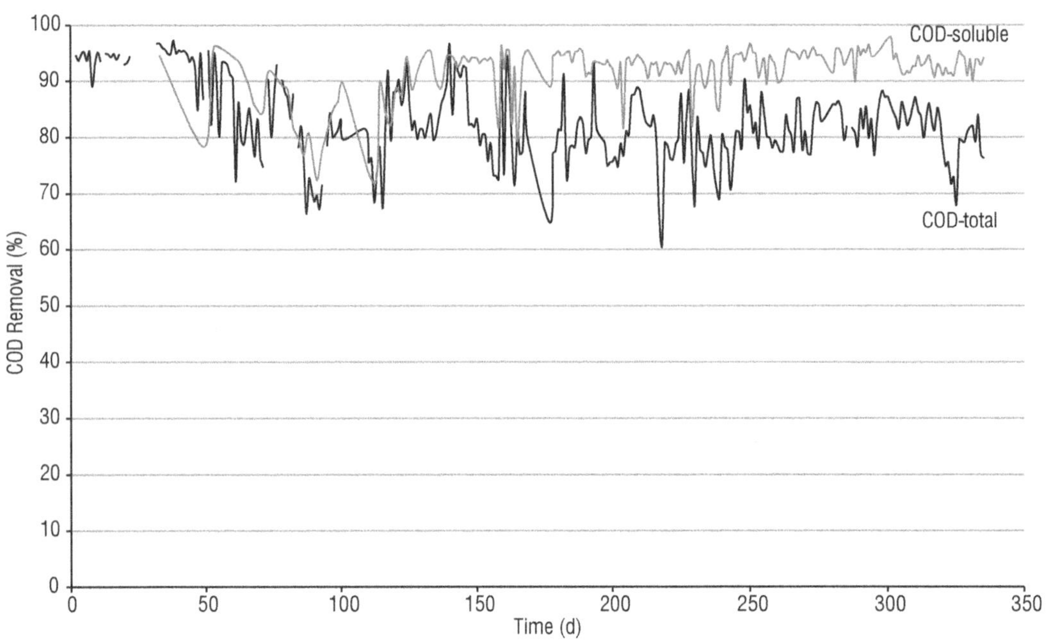

Figure 6. Soluble and total COD removal

References

Driessen, W. and P. Yspeert (2010) Biological treatment of distillery effluents comprising anaerobic processes; In: *Distilled Spirits: New Horizons: Energy, Environment and Enlightenment*. Edited by Walker, G.M. and P.S. Hughes, Nottingham University Press, Nottingham, UK, pp 141-146.

Yspeert, P., Yspeert, Y., Van der Heijden, P.C., Noordink, M., and R. Zapata Salas (2010) Anaerobi c treatment of tequila wastewater by the IC reactor, *Proceedings of the 12th world congress of anaerobic digestion*, Guadulajara, Mexico, 1p.

Chapter 43

Vegetation characteristics and associated conservation values in the watersheds of whisky distilleries in Scotland

Taro Asada and Takeshi Yonezawa
Whisky Blending and Planning Department, Suntory Liquors Limited
5-2-1 Yamazaki, Shimamoto-cho, Mishima-gun, Osaka, Japan 618-0001

Introduction

High quality Scotch whiskies cannot be produced without the pure natural water coming through their watersheds. There is anecdotal evidence that water that flows through peat covered by heather and underlain by granite is ideal for producing good quality whiskies (Cribb and Cribb, 1998). However, the natural ecosystem of such watersheds has not been studied well, and the importance of understanding the potential synergies between whisky production and nature conservation has been discussed infrequently.

In this paper, we aim to: (1) characterise the ecological landscape of the watersheds of the whisky distilleries in Scotland, mostly in Speyside, from the aspect of land-use and vegetation, (2) demonstrate the inter-relationships between human activity and the maintenance of these natural landscapes, and (3) discuss the conservation values required to protect the natural landscape in the distillery watersheds.

Materials and methods

Data collection and laboratory analysis

Eleven currently operating distilleries in Speyside and two from other areas in the Highland region of Scotland were selected, based on the ease of delineating their watersheds on topographical maps. Areas of watershed and land-use were estimated using 1:25,000 topographical maps (Ordnance Survey, 2007) and Google Earth Pro (Google Inc.; downloaded on March 16, 2010).

Peatland and heath vegetation were also sampled in eight distillery watersheds in Scotland including one on the island of Islay. Six of them were among the thirteen watersheds where land-use and bedrock were determined as described in the previous paragraph. 5 m × 5 m quadrats were placed so as to cover the most typical peatland and heath vegetation. Percent cover of each species was visually estimated within the quadrats. Nomenclature follows Stace (2010) for vascular plants, Daniels and Eddy (1990) for *Sphagnum*, and British Bryological Society (2009) for other mosses. Peat depth and slope were measured just beside the quadrats. Peat samples were collected at 10 cm below ground. Dry bulk density was obtained by drying samples at 105°C to a constant weight. Organic matter content was estimated as loss-on-ignition at 550°C for three hours.

Basal peat samples were collected using an Eijkelkamp peat sampler at five study sites where vegetation was sampled. Plant materials in the basal peat samples were submitted to Geoscience Laboratory, Nagoya, Japan, and AMS radiocarbon dating was carried out at Beta Analytic Inc. (Miami, Florida).

Data analysis

The vegetation data were subjected to two-way indicator species analysis (TWINSPAN; Hill, 1979) for the classification of plant communities. TWINSPAN was performed using the computer program TWINSPAN (CEP-41 Cornell Ecology Programs Series). The default options were retained for TWINSPAN. Detrended correspondence analysis (DCA; Hill and Gauch, 1980) was used for the ordination of vegetation samples. Species data were log-transformed and rare species were down-weighted. DCA was performed using the computer program CANOCO 4.5 (ter Braak and Smilauer, 2002).

Results

Land-use

The area of watershed and land-use ratios varies depending on the location of the distillery (Figure 1). Large areas of distillery watersheds are used for agriculture or silviculture, but peatlands (mostly blanket bogs) and heaths are the major watershed landscape for many distilleries in Scotland. ("Bog" is an ombrotrophic (precipitation-fed) peatland, and "blanket bog" is a type of bogs that cover large expanses of irregular terrains with a thin layer of peat.)

Peatland and heath vegetation

Six vegetation groups were classified by TWINSPAN (Table 1). All the groups except group 6 were characterized by the dominance

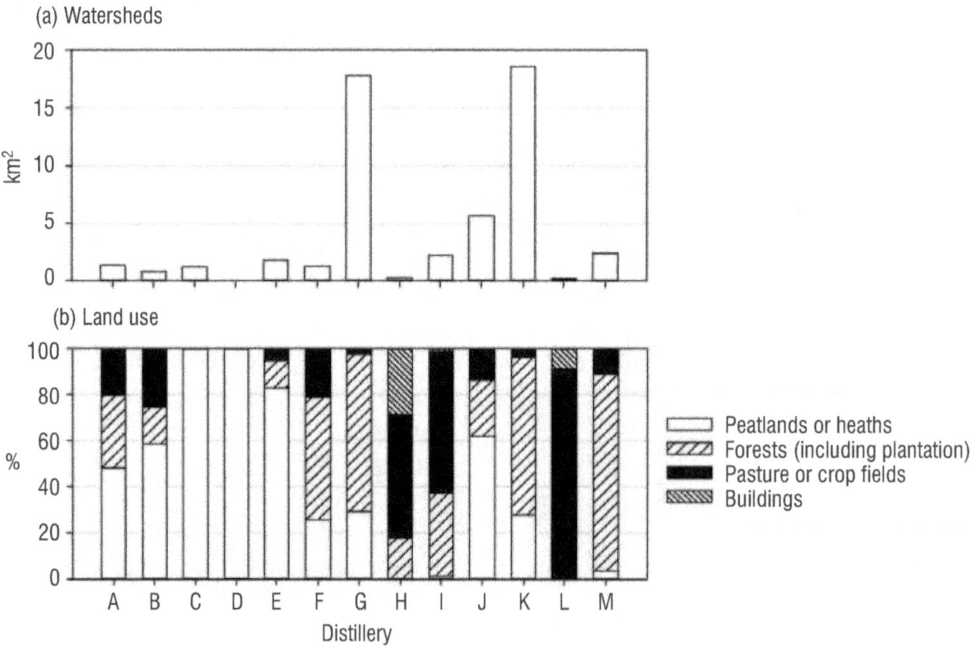

Figure 1. Area of watersheds and land-use ratios within the watersheds of the selected distilleries. A-K are distilleries in Speyside and L and M are from the other areas in Highland.

Table 1. Peatland and heath vegetation in the watersheds of the selected distilleries in Scotland classified by Two-Way Indicator Species Analysis (TWINSPAN). Values are means of categories of abundance within each vegetation group defined by pseudospecies cut levels of TWINSPAN. 1: *Calluna vulgaris - Eriophorum vaginatum - Pleurozium schreberi* community, 2: *Calluna vulgaris/ Vaccinium myrtillus - Hylocomium splendens* community, 3: *Calluna vulgaris - Trichophorum cespitosum* – Lichen community, 4: *Calluna vulgaris* - Grass/ Sedge - *Hylocomium splendens/ Sphagnum* spp. community, 5: *Erica tetralix/ Calluna vulgaris* - Grass - *Sphagnum capillifolium/* Lichen community, 6: *Pteridium aquilinum/ Juncus effusus - Sphagnum angustifolium* community.

	Vegetation group		*1*	*2*	*3*	*4*	*5*	*6*
Species		*n*	*20*	*10*	*3*	*2*	*2*	*3*
Trees	Species code							
Pinus sylvestris	Pin syl		0.1	0.2	0.3	-	-	-
Sorbus sp.	Sor sp		-	0.1	-	-	-	-
Larix decidua	Lar dec		-	0.1	-	-	-	-
Shrubs								
Calluna vulgaris	Cal vul		4.8	4.8	3.3	4.0	3.5	-
Vaccinium myrtillus	Vac myr		0.1	3.0	-	2.0	-	-
Vaccinium vitis-idaea	Vac vit		-	2.4	-	1.0	-	-
Empetrum nigrum	Emp nig		0.4	2.1	-	1.0	0.5	-
Erica tetralix	Eri tet		1.2	0.7	0.3	1.5	4.0	0.3
Erica cinenea	Eri cin		0.1	0.3	-	-	-	-
Rubus chamaemorus	Rub cha		-	0.4	-	-	-	-
Myrica gale	Myr gal		-	-	-	-	1.0	-
Herbs and Ferns								
Eriophorum vaginatum	Eri vag		2.3	1.5	-	-	1.5	-
Trichophorum cespitosum	Tri ces		1.7	0.3	2.3	-	0.5	-
Juncus squarrosus	Jun squ		0.6	0.4	1.7	-	0.5	-
Gramineae spp.	Gra spp		0.4	0.2	-	3.0	5.0	1.3
Pteridium aquilinum	Pte aqu		0.2	-	-	-	-	3.0
Carex binervis	Car bin		0.1	-	-	-	-	-
Carex spicata	Car spi		0.1	-	-	-	-	0.3
Carex spp.	Car spp		0.1	-	-	2.5	1.0	0.3
Deschampsia flexosa	Des fle		0.1	0.2	-	-	-	1.7
Drosera rotundifolia	Dro rot		0.1	-	-	-	-	-
Dryopteris carthusiana	Dry car		0.1	0.2	-	1.0	-	-
Potentilla erecta	Pot ere		0.1	-	-	1.0	0.5	0.3
Blechnum spicant	Ble spi		-	0.2	-	1.0	-	-
Carex nigra	Car nig		-	-	-	-	-	1.7
Cirsium palustre	Cir pal		-	-	-	-	-	1.3
Digitalis purpurea	Dig pur		-	-	-	-	-	0.3
Equisetum fluviatile	Equ flu		-	-	-	-	-	0.3
Galium saxatile	Gal sax		-	0.1	-	0.5	-	0.7
Juncus effusus	Jun eff		-	-	-	0.5	-	3.3
Narthecium ossifragum	Nar oss		-	-	-	-	1.5	-
Oxalis sp.	Oxa sp		-	0.1	-	0.5	-	0.3
Rumex acetosa	Rum ace		-	-	-	-	-	0.3
Trientalis europaea	Tri eur		-	-	-	0.5	-	-
Viola sp.	Vio sp		-	-	-	-	-	0.3

Table 1. Contd.

Species	*Vegetation group*	*n*	*1* *20*	*2* *10*	*3* *3*	*4* *2*	*5* *2*	*6* *3*
Bryophytes and Lichens								
Pleurozium schreberi	Ple sch		3.0	2.8	-	2.0	-	0.3
Sphagnum capillifolium	Sph cap		2.8	2.1	1.7	0.5	5.0	-
Hypnum cupressiforme (+ other brown mosses)	Hyp cup		2.2	0.3	-	1.5	-	0.3
Hylocomium splendens	Hyl spl		2.0	4.3	-	5.0	-	-
Cladina/*Cladonia* spp.	Cla spp		1.7	0.9	2.7	-	4.5	-
Polytrichum commune	Pol com		0.9	0.3	-	1.0	-	0.7
Sphagnum papillosum	Sph pap		0.5	-	-	-	1.5	-
Aulacomnium palustre	Aul pal		0.4	-	-	-	-	-
Sphagnum fallax	Sph fal		0.4	-	-	-	-	-
Sphagnum russowii	Sph rus		0.4	-	-	2.0	-	-
Plagiothecium undulatum	Pla und		0.4	0.2	0.3	0.5	-	-
Dicranum sp.	Dic sp		0.3	-	-	-	-	-
Sphagnum tenellum	Sph ten		0.2	-	1.0	-	-	-
Rhytidiadelphus loreus	Rhy lor		0.2	0.4	-	-	-	-
Sphagnum angustifolium	Sph ang		0.2	-	-	2.0	-	2.7
Sphagnum compactum	Sph com		0.1	-	-	-	-	-
Sphagnum cuspidatum	Sph cus		0.1	-	-	-	0.5	-
Liverworts spp.	Liv spp		-	0.2	-	-	-	-
Sphagnum girgensohnii	Sph gir		-	-	-	2.0	-	-
Sphagnum palustre	Sph pal		-	-	-	-	-	1.7
Sphagnum sp.	Sph sp		-	-	-	-	-	0.3

of *Calluna vulgaris* and the presence of other ericaceous shrubs and *Sphagnum capillifolium*. Differences in vegetation among the first 5 groups were explained by the presence/absence and/or dominance of species other than *C. vulgaris*. Vegetation group 6 is dominated by *Juncus effuses*, *Pteridium aquilinum*, and *Sphagnum angustifolium*. The cluster of the first five groups was clearly separated from the group 6 along the first axis of DCA which explained the 23.0% of the sum of all the eigenvalues (Figure 2).

Age of the peat accumulation

Age of the onset of peat accumulation varied depending on the sampled location (Table 2). Depth of the peat varied from 58cm to 524cm, and the relationship between the depth and the age was not linear. For example, the depth of peat was almost the same for the sample lab number 297470 and the 297471, but the age difference was more than 4000 years. Pieces of wood were found near the bottom of peat cores from one distillery watershed in Speyside and one in Islay (Figure 3), suggesting the area used to be covered by forests. Presence of charcoal just above the wood in the Speyside core suggests that fire was the reason that caused deforestation and paludification at the sampling site in the past.

Discussion

Characteristics of distillery watershed landscape

Our land-use research demonstrated that one of the major landscapes of the distillery watersheds is categorized as blanket bogs and closely-related heaths vegetation (Burnett, 1964; Rodwell, 1991; Goode, 1997). Distribution of

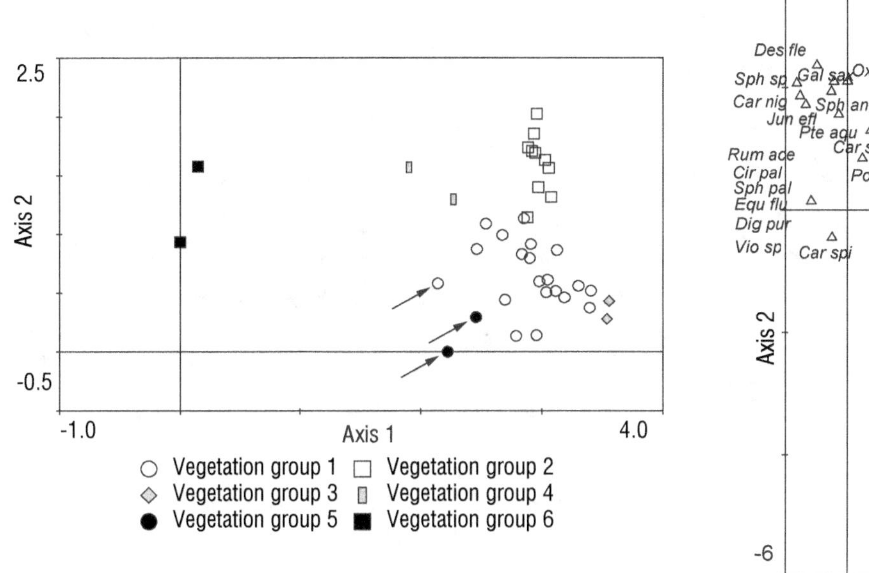

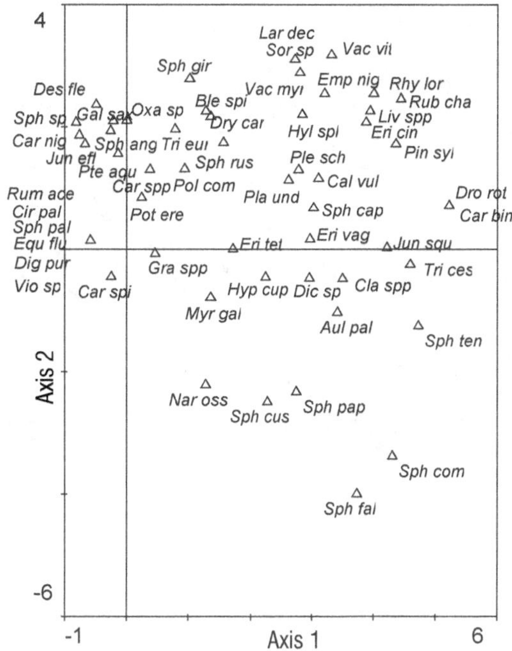

Figure 2. Ordination of the 40 sampling plots by Detrended Correspondence Analysis (DCA) superimposed by the plant communities classified by Two-Way Indicator Species Analysis (TWINSPAN). The three sampling plots pointed by the arrows are samples from Islay, and all the others are from Speyside. See Table 1 for the abbreviated plant species names.

Table 2. Radiocarbon ages of plant materials of the basal peat samples from some peatlands in the watersheds of whisky distilleries in Scotland.

Lab number	*Area*	*Sampled depth (cm)*	*Slope (%)*	*Calibrated age (^{14}C year BP with one sigma error)*
Beta- 297470	Speyside	55-60	3	4470 ± 40
Beta- 297471	Speyside	50-68	7	340 ± 40
Beta- 297472	Speyside	115-120	7	6610 ± 40
Beta- 297473	Islay	54-58	8	280 ± 40
Beta- 297474	Islay	522-524	0	8400 ± 50

such blanket bogs is not restricted to Scotland. They are typical in cool, wet oceanic regions in the world where the rate of precipitation is greater than that of evapotranspiration, including northwestern Europe, northern Pacific coasts, Canadian Atlantic coast, Tierra del Fuego, and New Zealand (Rydin and Jeglum, 2009). However, the blanket bogs in distillery watersheds in Scotland are still unique. One of the characteristics is the dominance of heather, *Calluna vulgaris*. Although *C. vulgaris* is almost ubiquitous in northern Europe and very common on heaths and peatlands, in no other country than Scotland does *C. vulgaris* occur on such an extensive scale (Scottish Natural Heritage, 1995). In general, the variety of peatland and heath vegetation in the distillery watersheds can be explained by the variable dominance of *C. vulgaris* with different combinations of other species such as *Sphagnum capillifolium*.

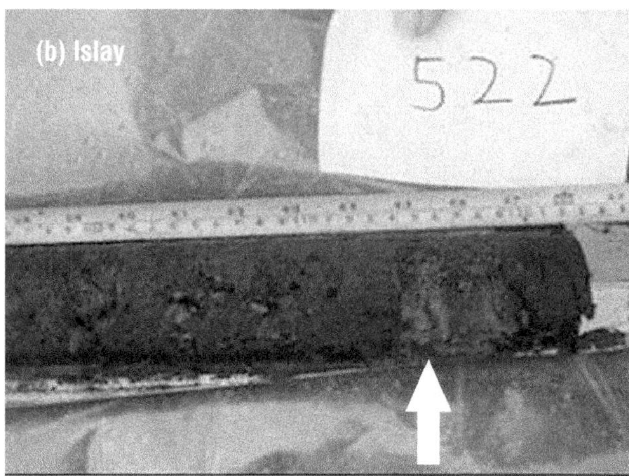

Figure 3. Pieces of wood found near the bottom of peat cores sampled from blanket bogs in distillery watersheds in Speyside (a) and in Islay (b). Charcoal was present just above the wood in the Speyside core. Arrow indicates the presence of wood in the peat cores.

Influence of human activities on the distillery watershed landscapes

Onset of peat accumulation would be triggered by regional/global climate change and local changes in hydrological conditions. More detailed studies are necessary to determine the reason at our study sites, but we found some evidence of deforestation in the past at two of our study sites, which would have caused paludification. Loss of tree canopy would have greatly reduced the rate of evapotranspiration and created wetter conditions suitable for expansion of peatland species such as *Sphagnum* and accumulation of peat (Moore, 1975; Asada *et al.*, 2004). Presence of charcoal just above the wood in the Speyside core suggests that fire caused the deforestation, which raises the possibility of burning by ancient people, as is the case in other studies (Moore, 1973, 1975). The varied results of the radiocarbon dating show that the onset of peat accumulation would have been caused by multiple factors. Other than the anthropogenic influence, the cooler and wetter climates during the early stages of the Holocene, and the Little Ice Age in more recent times, would be some of the other potential factors that triggered peat accumulation (Rydin and Jeglum, 2009).

As with their establishment, the maintenance of heaths and blanket bogs in Scotland can be largely artificial. Patchy vegetation landscapes of *Calluna*-dominated blanket bogs/ heaths in Speyside are the results of artificial burning (Figure 4). Most of the heaths are regularly burned for grouse hunting because new shoots of *C. vulgaris* attract grouse, not only because they are softer but also because they provide more nutritious diets than older stems (Miller, 1980). Some might argue that such heath-dominated blanket bog vegetation is already attuned to another equilibrium point after human disturbance and would not return back to the original forested vegetation even without burning, as explained in the ecological multiple stable states theory (Cornell and Sousa, 1983). Nevertheless, it is known that moderate fire contributes to the new shoot growth and germination of *C. vulgaris*, and maintenance of its dominance (Figure 4; Whittaker and Gimingham, 1962; Thompson *et al.*, 1995; Nilsen, Johansen and Velle, 2005). Both the onset and the maintenance of heaths and blanket bogs are closely related to the human activity in Scotland.

Figure 4. Various stages of the vegetation recovery of the *Calluna*-dominated heath after burning. The hill in the photograph A shows the typical vegetation patches of the fire-affected heath in Speyside. B shows the burned *Calluna*-dominated community, and the vegetation recovery proceeds from B, C, D, and back to E. Note that the dominance of *Calluna vulgaris* is variable, and the photographs show the idea of the community succession only.

Conservation values

Peatlands are the largest terrestrial carbon pool in the UK (Cannell *et al.*, 1999). Blanket bogs and heaths in whisky distillery watersheds store great amounts of carbon in their peat. Conservation of such watersheds helps to sequester carbon underground that contributes to the suppression of global warming. We have estimated the amount of carbon stored in the peat for some distillery watersheds in Speyside (Table 3). One of them stores as much as

Table 3. Estimated carbon stored in the watersheds of some whisky distilleries in Speyside, Scotland.

Distillery[1]	*Watershed (peatlands/ heaths) (km^2)*	*Mean dry bulk density*[2] *(g/cm^3)*	*Mean organic matter content*[2] *(%)*	*Mean peat depth (cm)*	*n*[3]	*Total carbon stored in peatlands/ heaths*[4] *(t)*
A	1.39 (0.67)	0.139	80.5	43.8	4	16,437
B	0.82 (0.48)	0.101	94.9	30.0	3	6,875
C	1.25 (1.25)	0.099	93.8	52.0	5	30,199
D	0.03 (0.03)	0.074	96.5	69.0	5	737
E	1.8 (1.49)	0.373	51.9	17.5	2	25,241
J	5.64 (3.50)	0.191	85.6	58.3	20	166,903

[1]: Distillery code is the same as in Figure 1.
[2]: Mean values approximately 10cm below ground.
[3]: Sampling number for mean dry bulk density, organic matter content, and peat depth.
[4]: Estimated assuming carbon concentration in peat is 50%.

approximately 170 thousand tons of carbon in its peat. This number roughly equates to 60 years of carbon emission from the whisky production processes in one of the largest distilleries in Japan. Assuming that the mean value from the distilleries A, B, C, D, E, and J is representative of all the distilleries in Speyside, the sum of carbon stored in the watersheds of all the distilleries in Speyside would amount to as much as two million tons. Carbon offsetting would be one of the important incentives to preserve peatlands in the distillery watersheds.

Conserving such natural landscape contributes to biodiversity as well. For example, the red grouse (*Lagopus lagopus scotica*) is a species virtually confined to heaths/ blanket bogs. The merlin (*Falco columbarius*) and hen harrier (*Circus cyaneus*) breed mainly on heaths/ blanket bogs in Scotland. Scotland boasts 70, 60, and 95% of the UK population of these species, respectively. As the numbers of these species are declining, protecting their natural habitats is an important initiative (Scottish Natural Heritage, 1995). There are many peatland restoration efforts underway in many places in the world including the blanket bogs in Ireland (Farrell and Doyle, 2003), which tells us that the possession of blanket bogs itself in distillery watersheds is a great asset.

Water is an essential ingredient for whisky. Protecting blanket bogs/ heaths in whisky distillery watersheds contributes not only to the maintenance of good water quality but also carbon sequestration and biodiversity. The wise use and conservation of blanket bogs/ heaths in whisky distillery watersheds is a good model for demonstrating positive synergies between human activities (history), culture (whisky), and environmental conservation.

Summary

Ecological landscapes in the watersheds of many whisky distilleries in Scotland are dominated by blanket bogs and wet heaths. These peatland-related ecosystems are maintained by the greater rate of precipitation than evapotranspiration under the cool, wet, and cloudy climate of the region.

Although Scotland is not the sole region in the world where blanket bogs are distributed, Scottish blanket bogs are quite vast and contain unique vegetation characteristics. The dominance of an ericaceous shrub, *Calluna vulgaris*, is one of such characteristics in Scotland, especially in Speyside.

The timing of the onset of peat accumulation varies depending on the locations, and human activities would be one of the factors that affected the developmental processes of such ecosystems. Maintenance of such ecosystems is also greatly controlled by human activities such as burning.

Blanket bogs/ heaths in distillery watersheds are type of ecosystems under continuous human influence; however, present day conservation of such ecosystems cannot be underestimated. They store great amounts of carbon in their peat and support important biodiversity. High quality Scotch whisky cannot be produced without the pure natural water coming through these blanket bogs/ wet heaths.

The negative influence of human activities on natural ecosystems is a global concern. The conservation of blanket bogs/ heaths in Scotland is a good model for demonstrating positive synergies between human activities (history), culture (whisky), and environmental conservation.

Acknowledgements

We thank Professor Barry G. Warner (University of Waterloo) for generously providing us with the laboratory facilities and other research resources for this work and Professor Paul Hughes (ICBD) for preparing the risk assessment for our fieldwork. We also thank Mr. Yushi Noguchi and our colleagues who helped us with this research.

References

Asada, T., Warner, B.G. and Banner, A. (2004). *Sphagnum* invasion after clear-cutting and excavator mounding in a hypermaritime forest of British Columbia. *Canadian Journal of Forest Research* **34**: 1730-1746

British Bryological Society (2009). *Checklist of British and Irish Bryophytes*. http://rbg-web2.rbge.org.uk/bbs/bbs.htm

Burnett, J.H. (1964). *The Vegetation of Scotland.* Oliver and Boyd, Edinbugh, UK, 613pp.

Cannell, M.G.R., Milne, R., Hargreaves, K.J., Brown, T.A.W., Cruickshank, M.M., Bradley, R.I., Spencer, T., Hope, D., Billett, M.F., Adger, W.N. and Subak, S. (1999) National inventories of terrestrial carbon sources and sinks: the UK experience. *Climatic Change* **42**: 505 –538

Connell, J.H. and Sousa, W.P. (1983) On the evidence needed to judge ecological stability or persistence. *The American Naturalist* **121**: 789-824

Cribb, S. and Cribb, J. (1998). *Whisky on the Rocks*. British Geological Survey, Keyworth, Nottingham, UK, 73pp

Daniels, R. E. and Eddy, A. (1990). *Handbook of European Sphagna*. Institute of Terrestrial Ecology. HSMO, London, UK, 263pp

Farrell, C.A. and Doyle, G.J. (2003). Rehabilitation of industrial cutaway Atlantic blanket bog in County. Mayo, North-West Ireland. *Wetlands Ecology and Management* **11**: 21-35

Goode, D. (1997). Types of Scottish bog vegetation. *Botanical Journal of Scotland* **49**: 441-446

Hill, M.O. (1979). *TWINSPAN - A FORTRAN Program for Arranging Multivariate Data in an Ordered Two-way Table by Classification of Individuals and Attributes*. Ecology and Systematics, Cornell University, Ithaca, NY

Hill, M.O. and Gauch, H.G., Jr. (1980). Detrended correspondence analysis: an improved ordination technique. *Vegetatio* **42**: 47-58

Miller, G.R. (1980). The burning of heather moorland for red grouse. *Bulletin D' Ecologie* **11**: 725-733

Moore, P.D. (1973). The influence of prehistoric cultures upon the initiation and spread of blanket bog in upland Wales. *Nature* **241**: 350-353

Moore, P.D. (1975). Origin of blanket mires. *Nature* **256**: 267-269

Nilsen, L.S., Johansen, L. and Velle, L.G. (2005). Early stages of *Calluna vulgaris* regeneration after burning of coastal heath in central Norway. *Applied Vegetation Science* **8**: 57-64

Ordnance Survey (2007). *OS Explorer Map. 1:25000 scale*. Southampton, UK

Rodwell, J.S. (1991). *British Plant Communities, Volume 2: Mires and Heaths*. Cambridge University Press, Cambridge, UK, 628pp

Rydin, H. and Jeglum, J. (2009). *The Biology of Peatlands.* Oxford University Press, NY, 343pp

Scottish Natural Heritage (1995). *The Natural Heritage of Scotland: An Overview.* Scottish Natural Heritage, Inverness, UK, 183pp

Stace, C. (2010). *New Flora of the British Isles, 3rd Edition.* Cambridge University Press, Cambridge, UK, 1232pp

ter Braak, C.J.F. and Smilauer, P. (2002). *CANOCO Reference Manual and CanoDraw for Windows User's Guide: Software for Canonical Community Ordination. (Version 4.5).* Microcomputer Power, Ithaca, NY, 500pp

Thompson, D.B.A., MacDonald, A.J., Marsden, J.H. and Galbraith, C.A. (1995). Upland heather moorland in Great Britain: a review of international importance, vegetation change and some objectives for nature conservation. *Biological Conservation* **71**: 163-178

Whittaker, E. and Gimingham, C.H. (1962). The effects of fire on regeneration of *Calluna vulgaris* (L.) Hull. from seed. *Journal of Ecology* **50**: 815-822

Chapter 44

The Sustainability Dilemma. Will this change the way we do business?

Andrew Bright
WSP Environment & Energy, 4/5 Lochside View, Edinburgh Park, Edinburgh, EH12 9DH

Introduction

The major question being considered in this paper is: how are we are going to create a more sustainable society? The overall theme of the WDSC conference is Science and Sustainability; with discussions focusing on Resources, Technology and Environmental Sustainability. This is extremely pertinent in today's global economy and the continuing sustainability of that economy.

In answering the question about how science can be used to drive changes to the way we do things that make a sustainable future a certainty, we can say that by understanding the science we can adapt and change to reflect the need to work within our environmental needs. Let me set the scene on the impact industry is having on the world and what the consequences of inactivity will be.

This conference has included areas such as the sustainability of grapes, reducing the need for virgin wood, sustainability of process design, and utilising green energy. These are truly global challenges for the distilled spirits industry that can be framed by illustrating the following key points:

- Why do we need to think about resources?
- What role is science and technology going to play in delivering a sustainable future?

These are important issues addressed during this conference and the distilling sector is clearly playing a role in trying to deliver a sustainable future. This paper will provide some further food for thought regarding future sustainability needs for the distilled spirits industry. Before the issue of resources is addressed, we need to understand the problem and understand what we mean by a sustainable future. Policy makers and government define sustainability as:

> *"The goal of sustainable development is to enable all people throughout the world to satisfy their basic needs and enjoy a better quality of life, without compromising the quality of life of future generations..."*
>
> (The UK Government Sustainable Development Strategy, 2005)

We are beginning to get an understanding of what this might look like and we are beginning to get a grasp of what it might take to achieve it.

Now, before we look to the future, perhaps we need to look to the past to see what we used to think it would look like.

50 years ago we had a vision of what the world would look like in the 21st Century. We would all have robots in the house, doing our domestic chores, automated vacuum cleaners and automated washing machines. There would be a robot "brain" that runs the house. We would be living in mega cities on Mars and we'd all have flying cars as our mode of transport.

This all shows what we considered would be the future, what would show a marked improvement in the quality of life. However, whilst some of that has happened, in many ways, not a whole lot has changed. For today's challenges, we need to look at the so called "mega trends" as this will inform what we need to be thinking about.

Resource constraint

The global population is forecast at 9 billion by 2050 (mid-range forecast), which will be mostly in developing countries. 50% of the 9 billion population will be middle class but we will still have great disparity. In 1994, there were 14 so-called "mega-cities," defined as cities with at least 10 million inhabitants. Their number is expected to double by 2015. Urbanization usually accompanies social and economic development, but rapid urban growth on today's scale strains the capacity of local and national governments to provide even the most basic of services such as water, electricity and sewerage. But 9 billion people will want things. They will want everything that you and I have. Cars, reliable electricity supplies, consumer goods [TV's, fridges], luxury products - more whisky! This presents some major challenges and threats for resources in the future (if not already apparent in many parts of the world – just look at available land) but for businesses, this threat is an opportunity. This gives business the drive to look at more sustainable practices to keep costs down and margins high.

To operate a sustainable future with 9 billion people and to be able to take advantage of the undoubted economic opportunity that this presents, we need to understand how big a challenge it is going to be. Can we decouple the economic growth and sustainability? How do we make a sustainable future a certainty? Let's take climate change and the level of CO_2 in the atmosphere as a benchmark to illustrate the size of the challenge. In 2009, the UK Sustainable Development Commission assessed the global CO_2 emissions against global economic output and used a measure of grams CO_2/$ globally. The number they came up with was 768g CO_2/$ globally. If we stabilise atmospheric CO_2 at 450ppm[1], that will still lead to significant climatic change and requirements for adaptation.

If we assume the 9 billion population and economic growth continues at an average of 1.4% per annum (Jackson, 2009), it would be necessary to decrease the grams CO_2/$ from 768g to 36g CO_2/$ by 2050. That is, a 95% reduction. If the population was 11 billion it would be 30g CO_2/$. If we include the fact that everyone wants to have a fridge and car and have an equitable standard of living to, for example, a per capita income equal to the EU in 2007, but no further per capita growth in the west, the number needs to fall to 14g CO_2/$. This demonstrates the size of the challenge. If this is considered in another way – from a resource perspective we are already in a scenario of living off more than the planet can sustain, at present - 1.5 planets. The WWF Living Plant Report (2010) states that by 2050 we will need 2 planets; or we will be using the resources twice as fast as the planet can replenish them.

Therefore, we are already seeing a massive constraint on resources. Just through the sheer size of the global economy and the demands for resources, this is going to present significant future challenges. In addition, businesses will

[1]Atmospheric CO2 is currently at 392ppm which is considered to be the maximum we can allow and locks us in to a 2 degree rise in average global temperature. This is considered by some scientists to be too much and that 350ppm is the upper safe limit.

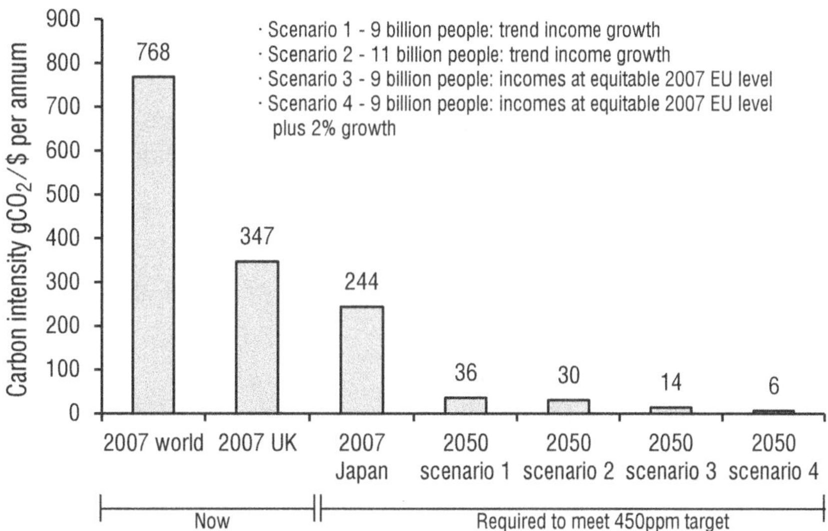

Figure 1. How the carbon intensity of our everyday life needs to change under a variety of scenarios to meet the desired CO_2 concentration level of 450ppm.

need to adapt. Supply chains will be more restricted and commodities will cost more. This may be due to the impact of environmental events. For example, the floods in Queensland last year resulted in a 10% increase in coking coal prices, impacting the price of steel, and if the decline in bee numbers continues, there could be major implications for pollination of 90% of commercial crops. Commodities may also cost more as a result of increased ownership of major commodity rights; for example, China is increasing the number of contracts it has with mining resources. This means businesses will need to adapt to the position that their supply chains' access to products may be more restricted. Developing an approach to maintaining ownership of your products for the entirety of their life and adopting a cradle to cradle approach may be the answer.

Sustainability is driving changes in the way business is done. We are seeing an increase in the move from product to service models. For example, B&Q – rent a power tool; Ecolab - the sustainable hotel laundry; InterfaceFlor – the "Evergreen Carpet" lease. In the Interface example, the customer pays for the service of having the floor covered. You never own your flooring! Interface is then incentivised to produce carpets in a way that minimises life costs, including making the materials recyclable and embedding a cradle to cradle business. Enabled by science; a deeper understanding of materials and the ability to recycle them ensures a low, if not zero, waste business. This is a significant example of resource efficiency.

Preparing today, through the initiatives apparent in the distilling sector, will be vital to a sustainable future to the spirits' industry. As the industry relies so much on natural resources, such as water and agricultural products, the sustainability of those natural resources is critical to its long term future. This is not a new consideration to the sector. In terms of the environmental pillar of sustainability, the sector has often been strongly focused on managing its resource use. In this regard, the sector has made significant strides over the years to improve resource efficiency and to embed a more sustainable way of working. Within in the whisky sector for example, an environmental strategy has been developed and has seen the evolution of an approach to measuring the life cycle of the product. Over time, this will no doubt drive initiatives for further improving efficiency.

Other mega trends

Technology is also driving change in the way we do business. 15 years ago, we *only* had paper airline tickets. Now you get charged £40 if you want one! The need for travel can be substantially reduced with the use of tele-presence technology. Not always a practical option, but given the impact the oil price will undoubtedly have on the cost of travel, it may well be the more sustainable option. We are therefore seeing immense pressure from a resource perspective and also pressures from a changing world, in the way business is carried out. But it is fair to say, that like most businesses, the industry often faces a dilemma, *The Sustainability Dilemma*. Quite often, in traditional terms, it is hard to see the economic benefit of sustainability. Innovations that have strong sustainability credentials, with robust scientific backing frequently just don't make economic sense. This is not unique to this sector, but consistent across the entire business community. New ways of working are often driven at their roots by science. For example, new technology can sometimes deliver greater productivity and reduce environmental impact, but this comes at a financial cost that does not provide an acceptable return. This may mean that if we are to be truly sustainable, the way we measure success may have to change.

Unilever Sustainable Living Plan

The following provides an illustration of how businesses are tackling these issues today and making significant revenue from the process. We need to embrace the realisation that we have to use resources better and create products and processes that have a positive impact. We are seeing some companies setting themselves very challenging targets that maybe 10 or 20 years ago would not have made it beyond a discussion in the bar. The following summarises key points from Unilever's Sustainable Living Plan:

- Help more than one billion people improve their health and well-being
- Halve the environmental impact of products
- Source 100% of our agricultural raw materials sustainably

Unilever's plan is perhaps considered to be different from many, as it addresses the entire value chain. The following represent key aspects which are pertinent to the distilling sector.

Sustainable sourcing

On resources, Unilever have identified 10 categories, ranging from Soya and palm oil to paper and board for packaging. They aim to achieve 100% sustainable sourcing by 2020.

That means requiring suppliers to use sources that are 'known and legal'- i.e. they can be traced back through every stage in their processing to a sustainable origin. And in the case of virgin fibres, they must come from forests that are not being converted to plantations or non-forest use, where traditional and civil rights are respected, and high conservation values are assured.

Water conservation

Unilever have identified reducing water use in agriculture as a key commitment. Water scarcity is already an acute problem in many parts of the world, with the United Nations estimating that 1.2 billion people live in areas of shortage, deprived in many cases of adequate supplies of drinking water. Unilever have identified seven countries which are water scarce and where access to an improved water source is an issue – China, Indonesia, India, Mexico, South Africa, Turkey and the US. They are working with suppliers and NGO's and working on different irrigation schemes and measurement techniques, as this is still an immense challenge.

Energy use & carbon emissions

- By 2020 CO_2 emissions from energy at the manufacturing facilities are targeted to be at or below 2008 levels despite significantly higher volumes. This represents a 63% reduction per tonne of production and a 43% absolute reduction (versus a 1995 baseline).
- They plan to more than double the use of renewable energy to 40% of their total energy requirement by 2020, recognising that this is only a first step towards a long-term goal of 100% renewable energy.
- All newly built factories will aim to have less than half the impact of current ones.

At present: -

- Manufacturing accounts for just 3% of total product GHG footprint
- 2009 compared to 1995: CO_2 from factories down by 2.26 million tonnes p.a. – equivalent to taking over half a million petrol-driven cars off the road annually
- 15.8% of their energy used is renewable

And the successful delivery of the plan forms part of the personal work objectives of the Chief Executive Officer!

DuPont

The final example business is DuPont. During the late 90's up to today, DuPont has undergone a significant transformation as a business. The company used to be targeted as the "world's biggest polluter" but it now brands itself as "... the world's most dynamic science company, creating sustainable solutions essential to a better, safer and healthier life for people everywhere." Their approach is based more around the development of products which enhance sustainability in use. R&D is focussed towards environmentally smart products with an emphasis on agricultural productivity, energy, renewably sourced materials, and safety. Whilst they have made significant progress on reducing the footprint of the business over the past 20 years, they have focused strongly on growing revenue from products with significant sustainability credentials. DuPont calculates that they have revenue from products that reduce greenhouse gas emissions and/or create energy efficiency totalling $731m in 2009. Looking at DuPont's progress on its own footprint, it is laudable, but not spectacular and its targets for improvement (in my opinion), do not look that stretching. However, the business has clearly set out on a "business opportunity" footing and is utilising the sustainability agenda to drive its revenue growth.

Conclusions

The examples I have highlighted show how differing industry sectors are embracing the sustainability agenda, either as a way to reduce their own footprint, but also to develop new ways of working and new products and services. The roots of what they are doing are driven by science but with a desire to make their businesses and products more sustainable. And it makes good business sense.

It is clear that the challenge to have a truly sustainable future is immense. The trends highlighted in this paper demonstrate the challenge, but also present an opportunity to deliver.

References

The UK Government Sustainable Development Strategy (2005). *Securing the future: delivering UK sustainable development strategy*, The Stationery Office, Norwich, UK: 16.http://www.defra.gov.uk/publications/files/pb10589-securing-the-future-050307.pdf

Jackson, T. (2009). *Prosperity without Growth: Economics for a Finite Planet*. Earthscan, UK.

WWF. Living Planet Report (2010): Biodiversity, biocapacity and development. http://assets.wwf.org.uk/downloads/wwf_lpr2010_lr_1_.pdf

Unilever's Sustainable Living Plan, http://www.sustainable-living.unilever.com/

Chapter 45

Sustainable Scotch: Will science deliver the industry's sustainability strategy or will the strategy deliver the science?

Julie Hesketh-Laird[1], Graham Hutcheon[2] and David Rae[3]
[1]Scotch Whisky Association, 20 Atholl Crescent, Edinburgh, EH3 8HA; [2]The Edrington Group Ltd, 2500 Great Western Road, Glasgow, G15 6RW; [3]The North British Distillery Ltd., Wheatfield Road, Edinburgh, EH11 2PX

Introduction

Scotch Whisky distillers are not newcomers to sustainability; quality raw materials, traditional production methods, and world famous brands rely on a pristine environment. In recent years, environmental sustainability has shot up the political and consumer agenda. Companies planning for the long-term will need to ensure not only that their impact on the environment is minimal and that their sustainable approach is communicated to ever-more engaged consumers and customers but that they can maintain the quality and availability of their raw material supplies (copper, cereals, water, energy, casks, packaging etc.). To stay on the front-foot, Scotch Whisky distillers launched an ambitious industry-wide strategy in 2009. It was the first of its kind in Scotland and, to our knowledge, the most ambitious forward-looking strategy in the UK. Commitments include sourcing at least 80% of primary energy requirements from non-fossil fuel sources by 2050; sourcing 40% of packaging from recycled materials; ensuring that 100% of packaging is recyclable or reusable by 2020; zero waste to landfill from packaging operations; and sustainable cask and water management policies. Delivery of the Strategy requires long-term commitment from a range of enablers (including companies, government, regulators and the supply chain). Inevitably with any stretching and enduring programme such as this, the industry does not claim to have all the answers to the challenges the industry will encounter on its delivery journey. This paper will explore what those challenges might be, potential knowledge gaps that science and research might help fill and other practical actions that will be needed to deliver on the industry's commitment in the long-term.

The Scotch whisky industry environmental strategy

Scotch Whisky trades on its environmental credentials and the industry has always had a good 'green' story to tell. Companies have for many years demonstrated individual successes but had never put forward their good-news collectively and cohesively. Together the individual examples of glowing best-practice seemed to add up to a significant story, bigger than the sum of its parts. Add to that the ambitions of a Scottish Government aspiring that Scotland becomes the 'Powerhouse of

Europe', oil prices peaking in 2008 at almost $150 a barrel, investor pressure demanding ethical decisions and increasing consumer expectations of branded goods, the case for industry collaboration on environmental improvement became overwhelming.

The Industry Strategy resulted from exceptional collaboration across a sector known for its fierce competition amongst its brands. Colleagues at the Scotch Whisky Research Institute (SWRI) were engaged to develop an assessment to evaluate the inputs, outputs and impacts of the whole sector taking into account all aspects of raw material use, production, manufacture and distribution[1]. The work was aligned with the British Standards Institution's Publicly Available Specification, PAS 2050[2] and with global ISO standards. And the industry provided detailed data to create a comprehensive inventory to underpin the assessment. This helped us understand where the industry could make the biggest difference and helped focus the strategy appropriately. The industry cannot maintain control over every part of the supply chain and has greatest influence over what they directly control, own or manage. However, companies can influence indirectly that which they procure, particularly when services to the Scotch Whisky industry are a key part of suppliers' business.

A synthesis of these issues resulted in the final agreed Strategy goals as follows:

- To mitigate greenhouse gas emissions and increased energy efficiency.
- By 2020 that 20% of primary energy requirements will be from non-fossil fuels with a target of 80% by 2050.
- To manage water requirements effectively.
- By 2020 to reduce by 10% the average unit weight of product packaging materials.
- By 2020 that 40% of product packaging will be made from recycled materials.
- By 2020 all product packaging will be reusable or recyclable.
- By 2020 no packaging waste from our packaging operations will go to landfill.
- All casks brought into the industry will be made from oak sourced from sustainable forests.
- Supply chain collaboration in areas which are not under the industry's direct control.
- Annual reporting.

The Scotch Whisky Association sought collective agreement to the targets from the very top of companies in its membership. The SWA's Council committed to a non-competitive approach to delivering the Strategy and openness in sharing best-practice. No individual distiller would be expected to meet every goal, but SWA members, big and small recognised that they could in a range of ways, contribute something in an area of importance or local relevance to them.

Looking ahead to 2020 and 2050

The Strategy is a long-term one with stretching targets up to 2050 when the world will look very different to the world today, not least in terms of the industry's product profile and market reach. Looking back only 30 years, the industry's primary focus was the sales of blends with malt sales being largely limited to the 'Blended Malt' category. Since the 1980's there has been a growing fondness from consumers for Single Malts and Premium Blends partly driven by the industry successfully raising consumer awareness of the flavour differences that can be achieved by clever blending.

By 2010 the industry was exporting to over 200 markets worldwide and global shipments were valued at a record £3.45bn[3] – a 60% increase in value since the turn of the millennium. Despite the marginal (-2%) drop in volume exported in 2010, export volume in 2010 was 7% (or 72m extra bottles) higher than in 2000. China has been the recent star market but figures for Brazil, South Africa, and Australasia are very encouraging. Although southern Europe has been

[1]SWA (2009). The Lifecycle Assessment of Scotch Whisky. http://www.scotch-whisky.org.uk/swa/files/LifeCycleAssessment.pdf

[2]PAS 2050: 2011 – Specification for the assessment of the life cycle greenhouse gas emissions of goods and services

[3]SWA (2010). Scotch at a Glance 2010. SWA, Edinburgh.

a difficult place to do business in recent years, other parts of Europe have demonstrated great growth potential. The popularity of Scotch in Poland alone has grown by over 33% in value since its accession to the EU in 2004.

With Whisky very much back in favour, even if the UK market remains sluggish, the SWA predicts that this trend will continue, not least helped by the work of its international team in progressing its trade agenda, including securing agreements for lower tariffs in South Korea, Geographical Indication (GI) registration in China and continuing focus on reducing import tariffs to the growing Indian market.

To meet the longer-term growing demand, large new malt Scotch whisky distilleries have been built at Roseisle and Girvan, Scotland. They add over 15m litres of pure alcohol per year to industry malt whisky supplies alone, with other distilleries being extended, some even doubled in size. Some grain distilleries are also being significantly expanded and a new grain distillery recently opened near Livingston, Scotland. This unprecedented investment equates to over around £1bn of new capital investment across the industry. This is activity not seen in the industry since the '70s, and all of this is rooted in the industry's own optimism in the long-term success for Scotch. The vast majority of the industry's staggering investment has been underpinned by sustainability considerations. All companies making investments will have procured competitively and a major drive will have been financial. But the bottom line ultimately has been to ensure that operations can thrive in the long-term. The new investments will inevitably present a more efficient operational environment, driving down the relative impact of distilling across the sector.

Meeting the Strategy targets

Since the Strategy launch, the Scotch Whisky Association (SWA) has collected detailed 2008 performance data. From the autumn of 2011, all participants (both SWA members and any non-member wishing to participate) will have access to an online environmental accounting system to manage safety, health and environmental information. This will help the SWA communicate the industry's overall performance more quickly and allow companies to benchmark themselves against the rest of the industry.

On the basis of 2008 industry data, the industry has already made impressive strides to meet its targets. The Scotch Whisky Association published data demonstrating that in 2008 98% of packaging used was recyclable or reusable against a 2020 target of 100%; 13% of industry packaging waste was sent to landfill against a 2020 target of zero and 42% of packaging was made from recycled materials, beating the 2020 target of 40%[4]. We will wish to review the stretch in these targets, no doubt, before long.

As expected, working towards the energy targets will be a slower burn. In 2008, only 3% of industry energy use was from non-fossil fuel sources, against a 2020 target of 20%. We recognise we have a long way to go. The SWA has however, over recent months undertaken a detailed analysis of the industry's planned investments in energy and energy efficiency schemes and fuel switching and has compared expected environmental improvements with the 2008 dataset in a comprehensive 'gap-analysis'.

On the basis of the current investments to using co-products for energy production, together with commitments for energy efficiency projects, wind, solar and green tariff energy, and with other board level commitments in the pipeline, we believe that the industry is not just on target to meet its 2020 energy commitment, but is likely to overshoot it. On the basis of announced investments since our Strategy was launched in 2009, we are confident that we will be well ahead of our 2020 target – comfortably so and expect that companies have even further plans that will set us in good stead to meet our 2050 targets.

---

[4]Scotch Whisky Industry Environmental Strategy Report 2010 (http://www.scotch-whisky.org.uk/swa/files/EnvironmentalReport2010.pdf)

Energy from biomass and anaerobic digestion and fuel switching are set to account for the majority of this. These are explored further in this paper.

No-one involved in developing the Strategy thinks for one minute that delivery will be straightforward. And we recognise that we don't know all of the answers. Neither do we control 100% of our environmental footprint. However, now we know where we might be in 2020, based on current investment plans, we can begin to consider what else needs to be addressed to give the industry the best chance of meeting its goals.

Given that a number of the largest distilleries in the Scotch whisky industry have already invested in or are commissioning improvements, focus will be on the remaining medium to large sites to make energy changes and for the smaller sites to make an appropriate contribution.

The challenges we face

The challenges ahead are varied. Surprisingly perhaps, some are posed by our own internal industry company structures.

Internal challenges

Companies that have made significant environmental investments report that internal company challenges are generally the first to become apparent when planning projects. Leaders in Scotch have taken a leap of faith that led them to sign up to the Strategy in 2009. There is a real desire to make a difference. The 'hearts and mind phase' of the Strategy has, by and large, been achieved, but detailed company knowledge and expertise has yet to follow. Not to say that company environmental managers are not knowledgeable and skilled, but in order for companies to make confident decisions, there remains a need for better understanding of technical and environmental matters within finance departments and senior management teams. This may be more acute for smaller companies with limited resource to engage easily in complex matters of proving environmental technology or challenging environmental regulatory barriers.

Even when company boards have been persuaded of the need to act, when it comes to the hefty financial commitments often required, it is the nature of our industry to take a long-term view. Significant investments can have good financial payback terms considering the long-term sustainability and energy security the plans offer. But if we are ever to break out of the cyclical production pattern that our industry follows, we will need to look to a longer term return on investment of 10 years plus. The current return on investment model with a simple payback hurdle rate of around 3 years should perhaps be challenged if we are to achieve step-changes in our energy sourcing and use.

The Scotch Whisky Association must also put some more effort into engaging non-SWA Members in the Strategy. Two sizeable grain distilleries and a number of small malt distilleries aren't represented in the Association's dataset or gap-analysis. We can assume that their trading environments and external pressures are similar to our Members and the solutions available to them will also be similar. So we are under no doubt that long-term sustainability and cost-savings will drive their behaviours towards sustainable investment as new equipment and infrastructure is required. Smaller players might lack the individual buying-power that comes with scale but collaboration with natural competitors in what the Association's members have deemed to be a non-competitive matter could pay dividends in terms of establishing influence over our supply chain from glass supply to rail freight operators.

External challenges

(i) Institutional and financial challenges

These are the most frequently quoted frustration to capital projects getting to the starting blocks. To illustrate these challenges, we can look at two significant industry environmental investments that hit institutional barriers very early in their planning stages.

The Combination of Rothes Distillers(CoRD) exists to process co-products from 16 malt distilleries. Owned by Edrington, Chivas, Diageo, Inverhouse, Campari and Ben Riach, it processes around 33,000 tonnes of distillers' dark gains annually. This is sold as high quality animal feed to dairy herds. Rising costs, the need for a bigger capacity to meet rising demands from the distilleries, an ageing 1970's plant together with a declining animal feeds market led to a strategic review and a decision to move to a duel-fuelled combined heat and power plant offering 6.25 megawatts of energy to the national grid and 40,000 tonnes of pot ale syrup for liquid animal feed. The joint venture company Helius CoRDE estimates that the project will displace 45,000t CO_2 and will reduce NoX and SOx emitted to the atmosphere whilst increasing the processing capacity of the plant from 85,000t per year to 130,000t.

The North British grain distillery (Edinburgh, Scotland) is one of the largest in the industry and is a joint venture between the Edrington Group and Diageo. To reduce the energy profile of the business and to reduce the environmental footprint of the spirit, the company committed to anaerobic digestion (AD) of its post-distillation liquid streams to create biogas that will be used to drive a combined heat and power plant to produce electrical energy. The project will produce 1 MW of renewable electrical energy, save 1 MW of energy and recycle 40% of the distillery's effluent. It will reduce the CO_2 emissions of the site by around 9,000t. North British aims to treble the size of this AD process producing approximately 3MW of electrical energy, making the distillery self-sufficient in power terms from renewable sources.

CoRDE was the first company to run into difficulties with the UK's bureaucratic interpretation of waste legislation by its desire to use distillery by-products as a fuel source. With considerable effort from the industry and SWA, we have worked with the Scottish Environment Protection Agency (SEPA) to develop a strong case that demonstrates the industry's long-term desire to fulfil Scotland's energy needs rather than focussing on the minutiae of technical waste rules. This partnership approach with SEPA has paid dividends as SEPA now allows companies to burn draff and pot ale without being hampered by waste legislation.

Separately, the project took around 10 months to gain planning permission from Moray Council largely because of discussions between the environmental regulator and the Council. Concerns ranged from farmers fears about loss of animal feed to concerns around the use of woodchips to co-fire the boilers. All of these delays took hold, despite the Government's stated commitment to encouraging fossil-fuel alternatives and particularly incentives for biomass projects.

So, what incentives exist for distillers wanting to harness their own by-products for energy? Little. Or so it appears. Whilst financial incentives exist for the biofuels industry which distils fermented food crops to produce fuel, potable alcohol producers, operating in a similar environment don't benefit from such incentives. They have even been denied access to the Government's much awaited Renewable Heat Incentive scheme due to the too-low thresholds for biogas schemes. Without available financial incentives to burn its biogas in a dedicated steam raising boiler for direct use in the distillery, The North British Distillery has been compelled to consider less efficient options for using their biogas such as electricity generation via a gas engine.

Governments and regulators must give clearer financial signals, equitable across all sectors if companies are to be able to successfully access incentives. And Government policies must be coherent to avoid the perverse environmental consequences demonstrated by the choices the North British has been compelled to make.

The current short-term financial squeeze we are experiencing is also of concern. Increasingly, risk-averse lenders are more focussed on guaranteed returns than ever. Demonstrating long-term payback from environmentally driven projects is straightforward, particularly when growth in Scotch Whisky has been historically so strong. But the short-term is harder, particularly with tough debt service coverage ratios expected. Banks and lending institutions are now so risk averse that it is commonly cited as the biggest barrier to progressing environmental investment projects.

The cost of capital is becoming a major issue for all companies wishing to invest and is increasingly driving companies to re-evaluate their expectations of the profitability of their potential investments.

And then there are the financial issues that will always remain out of our control. The Helius CoRDE project financing was developed during the build-up to the perfect financial storm. As the planning and permitting delays took hold, the value of sterling nose-dived at the same time that peak energy prices subsided and dark grains prices once again firmed up. A 4 to 5 month delay in signing contracts due to legal reasons drove the sterling cost of the investment up by over 30%.

(ii) Structural/geographical challenges

If fuel source switching is to become a real option for the whole of the industry, some serious structural and geographical challenges remain to be overcome. The vast majority of the industry bio-energy projects I have referred to so far are situated in the central belt of Scotland, with the exception of CoRDE, and connected to the gas grid.

A number of Scotch Whisky distilleries are located in remote parts of the country, away from the gas grid and rely on heavy fuel oil. These sites will not be able to benefit from the obvious synergies that come from offering waste heat to neighbours as in the cases of Morrison Bowmore on Islay whose waste heat warms the local swimming pool water or at the case of the North British Distillery whose waste heat warms the nearby Tynecastle High School. Diageo cracked the issue at Roseisle by building a 10m litre distillery in sight of its existing maltings which now takes excess heat for malt germination. That option is clearly not practical for most and setting up non-core activities to resolve energy challenges might not be of immediate interest to most distillers focused on spirit production first.

The remote distilleries tend to be much smaller in size and their potential to harness the energy embodied in distilling by-products is considerably reduced. Inability to access the grid in some areas reduces the incentive to generate from wind or wave for the feed in tariff. We'd like to see UK and especially Scottish Government's incentives and assistance being made available to operators in remote areas to investigate their potential renewable energy generation capacity.

(iii) Technological and scientific challenges

Whilst senior managers might view the introduction of new technologies with suspicion, technical managers will certainly have mountains to climb in order to prove even well known techniques in a distilling context. For example, whilst anaerobic digestion is established in a number of process industries, it is best proved in continuous processes. Although the physics and chemistry of AD is predictable, the biology will prove challenging to batch processing such as in malt distilleries – even at those sites with the dedicated resource to devote to such schemes. It will also be challenging to scale down existing technologies to fit a malt distilling model. Whilst we are starting to see AD applied in a small way capable of producing electrical energy from effluent streams, heat energy might only be available from by-product streams and that conversion is yet to be proved.

In the meanwhile, companies are being courted by suppliers with a range of potential other types of conversion technologies. In that context, which will be the first distillery to run its effluent through a microbial fuel cell?

As well as the obvious cost savings to be had from being an early adopter of a new technology in any industry, there are also downsides, which in a conservative industry like Scotch Whisky, often prove to be barriers capable of slowing the spread of new technologies and techniques.

In order to tackle these collective scientific and technological challenges, the industry must maintain its collective science base. We can rely on academics to develop the science we require to generate alternative forms of energy – that is a global matter. And we can possibly rely on other sectors to demonstrate the applicability of technologies to processes similar to our own. However, to prove the applicability of techniques and technologies to distilling is up to our industry. And we are seeing good leadership. But what of the challenges of biology and downscaling? In a non-competitive area such as environmental improvement, perhaps we need to review the level of collective support given by the industry to our scientific and research institutions in taking fundamental scientific knowledge into the realms of application. As an industry with a long-term view, there remains a palpable need for continuing strong support of these organisations even during difficult economic times. Scotland as a whole must protect its excellent science base. Despite Scotch's importance to the UK economy, we are not likely to be seen as critical players in terms of energy or environmental research. So we must also ensure that the UK, but especially the Scottish Government, maintains funding for Scottish institutions for both fundamental and applied research.

(iv) Political challenges

There are a number of political challenges that also require to be overcome to allow the industry to become 80% fossil-fuel free by 2050. The UK Government is taking a realistic medium-term position, maintaining a broad mix of secure energy generating sources as potential players in supplying the UK's base load energy capacity. The Scottish Government is currently relying on the development of renewables capacity as part of the UK energy mix. This is a welcome long-term goal but will take time to deliver. In the short-medium term, we look to the Scottish Government to be bolder in its energy agenda, to support our industry's investments in renewables by championing our case to the UK Government for better tailored incentives and fostering conditions for investments in innovative alternative renewable supplies. Our public commitment to move from reliance on fossil-fuels allows us to drive that debate more credibly than ever before.

Conclusions

There is presently great enthusiasm, backed up by significant financial commitment in the distilling industry to meet the goals of the industry's environmental strategy. In order to maintain momentum and ensure that sustainability is something ingrained into company thinking, current level of commitments must be maintained. There is no doubt that individual companies will continue to invest where there are obvious benefits (both bottom-line and sustainability benefits) to doing so. But much time and resource will be spent overcoming the various external barriers that remain. In the short-term, it is apparent that the challenges are more structural and institutional rather than technological though there is scope in the short term for innovative application of existing technologies to our sector. In the medium to long-term, however, sharper focus will be on the science to evolve and that can only be achieved by continuing commitment to Scotch Whisky and our Scottish science base.

References

British Standards Institution (2008) Specification for the assessment of the life cycle greenhouse gas emissions of goods and services. Milton Keynes, BSI.

SWA (2009). The Lifecycle Assessment of Scotch Whisky. http://www.scotch-whisky.org.uk/swa/files/LifeCycleAssessment.pdf

SWA (2010). Scotch at a Glance 2010. SWA, Edinburgh.

Chapter 46

Application of ultrasound in the bioconversion of distiller's spent grains to bioethanol

Jason Bennett, Graeme M. Walker and David H. Bremner
School of Contemporary Science, University of Abertay Dundee, Dundee, DD1 1HG, UK

Introduction

Bioethanol is one of the most easily utilised alternatives to current liquid transportation fuels, exhibiting the added benefits of being both renewable (Balat et al,.2008.) and environmentally friendly (Baras et al,.2002). Bioethanol derived from waste sources of lignocellulose represents one of the most attractive, yet challenging, opportunities to develop low-cost and sustainable bioethanol production systems, which do not detract from the human food supply (see Walker, 2011). Abundant sources of lignocellulosic biomass come in a variety of forms including residues from the brewing/distilling, forestry and paper industries.

Distiller's spent grains (DSG), the residual material remaining subsequent to starch hydrolysis, forms a readily available, low-cost source of lignocellulose, which has previously been shown to be a rich source of fermentable carbohydrate (White et al,.2008). DSG from the whisky distilling industry is currently sold as a low value animal feed, and new technologies which could generate value-added products from it, are of current topical importance.

Lignocellulose comprises mainly cellulose, hemicellulose, and lignin. Cellulose is a polysaccharide of β-1, 4 linked D-glucose subunits, which can be amorphous or crystalline in nature (Fan et al, 1982). Hemicellulose is a heteropolysaccharide consisting of various co-polymers; the pentoses xylose and arabinose, and the hexoses glucose, mannose and galactose (Saka, 1991). However, the exact composition of hemicellulose varies greatly between differing types of biomass. Lignin is a heterogeneous aromatic polymer containing phenylpropanoid monomers.

Whilst the composition of lignocellulose varies greatly between different types of biomass, spent grains typically consist of ~ 17% cellulose, ~ 28% non-cellulose polysaccharides (hemicellulose, mainly arbinoxylan) and 28% lignin (Mussato et al, 2006). Lignin characterises the biomass as being extremely resistant to hydrolysis and sugar extraction. As such, current approaches to extracting fermentable carbohydrate from lignocellulosic biomass rely heavily on chemical, mechanical or heat extraction pretreatment steps, or indeed a combination of all three (Sun and Cheng, 2002). The pretreatment degrades lignin bound to the cellulose fraction and partially hydrolyses hemicellulose resulting in the release of pentose sugars, chiefly xylose and arabinose. Coupled with this, the pretreatment increases the porosity of cellulose within the material, thus making it available to hydrolysing enzymes (Fan et al, 1982; Parisi, 1989). However, pretreatment is a trade off between efficient enzymolysis and fermentation. Whilst pre-treatment is required to enable efficient enzymolysis, the high temperatures usually employed in its application generate a number of chemical species which are inhibitory to yeast fermentation. For example, hemicellulose (arabinoxylan) hydrolysis yields acetic acid, in conjunction with this pentose and hexose sugars released during cellulose/ hemicellulose hydrolysis can be further degraded to furfural and hydroxymethyl furfural (HMF), respectively. Both of these compounds can be further degraded to formic and levulinic acid (Palmqvist and Hahn – Hagerdal, 1999). Lignin degradation products comprise a variety of phenolic compounds, the majority of which are inhibitory to yeast fermentation. A number of methods exist which have the potential to detoxify lignocellulosic hydrolysates including; overliming, filtration through activated charcoal and liquid-liquid extraction utilising an organic solvent.

Following pretreatment, lignocellulose is incubated with hydrolytic enzymes, typically a mix of cellulase, xylanase and β – glucosidase. Cellulase enzymes fall under two main classes; exocellulase and endocellulase. Endocellulase acts to cleave internal glycosidic bonds at random points along the cellulose chain, thus exposing individual chains to further hydrolysis. Exocellulase or cellobiohydrolase (CBH), comprises two enzymes - CBHI and CBHII, which cleave cellobiose subunits from the reducing and non-reducing ends of the cellulose chain, respectively (Bommarius et al.2008). Subsequent to cellobiose release, β – glucosidase hydrolyses the disaccharide to free glucose. Xylanase hydrolyses residual hemicellulose, not degraded during pre-treatment, to glucose, arabinose, xylose and low levels of galactose and mannose.

Ultrasound, defined as cyclic sound pressure wave with a frequency greater than the upper limit of human hearing i.e. 20 kHz. It has been shown to increase enzyme function in a number of different hydrolytic enzymes, such as amylase and amyloglucosidase (Barton *et al*, 1996, Bremner *et al* 2011). In terms of lignocellulose enzymolysis, few studies exist which examine the effects of ultrasonic irradiation upon the enzymes employed during lignocellulose degradation.

Many of the barriers to cellulosic bioethanol centre on the cost, efficiency and energy balance of the process techniques used in its production. In the past, cellulolytic enzymes have proved prohibitively expensive, causing the economies of production to be so adverse that the commercialisation of the technology remained unrealised. Recent developments in enzyme production techniques have improved this. However, research into technologies which can improve the cost:energy balance of bioethanol derived from lignocellulose are of significant importance.

This paper reports on the evaluation of the influence of ultrasonic irradiation, at a variety of frequencies, upon the function of the enzymes involved in lignocellulose hydrolysis. In addition, a variety of yeast species (*S.cerevisiae, P.stipitis, K.marxianus, P. tannophilus and C. shehatae*) were evaluated for their ability to ferment the spectrum of sugars produced during hydrolysis of distiller's spent grains.

Material and methods

Biomass preparation

DSG were sourced from North British distillery (Edinburgh, UK), consisting of spent grains from a mash of 86.4 % maize and 13.6% green malt.. Grains were dried at 50°C until constant weighting, followed by hammer milling utilizing a 2mm screen (Retsch, Germany). Spent grains were stored at room temperature within air tight containers until required.

Biomass pretreatment

DSG was mixed with sulphuric acid (0.2 mol l-1) at a loading of 10% total solids (w/w) in a total weight of 400g, followed by a thermal cycle of 121 °C at 30 PSI for 30 mins. After treatment, sample pH was adjusted to 5.5 using sodium hydroxide (10 mol l-1).

Ultrasonic setup

Treated samples were exposed to ultrasonic irradiation using a using a variable frequency sonicator (Meinhardt, Germany). Enzymatic digestions were carried out in jacketed ultrasonic reaction vessel with the temperature maintained at 50°C through the use of a thermostated circulator. (Fig.1.)

Ultrasonically irradiated enzymatic digestions

Pre-treated and pH adjusted DSG samples were dosed with cellulolytic enzymes obtained from Novozymes (Bagsvaerd, Denmark). The enzyme preparation consisted of Cellic ™ Ctec (cellulose/β-glucosidae) and Cellic ™ Htec (endoxylanase) at a dosing of 6% and 1% (w/w) total solids (TS). This equates to an activity within the hydrolysis mixture of; Ctec 6000 EGU and Htec 6000 FXU-S. Samples were exposed to ultrasound at a power of 46W and a variety of ultrasonic frequencies (584, 862, 998, 1174 kHz) in continuous sonication mode. Enzymatic digestions were allowed to proceed for 24 hrs with sampling occurring periodically.

Control enzymatic digestions

Two experimental controls were used to validate the data from enzymatic digestions exposed to ultrasonic irradiation. Positive control 1 consisting of enzymatic digestions in the absence of ultrasound and positive control 2 consisting of exposure of DSG to ultrasound in the absence of enzyme. Other than this, controls were exposed to an identical experimental method as the ultrasonically irradiated digestions documented previously.

Hydrolysate preparation

Subsequent to enzymolysis, the residual biomass was separated from the hydrolysate via a two stage vacuum filtration. Stage 1 through glass

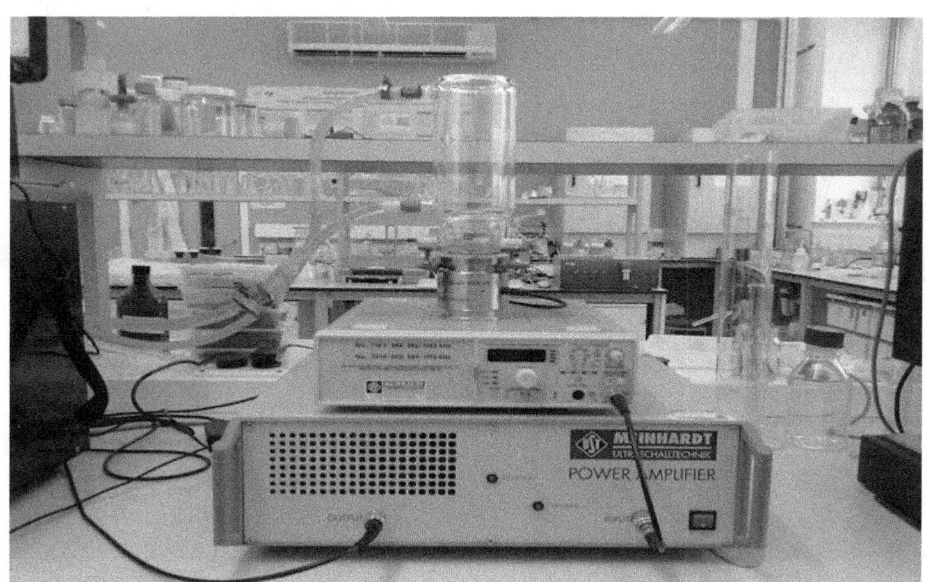

Figure 1. Overview of experimental setup used to expose enzymatic digestions to ultrasonic irradiation. From top to bottom; ultrasonic reaction vessel, signal transducer, signal generator, power amplifier.

micro-fibre filters and stage 2 through 0.2 μm membrane filters.

Yeast strains and growth conditions

The yeasts employed in this research were; *Saccharomyces cerevisiae* DCLM (Diageo, Menstrie, UK), *Pichia stipitis* NCYC 1542 (National Collection of Yeast Cultures, Norwich, UK), *Klyuveromyces marxianus* NCYC 1425, *Candida shehatae* var. *lignososa* NCYC 2389 and *Pachysolen tannophilus* NCYC 614. Yeasts were maintained on YPD agar slopes consisting of; 2% glucose, 2% bacteriological peptone, 2% technical agar and 1% yeast extract (Oxoid Ltd, New Hampshire, UK). Yeast slopes were used to inoculate 150 ml of liquid YPD (2% glucose, 2% bacteriological peptone, 1% yeast extract) in Erlenmeyer flasks. Cultures were grown at 30 °C on a rotary shaker at 150 r.p.m. (Electron incubator, Infors Ltd, Surrey, UK). Cultures were allowed to grow for 24 h at which point cells were washed in sterile distilled water, with the viability be determined, and used for fermentation of both crude and detoxified DSG hydrolysates.

Fermentation of DSG hydrolysates

Hydrolysate samples were separated 80 ml aliquots in sterile 100 ml Schott bottles. Yeasts were inoculated with an initial cellular density of 10 x 10^6 cells ml $^{-1}$. Fermentations were conducted at 30 °C and 100 r.p.m. and sampled periodically for 5 days. Samples were centrifuged at 13,000 xg and the supernatant was analysed for sugar and ethanol content. Yeast pellets were re-suspended in sterile water and analysed for viability and cell growth.

Analysis

Monosaccharide content

Samples taken during enzymolysis and fermentation were analysed via HPLC for total and specific monosaccharide content. The HPLC setup consisted of; a Thermoseparation Products Spectra Series AS100 autosampler installed with a Rezex ™ RHM Monosaccharide (Phenomenex, USA) ion exchange column. This was coupled to a SP6040XR refractive index detector (Spectraphysics, USA). The system was calibrated to quantify cellobiose, glucose, arabinose and xylose.

Ethanol content

Fermentation samples were analysed for ethanol concentration using a Shimadzu QP2010 gas chromatograph mass spectrometer (GC-MS) installed with an Agilent HP blood alcohol capillary column (ID: 0.32 mm, length 7.5m, film 25 μm). All samples were analysed using 1-propanol as an internal standard at a final concentration of 1%.

Yeast growth and viability

Fermentation samples were analysed for yeast cell growth and viability using a haemocytometer and staining with citrate methylene violet (0.01 % methylene violet, 2% sodium citrate).

Results and discussion

Ultrasonic acceleration of enzymolysis of DSG by ultrasound

Sugars hydrolysed during enzymolysis were analysed in terms of total and specific sugars. Fig. 2. shows the influence of ultrasonic irradiation, at varying frequencies, upon the total sugars released during enzymatic hydrolysis of DSG.

In terms of the enzymatic digestion of DSG, ultrasound had a significant beneficial effect upon enzyme function. This effect resulted in the increase in not only the rate of total sugar hydrolysis from DSG but also in terms of the total amount of sugar released into the liquid

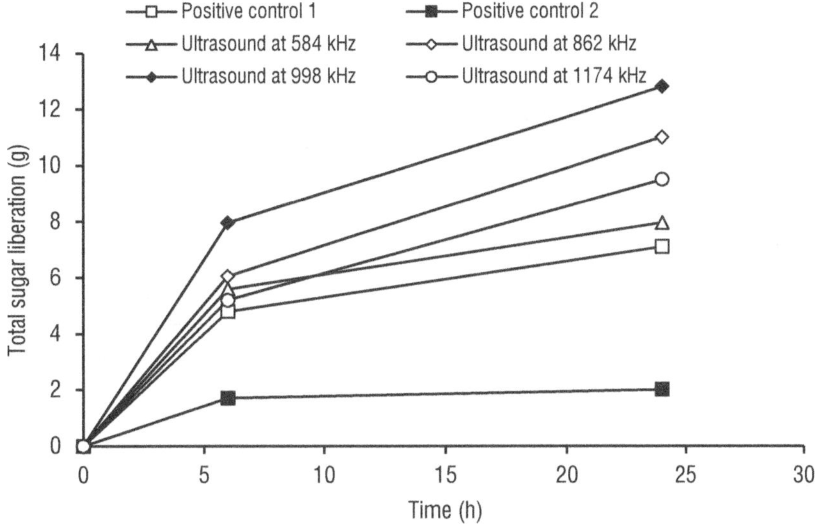

Figure 2. The impact of ultrasound upon total sugar release during enzymolysis of DSG (Positive control 1 – enzymatic digestion without exposure to ultrasound, Positive control 2- exposure of DSG to ultrasound without enzyme)

component of the hydrolysis mixture. Positive control 1 exhibited 7.06 g of sugar hydrolysed during the 24 h enzymolysis of DSG. This is in contrast to enzymatic digestions exposed to ultrasonic irradiation which exhibited values of 7.92, 11.05, 12.78 and 9.5 g at frequencies of ultrasonic irradiation of 582, 862,998, 1174 kHz, respectively. Clearly, ultrasound is accelerating the rate at which the enzymes employed in the study are acting upon their respective substrates. However, data from total sugars released during hydrolysis is insufficient to determine exactly which enzymes are being accelerated.

Ultrasound had a clear impact upon glucose released during enzymolysis of DSG (Fig. 3). Positive control 1 showed a glucose release of 5.77 g at the end of enzymatic hydrolysis. This compares to glucose values of; 5.97, 7.43, 7.95, and 7.01 g for enzymatic digestions exposed to ultrasound at 584, 862, 998

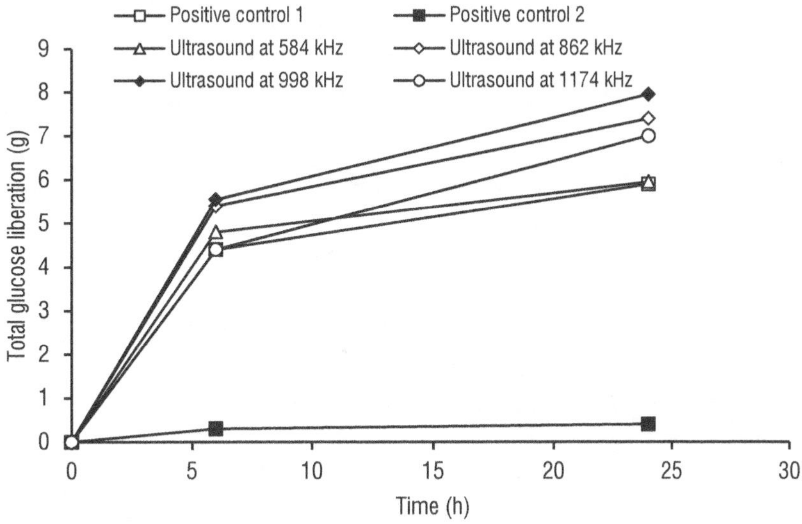

Figure 3. The impact of ultrasound upon glucose release during enzymolysis of DSG

and 1174 kHz, respectively. It is clear that ultrasound accelerated enzymatic hydrolysis of DSG to free glucose. In this study, the enzyme (Cellic Ctec) used to liberate glucose from the cellulose fraction of DSG has both cellulase and β-glucosidase activities. Cellulase hydrolyses cellulose to cellobiose, which is subsequently converted to glucose by β-glucosidase. Fig. 3 shows that ultrasound accelerated the release of cellulose hydrolysis to glucose. However, it is unclear whether ultrasound is affecting both cellulase and β- glucosidase, or one of the enzymes individually.

Fig 4 shows xylose release following enzymolysis of the arabinoxylan (hemicellulose) fraction within DSG. Positive control 1 exhibited a release of 1.13 g at the end of enzymolysis and this corresponded with values of 1.66, 2.85, 3.64 and 1.51g of xylose for digestions exposed to ultrasonic irradiation at frequencies of 583, 862, 998 and 1174 kHz, respectively. This relates to the data from arabinose release during enzymolysis (Fig. 5.), whereby the positive control exhibited 0.12 g of arabinose at the end of enzymolysis. This contrasts with results from ultrasonically treated samples which showed

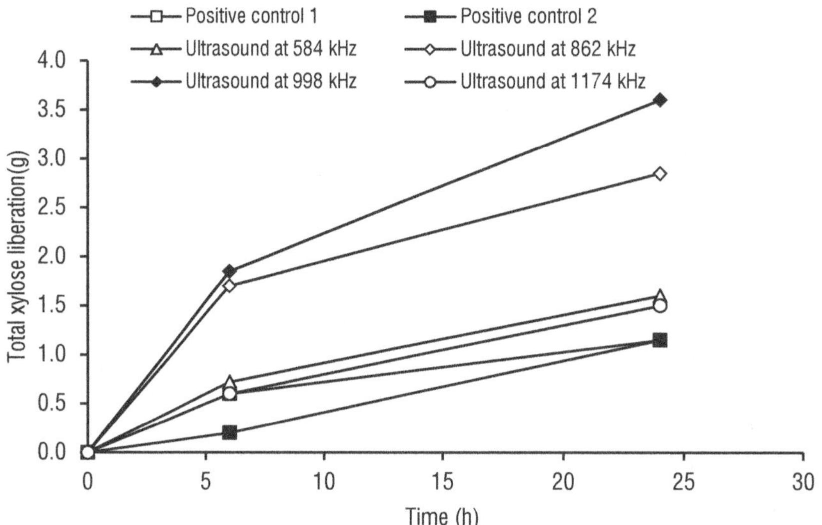

Figure 4. The impact of ultrasound upon xylose release during enzymolysis of DSG

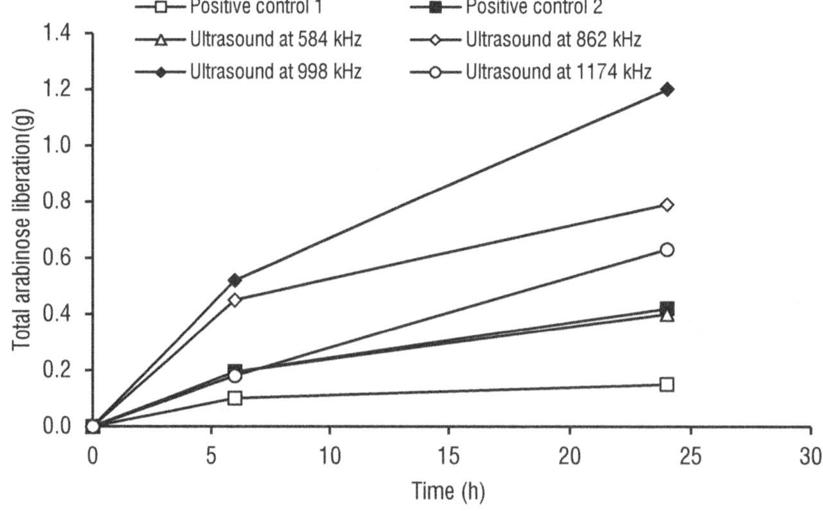

Figure 5. The impact of ultrasound upon arabinose release during enzymolysis of DSG

arabinose releases of 0.4, 0.78, 1.2 and 0.64 g at ultrasonic frequencies of 584, 862, 998 and 174 kHz, respectively. Cellic Htec, the enzyme used in this study for the hydrolysis of the arabinoxylan fraction within DSG, has xylanase activity. This results in the release of monomer xylose and arabinose during the enzymatic hydrolysis of arabinoxylan. Taking both xylose and arabinose data into account, thus suggests that ultrasound accelerates the rate at which xylanase hydrolyses arabinoxylan.

Whilst the presented data shows that ultrasound increases the function of enzymes important in the enzymolysis of DSD, as yet it is unclear as to what the exact mechanism for this increase in activity is. However, it is likely that ultrasound increases mass transfer during enzymatic hydrolysis, resulting in an increase in the rate at which the substrate binds to the active site of the enzyme.

Evaluation of yeast fermentation performance

Each 80ml aliquot of hydrolysate that was fermented contained; 2.13 g glucose, 2.08 g xylose and 0.81g arabinose. Each of the yeasts used in this study utilised different amounts of these sugars during the 120 hour fermentation (Fig. 6).

Yeast	*Sugar utilisation (g)*		
	Glucose	*Xylose*	*Arabinose*
S.cerevisiae DCLM	2.13	0	0
C. shehatae NCYC 2389	2.13	0.180	0
K. marxianus NCYC 1425	2.13	0.62	0
P. stipitis NCYC 1542	2.13	0.185	0
P. tannophilus NCYC 614	2.13	1.06	0

Figure 6. Sugar utilised during the fermentation by the yeasts evaluated

All five the yeast species under study metabolised all of the glucose present within the hydrolysate, however pentose utilisation varied greatly. As expected, S.cerevisiae showed good hexose utilisation, however following glucose depletion fermentation stopped. The remaining four yeast species all had a preference for glucose and upon depletion moved to metabolise xylose. That being said, consumption of xylose by the pentose utilising yeast was low, with *C.shehatae, K.marxianus, P.stipitis* and *P.tannophilus* metabolising 0.180, 0.62, 0.185 and 1.06 g, respectively. None of yeasts metabolised all of the available xylose and arabinose was not observed to be used by any of the yeasts used in the study.

Ethanol production varied between yeast species (Fig. 7), with *P.tannophilus* producing

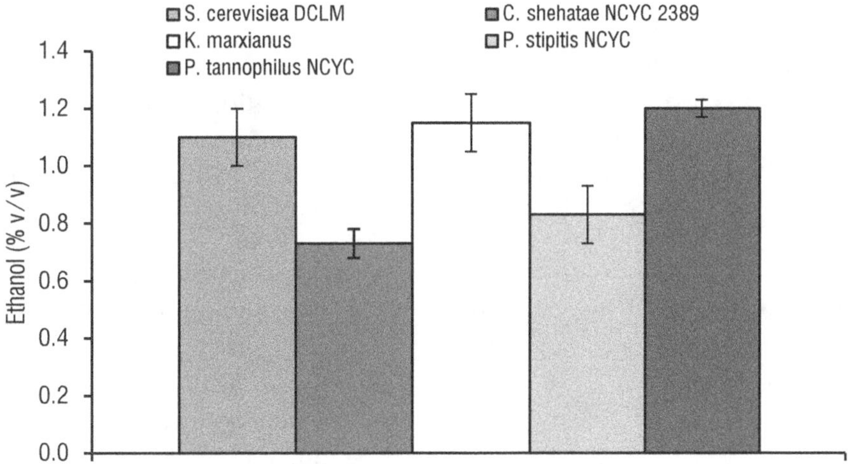

Figure 7. Ethanol produced during the fermentation of DSG hydrolysates

the largest levels of ethanol (1.2 %v/v) during the DSG hydrolysate fermentation. This compares with ethanol concentrations of 1.1, 0.72, 1.13, and 0.85 % v/v, for *S.cerevisiae, C.shehatae, K.marxianus* and *P.stipitis,* respectively. Taking into account both sugar utilisation and ethanol data, it is clear that inhibitory compounds generated during DSG pretreatment are leading to slow fermentations, with low levels of pentose metabolism and relatively low ethanol yields.

Conclusions

The main aim of this study was to evaluate the effects of exposing cellulolytic enzymatic digestions of lignocelluloses to ultrasonic irradiation. This was done with a view to developing novel bioethanol production systems that will help improve the cost: energy balance of bioethanol derived from waste materials. One of the main barriers to the commercialisation of cellulosic bioethanol is the costs associated with the enzymes utilised during enzymatic extraction of fermentable carbohydrate from lignocellulose. The results obtained during this study have demonstrated that ultrasound can increase cellulase/ β-glucosidase and xylanase enzyme function. This results in an increase of fermentable monosacchrides within lignocelluloses hydrolysates that can potentially be converted to bioethanol. Ultrasound has the potential to significantly improve this process.

It is clear from fermentation data that further work needs to be conducted to optimise the fermentation of DSG hydrolysates. Whilst ultrasound can improve the levels of fermentable carbohydrate seen within DSG hydrolysates, these increased levels of sugar are not being exploited sufficiently to produce higher ethanol yields. Current work is looking to optimise the fermentation process by detoxifying hydrolysates to remove fermentation inhibitors leading to utilisation of all available sugars.

Acknowledgments

The authors would like to express their thanks to Institute of Brewing and Distilling for funding. North British Distillery (Edinburgh, UK) for supplying stocks of DSG and Novozymes for providing samples of Cellic ™.

References

Balat, M., Balat, H. and Öz C., 2008. Progress in bioethanol processing. Progress in Energy and Combustion Science 34: 551–573.

Baras, J., Gaćeša, S. and Pejin, D. 2002. Ethanol is a strategic raw material. Chemical Industry 56: 89–105.

Barton, S., Bullock, C. and Weir, D. 1996. The effects of ultrasound on the activities of some glycosidase enzymes of industrial importance. Enzyme and Microbial Technology 18:190 – 194.

Bommarius, A.S. *et al*. 2008. Cellulase kinetics as a function of cellulose pretreatment. Metabolic Engineering. 10, 370-381.

Fan, L.T., Lee, Y.H., Gharpuray, M.M., 1982. The nature of lignocellulosics and their pretreatments for enzymatic hydrolysis. Adv. Biochem. Eng. 23, 158-187

Mussatto, S.I., Dragone, G. and Roberto, S.I. 2006. Brewers' spent grain: generation, characteristics. Journal of Cereal Science. 43, 1–14

Palmqvist, E., Hahn-Hagerdal, B. 1999. Fermentation of lignocellulosic hydrolysates: Inhibition and detoxification. Bioresoure. Technology.,

Parisi, F., 1989. Advances in lignocellulosic hydrolysis and in the utilisation of the hydrolysates. Adv. Biochem. Eng. 38, 53-87.

Saka, S., 1991. Chemical composition and Distribution. Dekker, NewYork, pp. 3-58.

Sun, Y. and Cheng, J. 2002. Hydrolysis of lignocellulosic material for ethanol production: a review. Bioresource Technology 83: 1-11.

Walker, GM (2011) Fuel alcohol: current production and future challenges. Journal of the Institute of Brewing **117**: 3-22

White, J.S., Yohannan, B.K. and Walker, G.M. 2008. Bioconversion of brewer's spent grains to bioethanol. FEMS Yeast Research 8:1175-1184.

Chapter 47

Recent advances in bioethanol production

W. M. Ingledew
University of Saskatchewan, c/o 1421 Saturna Drive, Parksville, B.C. V9P 2Y1, Canada

Starch/sugars to ethanol

In the early 1980's, a resurgence of bioethanol production occurred using production technology successfully used for centuries for beverages and used in the 20th century for fuel. However, economics of the biofuel process have been improved gradually through use of: enhanced substrates; alternate grinding and mashing methods; industrial enzymes for starch degradation; process optimization; refinements in gelatinization and solubilization of starch; new yeasts and yeast formats; understanding of yeast stress caused by nutritional deprivation; methods to reduce the effects of bacterial end products and harsh environments; production of very high levels of ethanol in fermentors up to and over 20% v/v; and improvements to increase yield. In addition, this industry has focused on improvement of production of uniform, consistent and high quality animal feed called distillers dried grain with solubles (DDGS). All these developments have aided the fuel alcohol industry to develop larger production facilities with high volume production using equipment of very high throughput, with more sophisticated distillation technology, improved molecular sieve technology to remove residual water, and significant improvement of water and energy use. The result of the advances made over more than 30 years and resultant expansion of the industry has led to an estimated 2011 production of about 53 billion L in North America from approximately 5 billion bushels (127 million tonnes) of corn. The conversion of sugar cane juice or small grains to ethanol along with corn-based ethanol totals about 88 billion L of ethanol/year in the world. Readers are directed to the newest and most detailed textbook (Ingledew *et al.*, 2009) describing production of fuel alcohol for information beyond the scope of this chapter or The Alcohol School - see www.ethanoltech.com for courses in Toulouse and Montreal each year.

Process alterations

In recent years, the baseline technology used in most fuel alcohol plants has been "jet cooking". This process grew from past practices of batch cooking using unit processes of cereals including the addition of ground corn or small grains to makeup water and thin stillage through a mixer, slurry tank and cook tank where the cooking was done by a hydroheater involving steam injection with concomitant agitation such that the grain slurry was discharged at over 100°C. A cook tube then supplied the residence time for gelatinization and was followed by a liquefaction tank employing a second dose of high temperature stable alpha-amylase. High molecular weight dextrins were made from starch. After temperature adjustment, saccharification of dextrins to glucose and some maltose was done – again in continuous tanks with added glucoamylase. The resultant mash was then cooled, inoculated, and allowed to ferment in large batch or continuous fermentation tanks. When fermentation was judged complete the spent mash was sent for distillation, with subsequent water removal from the distillate by molecular sieves, and concomitant processing of the stillage to DDGS with the thin stillage recycled in part to the next mash tank to reduce the use of fresh makeup water.

More recently, jet-less or no cook mashing has been used. Most production stages are the same, but no jet is used, and the slurry and liquefaction temperatures are held at approximately 80-85°C. A finer grind of grain is used – reducing 'blinded starch', a decreased Maillard reaction is seen, and no heat recovery at the side stripper is done. Savings occur in enzyme and heating costs. All enzymes are added to the slurry tank.

Even more recently, a commercial process pioneered by POET and Novozymes has enabled development and optimization of raw starch hydrolysis. Ultra finely ground corn and unique enzymes assist this process. The slurry tank is held at a temperature less than the gelatinization temperature of the grain used. This process has also been coupled to 'Very High Gravity (VHG) alcohol production achieving up to 20% v/v ethanol after fermentation.

Industrial enzymes aiding the total process have been developed in recent years. In addition to the heat stable amylases and cold cook amylases, pullulanases, mixed proteases, cellulases, phytases and other process aids have been described to reduce viscosity, increase solids in liquefaction, increase fermentation performance and ethanol yields and reduce fouling in heat exchangers and evaporators. Feed quality is also improved. A number of dry grind corn plants have now incorporated corn oil extraction into the process to bolster revenue.

A number of wet milling plants still produce significant volumes of ethanol but at a much lower percentage of annual ethanol production than ever before. This process is an offshoot of the production of starch and syrups for food use and has been well documented (Kohl, 2009).

Yeast manufacturers have also made significant advances to the *Saccharomyces* starter cultures available. New strains with better properties have been found in yeast culture collections and in nature that make higher alcohol concentrations. With these, fusel oils, esters and aldehydes are not a factor as they would be in beverage alcohol production. Many of these strains are therefore only recommended for fuel alcohol. A broader range of formats is also available including active dry yeast (really instant dry yeasts with an extreme shelf life of up to 3-4 years), compressed yeasts, liquid yeasts and stabilised liquid yeasts - available to dovetail to plant design and location. Some of these products can be used with minimal or no yeast acclimatization to the mash, and levels of alcohol up to 20% v/v can be obtained at end fermentation. Such yeasts should and usually do have very low levels of bacterial/wild yeast contaminants and very high viabilities. They normally leave only low levels of sugar at end fermentation, and are supported by manufacturers (but not by jobbers) with technical assistance, ongoing R&D, other products including yeast foods, and a broad knowledge of the effects of stress factors including bacterial end products, mash inhibitors, environmental stresses and how process changes such as temperature programming can prevent cessation of yeast activity and concomitant inability to consume residual sugars from mash.

A useful advance called Very High Gravity (VHG) fermentation was introduced in 1986 at the Alcohol School in Lexington Kentucky by this lab. However, it took almost 25 years for the technology to be introduced commercially for fuel production at alcohol levels of up to 20% v/v – first in approximately 20 industrial plants operated by POET (then Broin and Associates). The biological aspects of this advance are discussed in the scientific literature (Thomas and Ingledew, 1992; Thomas *et al.*, 1993; Thomas *et al.*, 1996, and many other publications) but it took some innovative steps in process flow engineering to successfully achieve the described levels of alcohol commercially that were previously seen in laboratory experiments. Plant 'bottlenecks' such as milling, viscosity, enzymology, yeast nutrition (especially usable nitrogen levels and other key nutrients), cooling, drying etc. had to be solved to allow the biology to be commercialized.

Yield improvements also have taken place in the industry. In the mid '90's, yields of alcohol per tonne of corn averaged about 372 L/tonne. In the last 15 years or so, these values have increased to 415-418 l/tonne, and now people talk about 446 L/tonne. Such increases obviously are related to one or more contributory factors including purchase of corn with increased starch content, lower moisture, low dockage and low levels of mycotoxin. Geneticists have also created new high starch varieties of corn (Haefele and Ross, 2009). However, increased yields also benefit by reduction of losses in mashing, reduction of microbial infection (eliminating lactic and acetic acids that affect yeast growth and metabolism), minimizing stuck fermentations, and lowering residual starches and sugars by mechanical or chemical means.

Control of bacterial and wild yeast infection is imperative. In the fuel alcohol industry, rather normal bacterial mash flora leads to production of acetic and lactic acids. These acids stress yeast and dramatically effect the growth and metabolism of yeasts when present at or over ~ 0.04% and 0.8% respectively (Ingledew, W.M., 2009). In North America antibiotics and other antimicrobials are used fairly routinely to suppress bacterial growth because infections can lead to alcohol losses that routinely range from 1-4% and can be higher than 17% when infections are severe. As antibiotics are removed from use or applied at lesser concentrations, more emphasis will be needed on the use of plant antimicrobials such as hop acids, and overall process applications like heat, cleaners and disinfectants (Narendranath and Brey, 2009; Richards, 2009) with a rigor more like that used in breweries, dairies and food plants. Minor equipment changes will also be required to facilitate such cleaning and sanitation steps.

Another significant factor leading to increased yearly production levels of alcohol has occurred due to the engineering of very large production plants able to make around 490 million L/year of alcohol. Modern equipment is available now to allow grinding, mashing, fermentation, distillation, dehydration and the manufacture of distillers dried grains with solubles to occur in very large scale. Engineers have also been able to conserve energy in a number of ways especially using heat and water recovery methodologies.

The future of the corn-to-ethanol industry is hard to predict. Research in corn and small grains will undoubtedly lead to strains with higher starch, and perhaps more easily obtainable starch. Already, an alpha-amylase corn has been described that contains its own enzyme to degrade starch to dextrins. Scientists will continue to reengineer plants that are less reliable on fossil fuel energy, and that require less water than is currently the case.

New technologies are developing – for example through the work of Butamax and Gevo, one relatively feasible new finding is the fermentation of starch to isobutanol rather than n-butanol - the latter an older fermentation with roots in WWII. The Agri-Energy fuel alcohol plant in Luverne has recently been purchased so that commercial quantities of isobutanol might be available as soon as next year. This fermentation product has some distinct advantages in that it contains more energy than ethanol per molecule and it can be shipped in pipelines without separation. It also can be used as a base chemical for production of other valuable products like plastics, rubbers, and solvents (http://www.argusleader.com/article/20110523/NEWS/105230310/

Luverne-ethanol-plant-highlight-market-expanding-technology?odyssey=nav%7Chead May 23, 2011).

It can be seen that dedicated transport for ethanol such as a 170 km pipeline just opened in Florida will be used. A pipeline of 2900 km from South Dakota to Linden NJ has been planned. An 850 km pipeline from Goias to Ribeirão Preto (near Saõ Paulo) continuing to Paulinia (near Rio de Janeiro) is under construction to help Brazil replace dedicated trucking. These and others will lower prices for transport, saving gasoline and ethanol while reducing traffic around plants and on highways.

As oil increases in price, the prices of gasoline continue to rise. As long as the price of corn does not increase at the same time as the price of gasoline (and ethanol) decrease in price, ethanol as a liquid fuel should remain in strong demand. Farming sectors around the world have been rejuvenated by the very large quantities of crops grown, the trucking of crop material and other consumables to the alcohol plants, and the positioning of most large distilleries in rural areas. The latter has led to jobs while the plants are constructed, stable jobs are created in and around the plant when it is operable, and there are improvements in rural life, economic spinoff, tax income for local and state governments, and rural development. Moreover, and most noticeable in Brazil and the USA, ethanol production has led to displaced oil importation, a reduction of payments to offshore foreign countries, and a stimulation of flex fuel automobile manufacture as well as hybrid and alternative fuel vehicles. It is certain that at the moment, the only other practical and available liquid fuel to blend with gasoline is ethanol.

Cellulosic to ethanol

The future expansion of fuel ethanol production by fermentation will likely lie with scientific advances in the degradation of cellulosic feedstocks leading to large amounts of sugar for the fermentative production of even larger amounts of ethanol. There are however, many problems that have not yet been addressed, and commercial production of ethanol at competitive price is not yet with us. So far reported yields of ethanol from cellulosics approach 170 L /tonne. Even small grains like wheat fall in the range of 373-385 L/tonne while corn is now well over 410 L/tonne.

A major problem in this author's view is that there are many possible substrates including corn stover, corn cobs, straw, grasses, woods, sawdust, newspaper, pulp, cardboard, cane bagasse, municipal solid waste, animal waste (to name a few). NO ONE MAJOR cellulosic substrate exists that is easily collected, processed and available broadly. Production, harvest, collection, the density of substrate and resultant transport costs are all a problem as is the consistency of collected material, its freedom from moulds, bacteria, their metabolic products and extraneous material. Consistency during storage, the limiting fermentation substrate concentration that will result from processing, as well as the variety of pretreatment steps and their uniformity from substrate to substrate will continue to occupy the minds of scientists. Each advance requires comparative reassessment. New uses and the value of released lignins and unused biomass will continue to be compared to the revenue stream obtained as DDGS in the corn-to-ethanol process.

Unfortunately, most processing steps for cellulosic substrates eliminate or drastically reduce soluble potential microbial nutrients from plant material. "Mashes" are therefore almost devoid of nutrition other than carbohydrate. Moreover, the microbes to be used for subsequent fermentation have not been chosen or fully studied so the nutritional needs of such microbes and their inhibition by any process residues (acetic acid, formaldehyde, hydroxymethyl furfural, and added chemicals) in the plant digests are not known. Suggested microbes include yeasts like *Saccharomyces, Pichia, Pachysolen* or *Candida*. Bacteria include *Zymomonas* (rejected by corn-to-ethanol industry due to growth problems and lack of tolerance to industrial substrates), *Escherichia coli, Klebsiella oxytoca,*

Clostridium thermocellum, C. phytofermentans or *C. ljungdahlii*. Virtually all of these lack the ability to make high amounts of ethanol, they produce other less desirable end products, and some are very hard to grow due to strictly anaerobic growth requirements and therefore low cell yields. Some if not all will need some degree of genetic manipulation to broaden substrate range, and any fibrous residues left after fermentation may not be easily used or disposed of.

For certain the technology needed to ensure availability of these highly viable microbes in active dry or liquid preparations suitable to initiate rapid fermentations will take additional research and time. At the moment, an investment of about $35 (US) will provide enough yeast to inoculate 50,000 L of corn mash to a cell number of approximately 4.6 million viable yeast cells/mL. This allows a relatively rapid start to fermentations. Such preparations are not available for bacteria or even other yeasts, and this will be a giant impediment for the cellulose-to-ethanol industry. Once the microbe is chosen, nutrients are determined, and fermentation is possible, work will be required to determine oxygen that may (or may not) be needed during semianaerobic metabolism, and the effect of osmotic pressure and incremental feeding of substrate. All of this is fairly well known for yeast in the starch-to-ethanol fermentation platform.

Eventually, the genetics of alternate microbes, their abilities to ferment a broad sugar spectrum, final alcohol concentrations suitable for distillation, stability, competition with usual microbial flora of plants, and resistance to stresses will all be relevant to study. Nutritional needs and thusly industrial nutritional packages for each selected microbe will need to be developed.

Cellulose-to-ethanol technology is still a daunting task – in part due to the remaining research needed and the difficulty of raising cash to fund commercialization. However, influx of money, expertise and government support appear to be aiding strategic ventures. It is sure that cellulosics are required to help reduce the amounts of imported oil and the resulting drain on the economies of the world. This approach will further stabilise farm economies and rural agriculture. There is a need to accelerate commercial production from cellulose as well as a need to reduce costs. Is it possible to focus on a designated crop with guaranteed price and sure market, a preferred treatment process, and a selected "engineered" microbe so that quicker progress can be made? There is so much to do in so little time. Even then, until commercial facilities are built, costs of construction and ethanol are difficult to estimate. Until we have costs and proof of economic viability, financiers will be reluctant to fund meaningfully sized new plants based on cellulose. The risk is just too high.

References

Haefele, D.M. and Ross A.J. In: Ingledew, W.M. (2009). Yeast stress in the fermentation process. In: The Alcohol Textbook. Edited by Ingledew, W.M., Kelsall, D.R., Austin G.D. and Kluhspies, C. (2009). *The Alcohol Textbook*. 5th Edition. Nottingham University Press. pp. 27-38

Ingledew, W.M., Kelsall, D.R., Austin G.D. and Kluhspies, C. (2009). *The Alcohol Textbook*. 5th Edition. Nottingham University Press.

Kohl, S. Wet milling and mash preparation. Edited by Ingledew, W.M., Kelsall, D.R., Austin G.D. and Kluhspies, C. (2009). *The Alcohol Textbook*. 5th Edition. Nottingham University Press. pp. 177-192

Narendranath, N.V. Bacterial contamination and control in ethanol production. In: The Alcohol Textbook 4th Edition. Edited by: Jacques, K.A., Lyons, T.P. and Kelsall D.R. Nottingham University Press. pp. 287-298

Narendranath, N.V. and Brey, S. Bacterial contamination and control. . Edited by Ingledew, W.M., Kelsall, D.R., Austin G.D. and Kluhspies, C. (2009). *The Alcohol Textbook*. 5th Edition. Nottingham University Press. pp. 337-356

Richards, C. Cleaning and Hygiene in a distillery. Edited by Ingledew, W.M., Kelsall, D.R., Austin G.D. and Kluhspies, C. (2009). *The Alcohol Textbook*. 5th Edition. Nottingham University Press. pp. 209-227

Thomas, K.C. and Ingledew, W.M. (1992). Production of 21% (v/v) ethanol by fermentation of very high gravity (VHG) wheat mashes. *Journal of Industrial Microbiology* **10**: 61-68

Thomas, K.C., Hynes S.J., Jones A.M. and Ingledew, W.M. (1993). Production of Fuel Alcohol From Wheat by VHG Technology. Effect of Sugar Concentration and Fermentation Temperature. *Applied Biochemistry and Biotechnology*, **43**: 211-226

Thomas, K.C., Hynes S.J. and Ingledew, W.M. (1996). Practical and theoretical considerations in the production of high concentrations of alcohol by fermentation. *Process Biochemistry*, **31**: 321-331

Chapter 48

Detectable limit of molasses-spirit mixed in rice-spirits using a SNIF-NMR method

Cheng-Hung Lai[1*], Wen-Ching Ko[1], Chang-Wei Hsieh[2]

[1] Department and Graduate Program of BioIndustry Technology, Da-Yeh University, 168 University Rd, Da-Tsuen, Changhua 51591, Taiwan, Republic of China; [2] Department of Medicinal Botanicals and Healthcare, Da-Yeh University, 168 University Rd, Da-Tsuen, Changhua 51591, Taiwan, Republic of China

Introduction

Rice spirits are common seasonings in Taiwanese cuisine and have been a unique feature of Taiwan dietary culture. Traditional Taiwanese rice-spirit was made by rice as the only ingredient and ethanol source. In order to increase production and decrease cost, some unscrupulous manufacturers often add edible alcohol made from cane molasses and declare the product as "pure rice-spirit" to deceive consumers (Hsieh, Wang, Chang and Ko, 2005). Assessing authenticity of foods, i.e., checking the botanical or geographical origin of a food (Ishida-Fujii, Goto, Uemura, Yamada, Sato and Yoshida, 2005), is becoming more important owing to the considerable price difference between products from specified regions and/or botanical source and "ordinary" food, which counterfeiters exploit. (Hermann, 2001).

Among the existing range of analytical tools applied to the characterization of foods and beverages, isotope analyses provide powerful authentication criteria (Charlton, Wrobel, Stanimirova, Daszykowski, Grundy and Walczak, 2010). Stable isotope ratio analysis (SIRA) methods have been recognized to provide the most innovative source of chemical information for authenticity assessment and for the origin assignment of agro-food products (Charlton *et al.*, 2010). The isotope ratio mass spectrometry technique (IRMS), which measures overall molecular isotope ratios of different elements, provides additional authenticity indicators (Ogrinc, Kosir, Spangenberg and Kidric, 2003). The ^{13}C content is especially efficient to distinguish organic products originating from C_3 and C_4 plants. Thus, addition of sugar syrups can be detected in fruit juices (Kelly, Rhodes, Lofthouse, Anderson, Burwood, Dennis and Brereton, 2003) and in honey (Cotte, Casabianca, Lhéritier, Perrucchietti, Sanglar, Waton and Grenier-Loustalot, 2007), for instance, and the carbon isotope ratios can be used for characterizing vinegars (Hattori, Yamada, Shibata, Hirano, Tajima and Yoshida, 2010). ^2H NMR determination of the site-specific $^2H/^1H$ ratios of fermentative ethanol in wine (Martin, Martin, Mabon and Michon, 1983) was initially adopted by the European Union as an official method for the proof of C_3 (sugar beet, orange, and grape) and C_4 plants (maize and sugar cane) sugar addition (EC Regulation 2676/90, 1990; Zhang, Fallourd, Role and Martin, 2003). Subsequently, the procedure was used to permit the detection of beet sugar in fruit juices (Martin, 1992) and to determine the authenticity of flavors (Martin and Remaud, 1993).

This project aimed to investigate the parameter indices of rice-spirits and molasses-spirit by the SNIF-NMR method. We hope to establish a standard of rice spirits authenticity determination and help to guarantee the quality of rice spirits for consumers.

Materials and methods

Materials

Five varieties of rice, Taikeng 8 (TK-8), Taikeng 9 (TK-9), Taichung sen 10 (TCS-10), Tainan 11 (TN-11) and Tainung 71 (TN-71) were obtained from the District Agricultural Research and Extension Station, Taichung, Taiwan. The 95% edible alcohol (a molasses-spirit; MS) produced from cane molasses was purchased from the Taiwan Sugar Corporation. *Rhizopus formosaensis* (BCRC 31150) and *Saccharomyces sake* (BCRC 20262) were obtained from the Food Industry Research and Development Institute (FIRDI) in Taiwan. Unless otherwise specified, all chemicals were analytical grade.

Fermentation of rice into rice spirits

Rice spirits was made with a 1:1 ratio of rice grains (10 kg) and water (10 kg). The rice/water mixture was simmered at 125°C for about 60 min and cooled to room temperature (25°C). *Rhizopus formosaensis* (BCRC 31150) was then inoculated 3×10^7 cells/mL into the rice to produce amyloglucosidase, α-amylase, and ß-glucuronidase. These enzymes broke down the starch polymers into smaller starch oligocarbohydrate polymers and monosaccharides, and also liquefied the rice for further and more complete fermentation. When the temperature reached 25°C after approximately 60 min, 2.8×10^7 cells/mL of *Saccharomyces sake* (BCRC 20262) were inoculated into the rice along with 30 kg water, with the temperature maintained at 25°C for fermentation. After fermentation was complete (12–14 days, depending on the alcohol content desired, it had 40 L 12% rice moromi in our experiment), 9 L of 40% alcohol rice spirits was collected via distillation, ready for the SNIF-NMR and authentication model (Que, Mao, Pan, 2006). The study flow chart is shown in Figure 1.

Results and discussion

SNIF-NMR index of ethyl alcohols from various sources

The stable hydrogen isotope ratio determinations were performed on fermentative ethanol. The SNIF-NMR index of ethyl alcohols from TK-8, TK-9, TCS-10, TN-11, TN-71 and MS are presented in Table 1. The parameters $(D/H)_I$ and $(D/H)_{II}$ value were notably different for spirits made from the five rice varieties and MS. The mean ratios found for these parameters in TK-8, TK-9, TCS-10, TN-11 and TN 71 were as follows: (D/H) I, 99.0 to 100.3 ppm (standard deviation = 0.5); $(D/H)_{II}$, 121.3 to 123.0 ppm (standard deviation = 0.7). And for MS the values were as follows: $(D/H)_I$, 108.7 ppm (standard deviation = 0.5); $(D/H)_{II}$, 125.8 ppm (standard deviation = 0.7). The values among five rice varieties were not notable different, but they obviously differed from that of MS.

Table 1. The ^{2}H fingerprints of fermentative ethanol in Taiwanese rice-spirits using different varieties of rice

Rice-spirits	*(D/H)I (ppm)*	*(D/H)II (ppm)*
TK-8	99.0 ± 0.5	122.8 ± 0.7
TK-9	99.1 ± 0.5	123.0 ± 0.7
TCS-10	99.5 ± 0.5	121.9 ± 0.7
TN-11	99.4 ± 0.5	122.3 ± 0.7
TN-71	100.3 ± 0.5	121.3 ± 0.7
MS	108.7 ± 0.5	125.8 ± 0.7

Each value represent mean ±SD (n = 3).

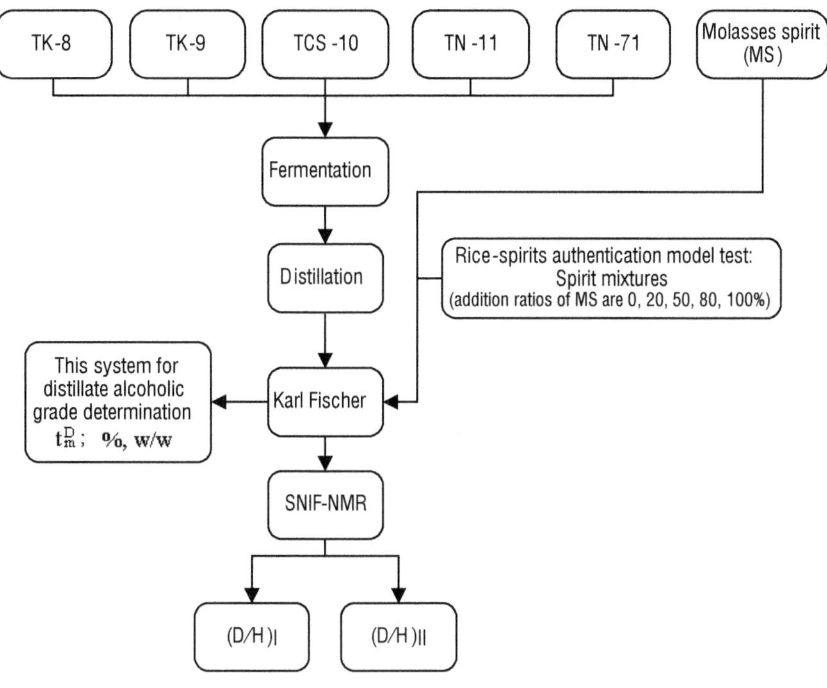

Figure 1. The flow chart of the experiment

Model test for rice-spirits mixed with molasses-spirit from cane

The ability of the developed method to detect an addition of MS was further confirmed by analysis of rice-spirits with known amounts of MS. Figure 2 and Figure 3 show the change of $(D/H)_I$ and $(D/H)_{II}$ for rice-spirits mixed with various ratios of molasses-spirit. As shown in Figure 2, a linear increase of the $(D/H)_I$ ratio occurs when increasing amounts of MS ratio are present in the rice-spirits (correlation coefficient $R^2 > 0.96$). The high coefficients ($R^2 > 0.96$) of linear correlation indicated that $(D/H)_I$ was an available index for identification. Conversely, addition of MS in rice-spirits resulted in irregular change in $(D/H)_{II}$. The observation that $(D/H)_I$ gave high coefficients ($R^2 > 0.96$) probably indicated that material sources are a key factor in SNIF-NMR determination.

Detectable limit of molasses-spirit mixed in rice-spirits

The regression lines for the rice-spirits mixed with MS are shown in Figure 2. The equations of these regression lines for $(D/H)_I$ are

$$y = 0.0962x + 98.711 \text{ [TK-8]},$$
$$y = 0.0865x + 98.856 \text{ [TK-9]},$$
$$y = 0.0878x + 98.97 \text{ [TCS-10]},$$
$$y = 0.0841x + 99.154 \text{ [TN-11]}$$

and

$$y = 0.0799x + 100.51 \text{ [TN-71]}.$$

The average precision value of the NMR measurement is 0.5 ppm for $(D/H)_I$. The experimental data for the detectable limit for rice-spirits mixed with MS are presented in Table 2. The $(D/H)_I$ value for various rice-spirits is over

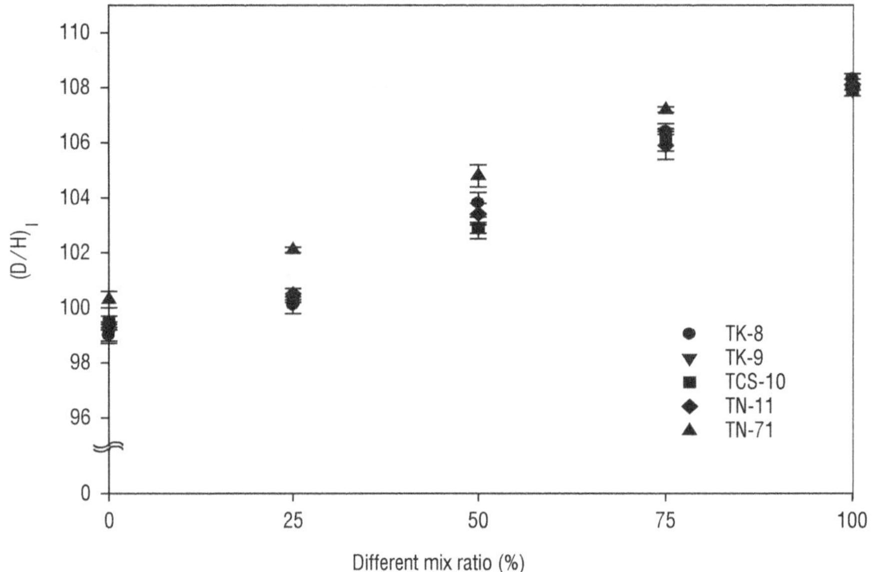

Figure 2. Changes in (D/H)I values of rice-spirits mixed with molasses-spirit

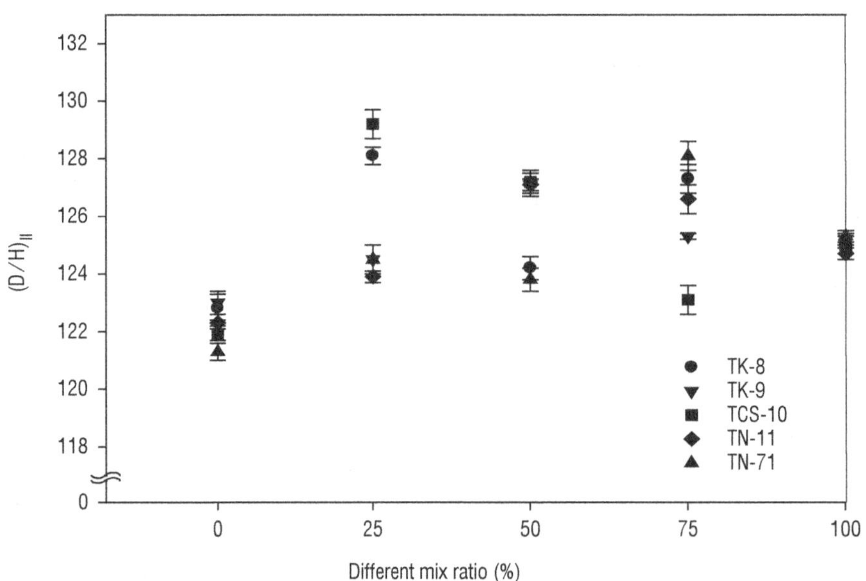

Figure 3. Changes in (D/H)II values of rice-spirits mixed with molasses-spirit

Table 2. Lower limit of detectability for molasses-spirit mixed in Rice-spirits

	TK-8	*TK-9*	*TCS-10*	*TN-11*	*TN-71*
Rice-Spirit With MS* (%)	8.20	8.60	11.73	8.87	3.62

*MS: Molasses spirit

0.5 ppm [$(D/H)_I$ value ~99.5 ppm for TK-8]. Also note from these Eq. that TN-71 shows sensitive a detectable limit of MS in rice-spirits of 3.62 %, whereas for TK-8, TK-9, TCS-10 and TN-11 the values ranged from 8.20 to 11.73 %.

Conclusions

The positional $^2H/^1H$ ratios allow a satisfactory discrimination between MS from rice-spirits. Ethanol obtained from different raw materials reveals significant differences in the D/H ratio of the methyl group. Our model test showed that SNIF-NMR is not only a potential method for the identification of pure rice-spirits [alcohol produced from rice has a $(D/H)_I$ ratio 99.0 ~ 100.3 ppm, and alcohol derived from molasses ~ 108.7 ppm], but also for distinguishing of rice-spirits mixed with molasses-spirit. Therefore, provided that a suitable database is available, the same approach will be applicable to any kind of rice-spirits containing MS. The next step of this research will validate the reproducibility of the method, to demonstrate its ability to become a standard procedure of rice spirits authenticity control.

References

Charlton, A.J., Wrobel, M.S., Stanimirova, I., Daszykowski, M., Grundy, H. and Walczak, B. (2010). Multivariate discrimination of wines with respect to their grape varieties and vintages. *European Food Research and Technology* **231:** 733-743.

Cotte, J.F., Casabianca, H., Lhéritier, J., Perrucchietti, C., Sanglar, C., Waton, H. and Grenier-Loustalot, M.F. (2007). Study and validity of ^{13}C stable carbon isotopic ratio analysis by mass spectrometry and ^2H site-specific natural isotopic fractionation by nuclear magnetic resonance isotopic measurements to characterize and control the authenticity of honey. *Analytica Chimica Acta* **582:** 125-136.

EC Regulation 2676/90. (1990). Detecting enrichment of grape musts, concentrated grape musts, rectified concentrated grape musts and wines by application of nuclear magnetic resonance of deuterium (SNIFNMR/RMN-FINS). *Official Journal of the European Communities* (L272) **33:** 1-192.

Hattori, R., Yamada, K., Shibata, H., Hirano, S., Tajima, O. and Yoshida, N. (2010). Measurement of the Isotope Ratio of Acetic Acid in Vinegar by HS-SPME-GC-TC/C-IRMS. *Journal of Agricultural and Food Chemistry* **58:** 7115-7118.

Hermann, A. (2001). Determination of D/H isotope ratio in acetic acid from vinegars and pickled products by ^2H-NMR-spectroscopy. *European Food Research and Technology* **212(6):** 683-686.

Hsieh, C.W., Wang, H.J., Chang, C.M. and Ko, W.C. (2005). Detection of added molasses-spirit in rice-spirits from TK-8 and TCS-10 by SNIF-NMR method. *Journal of Food and Drug Analysis* **13(3):** 251-255.

Ishida-Fujii, K., Goto, S., Uemura, R., Yamada, K., Sato, M. and Yoshida, N. (2005). Botanical and geographical origin identification of industrial ethanol by stable isotope analyses of C, H, and O. *Bioscience Biotechnology and Biochemistry* **69:** 2193-2199.

Kelly, S.D., Rhodes, C., Lofthouse, J.H., Anderson, D., Burwood, C.E., Dennis, M.J. and Brereton, P. (2003). Detection of Sugar Syrups in Apple Juice by δ^2H‰ and $\delta^{13}C$‰ Analysis of Hexamethylenetetramine Prepared from Fructose. *Journal of Agricultural and Food Chemistry* **51:** 1801-1806.

Kosir, I.J., Kocjancic, M., Ogrinc, N. and Kidric, J. (2001). Use of SNIF-NMR and IRMS in combination with chemometric methods for the determination of chaptalisation and geographical origin of wines (the example of Slovenian wines). *Analytica Chimica Acta* **429(2):** 195-206.

Martin, G.J., Martin, M.L., Mabon, F. and Michon, M.J. (1983). A new method for the identification of the origin of ethanols in grain and fruit spirits: high-field quantitative deuterium nuclear magnetic resonance at the natural abundance level. *Journal of Agricultural and Food Chemistry* **31:** 311-315.

Martin G.J., (1992). SNIF-NMR, a new method to detect added beet sugar to fruit juices and characterize their authenticity. *Fruit Process* **8:** 123-128

Martin, G. and Remaud, G. (1993). Isotopic methods for control of natural flavours authenticity. *Flavour Fragrance Journal* **8:** 97-107

Martin, G.G., Wood, R. and Martin, G.J. (1996). Detection of added beet sugar in concentrated and single strength fruit juices by deuterium nuclear magnetic resonance (SNIF-NMR[1] method): collaborative study. *Journal of AOAC International* **79:** 917-928.

Ogrinc, N., Kosir, I.J., Spangenberg, J.E. and Kidric, J. (2003). The application of NMR and MS methods for detection of adulteration of wine, fruit juices, and olive oil. A review.

Analytical and Bioanalytical Chemistry **376:** 424-430.

Que, F., Mao, L.C. and Pan, X. (2006). Antioxidant activities of five Chinese rice wines and the involvement of phenolic compounds. *Food Research International* **39:** 581-7.

Zhang, B.L., Fallourd, V., Role, C. and Martin, G. (2003). Comparison of isotopic fractionation in lactic acid and ethanol fermentations. *Bioorganic Chemistry* **31:** 227–236

Zhang, J.H., Huang, J.J., Tao, S.M. and Mao, Z.G. (2006). Study on the Application of Resin Absorption Technique to Reduce Higher Alcohols in Liquor. *Liquor-making Science & Technology* **7:** 27-30.

Chapter 49

Removal of higher fatty acid esters from Taiwanese rice-spirits by nanofiltration

Wen-Ching Ko[2], Yi-Hsiang Huang[2], Cheng-Hung Lai[2], Chang-Wei Hsieh[1]
[1] Department of Medicinal Botanicals and Health care, Da-Yeh University, 168 University Rd, Da-Tsuen, Chang-Hua, Taiwan, Republic of China
[2] Department and Graduate Program of BioIndustry Technology, Da-Yeh University, 168 University Rd, Da-Tsuen, Chang-Hua, Taiwan, Republic of China

Introduction

The brewing industry has used membrane filtration for many years, but it is only used to remove impurities in alcohols. Nanofiltration (NF) is a recently-developed process that is based on pressure-driven liquid separation and condensation procedures (Majumdar and Sirkar, 1992). The molecular weight cut off (MWCO) (150-1000 Da) of nanofiltration is within the nanometric scale, between reverse osmosis (RO) and ultrafiltration (UF) (Murthy, Sridhar, Sunder, Shankaraiah and Ramakrishna, 2005). Since NF can be performed at room temperature, it can be used to protect heat-sensitive and volatile substances. When applied to alcohols, NF maintains the quality of alcoholic drinks (Banvolgyi, Kiss, Bekassy-Molnar and Vatai, 2006). It is energy-efficient because it can be performed under relatively low pressures (Košutić, Novak, Sipos and Kunst, 1998). In recent years, nanofiltration has been widely applied to drinking water processing, food fermentation, medicinal condensation, and wastewater treatment (Košutić et al., 1998; Tessier, Bouchard and Rahni, 2005;Banvolgyi et al., 2006).

Some literature reports on nanofiltration and ultrafiltration are available; however, information regarding the application of nanofiltration and ultrafiltration to remove HFAEs from rice spirits is limited. The present study is the first attempt to remove HFAEs from rice spirits using nanofiltration and ultrafiltration under low temperature conditions (4°C). This study investigated the optimal operating pressure conditions and evaluated the efficacy of HFAEs removal by nanofiltration and ultrafiltration. The purpose of this study was to reduce the HFAEs content of rice spirits without affecting its quality and, ultimately, to improve rice brewing techniques.

Materials and methods

Materials

The membrane filtration system FT-150P, NF membranes DK (1812C-47P, GE Osmonics, MWCO 150-300 Da) and DL (1812C-47P, GE Osmonics, MWCO 150-300 Da), and UF membranes GE (2012C-28D, GE Osmonics, MWCO 1000 Da) and GH (1812C-47P, GE Osmonics, MWCO 2500 Da) were provided by Advanced Biotechnology Consultant Co.,

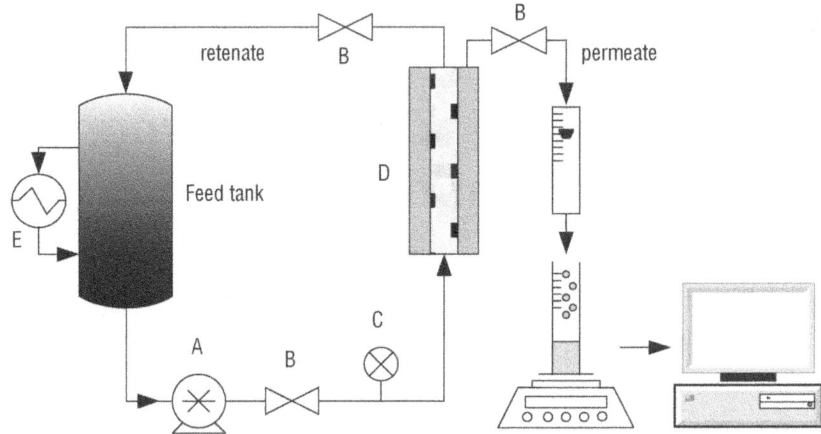

Figure 1. Schematic diagram of nanofiltration system
(A) feed pump, (B) regulation gate, (C) pressure gauge, (D) membrane, (E) constant temperature system

Ltd. (Taipei, Taiwan). The filtration system is illustrated diagrammatically in Figure 1.

The study flow chart is shown in Figure 2.

Results and discussion

Discussion of the removal effects of different filtration methods on higher fatty acid esters

The rejection rates of each HFAEs in rice spirits, achieved by the four filtration membranes (DK, DL, GE and GH), were evaluated at 30 psi and the results are shown in Table 1. In the control group, the rejection of ethyl palmitate, ethyl oleate and ethyl linolenate esters was 41.8, 23.3 and 17.1%, respectively, in rice spirits. The ultrafiltration membranes (GE and GH) effectively decreased the ethyl palmitate (27.8 and 28.4%), ethyl oleate (15.3 and 17.1%) and ethyl linolenate (9.9 and 10.8%), respectively. However, the HFAEs content of ethyl palmitate, ethyl oleate and ethyl linolenate were decreased 2.9 to 3.6 -fold using the nanofiltration membrane

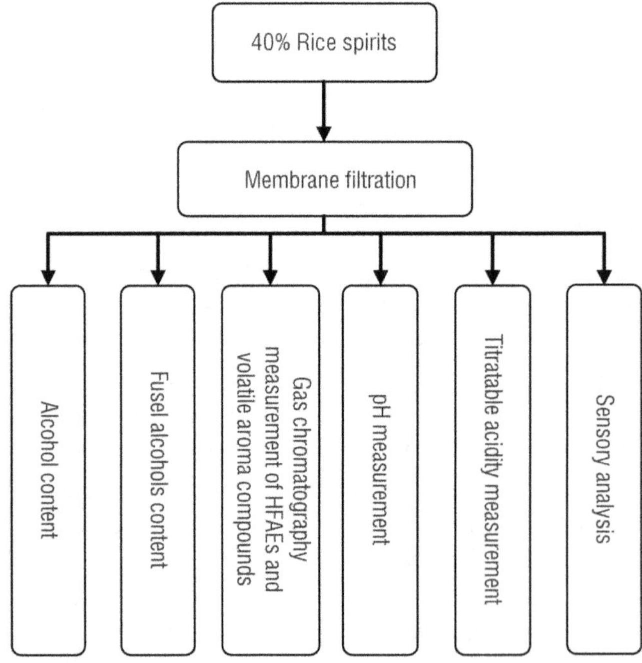

Figure 2. The flow chart of the experiment

Table 1. Per centage changes in rejection rate of HFAEs during membrane filtration of rice spirits carried out under 30 psi pressure using a pressure controller.

	ethyl palmitate	*ethyl oleate*	*ethyl linolenate*
Control	41.8 ± 0.3 [a]	23.3 ± 0.2 [a]	17.1 ± 0.2 [a]
GE membrane [a]	27.8 ± 0.2 [b]	15.3 ± 0.3 [b]	9.9 ± 0.1 [c]
GH membrane [b]	28.4 ± 0.4 [b]	17.1 ± 0.5 [c]	10.8 ± 0.3 [b]
DK membrane [c]	11.5 ± 0.3 [d]	7.6 ± 0.9 [d]	5.5 ± 0.5 [d]
DL membrane [d]	12.4 ± 0.4 [c]	7.9 ± 0.7 [d]	5.9 ± 0.6 [d]

Mean ± standard deviations from triplicate determinations
[a-c]Different letters in same column indicate significant differences at $P < 0.05$.
[a] GE membrane: Nominal MWCO 1000 Da
[b] GH membrane: Nominal MWCO 2500 Da
[c] DK membrane: Nominal MWCO 150-300 Da
[d] DL membrane: Nominal MWCO 150-300 Da

(DK and DL, respectively). These results show that ultrafiltration is not as effective as NF in decreasing the HFAEs content (the results show a significant difference ($p<0.05$)), as expected. Traditional ultra-filtration was unable to effectively separate HFAEs due to its large membrane pores and MWCO of 1000 Da to 100,000 Da.

Discussion on the removal effects of different pressures on higher fatty acid esters

The rejection rate results of each HFAEs at different operating pressures by nanofiltration are illustrated in Figure 3. These results indicate that the HFAEs content decreases as the operating pressure increases, as higher rejection rates are achieved. The DK membrane displayed the best removal results when operating at a pressure of 60 psi, and the ethyl palmitate, ethyl oleate, and ethyl linolenate rejection rates were 86.8, 82.1, and 83.6%, respectively. The DL membrane results show the ethyl palmitate, ethyl oleate, and ethyl linolenate rejection rates were 84.6, 80.2, and 81.9%, respectively, slightly poorer than for the DK membrane at the same pressure.

Effects of nanofiltration processing on other physiochemical indicators for rice spirits

The change in the concentration of ethyl acetate and ethyl lactate in rice spirits after nanofiltration is shown in Table 2. The ethyl acetate and ethyl lactate content in unfiltered 40% rice spirits (control group) is 108.2 and 69.9 ppm, respectively. The ethyl acetate and ethyl lactate content decreased only slightly via DK (99.4 and 57.5 ppm and DL (99.8 and 57.9 ppm) membrane filtration, respectively, avoiding a significant change of the aroma.

Table 2. Changes in concentration of ethyl acetate and ethyl lactate during membrane filter process of rice spirits in 60 psi at 4°C.

	ethyl acetate (ppm)	*ethyl lactate (ppm)*
Control	108.2 ± 0.2 [a]	69.9 ± 0.1 [a]
DK membrane [a]	99.4 ± 0.1[b]	57.5 ± 0.2 [c]
DL membrane [b]	99.8 ± 0.3 [b]	57.9 ± 0.1 [b]

Mean ± standard deviations from triplicate determinations
[a-c]Different letters in same column indicate significant differences at $P < 0.05$.
[a] DK membrane: Nominal MWCO 150-300 Da
[b] DL membrane: Nominal MWCO 150-300 Da

(a)

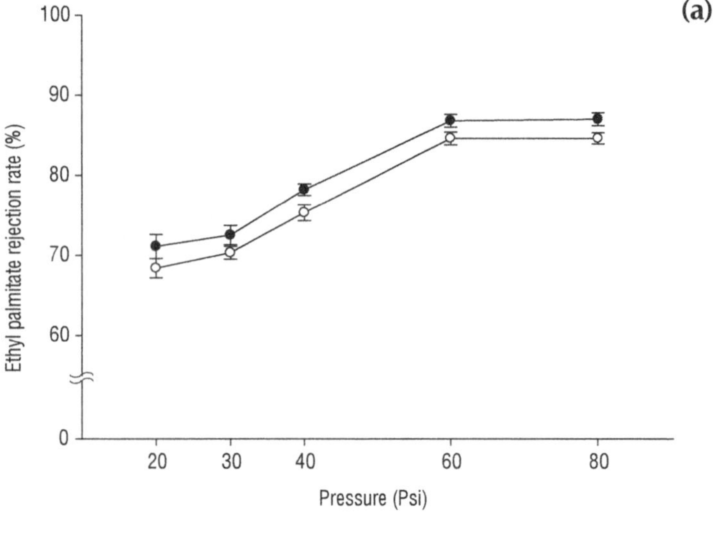

(b)

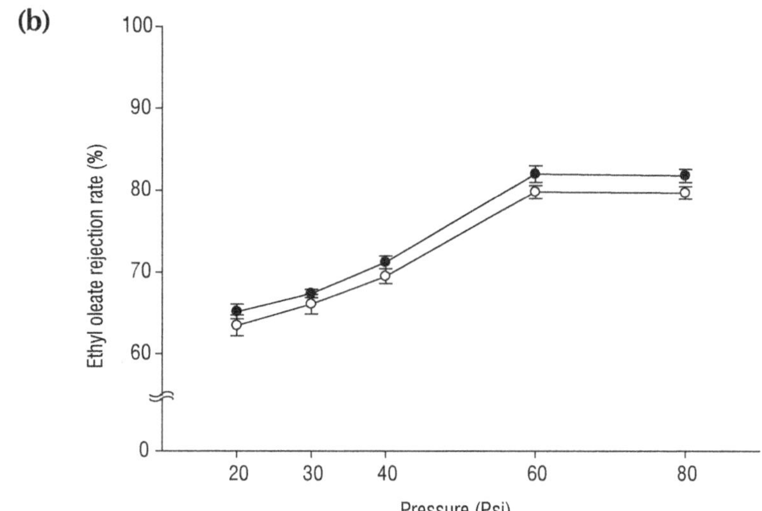

(c)

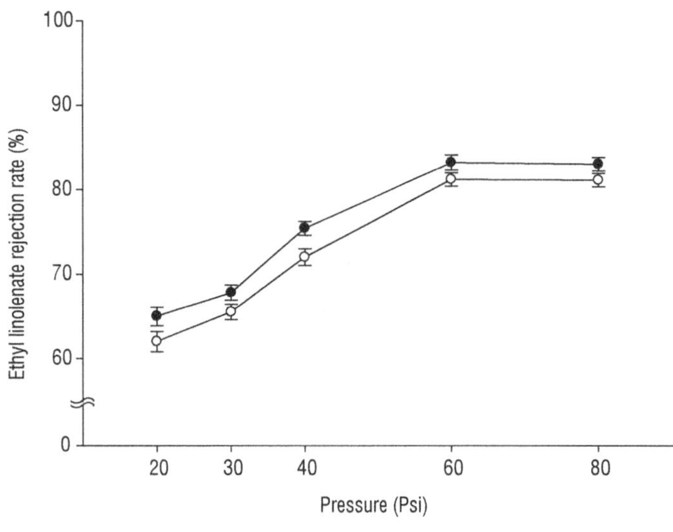

Figure 3 The HFAEs rejection rate of (a) ethyl palmitate (b) ethyl oleate (c) ethyl linolenate of rice spirits by nanofiltration at various pressure (20 to 80 psi) treatments at 4°C (● DK membrane, ○ DL membrane). Error bars represent ± SD (n = 3).

Assessment of nanofiltration with the DK and DL membrane was carried out using physiochemical indexes, such as alcohol concentration, total acidity, and fusel alcohols, and the results are illustrated in Table 3. After DK and DL membrane filtration, the alcohol concentration decreased slightly from 39.9% to 37.5% and 37.9%, respectively. In the control group, the original content of fusel alcohols was 4.5 g/L in rice spirit. However, the fusel alcohols content decreased to 2.5 and 2.9 g/L using the DK and DL nanofiltration membranes , respectively. As for the physiochemical indices after DK and DL membrane treatment, the ethanol concentration, flavor, total acidity varied slightly in rice spirits.

Sensory evaluation

Rice spirits, unfiltered and filtered by the DK and DL membranes, were compared and the results obtained at $p < 0.001$ revealed that 56% of the taster answers found differences. In order to analyze these difference in depth, two additional tests (flavour and colour) in accordance with ISO 4121-1987 and using a scale of three scores (undesirable, acceptable and desirable) were carried out. Based on the results of these two sensory tests (Figure 4), the rice spirits subjected to DK and DL membrane processing were judged acceptable in terms of flavour, in 62.1% and 58.5% of the taster answers, respectively, and the unfiltered rice spirits in 70.2%. In terms of colour (80% desirable in the unfiltered rice spirits), the desirable scores of DL and DL membranes were closer (93.8% and 90.2%, respectively). Overall, the sensory analyses revealed that rice spirits processed via nanofiltration was obviously of lower quality than unfiltered rice spirits in flavour, but still considered acceptable by the tasters.

Conclusions

Alcoholic beverages play an indispensable role in our daily life, and how to produce safe, quality products has been the goal of many studies. In this paper, nanofiltration has been used to investigate the removal of HFAEs in rice spirits. The results demonstrate the usefulness of this technique for removal of HFAEsat a low temperature and 60 psi pressure (not less than 82.1%). Also, nanofiltration could effectively remove fusel alcohol contents from rice spirits (not less than 35.5%), without significantly changing its physiochemical, flavor and quality. When applied to remove HFAEs, this technique could aid rice brewing techniques developed to optimise industrial performance.

References

Banvolgyi, S., Kiss, I., Bekassy-Molnar, E., & Vatai, G. (2006). Concentration of red wine by nanofiltration. *Desalination* **198:** 8-15.

Košutić, K., Novak, I., Sipos, L., & Kunst, B. (1998). Removal of sulfates and other inorganics from potable water by nanofiltration membranes of characterized porosity. *Separation and Purification Technology* **37:** 177-185.

Table 3. Physicochemical properties of membrane-filtrated rice spirits in 60 psi at 4°C.

	Total acidity (g/L)	*Ethanol (%)*	*fusel alcohols (g/L)*
Control	0.18 ± 0.02^{a}	39.9 ± 0.1^{a}	4.5 ± 0.1^{a}
DK membrane [a]	0.16 ± 0.01^{ab}	37.5 ± 0.1^{c}	2.5 ± 0.1^{c}
DL membrane [b]	0.15 ± 0.01^{b}	37.9 ± 0.1^{b}	2.9 ± 0.1^{b}

Mean ± standard deviations from triplicate determinations

[a-c]Different letters in same column indicate significant differences at $P < 0.05$.

[a] DK membrane: Nominal MWCO 150-300 Da

[b] DL membrane: Nominal MWCO 150-300 Da

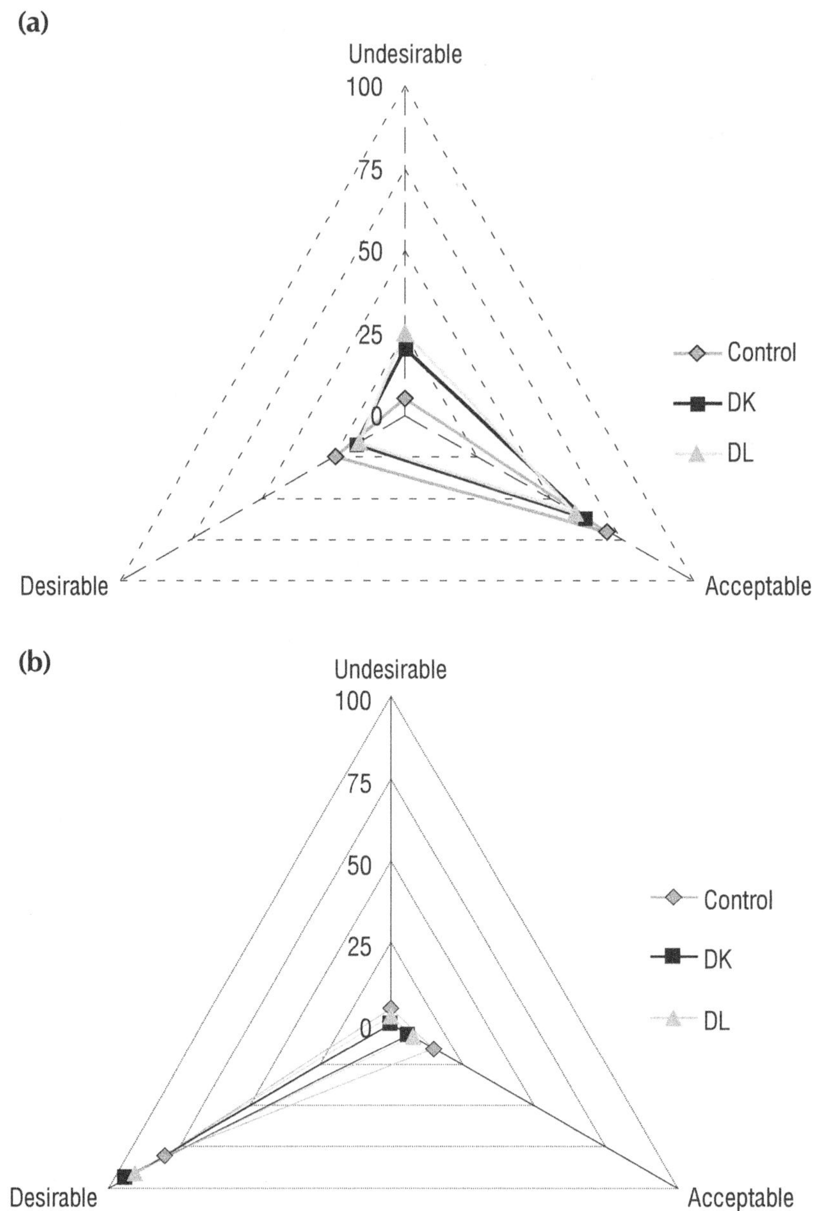

Figure 4. Sensory analyses of membrane-filtrated rice spirits by various membrane: (a) flavour and (b) colour.

Majumdar, S., & Sirkar, K.K. (1992). "*Hollow-Fiber Contained Liquid Membrane*," (pp. 704) in Membrane Handbook (W.S.W. Ho and K.K. Sirkar, eds.) Van Nostrand Reinhold, NY,

Murthy, G. S., Sridhar, S., Sunder, M. S., Shankaraiah, B., & Ramakrishna, M. (2005). Concentration of xylose reaction liquor by nanofiltration for the production of xylitol sugar alcohol. *Separation and Purification Technology* **44:** 205-211.

Tessier, L., Bouchard, P., & Rahni, M. (2005). Separation and purification of benzylpenicillin produced by fermentation using coupled ultrafiltration and nanofiltration technologies. *Journal of Biotechnology* **116:** 79-89.

Warczok, J., Ferrando, M., López F., & Güell C. (2004). Concentration of apple and pear juices by nanofiltration at low pressures. *Journal of Food Engineering* **63:** 63-70.

Chapter 50

Applications of flow cytometry in the distilling industry

Stephen Y. Pearson[1] and Jane W. Walker[1]

[1]*The Scotch Whisky Research Institute, The Robertson Trust Building, Research Avenue North, Riccarton, Edinburgh, EH14 4AP, UK*

Introduction

Scotch whisky production has undergone a number of changes in recent years to increase fermentation efficiency and reduce production costs. Consequently, today's whisky distillers are looking for a yeast that is of excellent quality, has a very high viability, is able to ferment rapidly, can compete with indigenous bacteria and tolerate a number of stresses. Distilling yeast (like brewing yeast) is subjected to a wide range of temporal stresses during industrial distillery processes, namely oxidative stress (Gibson *et al*, 2008), osmotic stress, temperature shock, changes in pH, wort acidification, ethanol toxicity and decreases in substrate availability, encountered as fermentation develops (Walker, 1999; Gibson *et al*, 2007).

In the past, distilleries have used traditional microbiological methods to assess yeast quality and monitor fermentation performance, but these techniques can be very time consuming and labour intensive. Flow cytometry provides a rapid and efficient alternative, which can be used to determine both fermentation performance and stress response (Sommer and Hutter, 2004; Sommer, Schuster and Hutter, 2004).

This chapter summarises the potential distillery application of flow cytometry, while also demonstrating the use of this technique as a research tool which will help to improve fundamental knowledge and understanding of yeast physiology and metabolism during the Scotch whisky fermentation process.

Application (1): Yeast viability and cell counts

Determination of yeast viability and cell counts using flow cytometry provides faster, more accurate results than current procedures such as the methylene blue method and plate counts. As well as measuring percentage viability, the flow cytometer is able to distinguish and enumerate live, dead and moribund cells (apoptotic cells, necrotic cells and cells with strongly compromised cell membranes) using two fluorescent dyes, fluorescein diacetate (FDA) and propidium iodide (PI). A typical example of yeast viability data obtained using the flow cytometer is illustrated in Figure 1 where quadrant *Q4* represents live cells, *Q1* denotes the dead cell population and *Q2* comprises moribund or compromised cells.

The information produced not only gives an accurate yeast viability (%) and cell count based on the number of live and dead cells

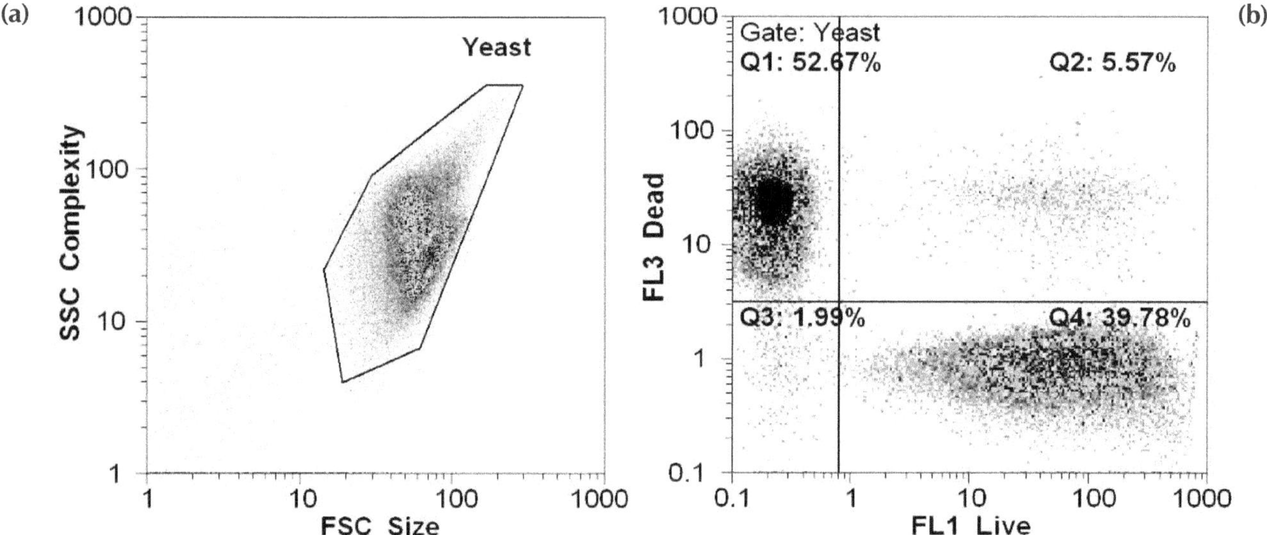

Figure 1. Example of viability data provided by the flow cytometer (a) Forward scatter (FSC, relative size) against Side scatter (SSC, relative cell complexity) dot plot, showing gated area (Yeast) representing yeast population; (b) Dot plot of Live (FL1, green channel (488nm - 527/30)) v Dead (FL3, red channel, 488nm – 630 red glass) fluorescence.

in the population but also gives a measure of apoptosis and necrosis that cannot be obtained using the conventional methylene blue method. This additional information on the moribund population provides information on yeast stress, thus enabling more detailed monitoring of the physiological status of *Saccharomyces cerevisiae* at different stages in the process.

Application 2: Yeast vitality measurements

Yeast vitality indicates the physiological condition and health of yeast cells and their response to various stressors. Vitality can be measured using flow cytometry with the application of selective fluorescent markers to measure intracellular levels of trehalose, neutral lipids and glycogen (Stewart, 2009).

Application 2.1: Yeast vitality measurement - Trehalose (intracellular)

Trehalose is a major indicator of stress tolerance in yeast and exposure to certain stressors such as temperature shock, ethanol toxicity and other stress factors result in increased levels of intracellular trehalose. Trehalose helps to protect proteins and lipids in the yeast cell membrane, contributing to the stability of the membrane under stressed conditions. Consequently, levels of trehalose vary during Scotch whisky production due to changes in fermentation conditions and yeast metabolism, with actively growing cells producing more trehalose than others. Therefore, the physiological state of yeast and the degree of stress tolerance will influence the amount of trehalose synthesised by yeast at different stages in the process.

In this assay, ethanol-fixed cells are labelled with a fluorescent marker Concanavilin A Fluorescein-isothiocyanate (Con A-FITC) which binds to the intracellular trehalose present in the yeast. The sample is then analysed using flow cytometry and the yeast cell population is defined according to relative size and complexity (Figure 2a). Yeast cells showing green (FL1) fluorescence are plotted in a histogram (Figure 2b) and the mean position of the green fluorescent peak is recorded to give intracellular trehalose values for stained cells.

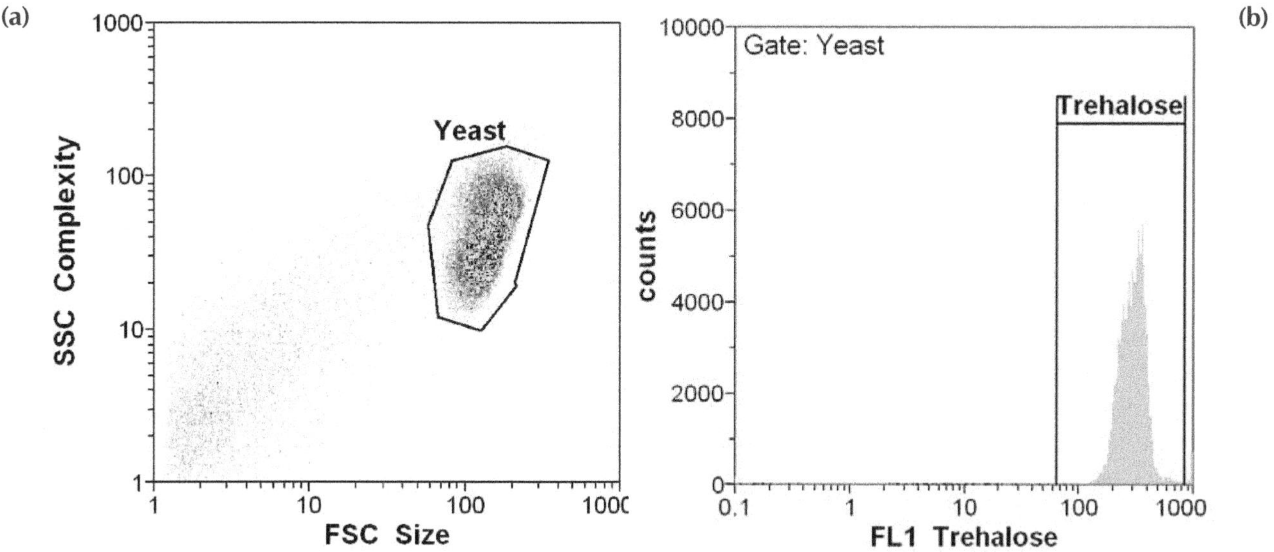

Figure 2. Typical set of data from the flow cytometer showing (a) Forward scatter (FSC, relative size) against Side scatter (SSC, relative cell complexity) dot plot; Figure 2(b) shows green fluorescence ((488nm - 527/30)) emissions relating to levels of intracellular trehalose in the yeast cell population.

Application 2.2: Yeast vitality measurement - Neutral lipids (intracellular)

Neutral lipids are membrane components but can also be stored inside the yeast cell vacuole. High levels of neutral lipids help to stabilise the yeast cell membrane conferring stress tolerance to yeast and protection against bacterial invasion. Neutral lipid levels vary depending on yeast metabolism and stresses encountered during fermentation.

In this assay, ethanol-fixed yeast cells are labelled with a hydrophobic fluorescent dye (Nile red) then assessed by flow cytometry where the yeast cell population is selected according to relative size and complexity (Figure 3a). Yeast cells showing orange fluorescence (FL2) are plotted in a histogram (Figure 3b) and the mean position of the fluorescent peak is recorded to give a value for intracellular neutral lipids level.

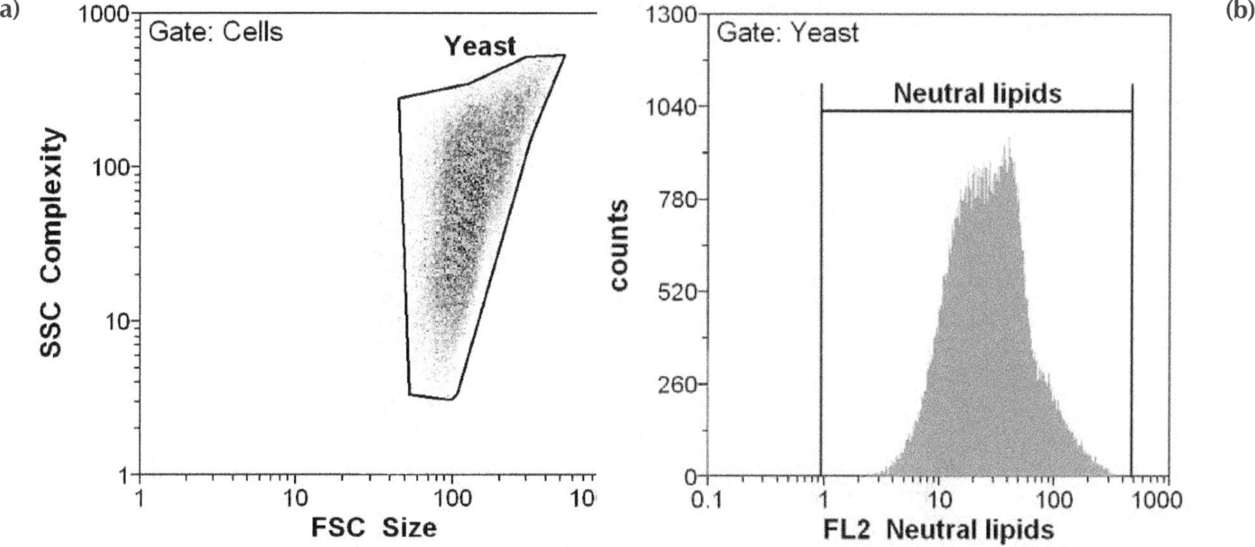

Figure 3. Typical set of data from the flow cytometer showing (a) Forward scatter (FSC, relative size) against Side scatter (SSC, relative cell complexity) dot plot; Figure 3(b) shows orange fluorescence emissions (488nm – 590 orange glass) relating to intracellular levels of neutral lipids in the yeast cell population.

Application 2.3: Yeast vitality measurement - Glycogen (intracellular)

Glycogen is a major reserve carbohydrate in yeast cells and its synthesis is dependent on yeast cell viability. It provides energy and carbohydrates for the synthesis of sterols and lipids during the aerobic phase of fermentation. Glycogen is accumulated in yeast cells during the early exponential growth phase and can be utilised by the cell at later stages in the process when nutrients in the media become depleted.

In this assay, a chemical reaction resulting in the production of reducing sugars is used to determine the amount of glycogen in the sample. Yeast cells fluorescently labelled with Acriflavin (Figure 4a) are presented in a histogram showing the green fluorescence (FL1) channel (Figure 4b) and the mean position of the fluorescence peak calculated to indicate the level of glycogen present in the yeast cells.

Application 3: Monitoring yeast performance (viability and vitality) during malt distillery fermentation

Performance of a distilling cream yeast strain (M Type, Kerry) was monitored during a normal malt distillery fermentation process. The fermentation was followed over a 96 hour period, with flow cytometry being used to determine the viability and vitality markers outlined in the previous sections. Results are recorded in Figures 5a – 5d.

It can be seen from Figure 5a that yeast viability remains high until 48–60 hours into fermentation when cells become stressed and die. This trend is reflected in the percentage of dead and moribund cells recorded. Figures 5b – 5d show that there are complex yeast vitality trends to be considered where levels of intracellular trehalose, neutral lipids and glycogen vary considerably during the course of fermentation.

In general, glycogen levels (Figure 5d) are high at the start of fermentation when yeast viability is high. Glycogen levels decrease as yeast cells become more stressed and substrate availability becomes limited. Trehalose (Figure 5b) and neutral lipid (Figure 5c) levels follow more complex patterns where levels decrease after the start of fermentation but rise as fermentation progresses and stress levels increase. These trends reflect complex dynamic interactions that take place during fermentation and relate to alterations in prevalent stress levels. Marked increases in trehalose and neutral lipid levels are observed between 36-48 hours and 48-60 hours respectively when yeast cells are

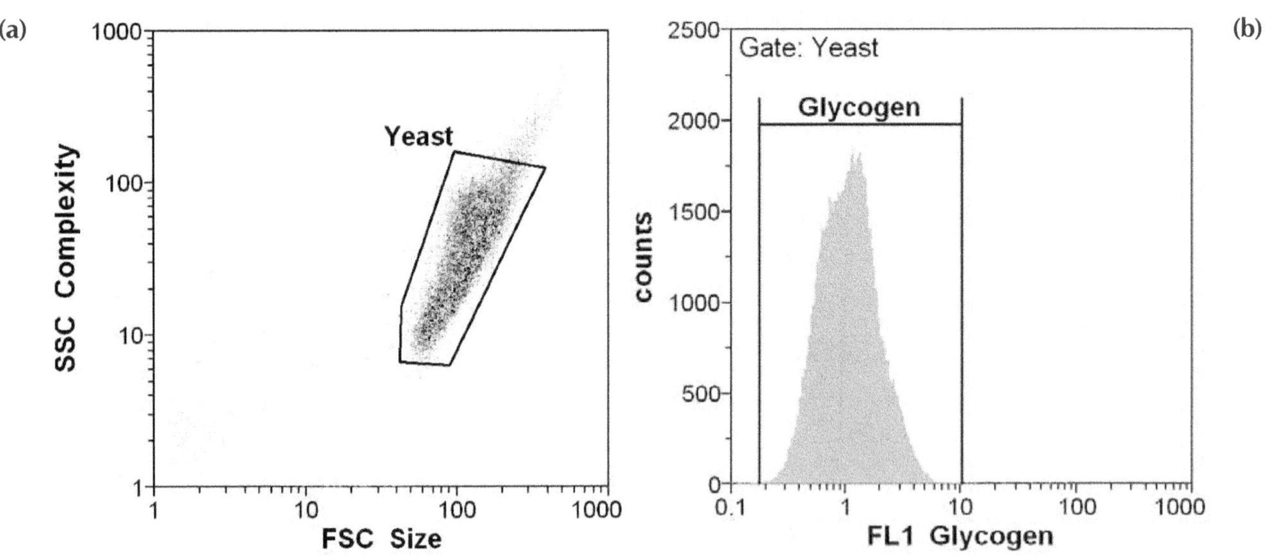

Figure 4. Typical set of data from the flow cytometer showing (a) Forward scatter (FSC, relative size) against Side scatter (SSC, relative cell complexity) dot plot; Figure 4(b) showing green fluorescence emissions (488nm - 527/30) relating to levels of intracellular glycogen in the yeast cell population.

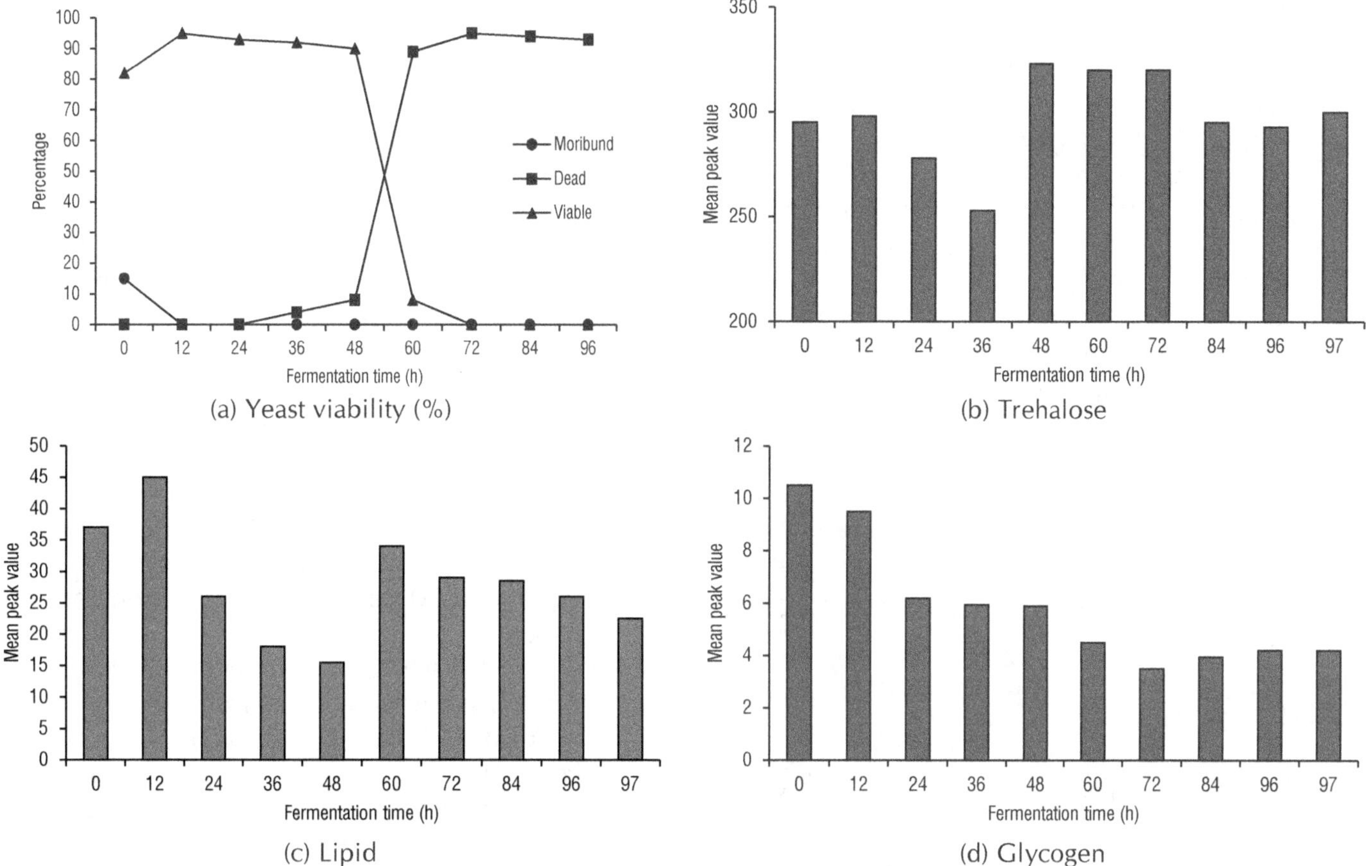

Figure 5. Yeast viability (Figure 5a) and vitality data (Figures 5b-5d) from a normal malt distillery fermentation monitored over a 96 hour period using M Type (Kerry) distilling yeast strain (cream).

stressed by a combination of factors, such as an increase in wash temperature and ethanol concentration, which ultimately result in yeast cell death. Hence, flow cytometry provides useful information on how yeast vitality levels alter in response to changing conditions and stress factors encountered during the distillery fermentation process.

Conclusions

To date, flow cytometry has been used successfully to determine percentage yeast viability and cell counts in populations from various stages of the Scotch whisky production process including; yeast delivery, storage, propagation (bubbing) and fermentation (data not shown). The cytometer has provided more rapid and accurate results for yeast cell counts, viability and vitality than can be obtained by traditional microbiological methods. Cytometry can also be used to demonstrate the presence of bacterial contamination e.g. from lactic acid bacteria in process samples (data not shown).

Not only does the flow cytometer provide better, more reliable information on cell counts and viability than previously obtained, it can also be used to determine the physiological status of yeast cells by using yeast vitality markers to determine intracellular levels of trehalose, neutral lipids and glycogen. This vitality data provides information on yeast cell condition and response to various stress factors encountered at different stages of the production process.

There are many other fluorescence markers commercially available which could potentially be used to determine additional parameters such as intracellular pH-value, membrane potential, mitochondrial activity, proteinase activity and bud scar index (Sommer, Rosenberger and Hutter, 2004) which may provide further information on yeast physiology and stress tolerance.

In conclusion, there is scope to use the flow cytometer for routine quality control measures and for more advanced research purposes. The main benefits of using flow cytometry are to obtain greater knowledge and understanding of yeast physiology and stress-tolerance in the distillery, helping distillers to optimise yeast performance during the Scotch whisky production process.

References

Chlup, P. H., Wang, T., Lee, E. G. and Stewart, G. G. (2007). Assessment of the physiological status of yeast during high- and low-gravity wort fermentations determined by flow cytometry. *The Master Brewers Association of the Americas, Technical Quarterly* **44** (4): 286-295

Diaz, M., Herreo. M., Garcia, L. A. and Quiros, C. (2010). Application of flow cytometry to industrial microbial bioprocesses. *Biochemical Engineering Journal* **48**: 385-407

Gibson, B. R., Lawerence, S. J., Leclaire, J. P. R., Powell, C. D. and Smart, K. A. (2007). Review article: Yeast responses to stresses associated with industrial brewery handling. *FEMS Microbiology Reviews* **31:** 535-569

Gibson, B. R., Lawerence, S. J., Boulton, C. A., Box, W. G., Graham, N. S., Linforth, R. S. T. and Smart, K. A. (2008). Research article: The oxidative stress response of a lager brewing yeast strain during industrial propagation and fermentation. *FEMS Yeast Research* **8:** 574-585

Hutter, K. J. (2002). Flow Cytometry – A new tool for direct control of fermentation processes. *Journal of the Institute of Brewing* **108** (1): 48-51

Macey, M. G. (2007). *Flow cytometry principles and applications*. Humana Press, Totowa, New Jersey, pp. 1-15

Sommer, S. and Hutter, K. J. (2004). Monitoring the functionality of yeast cells using flow cytometry. Presented at the *DGfZ-ESCC joint meeting*, 16-20 September 2008, Bremen, Germany

Sommer, S., Schuster, C. and Hutter, K. J. (2004). Monitoring fermentation performance and stress response of wine yeast (*Saccharomyces cerevisiae*) using flow cytometry. Presented at the *DGfZ-ESCC joint meeting*, 16-20 September 2008, Bremen, Germany

Sommer, S., Rosenberger, A. and Hutter, K. J. (2004). Cytonomics - Establishing an innovative fermentation control system based on flow cytometry. Presented at the *American Society for Enology and Viticulture*, 60th Annual meeting, 2009

Stewart, G. G. (2009). The Horace Brown Medal Lecture: Forty Years of Brewing Research. *Journal of the Institute of Brewing* **115** (1): 3-29

Walker, G. M. (1998). *Yeast physiology and biotechnology: Effects of physical and chemical stresses on yeast growth*. John Wiley and Sons Ltd, United Kingdom, pp. 149-168

Chapter 51

Impact of swallowing on the dynamics of aroma release and perception during the consumption of alcoholic beverages

I. Déléris[1], Y. Guo[1], A. Saint-Eve[1], P. Lieben[1], M. L. Cypriani[2], N. Jacquet[2], I. Souchon[1] and P. Brunerie[2]

[1] *INRA, UMR 782 INRA-AgroParisTech Génie et Microbiologie des Procédés Alimentaires, 1 avenue Lucien Brétignières, F-78850 Thiverval-Grignon, France*
Centre de Recherche Pernod-Ricard, 120 avenue du Maréchal Foch, F-94015 Créteil, France.

Introduction

Consumer preferences and choices depend largely on the sensory properties of food, and in particular flavour perception. The overall perceived flavour of a food is not only impacted by its composition but also by the way in which volatile aroma compounds are released in the mouth and transported to the olfactory receptors in the nose during food consumption. Among all the physiological and physical processes occurring in the mouth during food consumption, the key role of swallowing in the delivery of aroma compounds to the olfactory receptors has been extensively described (Buettner, Beer, Hanning and Settles, 2001). In the field of beverages, swallowing is particularly important, as these products require only limited oral manipulation, resulting in the product remaining in the mouth for a short period (Hodgson, Langridge, Linforth and Taylor, 2005; Normand, Avison and Parker, 2004; Rabe *et al.*, 2004). The development of analytical techniques, such as atmospheric pressure chemical ionisation mass spectrometry (APCI-MS) or proton transfer reaction mass spectrometry (PTR-MS), has provided new opportunities for determining the temporal release profile of volatile compounds and the study of their behaviour during the swallowing process (Buettner *et al.*, 2008).

Expert panels often taste alcoholic beverages without swallowing, to limit the effect of ethanol ingestion. Perceptions are thus evaluated in conditions that do not really represent actual consumption conditions. The known importance of swallowing for perception raises questions about the possible influence of tasting conditions on the perception of the sensory properties of the product.

In this context, the aim of this study was to quantify the impact of tasting protocol (with or without swallowing of the product) on both aroma release and perception of a commercial flavoured vodka. The originality of this work was to propose an integrated approach, through the simultaneous application of sensory and instrumental dynamic methods. This may help in improving our understanding of the relative roles of physiology and physicochemistry in flavour release and perception in the case of beverage drinking.

Materials and methods

Product

The alcoholic beverage used in this study was a commercial, flavoured vodka (750 mL bottle, 40% v/v ethanol). A three-fold dilution of the product was used to reduce the ethanol content of the samples to an ethanol concentration of 13% v/v (to ensure that the panellists experienced no discomfort and that instrumental constraints for analytical measurement were satisfied). GC-MS analysis of the product extract identified 23 key volatile components, belonging to several chemical families and having a wide range of physicochemical properties and sensory notes (Table 1).

Subjects

Ten panellists (7 men / 3 women, from 19 to 45 years of age, all members of the laboratory) were recruited for this study. They all volunteered and were specifically trained to perform sensory analyses in parallel with *in vivo* measurements.

Table 1. List and physicochemical properties of the aroma compounds used in this study

Aroma compounds	*CAS number*	*Molecular mass (g/mol)*	*Molecular formula*	*Air/water partition cœfficient (25°C)* [a]	*Sensory notes*
citronellyl acetate	150-84-5	198.20	$C_{12}H_{22}O_2$	2.82E-02	rose-like
hexyl acetate	142-92-7	144.20	$C_8H_{16}O_2$	2.58E-02	green, fruity, pear
ethyl hexanoate	123-66-0	144.20	$C_8H_{16}O_2$	2.58E-02	fruity
trans-3-hexenyl acetate	35926-04-6	142.20	$C_8H_{14}O_2$	6.76E-03	green, fruity
(Z)-3-hexenyl acetate	3681-71-8	142.10	$C_8H_{14}O_2$	6.76E-03	sweet
(Z)-3-hexenyl lactate	61931-81-5	172.22	$C_9H_{16}O_3$	5.41E-03	green
ethyl lactate	97-64-3	118.13	$C_5H_{10}O_3$	1.98E-03	buttery, creamy
methyl cinnamate	1754-62-7	162.18	$C_{10}H_{10}O_2$	1.05E-03	fruity
γ-decalactone	706-14-9	170.10	$C_{10}H_{18}O_2$	9.80E-03	fatty, peach-like
massoia lactone	51154-96-2	168.24	$C_{10}H_{16}O_2$	2.30E-03	sweet, creamy, milky, peach
β-citronellol	117-61-9	156.27	$C_{10}H_{20}O$	8.73E-04	rose-like
hexanol	111-27-3	102.17	$C_6H_{14}O$	7.95E-04	green, flowery
geraniol	106-24-1	154.25	$C_{10}H_{18}O$	4.59E-04	rose-like
maltol	118-71-8	126.11	$C_6H_6O_3$	2.68E-04	caramel-like
trans-3-hexenol	928-97-2	100.16	$C_6H_{12}O$	2.09E-04	green, flowery
(Z)-3-hexenol	928-96-1	100.16	$C_6H_{12}O$	2.09E-04	leaf-like
α-terpineol	98-55-5	154.25	$C_{10}H_{18}O$	1.29E-04	peach-like
linalool	78-70-6	154.25	$C_{10}H_{18}O$	1.73E-03	flowery
benzyl alcohol	100-51-6	108.14	C_7H_8O	1.91E-06	sweet
2-methylbutyric acid	116-53-0	102.13	$C_{15}H_{10}O_2$	5.25E-05	sweaty
butanoic acid	107-92-6	88.11	$C_4H_8O_2$	2.41E-05	sweaty, rancid
β-ionone	79-77-6	192.30	$C_{13}H_{20}O$	7.13E-03	violet-like
frambinone	5471-51-2	164.20	$C_{10}H_{12}O_2$	5.90E-09	fruity, sweet, raspberry

[a]: estimation with EPI Suite™ program

Consumption protocol for sensory and in vivo measurements

Panellists were served 5 ml of the beverage in a 70 ml hermetically sealed cup at room temperature (20°C). Panellists were asked to put the total amount of product in the mouth and to hold it there for 10 s while making tongue movements. Two consumption protocols were tested: they had to spit the product out (protocol 1) or swallow it (protocol 2). Between samples, panellists were asked to clean their mouths with unsalted crackers and water.

Sensory experimental procedure

Sensory analysis was performed by the temporal dominance of sensations method (TDS, Pineau *et al.*, 2009). Data were collected on a computer equipped with Fizz software (Biosystèmes, Couternon, France). A list containing three aroma attributes ("fruity", "green", "fatty") and one chemesthetic attribute ("warm") was proposed to panellists to describe product perception. The dominant attribute was defined as the sensation retaining the most attention during the drinking process. An attribute remained dominant until replaced by another attribute. During the evaluation of a product, panellists were free to select the same attribute several times.

Dominance rates (the percentage of panellists selecting a given attribute as dominant at a specific time) were calculated, by attribute, for each protocol and reported for each time of consumption, generating TDS curves. These graphs were interpreted with respect to two reference lines, the "chance level" and the "significance level" (Pineau *et al.*, 2009).

Fragmentation spectra of aroma compounds

The fragmentation patterns of aroma compounds from solutions of individual aroma compounds prepared in the reference product (a three-fold dilution of the spirit) were determined using a high-sensitivity proton transfer reaction-mass spectrometry (PTR-MS) instrument (Ionicon Analytik, Innsbruck, Austria) (Lindinger, Hansel and Jordan, 1998). Detailed operating conditions for PTR-MS *in vitro* analysis are described by Déléris *et al.*, (2011).

Measurements of in vivo aroma compound release kinetics

The *in vivo* release of aroma compounds was characterized by PTR-MS measurements simultaneously to TDS measurements. Nosespace air was sampled *via* the two inlets of a stainless steel nosepiece, which were inserted into the nostrils of the panellists (one on either side). Subjects were asked to taste samples according to a defined procedure to minimise interindividual variability (Déléris *et al.*, 2011). Four replicates were obtained for each protocol, each subject and each selected ion. Release curves were divided into two main periods: (i) the oral phase of consumption (phase 1); and (ii) the phase after the product had been swallowed or spat out (phase 2). Maximal intensities (I_{max1} and I_{max2}), times at which I_{max} occurred (t_{max1} and t_{max2}, which were calculated from the moment at which the product was placed in the mouth) and areas under the curve (AUC_1 and AUC_2) were extracted from each individual release curve and for each phase of product consumption (subscripts 1 for the phase before swallowing and 2 for the phase after swallowing):

Statistical analysis

Data analysis was performed with SAS software release 9.1 (SAS Institute Inc, Cary, NC) and Fizz data treatment software (Biosystèmes, Couternon, France). Analysis of variance with two factors (panellist and protocol) and their interaction and Student's t-tests were carried out on each parameter extracted from *in vivo* release curves and from TDS curves with the GLM (general linear model) and t-test modules of the SAS software package. When significant differences were highlighted ($p<0.05$), means were compared in Student-Newman-Keuls (SNK) full comparison tests.

Results

Determination of the fragmentation spectra of ethanol and aroma compounds

Concerning aroma compounds, results suggest that all molecules produce a large number of fragments under these PTR-MS operating conditions. Most of the fragments were common to several molecules (for instance, *m/z* 43, 46, 55, 83, 89 or 117). A principal component analysis was performed to highlight the existence of molecule clusters on the basis of their fragmentation patterns (Figure 1).

The first two principal components explained 31.85% and 18.01% of the total variance in the data sets. The diagram reveals three groups relating to molecules and fragments. However, no fragment specific for a chemical class of aroma compounds or for a particular sensory note was clearly identified. From PCA results and considering ions produced from the fragmentation of the most concentrated molecules in the initial product, three groups of three ions were selected to be monitored for the *in vivo* experiment: the first was more specific to the "green" note (ions *m/z* 55, 46 and 83), the second to the "fruity" note (ions *m/z* 61, 103 and 131) and the third reflected "overall" aroma (ions *m/z* 43, 89 and 117). In this selection, no fragment representing group B of the PCA plot was chosen for technical reasons of sensitivities.

Effect of swallowing on temporal perception

The sensory results obtained with the TDS method during the consumption of samples with the swallowing or spitting out of the product are shown in Figure 2.

First, the "fruity" note, identified as dominant very early in consumption (from 5 s), seemed to be the main characteristic note of this type of product, regardless of the protocol used. Yet, the

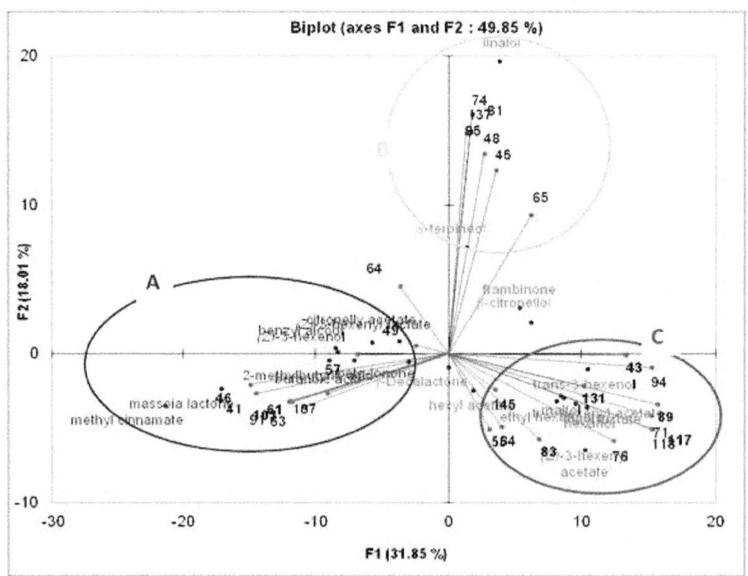

Figure 1. PCA plot on fragmentation data: scores on fragments and molecules are given on the first (horizontal) and second (vertical) principal component axes. Clusters A, B and C represent groups of molecules giving similar fragments during PTR-MS measurements. Bold numbers represent ions selected for further *in vivo* experiments.

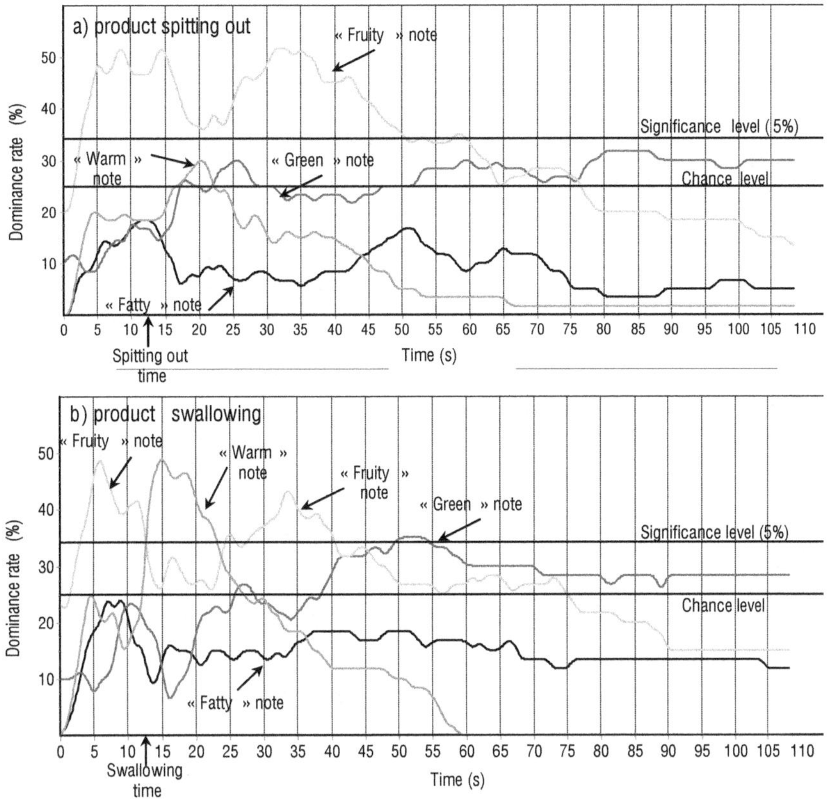

Figure 2. TDS curves evaluated during the consumption of diluted alcoholic beverage with a) spitting out of the sample or b) swallowing of the sample. The lower and upper horizontal lines indicate the chance and significance levels, respectively. Only TDS curves above the significance level are considered to be significantly dominant. Time 0 corresponds to the moment at which the product was placed in the mouth.

dominance rating of this "fruity" note was lower when the product was swallowed than when it was spat out.

When the product was spat out, the "fruity" note was perceived by the panel as the only dominant sensation, from the beginning of consumption and continuing for 47 s (Figure 2-a). Two peaks in the dominance rate of this attribute were detected, and a trough occurred just after the product had been spat out.

When the product was swallowed, perceptions became more complex, with the appearance of two other dominant sensations in addition to the "fruity" note (Figure 2-b). The "fruity" note was the first perceived, for a period of 10 s beginning at the start of consumption. Just after swallowing, a "warm" note was perceived as dominant by panellists for a period of 12 s, after which it was immediately replaced by a "fruity" note lasting 16 s. Finally, a "green" note was perceived as dominant after 50 s of consumption, over a period of 5 s. In neither protocol was a "fatty" note recorded as significantly dominant by the panellists at any time.

All these results suggest that the swallowing event affects sensory perceptions, particularly in terms of dominance rates and dominant attribute sequences (over time).

Effect of the swallowing event on in vivo release kinetics

Some examples of release kinetics obtained for one panellist (mean of the three replicates) are presented in Figure 3 for several ions and for both consumption protocols.

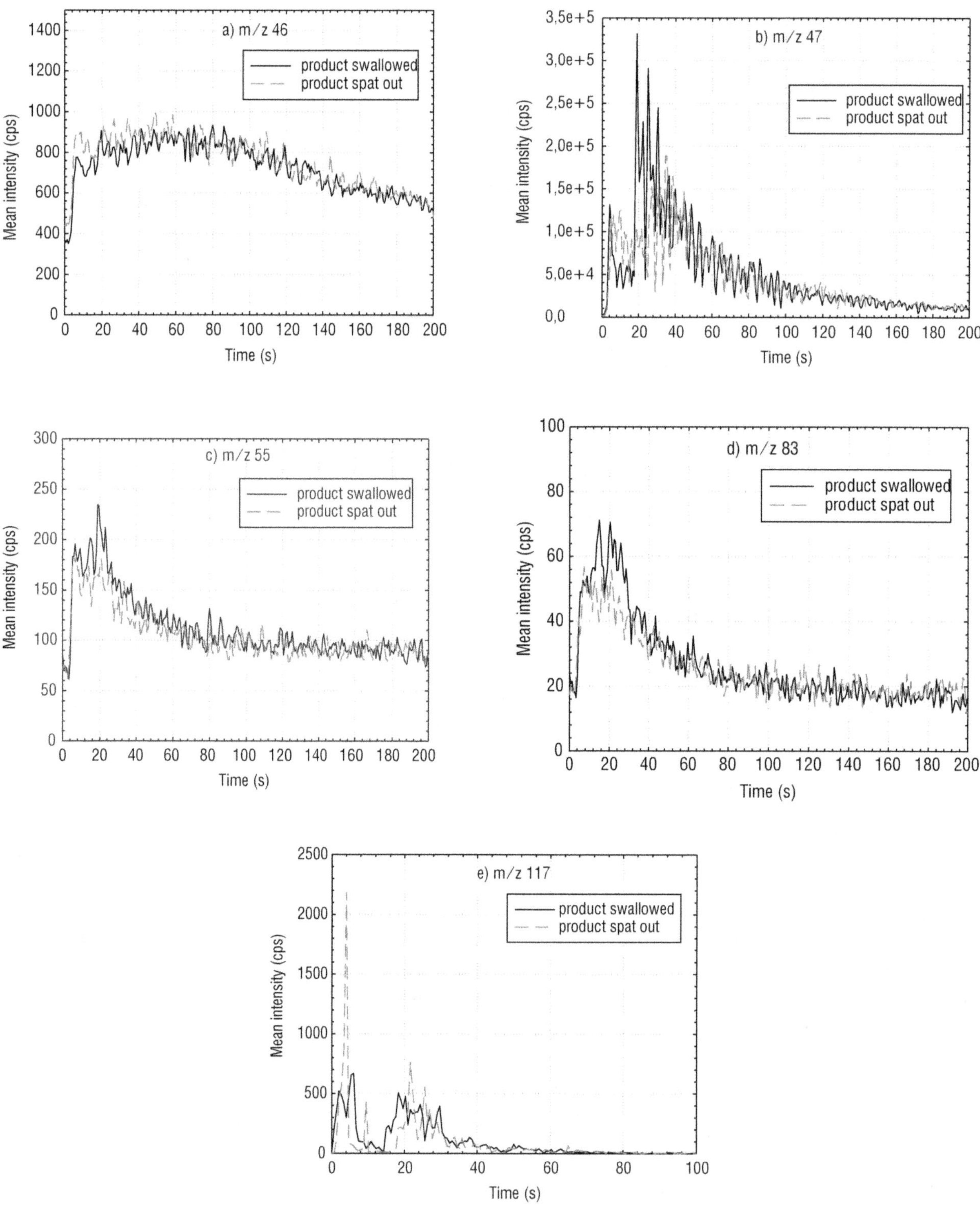

Figure 3. Release kinetics (1 panellist, mean of 3 replicates) obtained when the product was swallowed or spat out for a) *m/z* 46, b) *m/z* 47, c) *m/z* 55, d) *m/z* 83 and d) *m/z* 117. Time 0 corresponds to the moment at which the product was placed in the mouth.

The intensity of the signal was ion-dependent, with the ion *m/z* 47 the most strongly released (Figure 3-b) and the ion *m/z* 83 the least released (Figure 3-d). The shape of the release kinetics curve was ion-dependent, with differences observed in release intensity, release rate and persistence. The release of ion *m/z* 46 began immediately after the product was placed in the mouth and remained of limited intensity, but unlimited duration (signal persistence) (Figure 3-a). For ions *m/z* 47, 55, 83 and 117, a high initial rate of release was observed just after the swallowing event (Figures 3-b, -c, -d and -e, respectively). For these fragments, the shape of signal decrease after the start of swallowing was also ion-dependent. For some ions, the signal persisted, with a slow return to initial levels (ions *m/z* 47, 55 or 83, Figures 3-b, -c and -d respectively). For ion *m/z* 117, the decrease rate was high but further peaks appeared at each new swallowing event (whether the product was initially swallowed or not) (Figure 3-e). These patterns were observed for all panellists, but both the amount of aroma compounds released (I_{max} and AUC) and the shape of the release kinetics curve (I_{max} and t_{max}) were subject to high levels of inter-individual variability (not shown). This inter-individual variability in aroma release profile, already reported before (Buettner *et al.*, 2002), may be attributed to anatomical and physiological differences.

On the basis of the results of statistical analysis carried out on parameters extracted from individual release kinetics curves (all ions, all panellists and all replicates), no significant interaction between protocol and panellist was identified. Unsurprisingly, none of the parameters corresponding to the period before the swallowing/spitting out event differed significantly between the two protocols (data not shown). After the swallowing or spitting out of the product, only a few parameters were significantly affected, for which the swallowing effect (SE) was calculated as followed:

This ratio highlighted release differences between protocols whilst eliminating differences in the absolute intensity of release between panellists. An SE ratio value greater than 1.0 would indicate a more intense value of parameter with swallowing than with spitting out. Results are presented on Figure 4.

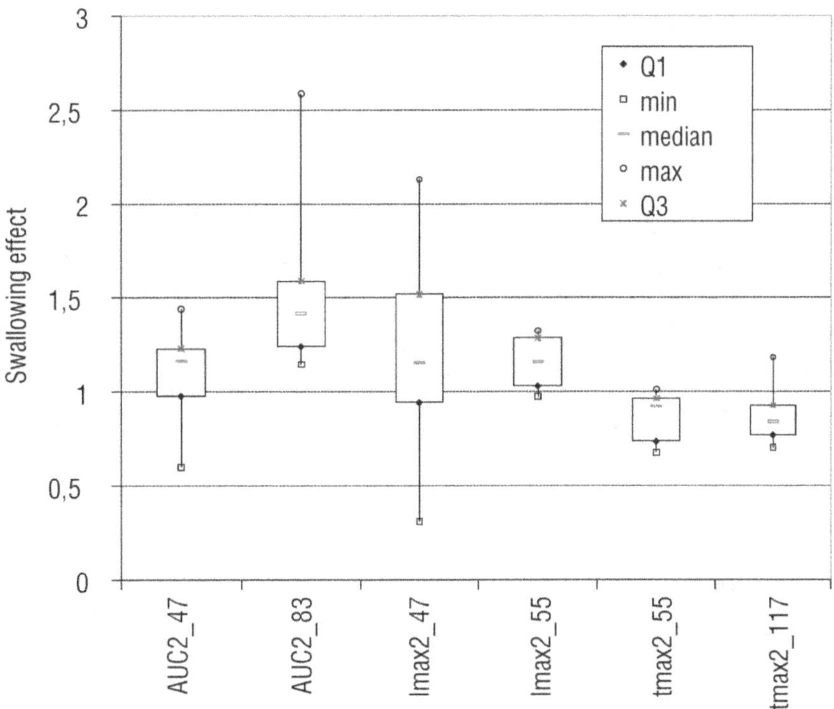

Figure 4. Values of the swallowing effect (SE) for discriminatory parameters extracted from *in vivo* release kinetics.

The swallowing of the product induced a higher and earlier release of larger amounts of aroma compounds than the one obtained with spitting out, but only for a limited number of ions (*m/z* 47, 55, 83 and 117). For ions *m/z* 47 (related to ethanol) and *m/z* 55, the maximal intensity after the swallowing/spitting out event (I_{max2}) was greater after swallowing than after spitting out (22% and 17% greater for *m/z* 47 and *m/z* 55, respectively). The quantity of ions released (AUC_2) was greater when the product was swallowed than when it was spat out for ions *m/z* 47 and *m/z* 83 (21% and 38% greater, respectively). Finally, the time t_{max2} at which intensity was maximal was significantly earlier with swallowing than with spitting out, for ions *m/z* 55 and *m/z* 117 (33% and 12% earlier, respectively).

Discussion

The application of dynamic methods, making it possible to acquire information about sensory and release kinetics over time, enabled the characterisation of the temporal dimensions of the phenomena involved and therefore their comparison. The main significant differences between the two tested protocols for both sensory and instrumental data are summarised in Table 2. Despite the lack of specific tracers for the main sensory attributes (except for ethanol), some relationships between release and sensory data can be proposed to account in part for the impact of swallowing on perception.

First, the "fruity" note, identified as dominant very early in consumption (from 5 s), has a quite broad definition and may relate to several aroma compounds present in the product (esters, lactones, ketones, etc) (Table 1). The rapid release of some fragments of these molecules just after the product was placed in the mouth as well as the subsequent release peaks after each swallow (examples on Figures 3-e for *m/z* 117) can explain the dominance of this sensory attribute at the beginning and all along the consumption time. The significant decrease in the dominance rate of the "fruity" attribute, noted when the product was swallowed, can be attributed to the apparition of the dominance of the "warm" perception just after swallowing, which probably masks or decreases the dominance rates of other attributes.

The "warm" dominance occurring at swallowing can be explained by physicochemical phenomena, as ethanol release (instrumentally traced by monitoring ion *m/z* 47) was significantly greater when the product was swallowed than when it was spat out. This "warm" perception may be partly due to the activation of the trigeminal nerve but also of other nerves in both nasal and oral cavities (notably cranial nerves) (Faurion, 2004).

Concerning the "green" note, despite the presence of a maximal release peak of fragments *m/z* 55 and 83 at around 20 s (originating

Table 2. Summary of the sensory and instrumental results obtained in this study. Only significant data are listed. Symbols "-" and "+" are used to compare signal level between the two protocols.

		Product spat out	*Product swallowed*
Sensory data	Dominant perceptions and sequence	"fruity"	"fruity"/"warm"/"fruity"/"green"
	Dominance rate	+ "fruity"	- "fruity" + "warm" + "green"
	Mean time and mean duration parameters	no signifcant difference	
Instrumental data	I_{max2} and AUC_2, *m/z* 47	-	+
	I_{max2}, *m/z* 55	-	+
	AUC_2, *m/z* 83	-	+
	t_{max2}, *m/z* 55 and 117	+	-

mostly from aroma compounds responsible for the "green" attribute, i.e. *(Z)*-3-hexenol, *(Z)*-3-hexenyl-acetate, hexanol) (Figures 3-c and 3-d), this sensory perception probably did not retain sufficiently the attention of panellists in comparison with other notes ("fruity" and/or "warm") to be evaluated as dominant at the beginning of consumption. The strongest release of fragments *m/z* 55 and 83 when the product was swallowed (increase in I_{max2} and AUC_2 values) can account for the significant dominant "green" note, even if it only occurred at around 50s. The signals for these fragments decreased slowly and seemed to be more persistent than the ones of other fragments, potentially accounting for the delayed perception of the "green" note. The existence of specific physicochemical interactions between aroma compounds responsible for the "green" note and pharyngeal and/or oesophageal mucosa may be proposed to explain the delayed release of these fragments and, thus, the delayed perception of this note when the product was swallowed (Buettner *et al.*, 2002; Normand, Avison and Parker, 2004; Hodgson, Langridge, Linforth and Taylor, 2005; Buettner and Beauchamp, J.., 2010).

The greater complexity perceived when the product was swallowed may be explained by the stimulation of a larger number of sensory receptors located in the mouth, the nasal cavity and the throat: product coating on throat and pharynx after swallowing increased the contact area between the air and the product, which favoured aroma release. With swallowing, this stimulation also happens over a longer period of time, notably because of the aforementioned specific interaction between aroma compounds and mucosa, which could induce retardation effects on aroma release. The greater complexity when the product was swallowed may also be due to the longer presence of ethanol in the nasal cavity, which can impact sensory perceptions both at receptor and neurological levels, as already mentioned in literature (Burgering, De Jong, Goorissen and Pepin, 2009; Meillon *et al.*, 2010). Sensory interactions between aromatic and trigeminal perceptions can also be assumed: the dominance rating of the "warm" note may imply an expectation of more complex aromatic perceptions (Reinbach *et al.*, 2007; Labbe, Gilbert and Martin, 2008; Kostyra, Barylko-Pikiena and Dabrowska, 2010).

These results confirmed the known role of the swallowing event on aroma perception and highlighted that both sensory and physicochemical phenomena were involved. These results could be useful to food industries to adapt and improve their tasting protocols during the phases of product development and characterization in order to better fit to consumer expectations in terms of sensory properties.

References

Buettner, A., Beer, A., Hanning, C. and Settles, M. (2001). Observation of the Swallowing Process by Application of Videofluoroscopy and Real-time Magnetic Resonance Imaging—Consequences for Retronasal Aroma Stimulation. *Chemical Senses,* 26(9): 1211-1219.

Buettner, A., Beer, A., Hannig, C., Settles, M. and Schieberle, P. (2002). Physiological and analytical studies on flavor perception dynamics as induced by the eating and swallowing process. *Food Quality and Preference,* 13(7-8): 497-508.

Buettner, A., Otto, S., Beer, A., Mestres, M., Schippa, C. and Hummel, T. (2008). Dynamics of retronasal aroma perception during consumption: Cross-linking on-line breath analysis with medico-analytical tools to elucidate a complex process. *Food Chemistry,* 108(4): 1234-1246.

Buettner, A. and Beauchamp, J. (2010). Chemical input – Sensory output: Diverse modes of physiology–flavour interaction. *Food Quality and Preference,* 21(8): 915-924.

Burgering, M., De Jong, C., Goorissen, H. and Pepin, L. (2009). Contrôle de la qualité sensorielle des vins à faible teneur en alcool préalablement à leur désalcoolisation. *Revue des oenologues,* 131: 39-42.

Déléris, I., Saint Eve, A., Guo, Y., Lieben, P., Cypriani, M. L., Jacquet, N., Brunerie, P. and Souchon, I. (2011). Impact of swallowing on the dynamics of aroma release and perception during the consumption of alcoholic beverages. *Chemical Senses, doi: 10.1093/chemse/bjr038*.

Faurion, A. (2004). *Physiologie sensorielle à l'usage des IAA*; Lavoisier: Paris.

Hodgson, M. D., Langridge, J. P., Linforth, R. S. T. and Taylor, A. J. (2005). Aroma release and delivery following the consumption of beverages. *Journal of Agricultural and Food Chemistry,* 53(5): 1700-1706.

Kostyra, E., Barylko-Pikiena, N. and Dabrowska, U. (2010). Relationship of pungency and leading flavour attributes in model food matrices - temporal aspects. *Food Quality and Preference,* 21(2): 197-206.

Labbe, D., Gilbert, F. and Martin, N. (2008). Impact of Olfaction on Taste, Trigeminal, and Texture Perceptions. *Chemosensory perception,* 1(4): 217-226.

Lindinger, W., Hansel, A. and Jordan, A. (1998). On-line monitoring of volatile organic compounds at pptv levels by means of proton-transfer-reaction mass spectrometry (PTR-MS) - Medical applications, food control and environmental research. *International Journal of Mass Spectrometry and Ion Processes,* 173(3): 191-241.

Meillon, S., Viala, D., Medel, M., Urbano, C., Guillot, G. and Schlich, P. (2010). Impact of partial alcohol reduction in Syrah wine on perceived complexity and temporality of sensations and link with preference. *Food Quality and Preferences,* 21(7): 732-740.

Normand, V., Avison, S. and Parker, A. (2004). Modeling the Kinetics of Flavour Release during Drinking. *Chemical Senses,* 29(3): 235-245.

Pineau, N., Schlich, P., Cordelle, S., Mathonniere, C., Issanchou, S., Imbert, A., Rogeaux, M., Etievant, P. and Köster, E. (2009). Temporal Dominance of Sensations: construction of the TDS curves and comparison with time-intensity. *Food Quality and Preference,* 20(6): 450-455.

Rabe, S., Linforth, R. S. T., Krings, U., Taylor, A. J. and Berger, R. G. (2004). Volatile Release from Liquids: A Comparison of In Vivo APCI-MS, In-mouth Headspace Trapping and In vitro Mouth Model Data. *Chemical Senses,* 29(2): 163-173.

Reinbach, H. C., Meinert, L., Ballabio, D., Aaslyng, M. D., Bredie, W., Olsen, K. and Moller, P. (2007). Interactions between oral burn, meat flavor and texture in chili spiced pork patties evaluated by time-intensity. *Food Quality and Preference,* 18(6): 909-919.

Chapter 52

Global counterfeiting detection

S Fisher
VP Pernod Ricard Brand Security, c/o Chivas House, 72 Chancellors Road, London, W6 9RS

The following is a transcript of the oral presentation given by Stephen Fisher at the 4th Worldwide Distilled Spirits Conference. It has been slightly adapted to fit into the format of these proceedings.

Introduction

As the Vice President of Pernod Ricard Brand Security and, as the group's senior executive in this field, one of my responsibilities is setting and implementing our strategy to protect our brands from criminal and non-criminal activity around the world. One significant element of this is to combat the counterfeiting of our brands wherever that occurs in the world.

It is my intention to provide you with an overview of the current situation in relation to the counterfeiting of our industry's brands around the world and the action we take to interdict this activity.

First, let me make it clear that counterfeiting is not a new phenomenon. One of the first examples of counterfeiting, a wine stopper for amphorae, dates back to 27 BC. In the 14th Century, Elector Palantine hanged a wine seller for attempting to sell counterfeit goods, and in 1564 France introduced the death penalty for counterfeiting. More recently, counterfeit parts were potentially to blame for the failure of the hostage rescue at the US Embassy in Iran in 1981; counterfeit parts were found in the US Military supply chain and may even have been fitted to Airforce One, the most secure and carefully looked after aircraft in the world.

Counterfeit activity affects not just distilled spirits but all premium luxury goods: prestige motor cars, oils, fuels, sporting goods, leatherwear, tobacco, pharmaceuticals, software, CDs, DVDs, washing powder and even firearms. Recently, in a city in China, enterprising counterfeiters even set up two completely counterfeit Apple stores.

Here in the UK in recent months some of the consequences of counterfeit alcohol production have been well publicised. Six men were convicted for running an operation that produced more than one million litres of illegal alcohol, costing the taxman £10 million in lost revenue; they were jailed for a total of 56 years. In Boston, Lincolnshire, five men were killed after a huge fireball ripped through an industrial building, which police identified as being used to produce alcohol illegally.

In terms of global trade, it is estimated that between 6 and 8 percent involves counterfeit goods. Trade in all counterfeit goods costs the global economy billions of US dollars annually. Some latest estimates include:

- The World Intellectual Property Organisation estimates counterfeiting is costing the global economy more than US$ 100 billion a year
- World Customs Organisation (WCO): estimates that pirated and counterfeit goods account for between seven and nine percent of global trade and therefore the value of counterfeit trade exceeds US$ 540 billion.

Counterfeiting poses a growing and significant threat to everyone involved in the production, marketing, distribution and sales of alcoholic beverage brands. The health of our consumers can be put at risk from counterfeit product, not only because of the quality of the spirit counterfeiters use or manufacture, but also because of the environment in which counterfeit spirit brands are often produced. Globally, over the past 10 years or so, more than 1200 deaths have resulted from the consumption of illegal alcohol. . Counterfeiting activity can, and on occasion does, seriously erode a premium brand's credentials, hence endangering the livelihood of those who make and market it and the investment of their shareholders. It also results in the loss of government revenues and increases the flow of financial resources to criminal networks. The presence of counterfeit spirits in a market may also mean our consumers' perception of the levels of counterfeit available may become distorted and reduce the likelihood of them buying affected brands.

Combatting the criminal activities of counterfeiters

Most, but not all, of Pernod Ricard's anti-counterfeit activity is conducted via the industry anti-counterfeit partnership, the International Federation of Spirits Producers Ltd (IFSP) of which I am a director and also the Chairman of IFSP Asia.

The global membership of IFSP currently comprises: Pernod Ricard SA, Diageo, Brown-Forman, Bacardi, Beam Global Spirits and Wines Inc., Moet Hennessey, Remy Cointreau. In addition to this, The Edrington Group and Cuervo are active in IFSP in selected markets around the world.

IFSP members' brands account for around a third of all global spirits sales most threatened by counterfeit, and include many of the industry's best-known names. The IFSP, a not for profit company, was formed in 1993, and is currently active in more than 40 countries.

The IFSP has investigation teams, either directly employed or 3rd party contractors, covering all of the key markets in Asia, the Middle East and Europe and Latin America where we are currently expanding our operational resources and capabilities.

The Federation's non-competitive basis means our members share information and resources to combat the counterfeiting of its members brands in order to:

- **Protect** consumers and brand-owners from the dangers of counterfeit products.
- **Promote** awareness of the economic harm caused by counterfeiting.
- **Support** trade partners and law-enforcement agencies in the fight against the counterfeiters.
- **Encourage** dialogue between all stakeholders so that the risks from counterfeit products are minimised.

Detecting criminal counterfeiting operations

Identifying the brands likely to be targeted by criminal counterfeiters in a specific counterfeit risk market is a simple process. Counterfeiters target the most popular brands, i.e. those with the most significant market share are their likely starting point as through such counterfeit activity the criminal can make significant profit.

In these markets it is necessary to identify the law enforcement agencies that are responsible for the enforcement of anti-counterfeit laws. For example, in the UK, Trading Standards are responsible for removing counterfeits from retail, whilst Customs and the Police will investigate those criminals involved in counterfeit production and distribution. In China, the Administration for Industry and Commerce (AIC) is responsible for enforcement at retail level and can issue administrative fines to those found selling counterfeit products, whilst the Public Security Bureau (PSB) will investigate those criminals involved in counterfeit production and distribution. In markets such as Singapore and Israel, the Police have their specific departments responsible for enforcing Intellectual Property laws.

In some markets, especially those where anti-counterfeit laws are complex or where such laws are not subject to regular use, it is often beneficial to offer support and training to law enforcement officers and/or prosecutors as well. This can be provided by in-house lawyers or by 3rd party lawyers who are experts in this field. This not only assists with the investigation, charging and criminal prosecution process but also shows to the government agencies the importance that brand owners put on protecting their consumers and brands.

I firmly believe that the best option to deter counterfeiters is via criminal prosecution and, where considered necessary, to lobby for appropriate sentencing. Therefore, having identified the law enforcement departments responsible it is necessary to provide them with Counterfeit Recognition and Education training. Training is designed to provide enforcement officers with some simple points to differentiate the genuine brand from the counterfeit; most counterfeit recognition training concentrates on the closure itself. When producing fake bottles of spirit. the counterfeiter has to either reuse a genuine closure or replace the original with a fake Reused closures usually show signs of being previously opened through integral tamper evident design, whilst counterfeit closures show to the trained eye small but significant differences to the genuine. Not only does Counterfeit Recognition and Education training enable trained officers to be able to identify counterfeit from the genuine product, it also enables brand owners directly, or through industry associations, to make enforcement officers and prosecutors aware of the dangers counterfeits pose to consumers and government revenues.

It is also necessary for us to provide law enforcement agencies evidence pertaining to the analysis of counterfeit sprits for use in criminal court proceedings. Whilst our own brand company scientists can analyse samples of seized counterfeit spirit and provide such evidence to court, if counterfeit activity in a certain market is high or local laws require such analysis to be conducted by their own government accredited laboratories, it will be necessary and more cost efficient for brand owners to provide local government scientists with information and training in relation to the analytical techniques for spirit brands and to monitor their activity in this respect. Analysis of the spirits used by counterfeiters will also serve to identify whether or not the spirit poses a health risk to our consumers.

At this juncture, it is important for me to stress the advantage of identifying and accrediting local in-market laboratories to conduct this analytical work on our behalf. Obviously it is necessary for a nominated senior industry scientist to monitor their activity. It is also necessary that the congener information provided to such (usually government) laboratories is limited, not only to protect brand information but also to ensure that the more sophisticated techniques used to discern counterfeit remains with the brand owners.

Subjecting counterfeit spirits for formal analysis is an investigational tool in itself. Where evidence is adduced, for instance, to show counterfeiters are using standard branded whiskey to refill a premium brand, it is often possible to identify those criminal groups who of course have no legitimate retail ability but are purchasing such brands in significant volume. Further, analysis of counterfeits that identifies illicit spirits are being used to refill branded product may reveal the source of the illicit spirit; the identification of almost identical spirit in more than one city may serve to identify the spread, scale of activity and perhaps distribution routes used by the criminals concerned. The same applies of course to counterfeit dry goods.

As an industry we have developed various Field Authentication Technologies. IFSP are currently working with 3rd party providers on the next generation of wet goods field and desktop authentication devices. The accuracy and efficiency of the devices being developed are currently being assessed and we would hope that they meet our stated needs and will be available for use both within the IFSP and by law enforcement agencies with whom we work around the world in the near future.

Last year IFSP:

- Organised over 800 training seminars in counterfeit recognition for law-enforcement agencies and their prosecution services and we, using our own industry scientists, trained or retrained scientists employed in government accredited forensic science laboratories in several markets.
- We assisted with more than 9,400 regulatory visits with law enforcement officers to wholesale and retail outlets. As this activity was targeted as a result of market inspections, in the vast majority of instances counterfeit products were seized.
- IFSP also conducted investigations that led to the closure of more than 1000 counterfeit production and distribution facilities. If these facilities had continued to operate, it is calculated that circa US$100m of revenue would have been diverted away from the spirits industry and tax authorities into criminal hands.

This activity resulted in the seizure and destruction of over 5.5 million counterfeit-branded items. This figure does not include counterfeiting equipment such as counterfeit and illicit spirits, capping machines, tools, vehicles, and related counterfeiting paraphernalia.

Many investigations are complex and take months to come to fruition, often using informants and undercover operatives. However, in simple terms, the obvious starting point to identify the presence of counterfeit in any market is at retail level, both in the on and the off premise. In this respect, close monitoring of consumer complaints received and of intelligence reported by our own sales teams will be of substantive assistance. Having identified the presence of counterfeit at retail level through the implementation of covert visits/inspections, consideration can be given to implementing comprehensive covert surveys to assess the level of counterfeit that exists by brand and/or by category in the market(s) concerned.

Having identified counterfeits in retail premises, usually through a surveillance operation, it is possible to identify those involved in distributing the counterfeit product and this should lead to the identification of the criminal's counterfeit storage and distribution facilities. From here, their counterfeit manufacturing sites can be identified. Subsequent investigation and surveillance is then conducted to identify those who are supplying the counterfeit manufacturers with empty genuine or counterfeit bottles, counterfeit closures, labels and of course wet goods. The evidence of this activity must of course then be put before the relevant law enforcement agency with a request that they act and pursue criminal prosecution against the perpetrators. It is here that the benefit of the prior provision of training and education by brand owners and industry partnerships becomes evident. This formation and maintenance of sound working relationships linked to the quality and accuracy of actionable evidence provided to law enforcement in relationship to criminal counterfeit enterprises builds a mutual trust that leads to the expeditious enforcement and prosecution of the criminals who attack our brands.

Targetted investigation into the activities of bottle collectors and the producers of counterfeit dry and wet goods also leads to the identification of those involved in the manufacture, distribution and sale of filled counterfeit branded spirits. The counterfeit dry goods producers are a primary target as the interdiction of these counterfeiters makes it much harder for the counterfeiter to produce counterfeit spirit brands.

Finally, it will come as no surprise to you that counterfeiters are using the internet to advertise the availability of counterfeit product. Not only do they advertise bottles of counterfeit spirit to retail but the counterfeiters also advertise the availability/production of counterfeit dry goods including glass, labels, closures and wet goods to the producers of counterfeit spirit brands. Some are even considerate enough to provide us with a map to ensure our investigation teams can find them easily.

Chapter 53

Anti-counterfeiting: Using LC-MS to detect and differentiate between caramels E150 a, b, c and d in whisky

S. Cubbon[1], D. McMillan[1], C. Owen[2], I. Goodall[2]
[1]: Waters, Atlas Park, Simonsway, Manchester, M22 5PP; [2]: SWRI, The Robertson Trust Building, Research Avenue North, Riccarton, Edinburgh, EH14 4AP

Introduction

The counterfeiting of spirits is reportedly increasing year after year as the worldwide market continues to expand, and poses serious risks to consumer safety. With the exports of Scotch Whisky worth £3.45 billion in 2010 (SWA, 2010), protecting the industry against losses through counterfeiting is key to ensuring brand reputation and job security.

The EU Whisky definition specifically requires that only E150a is to be used to colour Whisky, if required, and as a result the presence of other types of caramel would be prohibited (Regulation EC No 110/2008).

The analysis of Whisky using Mass Spectrometry (MS) has traditionally been performed using Gas Chromatography (GC) as the separation technique, and is often targeted at specific additives to identify a non-genuine product. With spirits such as Whisky being famed for their complex aromas, GC is an obvious choice for the separation of volatiles; the separation efficiency and reproducibility of the technique when combined with MS detection and the availability of searchable libraries have ensured that GC/MS is the dominant technique for mass spectrometric analyses.

There are very few publications that cite High Performance Liquid Chromatography (HPLC) MS for the analysis of spirits such as Whisky. The reasons behind the poor adoption of HPLC/MS could be the perceived poorer separation efficiency and reproducibility, combined with the lack of searchable libraries to aid in identification of components.

Both HPLC and MS techniques have improved greatly, with far superior separation efficiencies and reproducibility afforded by Ultra-Performance Liquid Chromatography (UPLC) combined with the ease of use of high-end time of flight (Tof) mass spectrometers which provide excellent mass accuracy (ppm); intuitive software and access to searchable on-line databases such as ChemSpider (www.ChemSpider.com contains over 26 million searchable structures) simplifies the processing of complex datasets, generating answers more rapidly.

Despite the dominance of GC/MS, UPLC/MS has a lot to offer for the analysis of Whisky and should be considered an important tool for the spirits industry in general. Not all compounds are volatile and amenable to GC/MS separation and analysis, with low molecular weight compounds or thermally labile compounds being easily degraded by the high temperatures involved during the injection and separation steps. In addition, the extensive fragmentation typically observed in the resulting mass spectra (whilst useful for library searching) can lead to ambiguous assignments of compounds due to the lack of precursor ion.

Whisky analysis using UPLC-Tof MS

For the analysis of caramels in Whisky, two separate experiments were designed: E150 caramels (E150a types 1 to 4, E150 b, E150 c and E150 d) were dissolved in ethanol (40 % v/v) at a concentration appropriate to match the absorbance of a standard Whisky blend (Whisky Blend C) and E150 caramels (E150a, E150b, E150c and E150d) were added to another Whisky Blend W (prior to any caramel addition) again at an appropriate concentrations to match the absorbance of Whisky Blend C.

The aim of adding caramel to ethanol was to determine if markers for E150a to d are present, and determine if there is any variation in E150a production evident (E150a types 1 to 4). The second experiment, where E150a to d were added to Blend W, was designed to establish whether the impact of the Whisky matrix overpowers any differentiations observed between caramels E150a to d observed in just ethanol (experiment 1).

All samples were analysed without any preparation, using a 10 minute gradient separation with water and methanol (both containing 0.1 % formic acid v/v) on a Waters ACQUITY UPLC®, using an ACQUITY HSS T3, 2.1 x 100 mm, 1.8 μm column; this resulted in less than 11 minutes cycle time. Each sample was analysed in triplicate (10 μL injection volume), with the order of analysis being randomised.

The Tof MS (Xevo™ G2 Tof) was operated in positive and negative electrospray ionisation (ESI) modes, with data being acquired over the range *m/z* 50 – 1200 using Waters' proprietary MS^E acquisition mode, which acquires full scan information in both low and high energy modes simultaneously, allowing fragmentation information to be obtained for all compounds.

All data were processed using MarkerLynx XS™, a multivariate data analysis tool which can take complex datasets and compare samples using both un-biased Principle Components Analysis (PCA) and biased Orthogonal Partial Least Squares - Discriminant Analysis (OPLS-DA).

Caramels in ethanol and whisky

The results for the analysis of caramels in ethanol using both positive and negative electrospray ionisation modes were compared using PCA, with the greatest separations between the different caramels being observed in negative mode.

Figure 1 shows that when caramels in ethanol are analysed using PCA (no knowledge of grouping is used), it is clear to see that the largest differences between caramels E150a, b, c and d can be observed by the separation along the x-axis, or principal component (PC) 1. Separation of caramel E150a, types I to IV, requires the second PC, meaning that the differences between the different types of E150a are more subtle.

As Whisky is a complex matrix, the concern that the separation between different caramels observed in ethanol would be overpowered when analysed in Whisky Blend W was addressed.

The analysis of caramels in Whisky Blend W shows that, despite the complex matrix, separation of each of the samples containing different caramels is still observed (Figure 2), even with no sample preparation being performed prior to injection.

With the differences between the caramel types being clear when using un-biased PCA, the components that cause the separation should be easily identifiable; each scores plot also has an associated loadings plot which contains all of the variables (components) responsible for the separation between each of the different caramels.

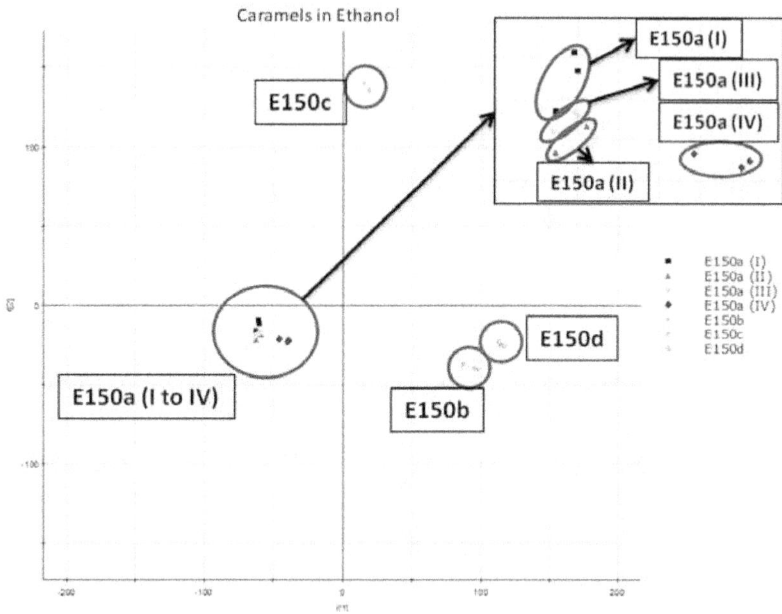

Figure 1. PCA scores plot of caramels E150a to d in ethanol. Using negative ESI, differences between the caramels E150a to d are clearly observed, with each set of triplicate injections clustering apart from one another. The region where E150a types I to IV cluster has been magnified to highlight subtle differences between each of the different types of E150a.

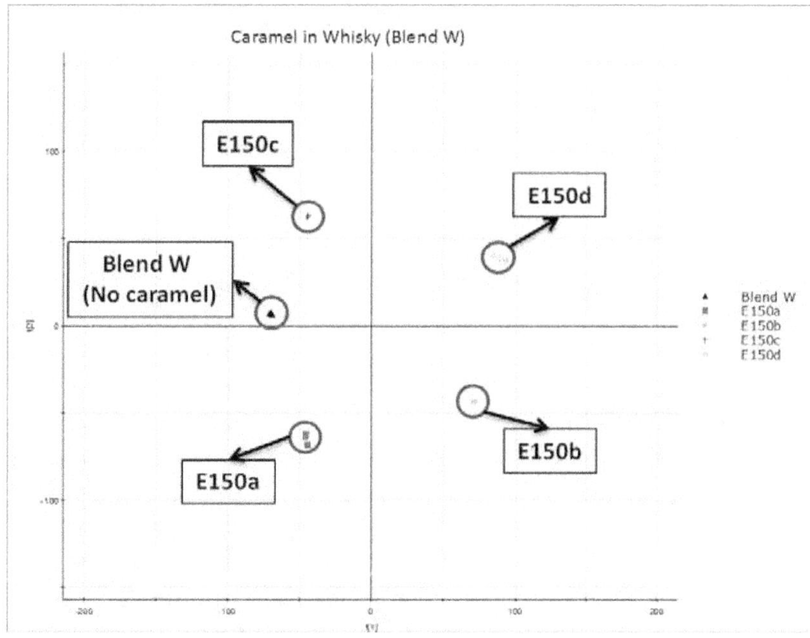

Figure 2. PCA scores plot of caramels E150a to d in Whisky. Again using negative ESI, differences between the caramels E150a to d are clearly observed, with each set of triplicate injections clustering apart from one another. The separation mirrors that seen in the PCA analysis of caramels in ethanol, but with greater differences now being seen between each of the four caramel types.

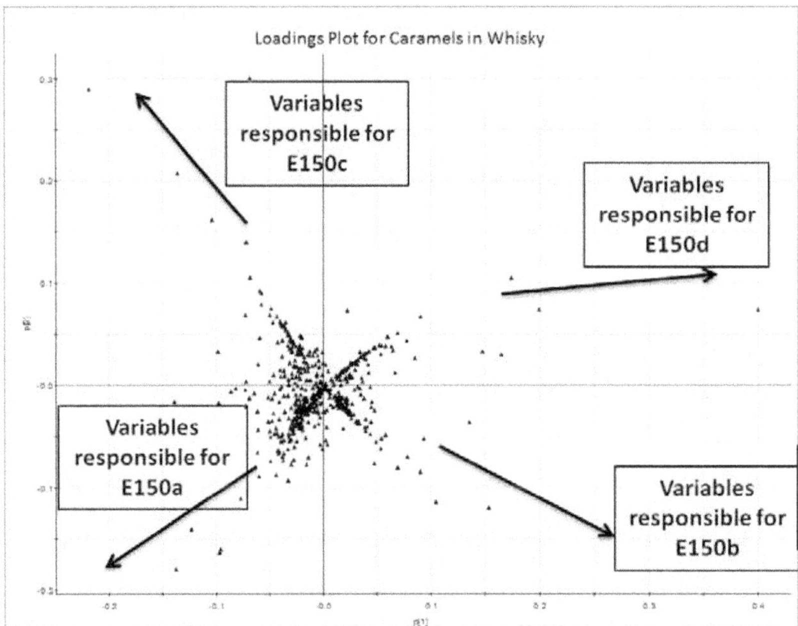

Figure 3. Loadings plot for the PCA of caramels in Whisky. Each triangle represents a unique mass and retention time. Variables which cluster around the origin give little contribution to the separation observed; variables that do contribute to the separations between each of the caramels are shown in the diagram, with variables further away from the origin having a greater contribution to the separation.

The variables shown in the loadings plot (Figure 3) can be used to determine the causes of any separation shown in the corresponding PCA scores plot, with the direction of any group from the origin in the PCA scores plot being mirrored by variables present in that region of the loadings plot, indicating higher concentrations or unique presence for those variables. Any variables that are present at the origin or in the opposite direction to any separation will be anti-correlating, meaning that they are present at lower concentrations or not present at all.

The variables can be selected and used to plot the intensity of each potential marker in the individual samples, or the average response for each variable in each sample group.

Using the loadings plot for caramels in Whisky Blend W, it is easy to plot the average intensity of the variables for each caramel vs. the remaining caramels (Figure 4). For each of the caramels E150a, b, c and d, there are several variables that appear to be unique (these are highlighted with arrows), with the remaining variables still contributing to the differentiation between each of the caramels but being unique to two or three caramels (for example, unique to E150b and c, and each permutation between E150a, b, c and d.)

The variables selected are then subjected to elemental composition calculation based upon their accurate mass, with the raw data being interrogated so that the isotopic peaks can also be used to increase the confidence in any elemental composition returned for the accurate mass. From the elemental composition returned, each variable can then be searched against user or online databases by its accurate mass or elemental composition; any tentative identification can immediately be viewed.

As the Xevo G2 Tof acquires fragmentation spectra simultaneously, any potential identification's structure can be used with software called MassFragment™; this software uses the structure and fragment ions from the original precursor ions and calculates potential fragments based on a series of novel chemically intelligent algorithms, using an approach based on systematic bond disconnection for the precursor structure instead of the usual rule-based approach. Therefore unlike rule-based

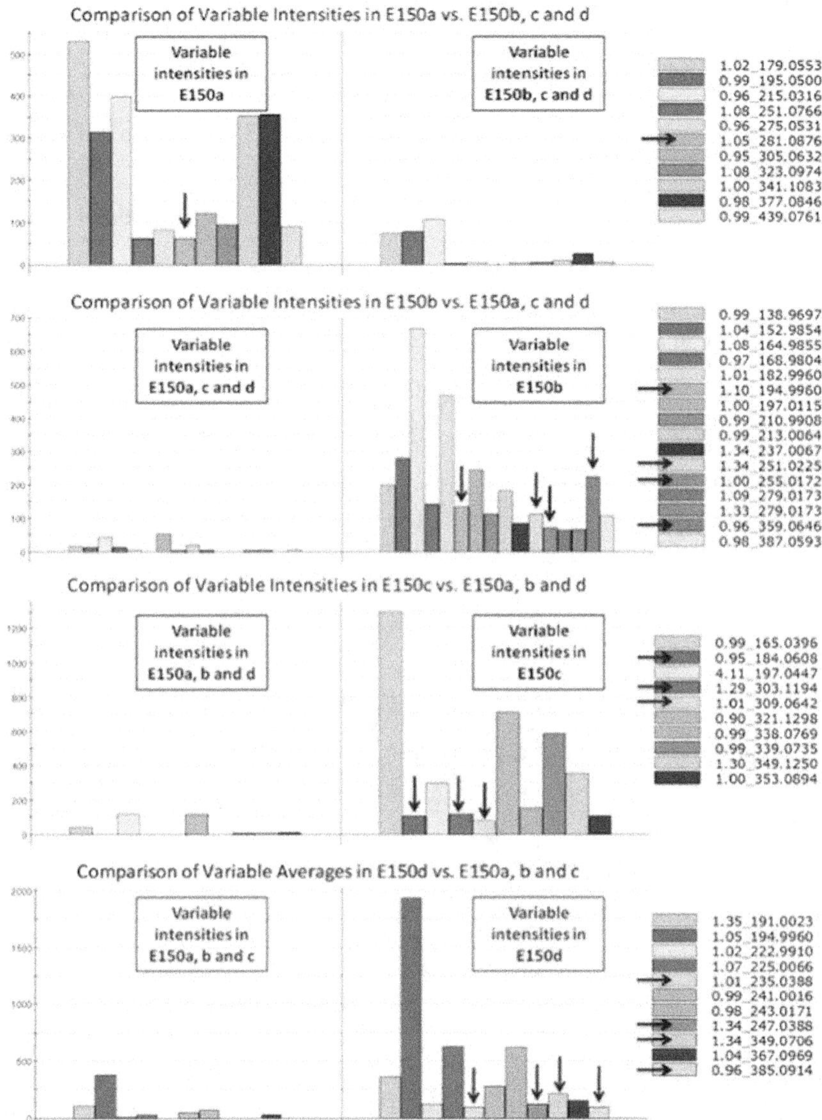

Figure 4. The variables with increased contribution for the separation of each of the caramels E150a, b, c and d are shown in the bar charts above, where each bar represents the average intensity of each variable for each caramel vs. the remaining caramels: E150a vs. E150b, c and d, E150b vs. E150a, c and d, E150c vs. E150a, b and d, and finally E150d vs. E150a, b and c. The legend to the right of each bar chart lists each variable as a retention time followed by *m/z* value (for example, the first variable is listed as 1.02_179.0553, which corresponds to a variable of *m/z* 179.0553 with a retention time of 1.02 min).

approaches, it is not limited to the extent of the rules coded. Each fragment is assigned a score based upon the bond disconnections used, which combined with accurate mass increases confidence in the assignment of that structure as a likely candidate for the variable.

The single variable highlighted as being unique for E150a has *m/z* 281.0876 with a retention time of 1.05 minutes. An elemental composition search returns $C_{10}H_{17}O_9$ as the top hit, with a calculated *m/z* of 281.0873 giving mass accuracy of 1.1 ppm (0.3 mDa); as this was negative ESI, the elemental composition requires the addition of a proton to give $C_{10}H_{18}O_9$. ChemSpider was searched using elemental composition, with the top hit being returned

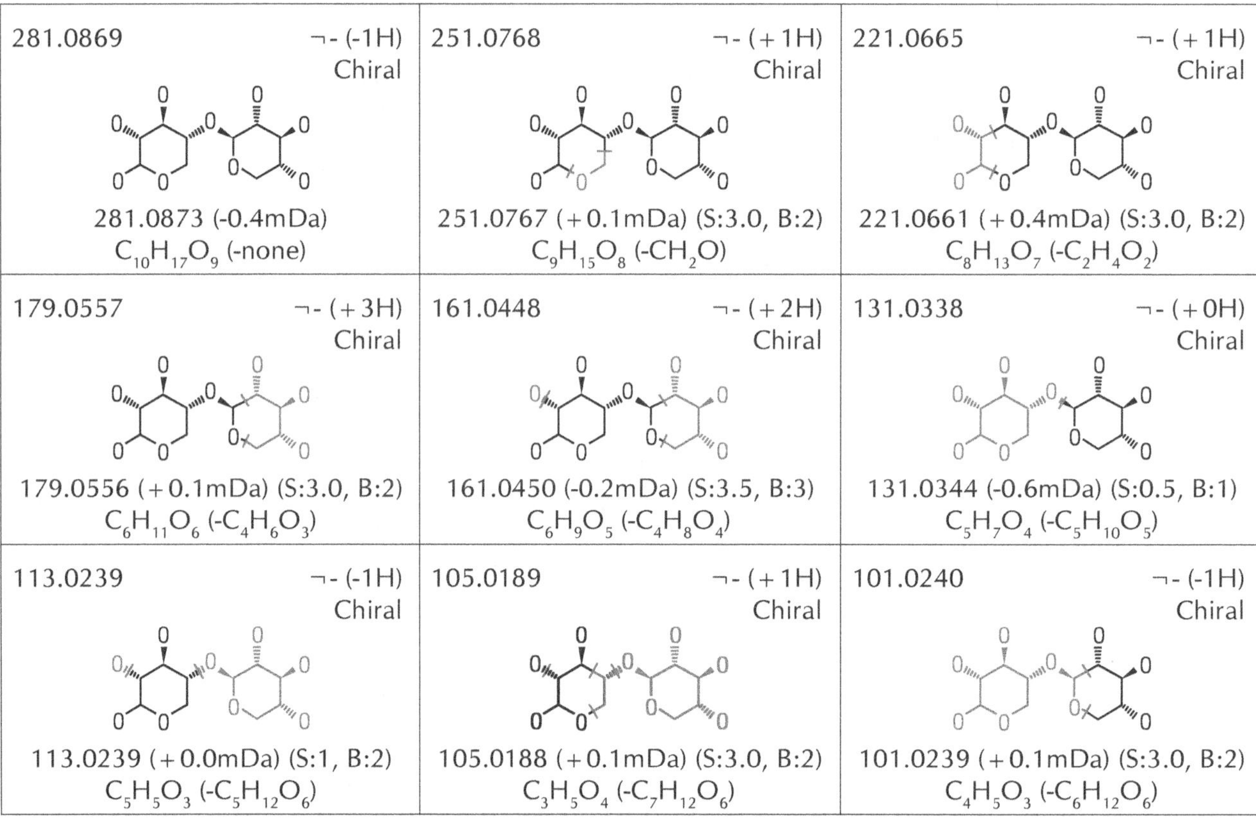

Figure 5. MassFragment results returned from the submission of 4-O-ß-D-xylopyranosyl-D-xylopyranose (structure top left) as a candidate for E150a. Each of the fragments has good mass accuracy. Given the near-symmetry of this compound, the fragments shown have several permutations which are not shown for clarity.

as 4-O-ß-D-xylopyranosyl-D-xylopyranose, a disaccharide (three other hits were also disaccharides of a similar structure).

The MS^E data (fragmentation spectrum) for *m/z* 281.0876 was submitted to MassFragment using the structure for 4-O-ß-D-xylopyranosyl-D-xylopyranose. The results shown in Figure 5 indicate a good fit, with the main peaks in the spectrum being able to have plausible structures with good mass accuracy assigned to them. However, to confirm 4-O-ß-D-xylopyranosyl-D-xylopyranose as the compound responsible, further fragmentation studies are to be performed (dedicated product ion fragmentation) and/or the injection of a standard to check that the retention time and fragmentation is identical. Further testing to determine the utility of this compound as one indicative of discriminating E150a from E150b, c and d would also increase the confidence in the assignment of 4-O-ß-D-xylopyranosyl-D-xylopyranose: analysing numerous known counterfeit (and genuine) samples and detecting 4-O-ß-D-xylopyranosyl-D-xylopyranose within the counterfeited samples and not in the genuine samples.

Summary

UPLC Tof MS and multivariate data analysis software were successfully used to determine potential markers related to the caramels E150a, b, c and d. The short analysis times, combined with excellent mass accuracy and the availability of on-line databases and fragmentation analysis software were shown as a simple workflow that can be applied to many other areas of research within the field of research into spirits.

Despite only focussing on one particular example in one polarity (negative ESI), many other experiments were performed. For example, detecting elevated levels of the common adulterants sucrose and vanillin in Whisky was simple, with both sucrose and vanillin easily detected and identified using accurate mass and fragmentation.

The potential for UPLC Tof MS was also highlighted for determining differences between blended Whiskies, compounds altered by fading, differentiation of cask types and research into maturation age as again, statistical analysis of the data allowed trends and potential markers to be easily highlighted.

Rapid analysis times, combined with simple to use instruments and software mean that UPLC Tof MS should be an analytical technique that is considered as a powerful tool for research into the growing problems of counterfeiting, as well as a tool for general research into numerous different aspects of the distilled spirits industry.

References

Regulation (EC) No 110/2008 of the European Parliament and of the Council of 15 January 2008 on the definition, description, presentation, labelling and the protection of geographical indications of spirit drinks.

SWA (2010) Scotch at a Glance. Available at:< http://www.scotch-whisky.org.uk/swa/files/ScotchataGlance2010%20low%20res.pdf> [Accessed 15th November 2011].

Index

www.ingramcontent.com/pod-product-compliance
Lightning Source LLC
LaVergne TN
LVHW081249100826
845148LV00009B/1179
* 9 7 8 1 7 8 9 1 8 2 7 5 0 *